Atlantic Islands

Azores, Madeira Group,
Canary Islands and Cape Verdes

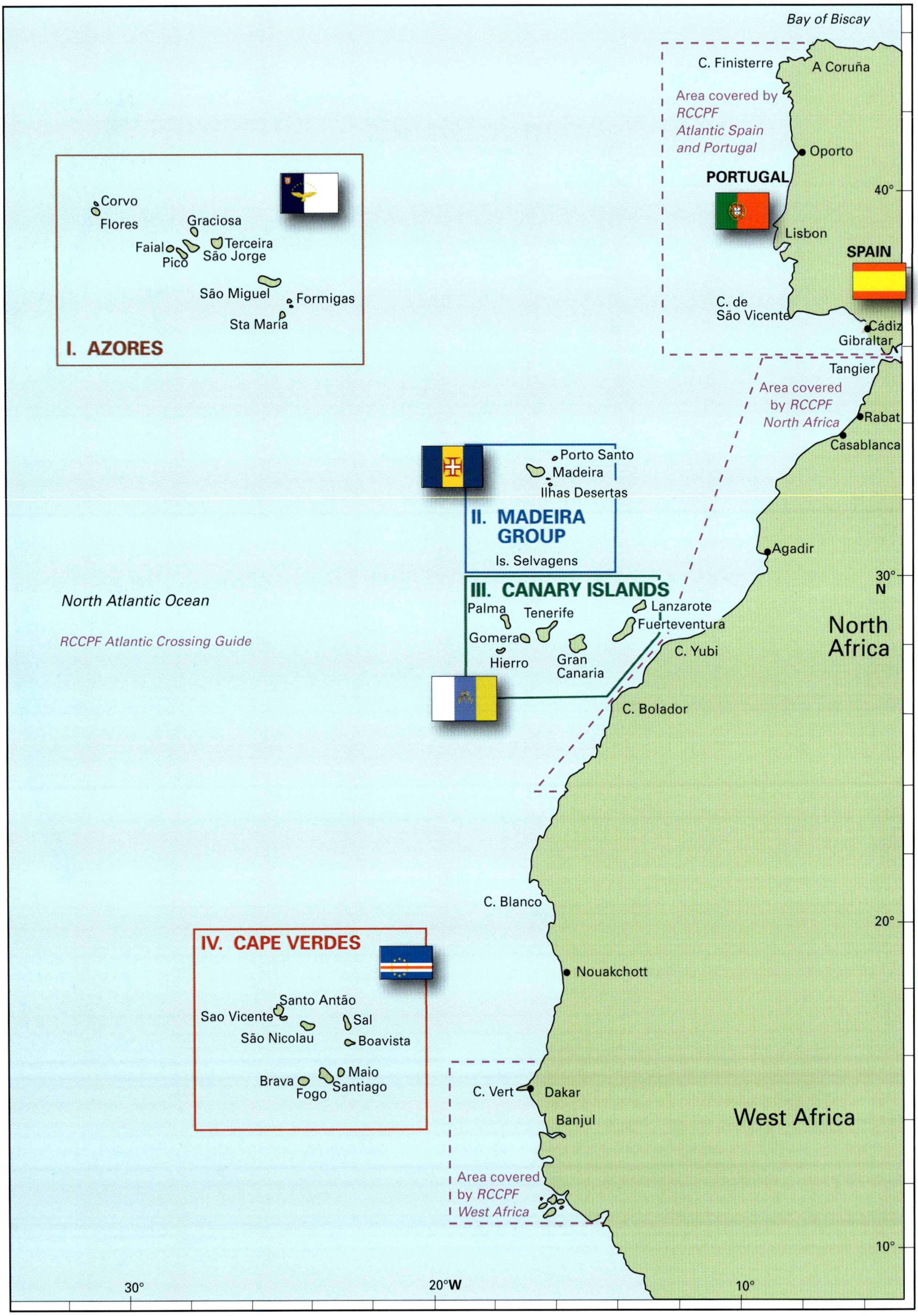
Bay of Biscay
C. Finisterre
A Coruña
Area covered by RCCPF Atlantic Spain and Portugal
Oporto
PORTUGAL
40°
Lisbon
SPAIN
C. de São Vicente
Cádiz
Gibraltar
Tangier
Area covered by RCCPF North Africa
Rabat
Casablanca
I. AZORES
Corvo
Flores
Graciosa
Faial
Pico
Terceira
São Jorge
São Miguel
Formigas
Sta Maria
II. MADEIRA GROUP
Porto Santo
Madeira
Ilhas Desertas
Is. Selvagens
Agadir
30° N
III. CANARY ISLANDS
Palma
Tenerife
Lanzarote
Fuerteventura
Gomera
Hierro
Gran Canaria
C. Yubi
North Africa
North Atlantic Ocean
RCCPF Atlantic Crossing Guide
C. Bolador
C. Blanco
20°
IV. CAPE VERDES
Nouakchott
Santo Antão
Sao Vicente
Sal
São Nicolau
Boavista
Brava
Maio
Fogo
Santiago
C. Vert
Dakar
Banjul
West Africa
Area covered by RCCPF West Africa
10°
30°
20°W
10°

Atlantic Islands

Azores, Madeira Group,
Canary Islands and Cape Verdes

RCC PILOTAGE FOUNDATION

Anne Hammick, FRIN

Azores
(Portuguese)

Portugal

Madeira
(Portuguese)

Spain

Canaries
(Spanish)

Republic of
Cape Verde

Imray Laurie Norie & Wilson Ltd

Published by
Imray Laurie Norie & Wilson Ltd
Wych House The Broadway St Ives Cambridgeshire PE27 5BT
England
✆ +44 (0)1480 462114 *Fax* +44 (0) 1480 496109
email ilnw@imray.com
www.imray.com
2011

Anne Hammick has asserted her right to be identified as the author of this work.

First edition 1989
Second edition 1994
Third edition 1999
Fourth edition 2004
Fifth edition 2011

ISBN 978 184623 336 4

British Library Cataloguing in Publication Data.

A catalogue record for this book is available from the British Library.

This work, based on surveys over a period of nearly 25 years, has been corrected to August 2011 from sea and land-based visits to the ports and harbours described, from contributions by visiting yachtsmen and from official notices.

British Library Cataloguing in Publication Data.
A catalogue record for this title is available from the British Library.

Printed in Singapore by Star Standard Industries (PTE) Ltd

CORRECTIONAL SUPPLEMENTS

This pilot book may be amended at intervals by the issue of correctional supplements. These are published on the internet at our web site www.imray.com (and also via www.rccpf.org.uk) and may be downloaded free of charge. Printed copies are also available on request from the publishers at the above address. Like this pilot, supplements are selective. Navigators requiring the latest definitive information are advised to refer to official hydrographic office data.

ADDITIONAL INFORMATION

Additional information may be found under the Publications page at www.rccpf.org.uk. This includes a downloadable waypoint list, links to Google maps, additional photographs and mid season updates when appropriate. Passage planning information may also be found on that website.

CAUTION

Whilst the RCC Pilotage Foundation, the author and the publishers have used reasonable endeavours to ensure the accuracy of the content of this book, it contains selected information and thus is not definitive. It does not contain all known information on the subject in hand and should not be relied on alone for navigational use: it should only be used in conjunction with official hydrographical data. This is particularly relevant to the plans, which should not be used for navigation. The RCC Pilotage Foundation, the authors and the publishers believe that the information which they have included is a useful aid to prudent navigation, but the safety of a vessel depends ultimately on the judgment of the skipper, who should assess all information, published or unpublished. The information provided in this pilot book may be out of date and may be changed or updated without notice. The RCC Pilotage Foundation cannot accept any liability for any error, omission or failure to update such information. To the extent permitted by law, the RCC Pilotage Foundation, the author and the publishers do not accept liability for any loss and/or damage howsoever caused that may arise from reliance on information contained in these pages.

POSITIONS

All positions in the text are to WGS 84 datum. They are supplied as aids to help orientation and to assist in locating and maintaining transits referred to in the book. As always, care must be exercised to work to the datum of the chart in use.

WAYPOINTS

This edition of the *Atlantic Islands* pilot includes waypoints. The RCC Pilotage Foundation consider a waypoint to be a position likely to be helpful for navigation if entered into some form of electronic navigation system for use in conjunction with GPS. In this pilot they have been derived from a variety of sources. They must be used with caution. All waypoints are given to datum WGS 84 and every effort has been made to ensure their accuracy. Nevertheless, for each individual vessel, the standard of onboard equipment, aerial position, datum setting, correct entry of data and operator skill all play a part in their effectiveness. In particular it is vital for the navigator to note the datum of the chart in use and apply the necessary correction if plotting a GPS position on the chart.

Our use of the term 'waypoint' does not imply that all vessels can safely sail directly over those positions at all times. Verification by observation, or use of radar to check the accuracy of a waypoint, may sometimes be advisable and reassuring.

We emphasise that we regard waypoints as an aid to navigation for use as the navigator or skipper decides. We hope that the waypoints in this pilot will help ease that navigational load.

PLANS

The plans in this guide are not to be used for navigation – they are designed to support the text and should always be used together with navigational charts. It should be borne in mind that the characteristics of lights may be changed during the life of the book, and that in any case notification of such changes is unlikely to be reported immediately. Each light is identified on the plans (where it appears in magenta) by its international index number, as used in the *Admiralty List of Lights*, from which the book may be updated. All bearings are given from seaward and refer to true north. Symbols are based on those used by the British Admiralty – users are referred to Symbols and Abbreviations (*NP 5011*).

Contents

THE RCC PILOTAGE FOUNDATION

In 1976 an American member of the Royal Cruising Club, Dr Fred Ellis, indicated that he wished to make a gift to the Club in memory of his father, the late Robert E Ellis, of his friends Peter Pye and John Ives and as a mark of esteem for Roger Pinckney. An independent charity known as the RCC Pilotage Foundation was formed and Dr Ellis added his house to his already generous gift of money to form the Foundation's permanent endowment. The Foundation's charitable objective is 'to advance the education of the public in the science and practice of navigation', which is at present achieved through the writing and updating of pilot books covering many different parts of the world.

The Foundation is extremely grateful and privileged to have been given the copyrights to books written by a number of distinguished authors and yachtsmen including the late Adlard Coles, Robin Brandon and Malcolm Robson. In return the Foundation has willingly accepted the task of keeping the original books up to date and many yachtsmen and women have helped (and are helping) the Foundation fulfil this commitment. In addition to the titles donated to the Foundation, new books have been created and developed under the auspices of the Foundation. The Foundation works in close collaboration with three publishers – Imray Laurie Norie and Wilson, Adlard Coles Nautical and On Board Publications – and in addition publishes in its own name short run guides and pilot books for areas where limited demand does not justify large print runs. Several of the Foundation's books have been translated into French, Spanish, German and Italian.

The Foundation runs its own website at www.rccpf.org.uk which not only lists all the publications but also contains free downloadable pilotage information.

The overall management of the Foundation is entrusted to trustees appointed by the Royal Cruising Club, with day-to-day operations being controlled by the Director. All these appointments are unpaid. In line with its charitable status, the Foundation distributes no profits; any surpluses are used to finance new books and developments and to subsidise those covering areas of low demand.

PUBLICATIONS OF THE RCC PILOTAGE FOUNDATION

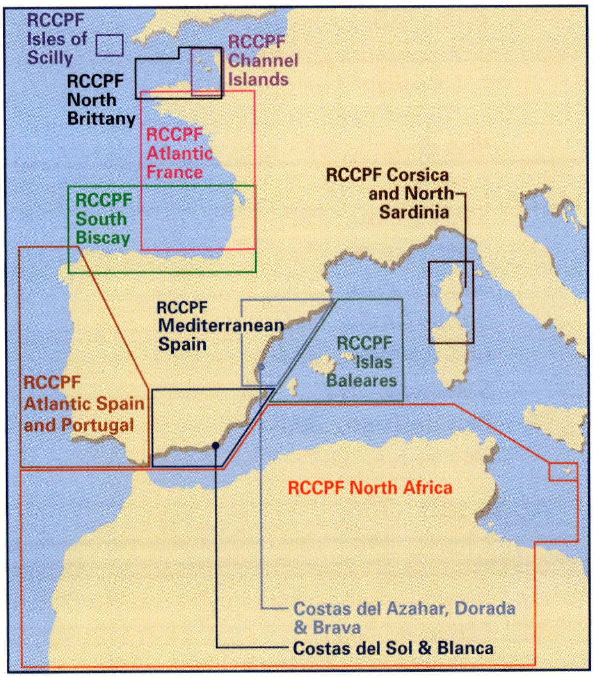

Imray
Faroe, Iceland and Greenland
Norway
The Baltic Sea
Channel Islands
North Brittany and the Channel Islands
Isles of Scilly
North Biscay
South Biscay
Atlantic Islands
Atlantic Spain & Portugal
Mediterranean Spain
  Costas del Sol and Blanca
  Costas del Azahar, Dorada & Brava
  Islas Baleares
Corsica and North Sardinia
North Africa
Chile
Black Sea

Adlard Coles Nautical
Atlantic Crossing Guide
Pacific Crossing Guide

On Board Publications
South Atlantic Circuit
Havens and Anchorages for the South American Coast

The RCC Pilotage Foundation
Supplement to Falkland Island Shores
Guide to West Africa
Argentina

RCCPF Website www.rccpf.org.uk
Supplements
Support files for books
Passage Planning Guides
ePilots - from the Arctic to the Antarctic Peninsula

Foreword

Four previous editions of the *Atlantic Islands* pilot book of the RCC Pilotage Foundation have informed and encouraged the transatlantic skipper for 22 years. It remains as popular as ever despite all the technical changes that have taken place in the cruising world over this time. Boats have tended to become larger, rigs easier to manage and engines more reliable. Ocean conditions themselves may not have changed but GPS and chart plotters have greatly simplified the navigator's role – helped further by the ability to obtain good weather information through easier communications.

The island groups covered in this book have also changed significantly with the provision of ever increasing facilities to meet the demands of the greater number of boats now sailing the Atlantic. Procedures have become simpler over time while the essential charm of the people and the diverse nature of the islands both remain unspoilt. All the islands groups may be regarded as places to cruise and visit and not used simply as stepping stones in an ocean passage.

Two things have remained constant. Firstly has been the meticulous research and compilation of information by the author, Anne Hammick, who has spent many months revisiting the island groups and ensuring that this 5th edition is as up to date as possible. Secondly, the team at Imray have worked tirelessly to ensure that this complex work is presented so clearly. The Pilotage Foundation is grateful to all involved. As always we will welcome feedback from those who sail these waters; this helps keep us up to date and may be published as supplements made available through www.imray.com and also via our own site www.rccpf.org.uk.

Martin Walker
Hon Director
RCC Pilotage Foundation
August 2011

Acknowledgements

I find it hard to believe that almost 25 years have passed since I began research for the first edition of *Atlantic Islands*. It was the third book to be published under the RCC Pilotage Foundation banner, and it says much for Oz Robinson, Director at that time, that he showed such faith in a young and unproven author. He answered my query 'what do you want me to include?' with 'whatever you'd expect to find in a pilot book', then left me largely to my own devices. Twenty-five years and five editions later I hope I have justified that confidence.

Coming closer to the present, I would like to thank those hundreds – possibly thousands – of yachtsmen and women who have taken the trouble to send corrections and updated information for inclusion in new editions and online supplements. To list all their names would take several pages, but please, keep the feedback coming!

Taking the archipelagos in sequence, Sr Carlos Adalberto Silva, Administrator of Portos dos Açores SA, and Carla Cook, who handles their PR, provided invaluable assistance during my research trip to their beautiful islands. Amongst the many who have provided feedback about the Azores since the previous edition was published, a few (in strictly alphabetical order) stand out in terms of the quantity and accuracy of their input: John Clementson (*Faustina II*); Thomas and Any Dargel of Boat & Sail Service, Ponta Delgada; Mark Holbrook (*Rain Again*); Roddy Innes (*Jessamy*); Keith Marshall of Lajes, Flores; Katherine and Stephen Paine (*Batrachian*); Harald Sammer (*Taniwani*) and Duncan Sweet of Mid Atlantic Yacht Services, Horta.

My researches in Madeira would have been much poorer – and certainly less fun – without the support and friendship of Cátia Carvalho of Quinta do Lorde Marina. Like Carla in the Azores, Cátia helped me chase up information unrelated to her own marina, and rightly considers herself an 'ambassador' for her native island. Looking through the list of those who have provided feedback over the past few years, Harald Sammer (*Taniwani*) and Andy and Lesley Scott (*Kodiak*) stand out, though there were many others whose input was also invaluable.

In the Canaries, Melanie Symes of Puerto Calero in Lanzarote is an ongoing tower of strength and support with an impressive network of contacts. Since my Spanish is even worse than my Portuguese, her willingness to ferret out the latest regulations affecting visiting yachtsmen, in addition to keeping me up to date regarding her own marina and adopted island, has been invaluable. Perhaps I should add that Mel, Cátia and Carla are all kept extremely busy by their own responsible jobs, which makes me even more grateful for their assistance. Among the many yachtsmen who took the trouble to send feedback – often going out of their way to respond to specific queries – were Iain Buchanan (*Ariadne*); Steve Burrows (*Cheng Feng*); Kate and John Crouch of Las Palmas, Gran Canaria; Nigel Mercier (*Dolcetto*); Pär and Nina Olofsson (*Osophine*); Andy and Lesley Scott (*Kodiak*) and Janet Wills of Club Yachting, Marina del Sur, Tenerife.

Feedback about the Cape Verde islands has always been more limited but, like his counterparts further north, Kai Brosmann of Marina Mindelo on São Vicente has always been ready to assist should I need it. In addition, Chris and Penny Bates (*L'Esprit de la Mer*); Henry Buchanan (*Spellbinder*); Len Hiley (*Scallywag*) and Chris Smith (*Avocette*) all provided feedback and invaluable photographs for this fascinating and rapidly-changing archipelago.

Moving on from the research to the writing stage, I was fortunate to assemble a particularly observant team of proof-readers, nearly all highly experienced cruising sailors and many familiar with the area for which they volunteered. Thus my thanks go to Brian Alexander, Dr David Bains, Hugh Clay, Kate Crouch, Anthony Fawcett, Liz Hammick, Gavin McLaren, Nigel Mercier, Dick Moore, John Power, Kit Power, David and Annette Ridout, Alex Scott-Bayfield, Chris Smith and Sandy Watson. Needless to say, any remaining errors rest at my door alone.

Finally, as always, my heartfelt thanks go to Willie Wilson and his team at Imray Laurie Norie & Wilson Ltd, particularly Elinor and Clare. All have shown great patience and good humour during the writing of a book which took far longer than anyone expected – not least because the number of marinas and yacht harbours has more than doubled since the previous edition.

Atlantic Islands was my first book and it may well be my last. It has been a privilege to follow the development of such a diverse and fascinating area, and one which offers so much to cruising yachtsmen and women.

Anne Hammick
Wrestler of Leigh
Falmouth, Cornwall
August 2011

For centuries Punta Orchilla formed the western limit of the known world, also serving as a prime meridian prior to 1884

Key to symbols used on the plans

English	Portuguese	Spanish
harbourmaster/ port office	*diretor do porto/ capitania*	*capitán de puerto/ capitania*
customs	*alfândega*	*aduana*
fuel (diesel, petrol)	*gasoleo, gasolina*	*gasoil, gasolina*
travel-lift	*e pórtico*	*grua giratoria*
yacht club	*clube náutico, clube naval*	*club náutico*
showers	*duches*	*duchas*
information	*informações*	*información*
post office	*agência do correio*	*oficina de correos*
anchorage	*fundeadouro*	*fondeadero*
chandlery	*fornecedore de barcos*	*efectos navales*

See Appendix IV, page 405, for further Portuguese and Spanish terms commonly used in a marine context.

Passages to and from the Islands

Passage planning

Whilst point of departure and arrival, timing and route are often dictated by outside factors, some basic rules should be observed when planning an ocean passage; most importantly that there are places and times which do not mix well, such as the western Atlantic during the tropical hurricane season and the northern Atlantic in autumn and winter when gales come with increasing frequency.

Other considerations to be taken into account, particularly for the longer passages, are the size and type of yacht, crew strength and experience, and range under power. Neither, at least with private yachts, should the important matter of crew happiness be neglected – for instance, most could easily make the passage from Bermuda to the European mainland without calling at the Azores, but only if the skipper wishes to risk a mutiny. Charter yachts, or others with paid crews, timetables and deadlines, clearly have other priorities.

Wind and current circulation

Weather systems revolve around the North Atlantic in a generally clockwise direction, powered by the permanent high pressure in mid-ocean and the relatively low pressures surrounding it. Though local winds can and do run counter to this general rule – the Azores in July, for example, frequently experience winds out of the eastern quadrant – the prevailing direction becomes more dominant as one heads south, until in November westerlies seldom occur in the Canaries on more than two or three days in the month while in the Cape Verde islands they are virtually unknown. Further information on the weather conditions likely to be encountered in each of the four island groups will be found in their respective Cruising sections, on pages 29, 139, 191 and 334.

Being largely wind-driven, current circulation around the North Atlantic is also clockwise. The Azores are affected by a branch of the North Atlantic Current (Gulf Stream) setting generally

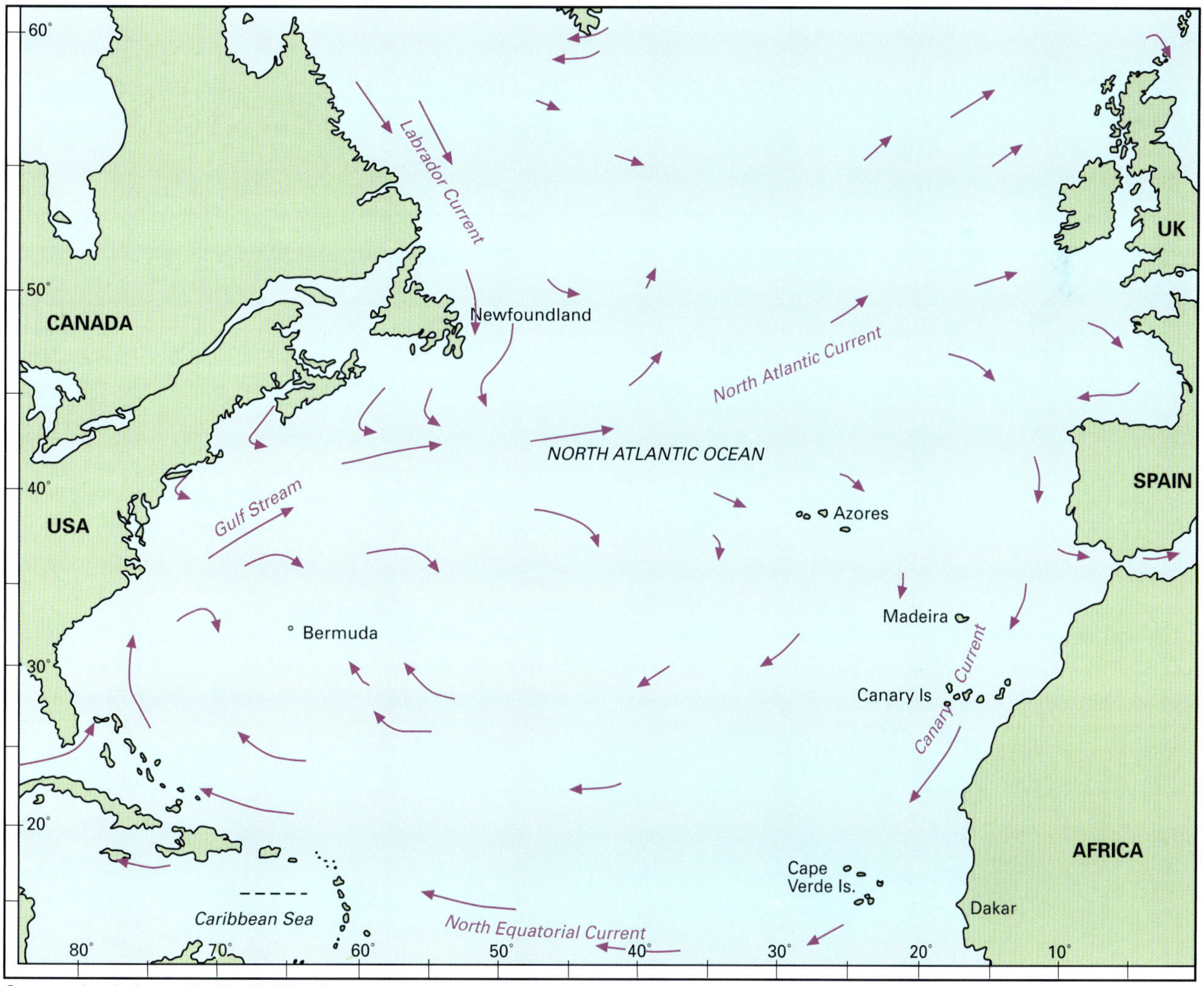

Current circulation in the North Atlantic

southeast or south, while the Madeira archipelago, the Canaries and the Cape Verde islands lie in the path of the southwest-going Canaries Current. Around the Azores currents seldom exceed 0·5 knots, but speeds tend to increase further south to one or 1·5 knots through the Cape Verde islands. Current flow in all areas may be increased following long periods of strong winds or where the general flow is obstructed, such as between, or around the ends of, islands. Equally it may be cancelled out or even reversed by strong, sustained opposing winds, but this is only temporary.

Sources of further information

A great deal of useful information will be found by reference to either the British Admiralty *Routeing Chart (North Atlantic Ocean) (NP 5124)* for the relevant month or the US NGIA *Atlas of Pilot Charts, North Atlantic Ocean (Pub 106)*, the latter containing individual charts for all 12 months and measuring 52cm x 71cm (20½in x 28in). The same information, if slightly less detailed, is to be found in smaller format – 43cm x 30cm (17in x 12in) – in James Clarke's *Atlantic Pilot Atlas*, now in its 5th edition, and on Imray Laurie Norie & Wilson Ltd's *Chart 100, North Atlantic Ocean Passage Chart*, the latter concentrating mainly on the months of April to July and October to December inclusive.

Passage charts

See Appendix I, page 396, for full details of large-scale charts

British Admiralty www.ukho.gov.uk

Chart	*Title*	*Scale*
3133	Casablanca to Islas Canarias (including Arquipelago da Madeira)	1,250,000
3134	Islas Canarias to Nouakchott	1,250,000
3135	Nouakchott to Bissau and Arquipelago de Cabo Verde	1,250,000
4011	North Atlantic Ocean – Northern Part	10,000,000
4012	North Atlantic Ocean – Southern Part	10,000,000
4014	North Atlantic Ocean – Eastern Part	10,000,000
4103	English Channel to the Strait of Gibraltar and the Arquipélago dos Açores	3,500,000
4104	Lisbon to Freetown	3,500,000
4114	Arquipélago dos Açores to Flemish Cap	3,500,000
4115	Arquipélago dos Açores to the Arquipélago de Cabo Verde	3,500,000

US National Geospatial-Intelligence Agency www.nga.mil

Chart	*Title*	*Scale*
121	North Atlantic Ocean (Northern Sheet)	5,870,000
120	North Atlantic Ocean (Southern Sheet)	6,331,100
125	North Atlantic Ocean (Southeastern Sheet)	5,281,950
126	North Atlantic Ocean (Northeastern Part)	3,619,020
103	English Channel to the Strait of Gibraltar including the Azores	3,500,000
104	Lisbon to Freetown	3,500,000

All the above give averages and extremes of wind strength and direction, current flow, wave and swell heights, visibility, temperature, barometric pressure, iceberg limits etc., and are based on data collected during many thousands of observations over the past 200 years. While the averages remain broadly correct, it appears that exceptional weather is becoming more frequent, more extreme and often more unseasonable.

The 5th edition of the *Atlantic Crossing Guide*, updated by Jane Russell for the RCC Pilotage Foundation, and *World Cruising Routes*, 6th edition, by Jimmy Cornell, are valuable at the planning stage and go into considerably more detail about many of the possible routes than can be included here. For online research, consult the RCC Pilotage Foundation's *Passage Planning Guide*, to be found on the Pilotage Foundation's website at www.rccpf.org.uk.

Finally, the British Admiralty Hydrographic Department's *Ocean Passages for the World (NP 136)* remains a classic in its 5th edition, though slanted more towards the needs of merchant shipping than towards yachts.

Routes to and from the Azores

Unlike islands in the trade wind belts, the Azores can be reached from almost any direction. Yachts arrive from Britain and Northwest Europe, Spain, Portugal, Gibraltar, Madeira, the South Atlantic, the Caribbean, Bermuda, the US East Coast and Canada. Departure is slightly more limited, with few yachts leaving the islands to head westwards though it is by no means unknown.

Note that recommended dates refer to departure rather than to the passage as a whole.

Possible routes with distances to nearest 50M

Falmouth to Ponta Delgada or Horta

1,150M and 1,200M respectively. May to August. Keep as near the rhumb-line as conditions permit. The current sets southeast and prevailing winds are between southwest and northwest. If faced with a limited weather window or prolonged, fresh southwesterly airstream consider sailing to southwest Ireland, possibly Crookhaven. When the wind veers the boat will be significantly up to windward, and the crew 'shaken down' and ready for the longer passage.

Ponta Delgada or Horta to Falmouth

1,250M and 1,300M respectively. May to August. Work north or north-northeast until approximately 47°N to make the best use of east-going currents and avoid Biscay. Prevailing winds are southwest through northwest. An alternative strategy is to break the passage in northwest Spain and pick one's weather for crossing the Bay.

Baiona or Lisbon to Ponta Delgada

800M. May to August. A rhumb-line course, allowing for south-going current and the likelihood of northerly winds, particularly in midsummer. If sailing the reverse leg it is vital to avoid making

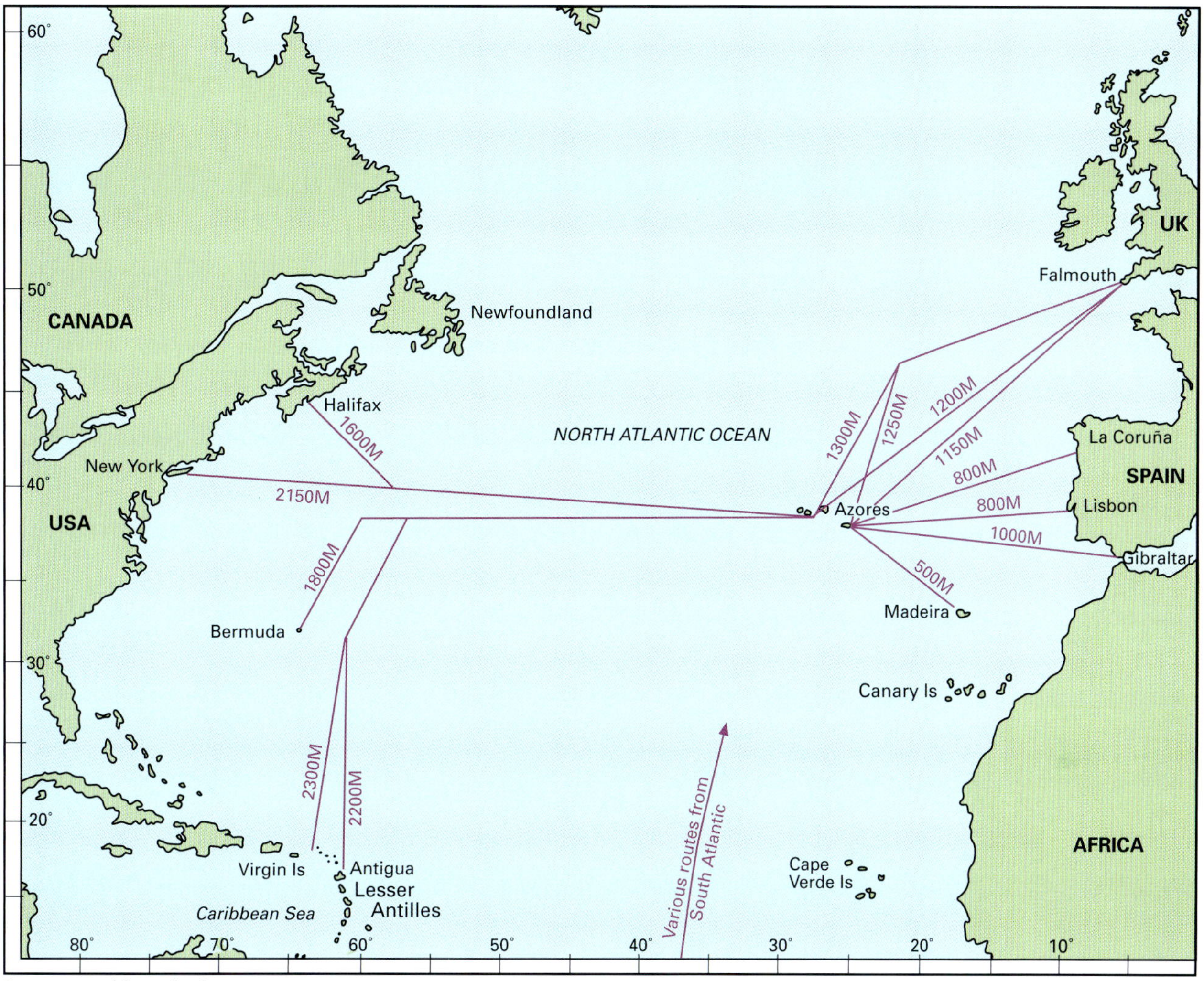

Routes to and from the Azores

landfall south of the intended destination, or the last part of the passage may degenerate into a tedious beat against both wind and current.

Gibraltar to Ponta Delgada

1,000M. May to August. Coastal or direct route to Cabo São Vicente, then as for Lisbon. Reverse leg similar.

Ponta Delgada to Madeira

500M. July to September. A rhumb-line course, with the current setting between southeast and southwest and winds likely to be northwest to northeast – probably a very pleasant passage. The reverse leg is possible but likely to be hard on the wind throughout.

South Atlantic to the Azores

Various distances. Pleasant passages from St Helena, Ascension Island or ports on the east coast of Brazil can be made leaving in April or May, especially if using the route recommended in *Ocean Passages for the World*. If followed closely this offers the shortest possible crossing of the inter-tropical convergence zone.

Antigua or the Virgin Islands to Horta

2,200M and 2,300M respectively (if sailed direct). April to June. Yachts with considerable range under power may risk the Great Circle route with its attendant calms. Others would be wise to work well north to within 200–300M of Bermuda (see below) but should still carry all possible fuel and water.

Bermuda to Horta

1,800M. April to June. The accepted route is to head northeast to 38° or 40°N in order to pick up heavier winds and stronger currents before running down the latitude for the Azores. Smaller yachts may prefer the lighter winds and flatter seas of the Great Circle route, but should anticipate a slow passage and carry all possible fuel and water.

Horta, Azores to Bermuda

1,800M. April or May. Adverse currents are inevitable, and yachts with good range under power may take the direct course through the high pressure and extensive calms which normally dominate this area. Those with less fuel should head due west to at least 50°W before altering course southwest, only ducking south earlier if forecasts indicate that reliable winds are likely to be found.

New York to Horta

2,150M. May or June. The rhumb-line course should enjoy prevailing southwesterly winds and a favourable current.

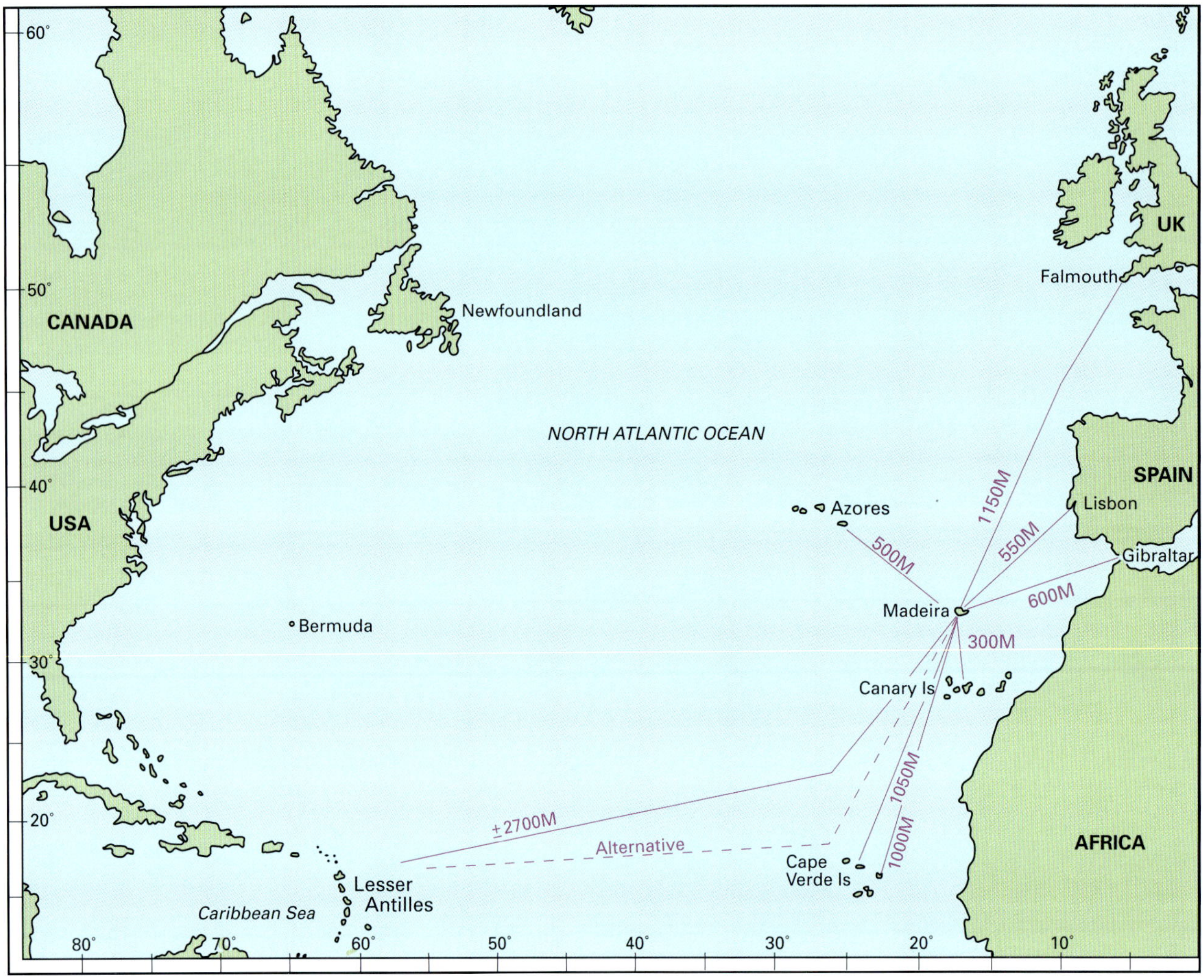

Routes to and from the Madeira Group

Halifax to Horta
1,600M. June or July. Definitely worth heading southeast to pick up a fair current around 40°N 57°W, then as for New York.

Routes to and from the Madeira Group

Most yachts arriving in the Madeiran group do so from the northeast, having come direct from mainland Europe, and continue south or southwest towards the Canaries or directly across the Atlantic. However, the passage from the Azores to Madeira has much to recommend it and occasionally a few yachts returning northwards from the Canaries also call in.

Note that recommended dates refer to departure rather than to the passage as a whole.

Possible routes with distances to nearest 50M

Falmouth to Madeira
1,150M. May to August. Basically a rhumb-line course with some extra westing early on to clear Ushant and Finisterre, but not keeping so far off the Iberian coast as to lose the Portuguese trades. There is an excellent chance of favourable winds and current once past the latitude of Finisterre. The reverse passage would probably be distinctly 'uphill' and best broken in Spain, Portugal or the Azores.

Lisbon to Madeira
550M. May to October. A direct course, allowing for the south-going current. Winds are generally northwest to northeast with occasional calm periods. The reverse passage would probably be to windward, with allowance for current necessary.

Gibraltar to Madeira
600M. May to October. A rhumb-line course, allowing generously for the south-going current once outside the Strait. It is usually possible to lay the course without problem, though westerly or northwesterly winds sometimes blow later in the year.

Ponta Delgada to Madeira
500M. July to September. Again a rhumb-line course, with the current setting southwest and winds likely to be northwest to northeast – probably a very pleasant passage. The reverse leg is possible but likely to be hard on the wind throughout.

Madeira to Gran Canaria
300M. All year. Another direct course with favourable wind and current. The reverse leg would almost certainly be to windward.

Madeira to Ilha do Sal or São Vicente, Cape Verdes
1,000 and 1,050M respectively. Most likely to be sailed in October to March or April, though feasible

at almost any season. A rhumb-line course, aided by the southwest-going current and prevailing winds between north and east. Attempting the reverse leg direct would be masochistic, though yachts occasionally do it.

Madeira to the Lesser Antilles
±2,700M. November to April. It is always necessary to head well southwest before altering course for the Caribbean, but the best latitude at which to turn varies with the position of the trade wind belt. The 'classic' turning point of 25°N 25°W is often successful, but some seasons it is much too far north and yachts may have to continue down to 20° or 18°N before finding good winds. A rhumb-line should then be possible, with favourable current and following winds.

Routes to and from the Canary Islands

Many yachts arrive in the Canaries from Madeira, others from mainland Europe or occasionally the Azores. The vast majority depart west or southwestwards across the Atlantic.

Note that recommended dates refer to departure rather than to the passage as a whole.

Possible routes with distances to nearest 50M

Falmouth to Gran Canaria
1,400M. May to August. Basically a rhumb-line course with some extra westing early on to clear Ushant and Finisterre, but not keeping so far off the Iberian coast as to lose the Portuguese trades. There is an excellent chance of favourable winds and current once past the latitude of northwest Spain. The reverse passage would probably be distinctly 'uphill' and best broken in Spain, Portugal or the Azores.

Lisbon to Gran Canaria
750M. May to October. A direct course, allowing for the south-going current. Winds are generally northwest to northeast with occasional calm periods. The reverse passage would probably be to windward, with allowance for current necessary.

Gibraltar to Gran Canaria
750M. May to October. A rhumb-line course, allowing generously for the south-going current once outside the Strait. It is usually possible to lay the course without problem, though westerly or northwesterly winds sometimes blow later in the year.

Madeira to Gran Canaria
300M. All year. Another direct course with favourable wind and current. The reverse leg would almost certainly be to windward.

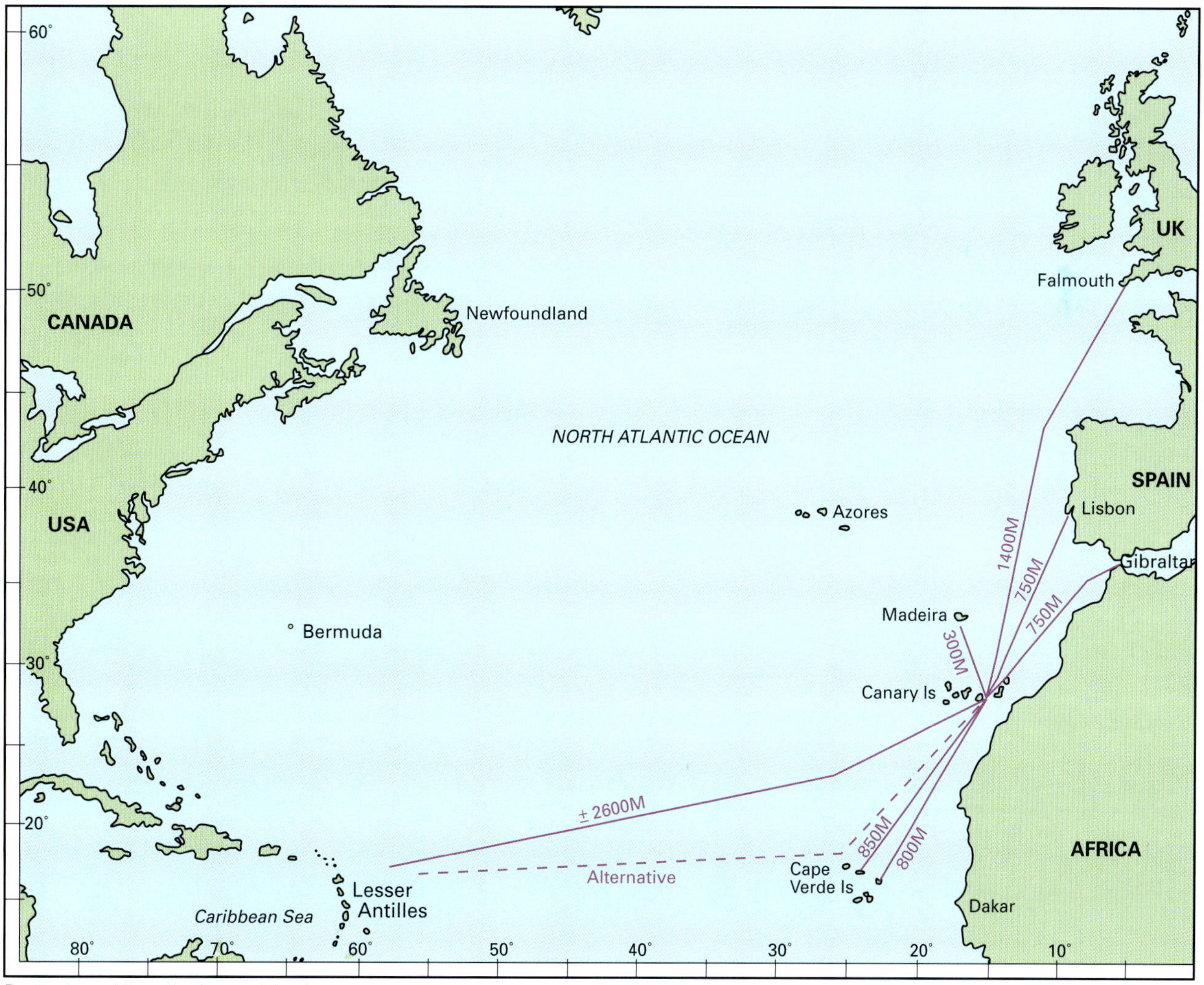

Routes to and from the Canary Islands

Gran Canaria to Ilha do Sal or São Vicente, Cape Verdes
800M and 850M respectively. Most likely to be sailed in October to March or April, though feasible at almost any season. A rhumb-line course, aided by the southwest-going current and prevailing winds between north and east.

Gran Canaria to the Lesser Antilles
±2,600M. November to April. As for Funchal to Antigua, though in some years it will not be necessary to sail very far southwest before picking up the trade winds.

Routes to and from the Cape Verdes

Lying squarely in the path of the northeast trades, the vast majority of yachts arriving in the archipelago do so from Madeira or the Canaries, with the occasional one from Gibraltar via West Africa. Equally, a very high proportion depart for the Caribbean or South America, though a few head south or southeast towards Africa.

Note that recommended dates refer to departure rather than to the passage as a whole.

Possible routes with distances to nearest 50M

Madeira to Ilha do Sal or São Vicente
1,000 and 1,050M respectively. Most likely to be sailed in October to March or April, though feasible at almost any season. A rhumb-line course, aided by the southwest-going current and prevailing winds between north and east.

Gran Canaria to Ilha do Sal or São Vicente
800M and 850M respectively. As for Madeira to Ilha do Sal or São Vicente.

Dakar to Ilha do Sal
350M. October to April. Northerly winds near the African coast may free to give northeasterlies nearer the islands, but as allowance must be made for the south-going current it would be wise to keep well to windward. The reverse leg is similar, but with the possibility of freer winds.

São Vicente or Santiago to Barbados
1,950 and 2,050M respectively. November to April. Without the need to search southwards for the trade winds, a rhumb-line is generally the best course for Barbados. With favourable winds and current this should be a fast and enjoyable passage.

São Vicente or Santiago to the Lesser Antilles
±2,150M. November to April. As for Barbados.

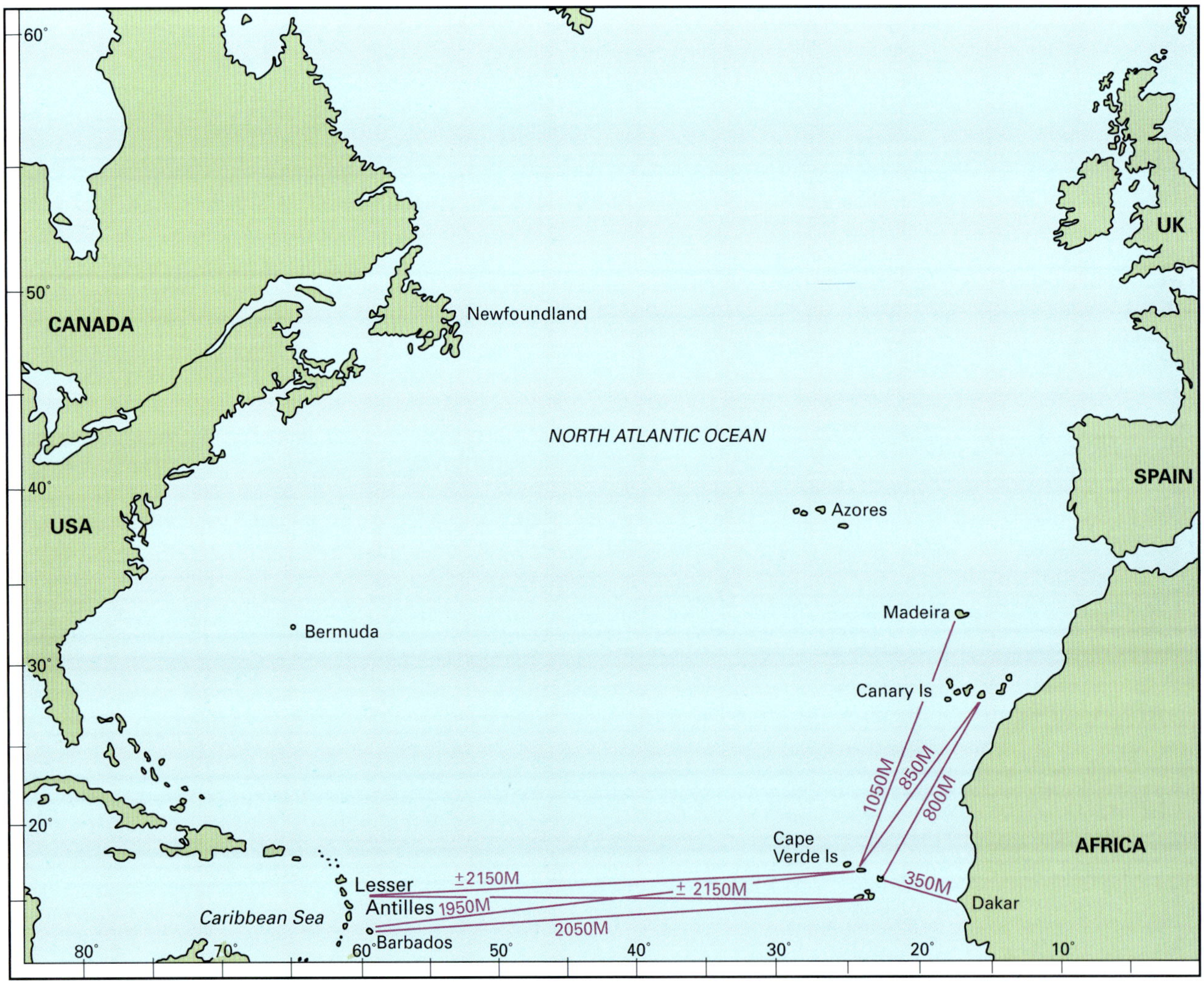

Routes to and from the Cape Verde Islands

Weather forecasts

Extremely comprehensive details of all official weather forecasts worldwide will be found in the *Admiralty List of Radio Signals, Volumes 3(1) and 3(2)*, the former covering Europe, Africa and Asia and the latter the rest of the world including the Americas. Thus the eastern Atlantic Islands are covered by *Volume 3(1)* and Bermuda by *Volume 3(2)*. Reprinted annually, they can be updated via the weekly *Notices to Mariners*, available online at www.ukho.gov.uk. The US equivalent is *Worldwide Marine Weather Broadcasts*, published by NOAA. Yachts equipped with Weatherfax or HF receivers are advised to carry the relevant volume(s). It should be noted that times quoted for weather messages, navigational warnings and traffic lists are normally given in Universal Time (UT or, previously, GMT). This contrasts with harbour and marina radio schedules, which are generally governed by office hours and are therefore quoted in Local Time (LT).

Most yachtsmen now receive the bulk of their weather information from the internet. Sites vary in their coverage and presentation and are very much a matter of personal choice, but those sites listed on page 9 are among the most used.

GRIB files

GRIB files (GRidded Information in Binary), which package data including wind speed, temperature, precipitation and sea state in a standardised form, have largely superseded Weatherfax as the favourite source of weather and sea state information for many yachtsmen, not least because they are often available as free downloads. As the name implies, these data are listed for grid points, often spaced as finely as half a degree and in intervals as small as two hours, for up to ten days ahead. The size of a GRIB file increases with the size of the selected surface area, the length of the forecast and the density of information, so when bandwidth is at a premium it makes sense to reduce all three.

They can be received in a number of ways, some of which allow the selection of a rectangular area as well as data type, interval, grid density etc.:

By email from Saildocs, www.saildocs.com – an excellent free site, or MailASail, www.mailasail.com, using Airmail software in conjunction with either Winlink or SailMail. (Airmail allows one to select the level of detail required and forwards a request to Saildocs);

By FTP (File Transfer Protocol) from UGrib, www.grib.us, or ZyGrib, www.zygrib.org;

By browser (easy to use, but requires greater bandwidth) from Weatheronline (www.weatheronline.co.uk), PassageWeather (http://passageweather.com), Windfinder (www.windfinder.com) another popular site, WindGuru (www.windguru.cz), MovingWeather (www.movingweather.com) and XCWeather (www.xcweather.co.uk) among others.

By iPhone App PocketGrib

As GRIB files merely comprise lists of data, programs are needed to display them except when viewed on a weather site via a browser. Airmail comes with a viewer, while others such as UGrib provide the necessary programs. Files normally display either as surface diagrams showing wind arrows, isobars etc. for a selected area at a given moment, or predict the developing situation over time for a given position. Advanced navigation programs may use GRIB data to plan optimal sailing routes.

GRIB data may be based on differerent computing models, but all are very dependent on the actual measured data – the finer and more comprehensive those are, the better the forecast. Luckily the northern Atlantic is probably one of the best-monitored weather systems. As with all forecasts accuracy diminishes the further the forecast projects into the future, and predictions are for averages, not extremes.

An extremely clear and comprehensive explanation of the subject by Frank Singleton will be found at http://weather.mailasail.com/Franks-Weather/Grib, and I would also like to thank Harald Sammer of yacht *Taniwani* for checking and expanding on my efforts regarding this technical subject.

Amateur forecasts

In addition to the official forecasts, several amateur or 'ham' nets transmit weather information for different parts of the Atlantic Ocean. Only licensed amateur operators may transmit, but all may listen and useful information can be obtained. All frequencies are USB (J3E). Nets come and go, but among the most long-standing, as well as the most useful, are:

Herb's Net – Herb Hilgenberg, often referred to as *South Bound II*, callsign VAX498
Email hehilgen@sympatico.ca
www3.sympatico.ca/hehilgen/vax498.htm
Broadcasts daily on 12359kHz from 2000UT. Now in his 25th year of assisting ocean-going yachts, Herb prepares a detailed five-day forecast for each yacht on his 'log', which in return is expected to report current conditions at their position. Those with receivers but no means of transmission are welcome to listen in and may well find that a forecast is given for a boat close to their own position.

Trudi's Transatlantic Maritime Mobile Net – run by Trudi in Barbados, callsign 8P6QM, broadcasts on 21400kHz at 1300UT, with weather on the half hour. Yachts throughout the Atlantic (but principally heading west on the trade wind route) check in, giving positions and actual weather conditions. The net may not operate for periods during the hurricane season.

Navtex

Three Navtex stations currently operate within the area covered by this book, with another three stations on the European mainland also covering Atlantic waters. A station has long been planned for Porto Santo but has yet to become operational. Much of the information is available online through either http://marine.meteofrancecom/ or http://weather.gmdss.org/ – see Meteorology on the internet on page 9.

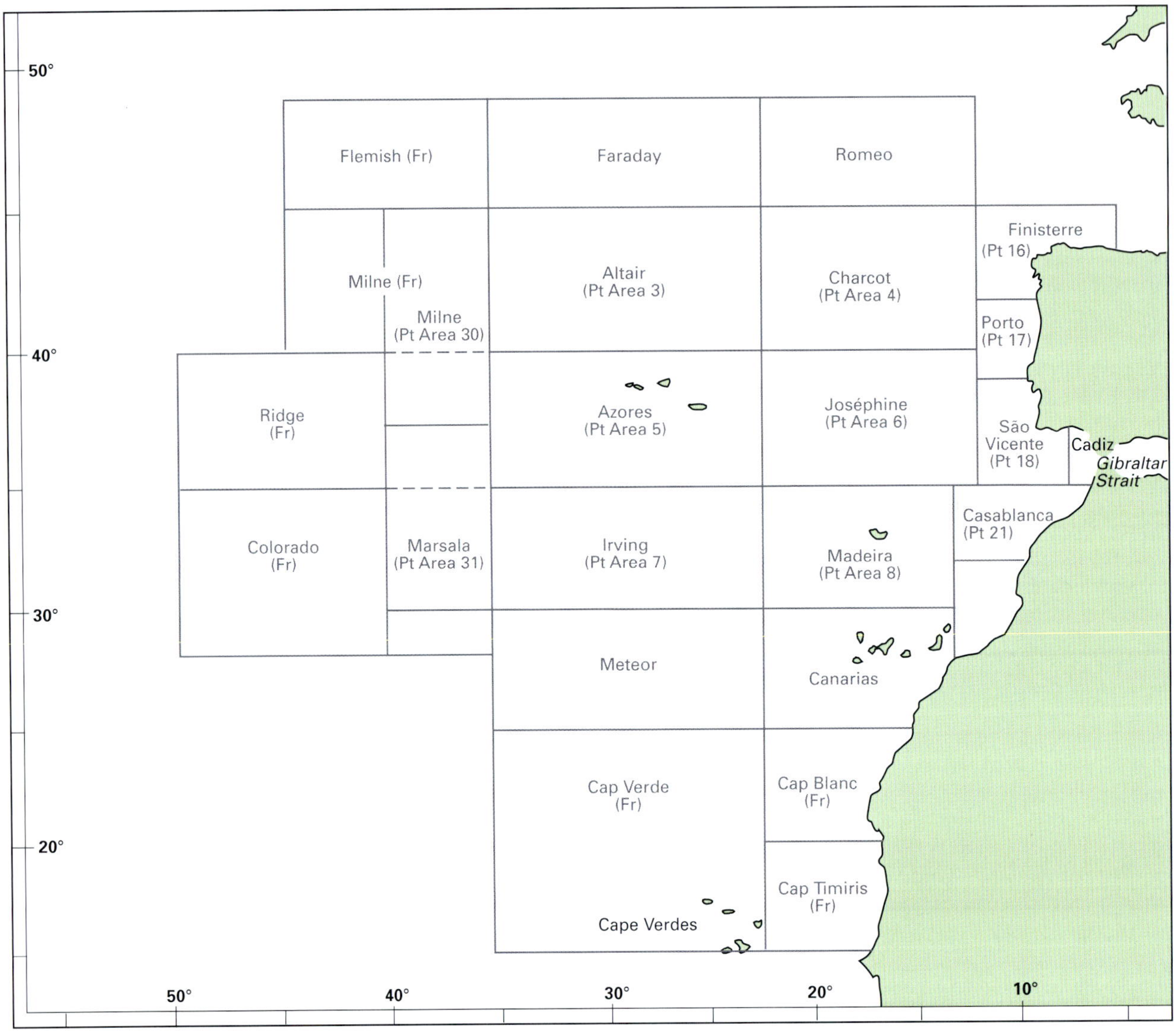

FRENCH, PORTUGUESE AND SPANISH WEATHER FORECAST AREAS

Horta transmits weather bulletins and navigational warnings in English (F) on 518kHz four-hourly from 0050, and in Portuguese (J) on 490kHz four-hourly from 0130.

Las Palmas transmits navigational warnings in English (I) on 518kHz four-hourly from 0120, with weather bulletins at 0920, 1320 and 1720. Equivalent transmissions in Spanish (A) on 490kHz are broadcast four-hourly from 0000, and at 0800, 1200 and 1600.

Ribeira de Vinha (São Vicente, Cape Verdes) transmits weather bulletins and navigational warnings in English (U) four-hourly from 0320. Equivalent transmissions in Portuguese (P) on 490kHz are broadcast four-hourly from 0230. (Several yachtsmen have commented on the unreliability of this station – see page 360.)

La Coruña (Spain) transmits in English (D) on 518kHz with weather bulletins at 0830 and 2030 and navigational warnings at 0030, 0430, 1230 and 1630. Equivalent transmissions in Spanish (W) on 490kHz are broadcast four-hourly from 0340, and at 1140 and 1940.

Tarifa (Spain) transmits in English (G) on 518kHz with weather bulletins at 0900 and 2100 and navigational warnings at 0100, 0500, 1300 and 1700. Equivalent transmissions in Spanish (T) on 490kHz are broadcast at 0710 and 1910, and at 0310, 1110, 1510 and 2310.

Monsanto (Portugal) transmits weather bulletins and navigational warnings in English (R) on 518kHz four-hourly from 0250 and Portuguese (G) on 490kHz four-hourly from 0100.

National forecasts

English language

BBC Radio 4 broadcasts its shipping forecasts at 0048, 0520, 1201 and 1754 LT (BST in summer, UT in winter) on 198kHz (1,515m). Coverage extends to 35°N and 15°W, relevant if sailing between mainland Europe and the Azores or Madeira.

Weather bulletins for local waters broadcast on VHF by Horta Radionaval, the Centro de Comunicações da Madeira in Porto Santo and Tenerife MRCC are all repeated in English – see pages 50, 143 and 264 for details.

Meteorology on the Internet

An ever-increasing amount of weather-related information can be found on the internet. As of March 2011 the following sites were all up and running, though much information is duplicated over several sites.

www.aemet.es – website of the Instituto Nacional de Meteorología Marítima (the Spanish Met Office), in seven languages including English (click on 'Welcome' at top right), though translations of forecasts themselves may need to be done via one of the online translation programmes. Surprisingly user-friendly

www.cnn.com/WEATHER/images.html – worldwide weather coverage with charts, satellite images and eight-day forecasts for hundreds of locations from US media giant CNN

www.ecmwf.int – billed as the 'European Centre for Medium-Range Weather Forecasts' and featuring pressure charts for up to twelve days ahead (as well as nine days into the past), plus dozens of useful links

http://marine.meteofrance.com/ – the marine section of the Meteo France site. Click on '*Bulletins grande large*' followed by the relevant area for a Navtex-style synopsis and forecast in English, and '*Cartes*' for plans showing the extent of each named sea area

www.meteo.pt – website of the Instituto de Meteorologia (the Portuguese Met Office), in Portuguese and English. Ten-day general forecasts and weather warnings for the Azores and Madeira in addition to mainland Portugal

www.metoffice.com – website of the UK Met Office, with marine (and aviation) forecasts for the UK and near Atlantic waters, and more general forecasts worldwide. Excellent animated pressure charts and satellite imagery

www.passageweather.com – described as 'Weather forecasts for Sailors and Adventurers', this user-friendly site features animated wind and pressure charts and tropical storm warnings amongst much else. Complete with low-bandwidth and mobile web versions

www.sat.dundee.ac.uk – the website of the Dundee Satellite Receiving Station at Dundee University, offering images from orbiting and geostationary satellites, plus some useful links. (Free) registration is necessary for full access

www3.sympatico.ca/hehilgen/vax498.htm – run by Herb Hilgenberg of *South Bound II*. Not weather information *per se*, but the background to Herb's Net as described under Amateur forecasts on page 7. Well worth visiting

www.weatherbase.com – a source of weather records and monthly statistics (not current forecasts) for more than 16,000 cities worldwide. Fascinating!

www.weather.bm – from the Bermuda Weather Service and including smallcraft warnings, long-term climate data, tropical storm warnings plus five-day general and marine forecasts

http://weather.gmdss.org/ – JCOMM Oceanography and Marine Meteorology, developed and maintained by Meteo France (see left), and again giving access to Navtex online but via a slightly different (and much more user-friendly) route. In English throughout

www.weather.mailasail.com/Franks-Weather/Grib – part of the site described below, but deserving an entry of its own for its remarkably clear and comprehensive explanation of GRIB files

www.weather.mailasail.com/Franks-Weather/Home – headed Frank Singleton's Weather and Sailing Pages, long-established and incredibly comprehensive. Believed to be the only meteorological website constructed by a yachtsman (and retired senior forecaster with the UK Met Office) for other yachtsmen. Contains links to many useful sites plus, crucially, advice on how to get the best out of them. The explanation of GRIB files and their use is particularly recommended

http://weather.noaa.gov/fax/otherfax.shtml – website of the US National Weather Service, and offering a wide range of surface analysis and forecast charts, though not all of them clear to the amateur at first glance

www.weatheronline.co.uk/ – detailed six-day synoptic charts for most parts of the world leading, via maps and clicking, to forecasts (1-day to 14-day) for individual areas and islands. Some advertising, but not too intrusive

www.wetterzentrale.de/topkarten – Wetter Zentrale, useful German site giving links to many key European weather sites, some of which charge if accessed directly

www.windfinder.com – an intuitive and user-friendly site claiming to offer 'Wind, waves and weather worldwide, For kitesurfers, windsurfers, surfers, sailors, paragliders and anybody who needs accurate wind data!' And it does, with seven-day forecasts for thousands of locations with particular emphasis on wave height and direction, including ocean swell. Recommended

www.windguru.cz – a subscription-based site originally intended mainly for windsurfers and kitesurfers though a favourite with many cruising yachtsmen

www.wmo.ch – website of the World Meteorological Organization, the branch of the United Nations tasked with promoting co-operation between national meteorological offices and hydrological services. No forecasts as such, but reams of interesting reading in English, French, Spanish, Russia, Arabic and Chinese – or possibly Japanese?

www.worldclimate.com – WorldClimate provides a fascinating archive of past weather data (no current or forecast information), though not specifically maritime

www.wunderground.com – Weather Underground was one of the first sites providing weather information online and still carries a vast range of marine and land-based weather information including local barometric readings and severe weather warnings

French language

Radio France International '*Le Meteo*' broadcasts at 1130 UT daily on the following AM (A3E) frequencies: 6175, 15300, 15515, 17570 and 21645kHz. Frequency varies according to reception area, as does the area covered in the forecast. The format is straightforward, being gale warnings, synopsis, development and 24-hour area forecasts and it is read clearly and at moderate pace (those with limited French may find it helpful to record it for translation).

Portuguese and Spanish language

Forecasts in the local language are broadcast on national radio throughout the eastern Atlantic islands, as well as on VHF by several stations in the Azores, Porto Santo in the Madeira group and by stations throughout the Canaries. See individual harbours for details.

Miscellaneous websites of interest

Of the thousands of websites of potential interest to yachtsmen cruising the Atlantic Islands, the following offer something for everybody.

www.amazon.org / www.amazon.co.uk – other than nautical charts there doesn't seem much that they don't supply. Check the FAQ section for details of international delivery times and costs

www.atlantic-islands.com/ – German retailer specialising in books and maps for the Azores, Madeira and Cape Verdes (not Canaries). Although most of the former are in German, a map is the same in any language. Site in German and English

www.bluewaterweb.com – website of Bluewater Books & Charts, one of America's largest nautical bookstores and chart agents, including Admiralty and Imray charts and publications. Online ordering

www.bradt-travelguides.com – publishers of *Azores: The Bradt Travel Guide* and *Cape Verde Islands: The Bradt Travel Guide* (both highly recommended) amongst many others. Online ordering

http://easytide.ukho.gov.uk – free tidal data for ports all over the world, including 38 in the islands covered in this book. Exceptionally user-friendly

www.imray.com – Imray Laurie Norie & Wilson Ltd – publisher of a wide range of cruising guides and charts (correctional supplements carried on the website), retailer for other publishers and Admiralty chart agent. Online ordering

www.maps.google.com – satellite images of much of the world, including excellent coverage of most parts of the Atlantic Islands. Although every image is labelled '© 2011 Google' (rolled on each year), this could be misleading as many of the images currently displayed are at least three years old

www.noonsite.com – originally created to carry updates and corrections for Jimmy Cornell's well-known *World Cruising Handbook* and *World Cruising Routes*, but now run by World Cruising Club Ltd and host to a vast amount of worldwide cruising information to which yachtsmen are invited to contribute

www.oceancruisingclub.org – a UK-based club with worldwide membership, backed by a network of port officers and representatives. Categories for Ordinary and Associate membership (the former requiring a port-to-port passage of 1,000 miles or more) ensure it remains THE club for ocean cruising sailors. Online application form

www.oceangrafix.com – website of OceanGrafix LLC, from whom US National Geospatial-Intelligence Agency charts (which are no longer available for public sale by the NGIA (see page 396), can be ordered on a print-on-demand basis

www.rccpf.org.uk – homepage of the RCC Pilotage Foundation, containing information about current and future PF titles, supplements etc., as well as access to its *Passage Planning Guide* (see page 2)

www.ssca.org – website of the Seven Seas Cruising Association, a US-based club for both serious cruisers and local liveaboards with a worldwide (though mainly American) membership, known for its informative monthly bulletin and 'clean wake' policy. Online application form

www.sunflowerbooks.co.uk – publishers of the highly recommended series of *Landscapes* walking and car touring guidebooks. No online ordering, but a comprehensive list of stockists. In English and German

www.ukho.gov.uk – website of the UK Hydrographic Office. Not as user-friendly as it used to be but, via the 'Products and Services' tab followed by 'Paper Charts', still the only source of weekly *Admiralty Notices to Mariners* (including an invaluable listing of relevant notices by chart). No online ordering, but a comprehensive worldwide distributor list

Horizontal chart datum and waypoints

Positions given by modern satellite navigation systems are normally expressed in terms of World Geodetic System 1984 (WGS84) Datum – in practice identical to the previously used WGS72, but sometimes differing by more than 500m from the datum of charts based on older surveys. New editions of British Admiralty charts are either based on WGS84 Datum or carry a note giving the correction necessary to comply with it, but charts published by other nations' hydrographic offices may use different datums when covering the same area.

Every effort has been made to relate the plans throughout this guide to WGS84 Datum, and all the waypoints use it. Thus while the waypoints are accurate in relation to the plans, a correction may sometimes be needed before a waypoint can be plotted on the chart in use.

Caution and request

Although considerably improved over the past decade, maintenance of lights and other navigational aids throughout the Atlantic Islands can still be poor and even major lights may occasionally be out of service for long periods. This is particularly true of remote areas such as the Ilhas Selvagens, where maintenance can be rendered difficult if not impossible by bad weather, and of the Cape Verde islands, where many lights simply do not work – ever.

The northern groups are for the most part accurately charted, though the rapid development of both tourist complexes and new harbours can prove confusing. The larger Cape Verdean harbours have also been surveyed relatively recently, but in other parts of the archipelago charts may be dangerously inaccurate.

In all the islands corrections may take many months to filter through the system before they appear in the weekly *Admiralty Notices to Mariners*, and in the case of the Cape Verdes a few of the changes described in the second (1994) edition of this book have yet to be officially recognised. For all these reasons, even a brand new chart, fully corrected, should not be assumed to be fully up-to-date in all respects.

Where changes come to the notice of the author and/or publisher they will be incorporated in the ongoing supplement to this book carried on Imray's website: www.imray.com. Feedback is very welcome, and should be sent by email to ilnw@imray.com. Alternatively, the feedback form available on www.rccpf.org.uk may be used. Thank you.

I. The Azores

Index to islands

The archipelago

The nine islands which form the Azores archipelago seem to have a uniqueness and appeal out of all proportion to their size – tiny, irregular pieces of land only 2,335km^2 in total, scattered over some 58,000km^2 of ocean and hardly more than dots on the North Atlantic chart. Perhaps this explains why many yachtsmen pass through the islands with only a brief stop at Horta for sleep, water and fresh food. Others may assume that there is only the one safe harbour in the archipelago, or that the islands must be so similar that there is little point in visiting more than one. Both those ideas could hardly be further from the truth. The islands form a varied, unspoilt and relatively uncrowded cruising ground waiting for any yacht – and crew – capable of the ocean passage.

The Azores lie about 750M west of mainland Portugal, somewhat to the east of the Mid-Atlantic Ridge and along the margins of the Eurasian and African Plates. Over millions of years these weaknesses in the earth's crust have allowed molten lava to seep through to the surface and form volcanoes, whilst at the same time new rock forming along the Mid-Atlantic Ridge pushed the older rock outwards – a process which is still continuing and causing the Atlantic Ocean floor to widen by 0·5cm each year. This accounts for the fact that the oldest lava in the Azores is a mere four million years old, whilst that in the Cape Verde islands, much nearer the African coast, is as much as 120 million years old. As the volcanoes grew, with later eruptions having to work upwards through ever greater thicknesses of older lava, the volcanic activity grew fiercer and more explosive, in many cases eventually disintegrating the entire cone to form a vast crater or *caldeira*. Only the massive Pico still retains most of its original height in one classic cone, but though apparently dormant it is now ringed with monitoring devices ready to detect the least hint of a build-up of pressure within.

Elsewhere in the Azores one finds vast lava fields – several formed within recorded history – sulphur caves, lava tunnels, boiling geysers and hot or cold mineral springs. Sterile pumice and ash still cover the western end of Faial, where a major eruption occurred off the Capelinhos peninsula in 1957, and all the islands have areas of dark, basaltic lava, though few are as spectacular as the imposing 'Organpipe Rocks' in Flores. With the high sea-cliffs laying much of the volcanic structure open to view, as well as the opportunity to study small-scale

The iconic cone of Pico, seen from Faial

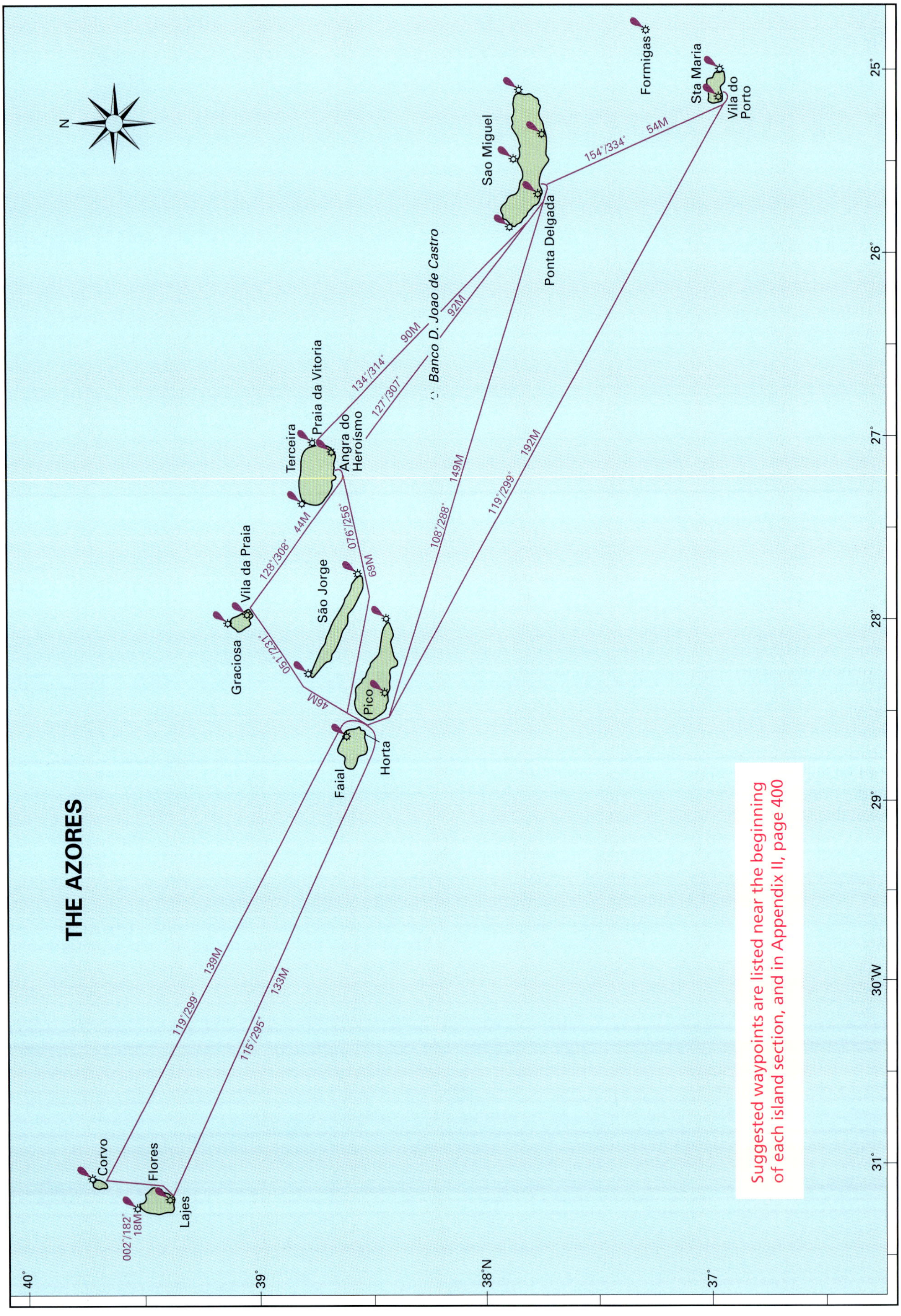
THE AZORES
N
Corvo
Flores
Lajes
002°/182°
18M
119°/299°
139M
115°/295°
133M
Faial
Horta
Pico
Graciosa
Vila da Praia
051°/231°
46M
São Jorge
128°/308°
44M
Terceira
Praia da Vitoria
Angra do
Heroísmo
076°/256°
69M
134°/314°
90M
127°/307°
92M
Banco D. Joao de Castro
108°/288°
149M
119°/299°
192M
Ponta Delgada
Sao Miguel
154°/334°
54M
Formigas
Sta Maria
Vila do
Porto
40°
39°
38°N
37°
25°
26°
27°
28°
29°
30°W
31°
Suggested waypoints are listed near the beginning
of each island section, and in Appendix II, page 400

Vines at Biscoitos on the north coast of Terceira, growing in the shelter of high lava-block walls

A traditional Azorean whaleboat at Cais de Barra in Graciosa

volcanic activity at first hand, it is hardly surprising that the islands have long been considered a geologists' paradise.

Volcanic soils become very rich and fertile after a period of weathering, particularly in warm, moist climates, allowing the Azores a vegetation which combines the best of European temperate and African tropical. Some areas of the original thick forest still survive, mostly as protected national parks, but the native plants such as myrtle, juniper, heather, holly and yew are now heavily outnumbered by naturalised newcomers including conifers, laurel, cedar, chestnut and eucalyptus. Bamboo and ferns thrive in the undergrowth and two unique species of orchid have evolved, found nowhere else in the world. The excellent *Açores Flores* (*Azores Flowers*) by Erik Sjögren details nearly 100 native and introduced plants and flowers and where they may be found, in four languages. It is understood to have been reprinted, and though not available outside the islands may sometimes be found in local tourist offices and bookshops – if a copy is encountered it should be snapped up without hesitation. The fauna side was originally less varied, with only seabirds, a few land birds and, surprisingly enough, bats. All the land mammals were brought by man, doubtless some unintentionally, whilst several of the introduced birds have gradually evolved into distinct subspecies over the centuries. *Birds of the Atlantic Islands* by Tony Clarke (Helm Field Guides) is a useful handbook.

The Azorean economy has changed little over the last 500 years. There is almost no industry – agriculture is still the mainstay, the most important

Courses and distances within the Azores

Harbour	*Course / Reciprocal*	*Distance*
Lajes, Flores – Vila Nova, Corvo	002° / 182° & by eye	18M
Lajes, Flores – Horta, Faial	115° / 295°	133M
Vila Nova, Corvo – Horta, Faial	119° / 299°	139M
Horta, Faial – Madalena, Pico	089° / 269°	4·5M
Horta, Faial – Velas, São Jorge	067° / 247°	22M
Horta, Faial – Vila da Praia, Graciosa	051° / 231°	46M
Horta, Faial – Angra do Heroísmo, Terceira	076° / 256° & by eye	69M
Horta, Faial – Praia da Vitória, Terceira	080° / 260° & by eye	80M
Horta, Faial – Ponta Delgada, São Miguel	108° / 288°	149M
Horta, Faial – Vila do Porto, Santa Maria	119° / 299°	192M
Vila da Praia, Graciosa – Angra do Heroísmo, Terceira	128° / 308°	44M
Vila da Praia, Graciosa – Praia da Vitória, Terceira	112° / 292°	48M
Angra do Heroísmo, Terceira – Ponta Delgada, São Miguel	127° / 307°	92M
Praia da Vitória, Terceira – Ponta Delgada, São Miguel	134° / 314°	90M
Ponta Delgada, São Miguel – Vila do Porto, Santa Maria	154° / 334°	54M

crops being grains, fruit and vines. Stock-raising of cattle, sheep and pigs is important on all the islands, with butter and cheese exported in quantity. Fishing, particularly of tuna for canning or freezing, is a fairly recent industry, though fishing for food must always have taken place. Big game fishing is an even more recent innovation and several world records for tuna, swordfish, ocean bonito and shark are held from Horta and Ponta Delgada.

The whaling industry, once the islands' second money-earner, is now a part of history and facilities to process the carcasses no longer exist. Whales have not entirely disappeared from the economy, however, with whale and dolphin-watching enterprises based in several of the islands. Having spent many years quietly rotting away on old slipways, a good number of the elegant double-ended whaleboats have been carefully restored for use in inter-island regattas, while new ones are once again being built. Santa Cruz das Ribeiras, west of Lajes do Pico, is particularly famous in this regard.

Tourism as a source of employment and income is on the increase in all the islands, particularly São Miguel, Terceira and Faial. A fair proportion of those visiting turn out to be Azorean expatriates and their children who, having emigrated during the 19th and 20th centuries, are now returning in increasing numbers to meet relatives and re-establish family roots. Most of the restaurants appear to cater largely for local people, with prices to match, other than in Terceira where personnel from the American air base provide a reliable source of custom. The lease on the base is also reputed to bring in sizeable funds, most of which stay in the islands.

The Azores must be amongst the few places in the world where as many foreign visitors arrive by yacht as by air. A single yacht passing through Horta in 1930 had increased to 59 in 1970, around 200 in 1978, over 800 in 1988, and at least 1,300 by 2010. The same figures revealed that, in the 24 years since Horta Marina welcomed its first yacht, some 25,826 boats and almost 100,000 yachtsmen and women had passed through the harbour. Even so, relatively few cruise the islands in detail and it would be rare to talk to a skipper who had visited all nine islands, or even the eight larger ones, in a single season. It is worth making the effort – despite ever-increasing numbers of yachts the friendliness of the islanders towards their crews remains unchanged, not only in Horta but throughout the Azores as a whole. Unless bound by a very tight schedule it is well worth taking the time to experience a cruising area with a fine climate, delightful people, stunning scenery and some excellent anchorages.

A windmill in Corvo

History

When the Portuguese claimed and colonised the Azores in the early 15th century they were uninhabited, with no human traces of any kind. However, it seems almost certain that although the Portuguese were the first to settle the islands, others had been aware of their existence centuries before. Various sources credit their discovery to the Phoenicians in the 6th century BC, the Carthaginians a few hundred years later, the Norsemen – though if they had known of the Azores why should they have chosen instead to settle in Iceland? – and even the Chinese. The earliest reliable reference to the islands dates back to 1154 when Sherif Mohammed al Edrisi, an Arab explorer and geographer at the court of King Roger II of Sicily, compiled a globe and descriptive manuscript entitled *El Rojari* which mentions nine islands lying to the northwest of the Canaries. They were next described by a Spanish friar writing in the early 14th century, and appear clearly on a Genoese chart of 1351, now in Florence.

History is less specific about the Portuguese connection, with some sources stating that Diogo de Silves, a pilot in the service of King João I of Portugal, rediscovered the islands in 1427 while others suggest that a copy of the Genoese chart was taken to Portugal in 1428 and given to King João's son, Prince Henry the Navigator. Either is possible – hemmed in by its powerful Spanish neighbour, Portugal was forced to look overseas to expand and colonise, with seaworthy caravels exploring the African coast and far out into the Atlantic. Prince Henry the Navigator (who rarely went to sea himself) spent much of his life at Sagres collecting and studying accounts of early voyages and such charts and maps as could be obtained, and would doubtless have paid well for such a valuable addition. Whatever his source, by 1431 Prince Henry was confident enough to send a small fleet commanded by Gonçalvo Velho Cabral in search of the elusive islands. With incredible bad luck, after crossing more than 700 miles of ocean Cabral and his men found only an isolated group of rocks, and one can imagine the disgust with which they named them the Formigas (the Ants) before turning for home. They must also have been dogged with exceptionally bad visibility not to have seen the 590m peak of Santa Maria just 20M to the southwest. Presumably Prince Henry was less than pleased with their lack of success, since Cabral was sent westwards again the following summer and on 15 August 1432 finally landed on Santa Maria.

Unlike many men of vision, Prince Henry was also practical and concerned with the settlement of his newly acquired islands. A Royal Edict dated 2 July 1439 is the oldest existing document regarding colonisation, at which time only Santa Maria and São Miguel were definitely known. The central group – Terceira, Graciosa, São Jorge, Pico and Faial – were added to the list around 1450, with Flores and Corvo far to the west not discovered until 1452. Cabral became the first governor or *capitão donatório*, based at Vila Franca do Campo in São Miguel, and work began on clearing the land for cultivation. Large areas of the dense natural forest were burned, volcanic boulders heaped into walls and windbreaks, and wheat, oranges, sugar cane and vines brought from the mainland. However, Portugal was unable to provide enough potential colonists, a difficulty partially solved by the intervention of Prince Henry's sister, the Infanta Isabella, Duchess of Burgundy and Countess of Flanders. Thousands of Flemings from her husband's estates were eager to escape the wars and persecution of the low countries (now Belgium and Holland) by emigrating to the Azores, as were Bretons from France and a scattering of Scots, Italians and Irish, all hoping for better lives. One of the early governors of São Miguel was Rui Gonçalves de Câmara, son of João Gonçalves Zarco who discovered Madeira. Why he left his father's island is not clear, but he almost certainly brought some Madeiran families with him, and very possibly Moorish and African slaves.

As the land was gradually cleared and cultivated, the small groups of thatched wooden huts built by the first settlers began to be replaced by stone cottages, usually built in the traditional style of the area from which each family had come. Even now this gives a valuable clue as to their origins – while low, whitewashed buildings with doors and windows outlined by broad stripes of colour are typical throughout all the islands, their chimneys vary dramatically, from the circular detached towers of Santa Maria to the sharp-edged wedges of Terceira. Many of the leading families of the 15th century still have descendants in the islands, and even more of the farmers and country dwellers are likely to have lived in the same cottages for generations, until recently most never leaving their own island throughout their entire lives.

Horses (and donkeys) are still used for working the land in the smaller islands

The restored *Misericordia* church which overlooks the marina at Angra do Heroísmo, Terceira

In contrast to this, as settlement and agriculture spread through the islands they gained importance as a port of call for ships exploring ever westwards. Columbus stopped briefly at Santa Maria in 1493 on his return from the 'new world', in 1498 João Fernandes Labrador left Terceira with the fleet of John Cabot to explore the land which still bears his name, the following year Vasco de Gama anchored briefly at Angra on his way back from India, and in the early years of the new century the Corte Real brothers, also from Terceira, led expeditions to Newfoundland and Canada. Its superior natural harbour soon led to Angra becoming the leading town in the Azores, particularly after the destruction of Vila Franca do Campo on São Miguel in 1522 by an earthquake and landslide. When, in 1534, Angra was granted a bishopric its dominant position was assured, even though each island still retained its own *capitão donatório* appointed by the King of Portugal.

Later in the 16th century Angra played an important part in Portuguese history when, in 1580, King Phillip II of Spain invaded mainland Portugal claiming the throne, the country and all its overseas territories, following the death of King Sebastão II. Dom António, Prior of Crato and claimant to the

Manueline-style carving around the church door at Santo Espírito in Santa Maria

Portuguese throne, fled to Terceira to organise his opposition with the help of the English and French, but after two years of resistance the island finally fell to the Spanish, the last Portuguese territory to do so.

The Spanish were quick to realise the value of the islands for their treasure galleons returning from the Americas, and within a few years the harbours at Angra and, to a lesser extent, at Horta had become magnets for pirates and privateers of all nationalities, including English, French and Venetian, traditional enemies of Spain who had supported the Prior of Crato. Castles were built to protect the two anchorages and provide secure storage for valuables (the Spaniards must have built well, as both have survived for more than four centuries), but even so Horta was attacked repeatedly by English fleets in the 1580s and 1590s, whilst raids by Moorish and North African pirates continued as they had done almost since the islands' discovery. Under Spanish rule Angra became capital of the archipelago, and although on the restoration of Portuguese independence in 1640 under the house of Bragança the system of independent governors was reintroduced, it never lost its position as the economic and commercial centre of the islands. Eventually, after a long period in the 17th and 18th centuries during which the islands largely went their individual ways remote from mainland Portugal, a central government under a single Captain General was again set up in Terceira in 1766 by the Marquês de Pombal, powerful adviser to King José I.

True to form, Terceira was also the island to become most heavily involved in Portugal's constitutional struggles between 1829 and 1832, when it supported the Liberals under Dom Pedro against the Absolutists led by his brother Dom Miguel. Dom Pedro established his Regency in Terceira and used the island as a base from which to plan his invasion of the mainland. After the successful Liberal revolution in 1832 the Azores became a province, with the islands grouped into three administrative districts based on the three main ports of Horta, Angra and Ponta Delgada, a situation which in modified form still exists today.

It was logical that the harbours should give their names to the administrative areas. Even with the improvements in farming and stock-rearing introduced in the 19th century, the sailing ships which filled the ports, always in need of provisions, labour and often crew, were a constant source of revenue and employment. Chief among these were the American whaling ships, about which Herman Melville wrote in *Moby Dick* in 1851:

> 'Not a few whalers come from the Azores, where the Nantucket ships often cast anchor to make up their crews with the solid peasants of these rocky islands... It is not known why, but the best whalers come from among these islanders.'

It is likely that the local whaling industry, which until thirty years ago hunted sperm whales with hand harpoons from lightweight open boats propelled only by oars, originated with seamen who had returned home after crewing on American whaling ships. Many, however, chose not to return, and from the early 19th century the Azores had very high emigration, with many islanders tempted to leave for New England, Bermuda, California or Brazil.

In 1855 the islands lost some of their remoteness when the first transatlantic cable was laid via Horta, soon to become a base for several big cable companies, and as the number of steamships increased the British-run Fayal Coal Company set up a bunkering station in the harbour. This would have been the scene which greeted Joshua Slocum when he arrived in May 1895, 21 days out of Boston, quite possibly the first singlehanded sailor ever to visit Horta. In *Sailing Alone Around the World* he recounted his impressions:

> 'Early on the morning of July 20 I saw Pico looming above the clouds on the starboard bow. Lower lands burst forth as the sun burned away the morning fog, and island after island came into view. As I approached nearer, cultivated fields appeared. Only those who have seen the Azores from the deck of a vessel realize the beauty of the mid-ocean picture... At 4.30pm I cast anchor at Fayal... It was the season for fruit when I arrived at the Azores, and there was soon more of all kinds of it put on board than I knew what to do with. Islanders are always the kindest people in the world, and I met none anywhere kinder than the good hearts of this place... I remained four days at Fayal, and that was two days more than I had intended to stay.'

In the same year that Slocum visited Faial the islands were granted limited autonomy, though no real economic independence – Slocum remarks how all mail had to go via Lisbon, even if the vessel carrying it put in at the Azores. By 1900 the population was reckoned to stand at just over a quarter of a million,

Paved pedestrian streets add to the relaxed atmosphere in Velas, São Jorge

the vast majority of whom were poor and uneducated, much as in Portugal itself. When the monarchy was overthrown in 1910 and the country became a republic little changed in the Azores throughout the long period of political instability before Dr Salazar took over, establishing a virtual dictatorship in 1932 with himself as head of a one-party state. During the First World War Portugal had remained neutral until 1916, when it joined the Allies and US naval bases were established in the islands.

A hint of the 20th century finally arrived in the Azores in the 1930s when American flying boats began to visit Horta en route for Europe. However, this can hardly have prepared the islanders for World War Two when, although Portugal again remained neutral, the strategic importance of the Azores was felt to be such that both Britain and the United States considered annexing them. Finally Portugal broke off diplomatic relations with Germany and allowed the Allies to build air bases in Santa Maria and Terceira, while British naval units fighting the Battle of the Atlantic used Horta as a base from 1943 until 1945. After the War Portugal became a founder member of NATO, enabling the US Air Force to retain their air base in Terceira, sharing runway facilities with the Portuguese Air Force and civilian airlines. The airport at Santa Maria was handed over to the Azores shortly after hostilities ended. Hopes that the airports might lead to increased agricultural exports proved optimistic, with air freight too expensive for bulk crops although such exotic items as São Miguel pineapples began to be sent abroad in increasing numbers. However, it has ruefully been said that the Azores' greatest export is people – more than 100,000 emigrated to the US alone in the first half of the 20th century, leaving approximately 320,000 islanders by 1950, nearly half of them in São Miguel. Of these another 74,000 left for the US and Canada during the 1960s, though many still send money back to relatives and some eventually return to settle, giving a much-needed boost to the local economy and particularly the building trade.

Portugal's right-wing dictatorship was finally overthrown in the 'Carnation Revolution' of 25 April 1974, which led to the Socialists gaining power. In the Constitution of April 1976 the Azores became an autonomous region with their own assembly and regional government, at the same time sending five members to the Portuguese parliament in Lisbon. An attractive flag was designed – which most visiting yachts fly together with their Portuguese courtesy ensign – and since 1980 the islands have issued their own stamps. There are still occasional demands for total independence, voiced by the *Frente de Libertação dos Açôres* amongst others, but it is difficult to see how the islands' economy could support such a move.

Perhaps the most obvious physical changes apparent to visiting yachtsmen are the many new or extended breakwaters which have turned dubious inlets into viable anchorages – often funded at least partially by EU grants. Also, after an apparently slow realisation of the economic benefits conferred by visiting yachts – not just in terms of marina fees, but in increased business to local shops, restaurants, taxi firms and even the local airline – by 2010 there were eight functioning marinas, with another nearing completion and several more at the planning stage. How many of the latter will come to fruition remains to be seen – it is, after all, less than 30 years since the islands' very first marina opened for business in Horta – and in any case not all yachtsmen will consider this a change for the better, but either way, there seems little doubt that the islands will retain their position as one of those magical destinations remembered with nostalgia and affection wherever ocean-going sailors gather.

Natural history

The banks surrounding the Azores are rich in marine life of all kinds, and many of the world's game fishing records are held from the islands. Of more interest to yachtsmen are likely to be the seabirds, mammals and other surface creatures which are sometimes to be seen.

Seabirds

Relatively few species of seabirds are common in Azorean waters, but amongst the most numerous are the common tern, herring gull, Cory's, Manx and little shearwaters, Wilson's, British, Madeiran and white-faced storm petrels, and the larger Bulwer's petrel.

Common tern (*Sterna hirundo*)
(Portuguese: *Garajau comum*)
Length 36cm. *Wingspan* 80cm.
Recognition Light grey with glossy back cap and wingtips. Long forked tail. Scarlet bill with dark tip, legs and feet also scarlet.
Call A drawn out 'kee-argh' or rapidly repeated 'kirri-kirri-kirri'.
Habits Gregarious. Breeds in colonies in open areas on coastal beaches and islands.

Roseate tern (*Sterna dougalli*)
(Portuguese: *Garajau rosado*)
Length 39cm. *Wingspan* 78cm.
Recognition Visually very similar to the common tern, but a lighter shade of grey and, during the breeding season (April to September), has a longer tail. A subtle rosy hue on the breast is distinctive and gives the tern its name. Bill black in early spring, gradually becoming red toward the tip, until by July it is much like that of the common tern (from August both species' bills begin to turn black). If seen with the common tern appears much more delicate and elegant.
Call A raspy 'ka-a-ak' and soft 'chivy'.
Habits Gregarious. Breeds in colonies among rocks or low vegetation on some of the smaller islets surrounding the main islands, especially Terceira, Santa Maria and Flores.

Common gull (*Larus canus*)
Length 40cm. *Wingspan* 100 cm.
Recognition Light grey or white above and below, with black and white tips to flight feathers. Bill and legs greenish yellow.

The endangered roseate tern nests, along with the common tern, on some of the smaller islets surrounding the main islands, especially Terceira, Santa Maria and Flores. Both species may be seen diving for fish miles away from the islands.
Researchers collect information on their whereabouts from October to March. Individuals ringed in the Azores in May and June have been found along the coasts of Bahía, Brazil and western Africa.
Matt and Grace Cormons

Call A strident 'kyou' and high 'gah-gah-gah'.
Habits Gregarious. Breeds on hillsides, islands and rough ground. Follows ships and fishing boats, but seldom yachts.

Cory's shearwater (*Calonectris diomedea*)
(Portuguese: *Cagarro*)
Length 49cm. *Wingspan* 111cm.
Recognition Greyish brown head, back and upper wing, largely white below with dark wingtips. Dull yellow bill, legs and feet pink. The largest of the Azorean shearwaters.
Flight Strong and purposeful but relaxed, with distinctly bowed wings. Several deep wing beats followed by a long glide.
Call Generally silent at sea, but loud and slightly irritable 'kaa-ouf', 'kik-kik-kik', 'ah-kee-kee-kee' or other variations on returning to breeding and nesting areas around dusk (as those who spend an evening in the anchorage at Velas, São Jorge will discover). Has been likened to a couple of old ladies having an argument…
Habits Follows ships and trawlers, sometimes circles yachts.

Manx shearwater (*Puffinus puffinus*)
Length 34cm. *Wingspan* 82cm.
Recognition Head, back, upper wing and upper tail black or brownish black. Chin, throat (extending upwards on sides of neck) and underside of body, wings and tail white. Bill black, legs and feet pink with black markings.
Flight Rapid, stiff shallow strokes followed by a low glide, banking to follow wave contours.
Habits Gregarious, often congregates offshore in late afternoon or evening.

Little shearwater (*Puffinus assimilis*)
Length 27cm. *Wingspan* 62cm.
Recognition Resembles a small Manx shearwater, with shorter wings and more white on the face. Brownish upper parts, wingtips and under tail, otherwise white. Black bill, legs and feet greyish blue.
Flight Four to six fast shallow wing beats followed by a short low glide. Feeds via shallow surface dives.
Habits Often follows ships, and sometimes yachts.

Wilson's storm petrel (*Oceanites oceanicus*)
Length 17cm. *Wingspan* 40cm.
Recognition Generally sooty brown, with lighter bands extending onto the wings. Extensive white area over rump, almost meeting underneath. Bill black, legs and feet yellow.
Flight Purposeful, with fast shallow wing beats. Skips over the surface when feeding, wings held vertically over back and feet trailing.
Habits Gregarious – flocks may reach several thousands. Readily follows ships, trawlers and yachts.

British storm petrel (*Hydrobates pelagicus*)
Length 15cm. *Wingspan* 37cm.
Recognition Smallest and darkest of the Atlantic

A fin whale, one of the many species of cetaceans to be seen in the Azores *Tony Gooch*

storm petrels. Generally sooty-black with a narrow grey bar on upper wings, white rump and lower flanks, and distinctive white bar on under wings. Bill, legs and feet black.

Flight Weak and fluttering, somewhat bat-like, with almost continuous wing beats and occasional short glides. Feeds with wings raised midway over back and feet pattering on the surface.

Habits Follows ships and trawlers.

Madeiran petrel (*Pterodroma madeira*)

Length 20cm. *Wingspan* 43cm.

Recognition Similar in looks to the British storm petrel, but slightly larger and lacking a white band under the wings. The tail is longer and slimmer.

Flight Generally buoyant, with quick beats and low glides somewhat like a small shearwater.

Habits Shy at sea – doesn't follow ships.

White-faced storm petrel (*Pelagodroma marina*)

Length 20cm. *Wingspan* 42cm.

Recognition Much more white on the body than other storm petrels likely to be seen in the area, from a distance appearing brown above and white below. On closer view the distinctive patterned face and pale rump are visible. Black bill, and legs and feet, which trail behind the tail in flight.

Flight Weaving and erratic, with jerky rhythmic wing strokes. Strong and direct flight when feeding, dancing on the surface between short glides.

Habits Five to 15 birds often seen together. Rarely follows ships.

Bulwer's petrel (*Bulweria bulwerii*)

Length 26cm. *Wingspan* 67cm.

Recognition Larger than the storm petrels, with a noticeably broader wingspan. Sooty-brown all over with a black bill, and pink legs and feet. The tail is long and pointed.

Flight Erratic and twisting, very low above the waves.

Habits Does not generally follow ships.

Mammals – whales and dolphins

A wide variety of cetaceans (whales, dolphins and porpoises) inhabit or pass through Azorean waters, ranging from the vast fin whale at up to 24m to the common dolphin at around 2m. It is worth stressing that no yacht in the area has ever reported being threatened or damaged by whales, though they can react violently if startled by a yacht under sail and experienced whale-watchers suggest running the engine at low revs if a whale is nearby. Changes of engine speed should be made as gradually as possible, and reverse gear not engaged unless absolutely essential. Try to stay at least 100m behind all whales and avoid crossing in front of them or separating group members.

Dolphins seldom seem to be interested in a yacht unless it is travelling at reasonable speed, and will then sometimes play in the bow wave apparently as much for our entertainment as their own.

Best known amongst the whales and the most likely to be seen in the vicinity of the Azores is the sperm whale, which was hunted from most of the islands until a few decades ago. However fin whales migrate through the islands and are occasionally seen, as are the smaller bottlenosed, killer and pilot whales. More common are the five species of dolphin: the spotted or stenella dolphin, bottlenose dolphin, common or saddleback dolphin, striped dolphin and Risso's dolphin or grampus.

Whale and dolphin watching enterprises are now run from several of the islands, including Faial and São Miguel.

Sperm whale (*Physeter macrocephalus*)

Length up to 20m.

Months May–July, large males only, generally alone (15–20m). August–September, joined by females, some with paler calves (10–12m). Groups of up to 24 have been recorded in the Azores.

Recognition Dark grey/brown all over. Huge, blunt box-like head, small rounded or triangular dorsal hump well aft, and broad triangular tail flukes which are thrown into the air on starting a deep dive. Mature males can be identified by a more pronounced bulbous head.

Dive When feeding may dive for 40–60 minutes (and to nearly 3,000m), with usual recovery time on surface seven to 15 minutes. When recovering from a dive and preparing for the next they generally blow around five times per minute. Socialising groups may spend several hours on the surface.

Blow Low and bushy, pointing forward.

Food Mainly squid plus some fish.

Fin whale (*Balaenoptera physalus*)

Length up to 24m.

Months Migrates northwards in June, often in pods of three to seven animals.

Recognition Dark grey to brownish black on back and sides, often with grey chevron behind head. Underside, including under flippers and tail flukes white. Lower lip white on right side, greyish on left. The head forms a V shape, with ridged back and large dorsal fin. Often presents a wheel-like silhouette on surfacing, but doesn't show tail flukes on diving.

Blow A tall and impressive jet reaching 4–6m, shaped like a long inverted cone.

Bottlenose whale (*Hyperoodon ampullatus*)

Length up to 10m.

Recognition Chocolate brown on back, lighter on sides and belly. Pronounced dolphin-like beak and bulbous forehead, but much bigger than any dolphin. Hooked dorsal fin, well back. May show tail flukes on diving. Usually in groups of four to 10.

Dive May dive for more than an hour, spend 10 minutes on the surface and then dive again.

Blow Bushy and projecting slightly forward. Up to 2m.

Killer whale (*Orcinus orca*)

Length up to 9m.

Recognition Unmistakable due to its striking black and white colour (think of a magpie on the grand scale). Generally black above and white or cream below, with a white patch behind the eye running up the sides of the belly, and a light-coloured 'saddle' behind the dorsal fin. Fin tall (up to 1·8m) and black, V-shaped in males, more hooked in females. Blunt nose and large rounded flippers. Pods of three to 20. Rarely seen in the Azores.

Food Will hunt almost anything, often in packs, including larger whales, dolphins, fish, birds etc. Very occasionally turns its attention to a yacht but soon loses interest (though have been known to attack a liferaft).

Pilot whale (short-finned)
(*Globicephala macrorhynchus*)

Length up to 7m.

Recognition Slate grey to black, lighter on throat and belly. Head thick and flattened, with bulbous forehead but no beak. Dorsal fin long and low with a distinctive hook, well forward on body. Pods of five to 75, often together with bottlenosed dolphins.

Food Mainly squid.

Atlantic spotted dolphin (*Stenella frontalis*)

Length up to 2·3m.

Recognition Generally dark grey with lighter spots above, silver grey below, sometimes with darker spots. The Azores stenellas are much less spotted than the same species found in the Caribbean. Long slim beak with whitish lips. Dark dorsal fin about halfway back.

Habits Often in large herds of several hundred, sometimes mixed with other dolphins. Vigorous swimmer, able to make high leaps. Often plays around yachts.

Common or bottlenose dolphin
(*Tursiops truncatus*)

Length up to 4m.

Recognition Brown or grey above, with lighter sides fading into a light grey belly, occasionally with spots or stripes. Short stubby beak and tall hooked dorsal fin about halfway back.

Habits Usually in pods of 10 to 100 animals, occasionally more offshore. Appears to enjoy riding bow waves – will intercept yachts and also surf in breakers.

Short-beaked or saddleback dolphin
(*Delphinus delphis*)

Length up to 2·7m.

Recognition Slender, streamlined and elegant. Dark above with an 'hourglass' effect on the sides formed by buff or cream stripes on front part, grey or black 'saddle' below dark dorsal fin, and white or light grey stripe running aft. Long beak with black lips, white throat and belly.

Habits Herds of 50 to 500 or more. Plays in bow waves, an acrobatic and powerful swimmer.

Striped dolphin (*Stenella coeruleoalba*)

Length up to 3m.

Recognition Generally dark on back, light grey on sides with a white belly, plus a wide grey blaze running from eye towards flippers and dark stripes from eye back towards tail.

Habits Usually in herds of several hundred to several thousand. Very active swimmer, often leaping clear of the water, riding bow waves etc.

Risso's dolphin or grampus (*Grampus griseus*)

Length up to 4m.

Recognition White or light grey with dark dorsal fin, flippers and tail flukes. Square blunt head with no beak. Tall hooked fin, often covered in whitish scars giving a generally battered appearance. May occasionally interbreed with common or bottlenose dolphins.

Habits Usually in herds of 10 to 20. Not very acrobatic, often just lies at the surface and seldom rides bow waves or takes an interest in yachts.

Both humpback and sei whales are also seen very occasionally on migration through the islands. The former can reach 17m, with a black or grey body, somewhat pointed nobbly head, very long white or greyish flippers, a distinct step in the dorsal fin, and broad or butterfly-shaped tail flukes very often with white patterns or scarring. The latter are very similar to fin whales but slightly smaller and with a single ridge down the head.

Other sightings which may add interest to a passage include turtles (most often the loggerhead, which may grow to 1·5m and can often be approached quite closely before it moves off), flying fish which use their surface skimming ability to evade predators (and make excellent eating when they land on deck), and various kinds of jellyfish. The latter are sometimes blown into harbours and onto beaches, and most sting to some degree.

Most dangerous of the jellyfish is the Portuguese man-of-war, so-called because of its pastel blue, pink or purple inflated 'sail' or float, and often to be seen during late summer by the dozen in all sizes from a few centimetres up to 30cm or more. Its long trailing tentacles can reach at least 4m in length and inflict a bad sting even after being detached from the body or when the animal is dead (wear gloves if recovering a fishing line or trailing log, as tentacles may adhere to it). If stung, bathe the area in alcohol – meths, gin or vodka will do if surgical alcohol is not available – not in water, which will make it worse. Medical attention should be sought if available following bad stings or if the victim is shocked.

Finally, although the Azores have no indigenous land mammals they do boast their own species of bat, the Azorean bat (*Nyctalus azoreum*), which is unusual in that it flies in daylight. Closely related to Leislers bat (*Nyctalus leisleri*), it is quite small at around 10–15cm and dark brown in colour. It has been positively identified on Faial, Pico and São Miguel and probably inhabits several of the other islands. It feeds from around midday until dusk, and is found in all habitats including over anchorages and over the sea close inshore.

General information

Nationality and language

The Azores are an autonomous region of Portugal and as such are part of the European Union. Portuguese is spoken with an accent which varies from island to island, with many Azoreans speaking French or English as a second language. Spanish is generally understood, though sometimes on sufferance (it is only 500 years since Spain invaded their country, and Portuguese memories are long).

Certain place names, including Praia (beach), Santa Cruz (Holy Cross) and Lajes (literally a paving stone, but in this case a flat lava shelf running out into the sea), are common throughout the Azores and could give rise to confusion if the island is not specified.

Portuguese representation abroad

Portuguese embassies and consulates

London: 11 Belgrave Square, London SW1X 8PP
☎ 020 7235 5331, 020 7291 3770
Fax 020 7245 1287, 020 7291 3799
Email london@portembassy.co.uk

Washington DC: 2012 Massachusetts Ave, Washington DC 20036
☎ 202 350 5400 *Fax* 202 462 3726
Email info@embassyportugal-us.org

Portuguese national tourist offices

London: 11 Belgrave Square, London SW1X 8PP
☎ 020 7201 6666 *Fax* 020 7201 6633
Email tourism.london@portugalglobal.pt
www.visitportugal.com

New York: 590 Fifth Avenue, 4th Floor, New York, NY 10036-4704 ☎ 800 767 8842, 646 723 0200, 646 723 0299
Email tourism@portugal.org, www.portugal.org

Diplomatic representation in the Azores

The following are consulates (embassies are to be found in Lisbon):

UK: British Honorary Consulate, Rua Domingos Rebelo 43A, 9500-234 Ponta Delgada, São Miguel ☎ 296 628175 *Fax* 296 628175
http://ukinportugal.fco.gov.uk/en

USA: Avenida Principe do Monaco, 6-2F, 9500-237 Ponta Delgada, São Miguel ☎ 296 282216
Fax 296 287216, www.usconsulateazores.pt/

Personal documentation

With the Azores the westernmost European Union border there is strong enforcement concerning visas and passports. Currently most EU nationals (including UK citizens) and those from the USA and Canada can visit for up to 90 days in a six-month period on a valid passport, no visa being required. Extensions are issued by the *Serviço de Estrangeiros* (Foreigner's Registration Service) which has a branch in most larger towns, or failing that by the local police.

Citizens of other states should inquire at a Portuguese embassy or consulate before departure.

Pets

There is no restriction on animals being allowed ashore from cruising yachts and there is believed to be no rabies in the islands, but all cruising pets should be inoculated and the certificates carried.

Those making a round tour should be aware that, although correctly 'chipped' and inoculated animals may enter Great Britain, Ireland or the Channel Islands through official entry channels, cruising pets are NOT admitted aboard yachts. For current regulations see the Pet Travel Scheme section at www.defra.gov.uk, the website of the UK's Department for Environment, Food and Rural Affairs.

Time

The Azores use UT –1, with local daylight saving (+1 hour) from late March until late October when the islands effectively revert to UT.

Money

Portugal, including the Azores, is part of the Eurozone. Most visitors rely on credit/debit cards, both for purchases and to withdraw cash – dispensers, often referred to as *Multibanco* – are widespread and accept all major cards. Most offer instructions in a choice of languages, including English.

Sterling, US dollars and other major currencies are readily exchangeable in banks, as are travellers cheques, but are less likely to be accepted by shops, hotels or restaurants. Banks normally open 0830–1500 weekdays only, though *Bureau de Change* offices may be open considerably longer hours, including all day Saturday.

Most restaurants, shops, car rental companies and other concerns welcome payment by credit card – principally Visa, MasterCard and American Express – but it is as well to confirm this in advance, particularly where fuel (for both yachts and vehicles) is concerned.

Shopping

Facilities for storing up have improved beyond all recognition since over the past few decades and it is difficult to think of any item – other than a few very local specialities – which would not be available in the large hypermarkets serving Horta, Angra do Heroísmo, Praia da Vitória and Ponta Delgada at prices comparable to those of mainland Europe. Shopping in other towns is necessarily more limited, and some indication will be found in the text for each harbour.

Regional specialities in the Azores include excellent cheese – traditionally from São Jorge and Pico though other islands, including Graciosa and Corvo, have now set up cheese factories – wine from Pico, Graciosa and Terceira, and pineapples from São Miguel. Superb plums, apricots, grapes and figs grow in nearly all the islands. Almost every town, together with many of the smaller villages, has a produce market selling fruit and vegetables which vary according to season.

Some notes regarding ships' stores – principally fuel, bottled gas and chandlery – will be found on page 28.

Communications

Mail

In theory all *Portos dos Açores* marinas are happy to hold mail for visiting yachts – though in practice it would be unwise to have anything important sent to either Lajes das Flores or Lajes do Pico as poor weather might well mean the yacht diverting elsewhere. So also are the Marina da Praia da Vitória, Terceira and, in Horta, both the Café Sport and Mid Atlantic Yacht Services. Few post offices (marked CTT or *correio*) now have *poste restante* counters and there have been reports of mail for foreign yachts being returned to sender, though doubtless this is not always the case. Incoming mail can be slow – up to a fortnight from the UK to the three islands with international airports, even longer to the more remote islands – though outgoing mail is usually much quicker. Finally, it is worth stressing that the word 'Portugal' should always be included on the envelope.

Post office opening hours vary, but stamps (*selos*) can also be bought at newsagents and souvenir shops where the green *correio* sign is seen, or from vending machines, which list current rates but do not give change. There are two classes of mail, *correio azul* and *correio normal* – effectively express and fairly slow – with the former also noticeably more reliable.

Incoming packages

Import problems may be encountered if ordering parts from outside the EU as dutiable goods usually require Customs intervention. If possible avoid using a courier service such as DHL, UPS, FedEx, TNT or the like – Customs will confiscate the goods at Lisbon airport, and getting duty and fees paid can be costly and time consuming. The addressee will also be expected to pay the forwarding costs to the Azores even though, as the original destination listed on the shipper's airway bill, this has already been paid for.

Importing goods from the USA to the Azores is best accomplished using the US Post Office and any of their overseas services – see www.usps.com/ for details. Packages sent this way normally transit Lisbon without hassle and clear through Azorean Customs in a day or two.

If in Horta and arranging the import of an essential item it would almost certainly be worth consulting Mid Atlantic Yacht Services – see page 56 – for advice.

Telephones

As in many countries, public telephones are seen as a lower priority with the widespread use of mobile (cell) phones. Even so, they are still to be found in most towns and details will be found under individual harbours. Not all, however, take coins, some requiring cards purchased from post offices, supermarkets and bars. Mobile (cell) phone coverage throughout the islands is generally excellent, with only a few 'holes' in the narrower mountain valleys and on the west coast of Flores.

Calls to the United Kingdom begin with the prefix 0044, followed by the area code (without the initial zero) and number. Calls to the United States and Canada begin with the prefix 001 and the area code plus number. The US access code for AT&T, www.att.com, is 800 800 128.

The international dialling code for Portugal, including the Azores, is 351. The islands share three area codes – 292 for Flores, Corvo and Faial, 295 for São Jorge, Graciosa and Terceira, and 296 for São Miguel and Santa Maria – the relevant numbers being included when dialing any landline number, even when calling from within the same island. Any telephone number not starting with one of these sequence can be assumed to be a mobile.

The costs incurred by using a mobile phone abroad are beyond the scope of this book, and individual phones may need 'unblocking' before they will work at all. If planning to spend some time in one country (remembering that the Azores and Madeira comprise a single entity in this context) it may be cheaper to buy a new phone or at least a new SIM card. The Portuguese have one of the highest rates of mobile phone – or *telemóvel* – ownership in Europe and most shops will have at least on salesman fluent in English.

Fax

Although declining in use with the ubiquity of email, most Azorean marinas will send and receive faxes for yachts – see individual harbours details. Many companies advertising photocopying also have a fax machine, as do most hotels.

Internet access

With email the communication method of choice for the majority of cruising sailors, free Wi-Fi is now available at or near all the archipelago's marinas, as well as in many town squares, libraries, etc. Mains power may not always be available, however, so reasonable battery life is essential. Cybercafés and other access points, some offering the use of computers, scanners, printers, etc. are also widespread – see individual harbours for details.

Electricity

Mains electricity is 220v 50Hz, as is standard throughout mainland Europe, and yachts from elsewhere should beware a probable difference in both volts and cycles. Mains power is provided in all the archipelago's marinas but is unlikely to be available elsewhere. 380v 3-phase current is available to yachts in some areas of Horta marina, including most of the south basin and parts of the north mole.

Transportation

International flights

Although all the islands have commercial airports, only Faial (Horta), Terceira (Lajes) and São Miguel (Ponta Delgada) receive regular international flights, handled either by TAP (*Transportes Aéreos Portugueses*) or SATA (*Sociedade Açôreana da Transportes Aérios*). Current timetables and fares will be found on their multilingual websites at www.flytap.com and www.sata.pt respectively. In summer it is possible to fly direct from the UK to Ponta Delgada with SATA, departing from Manchester on Saturday and Gatwick on Tuesday, but it may prove considerably cheaper to fly via Porto or Lisbon, generally possible without an overnight stop. SATA also runs regular schedules connecting Ponta Delgada with the US, Canada and eleven cities in mainland Europe, and Lajes with the US and Canada. If booking connections with inter-island flights it is important to remember that Azores time (UT –1) is one hour behind both UK and mainland Portuguese time (UT), irrespective of local summer time.

The airports at Horta and Ponta Delgada are both a short taxi ride from the harbour, whilst Lajes on Terceira is some 24km from Angra do Heroísmo but only 8km from Praia da Vitória. In July and August, when many expatriate Azoreans return to visit their relations, flights fill up early and it may be necessary to book well in advance.

Inter-island flights

SATA has for many years run the inter-island service and has offices at all the airports and in the larger towns. While it may be possible to get on a flight at short notice throughout most of the year, advance booking is generally necessary during the summer – and if a reserved ticket is being held until a stated time, be certain to redeem it by then or it is likely to be sold elsewhere. Current timetables and fares will be found at www.sata.pt.

Although SATA's booking procedures appear highly efficient the same cannot always be said of their luggage handling, and though items are seldom lost it is not unusual for checked-in bags to arrive up to 24 hours later than their owners. Be sure to pack overnight necessities (particularly medicines) in a carry-on bag. Do not worry unduly, however, as the errant luggage will almost certainly turn up next day, and may well be delivered to the marina by taxi.

If booking connections with international flights it is important to remember that Azores time (UT –1) is one hour behind both UK and mainland Portuguese time (UT), irrespective of local summer time.

Ferries

The Azores are served by two ferry companies, Atlânticoline and Transmacor. The former links all nine islands with their three ferries, which range from *Arial*, which carries twelve foot passengers between Flores and Corvo, to the 650 or so people plus cars carried by the *Santorini* and *Hellenic Wind*. See www.atlanticoline.pt, in Portuguese and English, for current timetable and fares.

The much smaller Transmacor (*Transportes Marítimos Açorianos Lda*) runs a frequent service between Faial, Pico and São Jorge. Again, timetables and fares will be found on their website at www.transmacor.pt, though as of early 2011 this was available in Portuguese only, the English version at www.transmacor.com having disappeared off the net.

Road transport

Cars can be hired on all the islands other than Corvo, though some of the roads may give pause for thought. The standard of driving in mainland Portugal leaves a great deal to be desired, and though driving on Azorean roads is generally much less fraught a good watch needs to be kept for suicidal quad-bikers who sometimes appear to forget the difference between roads and open fields. Azoreans also follow the mainland tradition of 'free range' parking and view blind bends, the brows of hills and even roundabouts as acceptable places to leave a car.

All car hire firms accept major credit cards and will require a credit (not debit) card number to be left as 'deposit', and most will encourage the hirer to take out further insurance beyond the CDW (collision damage waiver) which is normally included. Minor – but expensive – scrapes are relatively commonplace so this may be wise, though if hiring frequently it may prove more economic to take out annual car hire insurance. Either national or international drivers' licences are accepted, provided the former has been held for at least one year, and note that it is a legal requirement to carry one's passport and driving licence at all times when at the wheel. The majority of filling stations have attendant service, but even in the 21st century some still do not accept credit cards.

There are bus services on all the islands other than Corvo – where most things are within walking distance – and fares are generally cheap. However, being intended primarily for local people, they tend to run into town in the morning and back in the afternoon, the opposite of what the visitor wants, but it is generally possible to see something of the countryside if not around the whole island. Tourist

Further information

It took a surprisingly long time for the Azores to become the subject of a tourist guide, but David Sayers *Azores – the Brandt Travel Guide*, now in its 4th edition, fills the gap admirably and is a worthy addition to any cruising yacht's bookshelf. Walkers will also find *Azores* by Andreas Stieglitz in the *Sunflower Landscapes* series, currently in its 5th edition, invaluable.

Once in the islands, a variety of booklets are available from local tourist offices. *The Azores Guide for Tourists*, published annually since 1981 by Publiçor Lda, and the more recent *destinazores* guide both cover all the islands, containing a useful mixture of information, advertisements and photographs, plus maps of all the islands and plans of the bigger towns. Both are available free from tourist offices and, sometimes, supermarket checkouts. The *Guide to the Island of* ... series (one for each island, ranging from ten pages for Corvo to 94 pages for São Miguel) produced by the Direcção Regional de Turismo dos Açores can be bought individually at the tourist office in Ponta Delgada, though well worth the modest €12 or so charged for the entire set. The Tourist Office has also compiled free walkers' guides to a number of the islands in the *Trilhos Turísticos nos Açores* (Nature Trails in the Azores) series. Most of the above are available in several languages and it is worth checking that one has picked up the correct one. Others are multilingual within a single publication.

The Azores are well represented on the internet and the following sites (listed alphabetically) contain general information, some of which may be useful to the visiting yachtsman. Websites specific to each island or harbour are listed in the introduction to the relevant island.

www.acorestube.com – some great (and some not so great) video on a variety of subjects. Commentaries in Portuguese, though titles are in English, but most speak for themselves

www.andreas-stieglitz.de/ – homepage of the author of *Azores* in the *Sunflower Landscapes* series. Current information on the Azores and walking areas, in German only

www.atlanticoline.pt – website of Atlânticoline which, in summer at least, links all the Azorean islands with its three (very different) ferries. In Portuguese and English. See page 23 for further details

www.azoren.at – a beautiful, well-constructed site full of stunning photos, currently in German only

www.azores.com – a commercial site selling property and holidays in the islands, but also offering a great deal of detailed information on each individual island. In Portuguese and English

www.azores.dk – a private site devoted to the islands, with a mix of information and photographs, compiled by a regular visitor to the islands over the past 21 years. In Portuguese, English and Danish

www.azores.gov.pt – exactly what it says – the homepage of the Azorean Regional Government, in Portuguese only

www.azores-islands.info – run by Strawberry World, this site describes itself as 'the Azores' biggest holiday destination guide'. Whether or not that's true, it does contain some interesting information backed up by photos and maps. In Portuguese, English and Spanish

www.azoresrural.com – a commercial site promoting rural tourism throughout the islands, but containing much more than just accommodation details. In Portuguese and English

www.birdingazores.com/ – compiled by Steffan Rodebrand and The Birding Azores Team, who point out that 'the archipelago has become a popular destination for European birdwatchers in recent years'. Their site is enough to have anyone reaching for their binoculars – fascinating!

www.climaat.angra.uac.pt – features webcams showing not just the weather at a dozen places in the islands – Lajes das Flores, Corvo, Horta, Lajes do Pico, São Roque do Pico, Velas, Santa Cruz da Graciosa, Angra do Heroísmo, Praia da Vitória, Biscoitos (Terceira), Ponta Delgada and Vila do Porto (Santa Maria) – but in several cases the current state of harbour works or even whether berths are free! Other parts of the site repay investigation despite being in Portuguese only

www.destinazores.com – a model site covering all the islands (with downloadable PDF maps) and many topics of interest, in Portuguese and English, by the publishers of the *destinazores* guide mentioned above. Highly recommended, as it was in the previous edition of this book

www.drtacores.pt / www.visitazores.org – the homepage of the Azores Department of Tourism, in Portuguese and English. Includes travel details, a calendar of events, and an overview of each island

www.en.wikipedia.org/wiki/Azores – Wikipedia does its usual excellent job, with vast amounts of background material and related sites covering each of the individual islands ... even the Ilhéus das Formigas. If only this had existed when I started research on the first edition in 1987!

www.flytap.com – homepage of TAP (*Transportes Aéreos Portugueses*), Portugal's national airline. In Portuguese and English. See page 23 for further details

www.galenfrysinger.com – subtitled 'People and Places of the World' (once you get past the advertising-dominated homepage) and giving access to literally thousands of (undated) pictures, most with short but informative captions

www.galeriacores.pt.vu – ignore the homepage and click the Photos tab at right to access a vast collection of photos of all the islands, with the accent on Graciosa

www.geocities.com/giovannitosti/islands/Azores.htm – a non-commercial site featuring information and photographs of six of the nine islands (part of a larger site), in English only. Although apparently not updated since April 2006, much of the information is still relevant

www.hidrografico.pt – website of the Portuguese *Instituto Hidrográfico*, with details of charts, lights etc. In Portuguese only, but relatively easy to follow

www.library.csustan.edu/bsantos/azorean.html#3-33 – an authoritative site compiled by Robert L Santos, Librarian/Archivist at California State University, Stanislaus, detailing Azorean immigration, both from mainland Europe to the islands and then (often) onward to the United States

www.marinasazores.com – website of the branch of Portos dos Açores SA concerned with marina operation, in English, Portuguese and French. News and links as well as prices and facilities, plus some attractive photos

www.meteo.pt – the website of Portugal's *Instituto de Meteorologia*, which provides immediate, five-day and 10-day weather forecasts (and much more besides) for six cities across the archipelago, in Portuguese and English. In early 2011 'Marine Meteorology' pages were under construction

www.pierre.inazores.com – although headed 'Pierre Sousa Lima Motopage' the 'Azores' heading gives access to family-compiled pages containing information about and photos of all the islands

www.reocities.com/TheTropics/4338/ana.html – part of the website of the Sousa Lima family of São Miguel, this well-designed and entertaining section (in English and Portuguese) features Ana Taveira Lima's collection of Azorean recipes, including traditional Christmas, Easter and festival dishes, plus regional wines. Yum!

www.sata.pt – homepage of SATA (*Sociedade Açôreana da Transportes Aérios*) the archipelago's own airline, which started small but now offers services to destinations including the US and Canada, the UK and many cities in mainland Europe. In Portuguese and English. See page 23 for further details

www.semanadomar.net – website of Horta's famous Sea Week – see page 53 – in Portuguese only, but readily translated by Google translate or similar

www.theazores.net/ – cheerful, quirky site with a mixture of quotations, information, photographs and graphics. Quite limited as of early 2011, but with room for growth

www.transmacor.pt – website of Transmacor (*Transportes Marítimos Açorianos Lda*), which links Faial to Pico and São Jorge. In early 2011 it was available in Portuguese only, the English version at www.transmacor.com having disappeared off the net. See page 23 for further details

www.travel-images.com – hundreds of downloadable pictures of the Azores, but with little accompanying text

www.whalewatchazores.com/ – Whale Watch Azores has been in business since the early 1990s and in addition to pushing their whale watching trips there's also much information about the cetaceans they watch and research in progress. Great photos, of course

offices have bus schedules, which are seldom on display at bus stops (marked *Paragem* or *Paragem de Autocarro*).

Taxis are available almost everywhere. A taxi tour is an excellent way to see any of the islands, and there are many knowledgeable, English-speaking drivers whose commentary will add much to the interest. There are set tariffs for frequently-used routes, but as many taxis do not have automatic tariff counters the fare for a longer trip should be agreed in advance.

Walking and hitchhiking

There are many superb walks in the Azores along both footpaths and made-up roads, enabling the visitor to see a degree of detail missed by faster forms of transport. However, some of the most spectacular viewpoints are at the top of long, steep hills, when a taxi up and a downhill stroll may combine the best of both worlds. An alternative is to hitchhike – local people are generous in offering rides, though larger parties may have to be content with the back of a farm truck. A copy of *Azores* by Andreas Stieglitz in the *Sunflower Landscapes* series (www.sunflowerbooks.co.uk) will add to the enjoyment.

Medical

The only immunisation required is against yellow fever if coming from certain Central American and African countries, though many yachtsmen will also choose to keep vaccinations against tetanus and polio up to date. Medical facilities in the Azores are good, with at least one hospital on every island other than Corvo and no shortage of doctors and dentists (and veterinary surgeons) in all the larger towns. Many of those with medical training speak English, often fluently. Pharmacies abound, and usually appear to have good stocks of both non-prescription medicines and general items such as suntan creams and shampoo, often under familiar brand names. There are opticians in the larger towns, and wearers of glasses would be wise to carry a copy of their prescription (in addition to at least one reserve pair).

Consider taking out medical insurance, and if an EU citizen apply for a free EHIC (European Health Insurance Card) via www.ehic.org.uk. This covers the costs of medical treatment needed following illness or accident, though it may not be as comprehensive as would be the case in the UK and some contribution may be necessary. Neither does it cover the cost of repatriation, should that become necessary.

Needless to say, anyone with a chronic or recurring condition should take a good supply of medication with them even though, unlike its precursor the E111, the EHIC does cover the cost of treatment for a pre-existing condition. Every cruising yacht should, of course, carry a comprehensive first aid kit with instructions for its use.

National holidays

These are much the same as in mainland Portugal:

1 January	New Year's Day
moveable	Good Friday
25 April	National or Portugal Day
1 May	Labour Day
moveable	Corpus Christi
10 June	Portugal Day (Camões Day)
15 August	Feast of the Assumption
5 October	Republic Day
1 November	All Saints' Day
1 December	Restoration of Independence Day
8 December	Immaculate Conception
25 December	Christmas Day

In addition each island, town or area celebrates its own municipal holiday, and dates of these are given in the text. Almost everything except cafés and restaurants is likely to be shut, but there may be the bonus of a *festa* (festival) with processions, displays of Azorean folk dancing and singing, or perhaps one of the ever-popular firework displays.

Local festivals, such as the *Sanjoaninas* festivities at Angra de Heroísmo in Terceira during the third week of June, can lead to serious congestion in marinas and anchorages. If planning to attend it is wise to arrive several days in advance.

Creating decorations along a road in São Jorge, the route of a forthcoming religious procession (see page 71)

Sailing and navigation

Practicalities

Entry and regulations

The Q flag should be flown on arrival from outside the European Union, together with a Portuguese courtesy flag and, preferably, the archipelago's own flag – see the beginning of this section.

Despite Portugal having been a member of the EU since 1986, and the total lack of any overland border controls on the mainland, those arriving in or cruising the Azores by yacht can face some of the most irritating bureaucracy in western Europe. In addition to visiting the marina office with the usual ship's papers, passports and evidence of insurance, it is also necessary to clear into and out of each individual island with some or all of a bewildering array of officials – the *Serviço de Estrangeiros e Fronteiras* or *SEF* (Immigration), the *Alfândega* (Customs), the *Polícia Marítima* (the maritime police, who also have some coastguard duties), and the *Guarda Nacional Republicana* or *GNR* (effectively the local police). In most marinas the job is simplified by the necessary paperwork being copied to whichever officials wish to see it, who may then choose to visit a yacht or to call the skipper to their office. In other harbours it is still necessary to visit multiple offices, particularly in the case of a non-EU registered yacht, and some walking may be involved. Procedures differ from island to island, and though an effort has been made to describe these in the text, the best recourse must always be to ask the marina officials about local requirements.

In harbours with no marina the *Polícia Marítima* and/or *Guarda Nacional Republicana* are still likely to have a presence, though little English may be spoken. It may be helpful in this situation if a copy of the computer printout from one of the *Portos dos Açores* marinas is retained, as it carries answers to the standard questions and so pre-empts potential language difficulties. Alternatively, the *Yachtsman's Ten Language Dictionary* devotes several pages to Formalities.

Outward clearance – usually required between islands, and occasionally between harbours – generally involves revisiting the same officials. Not all work at weekends, and it may be possible to arrange inward and outward clearance in a single visit. If outward clearance, valid for 24 hours, has been obtained and then the passage is aborted after departure and the yacht returns to harbour even for a few hours, it will technically be necessary to re-obtain clearance – even when the second departure falls within the original 24 hours.

Finally, confusion frequently arises between the EU and the Schengen Area, which are not the same. Despite being members of the EU the UK and Ireland have never signed the Schengen Agreement, whereas a few countries, including Norway and Iceland, which are not EU members, are signatories (the same is true of Switzerland, but it is difficult to sail directly from Lake Geneva). This only affect yachts making landfall on Corvo, Graciosa or Santa Maria, which are not official 'border posts' under the Schengen Agreement. It is therefore not possible to clear into the Schengen Area at these islands, though a few days' rest before continuing to an 'official' port of entry is likely to be tolerated.

International Certificate of Competence

Portugal – and by extension the Azores – is among the European countries which in theory requires that visiting skippers carry an *International Certificate of Competence*. Though it is seldom inspected, lack of one could be a problem in the event of an accident or insurance claim. In the UK the ICC is administered by the Royal Yachting Association (www.rya.org.uk) at a cost of £40 (free to RYA members). An examination may have to be taken if an equivalent certificate is not already held.

Port limits

Formal port limits have been set up around many harbours in the Azores, inside which various local bye-laws may apply. Scuba diving is forbidden within these areas on security grounds, although swimming and snorkelling is generally permitted. If wishing to scuba dive – perhaps to check the yacht's hull or propeller – it is essential to seek permission from the authorities first. Limits for individual harbours are given in the text where known.

Marina fees (*Portos dos Açores SA* only)

All Azorean marinas other than those at Praia da Vitória (Terceira) and Vila Franca do Campo (São Miguel) are the responsibility of *Portos dos Açores SA*, as are all commercial and fishing harbours. The marinas at Praia da Vitória and Vila Franca do Campo each belong to their local *Câmara Municipal* (town or city council), as will the marina planned for Cais da Barra in Graciosa.

In 2011 the overnight berthing fees for visiting yachts of normal beam were standard throughout all six – soon to be seven – marinas administered by *Portos dos Açores SA*. They stood at €8.44 for yachts of 8–10m, €10.18 for 10–12m, €15.42 for 12–15m, €21.34 for 15–18m and €32.71 for 18-25m, which included water and electricity but not showers. Both IVA (VAT) at 16% and a 4% 'residue' charge (basically to pay for garbage disposal) were levied on the basic fees, bringing them up to €10.13, €12.22, €18.50, €25.61 and €39.25 respectively. Multihulls paid a 50% surcharge and discounts were available for longer stays. Visa and MasterCard were both accepted, but enquire on arrival if wishing to use another one.

Further information on *Portos dos Açores SA* tarifs, including charges for lifting and storage ashore etc., will be found at www.marinasazores.com, the website of the part of the company concerned with marina operation. Note, however, that different charges apply to yachts owned by residents and by non-residents.

For information about fees at Praia da Vitória and Vila Franca do Campo see pages 102 and 117 respectively.

Laying up

There are a growing number of harbours in the Azores with facilities to haul a yacht, though few have sufficient hardstanding for yachts to be stored ashore long-term. As of early 2011 there were travel-lifts equipped to lift yachts at Horta (20-tonne capacity), Angra do Heroísmo (50-tonne), Praia da Vitória (35-tonne) and Ponta Delgada (25-tonne). In addition Lajes das Flores had a 20-tonne harbour crane, the fishing harbour at Vila Franca do Campo on São Miguel boasted a 75-tonne travel-lift, and another of similar size (in order to lift fishing boats as well as yachts) is expected to be delivered to Vila do Porto Marina on Santa Maria in 2011. This latter will be a particularly welcome development, as it is backed up by generous hardstanding.

As of 2010 more foreign yachts laid up ashore at Praia da Vitória, Terceira than at all the other marinas combined, due not least to a combination of competent staff and excellent prices. Angra do Heroísmo also has an area of securely gated hard-standing, but both Horta and Ponta Delgada, despite having the largest marinas in the archipelago, having barely enough space to haul local boats, let alone visitors.

The prospects for laying up afloat are much better, with yachts regularly wintering in Horta and in Ponta Delgada's east marina, either unoccupied or with liveaboard crew. Smaller numbers overwinter in Angra do Heroísmo and Praia da Vitória, while Vila do Porto in Santa Maria has great appeal, though slightly more remote in terms of international travel. The Azores can and do suffer severe winter gales and it would be wise to organise *guardinage* (regular checking of lines, fenders and possibly battery state), but a well-secured yacht should encounter no more problems than if wintering in a British marina.

Owners of yachts registered outside the EU should note that no exemptions are made to the 18-month VAT limit (see below). The clock CANNOT be stopped while laid-up either ashore or afloat as it can be in some EU countries.

Value Added Tax (*Imposto sobre o Valor Acrescentado*, or IVA)

Value Added Tax, commonly referred to as VAT, is known in Portuguese as *Imposto sobre o Valor Acrescentado* (IVA). The Azores enjoy a reduced rate, which on 1 January 2011 increased from 15% to 16% on most items, as against 23% in mainland Portugal. Food, water, electricity, pharmacy items and – a little oddly – wine and restaurant meals are all taxed at a lower rate.

A boat registered in the EU and on which VAT has been paid, or which was launched before 1 January 1985 (and can be proved to have been inside the EU on 31 December 1992) and is therefore exempt on grounds of age, can stay indefinitely in any other EU country without further VAT liability. Evidence of status may occasionally be required – consult UK Customs and Excise on ✆ 0845 010 9000 or visit www.hmce.gov.uk (follow the link to forms, and then type 'yachts' into the search box).

The time limit for which 'Relief from Customs Duty and VAT' is available to non-EU registered yachts visiting the EU is now 18 months, while the length of time for which the yacht has to remain outside the EU before beginning a new 18 month period has never been specified. If VAT has not been paid the vessel may only be used by her owner and may not be chartered or even lent to anyone else.

If wishing to import a yacht into the EU, the Azores are a favourable venue in which to do so due to their 'concessionary' VAT rate of 16%, as against the 23% levied in mainland Portugal or 20% in the UK. It would, in theory, be possible to carry out the procedure oneself, but considerable time and a good knowledge of Portuguese would be required. Several companies, including Mid Atlantic Yacht Services in Horta – see page 56 – will assist with all the formalities involved in EU yacht importation. Contacting them at least six weeks before departure for the Azores will help streamline the process, which may then be achievable within five working days after reaching Horta, particularly if email is checked regularly whilst at sea. Alternatively Bensaude Shipping Agents Lda, ✆ 292 293031/33, *Fax* 292 292940, www.shipping.bensaude.pt, although primarily concerned with larger vessels, also handles VAT and importation through their offices in Horta, Praia da Vitória and Ponta Delgada.

'Long-stay' tax (*Imposto Unico de Circulação*)

Yachts which remain in Portuguese waters for more than 183 days in a calendar year, whether local or foreign-registered and afloat or ashore, may be liable to pay a tax known as *Imposto Unico de Circulação* (IUC). It is calculated according to engine capacity, with full exemption for vessels with engines of less than 20kw (26·8hp) and those registered before 1986. In 2011 the tax was set at €2.17 per kw. As 1hp equals 0·7457kw, this equates to €1.62 per hp.

It is the responsibility of the owner to notify the local *Finanças* (tax authorities), though a marina is legally obliged to supply a list of contracted berth holders to the authorities if requested. Payment of all Portuguese taxes is complicated, requiring a *Número de Contribuinte* (*Número Fiscal*), which cannot be obtained without a permanent address within the country. If intending to stay long-term it would be worth discussing the situation with the marina authorities who may be able to recommend a local lawyer or accountant willing to stand as 'Fiscal Representative'.

Note, however, that yachts which spend more than 183 days in the country spread over two calendar years – perhaps cruising the Azores from mid-July and then wintering in Madeira until the following May – are not liable. Ensure that initial clearance documents are retained should it be necessary to establish one's arrival date.

Lighthouse tax (*Taxa de Farolagem e Balizagem*)

In theory all yachts, including visitors, are liable to pay lighthouse tax. This is currently set at €2 for six months irrespective of the size of yacht, and is collected by the *Polícia Marítima*, usually from an office within the *Capitania*. In practice it does not appear to be actively collected in any of the islands other than Flores and Santa Maria, but if it has already been paid in mainland Portugal it would be worth retaining the receipt.

Ships' stores

As of mid 2011 the marinas at Horta (Faial), Velas (São Jorge), Angra do Heroísmo (Terceira) and Ponta Delgada (São Miguel), had fuelling berths where diesel (*gasóleo*, pronounced *gas-OH-leo*) and petrol (*gasolina*, pronounced *gas-ol-EE-na*) could be pumped directly into a yacht's tank. At the first two payment had to be made in cash, even for large quantities, as it still has to be at some roadside filling stations.

Where pumps were not installed diesel could sometimes be supplied by road tanker, as at Lajes das Flores, Lajes do Pico and Praia da Vitória (Terceira). However this could take several days to arrange and in most cases a minimum quantity (possibly shared between several yachts) was stipulated. Elsewhere it was a case of carrying cans from the nearest filling station, or preferably delaying refuelling until one reached somewhere more convenient. In both Horta and Ponta Delgada megayachts could be fuelled in their berths by road tanker, and in the former if more than 10,000 litres (about 2,250 UK gallons/2,800 US gallons) were required Mid Atlantic Yacht Services could arrange for it to be supplied duty free – see page 57.

If buying fuel at a filling station it is worth paying particular attention to pronunciation, as if the stress falls on the final vowels of *gasóleo* a Portuguese-speaker may well hear it as *gasolina*, with disastrous consequences. Confusion can also arise with paraffin or kerosene (*petróleo*, pronounced *petr-OH-leo*, though both *parafina* and *querosene* are likely to be understood) though less potentially dangerous than if the situation were reversed. Paraffin is available in two grades – poor quality from some filling stations (suitable for cleaning machinery but not for lamps or stoves) and a more expensive grade from chemists which burns well. Methylated spirits is *álcool metílico* (pronounced *AL-cool met-IL-ico*) and surgical spirits is *álcool etílico* (pronounced *AL-cool et-IL-ico*).

Most makes of gas cylinder can be refilled, with butane only, in Horta, Terceira (both marinas) and Ponta Delgada – see under individual harbour facilities. Camping Gaz exchanges are available on the same three islands and also in Santa Maria, but elsewhere only local bottles are on offer. Allow at least two working days though turnaround may often be quicker. Propane is not available, but no safety risk is incurred by refilling propane bottles with butane.

General chandlery is in short supply throughout the Azores other than in Horta and Ponta Delgada, though resources on Terceira are fast improving – see under individual harbour facilities. Due to transportation costs, prices tend to be high. Elsewhere some chandlery is to be found in both Lajes das Flores and Vila do Porto in Santa Maria, but almost nothing on the other islands. Good English is spoken in all the larger chandleries, where catalogues facilitate ordering specific items from suppliers in Europe or further afield. No duty is payable on spares or equipment ordered from within the EU, but importing parts from elsewhere (including the US) can be a lengthy process involving a variable import duty (usually 6–12%) plus administrative and handling charges – see Incoming packages, page 22.

Cruising

The Azores have been a favourite port of call for cruising yachtsmen since Joshua Slocum visited in 1895, but have only recently become a cruising ground in their own right. The busiest time for transients is May and June, when both Horta and Ponta Delgada marinas are likely to be busy. By July the crowds are beginning to thin out, and this is an ideal time for yachts based in northern Europe to cruise the islands, making their passage home across Biscay in August ahead of the autumn gales.

Summer temperatures are very pleasant – hot but seldom excessively hot – averaging 19°C in June rising to 23°C in August, though daily temperatures can occasionally reach 30°C for weeks at a time. Rainfall varies from island to island, much more falling in high areas than on the lower islands or at sea, but showers have a habit of appearing without warning when least appreciated. However, whole days of rain are rare in midsummer, the 'rainy season' occurring in September and October.

Fishing boats on the hard at Vila Franca do Campo, São Miguel

The nine islands are spread over a distance of almost 300M in longitude and 170M in latitude. Other than the passage from Flores or Corvo towards Faial or others of the central group and, for all but the fastest yachts, Faial to Terceira and Terceira to São Miguel, it is generally possible to leave and to arrive in daylight. All four of the islands' older marinas can, however, be approached at night with confidence, while both Velas (São Jorge) and Vila do Porto (Santa Maria) are perfectly viable in darkness if winds are light. The same should be true of Lajes das Flores, though many will prefer to drop a hook until daylight. Only Lajes do Pico and Vila do Porto should not be attempted in darkness.

Barometric pressure and winds

The sailing season in the Azores is at its best from June to the middle of September, by which time all but the largest yachts should have left to head east or southeast. Yachts leaving for the UK or northern Europe would be well advised to leave by mid August at the latest. Those intending to remain in the Azores outside these months must be prepared for sudden and drastic changes in weather conditions as the path of the North Atlantic depressions moves south during late autumn and winter.

During the summer the climate is governed to a great extent by the activity and strength of the Azores High. When this is strong and well established – with the barometer reading 1030mb or more – there may be days or even weeks of almost flat calm relieved by gentle land and sea breezes around the coasts. Equally, in years such as 2008 and 2010 when the high never forms or remains weak, changeable weather of the British summer variety is the rule. A sudden drop in barometric pressure accompanied by a south or southeast wind foretells the approach of a depression, which on arrival may produce gusts and squally conditions up to 30 knots (but seldom gale force) as the wind veers through southwest into the northwest or north as the depression passes. The most important, and least predictable, variant is probably the speed with which the low will approach and pass, sending southeast winds and swells into the many Azorean harbours open to that direction.

Prevailing winds in the early summer (May and June) are generally westerly, sometime veering northwest in the eastern part of the archipelago. Though winds average 11–16 knots and include a 4% incidence of calms, there is also a 1% chance of gales (30+ knots), at least until the end of May. During July and August southwest winds are most common in the western islands, while further east there is more chance of northwest or northerlies. Winds typically blow at 10 knots or less, with a 6% chance of calms and, according to published data, no gales at all (though some might dispute that). Prevailing wind direction stays much the same throughout September, though picking back up to 11–16 knots and again including a chance of gales, though also a 3% incidence of calms.

Island topography can greatly affect the strength and direction of winds in certain areas so that the true wind may not be found until up to 15M offshore. Katabatic squalls have been reported close to several of the higher islands, most notably along the north coast of Pico.

Visibility

Fog is uncommon in the Azores, particularly in summer, though low cloud can sometimes obscure the higher parts of the islands. Haze can sometimes reduce visibility to less than 5M although the horizon appears to be sharp, a phenomenon more common around Flores and Corvo than further east, and generally limited to southerly winds. More often visibility is near perfect, the higher islands occasionally being spotted at 50M or more and routinely at 30M. Heavy rain squalls, which may reduce visibility to 0·5M or less with very little warning, seldom last for long and if making an approach when overtaken by one it may be wise to stand off until it passes.

Sources of further information

Further statistics are available from a number of sources – the British Admiralty *Routeing Charts, North Atlantic Ocean*, the US National Geospacial-Intelligence Agency *Pilot Charts of the North Atlantic Ocean*, James Clarke's *Atlantic Pilot Atlas*, now in its 5th edition (see Further Reading, page 403) and Imray Laurie Norie & Wilson Ltd's *Chart 100, North Atlantic Ocean Passage Chart*.

Weather forecasts

The Azores are covered by Navtex transmissions from Horta in English as well as Portuguese (see page 50).

Various websites carrying worldwide weather information are listed on page 9. In addition, 3-day, 5-day and 10-day general forecasts for six cities across the archipelago are available from Portugal's *Instituto de Meteorologia* at www.meteo.pt, in English as well as Portuguese. In early 2011 specialised 'Marine Meteorology' pages were under construction.

In port, daily forecasts (normally comprising a synoptic chart and text in Portuguese, English or both) are displayed outside the marina or harbour office – see individual harbours for details.

Magnetic variation

Variation throughout the Azores decreases by about 2°40′ from west to east, in 2011 averaging just under 12°W and decreasing by 9′E annually. Exact figures will be found in the data heading for each harbour.

Tides and tidal streams

Admiralty Tide Tables, Volume 2: *The Atlantic and Indian Oceans including tidal stream predictions (NP 202)*, published annually, covers the Azores with Ponta Delgada as standard port. However, many more yachtsmen will turn to the internet and the UK Hydrographic Office's excellent *EasyTide* programme at http://easytide.ukho.gov.uk, which gives daily tidal data for at least one harbour on every island other than Pico and São Jorge. Following a suggestion from the author, the island name is now included in cases where the harbour name alone (Lajes, Santa Cruz) is insufficient.

Maximum mean spring range varies from 1·2m in Flores and Corvo to 1·4m in São Miguel and Santa Maria, with mean neap range increasing from 0·5m to 0·7m over the same area.

Tidal streams run north, northeast or east on the flood and reverse direction on the ebb, and are strongest in the Canal do Faial where 2 knots may be reached at springs.

Currents

The islands lie in the path of the Azores Current, an offshoot of the North Atlantic Current (Gulf Stream) which sets south or southeast at no more than 0·5 knots.

Navigational aids

Radio communications

Since the withdrawal of the very useful *NP289 – Maritime Communications, United Kingdom and the Mediterranean*, those wishing to carry details of all official radio communications in the Azores archipelago now need to invest in three volumes – *NP281(1) – Maritime Radio Stations*; *NP283(1) Maritime Safety Information Services* and *NP 286(1) Pilot Services, Vessel Traffic Services and Port Operations*.

Buoys and lights

The few buoys and many lights in the Azores adhere to the IALA A system, based on the direction of the main flood tide, as used throughout mainland Europe. If arriving after a transatlantic passage one should bear in mind that this is opposite to the IALA B system to be found throughout North America, Bermuda and much of the Caribbean.

Note that not every light listed in the text can be shown on the plans, in particular on the small-scale 'island' plans. Refer instead to the relevant – and preferably corrected – chart.

Charts

The most detailed charts of the Azores archipelago are those published by the Portuguese *Instituto Hidrográfico*, www.hidrografico.pt, which covers the islands on 13 sheets. These consist of a small-scale chart of the entire archipelago, three medium-scale charts covering the western, central and eastern groups, and nine showing either an island plus several inset harbour plans or harbour plans alone. A catalogue can be downloaded from the *Instituto's* website at www.hidrographico.pt, from which it may soon be possible to buy online.

It is a legal requirement for Portuguese-owned boats to carry relevant charts, but even so it is difficult to source them once in the islands. Teófilo SA in Horta, Flores & Parreira near Angra do

Waves break inside 'whale rock', near Punta da Barca on Graciosa's north coast

Heroísmo and MAP in Ponta Delgada all carry limited stocks, and may be willing to order from the Institute's *Catálogo de Cartas Náuticas*, as indeed may either Mid Atlantic Yacht Services in Horta or Boat & Sail Service in Ponta Delgada – see under individual harbours for contact details.

British Admiralty charts (www.ukho.gov.uk) cover the archipelago on five sheets, with five small-scale plans and 10 approach and harbour plans. They are stocked by Mid Atlantic Yacht Services in Horta and MAP in Ponta Delgada, but it would make sense in economic as well as safety terms for a British yacht to buy before departure, as prices are approximately double those in the UK. Alternatively, Imray Laurie Norie & Wilson Ltd (www.imray.com) are official agents and will mail corrected Admiralty charts worldwide.

The US National Geospatial-Intelligence Agency devotes five sheets to the islands. Though no longer available directly from the NGIA, they can be ordered online from approved suppliers. See page 396 for further details. Finally, Imray Laurie Norie & Wilson Ltd's *Imray-Iolaire* series covers the archipelago on a single sheet, *E1*, at scale of 1:750,000, with 10 inset approach and harbour plans, and is stocked by MAYS in Horta.

See Appendix I, page 396, for chart lists.

Chart datum and satellite derived positions

All current editions of British Admiralty charts of the Azores are based on WGS84 Datum, allowing satellite-derived positions to be plotted directly onto them without further correction. For a fuller explanation see Horizontal chart datum on page 10 of the Passages section.

Guides, pilots, etc.

The archipelago is covered in the British Admiralty's *West Coasts of Spain and Portugal Pilot (NP 67)* and in the US National Geospacial-Intelligence Agency's *Sailing Directions for the West Coast of Europe and North West Africa (Pub 143)*, both of which are of course written with very much larger vessels in mind. In addition, the 6th edition of *The Atlantic Crossing Guide* includes brief passage planning notes, with additional harbour details for Lajes das Flores, Horta and Ponta Delgada and other information. They are also mentioned – even more briefly – in Rod Heikell and Andy O'Grady's *Ocean Passages and Landfalls*, and in *World Cruising Routes* and *World Cruising Destinations* by Jimmy Cornell.

Caution and request

A great deal of harbour and marina building has taken place in the Azores since the 4th edition of this book was published in 2004, and though undoubtedly slowing down – if only because there are few reasonably sheltered places remaining in which to build – several projects remain unfinished, and one or two unstarted, at the time of going to press. Works in progress frequently remain unlit, posing a hazard to those approaching after dark, while changes are often slow to be reported through the official channels. Thus even a brand new chart, fully corrected, should not be assumed to be fully up-to-date in all respects.

Where changes come to the notice of the author and/or publisher they are normally incorporated in the interim supplements carried on the websites of both Imray Norie Laurie & Wilson Ltd (www.imray.com) and the RCC Pilotage Foundation (www.rccpf.org.uk). The author and publisher are therefore indebted to the hundreds of yachtsmen and women who have taken the trouble to send in corrections, comments and photographs for these supplements, either by email to ilnw@imray.com or by post to Imray Laurie Norie & Wilson Ltd, Wych House, The Broadway, St Ives, Cambs PE27 5BT. Even in these days of information overload there is nothing to compare with direct feedback from someone who is actually on the spot – thank you, and long may it continue!

Flores

Between 39°22'N–39°32'N and 31°07'W–31°16'W

Introduction

Many yachtsmen remember their visit to Flores as the highlight of their time in the Azores. Only 17km long by up to 14km wide, it has a land area of some 143km², almost all of it magnificent scenery. The second memory of Flores will be of the people. Even amongst the friendly Azoreans they stand out in their readiness to help others which, until Porto das Lajes took over from Santa Cruz as the main harbour in 1994, was essential to a safe landfall. The sight of a yacht approaching the narrow rocky entrance to Santa Cruz would immediately bring the ferryman or his son, or perhaps a local fisherman, rowing out in a heavy dinghy to escort the newcomer in – and all with no thought of payment. As one 1998 visitor put it: 'the friendliness of the people of Flores outweighs any possible shortfall in facilities'.

Flores and Corvo, separated by less than 10M of Atlantic Ocean, lie 120M west-northwest of Faial and were the last of the Azores to be discovered by the Portuguese, who arrived in 1452. However, several atlases and charts of the previous century had identified the '*islas de corvos marinis*' – the islands of the sea crows – or in one case '*de raca*' – of eagles. Amongst the early colonists were the three brothers of Jobst van Huerta who settled Faial, attracted by rumours of silver and tin, and one Wilhelm van der Haegen, also a Fleming, who in 1470 lived at Ribeira da Cruz, before leaving Flores in favour of São Jorge. Settlement began in earnest in 1504 under Captain João da Fonseca, with immigrants from Madeira and Terceira as well as mainland Portugal, its success being attested in the town charters granted to Santa Cruz and Lajes soon after. Later in the 16th century Flores became a base for resistance to the Spanish domination of Portugal – aided, amongst others, by Sir Walter Raleigh – but after the Spanish victory of 1580 it became a favourite target for pirates and privateers of all nations attracted by the rich treasure galleons returning from the New World. In 1587 Santa Cruz was attacked by the English fleet, at war with Spain, whilst Tennyson's stirring lines beginning 'At Flores in the Azores Sir Richard Grenville lay', and recounting the battle in 1591 between the *Revenge* and a large Spanish squadron, will constitute many yachtsmen's sole previous knowledge of the island.

Until comparatively recently the inhabitants lived a very isolated existence, exporting some whale oil, honey and cedar wood to Faial and Terceira via the occasional sailing ship and, during the 18th and 19th centuries, often supplying crew for the American whalers, who prized Azoreans as amongst the finest seamen and harpooners. The 20th century brought better communications with the outside world, including telephones, television and, of course, most recently the internet. The French meteorological observatory set up in the 1960s became a satellite tracking station before its closure in July 1993 – the buildings have now been converted into a hotel – and the much-enlarged airport handles several dozen civilian flights each week, many passengers being emigrants to the USA and Canada returning to visit relatives, and vice versa. The already good road system is expanding, and the breakwater at Lajes, completed in 1994, not only allows cargo to be unload alongside instead of via lighters, but also shelters the small marina which opened in July 2011.

Even so, life for many of the 4,500 or so islanders appears to be changing relatively slowly. Many still make a living from farming and stock-raising – Flores gives the impression of being able to grow almost anything in its rich volcanic soil, a reddish tan where recently disturbed, weathering to a gritty

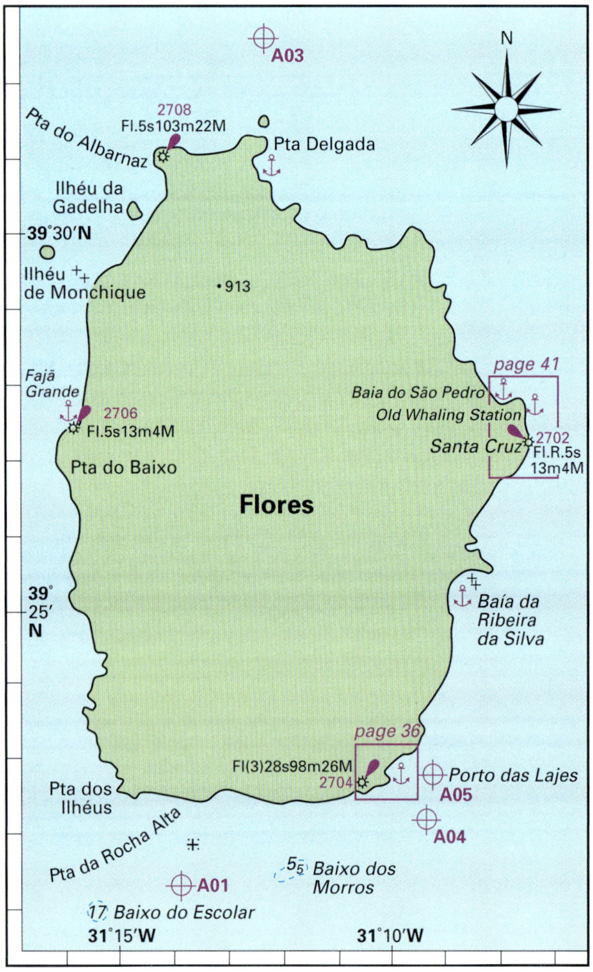

Navigation

Waypoints
⊕ A01 – 39°21'·3N 31°13'·9W (1M S of Pta da Rocha Alta : light weather)
⊕ A02 – 39°19'·3N 31°15'W (3M S of Pta dos Ilhéus : heavy weather)
⊕ A03 – 39°32'·6N 31°12'·4W (1M N of Pta Delgada)
⊕ A04 – 39°22'·2N 31°09'·4W (0·5M SE of Lajes)
⊕ A05 – 39°22'·8N 31°09'·3W (0·5M E of Lajes)

Courses and distances
⊕ A01 – ⊕A05 via ⊕A04 = 4·2M, 076° & 007° / 187° & 256°
⊕ A02 – ⊕A05 via ⊕A04 = 5·6M, 058° & 007° / 187° & 238°
⊕ A03 – ⊕A05 = 12M, by eye
⊕ A03 – ⊕A09 (0·5M SE of Vila Nova, Corvo) = 9M, 033° / 213°
⊕ A05 – ⊕A10 (1M W of Pta dos Capelinhos, Faial) = 117M, 113° / 293°

Magnetic variation
12°15'W (2011), decreasing by 8'E annually.

Tidal Streams
Tidal streams set north or east on the flood and south or west on the ebb at up to 1·5 knots. At springs the tidal current between Flores and Corvo can run strongly enough to give rise to noticeable wind over tide conditions.

Charts
Admiralty *1959* (1:150,000)
Portuguese *43101* (1:300,000), *46401* (1:75,000)
US *51041* (1:250,000)
Imray-Iolaire *E1* (1:750,000)

Lights
2708 **Ponta do Albarnaz** Fl.5s103m22M
035°-vis-204°, 214°-vis-258°
Grey tower and buildings, red lantern 15m
2702 **Santa Cruz (Pedra Açucareiro)**
Fl.R.5s13m4M 156°-vis-308°
White column, red bands 6m
2704 **Ponta das Lajes**
Fl(3)28s98m26M 263°-vis-054°
Square white tower and building, red lantern, 16m
2706 **Fajã Grande** Fl.5s13m4M
White post, red bands on white base 6m

Coast Radio Station
Flores 39°23'N 31°11'W, remotely controlled from Lisbon
VHF Ch 16, 23 (24 hours)

Banks of blue hydrangeas have long been synonymous with the Azores, despite not being a native species

Organpipe Rocks in southwest Flores, witness to volcanic activity long ago

grey or black. It must be amongst the loveliest places in the world, the scenery a succession of stunning panoramas, albeit often shrouded in mist. Rolling hillsides end in vertical cliffs, with silver ribbons of water cascading hundreds of feet into valleys where whitewashed cottages cluster amongst meadows full of piebald cows and waving sweet corn. Narrow roads lead up to the 914m mass of Morro Alto and overlook deep green lakes – seven in all – lying in the craters of extinct volcanoes, their sides thick with blue hydrangea, pine, cedar and eucalyptus.

Thousands of flowers line the roadsides – red and yellow canna lilies, blue agapanthus, orange montbretia, pink climbing roses, and thick banks of deep green fern. Smooth grassy hills reminiscent of England's West Country sport granite ridges like spines along their crests and bare volcanic plugs on their summits, whilst dwarfing the village of Mosteiro are the Rochas dos Bordoes – Organpipe Rocks – a black basalt crag formed of vertical columns full of angles and facets, a mosaic of sunlight and shadow. The lasting memory, though, is of lush vegetation – in the deep valleys, edging the tiny fields, and stretching up the sides of the hills. It's easy to see why, after a short time as Ilha de São Tomás, the early settlers renamed their new home 'the Isle of Flowers'.

Holidays and festivals

In addition to the national holidays listed on page 26, Lajes celebrates its official holiday on 17 June, with that of Santa Cruz following a week later. The Festival of *Espírito Santo* is celebrated about six weeks after Easter, with the Feast of St John on 24 June. An Emigrants' Festival, to which islanders return from all over the world, takes places in Lajes on the third weekend in July.

Telecommunications

Mobile (cell) phone reception is excellent on the east coast and also around Fajã Grande, but is patchy along some parts of the west coast. The country code for the Azores is 351, as it is for mainland Portugal, and the area code for Flores – which must be included even when dialling from within the island – is 292, shared with Corvo, Faial and Pico.

By 2011 free Wi-Fi was available in several locations in both Lajes and Santa Cruz.

Websites

The internet currently offers no website devoted to Flores as a whole, other than Wikipedia's www.en.wikipedia.org/wiki/Flores_Island_(Azores) though www.cmlajesflores.com/ brings up the attractive website of the *Câmara Municipal das Lajes das Flores* (effectively the town council), complete with musical accompaniment. The island also features on several of the general Azores sites listed on pages 24–5.

Approach

Situated almost exactly halfway between mainland Portugal and Newfoundland, Flores is the most westerly of the Azores, whilst the off-lying Ilhéu de Monchique qualifies as the westernmost land in Europe at 31°16'·2W. Thus for yachts arriving from Bermuda, the USA and Canada, Flores is likely to be the first island sighted and in clear weather may be spotted from at least 40M off. However, clouds blanket the higher areas for much of the time and the whole island may be completely hidden by mist at 5M although the yacht is in bright sunshine.

If approaching around the south of the island in light weather allow an offing of at least mile, (⊕A01) to be sure of clearing the breaking rocks just over 0·5M south of Ponta da Rocha Alta. In heavier weather it would be prudent to remain south of Baixo do Escolar, as although it carries a reported 17m the water shoals very sharply from around the 80m mark. ⊕A02, three miles south of Ponta dos Ilhéus, gives good clearance of both Baixo do Escolar and the 5·5m Baixo dos Morros.

Possible hazards on approaching from the west or northwest are the small island and rocks off Ponta Delgada at the northern tip of the island and Ilhéu de Monchique approximately 1M west-northwest of Ponta dos Fenais. There are no off-lying hazards on approach from the east, but it would be unwise to close the island in darkness from any direction without local knowledge. Much of the coast consists of high volcanic cliffs and headlands with vicious fringing rocks, and even in daylight an offing of at least 0·5M should be maintained.

Lagoa Funda, one of Flores's many beautiful lakes

Harbours and anchorages

Porto das Lajes

39°22'·74N 31°09'·94W (breakwater head)

Waypoints
⊕A04 – 39°22'·2N 31°09'·4W (0·5M SE of Porto das Lajes)
⊕A05 – 39°22'·8N 31°09'·3W (0·5M E of Porto das Lajes)

Tides
Predictions for Porto das Lajes are available via Admiralty *EasyTide* – see page 30
Time difference on Ponta Delgada: –0006
Mean spring range 1·2m
Mean neap range 0·5m

Plans
Admiralty *1959* (1:20,000)
Portuguese *46401* (1:5,000)
US *51041* (1:20,000)
Imray-Iolaire *E1* (1:20,000)

Lights
2704 **Ponta das Lajes** Fl(3)28s98m26M 263°-vis-054°
Square white tower and building, red lantern, 16m
2705 **Breakwater** Fl(2)R.10s9m2M White post
Note Work was taking place on the breakwater at the time of writing. When finished, a new light structure will be built which may display different light characteristics
2704·5 **Ldg Lts on 251°** *Front* Fl.G.7s17m2M
Grey post close to large white chimney on building
Rear, 267m from front, Oc.G.4s65m2M
Grey post at NE corner of white church 2m
Note Expected to be replaced by a red, white and green sectored light positioned on the shore northwest of the marina
Marina, east mole Fl.R.5s
White post, red bands 6m
Marina, west (inner) mole Fl.G.5s
White post, green bands 4m
Note A mobile phone mast marked by red lights stands on the cliffs close north of the harbour

Harbour communications
Harbour Authority ✆/*Fax* 292 593437
Email lajes.flores@aptosa.com (0900–1700). There is currently no permanent VHF watch, though Ch 16 may be monitored at times and the English-speaking ships' pilot uses Ch 14 to communicate with incoming ships
Lajes das Flores Marina ✆/*Fax* as above. The marina is not yet featured on the *Portos dos Açores SA* website at www.marinasazores.com, but will doubtless be added in due course. VHF Ch 10 is expected to be used

Harbour anchorage with small marina

Formerly an open bay with a small stone quay, a substantial breakwater some 450m in length was completed in 1994. Whilst its primary purpose was to provide an alongside berth for the supply ship and large fishing vessels, it greatly improved shelter in the bay which now offers protection from all quarters other than northeast. After many years of discussion, in early 2009 work finally began on a small marina, the seventh in the *Portos dos Açores SA* chain, which was formally opened in July 2011. Between 20 and 30 yachts are normally to be seen in the harbour during the summer, and several hundred pass through Lajes each year, some of them staying a considerable time.

The sudden elevation of the small town of Lajes to the position of premier port of the island is reflected in much improved facilities and communications, though Santa Cruz remains the island's principal town with airport, hospital and government buildings and no visit to Flores is complete without some time spent there – but arriving by land, not water.

Lajes is also attractive, though other than the church it has relatively few old buildings. The town has expanded considerably over the past decade, both around the well-kept central gardens and along the main road to the west, but one does not need to go far out of town to find a countryside little changed for many years. An excellent view over the harbour can be enjoyed by crossing the bridge on the road out of town to the north and taking the cobbled track which leads off to the right just beyond. At the end of the track is a small public garden complete with stone benches and a barbecue – not a bad place for a sundowner or even supper on a calm evening.

Although Lajes has no tourist office its role is largely filled by the *Câmara Municipal* (town hall, open 0830–1230, 1320–1630 weekdays only) where maps, guides and even bus timetables are available at the reception desk.

Approach and entry

If approaching Lajes other than from elsewhere on the east coast of Flores, see the island Approach opposite.

The final approach to the harbour is straightforward and there are good depths off the breakwater, but its end – which was being widened and reinforced in July 2011 – should be given at least 50m clearance as it is buttressed by a protective cone of large boulders. Evidence of repeated storm damage is clearly visible, and the outer section should be given a wide berth.

Berthing

Lajes das Flores Marina had only been open for a few weeks at the time of writing, and feedback has been mixed. A skipper who arrived in strong southeasterlies reported a major problem with swell resulting in 'much talk of damage and broken lines', a particular problem being that 'when rafted two or three deep along the east wall boats surge in opposite directions.' On the other hand, an experienced cruising family who spent much of June and July alongside the same wall, having 'fallen in love with the island', described the situation with three yachts rafted abreast and surge coming in as 'manageable'. The quietest spot was said to be alongside the southern (inner) end of the east breakwater, but in any position long nylon warps and/or springs or 'rubber-snubbers' would be advisable.

No one denies that the marina is small, and once local boats have taken up residence the space for visitors will be even more limited. Although all 45

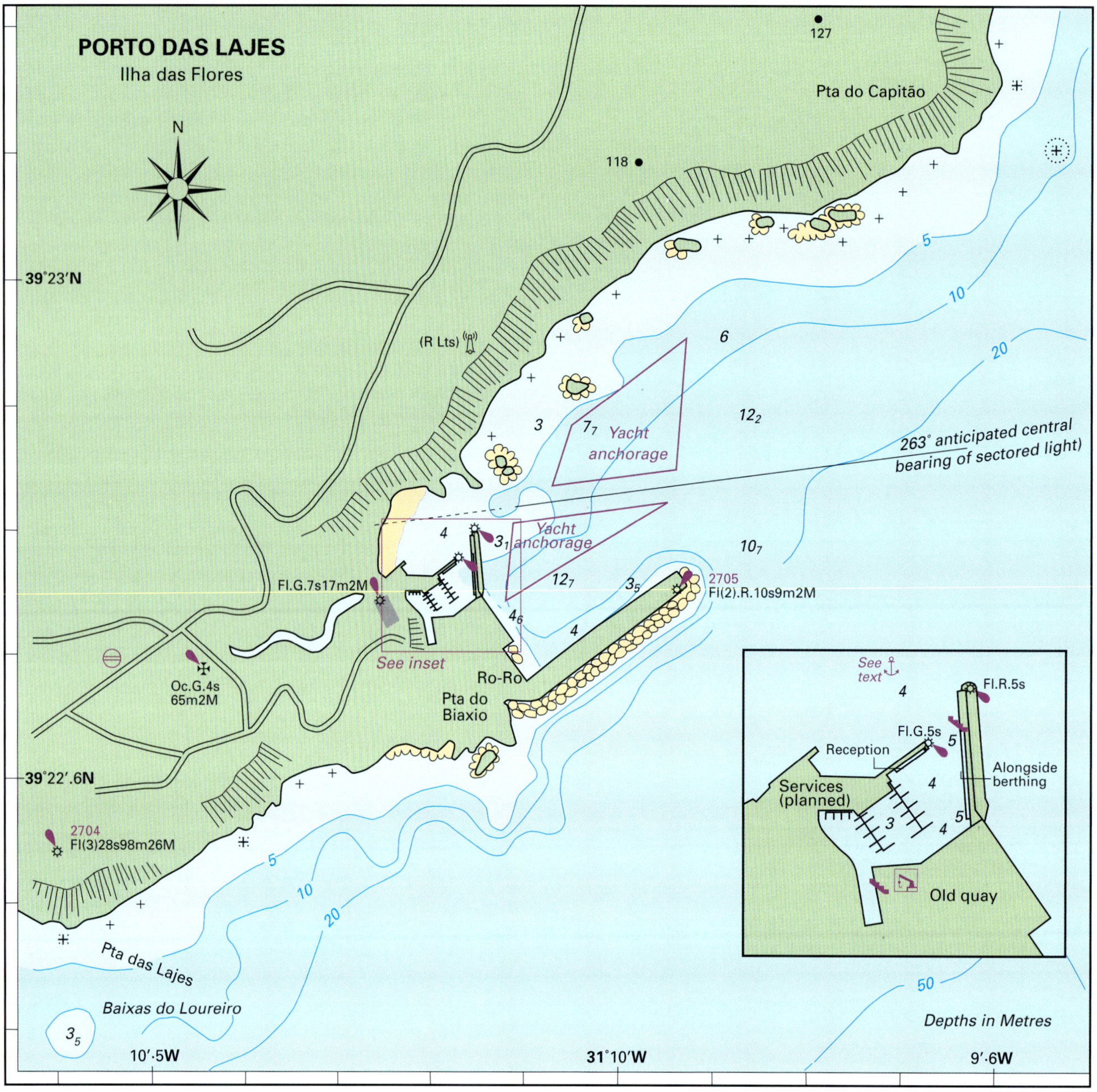

pontoon berths are alongside fingers, none – other than the single hammerhead – are designed to take craft over 10m. Visitors are likely to be restricted to the 60m pontoon inside the east mole (where it is normally possible to raft two or three abreast) and possibly the 40m wall along the northwest edge of the old quay, though this may remain the preserve of fishing boats returning to unload their catch. The 25m reception/fuel pontoon on the southeast face of the inner quay (see plan) will presumably be kept clear for its designated purpose.

While depth is not a problem, with 5m along the east mole, 4m at the outer finger pontoons and 3·5m at the inner pontoon, the marina has an entrance width of 20m and a 30m diameter turning area, so skippers of larger and less manoeuvrable yachts may prefer to anchor on arrival and investigate by dinghy. Yachts should not secure to the outside of the marina's west mole, as this is reserved for the Corvo ferry. This wall is also reported to be rendered only down to low water level, below which steel reinforcing rods project outwards.

In the past, two or three yachts of up to 15m have normally been permitted to berth alongside the outer part of the main breakwater in 3·5m or more, if it is not required for commercial vessels. However, as permission must first be obtained from the harbourmaster, Sr Carlos Avelar, it is necessary to anchor on arrival. It is understood that yachts will no longer be allowed to anchor bow or stern-to the old inner quay.

Anchorage

There are now two designated anchorage areas – see plan – in addition to which a single yacht may be able to tuck in north of the marina's west mole. The main anchorages straddle the 10m line over sand, gravel and rock, while the inner one (where a riding light should be displayed) is in about 4m over sand. In due course moorings may be laid in the latter spot. A Ro-Ro berth has been created in the angle formed by the breakwater and the old quay, and its approach channel must not be impeded.

Considerable swell works into the harbour during winds from the east or southeast and, whilst protected by the cliffs from northerly winds, a northerly or even northwesterly groundswell may work around the island to make the anchorage uncomfortably rolly. This is aggravated by the surrounding topography which conspires to send a light southwesterly across the anchorage, thus encouraging yachts to take the swell beam-on. Good chafing gear will be needed if relying on a rope anchor rode.

There is no charge for anchoring, and dinghies can be left at the steps inside the marina.

Formalities

As of 2011 the harbourmaster, Sr Carlos Avelar, who is also to be marina manager, had a small office a little way up the hill from the harbour, while other officials completed their paperwork in the open air. However, by 2012 a new *Delegação Marítima* building – to provide office space for him, the *Polícia Marítima* (maritime police), *Serviço de Estrangeiros e Fronteiras* (Immigration), *Guarda Nacional Republicana* (local police) and *Alfândega* (Customs) – should be operational on the quay. It seems unlikely that all the above officials will be there throughout the entire day, in which case Sr Avelar will handle the paperwork and tell skippers if, and when, they need to visit the other offices.

Clearance is treated in a rational manner as befits an island people accustomed to the dictates of the weather, and should a yacht arrive at the weekend and be unable to remain until Monday there will be no repercussions if formal clearance is delayed until its next port of arrival, most often Horta.

The narrow though protected entrance to Lajes das Flores Marina *Keith Marshall*

Charges

As the latest addition to the *Portos dos Açores SA* chain Lajes das Flores Marina will share their basic price structure, although in 2011 yachts were not being charged. From 2012 those of 10–12m LOA are expected to pay €12.22 per night and those of 12–15m €18.50, to include water, electricity and tax. For further details see page 27 and/or www.marinasazores.com, the website of the branch of *Portos dos Açores SA* concerned with marina operation.

Lighthouse tax – *Taxa de Farolagem e Balizagem* – is sometimes collected by the *Polícia Marítima*. At just €2 for six months one has little to complain of, but it is worth keeping the receipt.

As mentioned above, there is no charge for anchoring.

The new marina at Porto das Lajes soon after completion in June 2011, seen from the west *Mark Holbrook*

I. THE AZORES

The interior of Lajes das Flores Marina in July 2011. In the longer term all pontoon berths are likely to be occupied by local boats *Harald Sammer*

Facilities

Most goods and services are available, though as many businesses are poorly advertised it helps to have local advice. Paula Andrade, *Email* paulas-place-flores@hotmail.com, mentioned in the previous edition of this book as a friend to all visiting yachtsmen, is now back in Flores after a period away and will assist whenever possible. Most evenings she is to be found at Paula's Place (see *Cafés, restaurants & hotels*, opposite). She speaks fluent English and has wide-ranging contacts.

Boatyard No yard as such, but welding is available as are repairs to GRP and timber. Enquire at the office of the *Capitão do Porto* or consult Paula (see above).

Travel-lift Although a travel-lift has not been ruled out, the necessary dock does not feature in current plans.

Crane Large mobile crane capable of lifting 12 tonnes with mast up, or up to 22 tonnes without, though the 2·5m spreaders (to keep the strops apart) would be too narrow for a yacht of any size. There is a strong 'can do' ethos in Lajes, however, and if a yacht arrives with a serious underwater problem the *Capitão do Porto* insists that "anything is possible".

Diving services Nothing official, though several people in the town have diving equipment – ask at the office of the *Capitão do Porto* or consult Paula. Permission to dive (though not to snorkel) within the port must be obtained from the *Capitão do Porto* before going ahead.

Engineers, electronic & radio repairs Skilled mechanics and electricians are available, together with a number of well-equipped workshops, but spares of any kind would be a problem and would probably have to be ordered via MAYS in Horta (see page 56).

Sail repairs Paula may be able to organise simple repairs, but anything serious will have to await arrival in Horta.

Chandlery An electrical appliance store near the supermarkets (see below) has a hardware store upstairs, where some chandlery is also sold. A very limited range is also held in a small shop adjacent to one of the supermarkets.

Water On the marina pontoons, including reception, and included in the berthing fee.

Showers Available free in the facilities block on the quay (cold water only, but very clean). A block housing showers, toilets and a launderette may form part of the marina complex, or alternatively the old *clube naval* buildings may be refurbished.

Launderette There is a launderette in the town, but it is reported to be expensive, particularly for drying, so it would be advisable to check prices in advance. A laundry is among the facilities on the wish list for the new marina.

Electricity On the marina pontoons, and included in the berthing fee.

Fuel The marina reception pontoon is intended to double as a fuel pontoon, but it may well be several years before a pump is installed. In the meantime order via Paula Andrade who (among her other enterprises) runs the AZORIA filling station, ✆ 292 593813, on the Santa Cruz road, open 0830–1800 Monday to Saturday, 1100–1300 Sundays and holidays. Up to 500 litres can be brought down to the harbour in cans; much more and she will organise delivery by road tanker. Fuelling normally takes place alongside the northwest wall of the old quay, now well sheltered inside the marina. Pay in cash or by Visa card.

Bottled gas One of the supermarkets exchanges GALP cylinders, but there is no chance of getting other bottles filled while in Flores.

Banks Two, both with cash machines, plus several more in Santa Cruz.

Shops/provisioning There are two supermarkets in Lajes itself, close to each other near the top of a steepish hill (go straight over the little roundabout beyond the church and keep on until you reach a T-junction). One lies on the left just before the T-junction, beyond a large hardware store. It is the better stocked of the two and impressively clean. Opening hours are 0830–1230, 1330–1730 weekdays, 0830–1300 Saturday. The other lies a short distance down the road to the right, and as well as foodstuffs sells household goods at the rear and clothes and shoes upstairs. A hardware store, which stocks tools and a limited range of chandlery, is accessed through an unmarked door to the left of the supermarket entrance. Both parts of the shop are open 0900–1800 Monday to Saturday inclusive.

If arriving on Sunday and desperate to stock up, one of the two supermarkets in Fazenda, a mile or so up the road towards Santa Cruz, is open 0800–2000 Monday to Saturday, 1400–2000 Sundays and holidays.

For fresh organic vegetables visit Sylke and Uwe Steiner, ✆ 292 593839. Head west out of Lajes and follow the signs to Fajã Lopo Vaz, turning turn right up the last street, Rua Assumada. Sylke makes fresh bread, goat's cheese, marmalade and chutneys, and also sells fresh and dried herbs.

Cafés, restaurants & hotels Small hotel, plus self-catering cottages run under licence from the *Câmara Municipal*, together with numerous bars and restaurants. The Beira Mar bar/restaurant will be found just up the road from the harbour, though no longer run by Paula Andrade who now has the smaller Paula's Place overlooking the harbour. A new restaurant, Rigosom, was due to open in the harbour area in August 2011 (the proprietors both speak good English).

Medical services Health centre just beyond the town hall, with pharmacy in the same building, both open weekdays only. For serious medical attention it is necessary to go to the hospital in Santa Cruz.

Communications

Post office On the main square, open 0900–1230, 1400–1730 weekdays only.

Mailing address A visit to Flores by yacht remains weather dependent, making it wise to have mail sent direct to Horta for collection.

Telephones Two public phones near the harbour (one coin-operated, one card) and others in the town. Cards are obtainable at the post office.

Internet access Free Wi-Fi in the harbour area, covering the marina and adjacent anchorage, as well as the terrace at Paula's Place where patrons can access mains power. Also at the public library (a few blocks beyond the town hall, open 0900–1230, 1330–1700, weekdays only), where there are six computers for general use or one can bring one's own, with plenty of power sockets available.

Car hire Paula operates a car hire business with a fleet of economical small cars, all purchased new in 2010. Other companies operate from the airport in Santa Cruz.

Taxis Several based locally, with a taxi rank conveniently placed between the two supermarkets at the top of the town.

Buses The very limited bus service had been much improved by mid-2011, with daily services to Santa Cruz and Fajã Grande. In late July a bus left Lajes for Santa Cruz at 0900 every day, returning at 1650, with more services in school term time. Check the current timetable at the *Câmara Municipal* (see page 35).

Ferries Atlânticoline (see page 23) runs a frequent service between Flores and Corvo for foot passengers only.

Air services Inter-island airport at Santa Cruz, with daily flights to Faial and Terceira.

Baía da Ribeira da Silva

39°25'·38N 31°08'·7W (anchorage)

Anchorage protected from northerly swell

In the light northerlies which follow a frontal passage the anchorage at Lajes becomes rolly, and much better shelter is reported to be found in the Baía da Ribeira da Silva, about 3M north of Lajes and 2M south of Santa Cruz. The bay lies north of Ponta da Fora – a spectacular volcanic headland, riven with bright red strata and vented by lava tubes – and immediately south of Ponta Caveira. The Baixa do Bezerro shoal lies in the northern part of the bay but is said to be visible nearly all the time and the bottom, of sand with very large boulders, is clearly visible at depths of 5–10m.

The anchorage is surrounded by a boulder beach, the Fajã de Pedro Viera, across which flows the Ribeira da Silva, from which ships filled their water tanks in the early 19th century. It is possible to wade up the river through a beautiful gorge to a waterfall in a cylindrical chamber. Paths can be followed through the undergrowth and trees to the village of Caveira, but the bay itself remains totally unspoilt.

Looking south across Baía da Ribeira da Silva on the east coast of Flores *Steve Burrows*

Santa Cruz (Porto das Pocas)

39°27'·08N 31°07'·54W (quay)

Plans
Admiralty *1959* (1:25,000)
Portuguese *46401* (10,000)
US *51041* (1:25,000)

Lights
2702 **Santa Cruz (Pedra Açucaeiro)** Fl.R.5s13m4M 156°-vis-308° White column, red bands 6m
Note Two pairs of leading lights guide local smallcraft into Porta das Poças and the nearby Porto Velho, but neither should be entered by yachts, day or night. FR on airport control tower 570m NW

Harbour communications
Harbourmaster ✆ 292 592224 *Fax* 292 542149 *Email* cp.flores@mail.pt VHF Ch 11, 16 (call *Capimar Flores*) (0900–1230, 1400–1730)
Harbour Authority ✆ /*Fax* 292 593437 (0900–1700)

A harbour to be seen but not entered

One of the smallest and most nerve-racking of harbours, prior to the construction of Lajes breakwater in 1994 yachts wishing to visit Flores had little choice other than Santa Cruz. Once inside protection is good, but both entry and exit are hazardous in the extreme and more than one yacht has been lost in the attempt. For many years the standard practice was to wait outside until a local man came out in an open boat to guide one in, the same process happening in reverse on departure. However, yachts are no longer welcome at Santa Cruz and entry should not even be considered in anything larger than a RIB, perhaps on a visit from Lajes some 5·5M down the coast.

If entering by RIB or dinghy take it very slowly and stick carefully to the leading line on 285°, marked by two red and white poles, one halfway up the cliff and one on the cliff top. Watch out for buoys and floating lines, and take care to avoid the shoal in the centre of the harbour, particularly at low tide or if surge is affecting water levels. Although a RIB would probably be permitted to lie alongside for an hour or two – the quay has been enlarged at the expense of the old slipway – take care not to impede local craft wishing to use the crane or steps.

Even if all formalities have been completed at Lajes, it would be wise to carry passports and copies of other documentation, if only to confirm ownership of one's arrival vessel.

The town of Santa Cruz is pleasant but not outstandingly attractive and the older part can be circumnavigated in ten minutes. The baroque parish church of São Pedro is worth a visit as is the town museum, due to move to new premises near the old whaling station at São Pedro (see below).

Facilities include water from a tap on the quay and fuel by can from a filling station a short walk away. There are several banks and three or four supermakets, the largest of which also sells hardware in the basement and clothing etc. upstairs. No shortage of hotels together with a good choice of cafés and restaurants, plus a small hospital with pharmacy next door. There is a post office, open 0900–1230, 1400–1730 weekdays only, and free Wi-Fi is available in the airport foyer and elsewhere. There is an infrequent bus service to all parts of the island, including Lajes, Ponta Delgada and Fajã Grande, but taxis are readily available and there are several car rental companies. Nearly all of these have offices at the airport, which handles inter-island flights, mostly via Faial.

The Corvo ferry leaves the tiny harbour of Porto das Pocas, Santa Cruz, viewed from just north of west

Anchorages on the northeast coast of Flores

Old Whaling Station (Boqueirão)

39°27′·79N 31°07′·69W (quay)

Narrow inlet open to the east

This deep narrow inlet approximately 0·75M north of Santa Cruz was once popular with yachts too large or deep to enter the tiny harbour further south, and vessels of more than 25m are reported to have used the cove. However, it is several years since a yacht last visited, nearly all preferring the open anchorage and cameraderie to be found at Lajes – and with good reason.

Rocks lie up to 200m off the headland north of the inlet, but the entrance is reasonably wide and may be taken on a bearing of 235°. With no room for proper scope in the 15m depths, normal practice was to secure 'all-fours' between the steps and rings on the rocks opposite, about one-third of the way across. Protection is good from all winds other than east, when the cove quickly becomes untenable, and visitors were always advised to warp their boat around and lie facing outwards so as to facilitate hasty departure if necessary. The old steps and ramp – up which whale carcasses were dragged for processing – provide a convenient landing, with a 15 minute walk into the centre of Santa Cruz.

A four-star hotel has recently opened at the top of the steep hill leading up from the cove, and a fascinating Interpretation Centre covering both the history of local whaling and the island's marine ecology has been built on the site of the old whale oil tanks. When visited in 2010, shortly after opening, the captions were in Portuguese only, but English is expected to be added and in any case the stunning photographs need little explanation. The extensive buildings of the old whale processing factory just uphill from the Interpretation Centre were being renovated to become the town's new museum.

Yachts occasionally use the Old Whaling Station inlet northeast of Santa Cruz

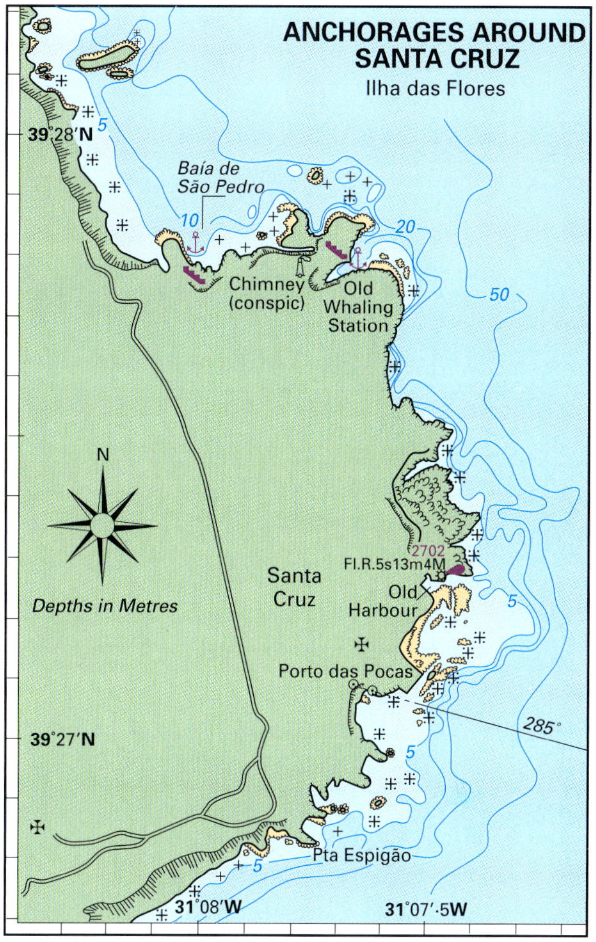

Baía do São Pedro

39°27′·74N 31°08′W (steps)

Anchorage open to the north and east

The Baía do São Pedro is perhaps the safest anchorage in the area in winds from southeast through southwest to northwest, being easy to enter and equally easy to leave if necessary. The faded white bridge at the head of the inlet and chevrons marking the northern end of the runway can be seen from some distance. At spring tides the current sweeps quite strongly into the bay.

Approach on a course of between 170° and 220°, giving reasonable clearance to Baixa Vermelha to the north and the rocks lying up to 200m off Ponta São Pedro to the east. Although very clear, the water is deep and the bottom largely rock, making a tripline on the anchor advisable. Depths of around 10m may be found well in, though some may prefer to stay further out in 15m or more and it is clearly essential not to impede the line of the runway.

Steps and a ramp provide convenient landing, but due to almost constant swell the dinghy should be carried well back. It takes about 15 minutes to walk into Santa Cruz.

Baía de São Pedro, north of Santa Cruz, looking southeast

Porto do Ponta Delgada

39°31'·17N 31°12'·42E (quay)

Interesting but exposed anchorage

Tucked under high cliffs near the northern tip of Flores, Porto do Ponta Delgada – a tiny corner of a larger bay – has a small quay and a crane used by local fishing craft. The bay, which is open from northeast to southeast, appears deep and there are no known hazards in the approach, though large rubble blocks extend well beyond end of the recently extended mole (which remains unlit). The bottom is rock and large stones, making a tripline advisable. There is nothing at the landing, but by following the steep road inland first a public tap and then a village (with basic facilities including a small supermarket and several bars) will be found.

The coast between Santa Cruz and Porto do Ponta Delgada is a protected area, particularly as regards wildlife and nesting birds, none of which must be disturbed.

'Porto' do Ponta Delgada in the extreme north of Flores – not to be confused with the true port of that name on São Miguel *Harald Sammer*

Anchorages on the west coast of Flores

Fajã Grande

39°27'·58N 31°15'·72W (quay)

Waypoint
⊕A06 – 39°28'·2N 31°16'·8W (1M WNW of Fajã Grande)

Lights
2706 **Fajã Grande** Fl.5s13m4M
White post, red bands on white base 6m
2706·3 **Ldg Lts on 156 4°** Oc.G.6s
Concrete posts 28m apart

The most westerly anchorage in Europe

This wide bay, sheltered by towering cliffs from the northeast through east to south, provides an attractive and viable anchorage in settled easterly weather. (In August 2000 one yachtsman praised it as: 'a paradise off a weather shore when the wind was howling from the east-southeast'). However, it is prone to swell running down the coast from the north, as well as anything coming in from the Atlantic, possibly generated by a weather system hundreds of miles away. It is the most westerly village, and the most westerly anchorage, in Europe.

If approaching other than from directly offshore give a generous berth to the rocks which run out from both ends of the bay, and do not venture much beyond the line of the inner quay face without careful eyeball navigation as there are several awash rocks off the beach. Fortunately the water is very clear. Anchor in 7–8m over boulders, with a tripline advisable. Dinghies can be landed at the small quay (with steps) or at the wide slipway/sunbathing area. Although lit, Fajã Grande is suitable for daylight approach only – in fact the entire west coast of Flores should be given a wide berth in darkness or poor visibility.

There is a café/restaurant immediately behind the slipway where swimmers' (ie. cold) showers are available and water cans may be filled. The village boasts three small supermarkets, two on the main street (the larger of which also sells a small range of hardware, clothes, shower gel, etc.) and a third which receives a delivery of fresh bread every morning) down a sideroad to the left. Both are open until late in the evening and accept most credit/debit cards – potentially very useful, as there is no bank or cash dispenser in the village. A public telephone and an infrequent bus service link Fajã Grande to other parts of the island. Excellent walking can be enjoyed in almost any direction, with surf, waterfalls and birdsong the only sounds.

Looking northwest over the wide bay at Fajã Grande on the west coast of Flores, with Ilhéu de Monchique visible in the distance

Towering cliffs and waterfalls, backdrop to the rocky bay at Fajã Grande

Corvo

Between 39°40'N–39°44'N and 31°05'W–31°07'W

Introduction

Corvo is the most northerly and by far the smallest of the Azorean islands with an area of only 17·5km², being 7km long by up to 4·5km wide. It consists of a single oval volcanic cone, Monte Gordo, which reaches 770m and contains a crater 1·5km in diameter and over 300m deep. Two small lakes and seven tiny islands lie inside the caldeira.

Corvo was discovered together with Flores in 1452, although their existence as the '*ilhas dos corvos marinis*' was almost certainly known prior to that date (see Introduction to Flores). Due to its remoteness colonisation did not take place until 1548 when a small settlement was established at Vila Nova do Corvo, the only landing place amongst the island's high cliffs and rocks. A self-sufficient pastoral community developed, living by stock-raising, limited arable farming and fishing, a pattern which still continues. Bonfires were used to communicate with passing ships and with Flores, using a code to indicate particular needs such as a priest or doctor, and limited only by the haze which often surrounds both islands cutting Corvo off for weeks at a time.

Emigration has been high since the 18th and 19th centuries when American whaling ships called in search of crew, and the current population of around 400 is only half that of 60 years ago. Vila Nova do Corvo – sometimes referred to as Vila do Corvo or simply Vila – has remained the island's only settlement. Created a borough in 1832, it is proud of

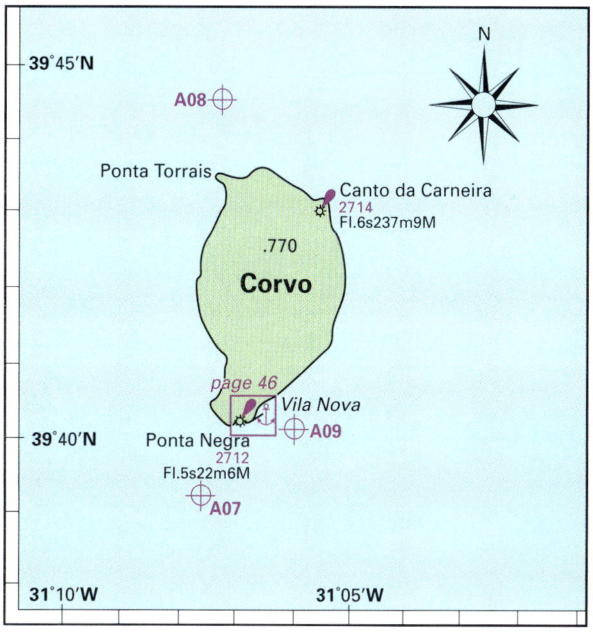

its status as the smallest town in Portugal. The old quarter is now a conservation area where ancient cottages fringe narrow streets and steep pathways, many of the tiny front yards also housing two or three pigs. There are few locks to be seen, no jail, and crime is almost unknown. Be wary, though, of straying off the beaten track and onto private property – for its size, Corvo has a disproportionate population of large dogs. Though most are chained up, a few are not and all take their guard duties seriously – and very loudly.

Over the past few decades communication with the outside world has improved markedly, first with a meteorological and radio station, then a telephone system, and most recently a passenger airport with regular flights to Flores and Faial. Weather permitting, ferries run a regular service between Corvo and Flores during the summer. Many local people have spent some time abroad, usually in America or Canada, and thus speak English, but a smile and a wave means the same in any language and visitors are made to feel particularly welcome.

Holidays and festivals

In addition to the national holidays listed on page 26, Corvo celebrates the Festival of *Espírito Santo* about six weeks after Easter and holds its official holiday on 20 June. However, the greatest celebrations are reserved for the Feast of Nossa Senhora Milagres on 5 August.

Telecommunications

Mobile (cell) phone reception in Vila Nova do Corvo is excellent, though this may fade on ascending towards the *caldeira*. The country code for the Azores is 351, as it is for mainland Portugal, and the area code for Corvo – which must be included even when dialling from within the island – is 292, shared with Flores, Faial and Pico.

By 2011 free Wi-Fi was available in several locations, including the airport.

Corvo's peaceful *caldeira* on a misty day. The seven islands within the two small lakes are claimed to resemble those of the Azores archipelago in miniature

Websites

The internet currently offers no website devoted solely to Corvo other than Wikipedia's www.en.wikipedia.org/wiki/Corvo_Island. However, the island does feature on several of the general Azores sites listed on page 24–5.

Approach

With a maximum height of 770m Corvo may be visible from 30M or more in clear weather, appearing from all directions as a single flat-topped mass, largely edged by steep cliffs. However clouds frequently cover the island, and sea mist may obscure it (and its light) until little more than 5M off in apparently good visibility.

Although most of the coast consists of sheer cliffs, with close off-lying rocks and no hazards extending more than 500m from the shore, depths generally shoal steeply and the echo sounder gives little advance warning.

Navigation

Waypoints

⊕ A07 – 39°39'·3N 31°07'·7W (1M SSW of Pta Negra)
⊕ A08 – 39°44'·5N 31°07'·2W (1M N of Pta Torrais)
⊕ A09 – 39°40'·1N 31°06'W (0·5M SE of Vila Nova)

Courses and distances

⊕ A07 – ⊕A09 = 1·5M, 059° / 239°
⊕ A08 – ⊕A09 = 6M, by eye
⊕ A09 – ⊕A03 (1M N of Pta Delgada, Flores) = 9M, 213° / 033°
⊕ A09 – ⊕A10 (IM W of Pta dos Capelhinos, Faial) = 223m, 121° / 301°

Magnetic variation

12°15'W (2011), decreasing by 8'E annually.

Tidal Streams

Tidal streams set north on the flood and south on the ebb at up to 1·5 knots.

Charts

Admiralty *1959* (1:150,000)
Portuguese *43101* (1:300,000), *46401* (1:75,000)
US *51041* (1:250,000)
Imray-Iolaire *E1* (1:750,000)

Lights

2712 **Ponta Negra** Fl.5s22m6M
Hexagonal grey tower near white windmill 3m
2714 **Canto da Carneira** Fl.6s237m9M
White column, red bands 4m

Harbours and anchorages

Vila Nova do Corvo (Porto da Casa)

39°40'·31N 31°06'·58W (molehead)

Waypoint
⊕A09 – 39°40'·1N 31°06'W (0·5M SE of harbour)

Tides
Predictions for Vila Nova do Corvo are available via Admiralty *EasyTide* – see page 30
Time difference on Ponta Delgada: –0010
Mean spring range 1·2m
Mean neap range 0·5m

Plans
Portuguese *46401* (1:5,000)

Lights
2712 **Ponta Negra** Fl.5s22m6M
Hexagonal grey tower near white windmill 3m
Molehead Fl.R.4s7m3M
White post, red bands 4m

Anchorage off Portugal's smallest town

An open bay, sheltered by Corvo itself from the west and north, Porto da Casa at Vila Nova do Corvo is the only possible landing on the island. A concrete mole about 90m in length faces a boulder beach, providing some additional shelter plus convenient dinghy landing. It may be possibly to lie alongside in calm conditions if the mole is not required for unloading cargo or by the Flores ferry. Even so, Porto da Casa remains very definitely a fair weather port-of-call which usually experiences some swell, and is untenable in any easterly wind or swell, even if very light. Relatively few yachts visit Corvo so the reception is welcoming. The more usual way to visit is via the ferry from Flores – much better than nothing, but necessarily more limited regarding time.

Approach and anchorage

Give the southeast tip of the island at least 500m clearance – thus remaining well outside the 10m contour – and do not close the end of the mole until it bears around 300°. There are no hazards in the final approach, but it would be wise to proceed slowly in order to assess the situation at the mole – ie. whether it will be possible to lie alongside or not. The mole remains unlit and night approach is not advised.

If anchoring, a tripline is essential as a chain (to which a mooring may be attached) lies on the seabed near the end of the mole. Holding is poor amid the same ostrich-egg sized boulders which line the beach, though a weight slung from the chain or rode will encourage the anchor to work in. The water is crystal clear, making it easy to see what the anchor is up to many metres below. If remaining overnight an conventional anchor light in the forward rigging is essential, as fishing boats come in at all hours and do not expect to find yachts already in residence. A second light suspended from the boom may be unofficial but will provide additional peace of mind.

Dinghies can be landed on the slipway or at steps near the root of the mole.

Berthing

Yachts are welcome to berth alongside the mole if it is not required for unloading cargo or by the Flores ferry. The outer third (ie. about 30m) carries at least 4m, but long lines will be needed as the massive bollards are some 25m apart. Shore access may also be difficult at times, as there are no ladders and the mole stands nearly 3m above the water at low tide. There is generally some surge even in offshore winds, so good fendering will be required together with anti-chafe protection where warps come in contact with the concrete mole.

Formalities

Officials from both the *Guarda Nacional Republicana* (*GNR*) and the *Polícia Marítima* come down to the mole when a yacht arrives (though the latter is not on duty at weekends). If, as is usual, the yacht has arrived from Flores or Faial there are few formalities, but if it has arrived from outside the Azores some paperwork will be necessary pending full clearance on reaching one of the larger islands. Corvo is not an official 'border post' under the Schengen Agreement.

Facilities

Facilities are inevitably limited, but as in most island communities there is a strong ethos of assisting those in difficulties and a variety of skills (and tools) are available – they are simply not advertised.

Engineering No marine engineer, but local experience with diesels of all sizes is necessary to keep both the electricity generating plant and a variety of road and agricultural vehicles in working order. Getting spare parts (probably via MAYS in Horta, see page 56) would take time.

The quay at Vila Nova do Corvo, also known as Porto da Casa

I. THE AZORES

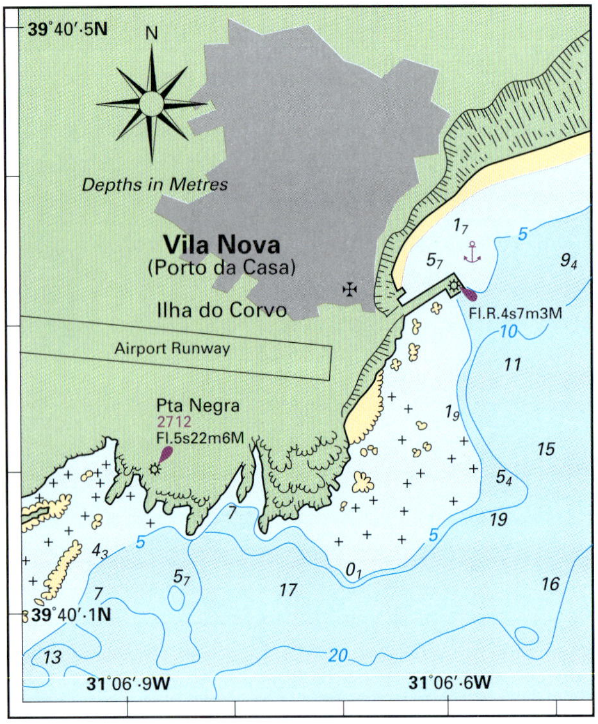

Water Fresh water from a tap at the root of the mole.

Showers Swimmers' (ie. cold) showers near the island's only beach, at the west end of the very short runway.

Fuel By can from the filling station near the root of the mole.

Bank Next to the post office, with a cash dispenser.

Shops/provisioning Small supermarket on the road leading out of the town (where some English is spoken), plus several tiny general stores in the old village. Bakery on the main road leading up from the harbour, and tasty island cheese direct from the factory – the last building on the left past the (somewhat noisy) electricity generating plant.

Cafés, restaurants & hotels Two guesthouses (not really hotels) plus several restaurants and café/bars. The O Caldeira restaurant, ✆ 292 596018, south of the runway on Caminho dos Moinhos, was recommended several times in the four years preceding publication. Outside the busy summer season it would be wise to visit a few hours in advance to check opening times and possibly to order one's meal.

Medical services Small health centre – emergency cases are evacuated to the hospital in Flores.

Communications

Post office On the main road, open 0900–1230 and 1400–1730 weekdays only.

Telephones Card and coin-operated phone outside the post office.

Internet access Free Wi-Fi in several locations, including at the airport and in the town's tiny main square.

Car hire & taxis None as such, though a privately-owned minibus may be available for a trip up the to *caldeira* – ask at either of the guesthouses. The walk back down is enjoyable, even for boat-softened feet.

Ferries Atlânticoline (see page 23) runs a frequent service between Corvo and Flores for foot passengers only.

Air services Regular, but not daily, flights to/from Flores, Faial and Terceira.

Canto do Pão de Açúcar

39°40′·83N 31°07′·15W (anchorage)

Dramatic anchorage for calm conditions only

A viable day stop and, in very settled conditions, a night one as well, has been reported in the small bay at Canto do Pão do Açúcar (literally, the 'corner of the sugar loaf') on the west coast of Corvo, most easily identified by the tall rocks which fringe the bay to the north. About 8m will be found over a bottom consisting of enormous boulders with only the occasional free area of sand, and an anchor tripping line is recommended. Landing beyond the narrow beach is not possible in the immediate vicinity, though a dinghy with a reliable outboard could go to the bathing area at the west end of the runway.

Huddled houses at Vila Nova do Corvo contrast with the runway behind. The latter may look lengthy, but does not feel it!

Scenic anchorage at Canto do Pão do Açúcar on the west coast of Corvo *Mike Gill*

Faial

Between 38°31′N–38°39′N and 28°36′W–28°50′W

Introduction

Faial is the most westerly of the central group and, though the competition is growing, still has the best facilities for yachts to be found in the Azores. It has always been the most popular landfall for yachtsmen arriving after an Atlantic crossing, many of whom stay so long that no time is left for exploring the other islands. In fact a surprising number of visitors never venture outside Horta, a great pity on an island with so much to offer.

Faial is one of the smaller islands, with maximum dimensions of around 22km by 15km giving it a land area of 173km². Its highest point is Cabeco Gordo on the rim of the *caldeira*, at 1,043m. Many of the 16,000 or so inhabitants still live by farming, though fishing and trade at all levels are also important and the service industries, particularly cafés and restaurants, provide seasonal employment in Horta itself.

Approaching by yacht, Faial appears an island of contrasts. Few landscapes could look more barren and uninviting than the sterile volcanic cliffs of Ponta dos Capelinhos in the extreme west, but further east the island is green and lush, its roads lined with flowers and the cottages white or pastel with square sash windows and doors heavily outlined, usually in blue. Blue also are the massed hydrangeas which earned Faial its nickname of *Ilha Azul* – 'Blue Island'. Introduced from China in the 18th century, they have since become naturalised and are perhaps one of the best known features of the Azores as a whole.

The Latin name of the plant, *Hydrangea hortensia*, often causes understandable confusion. Horta actually owes its name to an early settler, one Joste van Huerter (or Josse van Hurtere), a Fleming who became the first '*donee*' of the island under the patronage of Isabella, Duchess of Burgundy and sister of Prince Henry the Navigator. By 1468 when the Flemings arrived the island had already been inhabited by Portuguese immigrants for nearly ten years, but:

> 'In those days Flanders was visited with great wars and dire distress and the Duchess sent men and women of all sorts and conditions, eke (also) men of religion and ships loaded with furniture and tools for husbandry and building homes ... the which folk were two thousand in number ... in company with the noble Knight Josse Van Hurtere, Lord of the Manor at Moerkirchen in Flanders.'

In fact van Huerter and his three brothers seem to have had other reasons for coming to Faial, after hearing rumours of rich silver and tin deposits. These turned out to be no more than travellers' tales, but silver or no silver van Huerter and his

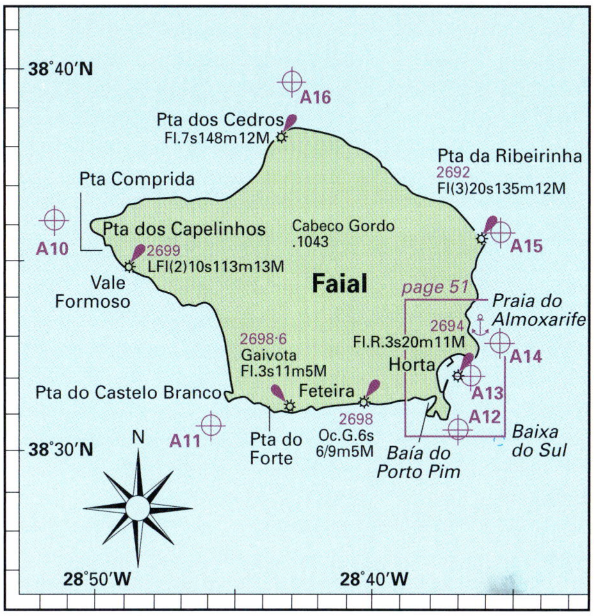

Portuguese wife, previously a lady-in-waiting to the Infante, did well in their new home. Corn, sugar, grapes and woad grew readily in the fertile soil and soon the van Huerter family were wealthy enough to build a fine house at Porto Pim, near the bay which constituted Faial's main harbour. There their daughter married Martin Behaim, traveller and creator of the Nuremberg Globe, who undoubtedly used his sojourn in Faial in the late 1480s to collect information from passing seamen.

In common with the rest of the Azores and mainland Portugal, Faial was occupied by Spanish forces from 1580 until 1640, during which time the island saw both prosperity and bloodshed. Although the fort of Santa Cruz had been established in 1565 it was unable to withstand the invaders, and defences were strengthened under Spanish rule – the fort of São Sebastião and the Spanish Gate, both at Porto Pim, date from that period – but even so the busy harbour was a tempting target for privateers, particularly the English who regarded Spain as their enemy. In 1589 the Earl of Cumberland attacked and burnt the town, and in September 1597 Sir Walter Raleigh landed with 500 men and again burnt Horta to the ground.

The 17th and 18th centuries appear to have been fairly peaceful, other than a serious earthquake in 1672, one of at least seven since the island has been inhabited. Faial was already becoming known as 'the garden of the Azores' and when Captain Cook, no stranger to lush and exotic landscapes, visited in 1775 he noticed the 'hills studded with handsome abodes, gardens and coppices'.

The island supported the Liberals in the political struggles of the early 19th century and was visited by King Pedro IV in 1832. Horta was granted city status the following year, and in 1876 the building of the 750m breakwater began. Although the harbour had declined with the coming of steam, it saw renewed prosperity as a base for American whaling ships, as many as 400 being anchored in the harbour at once, as witnessed by old photographs. Many carried local men among their crews, leading indirectly to growing emigration to the United States and Canada. The little raised turrets on the roofs of many of Horta's older homes, built to watch for approaching ships, probably date from this time.

The Azores have long been established as an important source of meteorological data, the first observatory being built on the hill of Monte das Mocas overlooking Horta. The need to transmit meteorological information to the mainland led in 1885 to the laying of the first of many cables, the Azores' first direct link with Lisbon and the outside world. By the early years of the 20th century transatlantic cables were being laid via Horta, with British, American, German and Italian companies involved. The buildings they commissioned to house their offices and equipment still line the road behind the town, looking more like country houses than one-time offices, and within a few years more than 300 foreigners were employed by the cable companies. Further links were laid in the 1920s, and even thirty years later cable was still considered more reliable than radio. However, greater automation had cut the numbers needed for maintenance and operation, and even before the advent of satellite communications the era of bridge evenings, garden parties and dances amongst the expatriate community was on the wane, with the last cable company leaving the island in 1969.

Of equal importance in the early 20th century were the beginnings of air travel, heralded in 1919 when the American Navy pilot Albert C Read landed his tiny NC4 seaplane in Horta harbour at the end of the first transatlantic flight ever made (a photograph can be seen in the SATA office in Horta). Others followed his lead – in 1929 the massive 12-engined Dornier DOX visited, as did Charles Lindbergh in 1933 on behalf of Pan Am, who used the harbour for their Pan Am Clippers between 1939 and 1945. The first foreign airline to establish a base was Lufthansa, with Imperial Airways (later to become British Airways) and Air France following between 1937 and 1939. The island's first airfield was not opened until 1971, but has been enlarged several times since.

Horta harbour was used by Allied fleets during both world wars, but perhaps of even greater danger to the islanders than war was the first major volcanic eruption for nearly three centuries. It began in mid-September 1957 with a series of earthquakes which themselves caused damage, and week or two later submarine eruptions were noticed about 1km off Ponta dos Capelinhos at the western tip of the island, growing until steam, ash and pumice fragments were being hurled hundreds of metres into the air. By mid-October an island nearly 100m high had been formed and layers of ash and pumice covered much of western Faial. A quiet spell at the end of the month proved brief, and by mid-November the former island was attached to Faial by a narrow isthmus. The cycle of alternating active and quiet periods continued into 1958, the loose ash being reinforced at intervals by lava flows until by August the cone had grown to 144m. At least 300 houses were destroyed by the associated earthquakes or buried by ash, and the noise of the eruption could often be heard in Flores 130 miles away. The island's cattle had long since been moved to mainland Portugal and many children were temporarily evacuated to the relative safety of Pico. Some 15,000 people – nearly half the island's population – took the decision to emigrate, many to the United States.

Volcanic activity had largely ceased by the end of October 1958, leaving a new headland 160m in height and Faial 2·5km^2 larger than a year earlier. It was calculated that at least 140 million cubic metres of material had been ejected, and on one occasion nearly 2m of ash fell in a single night. Steam rose at intervals for several years, but none has been seen since 1979 and the volcano is thought to be extinct. The newly formed cliffs, mostly of loose ash and pumice, have been eroded by winter storms and less than 1km^2 of the extra area remains. Thirty years ago the old Capelinhos lighthouse, now almost invisible from seaward and with its roofless buildings half covered, appeared to be standing on the edge of a desert, and even 50 years after the last eruptions much of the area is still barren, with clumps of bamboo, tamarisk and tough grasses still fighting to colonise the loose sand and ash. The whole complex, including the excellent new underground Interpretation Centre, demands a minimum of two hours' exploration which may include the chance to climb to the top of the old lighthouse. Summer opening hours (1 June to 30 September) are 1000–1900 Tuesday to Friday, 1100–1800 weekends, closed Monday, with shorter hours in winter. However, for all the interest of the new Centre with its photographic displays and films of historic volcanic activity, not to mention captioning in English as well as Portuguese, returning visitors may regret the loss of the surrounding area's unique, somewhat eerie, atmosphere.

Volcanic activity may have ceased, at least for the time being, but seismic shifts continue and in the early hours of 9 July 1998 Faial suffered a major earthquake which left at least five people dead, three villages almost completely demolished and nearly 3,000 homeless. Although the epicentre, measuring 5·8 on the Richter scale, is estimated to have been under the sea some 9M northwest of Faial, villages near the fault line which dissects the island (said to be where the Eurasion and North African plates abut) were particularly badly hit. Yachtsmen asleep in Horta marina were awakened by violent shaking, as though a sail was flogging in the wind, but the town suffered relatively little damage. Relief operations began almost immediately, though hampered by the aftershocks which continued for several months.

For a short while after both the Capelinhos eruption and the 1998 earthquake the central *caldeira*, which dominates the island, was declared a possible danger area – at the time of the Capelinhos eruption fumaroles in the interior began to steam and the lake partially drained away. The crater is nearly 2km in diameter and 400m deep, with a tunnel at the end of the road giving access to the steep interior. A path runs around the rim, providing magnificent views over the island and towards Pico and Faial, and normally the area is a favourite picnic spot for locals and visitors alike – it should certainly be high on the list of places to visit. The exterior slopes are almost bare except for short grass on which sheep and cattle graze, whilst the crater, which is partly covered with natural forest, has been declared a nature reserve.

A second reserve has been set aside nearer Horta, on the slopes of Monte da Guia and Monte Queimado just south of the town. Both hills are protected areas where the indigenous vegetation including Azores heath, Azores candleberry myrtle and Azores cedar still flourish. It was the candleberry myrtle, which can reach 6m, that gave the island its name when the early settlers mistook it for beech – *faya* – indicating how prevalent it must once have been. Monte da Guia, ascended by a winding road, is a miniature horseshoe crater enclosing the tiny Caldeira do Inferno, which although open to the sea is also part of the nature reserve and forbidden to all power-driven boats. The lower Monte Queimado ('burnt hill'), its summit crowded with tiny fields unsuspected from below, is worth climbing simply for the view it affords over Horta – though the bottom of the path, hidden behind the cottages overlooking Porto Pim, can be difficult for the visitor to find.

No one island can be said to typify the Azores but, if time is limited and only one harbour and island can be visited, a few days in Horta and a taxi-tour around Faial will probably create an ambition to return with a more leisurely schedule.

Holidays and festivals

In addition to the national holidays listed on page 26, Faial holds its official holiday on 24 June. The Festival of *Espírito Santo* and Feast of *Nossa Senhora das Angústias* are celebrated about six weeks after Easter, and the Feast of St John on 24 June. Sea Week – *Semana do Mar*, see page 53 – starts on the first Saturday in August.

Telecommunications

Mobile (cell) phone reception throughout the island is good. The country code for the Azores is 351, as it is for mainland Portugal, and the area code for Faial – which must be included even when dialling

The disused Capelinhos lighthouse near the western end of Faial

from within the island – is 292, shared with Flores, Corvo and Pico.

By 2011 free Wi-Fi was available in many parts of Horta and elsewhere throughout the island including at the airport.

Websites

Faial has several websites specific to the island including www.cmhorta.pt, a well-designed site maintained by the *Câmara Municipal de Horta* (effectively the town council) in Portuguese only, but relatively easy to follow in search of the dates of local festivals etc.; www.semanadomar.net/, the homepage of Horta's famous Sea Week, Portuguese only but readily decoded by Google Translate or similar; and finally www.petercafesport.com, devoted to the famous Café Sport, the Scrimshaw Museum, the Azevedo family and a good deal else besides, in Portuguese, English and French.

Faial is also covered by Wikipedia at www.en.wikipedia.org/wiki/Faial_Island, as well as featuring on several of the general Azores sites listed on pages 24–5.

Approach

Approached from west or northwest Faial appears relatively low and rounded, and although visible at up to 30M in clear weather will often not be seen until after the summit of Pico, some 15M beyond, has been identified.

Prominent headlands at Ponta dos Capelinhos and Ponta do Castelo Branco make a landfall on the southwest coast reassuringly simple after a long passage, though care must be taken not to confuse the two lighthouse towers. The old lighthouse, close northeast of Ponta Comprida, is of grey stone and can be seen on the skyline when southwest of Faial. The replacement lighthouse at Vale Formoso is seen against the hillside, and is thus considerably less conspicuous in daylight.

There are few off-lying dangers and clearance of 0·5M is plenty, though much of the coast may be approached closer in safety. Rocks in the bay north of Ponta do Castelo Branco and around Ponta do

Forte should be given a wide berth. The approach from north and northeast is clear, other than rocks close inshore around the headlands where tide rips can also build up. If approaching from southeast the Baixa do Sul (also known as Chapman's Rocks) with 7m depths should be avoided if any sea is running. A conspicuous white conical building with a circular dish stands on Monte da Guia, south of Horta and a windfarm (six towers) on hills to the north.

Caution

In May 2010 intense underwater seismological activity was detected about 8·5M northwest of Faial in an area stretching from 38°39'·1N to 38°46'·9N and 28°52'·8W to 29°01'·7W – close to the probable epicentre of the 1998 earthquake described on page 49. Although no further activity has been reported it would be wise to avoid the area if possible. Those who do pass through it are asked to report anything unusual to the *Centro de Informação e Vigilância Sismo Vulcânica* ✆ 296 654471
Email cvarg.macrosismica@azores.gov.pt

Navigation

Waypoints

⊕ A10 – 38°36'·1N 28°51'·4W (1M W of Pta dos Capelinhos)
⊕ A11 – 38°30'·7N 28°45'·8W (1M SW of Pta do Castelo Branco)
⊕ A12 – 38°30'·5N 28°37'W (0·5M SE of Monte da Guia)
⊕ A13 – 38°32'N 28°36'·6W (0·5M E of Horta)
⊕ A14 – 38°32'·8N 28°35'·5W (0·5M E of Pta de Baía do Cavalo)
⊕ A15 – 38°35'·8N 28°35'·4W (0·5M E of Pta da Ribeirinha)
⊕ A16 – 38°39'·7N 28°42'·9W (1M N of Pta dos Cedros)

Courses and distances

⊕ A10 – ⊕A05 (0·5M E of Lajes, Flores) = 117M, 293° / 113°
⊕ A10 – ⊕A09 (0·5M SE of Vila Nova) = 223m, 301° / 121°
⊕ A10 – ⊕A11 = 7M, 141° / 321°
⊕ A13 – ⊕A17 (0·5M NW of Madalena, Pico) = 3.3M, 099° / 279°
⊕ A13 – ⊕A20 (0·5M W of Lajes do Pico) = 19M, by eye
⊕ A13 – ⊕A22 (0·5M SSW of Velas, São Jorge) = 20·6M, 067° / 247°
⊕ A13 – ⊕A24 (1M ESE of Ilhéu do Topo, São Jorge) = 42M, by eye
⊕ A13 – ⊕A38 (1M S of Santa Clara, São Miguel) = 149M, by eye & 108° / 288° & by eye
⊕ A13 – ⊕A45 (1M WNW of Pta do Lobaio, Santa Maria) = 187M, by eye & 120° / 300° & by eye
⊕ A11 – ⊕A13 via ⊕A12 = 8·5M, 091° & 012° / 192° & 271°
⊕ A15 – ⊕A13 via ⊕A14 = 4M, 181° & 227° / 047°, 001°
⊕ A15 – ⊕A21 (1M WNW of Pta dos Rosais, São Jorge) = 15·4M, 050° / 230°
⊕ A16 – ⊕A15 = 7M, 124° / 204°

Magnetic variation

11°25'W (2011), decreasing by 7'E annually.

Tidal Streams

Tidal streams can run strongly in the Canal do Faial, the flood setting northwards at up to 1·5 knots and the ebb setting southwards, with an eddy on the ebb setting strongly into the Baía da Horta. The Canal do Faial (which is relatively shallow) can become extremely rough at times, with tidal races off all headlands and in particular off Ponta da Baía do Cavalo just north of Horta itself.

Charts

Faial and the Central Group
Admiralty *1956* (1:175,000)
Portuguese *43102* (1:300,000)
US *51061* (1:250,000)
Imray-Iolaire *E1* (1:750,000)

Canal do Faial and Approaches to Horta
Admiralty *1957* (1:37,500)
Portuguese *46403* (1:50,000)
US *51062* (1:50,000)

Lights

2699 **Vale Formoso** LFl(2)10s113m13M
White tower, small red lantern 14m
Note Repeatedly observed to have considerably less than the stated range
2698 **Feteira Ldg Lts on 341°** Oc.G.6s6/9m5M
White posts, red bands 3/5m
2698·6 **Gaivota (Faial Airport)**
Fl.3s11m5M Yellow column
2694 **Horta breakwater** Fl.R.3s20m11M
Red lantern on white framework tower 15m
2692 **Ponta da Ribeirinha** Fl(3)20s135m12M
133°-vis-001° Metal post 6m
2700 **Ponta dos Cedros**
Fl.7s148m12M White tower 4m

Coast Radio Station

Faial 38°35'N 28°43'W, remotely controlled from Lisbon
VHF Ch 16, 25, 26, 28 (24 hours)

Radionaval

Horta 38°32'N 28°38'W
DSC MF MMSI 002040200 ✆ 292 208620 *Fax* 292 208669
(This station does not accept public correspondence other than distress and safety traffic)
VHF Ch 11, 16 (24 hours)
Weather bulletins Ch 11 at 0900, 2100 (storm and bad weather warnings, synopsis and 24-hour forecast for waters within 20 miles of Faial, Graciosa, Pico, São Jorge and Terceira); Ch 11 at 1000, 1900 (storm and bad weather warnings, synopsis and 24-hour forecast for waters within 20 miles of Flores and Corvo). Both transmissions in Portuguese and English
Navigational warnings Ch 11 at 0900, 2100 (local warnings for Faial, Graciosa, Pico, São Jorge and Terceira); Ch 11 at 1000, 1900 (local warnings for Flores and Corvo). Both transmissions in Portuguese and English

Navtex

Identification letters 'F' and 'J'. The Azores fall within NAVAREA 11. Transmissions in English (F) are on the standard Navtex frequency of 518kHz, those in Portuguese (J) are on 490kHz. Horta 'F' transmits storm and gale warnings, synopsis and 24-hour forecast in English for Areas 3, 5, 7, 30, 31 (see plan page 7) on receipt and at 0050, 0450, 0850, 1250, 1650, 2050. Navigational warnings follow the weather bulletin. Horta 'J' transmits the same information in Portuguese on receipt and at 0130, 0530, 0930, 1330, 1730, 2130.

Harbours and anchorages

Horta

38°32′·03N 28°37′·28W (breakwater head)

Waypoint
⊕A13 – 38°32′N 28°36′·6W (0·5M E of Horta breakwater)

Tides
Predictions for Horta are available via Admiralty *EasyTide* – see page 30
Time difference on Ponta Delgada: –0002
Mean spring range 1·2m
Mean neap range 0·5m

Plans
Admiralty *1957* (1:10,000)
Portuguese *46403* (1:7,500)
US *51062* (1:10,000)
Imray-Iolaire *E1* (1:12,500)

Lights
2694 **Breakwater** Fl.R.3s20m11M
Red lantern on white framework tower 15m
2696 **Boa Viagem** Iso.G.1·5s12m9M
Square black column, red top 7m
buoys **Temporary buoys**
In 2010 three small yellow buoys, all Fl(4)Y.10s2M and with × topmarks, were positioned from 38°32′·5N 28°37′W to 38°32′·2N 28°37′·5W. They lay outside the new north breakwater and are likely to be moved as work progresses
buoy **Wave recording buoy**
Fl(5)Y.20s3M Spherical yellow buoy
Expected to remain in place until late 2012
2697 **Ldg Lts on 196°** Iso.G.2s13/15m2M
White posts, red bands and × topmarks 8/9m, 12m apart

Harbour communications
Harbourmaster ✆ 292 208010 *Fax* 292 208019
Email capitania.horta@marinha.pt VHF 11, 16 (call *Capimar Horta*) (0900–1230, 1400–1700)
Port Authority ✆ 292 208300 *Fax* 292 208315
Email portohorta@mail.telepac.pt
www.portohorta.com VHF Ch 11, 16 (0800–1200, 1300–1700)
Horta Marina ✆ 292 391693 *Fax* 292 293986
Email hortamarina@aptosa.com
www.marinasazores.com VHF Ch 10, 16 (0800–1200, 1300–2000 daily from 1 May to 15 August, otherwise 0800–1200, 1300–2000)
Mid Atlantic Yacht Services ✆ 292 391616
Fax 292 391656 *Email* mays@mail.telepac.pt
www.midatlanticyachtservices.com VHF Ch 77 (1000–1300, 1400–1700 weekdays, 1000–1300 Saturday)

Port limits
A circle, radius 4M, centred on Horta breakwater light – see Port limits, page 27.

The crossroads of the Atlantic

The marina at Horta first opened in 1986, to the general approbation of visiting yachtsmen, and has been followed up by a systematic programme of harbour and marina improvements. First the main breakwater, built in 1876, was reinforced with steel and concrete and a container area created at its root to ease cargo handling, soon followed by a short mole in the southeast corner – apparently built partly of masonry rubble from the 1998 earthquake – to create a fishing and smallcraft area. Then, after several years in the planning and building stages, the marina's new 'south basin' was officially opened in 2002, increasing berthing to a maximum of 300 yachts, though the north basin, with its narrow entrance, remains probably the safest place in the archipelago to ride out storm or hurricane force winds. Both the reception quay and the building overlooking it – which houses all the relevant authorities – have been enlarged, and the entire facility is run with efficiency and friendliness.

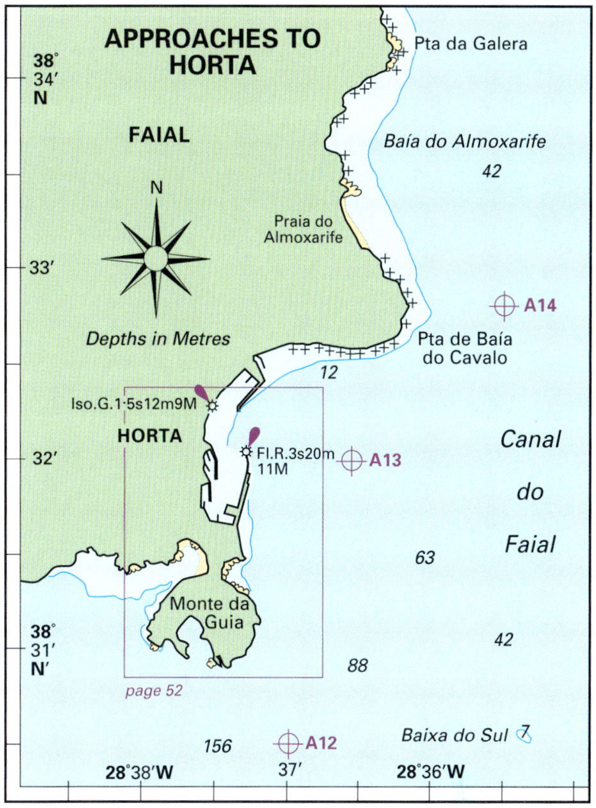

Visitor numbers have increased steadily over the years, with 1,135 yachts of over 30 nationalities passing through in 2000, rising to 1,300 boats and around 5,000 people by 2009. Records show that in the 24 years from 1986 to 2009 inclusive 25,826 boats and almost 100,000 yachtsmen and women visited Horta, making it one of the four busiest yacht transit harbours in the world. Every year sees a higher proportion of seriously large yachts, both sail and power, and as early as 2002 more than 150 yachts of over 21m (70ft) called in. The growing proportion of large cruising catamarans also poses problems when space is at a premium. Cruising yachts of under 10m are becoming a rarity, and though no statistics are available it is estimated that average cruising yacht size had grown from around 11m (36ft) in 1990 to at least 13·5m (44ft) by 2010 – with beam to match. The authorities are rightly proud that, despite the enormous rise in numbers, Horta has never lost its EU 'Blue Flag', indicating an outstandingly clean harbour, since this was first awarded in 1987.

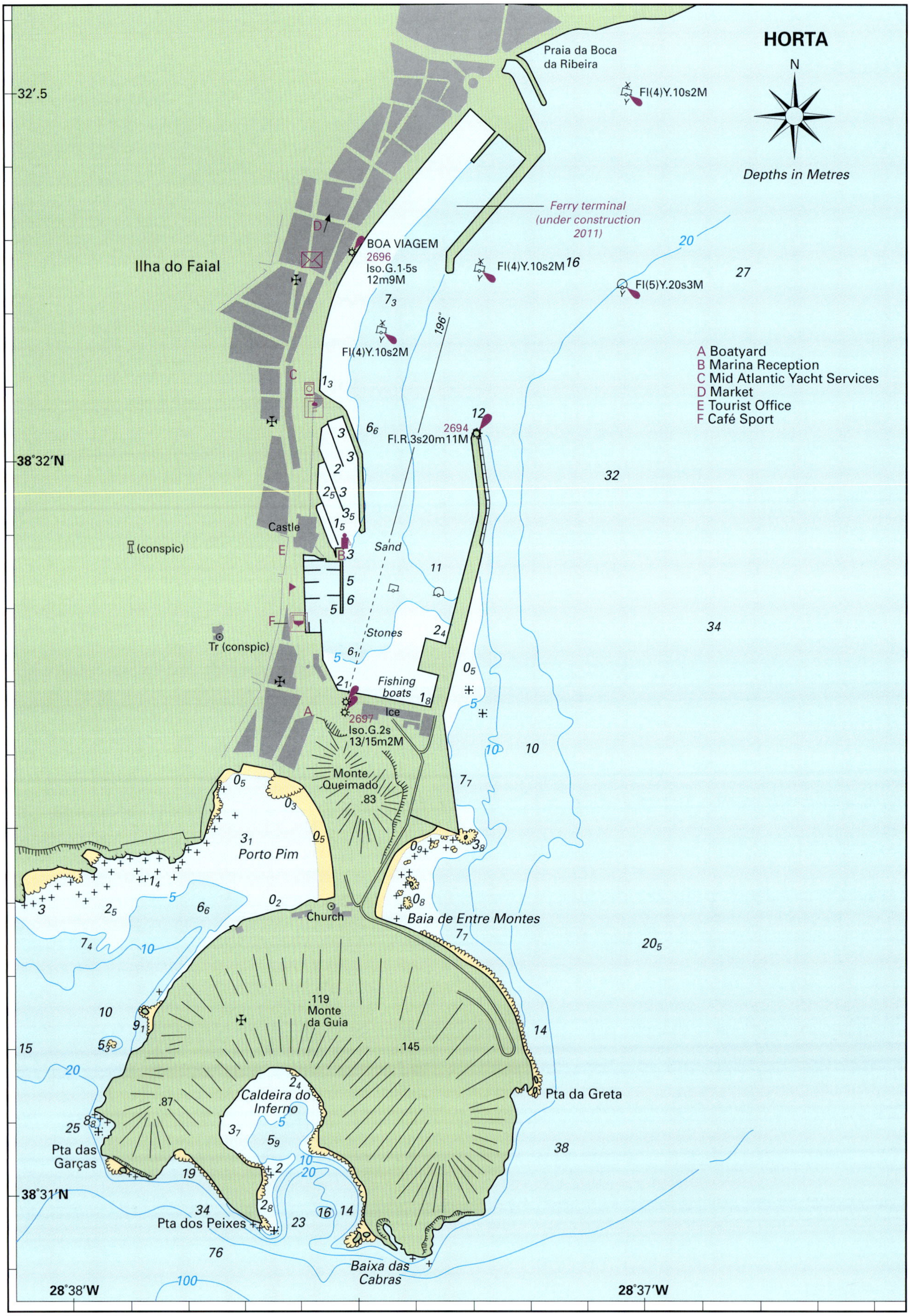
HORTA
N
Depths in Metres
Praia da Boca da Ribeira
Fl(4)Y.10s2M
Ferry terminal (under construction 2011)
BOA VIAGEM
2696
Iso.G.1·5s
12m9M
Fl(4)Y.10s2M
Fl(5)Y.20s3M
Ilha do Faial
A Boatyard
B Marina Reception
C Mid Atlantic Yacht Services
D Market
E Tourist Office
F Café Sport
2694
Fl.R.3s20m11M
Castle
(conspic)
Sand
Stones
Tr (conspic)
Fishing boats
Ice
2697
Iso.G.2s
13/15m2M
Monte Queimado
Porto Pim
Church
Baia de Entre Montes
Monte da Guia
Caldeira do Inferno
Pta da Greta
Pta das Garças
Pta dos Peixes
Baixa das Cabras
32′.5
38°32′N
38°31′N
28°38′W
28°37′W

The latest project – and by far the most ambitious to date – is the construction of an entirely new breakwater extending southeast from a point north of Boa Viagem light (see plan). This will handle ferry traffic and smaller cruise ships, freeing the southwest corner of the 'old' harbour for other use, possibly by superyachts. Work on the new facility was progressing well during the summer of 2010 despite poor weather, and is scheduled for completion by June 2012.

Once ashore, the long narrow town is attractive with good shopping, and the local people still friendly and helpful towards yachtsmen despite the vastly increased numbers. The Café Sport, overlooking the harbour, has been a meeting place for yachtsmen for well over half a century. Founded by Henrique Azevedo in 1918 and run for many years by his son José – always known as Peter, who died in November 2005 at the age of 80 – it is now in the care of Peter's son José Henrique. The single café has expanded since the late 1990s, with associated shops in Horta, Ponta Delgada and elsewhere, and other Café Sports in Lisbon and on the Algarve. Local recognition includes the renaming of the western part of Rua Vasco da Gama, on which the original café stands, as Rua José Azevedo (Peter). In the rooms above the café an impressive museum of Azorean scrimshaw has been assembled, comprising nearly 1,000 exhibits and representing the work of some 20 different scrimshanders. Highly recommended.

Back downstairs, the walls of the world-famous café are hung two and three deep with burgees bearing the names of some of the best known yachts in the annals of ocean cruising. The same names once appeared on the famous breakwater wall, where the crews of visiting ships and yachts have been painting their names and insignia for many decades, and such was the pressure on space that old paintings were often obliterated to make way for new. The marina's concrete walls offered a new and much more convenient venue, but within two seasons they were completely covered, with boats, birds, whales, charts, burgees, cartoons and abstract designs providing an outdoor art gallery. When wall space ran out crews began painting on the marina mole itself, so that from any vantage point the entire area resembles a brightly coloured patchwork – generally including several figures absorbed with brush and paint pot. The tradition has grown up that it is unlucky to leave Horta without making one's mark, and it would seem that cruising yachtsmen are a superstitious breed.

Horta's third claim to fame amongst cruising yachts is its annual Sea Week, *Semana do Mar*, which starts on the first weekend in August. Long a local festival with music, dancing and craft displays ashore, dinghy and swimming races in the harbour,

Horta's large bay seen from the north, with the new ferry terminal taking shape in the foreground

Horta marina's 'south basin', with the 'north basin' beyond. The white office building can be seen on the reception quay

and culminating in the 'Canal Race' for visiting yachts on the final Sunday, for the past 30 years or so the *Clube Naval de Horta* has included a number of other races in its programme. Handicapping is necessarily something of a lottery, protests are firmly discouraged, and yachts of all types and nationalities take part in a spirit of competitive entente. The week finishes with a prizegiving and party to which all competitors are invited. Unfortunately it sometimes falls a little late in the season for yachts returning to northern Europe, but is very definitely worth staying for if the schedule permits.

Approach and entrance

In early 2011 a spherical yellow wave recording buoy was deployed at 38°32'·26N 28°37'·02W, about 0·3M northeast of the main breakwater head. It is lit as described above, and is expected to remain in place until late 2012.

By day quite straightforward, though the harbour cannot be seen until the last headland is cleared and a course can be steered for the white tower structure on the end of the breakwater. There are good depths directly off its end, which should not be rounded too closely in case of the Pico ferry or a fishing boat leaving at speed. On rounding the main breakwater the marina mole and reception berth will be seen dead ahead. Work is taking place in the northern part of the bay – see plan – and yachts should avoid this area.

By night the town lights of Horta are very bright and, if approaching along the south coast of Faial, will be seen over the Baía do Porto Pim before Monte da Guia is rounded. The breakwater light will probably be identified first. Boa Viagem is difficult to identify against the town lights and in any case is of little use to yachts. During Sea Week in early August thousands of coloured lights illuminate the town and harbour and could make identifying navigation lights more difficult than usual. The construction work in the northern part of the harbour – see plan – is well lit and is, in any case, well off the approach line normally taken by yachts.

The south end of the marina wall carries a large angular sculpture lit by white floods, but no navigation light. Two ship's mooring buoys are currently laid in the harbour, together with a few local moorings, and during the busy summer season there are likely to be several yachts lying at anchor, possibly unlit.

Berthing

On arrival, yachts of up to 15m or so should go alongside the reception quay (least depth 3m) to be allocated a berth. If the quay is full, however, and there is any swell running, rafting up is not recommended due to surge and anchoring will be found preferable while awaiting one's turn.

It is helpful if yachts of more than 15m LOA call on VHF during their approach, while the very large indeed should notify the marina of their ETA on departing their previous harbour. In both cases they are likely to be directed straight to a berth in the south basin. This can take five yachts of 30–35m LOA and 5–6m draught on the southernmost fingers, with another seven of 18m LOA and 4–5m draught inside (see plan). The very largest generally berth on the outside of the 120m south mole in 5–6m, and only when this is already occupied is the main breakwater pressed into service. In 2006 a patch carrying no more than 3·5m was reported just off the ferry berth, approximately parallel with the root of the short mole and around 30m offshore, but this has not been confirmed.

Visitors of more modest size are usually allocated a berth in the older north basin, either alongside a finger or rafted up against the wall. If directed to the shoreward side of C pontoon (the northernmost), note that the wall slopes down steeply to the waters edge. Beyond this lie a band of loose black lava rocks which extend outwards about 2m and are barely awash at low tide. Further out there are a few larger rocks or piles of rocks, some as much as one-third of the way across the channel, which could pose a particular hazard to the rudder if going astern. The very clear water does help in locating them, however.

Yachts taking part in a rally will be grouped together if the marina office is notified in advance by the organisers.

Anchorage

After many years during which anchoring was discouraged, it is now accepted as necessary during the busier parts of the year, in particular for multihulls. Holding is generally poor over large stones, though there are some sand patches. The daily charge (see below) includes unlimited water, either from the reception quay or by can from elsewhere in the marina, and those at anchor are welcome to leave dinghies at any convenient point in the marina and to use the toilets, showers and launderette on payment of the usual fees.

Formalities

Marina manager is Armando Castro, who has an office on the upper floor of the marina administration building overlooking the reception quay. The formalities are generally completed on the ground floor, however, often by José Lobão who, in June 2011, will have manned the marina's front office for exactly 25 years. Both men speak good English and know their marina inside out. Office hours are 0800–1200 and 1300–2000 daily from 1 May to 15 August, otherwise 0800–1200 and 1300–2000.

The *Serviço de Estrangeiros e Fronteiras* or *SEF* (Immigration), *Alfândega* (Customs) and *Polícia Marítima* all have offices in the marina reception building, and must be visited even if clearance has already been obtained elsewhere in the Azores. The *SEF* keep the same hours as the marina office; the *Alfândega* and *Polícia Marítima* are both open 0900–1200 and 1300–1700 daily. In Horta the *Guarda Nacional Republicana* (*GNR*) are not directly involved, although copies of the paperwork is forwarded to them.

On departure the marina office must be visited first to settle the bill (most major credit cards are accepted, though not American Express), and copies of the receipt presented at all three offices. There is no requirement to move the yacht herself back to the reception quay. If any of the crew are leaving by air it is necessary to advise the *Alfândega* a day or two in advance in case they should wish to come and inspect the yacht.

If planning to visit any of the smaller islands it will be worth preserving the computer printout which one receives. This carries answers to all the standard questions, so avoiding potential language difficulties.

The picturesque waterfront at Horta, Faial

Just a few of the many hundreds of paintings which adorn the marina walls at Horta

Charges

Horta Marina is one of the Portos dos Açores SA chain, and shares their basic price structure. As of 2011 yachts of 10–12m LOA paid €12.22 per night and those of 12–15m paid €18.50, inclusive of everything except showers (see below). For further details see page 27 and/or www.marinasazores.com, the website of the branch of Portos dos Açores SA concerned with marina operation (though note that different charges apply to yachts owned by residents and by non-residents).

There is a flat rate for anchoring, applicable all monohulls and multihulls irrespective of length. As of 2011 this stood at €6.08 per day and included unlimited water and other use of other marina facilities – see Anchorage, above.

Facilities

Horta undoubtedly has the best facilities for yachts in the Azores, and in particular the continuing success of Mid Atlantic Yacht Services (MAYS) ✆ 292 391616 *Fax* 292 391656 *Email* mays@mail.telepac.pt www.midatlanticyachtservices.com, has eased the situation for visiting yachtsmen needing to get work done. In addition to English, owners Duncan and Ruth Sweet speak French, German and Portuguese and have good contacts in mainland Portugal. MAYS, which is to be found opposite the root of the marina mole, is Azorean agent for over a dozen international manufacturers (including Raymarine – for which it is a licensed Service Centre – Volvo Penta, Yanmar, Vetus, Magellan, Jabsco, ICOM, Frigoboat) and can organise importation and fitting of most items. The company specialises in engineering, electronics, rigging and deck hardware, but amongst its other services will assist with EU yacht importation (see page 28), send and receive faxes and email, and handle cruisers' mail. They also run a free book-swap, and display a four-day weather forecast updated daily. Office hours are 1000–1300, 1400–1700 weekdays, 1000–1300 Saturday.

Boatyard There is a small, open lay-up area in the southwest corner of the harbour where DIY repairs and other work can be carried out. Water and electricity are laid on, and workmen can be employed if required. Consult the marina office regarding timing and prices though space is at a premium and, other than in a real emergency, a long wait is likely. As of 2010 there appeared to be the usual problem of semi-derelict (and possibly abandoned) yachts occupying a large part of the available space, and in the longer term a suitable long-term storage site away from the harbour is likely to be acquired.

Travel-lift A 20-tonne capacity hoist stands in the southwest corner of the harbour. Book via the marina office, whose personnel operate the hoist and where suitable supports (chocking) can be organised if needed. Proof of insurance will be required. A second 75-tonne capacity travel-lift is due to be installed on the spur in the southeast corner of the harbour, probably in 2014.

Diving services Norberto, ✆ 292 293891, 962 824028 *Email* norbertodiver@mail.telepac.pt or norbertodiver@mail.telepac.pt, with premises near the *clube naval*, primarily offers sport diving and whale-watching but can also handle underwater repairs or assessments. Central Sub ✆ 292 249870 *Email* centralsub@sapo.pt www.centralsub.com, also offer tuition, sport diving and whale watching, in addition to underwater inspection, hull cleaning and other work. Official permission should first be sought – see Port limits on page 27.

Engineers MAYS is agent for various international manufacturers (see head of this section) and has a long-established reputation. Jean Pierre Paulus Dhondt can also be contacted direct on ✆ 962 669856 or *Email* jeanpierre-repair@sapo.pt and specialises in engines and gearboxes.

Helitractores Lda ✆ 292 208500 *Fax* 292 208505 offers diesel injector and pump servicing in addition to general welding and other metalwork, while RY Marine Yacht Services ✆ 964 124053 carry out welding and other repairs from a small workshop near the lay-up area.

Engineering is also among the services offered by the newly-established Horta Yacht Center ✆ 966 531002, 965 648559 *Email* maresemarinheiros@hotmail.com which opened on Rua Vasco da Gama (opposite the Forte de Santa Cruz) in May 2010.

Electrical & electronic repairs Once again MAYS heads the field, with competition from Horta Yacht Center (see *Engineers*, above) and João Neves ✆ 918 063427.

Sail repairs & canvaswork Ralf Holzerland ✆ 292 293149, 914 922111 will collect, repair and return sails, but does not normally make them from scratch. His work has been highly praised by a number of visiting skippers. Also among the services offered by Horta Yacht Center (see *Engineers*, above)

Rigging MAYS stocks 1x19 wire plus a broad range of swageless fittings up to 12mm and some rigging components for larger dimensions. Also among the services offered by Horta Yacht Center (see *Engineers*, above).

Liferaft servicing A technician/inspector from mainland Portugal visits Pico annually, usually in March or April, to service liferafts for local commercial craft. Over-wintering yachts may wish to have theirs serviced at the same time – consult MAYS regarding timing and transport. Most major brands can be handled.

Chandlery By far the widest range is available at MAYS, who manage to pack an impressive variety into their small premises and will order parts and equipment not in stock (open 1000–1300, 1400–1700 weekdays,

1000–1300 Saturday). Much smaller quantities of chandlery and sailing clothing will be found at Horta Yacht Center (see *Engineers*, above) open 1000–1400, 1600–1900 weekdays only) and Horta Sub on Rua Vasco da Gama, which has limited chandlery, clothes and outboard motors amongst its large choice of fishing equipment.

While not really a chandlery, Teófilo SA (open 0900–1800 Monday to Saturday), ✆ 292 200000 *Fax* 292 391392, near the Café Sport, stocks an impressive range of tools and general electrical and DIY items, as well as paint, batteries, lubricants and a very limited range of chandlery. Other hardware stores throughout the town sell reinforced hose, electrical fittings, etc. in addition to hand and power tools of all kinds.

Charts MAYS have a good range of Imray books and charts, plus a selection of Admiralty charts and publications, independently printed almanacs, etc. and will order items not in stock. In 2010 Teófilo SA (see above) also had a few elderly Portuguese charts for sale, though none for outside the Azores.

It should be noted that neither of the above are cheap options for a boat sailing from the UK – an Admiralty chart will cost about half as much in Britain as the same chart, or the Portuguese equivalent, would if bought in the Azores.

The João Luis Copy Centre on Praça da República ✆ 292 391381 *Email* joaoluiscentrocopia@sapo.pt offers large-sized photocopying in addition to computer printing, etc. Note, however, that most charts and all pilot books – including this one – are subject to copyright.

Water Supplied to each marina and mole berth and included in the daily charge, though hoses are not provided.

Showers In the semi-circular building in the northwest corner of the marina area, open 0800–1145, 1300–1900, 2100–0700 from 1 May until 15 August, otherwise 0800–1145, 1300–1630. In 2011 a shower cost €2, which included soap and a towel.

Laundry There is a large laundry room in the shower and services block of the marina. Normally attendant service by machine or DIY at large sinks, though it may sometimes be necessary to return to move one's load from washing machine to dryer. Open 0800–1145, 1300–1900 from 1 May until 15 August, otherwise 0800–1145, 1300–1630, but go early as there are only five washers and two dryers to serve the entire marina and a queue often builds by mid-morning. In 2011 it cost just under €8 to wash and dry a 5kg load.

Alternatively call either the Lavandaria Rosa ✆ 292 391557, 962 821723 which will collect and return laundry to the marina seven days a week, or visit the Horta Laundry ✆ 292 391911 on Rua Conselheiro Medeiros (the road leading towards the market), which also offers dry cleaning.

Electricity At all berths and on the marina wall, and included in the daily charge. Yachts must provide their own cable and standard European plug, plus adaptor if needed (all components are available from MAYS, assembled or separately). 220v is available in both basins, with 380v 3-phase in the south basin and on parts of the north wall. Electricity throughout the Azores is 50Hz.

Fuel Both diesel and petrol are available at the marina reception quay, and yachts are encouraged to fill up on arrival to avoid a return visit. The concession is run by the *Clube Naval de Horta*, and from mid-April to mid-August operates the same hours as the marina office (0800–1200 and 1300–2000 daily). Payment must be made in cash, but MAYS will process payment by credit/debit card (in any currency) for a small service charge.

If more than 5,000 litres (about 1,130 UK gallons / 1,400 US gallons) are required, arrange bunkering via MAYS (see above) or Bensaude Shipping Agents Lda ✆ 292 293031/33 www.shipping.bensaude.pt who have an office at Rua Vasco da Gama 42. Delivery is by truck, to the outer wall of the south marina basin or to the main breakwater. Duty free diesel is available in quantities of 10,000 litres (about 2,250 UK gallons / 2,800 US gallons) or more by arrangement with MAYS. Two working days' notice is required and delivery is by truck as above.

Bottled gas Camping Gaz exchanges are readily available. Calor Gas and other non-standard cylinders can be refilled with butane, either via the attendant at the marina fuel pumps, Teófilo SA or MAYS. For the former allow at least one working day, though if bottles are taken to MAYS by 1100 they will normally be ready for collection by 1500.

The summit of Pico seen over Horta's north marina basin

Whaleboats lined up on the slipway at Horta. Both sailing and rowing races are popular features of local regattas

Weather forecast The marina office and Café Sport display Portuguese three-day forecasts and synoptic charts; Mid Atlantic Yacht Services offers the US NOAA current, 48-hour and 96-hour forecasts and charts (with copies available at nominal charge).

Clube naval The *Clube Naval de Horta* occupies the glass-fronted building on the water front south of the marina. Although mostly concerned with dinghy sailing, it organises the yacht races during Sea Week and scuba equipment is available for hire. There is a café/bar, and a limited restaurant service.

Banks Numerous, all with cash dispensers. There is also a cash machine in the marina reception building.

Shops/provisioning Several reasonably well-stocked supermarkets in the town centre, plus a vast MODELO hypermarket on Rua Princípe Alberto do Mónaco (which leads uphill from opposite the old church at the south end of the harbour). Open 0830–2100 Monday to Saturday, 0830–1300 Sunday and holidays, and normally willing to deliver larger orders to the marina. A branch of Worten (a Portuguese-wide retailer of electrical and electronic goods) shares the same entrance on the right.

Closer to home, Horta Yacht Center's 'Yachts Pantry' is conveniently located just behind the public gardens and is open 0830–2000 weekdays, 0900–1300 Sunday. Trolleys can be borrowed to transport purchases to the boat, but they *must* be returned. Alternatively Loja do Triangulo, a locally-owned shop selling fresh goods (grown and baked) as well as wine and handicrafts, sourced entirely from Faial, Pico and São Jorge operates from premises on Rua Conselheiro Medeiros.

A good selection of souvenir, clothing, chemists and other shops will be found in the older part of the town, though see the note on page 67 if considering a piece of scrimshaw. Books on Azorean subjects in a number of languages can be purchased at Base Peter Zee and elsewhere, while the MAYS office houses an extensive book-swap, again in several languages.

Produce market A small fruit and vegetable market, with a fish market behind, lies towards the northern end of town. The best variety is generally to be found on Friday, but it is always necessary to go early for a good selection, particularly of fish. Some of the produce is brought over on the ferry from Pico – Horta plums and Pico cheese are mentioned by Joshua Slocum, who found that the two do not mix.

Hotels, restaurants & cafés Hotels range from four star downwards. A wide variety of restaurants, snack bars and cafés serve food at very reasonable prices, including the Internacional Café – see under Internet access, below – and the somewhat anonymous, though long-established, Papa Pizza opposite the public gardens (look for the Nestlé sign).

Medical services Hospital outside the town – many of the staff speak some English – plus dentists and opticians.

Communications

Post office On Rua Serpa Pinto at the northern end of the town, open 0830–1830 weekdays only. Stamps can be bought at any shop displaying the green *correio* sign as well as in MAYS or at the Café Sport.

Mailing addresses C/o Horta Marina, Cais de Santa Cruz, 9900-017 Horta, Faial, Açores, Portugal; Mid Atlantic Yacht Services, Rua Conselheiro Medeiros da Silveira 3, 9900–144 Horta, Faial, Açores, Portugal; or the Café Sport, Rua José Azevedo (Peter) 9, 9900-027 Horta, Faial, Açores, Portugal.

Telephones At the main post office, outside the marina bar, opposite the *clube naval* and elsewhere. Most are card-operated, using cards available at the post office.

Internet access Horta is extremely well served, both for those with their own computers and those without. For the former group, free Wi-Fi is available throughout the marina and may cover yachts at anchor. Ashore, it is available in the park overlooking the north marina, complete with electrical sockets (look on the trees...), and at the marina bar, though without power sockets. The Internacional Café, on the corner opposite, offers patrons free Wi-Fi and mains power (a four-way adaptor is provided), as well as having its own computer/printer combination available for rental by the hour.

For those dependent on static computers Base Peter Zee, close to the Café Sport, has four internet computers plus a printer, and is open 0830–2200 daily from June until August, closing at 1730 at other times. Navig@te, ✆ 292 207278, on Rua Conselheiro Medeiros (the town's main shopping street), offers computer services, including repairs, as well as access to the internet, and is open 0900–1300, 1400–1800 weekdays, 0900–1300 Saturday. Finally AZIP ✆ 292 292288 www.azip.pt on Rua das Augústias in the southern part of the town, has three computers connected to the internet, offers a repair service and sells computer consumables including a range of inkjets.

Car hire A choice of at least four companies, three of them situated on the Rua Conselheiro Medeiros, one street inland from the marina. Book in good time if possible, particularly during July and August, possibly via MAYS in advance of arrival.

Taxis Taxi ranks outside the Estalagem de Santa Cruz and near the market.

Buses Circular route around the island – timetable from the tourist office.

Ferries Several times daily to Pico, and also to the other islands of the central group – details and timetable from the tourist office, or see Transportation, page 23.

Air services Daily services to the UK via Lisbon, and to the other islands. See Transportation, page 23.

Praia do Almoxarife, looking a little east of north with Graciosa and São Jorge just visible on the horizon

Praia do Almoxarife

38°33'·4N 28°36'·55W (quay)

Lights
2693 **Almoxarife cables**
Dir.Fl(2)R.8s6m9M (daylight range 5M)
Directional on 224·5°
White column, red bands 4m. Marks submarine cables

Beach anchorage open to the east

An open bay 1·5M north of Horta, which can also be reached by bus, Praia do Almoxarife has a pleasant dark sand beach with clear water for swimming and a short mole with steps suitable for dinghy landing. It is protected from south through to northwest, but is recommended as a daytime anchorage only and following the completion of formalities at Horta.

Ponta da Baía do Cavalo to the south is fringed by off-lying rocks to a distance of about 200m. However the prominent church almost on the beach can safely be approached bearing between 256° and 296°. Good anchorage in 7–8m over sand and rock is to be found both south of the small quay, which has a water tap and a café at its root, and in a small indentation about 0·25M further north, beyond Pta do Areal and the Baixa do Feno. Public gardens (including a children's play area), a campsite and the impressive grey and white church lie behind the beach to the south of the quay, with a few shops a short walk inland.

Baía do Porto Pim

38°31'·48N 28°37'·67W (centre of bay)

Lights
2697·5 **Porto Pim cables**
Fl(2)R.8s8m9M (daylight range 1·7M) 345°-vis-013°
White column, red bands 4m.
Marks submarine cables

Enclosed bay where anchoring is forbidden

Anchoring in the Baía do Porto Pim is now forbidden, for fear of damaging the optical cables marked by the above light. (The same is true off all the other newly laid, and lit, cables throughout the Azores.) It is mentioned here largely to emphasise that point, though there is nothing to prevent the crews of yachts berthed in Horta Marina visiting by a dinghy which can be hauled up on the sand. Such a trip could include a turn inside the Caldeira do Inferno, the perfect double crater inside Monte da Guia – though it would have to be under oars rather than power, and landing is forbidden.

The northern edge of the Baía do Porto Pim is fringed with volcanic rocks, but in the centre the fine sandy bottom shoals evenly towards the beach, a popular spot for swimming with local people and visitors alike where a bar and (cold) swimmers' showers are to be found. Alternatively, if berthed in the marina the beach at Porto Pim is only 10 minutes away on foot.

Perhaps the best reason to visit Porto Pim is to visit the *Fábrica da Baleia* (the old whale processing factory, now a museum, which should be open again in 2011 following restoration. Summer opening hours are 1000–1800 weekdays (guided tours 1100, 1500 and 1630) and 1500–1900 weekends (guided tour 1630), with shorter hours in winter.

Looking southwest over Baía do Porto Pim, southwest of Horta

Pico

Between 38°23'N–38°34'N and 28°02'W–28°33'W

Introduction

Pico is dominated by the 2,351m volcanic peak after which it is named and which lies approximately one-third of the way along its west to east axis, and for most visitors the sight of this perfect volcanic cone reaching into the clouds will be one of the most enduring images of the entire Azores. However, the mountain – often referred to as Pico Alto – comprises only part of the island, which is approximately 48km long by up to 15km wide, its area of about 445km² making it the second largest in the group after São Miguel. Neither is it the only volcano on the island. Small, isolated cones and craters dot the uplands, particularly in the western part, while eight small lakes lie further east towards Pico Topo, at 1,633m the second highest peak. Other evidence of volcanic activity are the lava beds known as *mistérios* (mysteries), legacies of eruptions in the 16th and 18th centuries and only now beginning to support vegetation. There are long galleries and caves in the slopes above Madalena and Lajes, caused by escaping gas bubbles as the lava cooled. The *Gruta das Torres* (Cave of the Towers), discovered in 1990 and just a few kilometres from Madalena, is the largest of these – in fact the largest lava tunnel in the entire archipelago – and has been open to visitors since 2005. Hard hats and lamps are provided, after which small groups are taken on guided tours (in several languages, including English) through the first 450m of the cave. Check opening times at the tourist office in Horta, then ask directions or get a taxi from Madalena.

Pico wine was famous in the 18th century and is gradually making a comeback

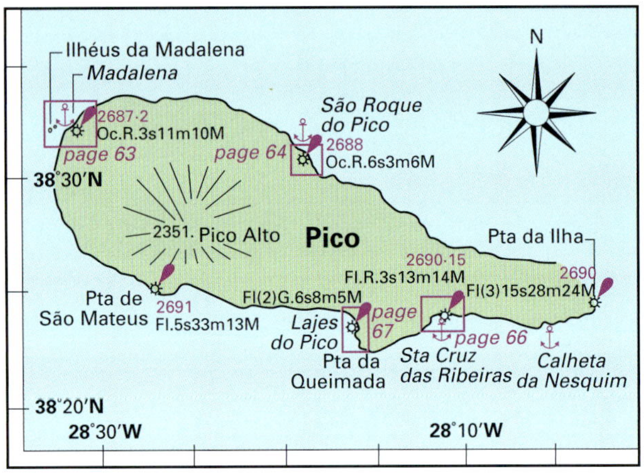

A guide is no longer mandatory if wishing to climb Pico. Instead one checks in at the interpretation centre at the top of the single road, sign a disclaimer and are given an electronic tracker to return on the way down. The lower slopes are forested up to about 1,500m with shrubs reaching a further 500m, but the final 300m or so is bare lava, snow-covered in winter, rendered even more difficult by the 40° ascents and loose footing of ash and pumice. Pico Alto is crowned by a crater some 300m in diameter and 30m deep. Within lie steaming fumaroles – it must be remembered that whilst semi-dormant the volcano is by no means extinct – and the 70m cone of Pico Pequeno (Little Pico), the highest point not only in the Azores but in all of Portugal. As might be expected, on a clear day the views from the summit are superb, though often the peak is blanketed by cloud. Certainly the ascent is only for the fit and energetic, with some parties opting to spend the night in the crater itself in order to watch both sunset and sunrise. The mountaintop gets extremely cold at night, even in summer, and warm clothes and sleeping bags are essential.

It would be a mistake to assume that Pico Alto is the island's only attraction, and other than perhaps São Miguel it is probably the most popular of all the islands for touring by hire car or taxi. The scenery is surprisingly varied. As the road along the south coast leaves Madalena and winds through the heart of the wine area it seems to run between a maze of black lava walls, built with vast toil over the centuries to protect the vines from the Atlantic winds. Until recently many of the tiny vineyards which they enclose lay deserted and derelict, but now areas which have plainly been untended for decades are being brought back into use, such is the resurgence in popularity of Pico wine. In the 18th century *Vinho do Pico* was exported to America, England and even the imperial court of the Russian Tsars, but the vines were attacked by disease in the

Navigation

Waypoints

⊕ A17 – 38°32′·5N 28°32′·5W (0·5M NW of Madalena)
⊕ A18 – 38°32′·1N 28°18′·6W (0·5M NE of São Roque)
⊕ A19 – 38°24′·3N 28°00′·6W (1M ESE of Pta da Ilha)
⊕ A20 – 38°24′N 28°16′·2W (0·5M W of Lajes do Pico)

Courses and distances

⊕ A17 – ⊕ A13 (0·5M E of Horta) = 3.3M, 279° / 099°
⊕ A18 – ⊕ A13 (0·5M E of Horta) = 15M, by eye
⊕ A18 – ⊕ A22 (0·5M SSW of Velas, São Jorge) = 9·4M, 031° / 211°
⊕ A20 – ⊕ A13 (0·5M E of Horta) = 19M, by eye

Magnetic variation

11°25′W (2011), decreasing by 7′E annually.

Tidal Streams

The flood tide sets north in the Horta channel at up to 1·5 knots, and east in the Pico-São Jorge channel, maximum 1 knot. The ebb sets west and south at similar rates. Quite severe tide rips can build up around headlands in wind against tide conditions.

Charts

Admiralty *1956* (1:175,000)
Portuguese *43102* (1:300,000), *46201* (1:75,000)
US *51061* (1:250,000)
Imray-Iolaire *E1* (1:750,000)

Lights

2687·2 **Madalena breakwater** Oc.R.3s11m10M
White tower, three red bands 7·5m
2688 **São Roque do Pico (Cais do Pico)** Oc.R.6s3m6M
White structure containing red lantern, on wall, 5m
2690 **Ponta da Ilha** Fl(3)15s28m24M 166°-vis-070°
Square white tower and building, red lantern 19m
2690·15 **Santa Cruz das Ribeiras** Fl.R.3s13m14M
Red lantern on red and white post (the latter almost totally masked by the breakwater) 8·5m
Lajes do Pico Fl(2)G.6s8m5M
Green and white banded column 3·5m
2691 **Ponta de São Mateus** Fl.5s33m13M 284°-vis-118°
White truncated conical tower, red lantern 13m
2690·9 **Galeão cables**
Fl(2)R.8s8m9M (daylight range 1·7M) 315°-vis-010°
White post, red bands 4m. Marks submarine cables
Note The leading lights of five small Pico harbours – Manhenha, Porto do Calhau, Areia Larga, Prainha de Baixo and Santo Amaro – are not included here as being suitable only for local fishing craft

Coast Radio Station

Pico 38°24′N 28°44′W, remotely controlled from Lisbon
VHF Ch 16, 24, 26, 27 (24 hours)

late 19th century and although replaced by more resistant plants from California have never recovered their international fame. While in the Azores be sure to sample the full range – a rich, pale gold wine slightly reminiscent of Madeira, light reds and *verdes* – all serving admirably to wash down a picnic lunch of the fruit and cheese for which Pico is also renowned.

Sometimes called 'the orchard of the Azores' – though this seems not entirely fair to its neighbours – Pico supplies much of the produce in Horta's market, including apples, pears, apricots, peaches, plums, oranges and, for those able to stay until late August or September, almost more figs than anyone can eat. Where the land is too rugged for vines or fruit trees cattle are pastured, particularly toward the eastern end of the island on the lush slopes of Pico Topo and its fellows. The result is several varieties of cheese – one dry, white and somewhat crumbly, one yellow, harder and reminiscent of a mature Cheddar, and finally what appears to be the only soft, French-style cheese produced in the entire Azores.

Until relatively recently Pico was the centre of Azorean whaling, with at least 300 carcasses a year processed at the factory near São Roque before it closed in 1984. There was also a factory near Lajes, the chief harbour for the open whaleboats, where a whaling museum has been created in the *Casa dos Botes* and the Whalers' Festival is celebrated each year on the last Sunday in August. At Santa Cruz das Ribeiras a few miles east of Lajes, the building of whaleboats has taken on a new lease of life, something undreamed of a few decades ago. Not surprisingly most of the best scrimshanders in the Azores now work from Pico, producing intricate designs and carvings on whalebone or teeth, though the latter are becoming scarce and expensive. Lajes was the first town on the island and once its capital, receiving its town charter in 1502 more than 200 years before Madalena, and is now home to the island's only – if fairly diminutive – marina.

The north coast of Pico is generally more spectacular than the south, from the lava arches, stacks and sea caves at Cachorra near Madalena in the west to the almost sheer 415m cliffs at Terra Alta in the east. A few miles down the road from Terra Alta – a road banked with hydrangeas, wild roses and yellow ginger lilies (known locally as *conteira*) – heavy wooden fishing boats are built behind the stony beach at Santo Amaro. Massive timber frames are left to season and then planked up as they have been for centuries, but there tradition ends. By the time launching day arrives the larger vessels will be fully equipped with the latest in GPS, radar, fish-finders and all kinds of radio. More evidence of the 21st century lies near Madalena in the guise of Pico's airport, built nearly 20 years ago but still able to take only small, inter-island planes. The vast majority of visitors arrive via the ferry from Horta, past the Ilhéus da Madalena, otherwise Ilhéu Deitado and Ilhéu em Pé (Sleeping Isle and Standing Isle), and into the sheltered waters behind the tall breakwater. Until this was completed in the late 1980s disembarking from the ferry could be hazardous, and in bad weather the island was occasionally cut off for days or even weeks at a time. If the silhouette of Pico has been likened to something out of a Japanese painting, perhaps Hokusai's famous picture of the white-crested, curling wave might sum up the islanders' relationship with the sea.

Holidays and festivals

In addition to the national holidays listed on page 26, Lajes celebrates its official holiday on 29 June, Madalena on 22 July (when the Horta–Madalena ferry may run until 0130 or 0220), and São Roque on 16 August. The Festival of *Espírito Santo* is celebrated about six weeks after Easter, with the Feast of Saint Mary Magdalen on 20–23 July, Whalers' Week on 20–26 August and a Harvest Festival in September.

Telecommunications

Mobile (cell) phone reception around the coast is good, though this has not been verified for the upper slopes of the mountain itself. The country code for the Azores is 351, as it is for mainland Portugal, and the area code for Pico – which must be included even when dialling from within the island – is 292, shared with Flores, Corvo and Faial.

Free Wi-Fi is available in the new marina at Lajes do Pico.

Websites

All Pico's websites appear to be inspired by the island's natural wonders. They include www.ewpnet.com/Pico.htm, a commercial site offering guided walks on Pico (as well as several of the other islands), with some good photos; www.whales-dolphins.net/index.html, homepage of Pico Sport Lda, who run a diving and whale-watching centre from a base near Madalena, in English, German and Italian; and www.wild-wonders.com/blog/?p=6221, a page on the Wild Wonders of Europe site with some great underwater shots from photographer Magnus Lundgren.

Pico is also covered by Wikipedia at www.en.wikipedia.org/wiki/Pico_Island, as well as featuring on several of the general Azores sites listed on pages 24–5.

Approach

The 2,351m volcanic peak after which the island is named lies approximately one-third of the way along its west/east axis. Lower peaks and craters form a secondary area of high ground (over 1,000m) further east. In good visibility Pico can be visible from well over 50M and forms a spectacular backdrop on approach to Faial – once seen it is quite unmistakable. However, the topmost part is frequently lost in cloud even when the sky is otherwise clear.

Other than the Ilhéus da Madalena and associated rocks almost 1M offshore due west of Madalena harbour there are no serious off-lying dangers, and 0·5M clearance when coastal sailing is a safe margin.

In 2009 an experimental marine farm was established in the Canal do Faial, centred on 38°32′·5N 28°33′·9W (very close to the Madalena Rocks). Although 6m below chart datum, vessels should give generous clearance both to it and to its associated (and apparently unlit) bright blue buoys.

Harbours and anchorages

Madalena

38°32′·18N 28°31′·98W (breakwater head)

Waypoint
⊕A17 – 38°32′·5N 28°32′·5W (0·5M NW of Madalena)

Tides
Time difference on Ponta Delgada: +0003
Mean spring range 1·2m
Mean neap range 0·5m

Plans
Admiralty *1957* (1:37,500)
Portuguese *46403* (1:7,5000)
US *51062* (1:50,000)
Imray-Iolaire *E1* (1:37,500)

Lights
2687·2 **Breakwater** Oc.R.3s11m10M
White tower, three red bands 7·5m
Note Reported in 2011 to be working with reduced height and range
2687·5 **Ldg Lts on 139°** Fl.G.6s15/20m5M
White posts, red bands 8m, 128m apart

Harbour communications
Harbour Authority ✆ 292 623303 VHF Ch 16, 11 (call *Policiamarmadalena*) (0900–1200, 1400–1700, weekdays only)

Port limits
A circle, radius 1M, centred on Madalena molehead light – see Port limits, page 27.

Small commercial and ferry harbour

Originally little more than an open bay, the construction in 1987 of a long breakwater turned Madalena into a small but pleasant harbour protected from northwest through east to southwest, though any swell from the westerly quadrant will find its way inside. Even so, most yachtsmen continue to leave their boats in Horta and visit Pico by ferry, touring the island by taxi or hire car without any worries about a yacht left at anchor.

The snorkelling inside the harbour is particularly good, and there is also a small seawater swimming pool amongst the rocks at Ponta do Arieiro with a larger and more conventional pool close by. A path runs south to the small harbour at Areia Larga, and with a southerly wind the nearby fish cannery may make its presence smelt.

There have been persistent rumours that a small marina may be built at Madalena, but if so it is likely to be a local initiative intended for smallcraft rather than visiting yachts. In May 2011 it was reported that work was taking place in the harbour, though no further details are available. The breakwater light was functioning, but with reduced height and range.

Approach

Approach can be made from north or south of the Ilhéus da Madalena, which in the latter case should be left close to port until the breakwater end bears about 085° in order to avoid Baixo do Cação off Ponta do Arieiro. The approach from north or northwest is straightforward. The leading marks transit on 139° but

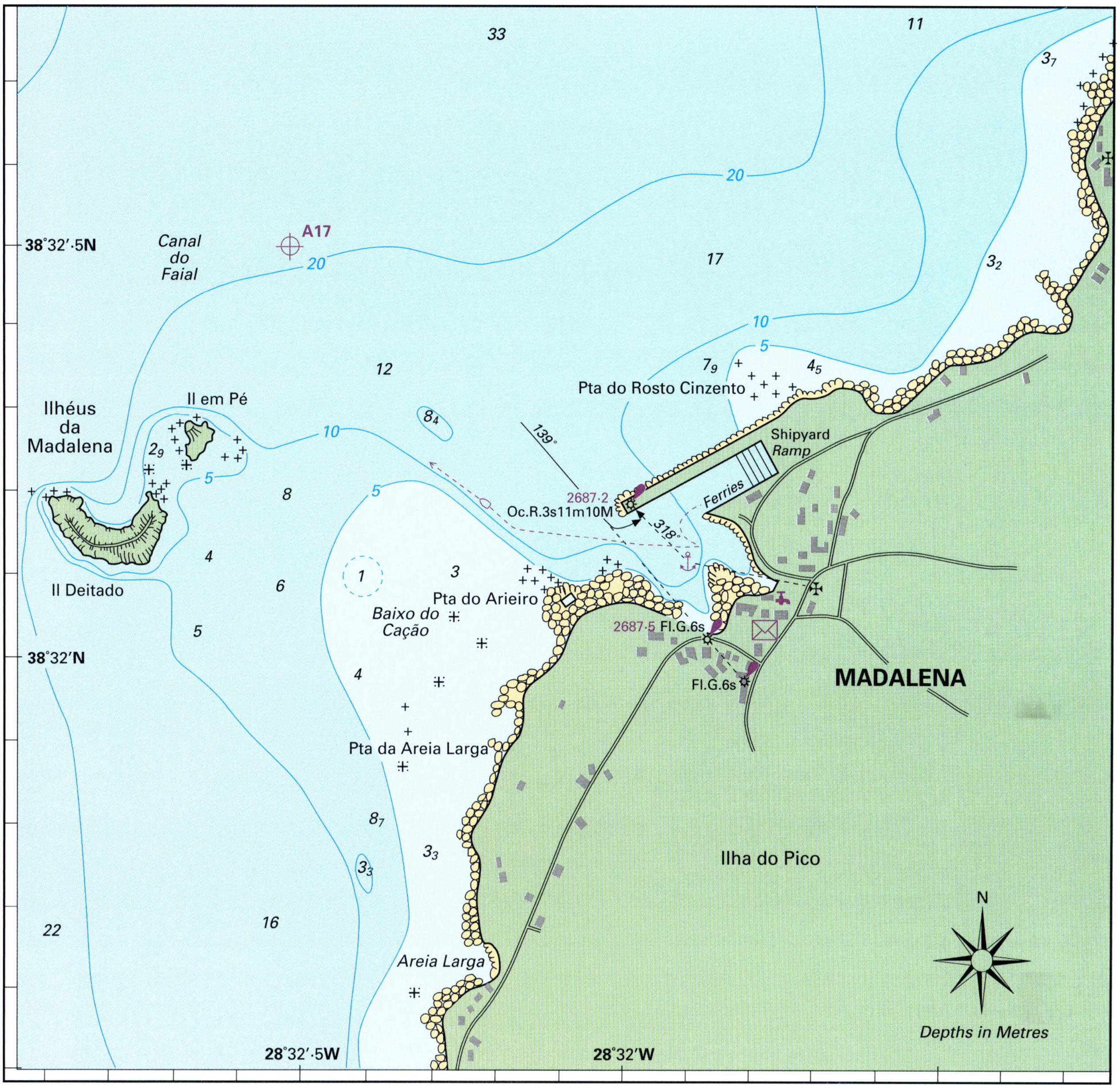

Looking southeast into the harbour at Madalena from a commercial aeroplane

should not be followed once inside the line of the breakwater. The Horta ferry tends to depart at speed, as do some fishing boats, in which case hasty evasive action may be necessary.

In 2009 an experimental marine farm was established in the Canal do Faial, centred on 38°32′·5N 28°33′·9W (very close to the Madalena Rocks). Although 6m below chart datum, vessels should give generous clearance both to it and to its associated (and apparently unlit) bright blue buoys.

Anchorage, moorings and berthing

Anchor in the southern part of the harbour in 9–10m over sand, with the breakwater light and the church bearing 318° and 098° respectively. It is essential to keep well clear of the approach used by ferries berthing at the central terminal – remembering they leave the quay going astern, and turn within the harbour. Dinghies can be landed at steps in the old inner harbour under the church.

In settled weather yachts sometimes berth alongside in the northeast corner of the harbour. However, this area tends to be noisy and gritty, and is subject to considerable wash from ferries berthing opposite.

Formalities

If arriving from within the Azores formalities appear to be non-existent. Neither the *Guarda Nacional Republicana* (*GNR*) nor the *Polícia Marítima* maintain a permanent presence in town – both are based along the coast in São Roque. However, a *Polícia Marítima* van may been seen in the vicinity of the ferry terminal around departure time, and it would be wise to bring the usual documents ashore just in case.

Facilities

Boatyard Situated near the root of the breakwater, with two marine railways on which large wooden fishing vessels are brought ashore and considerable undercover space. No provision for hauling deep-keel yachts.
Water By can from taps at the small fish market overlooking the inner harbour and elsewhere.
Showers Swimmers' (ie. cold) showers beside the pool at Ponta do Arieiro. Both facilities are free.
Fuel By can from a filling station about 1km along the road towards São Roque.
Banks Several, with cash dispensers.
Shops/provisioning Small but quite well stocked supermarket close west of the old inner harbour, plus several small grocery stores selling basic foods including the excellent Pico cheese. The souvenir shops have an unexpectedly wide selection including attractive Azorean pottery and whalebone items.
Cafés, restaurants & hotels A growing number of all three.
Medical services Small hospital just south of the town.

Communications

Post office Just behind the church, open 0900–1730 weekdays.
Telephones At the ferry terminal and elsewhere.
Car hire At least four companies.
Taxis In profusion, though a longer trip such as an island tour is best booked in advance.
Buses Daily services along the north and south coasts of the island.
Ferries Regular service to/from Horta, São Roque etc.
Air services Inter-island airport on the road to São Roque.

São Roque do Pico (Cais do Pico)

38°31′·85N 28°19′·14W (breakwater head)

Waypoint
⊕A18 – 38°32′·1N 28°18′·6W (0·5M NE of São Roque)

Plans
Portuguese *46201* (1:75,000), *47501* (1:5,000)

Lights
2688 **São Roque do Pico (Cais do Pico)** Oc.R.6s3m6M
White structure containing red lantern on wall 5m
2688·2 **Breakwater** Fl.G.3s6m2M 120°-vis-030°
White tower, green bands 4m

Harbour communications
Harbourmaster ✆ 292 642326 *Fax* 292 642948
Email delmar.sroque@mail.pt VHF Ch 11, 16 (call *Delegmar Roque*) (0900–1230, 1400–1630)
Port Authority ✆ 292 642466 *Fax* 292 642134 (0800–1200, 1300–1700)

Port limits
A circle, radius 1·5M, centred on São Roque do Pico breakwater light – see Port limits, page 27.

Harbour anchorage open to the east

Until the late 1970s the site of Pico's largest whale-processing factory, a 200m breakwater was built a few years later to provide the island with a deep-water harbour and container port. Shelter is good from south through west to northwest, though strong katabatic gusts can pour down off the slopes of Pico, almost doubling the prevalent windspeed.

The view of the mountain is superb, making the volcano appear almost symmetrical, and there are attractive walks in the hills behind the village. The old whaling factory is now a museum, with much of

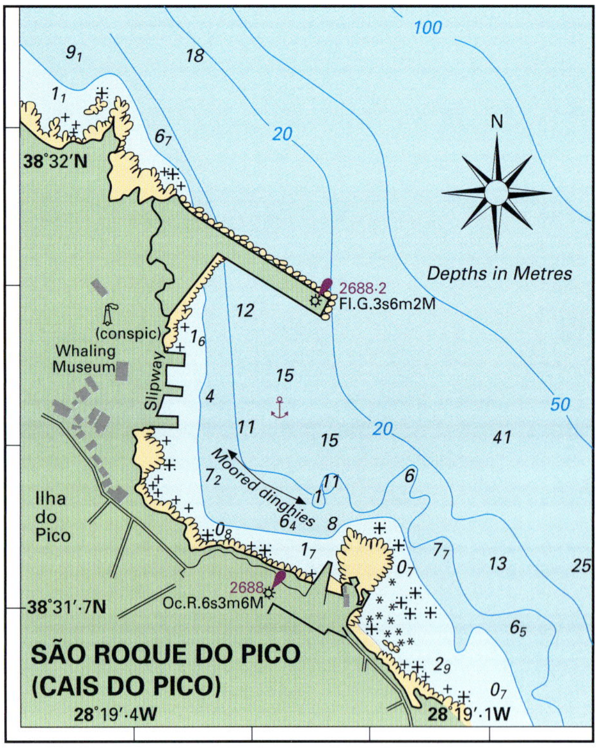

the original machinery still in place (open 0915–1230, 1400–1730 Tuesday to Friday, 0915–1230 weekends, closed Monday.

Approach

By day Straightforward. If coming from the northwest the green and white banded column on the breakwater end is visible from a distance against the town; from the east the dark chimney of the old whale processing factory is distinctive. There are no hazards if approaching from offshore, but if approaching from the east or southeast the Baixo do Cais and off-lying rocks must be given at least 200m clearance.

By night The breakwater light can be approached bearing between 130° and 295° and rounded at least 50m off.

Anchorage and moorings

It is possible to anchor anywhere in the centre of the harbour, avoiding moored fishing boats and traffic to and from the breakwater wall. However, depths are great – 15m or more – and the bottom rocky, so a tripline is strongly advised. The water is usually very clear.

In June 2010 there were four moorings in the harbour, one occupied by a yacht of 12m or more and others by smallcraft, but few would care to leave their yacht on an unknown mooring even to visit the whaling museum.

Dinghies can be left at one of the small inner quays or adjoining slipways where whales were once hauled ashore.

Formalities

Visit the *Polícia Marítima* in the *Delegação Marítima* (harbour office) at the west end of the seafront and the *Guarda Nacional Republicana* (*GNR*) who occupy a building marked *Poste de Despacho* at the other end of the town, with solid arched doorways and a single turret topped by a handsome whale weathervane. It may well ease clearance if the computer printout which one is given in Horta or Ponta Delgada is available. This carries answers to all the standard questions, so avoiding potential language difficulties.

Facilities

*Boatyard/*engineers Nothing specifically for yachts, though local skills clearly exist – witness the beautifully renovated and maintained whaling boats (now used for racing) and their original tow-boats.

Water By can from a tap at the rear of the *clube naval* boat store (it would be courteous to ask before helping oneself). Alternatively there is a tap let into the wall near the São Roque light structure.

Showers At the *clube naval*. Generally kept locked, but available for a small fee on request.

Fuel By can from a filling station on the road leading inland from near the São Roque light structure.

Weather forecast Sometimes to be found in the entrance to the *clube naval*, though not posted daily.

Clube naval The *Clube Naval de São Roque* have premises near the whaling museum, with a large store full of sailing dinghies in addition to a busy waterfront restaurant.

Banks Several, all with cash dispensers.

Shops/provisioning Several small supermarkets at the eastern end of the town.

Cafés & restaurants Along the seafront.

Medical services Hospital outside the town.

Communications

Post office Overlooking the harbour.

Telephones In the entrance to the *clube naval* and elsewhere.

Car hire One company (though not a place to leave a yacht unattended whilst exploring the island).

Taxis Available, though it might be necessary to order by phone from Madalena.

Buses To Madalena and elsewhere.

Ferries Regular service to Madelena and Horta in one direction and Velas (São Jorge) in the other.

Air services Inter-island airport on the road to Madalena.

São Roque de Pico seen from the northeast, with the end of its substantial breakwater at right

Calheta da Nesquim

38°24′·13N 28°04′·71W (molehead)

Lights
2690 **Ponta da Ilha** Fl(3)15s28m24M 166°-vis-070°
Square white tower and building, red lantern 19m
2690·1 **Ldg Lts on 000°**
Front Fl.R.5s13m7M Red lantern on white post near church 1m
Rear, 30m from front, Fl.R.5s17m7M Red post 6m

Scenic but open anchorage

An attractive bay protected from west through to northeast, Calheta da Nesquim would make an interesting daytime anchorage in settled northerly weather. A large white church stands above the chequered sea wall and small stone mole, with gently sloping woodland behind.

The initial approach is clear, other than rocks close around the low headland to the west. However, good light is necessary to enter the bay itself due to isolated rocky patches, particularly in the eastern part. Anchor south or southeast of the mole, well outside the rocks, or in the bay further east. There are steps and a slipway in the shelter of the mole. A water tap will be found on the mole and a small café at its root, but there are no other facilities.

Santa Cruz das Ribeiras

38°24′·34N 28°11′·15W (molehead)

Plan
Portuguese *47501* (1:5,000)

Lights
2690·15 **Santa Cruz das Ribeiras** Fl.R.3s13m14M
Red lantern on red and white post (the latter almost totally masked by the breakwater) 8·5m

Small, attractive harbour anchorage

One of the oldest settlements on Pico, Santa Cruz das Ribeiras has a small fishing harbour protected from the southwest by a short breakwater and from west through to northeast by steep terraced and wooded slopes. In addition to being one of the main centres of whaleboat building in the Azores, several restored craft are kept, fully-equipped, in a boathouse at the head of the habour. Their elderly guardians appear happy for visitors to look around, while a stroll along the road to the west will often be rewarded by the chance to examine new hulls under construction.

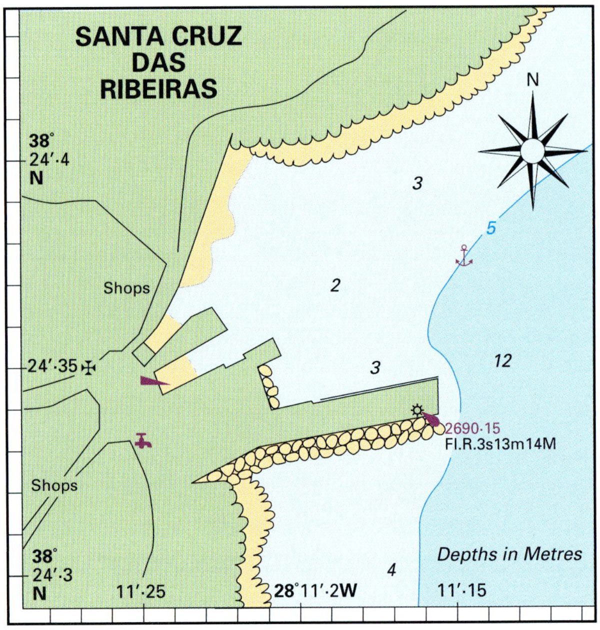

The short mole at Santa Cruz das Ribeiras, seen from hills to the northwest

Another of Pico's traditions, cheesemaking, is a speciality of the area. Most of that produced is hard and quite strong, similar in taste and texture to a mature Cheddar. It keeps well – assuming it gets the chance – and a 5kg (11lb) truckle would keep most crews munching for weeks.

Approach

No problems from either direction, though if coming from the southwest the dark grey concrete breakwater may be difficult to identify against the rocks behind until bearing at least 010°.

Anchorage, mooring and berthing

Anchor in line with the end of the breakwater in about 5m over sand, rock and stones. A tripline is advisable. There are several sets of steps at which a dinghy could be landed.

At least 2·5m should be found along the outer half of the breakwater, but it may be difficult to confirm that no larger vessels are expected in. There is nearly always some surge.

Facilities

Water Tap near the small crane on the inner quay.
Showers Cold shower in a building near the root of the breakwater.
Shops/provisioning Small general store in the village.
Cafés & restaurants Two cafés near the harbour, and a restaurant about 10 minutes' walk westward.

Communications

Telephone About 200m beyond the church.
Taxis Available, though it might be necessary to order by telephone from Madalena.
Buses Services to Madalena and elsewhere along the main road, a steep walk up from the harbour and village.

Lajes do Pico

38°23′·94N 28°15′·47W (breakwater head)

Waypoint
⊕A20 – 38°24′N 28°16′·2W (0·5M W of Lajes do Pico)

Plans
Portuguese *47501* (1:5,000)

Lights
Breakwater Fl(2)G.6s8m5M
Green and white banded column 3·5m
buoy **Port hand buoy No.2** Fl(2)R.5s3M
Red buoy, ■ topmark
buoy **Port hand buoy** No.6 Fl.R.3s2M
Red pillar buoy, ■ topmark
2690·4 **Inner quay** Fl.G.5s6m3M
White post, green bands 4m

Harbour communications
Harbourmaster ✆ 292 672289 VHF Ch 11, 16 (call *Delegmar Lajes*) (0900–1230, 1400–1630)
Port Authority ✆ 292 642466, *Fax* 292 642134 (0800–1200, 1300–1700)
Lajes Marina ✆/*Fax* 292 672121, 917 289369 *Email* nrecreio.lajes@sapo.pt VHF 16 (0800–1200, 1300–2000 weekdays from 1 June to 15 August, otherwise 0800–1200, 1300–1700, with flexible hours at weekends throughout the year). Mentioned but not described in detail on the *Portos dos Açores SA* website at www.marinasazores.com

The Azores' smallest marina

Lajes was the earliest settlement on Pico and its first capital. Hints of its past importance can be detected in some of the older buildings, including the two churches, and particularly in the engineering of the impressive hillside road running southwards out of the town. It was also the centre of Pico's whaling fleet, which operated out of the small inner harbour (the factory buildings are about 1km further north) now occupied by the archipelago's smallest and – pending the completion of its namesake in Flores – newest marina. Conversely, it is home to the island's oldest whaling museum, the *Museu dos Baleeros*, appropriately situated on Rua dos Baleeros almost opposite the harbour, open 0915–1230, 1400–1730 Tuesday to Friday, 1400–1730 weekends, closed Monday. In addition to the *Santa Terezinha*, a 10·75m whaleboat built in 1928 and on display complete with harpoons, lances and other whaling implements, the museum has a valuable collection of scrimshaw and whalebone items and a growing library on the subject, and is worth a visit whatever one's feelings are regarding whaling. Several nearby concerns offer whale and dolphin-watching excursions.

Most of the best scrimshanders still working in the Azores live on Pico, several running small workshops in Lajes where scrimshaw and whalebone items can be bought. However, before choosing a souvenir note that many countries have introduced legislation to control the import of whale-derived products. Both producer and vendor should display certificates permitting them to deal in such goods, and if this is done it is then legal for an EU citizen to buy and own scrimshaw or whalebone items and to transport them between EU countries. Non-EU citizens would be wise to check the situation regarding their home country. Note also that with the growing scarcity of teeth some scrimshanders are now engraving on hard plastic as an alternative to tooth or bone, while mass-produced pieces may occasionally be moulded rather than engraved. While there is clearly much to be said for the former, which may exhibit just as much skill as 'traditional' scrimshaw, most people would rather avoid the latter. It should be easy enough to tell the difference on close inspection.

Approach and entrance

The approach from the west is clear, but if coming from the south the banks between Ponta do Castelete and the breakwater are best given clearance of at least 600m (outside the 20m contour), until the breakwater head bears due east. Look for a red and white radio mast on a small hill,

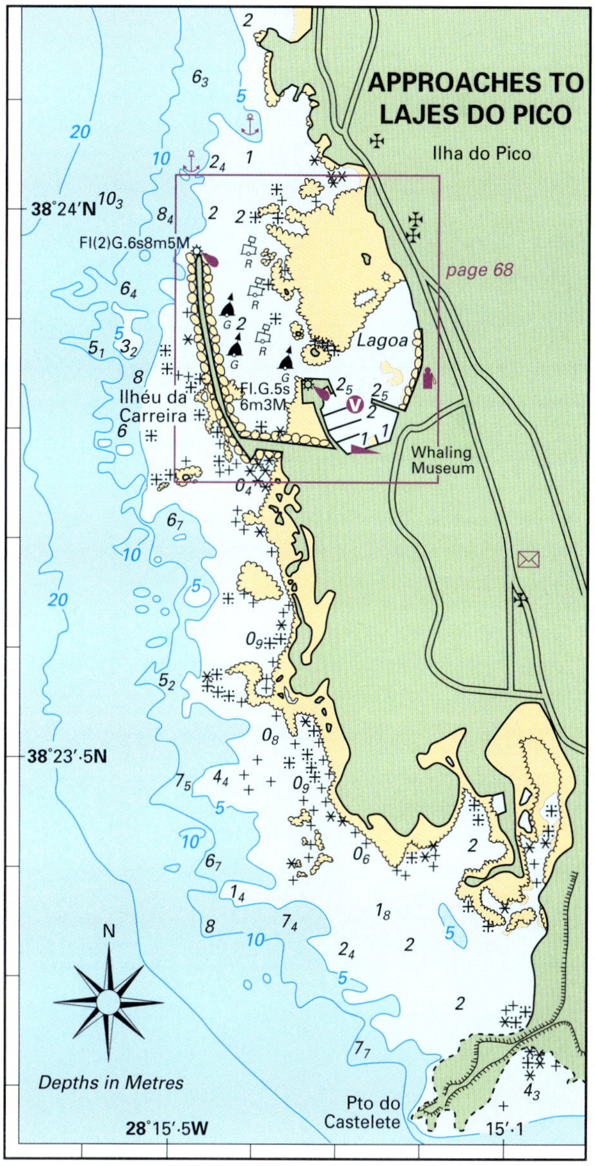

Approaching Lajes do Pico from due west, with the new breakwater at right *Dick Moore*

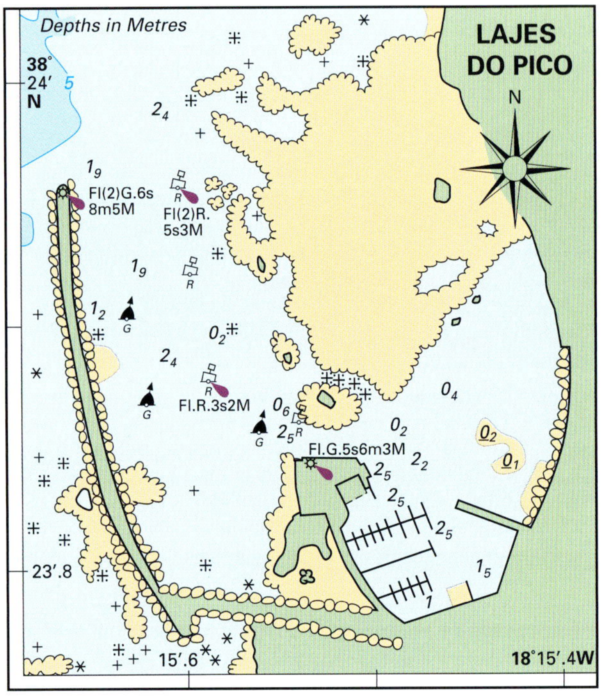

bracketed by a blue building with a grey roof to the left and a low white building with a brown roof to the right – the breakwater will come into view in front.

The breakwater and its inconspicuous light structure should not be rounded too closely (rubble lies off it following storm damage in the winter of 2009/10), after which one turns south to follow the buoyed entrance channel. In all but the lowest of tides – best avoided, in any case – at least 3m should be found as far as the reception quay, but it is essential to stay well within the channel, particularly at the final port turn – swing wide and on no account cut the corner. It goes without saying that first-time entry should be made at very slow speed, with a crewmember on the bow if possible. The water is extremely clear.

Approach at night, other than possibly to anchor off, is not feasible.

Anchorage

The seabed north of the breakwater head is relatively clear of dangers outside the 5m contour. About 6m will be found over sand and rock some 200m north of its head, and there are other viable spots further northwest. A tripline is advisable.

Berthing

Lajes Marina officially opened on 8 June 2008 and, like most in the Azores, is owned and run by *Portos dos Açores SA*. As mentioned above it is very limited size, and although there are nominally 48 berths most are only suitable for very small, shallow runabouts. The north side of northernmost pontoon provides berthing for no more than six yachts in the 10–14m range, all alongside finger pontoons and in depths of 2·5–3m. Only four of those berths can accommodate 14m, and in 2010 two of these were

The interior of Lajes harbour at low tide, before all the buoys were in place *John Clementson*

Lajes from the southeast, with six of the seven buoys in place
Andy Scott

occupied long-term while two were reserved for visitors. The hammerhead and the south side of the pontoon are normally occupied by whale-watching RIBs. A further two yachts may be permitted to lie alongside the reception quay, though this is frequently needed for the fuel trailer.

In light of the above it would be wise to make contact before leaving one's previous harbour to check whether there is likely to be a space, but even failing that an approaching yacht will usually be met by one of the marina staff and directed straight into a berth if available. Otherwise secure to the pontoon alongside the reception quay in about 2·5m, as depths shoal rapidly further in.

Protection inside the inner harbour is excellent, but high winds and seas from the west or southwest could make leaving a very dicey prospect indeed.

Security is provided by individual gates giving access to each pontoon. Beware getting locked out only to discover that no marina staff are on duty!

Formalities

Visit the marina office with the usual ship's papers, passports, etc. Turn left on leaving the quay and walk a short distance up Rua do Baleeiros. The well-marked *Polícia Marítima* is on the left, with the marina office almost opposite.

The *Polícia Marítima*, *GNR* and *Serviço de Estrangeiros e Fronteiras* (Immigration) will be informed of a foreign yacht's arrival by the marina authorities and may visit the yacht. However, despite the presence of the latter Lajes do Pico is not a port of entry into the Azores (or into the Schengen area) and clearance should first be obtained at a larger harbour.

Charges

Lajes Marina is one of the *Portos dos Açores SA* chain, and shares their basic price structure despite its current lack of facilities. As of 2011 yachts of 10–12m LOA paid €12.22 per night and those of 12–15m paid €18.50. For further details see page 27 and/or www.marinasazores.com, the website of the branch of *Portos dos Açores SA* concerned with marina operation (though note that different charges apply to yachts owned by residents and by non-residents).

Facilities

Boatyard, travel-lift, etc. Nothing at all, and nothing planned – another reason for being extremely careful on entry and departure...

Water On the pontoons.

Toilets Until the marina services block is operational (see below), yachtsmen must use public toilets about 100m away (underground, in the centre of the nearby grassy area). They are said to be poor.

Showers A service block is planned for the quay, hopefully by 2012. In the meantime showers are available at the *Clube Náutico*.

Laundry Likely to be included in the service block mentioned above.

Electricity On the pontoons.

Fuel A small fuel trailer is brought down to the reception quay most evenings to refuel fishing and whale-watching boats, and marina officials can arrange for yachts to refuel at the same time. There is a filling station near the root of the mole from which small quantities can be collected by can.

Bottled gas Nothing available other than GALP's own cylinders, not even Camping Gaz.

Banks Several in the town, with cash dispensers.

Shops/provisioning Most daily needs can be met in the town, otherwise visit the large new shopping centre on Rua São Francisco (the road north out of town).

Cafés, restaurants & hotels A growing number of all three.

Medical services Small hospital on Rua São Francisco.

Communications

Post office At the back of the town.

Telephones At the post office, near the whaling museum and elsewhere.

Internet access Free Wi-Fi in the harbour area, including the marina.

Car hire There is no rental company in Lajes, but the Futurismo whale-watching concern can usually arrange a deal through one of the companies in Madelena (or do so direct, of course).

Taxis Taxi rank on Rua São Francisco (the road north out of town).

Buses To Madalena and elsewhere from the bus station on Rua dos Baleeiros.

São Jorge

Between 38°32′N–38°45′N and 27°45′W–28°19′W

Introduction

Variously said to resemble a sword blade, a cigar and a sleeping animal, São Jorge is a long, narrow island and literally the central island of the central group. It suffers the physical misfortune of being eclipsed by its neighbour Pico, even though it is itself something of a geological oddity. Nearly 54km long by only 7·5km wide, almost all the coast consists of steep volcanic cliffs, with low tongues of lava (*fãjas)* extending out to sea in a few places, and a high percentage of its 246km^2 lies above the 300m contour. Unlike Pico, São Jorge consists of a whole string of volcanic peaks, lower to the northwest, reaching their greatest height of 1,053m at Pico do Esperança roughly halfway down the chain, and then gradually losing height to the southeast so that the 942m Pico dos Frades stands well above its neighbours.

From a distance São Jorge reminds one of the serrated backbone of a sleeping brontosaurus, but this impression of a mountainous island is not entirely correct. The high land above the steep and rugged coast forms a rolling plateau, dotted with small white villages set amongst rounded hills, though from deck level this can be hard to believe. Sections across ancient volcanoes stand like plates from a geology textbook, with dipping and swooping strata of brick red, yellow, tan, olive green and grey, each with its range of tones and shadows. Bright green bushes of Azores heather (*Erica azorica*) cling dangerously to every niche, and narrow waterfalls tumble into the sea below. São Jorge is seldom without its long, narrow cloud, whose dampness keeps the island moist without great rainfall. Vines grow on some of the gentler southern slopes, oranges, bananas and plums thrive, and the thousands of fig trees produce more fruit than can be harvested.

However, the real wealth of São Jorge lies in its fertile upland plateau where animals have grazed for well over 500 years. Although the early villages were built on the low-lying *fãjas* along the south coast, the clifftop land was slowly cleared, its timber valuable in itself. A small part of that native forest still survives as the Forest Reserve of Sete Fontes (Seven Fountains) near Rosais, one of three protected areas on the island. (The other, contrasting, areas are the tiny lagoon of Caldeira de Santo Cristo in the Ribeira Grande region, and the low-lying Ilhéu do Topo off the southeast tip of São Jorge, once used as summer pasture but now a nature reserve and seabird nesting sanctuary.)

Such a forward-looking attitude might seem unexpected, until one realises that for decades the dairy and stock-rearing industries have been run according to the most modern Danish co-operative farming methods, with carefully bred Holstein, Shorthorn and Frisian herds. With the whole

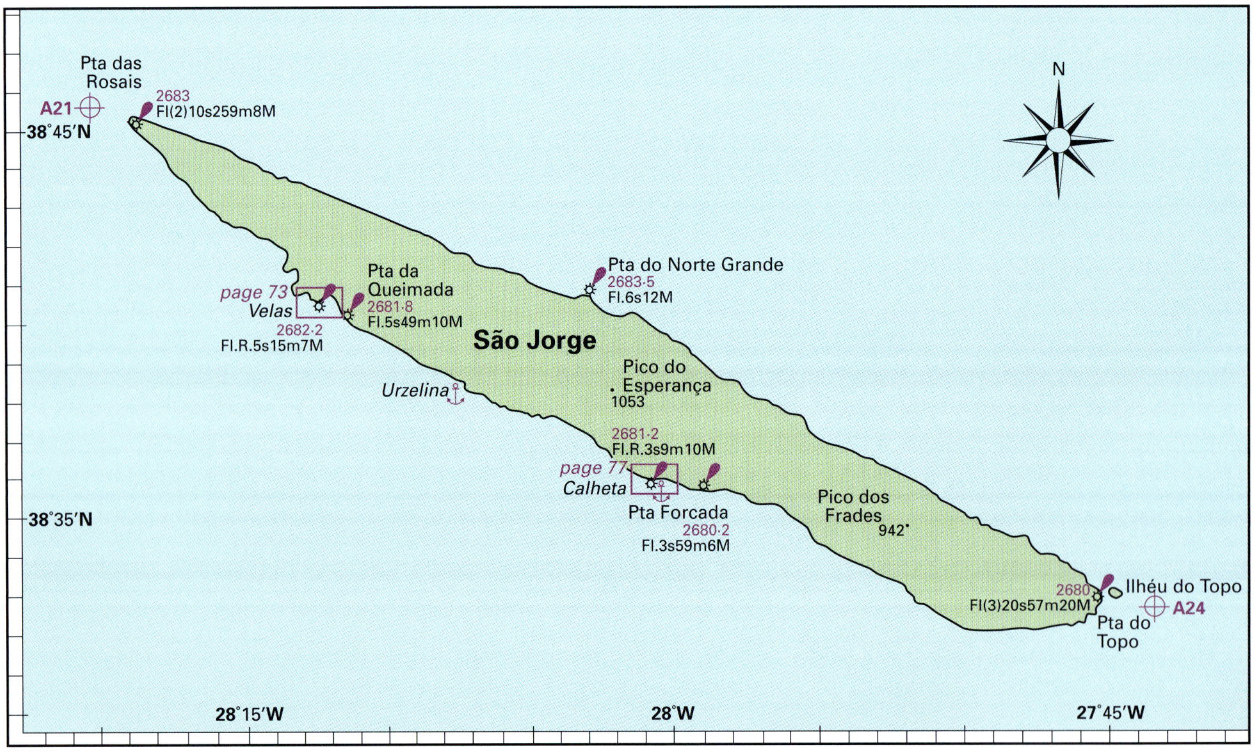

Navigation

Waypoints

⊕ A21 – 38°45'·7N 28°20'·3W (1M WNW of Pta dos Rosais)
⊕ A22 – 38°40'·2N 28°12'·5W (0·5M SSW of Velas)
⊕ A23 – 38°35'·5N 28°00'·8W (0·5M SSW of Calheta)
⊕ A24 – 38°32'·8N 27°43'·4W (1M ESE of Ilhéu do Topo)

Courses and distances

⊕ A21 to ⊕A15 (0·5M E of Pta da Ribeirinha, Faial) = 15·4M, 050° / 230°
⊕ A21 to ⊕A22 = 8·5M, by eye
⊕ A21 to ⊕A25 (1M SE of Ilhéu de Baixa, Graciosa) = 23M, 054° / 234°
⊕ A22 to ⊕A13 (0·5M E of Horta, Faial) = 20·6M, 247° / 067°
⊕ A22 to ⊕A18 (0·5M NE of São Roque, Pico) = 9·4M, 211° / 031°
⊕ A22 to ⊕A24 = 25M, by eye
⊕ A24 to ⊕A29 (0·5M S of Monte Brasil, Terceira) = 24M, 078° / 258°
⊕ A24 to ⊕A38 (1M S of Santa Clara, São Miguel) = 109M, 117° / 297°

Magnetic variation

11°25'W (2011), decreasing by 7'E annually.

Tidal Streams

Tidal streams generally set east on the flood and west on the ebb at up to 1 knot, though countercurrents may sometimes run close inshore south of São Jorge. Tide rips can build up around Ponta de Rosais and Ponta do Topo in wind against tide conditions.

Charts

Admiralty *1956* (1:175,000)
Portuguese *43102* (1:300,000), *46201* (1:75,000)
US *51061* (1:250,000)
Imray-Iolaire *E1* (1:750,000)

Lights

2683 **Ponta de Rosais** Fl(2)10s259m8M 320°-vis-283°
Futuristic concrete tower with vertical ribs 27m
2683·5 **Ponta do Norte Grande** Fl.6s12M
White tower, red bands 6m
2680 **Ponta do Topo** Fl(3)20s57m20M 133°-vis-033°
White tower, red lantern and buildings 16m
2680·2 **Ponta Forcada (Ribeira Seca)** Fl.3s59m6M
Red column, white bands 4·5m
2681·8 **Ponta da Queimada** Fl.5s49m10M
White column, red bands 5m

economy relying on cattle the flowery meadows of the upland *serra* form one vast pasture, the large fields divided by low stone walls or the familiar hydrangea hedges, served by modern dairies where milk from the entire district can be collected and processed. Perhaps it was the many Flemish immigrants who first began making the delicious, slightly sharp cheese for which São Jorge is famous. Large flattened footballs weighing up to 5kg (11lb), a sizeable wedge makes an excellent edible souvenir which will keep without chilling for as long as it remains uneaten.

It may also have been the Flemish who introduced the island's characteristic thick coverlets and rugs, woven out of unbleached wool on hand looms and distinguished by their raised and textured patterns, second cousin to the Aran sweater. Another way in which the islanders employ their artistic talents is by decorating the island's quiet roads for the many religious festivals. A wooden pattern is placed on the road, leaves and different coloured petals carefully placed inside it, the pattern removed, and water used to keep the design fresh and in place. Hundreds of squares and oblongs may snake down the centre of the road for several kilometres before one encounters a busy knot of islanders slowly working their way forward – and woe betide any driver who runs his or her wheels over their handiwork!

A good deal of effort has been put into São Jorge's growing tourist industry and there is a small airport for inter-island flights, but most visitors still take the ferry from Faial to Vila das Velas, the imaginatively named 'Town of the Candles' or possibly 'of Sails' – either would be appropriate. Many arrivals are returning emigrants – the population dropped by a third during the latter part of the 20th century, but is now starting to recover – perhaps inspired by the story of the barefoot local boy who became an American ranching millionaire and returned to his native island as a major benefactor. His statue still stands in the main square at Velas.

One by-product of this returning wealth has been a building boom, with many new houses on the outskirts of the town positioned on the slopes to enjoy the imposing views of Pico, while from seaward the ultra-modern Estalagem das Velas hotel looks oddly out of place as though it might be happier in a Mediterranean resort complete with amplified music and crowded beaches. Another sign of increasing local wealth must be the number of runabouts and sportsboats kept in Velas Marina. Local people have always owned small fishing craft, but boats kept purely for recreation are a luxury which is still fairly new.

Holidays and festivals

In addition to the national holidays listed on page 26, Velas celebrates its official holiday on 23 April with that of Calheta following unusually late in the year on 25 November. As elsewhere, the Festival of

An intricate design in stone in Velas town centre

Espírito Santo is celebrated about six weeks after Easter. Velas Cultural Week takes place early in July, with a 'July Festival' following during the second fortnight of the month.

Telecommunications

Mobile (cell) phone reception throughout the island is good. The country code for the Azores is 351, as it is for mainland Portugal, and the area code for São Jorge – which must be included even when dialling from within the island – is 295, shared with Graciosa and Terceira.

By 2011 free Wi-Fi was available in the harbour area at Velas. The internet could also be accessed from at least one place in Calheta.

Websites

The internet currently offers no website devoted to São Jorge as a whole, other than Wikipedia's www.en.wikipedia.org/wiki/Sâo_Jorge_Island. The *Câmara Municipal de Velas* (effectively the town council) has a site at http://cm-velas.azoresdigital.pt, though in Portuguese only. It requires one to log in (though it does not say how) to access some parts of the site. São Jorge also features on several of the general Azores sites listed on pages 24–5.

Approach

Viewed from north or south São Jorge appears as a regular if rather serrated plateau almost entirely fringed by steep cliffs. However, if approaching 'end on' from east or west the island appears much smaller, with little of the plateau to be seen. The heights of Pico can often be seen over São Jorge if coming from the direction of Graciosa.

There are few off-lying hazards, and depths shelve steeply except around the *fãjas* (the lava flows running out into the sea) and at either end of the island, where at least 0·5M clearance should be allowed.

Stress-free milking on a small farm in northern São Jorge

Harbours and anchorages

Vila das Velas

38°40'·68N 28°12'·17W (breakwater head)

Waypoint
⊕A22 – 38°40'·2N 28°12'·5W (0·5M SSW of Velas)

Tides
Time difference on Ponta Delgada: –0003
Mean spring range 1·3m
Mean neap range 0·5m

Plans
Portuguese *46201* (1:75,000), *47501* (1:5,000)
Imray-Iolaire *E1* (1:7,500)

Lights
2682·2 **Breakwater** Fl.R.5s15m7M
White tower, three red bands 3m
2682·3 **Velas cables**
Fl(2)R.8s15m9M (daylight range 1·7M) 033°-vis-061°
White post, red bands on breakwater 4m. Marks submarine cables
2682·4 **Ship anchorage Lts in line on 304 3°**
Front Iso.R.5s12m6M Red post, white band 9m
Rear, **Ermida do Livramento**, 803m from front, Oc.R.6s49m7M Lantern on small grey chapel 8m
Important These lights indicate the offshore ship anchorage and are NOT leading lights
2682·1 **Marina southeast mole** Fl(3)G.9s8m3M
White column, green bands 2·5m
2682·15 **Marina west mole** Fl(3)R.9s4m3M
White post, red bands 3m
buoys **Temporary buoys**
In 2010 three small yellow buoys, all Fl(4)Y.10s2M, marked work on an extension to the fishing quay close west of the marina entrance

Harbour communications
Harbourmaster ✆ /*Fax* 295 412336
Email delmar.velas@mail.pt VHF Ch 11, 16 (call *Capimar Velas*) (0900–1230, 1400–1730)
Port Authority ✆ 295 412047 *Fax* 295 412306 (0800–1200, 1300–1700)
Velas Marina ✆ 295 412047, 963 698900 *Fax* 295 412306
Email velasmarina@aptosa.com
www.marinasazores.com VHF Ch 10, 16 (0800–1200, 1300–2000 daily from 15 May to 15 August, otherwise 0800–1200, 1300–1700)

Small marina in attactive bay

Velas has long been a favourite spot with visiting yachtsmen, though prior to the opening of the marina in 2008 visits ashore always required a weather eye open for southerly windshifts. With one's boat safe in the marina it is now possible to spend days exploring this beautiful island – and very well worth it. The breakwater, which is becoming ever more busy with container ships and ferries, provides protection from the west and southwest, while dramatic 200m cliffs behind the harbour encircle it from northwest through to southeast. In 2010 sources in Horta stated that the breakwater was likely to be extended by about 150m, probably in 2012 or 2013, but this should not affect visiting yachts.

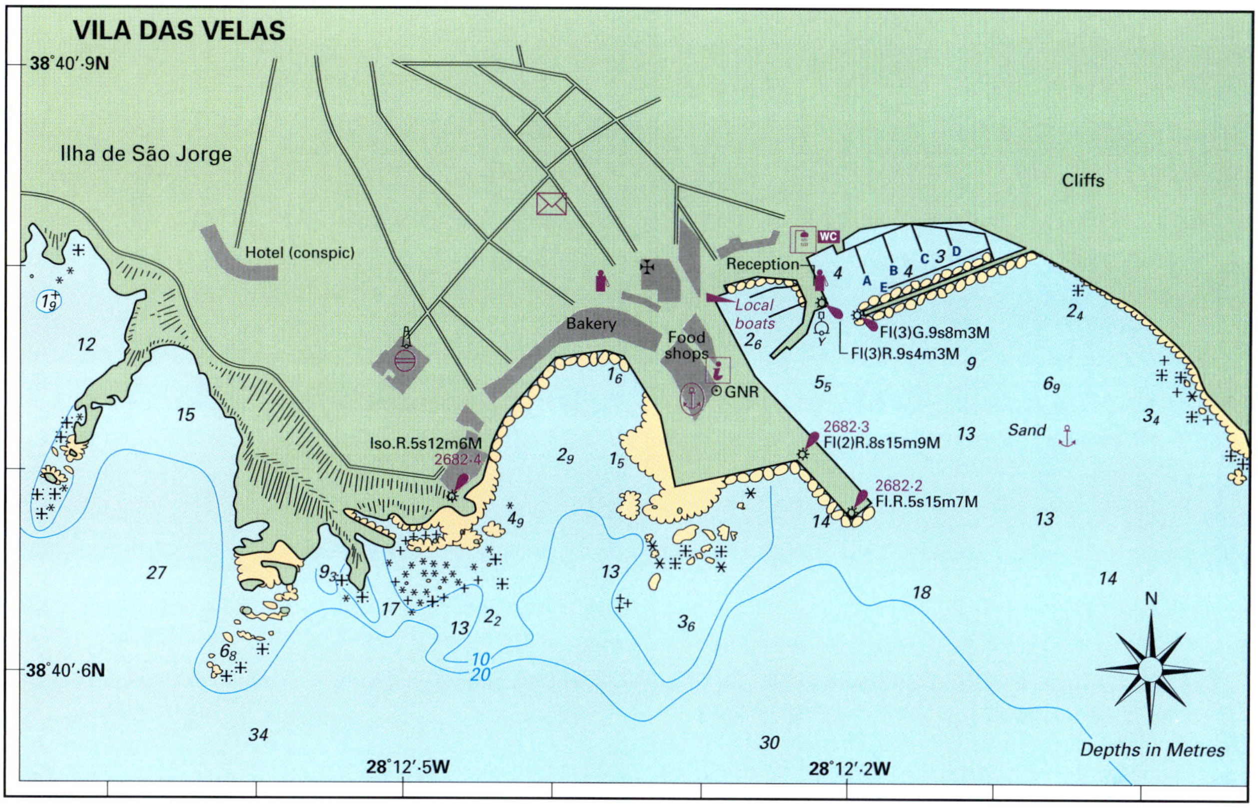

The vast amount of new building in and around the town of Velas threatens to swamp the old town though the superb view of Pico forms an understandable attraction. A high stone wall dating from the days of the pirate threat surrounds the harbour, its 18th-century baroque gateway unique in the Azores. Also of interest are the 17th-century parish church, where the usual black on white stonework is surmounted by an almost oriental dome, and the solid 18th-century town hall with its twisting basalt columns facing the public gardens. Much of the town centre is pedestrianised, and in an archipelago noted for its intricate stone pavement designs Vila das Velas has some of the most impressive.

An inexpensive taxi ride takes one to the *miradouro* (viewpoint) on the cliffs above the harbour, from which it is worth strolling down the old road, now a footpath, to appreciate fully the ever-changing scenery. If there is a swell running it is also worth walking along the seafront west of the *Estalagem das Velas* hotel to watch the lava arch blow-hole in action. About an hour after sunset the hundreds of Cory's shearwaters which nest on the cliffs above the harbour exchange their usual brief call for a peculiar 'ah-kee-kee-kee' at considerable volume whilst circling the anchorage. This tails off after a few hours, but may be heard at intervals all night and again at dawn.

A yacht race from Horta to Velas and back is organised annually for a weekend in early July. The racing itself is informal but the hospitality memorable, and entertainment laid on has included bull running on the quay (no injury to the bull), regional meals, coach tours of the island, displays of Azorean dancing and singing and impressive fireworks. If in the area round this time the Horta–Velas race should not be missed.

Approach and entrance

By day If approaching from westwards, 400m offing should be maintained until the end of the breakwater bears at least 025°. There are no dangers from eastwards other than rocks close inshore around Ponta Queimada. The marina is hidden from the south until the breakwater has been rounded, when its narrow entrance comes into view straight ahead. Even with a ship alongside the breakwater, there is ample space to circle in the harbour if necessary.

One or more small, unlit orange spar buoys mark rubble which extends from the end of the old quay, now site of the marina office – favour the starboard side where at least 4m should be found. The small harbour west of the marina, completed in June 2011, is for local craft only.

By night Approach may be made with the breakwater light bearing between 333° and 025° – allow generous clearance as rocks extend some distance beyond its base. The marina is lit on either side and, with the considerable ambient light from town and harbour, night entry should not pose problems in calm conditions.

Berthing

Velas Marina has been highly praised ever since it opened early in 2008. It is, however, quite small – only a dozen or so of its 79 berths can take visiting yachts in the 12–15m range – making it wise to

Looking into Velas Marina from the south, with the new office building just left of centre

phone from one's previous harbour to check that space will be available. Depth is not likely to be a problem, with at least 3–4m throughout. It is advised, though not essential, to call on VHF or mobile phone before arrival, allowing the staff to direct you straight to your berth. Otherwise secure at Reception (see plan), though this position experiences the worst of any swell and is generally too uncomfortable for a long stay.

Visiting yachts are normally berthed on 'A' pontoon (see plan), which has three bights between four 10m fingers on its west side, shorter fingers to the east, plus a hammerhead. The fingers are substantial with pillars at their ends allowing them to berth longer and heavier boats, though beam may become a limitation, and two or even three yachts – the largest around the 17m mark – may be rafted against the hammerhead in light conditions. If larger visitors have to use the berths on the east side of the pontoon a very tight turn becomes necessary, in which case willing helpers and old-fashioned warping seem to be the rule. The hammerhead of 'B' pontoon can also take at least on 15m yacht.

Visitors may also be placed on 'E' pontoon, which parallels the southeast wall. The outer part carries around 4m, and though this decreases along its length all berths have at least 3m. It experiences least surge, offset by a longer walk into town. The inner parts of 'A' pontoon plus all of 'B', 'C' and 'D' are apparently reserved for local boats, many quite small, though a visitor of 10m or less might well be tucked into a vacant 'local' berth.

On the face of it the marina appears vulnerable to strong southeasterlies, in terms of both wind and swell, but as a primarily 'summer only' haven, at least for visitors, any problems have yet to surface. Security is good, with the marina gates locked at night and a key provided to berth holders, even though the risk of crime in Velas is low.

Anchorage

Moorings are no longer laid anywhere in the harbour, the marina clearly being much preferable for locals as well as visitors. This has both enlarged the anchorage and improved one's chances of gaining some shelter, at least from the west. Even so, it remains highly weather-dependent, with the ever-present possibility of having to leave at short notice. There is a reasonably wide shelf within the 10m line, and in any case it is essential to keep well north, out of the way of manoeuvring ferries and other ships. An anchor light should be displayed if remaining overnight and a tripline would be a wise precaution.

Dinghies can be left inside the marina provided they do not impede other users – ask the marina staff where to secure – and those at anchor are welcome to use the toilets, showers and launderette.

Formalities

Visit the marina office on the west mole with the usual ship's papers, passports and insurance documents, though it is likely that marina master José Dias will already have come by to introduce himself. In common with all his colleagues throughout the Azores he speaks excellent English and is unfailingly helpful and polite, and until the administration block was ready in 2010 he normally left his office on the main quay to come and welcome every arriving yacht, despite other staff being on duty.

Other offices in the administration block are occupied by the *Polícia Marítima*, *Guarda Nacional Republicana* (*GNR*) and *Alfândega* (Customs), even though Velas is not a port of entry into the Azores (or into the Schengen area) and clearance should first be obtained at a larger harbour. Of the three, only the *GNR* need to be visited on departure.

Charges

Velas Marina is one of the *Portos dos Açores SA* chain, and shares their basic price structure. As of 2011 yachts of 10–12m LOA paid €12.22 per night and those of 12–15m paid €18.50, inclusive of everything except showers (see below). For further details see page 27 and/or www.marinasazores.com, the website of the branch of *Portos dos Açores SA* concerned with marina operation (though note that different charges apply to yachts owned by residents and by non-residents). There is no charge for anchoring.

Facilities

Boatyard Nothing suitable for yachts, although work is carried out on local smallcraft. In all but the direst emergency it would be far preferable to limp over to Horta.

Travel-lift No travel-lift or bay for one, though in an emergency yachts of up to 12m can be lifted by the harbour crane.

Chandlery Limited stock among the fishing tackle in a yellow building behind the quay (look for the Yamaha sign).

Water At all marina berths.

Showers The purpose-built block which opened on the north side of the marina in 2010 is reported to be excellent, with three showers each for men and women plus one with wheelchair access. All have both wet and dry areas, complete with a bench for clothes in the latter. In 2011 showers cost €1.50 each, whether berthed in the marina or at anchor.

Launderette In the same block as the showers, with two 7kg washing machines and one dryer. In 2011 both washing and drying cost €3.90 per load, again accessible (and similarly priced) whether berthed in the marina or at anchor.

Electricity At all marina berths.

Fuel Newly-installed pump near the marina reception building.

Bottled gas No Camping Gaz exchanges or refills of other cylinders in São Jorge.

Weather forecast Displayed in the window of the marina office.

Clube naval The prominently labelled *Clube Naval de Vila das Velas*, ✆ 295 432169, is very friendly and contains one of the best restaurants in Velas. It is said to be a keen sailing-orientated club which provides lectures and tuition.

Banks Numerous banks in the town, all with cash dispensers.

Shops/provisioning Several supermarkets in the town centre plus a larger one on Avenida do Livramento to the west of the town centre, plus a good variety of other shops.

Cafés, restaurants & hotels Throughout the town, with the large (and expensive) *Estalagem das Velas* on the seafront.

Medical services Small hospital.

Velas Marina seen from a vantage point to the northeast, with the completed smallcraft harbour beyond. The main photograph on the front cover was taken from very close by *Chris Smith*

Communications

Post office Near the main square.

Telephones Numerous kiosks as well as at the post office.

Internet access Good Wi-Fi at the *clube naval*, and elsewhere in the town. The public Wi-Fi provided in the harbour area is usually accessible from the marina and even the anchorage if the yacht has a good antenna, but laptops in use below (and relying on built-in receivers) may struggle.

Car hire Several companies in the town – a day spent exploring the island is particularly recommended.

Taxis Taxi rank on the square close west of the harbour. Some also arrive on spec to meet ferries and other ships.

Buses Routes along the south coast and elsewhere, but not all returning to Velas the same day.

Ferries Regular service to/from Faial and Pico, with less frequent links to Terceira.

Air services Inter-island flights from the small airport east of the town.

Urzelina

38°38'·63N 28°07'·72W (quay)

Lights
2681·5 **Urzelina** Fl.R.6s9m6M
Red support on white and yellow banded wall 4m

Fair-weather anchorage

A small bay lying between Velas and Calheta, protected from northwest through north to southeast but heavily fringed with rocks, Urzelina offers an attractive daytime anchorage with very clear water but could quickly become untenable in onshore winds.

Several small wooden windmills stand on the low promontory to the west amongst overgrown vineyards, and there is a large sea cave a short distance east to explore by dinghy. Inland, the old church tower is the only survivor of the 1808 eruption of Pico da Esperança when the rest of the village was buried beneath lava and ash.

The coast on either hand should be allowed 400m clearance, heading in for the centre of the bay only when it is fully open. Anchor south or southeast of the small quay in about 10m over rock and sand. The quay has steps, a ramp and a small crane.

Water is available by can and there are several cafés and restaurants serving the village and nearby campsite, a small supermarket, a bank with cash dispenser and a public telephone.

Looking northeast across the small bay at Urzelina from its western quay

Calheta

38°35'·98N 28°00'·56W (breakwater head)

Waypoint
⊕A23 – 38°35'·5N 28°00'·8W (0·5M SSW of Calheta)

Plans
Portuguese *47501* (1:5,000)

Lights
2681·2 **Breakwater** Fl.R.3s9m10M
Red column, white bands 6m

Quiet harbour behind short breakwater

Formerly a small rocky bay sheltered by high cliffs from northwest through north to east, the completion of an entirely new outer breakwater in 2003 provides both ferry landing and much improved shelter from the southwest. Even so, some swell is nearly always present, especially at high tide.

The otherwise pretty Baía da Calheta is somewhat marred by the very derelict fish cannery at its head, though this is becoming ever more overgrown and will soon be totally engulfed by vegetation unless renovated, possibly as a hotel or restaurant. Coincidentally, the largest tuna cannery in the Azores – the Santa Catarina Cannery – occupies a modern factory at the other end of town. Its produce is recommended.

The terraced and wooded slopes behind the old factory are most attractive and seem to be the haunt of many songbirds, while a fine view over the harbour and the Pico channel may be had from the conspicuous cross, a short, steep walk up the *Ladeira Velha* – an ancient cobbled lane between high, lava-block walls.

Walking westwards into town along the seafront road one passes Calheta's two most important landmarks, the 16th century *Matriz de Santa Catarina* and the *Museu de São Jorge*. Although victim of numerous fires and earthquakes over the years, the church's stone-bordered doors are a beautiful example of local baroque architecture. The museum (open 0900–1730 weekdays) is located inside a large and handsome house built in 1811. It contains two exhibition halls, a library covering the island's history and traditions, a bookshop and several computers.

In 2010 sources in Horta suggested that a small marina might be built at Calheta in the next few years, though probably intended for local smallcraft rather than for visiting yachts.

Approach and anchorage

The coast on either side is clear to within 200m of the shore, but rocks fringe the eastern side of the entrance which should not be approached until the end of the breakwater bears at least 290°.

Many yachts have, over the years, enjoyed good anchorage over sand and boulders east of the old inner quay, but as the inter-island ferries which use the breakwater turn inside the harbour, it would be

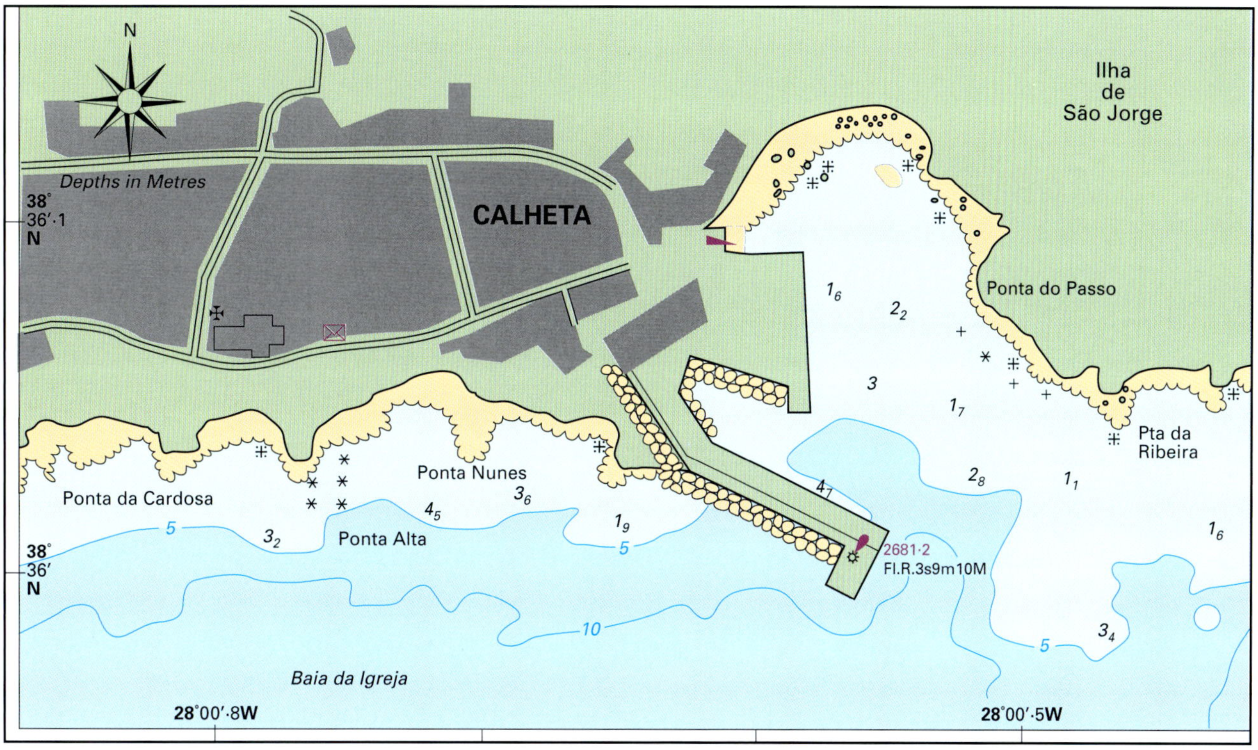

Blue sea surrounds the quay and breakwater at Calheta, viewed from high ground to the northwest

unwise to anchor south of its southern extremity. Unfortunately much of the sand appears to have been covered by rocks and rubble, possibly detritus from the construction works, and the single bright pink buoy which is sometimes laid in the middle of the harbour is used by local boats. Dinghies can be left on the slipway north of the old quay, or at the nearby steps.

Berthing

Visiting yachts are normally permitted to secure to the breakwater, though larger yachts may need to move if a ferry is due – see page 23 for timetable sources. Large bollards are situated at intervals, together with black rubber vertical cylindrical fenders intended for ships (and likely to mark a yacht's hull). At least 4m should be found all along its length other than in the extreme west. The breakwater does not appear to be used by any ships other than the ferry.

In settled conditions the old inner quay might be a better bet, but inspect first by dinghy as although around 2·5m should be found along its eastern side there is an underwater ledge where storm damage in the early 1990s caused some blocks to shift.

Almost the reciprocal of the photo overleaf – the inner quay at Calheta, backed by high wooded hills

Formalities

Not a port of entry, though if going ashore it might be wise to take ship's papers and passports as in the past skippers have occasionally been sent back aboard to collect them – even when the yacht has only sailed from Velas.

Facilities

Water From a tap on the old quay.
Electricity Not available on either breakwater or quay.
Fuel The filling station on the quay has closed, and although diesel is supplied to fishing boats by road tanker it is unlikely that a yacht could join the queue at short notice.
Bank Several in the town, with cash dispensers.
Shops/provisioning Small supermarket on the waterfront west of the church, with a bakery further on. The café/bar facing onto the old quay has a small grocery shop behind.
Cafés, restaurants & hotels Numerous restaurants and cafés plus two or three small hotels.
Medical services Health centre at the west end of the town and hospital on the main road above.

Communications

Post office with telephones On the waterfront west of the harbour.
Internet access Several (free) computers at the Museu de São Jorge (see above), open 0900–1730 weekdays. Staff may also know whether Wi-Fi is available in the town.
Car hire At least one company in the town, with others in Velas.
Taxis Taxi stand on Rua Domingos d'Olivera, just west of the harbour.
Buses Daily service to Velas and elsewhere.

Fajã do Ouvidor

38°40'·68N 28°03'·03W (quay)

Pretty bay open to the north

In settled light southerlies intrepid cruisers may be tempted to visit Fajã do Ouvidor, believed to be the only viable anchorage on the north coast of São Jorge. Little more than a quay overlooked by a summer café, the surroundings are particularly beautiful even by the high standards of the Azores. Some swell is almost certain, ruling out the possibility of lying alongside, but there are ladders and steps at which a dinghy might be secured. The rocks close west of the harbour have been joined to form a seawater swimming pool, making Fajã do Ouvidor worth a detour if touring the island by car in hot weather. There are toilets on the quay but, apparently, no tap, and no other facilities except for the café mentioned above.

The pretty bay at Fajã do Ouvidor on the north coast of São Jorge, looking a little west of north

Graciosa

Between 39°00'N–39°06'N and 27°56'W–28°04'W

Introduction

The most northerly, and isolated, of the central group, Graciosa is a small oval island approximately 13km long by 7km wide with an area of 62km^2 – only Corvo is tinier. It is also the least mountainous of the Azores, Alto do Sul on the rim of the *caldeira* and Pico Timão in the centre both reaching around 400m and Pico do Facho a mere 350m. Thus it does not possess the drama of Flores or Pico, though the lower, rounded hills, covered in woodland or large regular fields and separated by wide fertile valleys, are indeed 'gracious' and at one time supported a population second only to São Miguel's in density.

Clearly visible from Terceira, by tradition the first Portuguese settlers came from there and landed at Carapacho on the southeast coast, probably in May 1450. From the first the island was prosperous, Santa Cruz receiving its town charter in 1485 and Vila da Praia some 60 years later, with the hardworking immigrants from Portugal and Flanders cultivating wheat and barley and growing vines on the *biscuitos* (lava fields) to produce high quality wines and brandy for export. Little seems to have changed – maize is grown in place of wheat, and cattle-rearing has become an important part of the economy, but 'Graciosa White' is still reckoned among the best wines produced in the Azores, though with the shrinking population (down from 12,000 in 1900 to less than half of that 100 years later) many of the tiny fields and terraces lie neglected.

Until very recently the timelessness of Graciosa's way of life was most obvious in the number of horses and donkeys, and occasionally even cows, used for both work and transport. Walking in the countryside in the late 1980s at least half the 'traffic' one encountered was fuelled by grass – only logical in an island where it grows in abundance whilst every drop of petrol must be imported. A decade later, by which time the 5,500 or so islanders were said to own some 2,500 vehicles, no more than 10% of traffic had hooves and by 2010 it was rare to see an animal in use on the roads. Even so there were still more water troughs than filling stations and many doorways offered a ring, or simply a hole in a projecting stone, to solve the parking problem. (Glancing upwards, though, the roof was quite likely to be adorned with a reception dish for satellite television … .)

Almost all this fertile island is or has been cultivated, although there are few springs and fresh water has always been in short supply. The damp sea air and wells up to 60m deep combine to keep the lower fields green, but stone walls rather than thirsty hydrangeas mark out the dry hill pastures and banks of tamarisk fringe the sandy coastal roads, and as a result Graciosa often appears browner from seaward than its sister islands. Also, and possibly due to the long years of intense cultivation, Graciosa does not seem to have the profusion and variety of wild flowers to be seen on some of the other islands.

Windmills dot the landscape, and though only one is still in working order many of their sturdy stone trunks have been converted into barns or houses.

Graciosa, the lowest island in the Azores, seen from Terceira

Navigation

Waypoints
⊕ A25 – 38°59'·7N 27°55'·4W (1M SE of Ilhéu de Baixa)
⊕ A26 – 39°02'·7N 27°56'·8W (1M SE of Vila da Praia)
⊕ A27 – 39°05'·2N 27°59'W (0·5M ESE of Cais da Barra)
⊕ A28 – 39°06'·6N 28°03'·8W (1M NW of Pta da Barca)

Courses and distances
⊕ A25 – ⊕A21 (1M WNW of Pta dos Rosais, São Jorge) = 23M, 054° / 234°
⊕ A25 – ⊕A26 = 3·2M, 340° / 160°
⊕ A26 – ⊕A33 (1M NE of Ilhéu do Norte, Terceira) = 44·5M, 110° / 290°

Magnetic variation
11° (2011), decreasing by 7'E annually.

Tidal Streams
Tidal streams set northeast on the flood and southwest on the ebb, seldom exceeding 1 knot.

Charts
Admiralty *1956* (1:175,000)
Portuguese *43102* (1:300,000), *46404* (1:50,000)
US *51061* (1:250,000)
Imray-Iolaire *E1* (1:7509,000)

Lights
2676 **Ponta da Barca** Fl.7s70m20M
029°-vis-031°, 035°-vis-251°, 267°-vis-287°
White tower, black bands and building, red lantern 23m
2672·5 **Vila da Praia** Fl.G.3s15m9M
White tower, green bands 4m
Note Obscured 231°–264° by Ilhéu da Praia when seen from offshore
2670 **Ponta da Restinga (Carapacho)**
Fl(2)10s190m15M 165°-vis-098°
White tower and building, red lantern 14m

Each island has its typical style, those in Graciosa having a pointed wooden dome reminiscent of a giant onion to which the lattice sails are attached. A long pole allows this upper part to be manoeuvred towards the wind. Surprisingly, these very Dutch buildings did not arrive with the early Flemish settlers and were only introduced in the early 19th century when milling ceased to be a licensed activity using machinery driven by water or animal power. The waters around Graciosa seem almost as productive as the land, and a good number of larger fishing vessels are based in Praia. The stretch of rocky coast running south to the Ilhéu de Baixo is a favourite place for smaller craft using hand lines.

Ponta da Barca lighthouse keeps guard at the far northwest of the island

Tourists are not yet an industry in Graciosa. Apart from the new Graciosa Hotel at Portinho da Barra there are only a few *residencials* (guest houses) on the island, plus a few rooms available in private houses, and visitors are treated with polite interest. Offers of assistance and information may be proffered in strong American or Canadian accents, and on enquiry it generally turns out that the helpful local is a returned emigrant, who left as a young man to make his fortune in the New World. Otherwise less English is spoken than in most of the larger islands, and one gets the impression that many of the educated young people leave to seek wider horizons.

One of the first yachtsmen to call at Graciosa, in 1879, was Prince Albert of Monaco, who led several hydrographic expeditions to Azorean waters in his yacht *Hirondelle*. Like many later visitors he was intrigued by the Furna do Enxofre (sulphur springs), a rare geological phenomenon inside the *caldeira* in the southwest of the island. A hundred years ago the crater could only be gained by a steep climb over the rim and an even steeper descent inside, but the modern visitor passes through a tunnel to emerge deep in the beautiful *caldeira* on a road which winds amongst pine and eucalyptus down to the floor of the old volcano some 300m below its rim. One may often see, hovering around the crater rim, the hawks or buzzards – *açôres* in Portuguese – from which the islands took their name.

Inside the *caldeira* several dark fissures cut into the earth, one guarded by a locked gateway giving access to a stone staircase spiralling 75m down the rock face to the mouth of a huge cavern. It must have been a tiring climb for the adventurous prince, for whom a rope ladder was provided. The cave, probably formed by a lava collapse, is immense – some 150m by 100m and over 20m high – and contains a lake 130m across and at least 15m deep. Until recently visitors could paddle around the lake in a small rowing boat, but sadly the whole area is now cordoned off following a accident in which two people died. Several fumaroles emit a strong smell of sulphur, which has condensed into yellowish patches on the surrounding rock, and there are cauldrons of hot, bubbling mud, although the lake is cold and tasteless and presumably fed by rainwater.

There is a small charge for entry to the cavern, which is open 1000–1800 daily between mid June and mid September, otherwise 0930–1630 weekdays, 1400–1730 weekends and holidays. It is best visited around noon when sunlight streams down the narrow entrance to light the cave mouth, though electric lighting has now been installed. In April 2010 a new Visitors' Centre opened (with information in English as well as Portuguese), both to explain how the Furna do Enxofre came into being and to give some background regarding the dramatic geology of the Azores as a whole.

On the south coast, near Ilhéu de Baixo, is the little spa of Carapacho, whose subterranean mineral springs must be associated with those of the Furna. Many years ago a medicinal bathhouse was built on a natural terrace overlooking the sea where the hot yellowish water wells up. That this is still not merely functioning as a spa, but has recently been renovated at considerable expense, is surely an anachronism in the 21st century – but then so, in many ways, is Graciosa.

Holidays and festivals

In addition to the national holidays listed on page 26, Graciosa celebrates the Festival of *Espírito Santo* about six weeks after Easter, the Feast of *Senhor Santo Cristo Milagres* on 8 August and its official holiday four days later.

Telecommunications

Mobile (cell) phone reception throughout the island is good. The country code for the Azores is 351, as it is for mainland Portugal, and the area code for Graciosa – which must be included even when dialling from within the island – is 295, shared with São Jorge and Terceira.

By 2011 free Wi-Fi was available in the library and the adjacent main square at Santa Cruz though apparently not in Vila da Praia.

Websites

Graciosa is the home of www.galeriacores.pt.vu, originally set up by a local man who ran a computer club in Santa Cruz. It is also covered by Wikipedia at www.en.wikipedia.org/wiki/Graciosa, as well as featuring on several of the general Azores sites listed on pages 24–5.

Approach

Although Graciosa is the least mountainous island of the archipelago it is often visible from 40M or more when, from almost all directions, its three major peaks (which form a rough triangle) give the impression of at least two separate islands. Much of the coast consists of high cliffs fringed by inshore rocks, and an offing of 0·5M leads clear of all dangers other than the two islands of Ilhéu da Praia and Ilhéu de Baixo. A deep-water passage more than 0·5M wide runs between Ilhéu da Praia and Graciosa on a heading of 329°/149°, parallel to the trend of the coast. A passage some 650m wide leads inside Ilhéu de Baixo, with greatest depths about two-thirds of the way towards the smaller island. If staying outside either island maintain at least 0·5M clearance. The Baixa do Pesqueiro Longo, with 5m depths, lies between 0·5M and 0·75M off the north coast of Graciosa and should be avoided if any sea is running.

Harbours and anchorages

Vila da Praia (São Mateus)

39°03′·16N 27°57′·95W (breakwater head)

Waypoint
⊕A26 – 39°02′·7N 27°56′·8W (1M SE of Vila da Praia)

Tides
Time difference on Ponta Delgada: +0001
Mean spring range 1·3m
Mean neap range 0·6m

Plans
Admiralty *1957* (1:12,500)
Portuguese *46404* (1:5,000)
Imray-Iolaire *E1* (1:10,000)

Lights
2672·5 **Breakwater** Fl.G.3s15m9M
White tower, green bands 4m
Note Obscured 231°-264° by Ilhéu da Praia when seen from offshore
2672·3 **Ldg Lts on 307°** *Front* Fl.R.2s8m6M
Red tower, white bands on root of breakwater 4m
Rear, 70m from front, Iso.R.4s14m6M
Red column, white bands 9m
2672·4 **Fishing harbour breakwater**
Fl.R.3s10m6M Red column, white bands 4m
2672·42 **Fishing harbour north quay**
Fl(2)G.6s5m3M Green column, white bands 4m
2672·7 **Praia cables**
Fl(2)R.8s13m9M (daylight range 1·7M) 264°-vis-292°
Red lantern on terrace of building. Marks submarine cables
buoy **Pillar buoy** Q(3)10s3M
East cardinal buoy, ⧫ topmark 5m
buoys **Red can buoys** Q(3)R.4·5s3M
Two red buoys with identical characteristics have recently been placed in the harbour, possibly to mark the extent of the cables

Harbour communications
Harbourmaster ✆ 295 712128 *Fax* 295 732002
Email delegmar.graciosa@marinha.pt VHF Ch 11, 14, 16 (call *Delegmar Graciosa*) (0900–1230, 1400–1730)
Port Authority ✆ 295 712257 *Fax* 295 712206
Email aptg.graciosa@aptg.pt www.aptg.pt

Port limits
A rectangle extending 2·5M from Vila da Praia breakwater light – see Port limits, page 27

Fishing harbour with anchorage

Until the main breakwater was completed in the early 1980s Vila da Praia was a small isolated fishing village – as in some ways it still is, despite the new fishing harbour which, is should be stressed, is NOT a marina. (Rumour has it that it was originally planned as a double facility with a marina outside the fishing harbour, but that this idea was later shelved.) In 2010 a fish market was nearing construction on the west quay. Neither is the town particularly attractive, with many of its frontage of terraced white houses with pink tiles now holiday or weekend homes – perhaps not surprisingly, since

The view northeast over Vila da Praia from the vantage point of Senhora da Saúde

they overlook the island's only sandy beach. It appears to have expanded very little over the past thirty years, and still offers very limited shopping and restaurant facilities, though a visit to Santa Cruz will supply all day-to-day shopping needs.

Vila da Praia's principal charms are its total lack of sophistication and its people – it would be rare to pass anyone in the street without exchanging a smiling *bom dia* (good morning) or *bõa tarde* (good afternoon). In summer the streets, walls and pavements are often covered in (fortunately odourless) seaweed, which after drying is exported for use in medicines and cosmetics. Presumably it is collected up before festivals, when one of the favourite diversions is the *tourada da corda*, running bulls through the boarded-up streets of the town. More details of this favourite Azorean entertainment will be found in the introduction to Terceira.

The surrounding countryside is also unspoilt, with superb views from the little hill of Senhora da Saúde southwest of the town, a two hour stroll between fields of maize and piebald cattle. The fascinating Furna do Enxofre (see Introduction, page 80) entails a short taxi-ride or pleasant walk – probably the majority of yachtsmen take a taxi up and walk back.

Approach

By day Vila da Praia lies directly inside the small island of Ilhéu da Praia, some 500m long and up to 51m in height, which may be left on either hand if approaching from eastwards allowing at least 300m clearance. If approaching from the south via Ilhéu de Baixo, care must be taken to avoid the Baixa dos Remédios south of the harbour. The green and white banded column on the breakwater end can be difficult to pick out if seen against cultivated land, but the white houses along the front are distinctive.

By night The breakwater light may safely be approached from the north or northeast when bearing between 159° and 220°, while from the south it would be wise to remain 0·5M offshore until one has picked up the leading lights on 307°. These should be followed until the breakwater light is abeam, after which a turn to port will bring one into suitable depths to anchor (but watch out for mooring buoys and semi-submerged fish cages).

The main breakwater has been widened and infilled along most of its length, and yachts are no longer permitted to lie alongside. It would be unwise to enter the fishing harbour at night.

A potentially dangerous wreck has recently been reported at 39°02'·99N 27°57'·6W.

Looking into the fishing harbour from the main breakwater. Both light structures stand out prominently

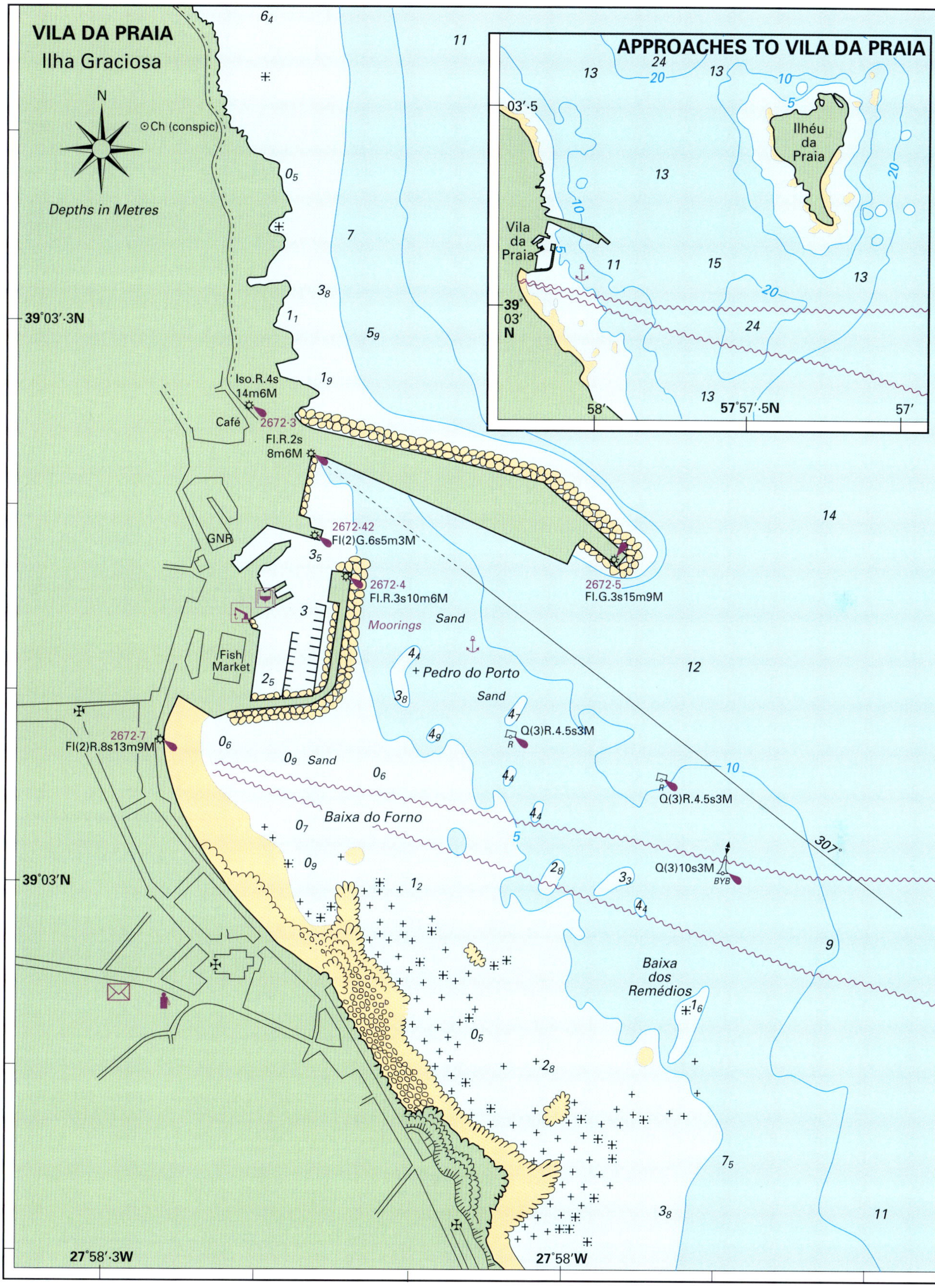

Anchorage

Formerly an exposed bay, a breakwater was built in the early 1980s and protection now runs from south through west to northeast. However, swell from either north or south may run along the coast, in which case a stern anchor to hold the bow into the

The inner harbour at Vila da Praia from the southwest

swell may prove its worth. Yachts must be sure to anchor well clear of the leading line on 307°. The front mark is conspicuous by day as well as night, positioned at the root of the mole with red and white stripes extending down the concrete below. In addition, most ships turn inside the harbour on arrival to berth port side-to against the breakwater, and generous room must be allowed for this.

Large areas of sand alternate with smaller patches of darker rock – the water is very clear – so arrival in daylight is preferable. If arriving in darkness safe anchorage will be found in 10m, though greater protection is to be had further inshore in 5–7m. A number of small boat moorings (apparently seldom occupied, but not up to the weight of a cruising yacht) are usually laid in the centre of the harbour.

A loop of armoured cable is said to lie near the inner of the two red buoys, and two more cables cross the harbour from a point just south of the fishing harbour (see plan).

Berthing

It should again be stressed that the inviting inner harbour is intended for fishing boats, not yachts – it is NOT a marina. However, yachts are normally permitted to enter if space is available and, although in theory all the berths are allocated to local boats, in practice one or two visitors can normally be squeezed in. The attitude of local fishermen is reported to vary from cheerful welcome to faint hostility. The best approach would almost certainly be to anchor off, going ashore by dinghy to visit the authorities and assess prospects.

There are two possibilities: two yachts (but no more) are usually permitted to raft up against the wall southwest of the travel-lift dock, keeping well clear of the crane at its root; otherwise go to the fish market and ask for the travel-hoist driver, who has a list of fishing boats at sea and may be able to allocate a vacant pontoon berth for a limited period.

On several occasions larger yachts have been asked to leave when easterly wind and swell are forecast, as although the finger pontoons are reasonably long and appear sturdy, their attachment points were apparently not designed to bear a yacht's weight in these conditions. Neither is berthing alongside either of the quays likely to be feasible, as that below the port hand light is normally occupied by the pilot boat, while a 45ft yacht which lay alongside the old northern quay in light easterlies experienced a most uncomfortable night.

There is no security around the harbour, other than a barrier for incoming cars, probably because the crime rate is so low.

Formalities and charges

Whether at anchor or in the fishing harbour, visit the *Guarda Nacional Republicana* (*GNR*) in their office opposite the old fishing harbour bearing the usual ship's papers and passports. They remain the only officials in the village, though the *Polícia Marítima* may drive over from their office in Santa Cruz. Formalities are typically pleasant and relaxed, though it may simplify things if a computer printout from one of the islands' true marinas is available, as this carries answers to all the standard questions so avoiding potential language difficulties. There is currently no need to visit again before departure.

Graciosa is not an official 'border post' under the Schengen Agreement, and if coming from outside the Schengen area clearance should first be obtained at a larger harbour. Note that, although part of the EU, the UK and Ireland are not signatories to the agreement.

No fees are charged for short-term berthing in the fishing harbour, presumably because visitors were not catered for in the original game-plan. This situation could change at any time, of course.

Facilities

Travel-lift An 80-tonne capacity hoist arrived in 2011 but had not yet been used at the time of writing, and neither were any props to be seen. (Local fishermen still appeared to prefer their 10-tonne crane.)

Water On the pontoons in the fishing harbour, as well as several taps. Further taps behind the fishermen's chapel and outside the public showers (see below).

Showers Free cold showers and toilets for beach users on the small quay which backs onto the fishing harbour wall. Further toilets (but no showers) in the building behind the fish market.

Electricity Sockets on the pontoons, though even if permitted to occupy a berth it would be tactless to help oneself.

Fuel In cans from the filling station just outside the village on the road towards the *caldeira*. Fishing boats are refuelled by a road tanker, but it is unlikely that it would supply a yacht.

Bottled gas The only bottled gas on Graciosa appears to be Butagas, distributed by Shell.

Bank Single bank, with cash dispenser.

Shops/provisioning Small general store plus café/bakery on the front, with the larger Supermercado Melo a few minutes further south. Several hardware and other shops, but for anything else it is necessary to visit Santa Cruz.

Café & restaurant The café/bakery mentioned above plus several other café/restaurants, but no hotel.

Medical services Hospital in Santa Cruz.

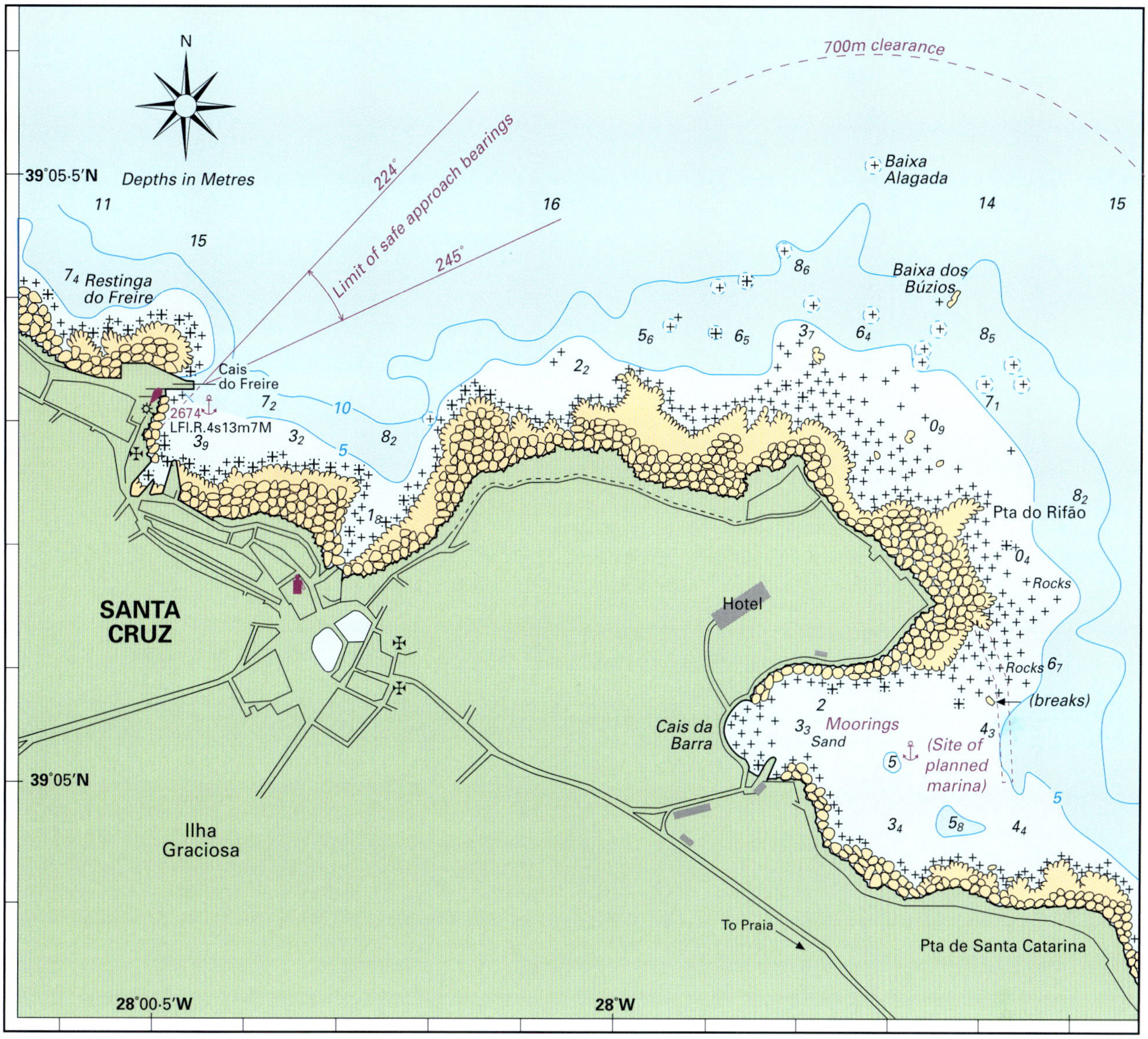

Communications

Post office Near the filling station. Open 0900–1145, weekdays only.
Telephone Public telephone opposite the old slipway.
Internet access Only in Santa Cruz (see page 87).
Car hire Two companies in Santa Cruz, both willing to deliver and collect throughout the island.
Taxis Can be ordered by telephone to come from Santa Cruz. A visit to the *caldeira*, or preferably a full island tour, is highly recommended.
Buses To Santa Cruz (though a lift may well be offered before the bus appears).
Ferries An inter-island cargo ferry, which may also carry some passengers, calls a couple of times a week.
Air services Small airport close west of Santa Cruz.

Cais da Barra

39°05′·03N 27°59′·82W (quay)

Waypoint

⊕A27 – 39°05′·2N 27°59′W (0P5M ESE of Cais da Barra)

Shallow bay and planned marina site

A small, shallow bay at the extreme northeast of Graciosa, once a whaling station and barely 10 minutes' walk from Santa Cruz. The *Clube Naval do Ilha Graciosa* have a workshop on the south side of the harbour although their main premises are at Barro Vermelho some distance west of Santa Cruz. In 2010 two whaleboats – or *canoas* – were stored undercover, with another whaleboat plus traditional

Cais da Barra, the site of Graciosa's proposed marina, seen from a little south of west

towboat outside. Since 2009 the north side has been overlooked by a frankly hideous hotel and conference centre – an almost inexplicable lapse, when so much Azorean architecture is notably harmonious and beautiful.

Cruising yachts have occasionally used the bay as a fair-weather anchorage but, despite giving good protection other than from the east, it is not place where any skipper would want to leave a yacht unattended for very long. However, this is due to change. After years of speculation and rumour, by 2010 plans for the Marina da Barra were well in hand. Plans had been submitted for official approval, although not all the necessary funding – estimated at €11 or €12 million – was yet in place. The marina will be owned and run by the *Câmara Municipal da Santa Cruz da Graciosa* (effectively the town council) as at Praia da Vitória, Terceira and Vila Franca do Campo, São Miguel.

Work may start in 2012, though 2013 seems more probable, and should take about two years – though progress will be very weather-dependent, at least until the outer breakwater is complete. Plans are not yet available, but it seems likely that the main breakwater will make use of the rocks which already give some protection from the northwest – the '*barra*' from which the bay takes its name. There are likely to be around 120 berths, all alongside finger pontoons and supplied with water and electricity, with showers and laundry facilities ashore.

Approach and entrance

From the south, an offing of 400m clears all dangers; from north and northwest about 700m is necessary to clear the Baixa Alagada. Enter when the tall white crane on the quay bears due west, by which time it should be quite clear whether work has started on the marina described above making it wiser to pass on by.

Anchorage

Although a crescent-shaped patch of sand with 3m depth lies well into the bay, this has been reported to cover the underlying rock so thinly as to afford scant holding. An iron eye let into the rock (dating back to Cais da Barra's whaling days) may be recommended by local people, but the metal is old and sharp and if a warp is used it must be checked frequently for chafe. In early June 2010 nine or 10 moorings were in evidence, none of them occupied, but it is unlikely that any would be up to the weight of a cruising yacht, even if offered.

Facilities

None, other than water from a tap beside the gateway opposite the *clube naval* workshop. However, Santa Cruz is no more than 10 minutes' walk away.

Santa Cruz

39°05'·33N 28°00'·46W (northwest mole)

Tides
Predictions for Santa Cruz are available via Admiralty *Easytide* – see page 30

Plans
Portuguese *46404* (1:5,000)
US *51062* (1:50,000 & 1:10,000)

Lights
2674 **Santa Cruz** LFl.R.4s13m6M
Red lantern on post 6m
Important For information only – Totally unsuitable for night entry

Pretty town best visited by land

With the building of first the airport and then the breakwater at Vila da Praia, Santa Cruz's importance as a port has largely died, leaving the picturesque little harbour with its four tiny boat quays deserted except for a few small fishing craft. Even the whaling industry is a thing of the past. A small, traditional harbour open to the north and east and almost always affected by swell, it cannot be recommended other than as a daytime stop in exceptionally calm weather. Most yachtsmen will prefer to leave their boats at Vila da Praia and visit by road.

The pretty pink and white town is laid out around two small lakes – originally for watering animals – and a spacious tree-lined square, giving Santa Cruz an almost Mediterranean air. Parts of the *matriz* (parish church) date back to the 16th century, though the rest is 18th century as are most of the surrounding houses with their distinctive wrought-iron balconies. There is a particularly good museum of island life, as well as a whaling museum in an old boathouse on the waterfront.

A steep road zigzags up the 130m Monte d'Ajuda behind the town, where three tiny chapels perch on the rim of a miniature crater in which nestles the island's equally miniscule bull ring. If driving, follow the signs and don't take fright at the short stretch of rough cobbles, which soon give way to tarmac. If walking, turn left off the cobbled stretch and take the old path – part steps, part steep slope – to the summit from which, until only three decades ago, a permanent watch was kept for whales. As so often in the Azores, any effort is rewarded by lovely views.

Approach

From south and east an offing of 700m clears all dangers including the breaking Baixa Alagada. The Cais do Freire (which is inconspicuous from seaward) may be approached when bearing no more than 245°. From west or north the 5m Baixa do Pesqueiro Longo is best avoided, but 400m clearance is sufficient for all other hazards. The dangerous Restinga do Freire rocks north of the Cais do Freire will be cleared if the latter is not closed until bearing at least 224°, when the tiny Santos chapel will be seen just clear of the mole end.

The pretty town and rocky harbour at Santa Cruz, seen from the southeast

Berthing and anchorage

In very calm conditions it would be possible to lie alongside near the outer end of the Cais do Freire, but depths shoal rapidly near the steps. Yachts have secured 'all-fours' south of the quay (with lines to it and to rocks under the fort, and an anchor to the southeast) but this blocks access to the manual crane used to launch and recover small fishing boats and would be impossible with any swell running.

Alternatively anchor southeast of the mole end in 7–10m. The bottom is very rocky with poor holding and a tripline is essential.

Facilities

Water Tap at the root of the Cais do Freire.
Fuel By can from the filling station in town.
Bottled gas Nothing available other than GALP's own cylinders, not even Camping Gaz.
Banks Three, all with cash dispensers outside.
Shops/provisioning Three or four small but adequate supermarkets in the town, plus a larger one on the road to the airport. Bakery and cheese factory, both on the west side of the town. Although shopping and other facilites cannot compare with those of the larger islands, they are very much better in Santa Cruz than throughout the rest of Graciosa.
Produce market Small and rather sleepy market next to the Cultural Centre.
Cafés, restaurants & hotels Numerous cafés and restaurants, and several *residencials* (guest houses), in addition to the new hotel overlooking Portinho da Barra.
Medical services Small hospital in the town.

Communications

Post office Open 0900–1230 and 1400–1730 weekdays only.
Telephones Public phones on the main square and elsewhere.

An old man drives his donkey cart through the streets of Santa Cruz. The town's two lakes were originally built to water working animals

Internet access Free Wi-Fi plus power sockets in the *Biblioteca Municipal* (public library) overlooking the main square, where there are also four computers for general use (also free, but limited to 30 minutes at busy times), open 0900–1700 weekdays only. The Wi-Fi covers the entire square and is believed to be on 24/7, but there is no outdoor power source.

For computer hardware, software and consumables such as inkjets try Inforclick ✆ */Fax* 295 732325 *Email* geral@inforclick.com on Rua Dr. João de Deus Vieira near the parish church, open 0900–1230, 1400–1800 weekdays only. Staff speak good English and are particularly helpful.
Car hire At least three companies, with offices at the airport.
Taxis Taxi rank on the main square.
Buses Services to Vila da Praia and elsewhere.
Air services Small inter-island airport west of Santa Cruz. Most services are routed via Terceira.

Folga

39°01′·06N 27°59′·99W

Plans
Portuguese *46404* (1:5,000)

Lights
2677 **Folga** LFl.5s30m4M
White column, red bands on hut 5m
Important For information only – Totally unsuitable for night entry

Port limits
A rectangle extending 1·5M from Folga light – see Port limits, page 27

The exposed bay at Folga in southwest Graciosa

Rocky bay exposed to the west

A deep rocky bay on the southwest coast of Graciosa which used to be a regular port of call for the steamer from Terceira, Folga provides protection of a sort from northwest through northeast to southeast. Definitely a fair weather daytime stop only, usually with some swell, where a yacht should not be left unattended. Waves break on the rocky beach in even the calmest weather and it is hard to imagine how the steamer ever unloaded its passengers and cargo without mishap.

Folga is easily recognised by the village and windmills on the slopes behind. Once identified the approach is quite straightforward and the light structure can be closed on a bearing of between 353° and 095°. Anchor southeast of the slipway in 10–15m over rock – a tripline would be a wise precaution. There is a small stone landing with steps, but no possibility of lying alongside. The buoys in the harbour are understood to mark fish pots, and in no circumstances should a yacht be attached to one of them.

A seasonal restaurant overlooks the landing, where there is a water tap and some rubbish bins but nothing else. The village of Folga, some distance inland, has basic shops.

Carapacho

39°00′·75N 27°57′·53W (baths)

Attractive open anchorage

An attractive, settled-weather anchorage is reported close west of Ponta da Restinga off the *Termas de Carapacho* (thermal baths) a low white building slightly east of the town of the same name (see also page 81), where 7–8m will be found over sand. The baths have been closed for several years for extensive refurbishment, but are expected to reopen by 2011.

Landing at the steps below the baths is not permitted, as the area is reserved for swimming, but is possible in flat weather at steps let into a small quay, identifiable by its white-painted walls, about 400m to the southwest. There is a tap at the campsite overlooking the thermal baths and a café/restaurant nearby, with basic shopping in the village near the dinghy landing, but little else.

Looking east along the coast at Carapacho, with Ponta da Restinga lighthouse high on the hillside and Ilhéu de Baixa in the distance

Terceira

Between 38°38'N–38°48'N and 27°02'W–27°23'W

Introduction

Meaning 'third' in Portuguese, Terceira was the third island to be discovered and is also the third in order of size, approximately 30km long and 18km wide with an area of just under 400km². Its western end is composed of a high volcanic peak, the Caldeira de Santa Barbara, with a height of 1,020m. It has a large deep crater – the largest *caldeira* in the Azores – and a lower plateau and fringing ranges lying further east. High cliffs and rocky bays comprise much of the coastline. The last major volcanic eruption occurred in 1761 when lava poured northwards towards the village of Biscoitos, but earthquakes have been a recurring problem with severe destruction in 1641, 1841 and latterly on New Year's Day 1980 when the capital city, Angra do Heroísmo, was particularly badly hit.

Terceira was first recorded in 1450 and soon afterwards settled by immigrants from the Low Countries whose fair-haired descendants can still be seen. The first villages were built in the southeast and the parish churches at Praia da Vitória and São Sebastião both date back to the 15th century. However, Angra do Heroísmo rapidly grew in population and prosperity due to its superior natural anchorage, for centuries being the most important town in the Azores and capital of the archipelago until 1832. From it Martin Homem and João de Cortez-Real sailed to discover Newfoundland, Barcelos for Greenland, and João Fernandez

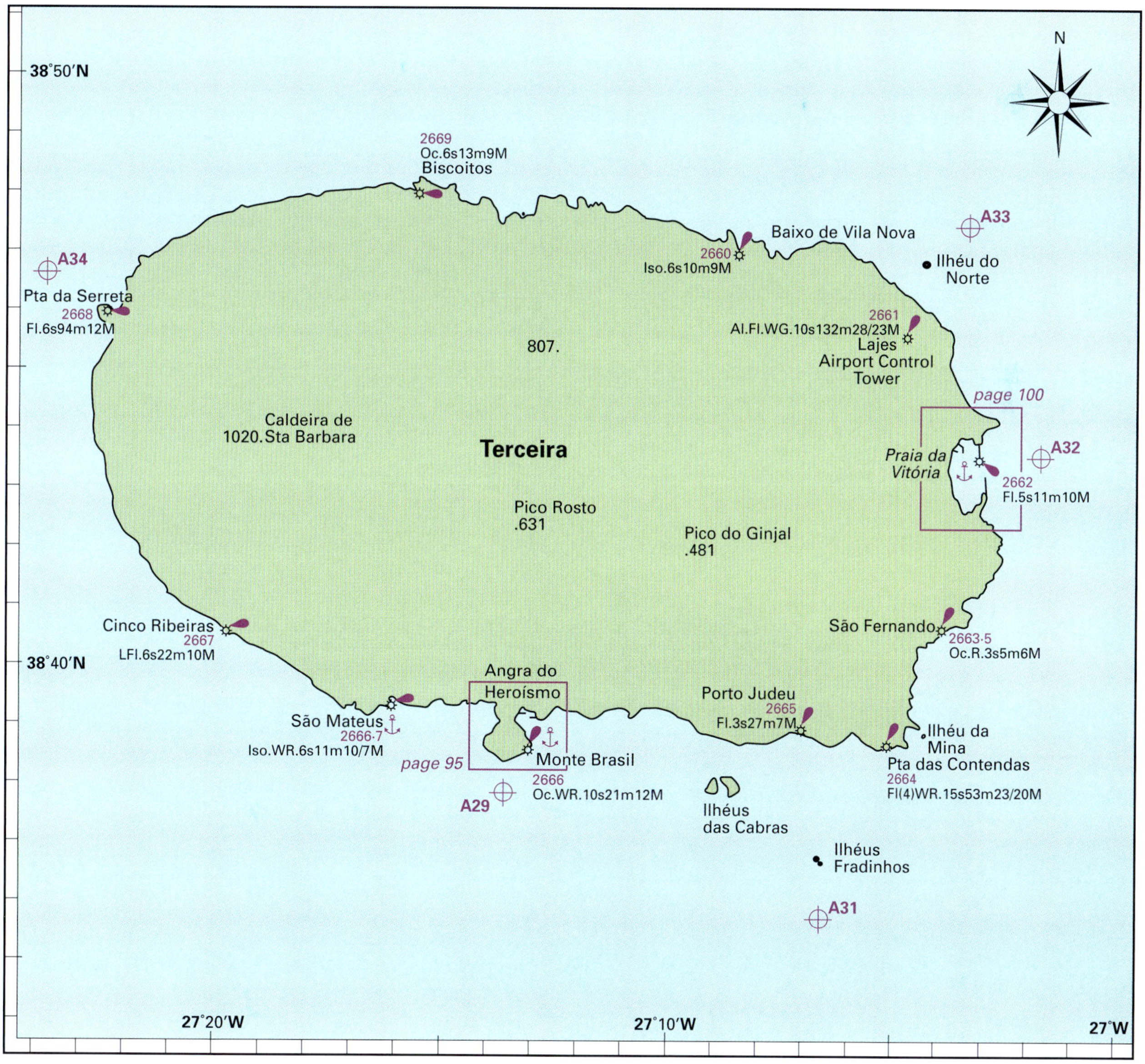

I. THE AZORES

Labrador as pilot with the English fleet led by John Cabot in the discovery and exploration of Labrador. In 1499 Vasco de Gama stopped briefly to bury his brother on their return voyage from India. Only very recently has the harbour of Angra do Heroísmo been rivalled by that at Praia da Vitória.

During the 16th century Angra continued to grow, being granted city status in 1534, the same year that a bishopric was set up by Pope Paul III. In 1580, when mainland Portugal was dominated by Spain, Terceira became the last major centre of resistance. A Spanish force was prevented from landing on the beach at Praia in 1581 when the locals, lacking proper weapons, drove their wild cattle down from the hills and against the invaders, but the island finally fell in 1583. Phillip II of Spain quickly built the impressive fortress of São João Batista, commanding both the town of Angra and its harbour, to provide safekeeping for the gold and silver brought to the island by galleons returning from the New World, always a tempting target for pirates and privateers. Amongst the latter were Sir Francis Drake, who attacked Angra in 1587, and the Earl of Essex who attempted to seize an entire fleet of Spanish treasure ships at anchor in the harbour.

Even after Portugal regained her independence in 1640 and the Spaniards were expelled, small forts continued to be built around the island as a defence against the pirates – Spanish, French, English, Dutch and North African – who plagued all the Azorean islands in the 16th and 17th centuries. The deposed King Alfonso VI was imprisoned in the fortress of São João Baptista in the 1660s, a foretaste of its much later use as a prison for captured German troops during the First World War. Terceira's last major role in Portuguese politics was its support of the Liberalists in 1829. The right-wing Absolutists were prevented from landing at Praia – earning its *da Vitória* title – swiftly followed by the award of *do Heroísmo* to the city of Angra by the Liberalist Regency established there.

The well-kept public gardens at Angra do Heroísmo

The lessening importance of Angra as a port was to some extent compensated by the construction at Lajes of the Azores' first major airport, built by the RAF in 1943. Part was leased to the US in 1947 when the airport at Santa Maria was returned to the Portuguese and many American servicemen are still based on the island. As well as being an important NATO airfield it serves as the headquarters of the Portuguese Azores Air Command and as Terceira's civil airport.

Although Terceira, with a population of around 60,000, is one of the more densely populated islands, the impression from a distance – and particularly from the sea – is one of spaciousness. This may be partly due to the wise decision, taken some years ago, not to permit unnecessary building above the 200m contour. The south and east have long been cleared for farming, while the upper slopes were unfenced grazing until the 18th century when walls were built by government order – and promptly destroyed by the locals. As a result the fields are large and regular, in contrast to the small and generally random effect prevalent in the other islands. Pastoral farming remains an important industry.

Further north and west more of the native forest of pine, laurel and eucalyptus survives, with moorland and scrub on the upper slopes which are often blanketed by mist or low clouds even though at sea level it may be pleasantly sunny and warm. Thus the majority of villages are near the coast, characterised by low whitewashed cottages with odd wedge-shaped chimneys vented near the top by a few missing bricks. Particularly around Angra, casement windows give way to sash frames, often in three overlapping parts, while cottage gardens are obviously a source of pride with roses and chrysanthemums vying for space with hibiscus and bougainvillaea.

On the north coast around Biscoitos vines are grown in tiny plots surrounded by protective lava-block walls. Even the soil seems to be mostly pumice, and apparently it is the iron oxide in the stone which gives the wine its distinctive smell and flavour – making it something of an acquired taste. The wine museum, set up in an old farmhouse and displaying tools, documents, photographs and even dried rootstocks, is well worth a visit.

Also worth visiting are the caverns at Algar do Carvão, about 14km north of Angra do Heroísmo, and the nearby fumaroles at Furnas do Enxofre. Not fully explored until the 1960s, the caves extend at least 100m underground and, as in Graciosa, contain a small subterranean lake. Originally access was via a narrow vertical shaft, but in 1996 a tunnel was dug and electric light laid on. Steps and galleries allow the visitor to move around easily, though since the earthquake of 1980 it has not been possible to reach the further part of the system. The caves are open daily from June to September inclusive, with a small entrance fee.

All over Terceira one sees brightly painted *Imperios do Espírito Santo* – literally Empires or Theatres of the Holy Ghost – tiny chapels with windows on three sides and often a balcony, used for displaying the silver crown, dove and sceptre associated with the festivals of *Espirito Santo* which mainly take place during June. The other typically Azorean entertainment is the *tourada da corda*, the local version of the Portuguese bullfight, when the animals are allowed to career through the village streets whilst the local youths show off their courage and daring, cheered on by spectators from safe vantage points. Two or three men check the bull's movements by means of a long rope, and although it is teased to the point of exhaustion – brightly coloured umbrellas are the modern substitute for the cape – no bull is ever killed or seriously injured. It has been suggested that the *tourada da corda* goes back to the day over 400 years ago when the Spanish invaders were driven back into the sea from the beaches at Praia da Vitória. *Tourada da corda* can be held any time from May until October, with dates and venues available from tourist offices.

Certainly Terceira is an island with a proud history, and it was a tragedy that so many of its ancient buildings were severely damaged by the earthquake referred to previously. Fortunately most people were outside celebrating the New Year and escaped injury, but 64 people died and three-quarters of Angra's buildings were affected. Now all are repaired and the atmosphere is prosperous, perhaps due partly to the American presence on the island, though this is unobtrusive. Rather more people speak English (or American) than elsewhere and there are more new, large cars to be seen on the roads. Having written back in 1987 that '... even they may have to wait while an old man seated sideways on a donkey follows his herd of cows down a cobbled country lane' the modern equivalent, observed with wonder well into the 21st century, was a large herd of dairy cows being walked unhurriedly along three lanes of the island's busiest dual carriageway as though they owned the place. Which of course they do...

Holidays and festivals

In addition to the national holidays listed on page 26, Angra do Heroísmo celebrates its official holiday on 24 June. Known as *Sanjoaninas*, these festivities can lead to serious congestion in the marina, which does not accept advance reservations. If planning to attend it is wise to arrive several days in advance.

The local holiday at Praia da Vitória occurs on June 20th, with the Mid Atlantic Gastronomic Festival taking place over 10 days in early August, complete with bands on the promenade and events on the beach.

Festivals of *Espírito Santo* take place all through the Azores about six weeks after Easter, but are particularly popular in Terceira where the *Imperios do Espírito Santo* are decorated and filled with offerings, and bread and wine offered to passers by.

Every country village in Terceira has its *Imperio do Espírito Santo*, often painted in bright primary colours

Telecommunications

Mobile (cell) phone reception throughout the island is excellent. The country code for the Azores is 351, as it is for mainland Portugal, and the area code for Terceira – which must be included even when dialling from within the island – is 295, shared with São Jorge and Graciosa.

Eel, anybody? The fishmarket at Angra do Heroísmo

Navigation

Waypoints
⊕ A29 – 38°37'·8N 27°13'·6W (0·5M S of Monte Brasil)
⊕ A30 – 38°38'·7N 27°12'·5W (0·5M SE of Angra do Heroísmo)
⊕ A31 – 38°35'·7N 27°06'·6W (1M S of Ilhéus Fradinhos)
⊕ A32 – 38°43'·5N 27°01'·7W (1M E of Praia da Vitória)
⊕ A33 – 38°47'·4N 27°03'·3W (1M NE of Ilhéu do Norte)
⊕ A34 – 38°46'·6N 27°23'·7W (1M NW of Pta Serreta)

Courses and distances
⊕ A29 – ⊕A24 (1M ESE of Ilhéu do Topo, São Jorge) = 24M, 258° / 078°
⊕ A29 – ⊕A30 = 1·2M, 044° / 224°
⊕ A30 – ⊕A32 = 12M, by eye
⊕ A31 – ⊕A38 (1M S of Santa Clara, São Miguel) = 86M, 128° / 308°
⊕ A33 – ⊕A26 (1M SE of Vila da Praia, Graciosa) to = 44·5M, 290° / 110°
⊕ A33 – ⊕A32 = 4M, 072° / 242°
⊕ A34 – ⊕A33 = 16M, 087° / 267°

Magnetic variation
11° (2011), decreasing by 7'E annually.

Tidal Streams
Tidal streams set north or east on the flood and south or west on the ebb, but seldom reach 1 knot.

Charts
Admiralty *1956* (1:175,000)
Portuguese *43102* (1:300,000), *46405* (1:75,000)
US *51061* (1:250,000)
Imray-Iolaire *E1* (1:750,000)

Lights
2668 **Ponta da Serreta** Fl.6s94m12M
White tower, red bands 14m
2661 **Lajes Airport** Aero
Al.Fl.WG.10s132m28/23M
Wooden framework tower 19m
2662 **Praia da Vitória, north breakwater** Fl.5s11m10M
White column, black bands with 'basket' top 9m
2664 **Ponta das Contendas** Fl(4)WR.15s53m23/20M
220°-W-020°-R-044°-W-072°-R-073° 079°-R-093°
(Obscured 073°-079° by Ilhéu das Cabras)
Square white tower and building, red lantern 13m
2666 **Monte Brasil (Ponta do Farol)**
Oc.WR.10s21m12M 191°-R-295°-W-057°
White column, red bands 5m
2667 **Cinco Ribeiras** LFl.6s22m10M
White pyramid, red bands 2m
Note The lights of Porto Judeu and São Fernando (Ribeira Seca), both on the southeast coast, are omitted due to their total unsuitability for yachts

By 2011 free Wi-Fi was available in many places in both Angra do Heroísmo and Praia da Vitória, as well as at the island's international airport.

Websites

Terceira has several websites of potential interest to yachtsmen, including www.cm-ah.pt/ – the impressive website of the city council of Angra do Heroísmo, currently available in Portuguese only, but with built-in 'auto translation' into English, French and Spanish; http://museu-angra.azores.gov.pt/ – homepage of Angra do Heroísmo's city museum, in Portuguese only but with useful information including opening times etc.; www.cmpv.pt – the website of the *Câmara Municipal* (town council) of Praia da Vitória, with various links including one to the marina, in Portuguese only; www.lajes.af.mil – website of the US Airbase at Lajes, including an interesting history of the base – in American English, of course!

Terceira is also covered by Wikipedia at www.en.wikipedia.org/wiki/Terceira_Island, as well as featuring on several of the general Azores sites listed on pages 24–5.

Approach

Terceira is one of the higher islands in the Azores, and the hills which lie close behind much of its coastline make it visible from a considerable distance. Even before the advent of GPS Terceira was considered a relatively easy landfall, although there are a few offlying hazards, most unlit. When closing the southeast coast the Ilhéus Fradinhos, some 10m in height and lying about 2M offshore at 38°36'·66N 27°06'·64W, are clearly visible by day but unlit at night though covered by a red sector of Ponta das Contendas light, as are the Ilhéus das Cabras. (A passage exists between the two Ilhéus das Cabras carrying a least depth of some 8m, but caution should be exercised due to strong and unpredictable currents). Other possible hazards are the Ilhéu da Mina, close off the headland of that name, the Ilhéu do Norte just over half a mile offshore from Lajes on the northeast coast, and the rocks forming the Baixa de Vila Nova off the town and tiny inlet of that name a few miles to the west. In rough weather it would also be wise to avoid the Baixa da Serreta, 2M off Ponta Serreta on the west coast and shoaling to 8m, where bad seas might be expected.

Careful navigation is essential if on passage towards Terceira from São Miguel, particularly in poor weather, as the unmarked Banco Dom João de Castro shoal lies only 5M west of the direct course between the two. Although the shoal – the tip of a subterranean volcano – has broken the surface at least once during the last 500 years it is currently charted at 12m, confirmed in 1999 by the crew of a yacht who carried out several dives on the bank, but as there is ongoing seismic activity in the area depths could decrease at any time. They pinpointed the least depth to be at 38°13'·37N 26°36'·36W, and within 100m of this spot were off soundings. As one might expect, seas break heavily on the bank in strong winds.

Finally, Admiralty chart *1956* bears a note that 'Aircraft may occasionally jettison external loads within the area indicated on this chart', the area concerned being a circle 10M in diameter centred just over 10M north of the eastern end of Terceira. Exactly what these 'external loads' may consist of it not specified, but it might be as well to avoid the area on principal.

Harbours and anchorages

Angra do Heroísmo

38°39'·05N 27°12'·93W (Porto das Pipas molehead)

Waypoint

⊕ A30 – 38°38'·7N 27°12'·5W (0·5M SE of Angra do Heroísmo)

Tides

Predictions for Angra do Heroísmo are available via Admiralty *EasyTide* – see page 30
Time difference on Ponta Delgada: –0004
Mean spring range 1·4m
Mean neap range 0·6m

Plans

Admiralty *1957* (1:12,500)
Portuguese *46405* (1:10,000)
US *51064* (1:12,500)
Imray-Iolaire *E1* (1:12,500)

Lights

2666 **Monte Brasil (Ponta do Farol)**
Oc.WR.10s21m12M 191°-R-295°-W-057°
White column, red bands 5m
2666·2 **Ldg Lts on 341°** *Front* Fl.R.4s29m7M
Red post near church 2m
Rear, 505m from front, Oc.R.6s54m7M
Yellow metal structure, red top 2m
2666·5 **Porto das Pipas molehead** Fl.G.3s14m6M
White column, green bands 5m
2666·3 **Marina south mole** Fl(2)R.6s8m3M
White cone, red bands 3m
2666·1 **Silveira cables**
Fl(2)R.8s29m9M (daylight range 1·7M) 024°-vis-052°
White post, red bands 4m. Marks submarine cables
Note Situated west of Monte Brasil

Harbour communications

Harbourmaster ✆ 295 540500 *Fax* 295 540502
Email capitania.pvitoria@marinha.pt VHF Ch 11, 16 (call *Capimar Angra*) (0900–1230, 1400–1730)
Port Authority ✆ 295 540000 *Fax* 295 540019
Email aptg.sa@aptg.pt www.aptg.pt
VHF Ch 11, 14, 16 (0900–1200, 1300–1700)
Marina d'Angra ✆ 295 540000 *Fax* 295 216309
Email marina.angra@aptg.pt
www.marinasazores.com VHF Ch 09, 16
(0800–2000 from 15 May to 15 September, 0800–1700 at other times)

Port limits

A rectangle extending 2·5M from Porto das Pipas molehead light – see Port limits, page 27.

Marina adjoining UNESCO World Heritage city

One of the most handsome natural harbours in the Azores, Angra do Heroísmo is protected by high land from all directions other than southeast, though swell sets in with winds from anywhere between south and east. Yachts at anchor had always to be ready to leave the harbour at short notice, often curtailing exploration beyond the immediate city, but that is now a thing of the past thanks to the long, narrow marina which lies directly beneath the old sea wall. Plans for the marina were approved in the mid-1990s, but work had barely started when a historic wreck – thought to be that of a 16th- or 17th-century galleon – was discovered on the harbour bed and operations were suspended while archaeologists investigated the site. Construction resumed in 1999 and by June 2001 it was effectively complete, though without much of its shoreside infrastructure.

From early days the harbour was used by vessels trading to Africa, India and the Americas, bringing wealth and importance to the settlement which was raised to city status in 1543. During the Spanish occupation in the 16th century it was twice attacked by British fleets, one commanded by Sir Francis Drake, and the fort of São João Baptista was built for harbour defence and the safekeeping of valuable cargoes – as well as to keep the townspeople in a suitably submissive frame of mind.

Plans to further extend the harbour further have been under consideration for at least a decade. A cruise ship terminal has been suggested, though it seems more likely that the Porto das Pipas mole may be extended, perhaps with a small harbour created outside the current south wall (see plan). Commercial traffic no longer calls, going to purpose-built wharfs at Praia da Vitória instead, though a catamaran ferry visits three times a week during July and August and berths against the inner side of the Porto das Pipas mole. The harbour is noticeably clean with very clear water, recognized by the award of an EU 'Blue Flag' each year since 2006.

The city is notable for its fine buildings and well-kept public gardens, and a particularly informative city guide is available free from the tourist office on Rua Direita (open 0900–1200, 1400–1700

Angra do Heroísmo city and harbour, seen from Monte Brasil to the southwest

I. THE AZORES

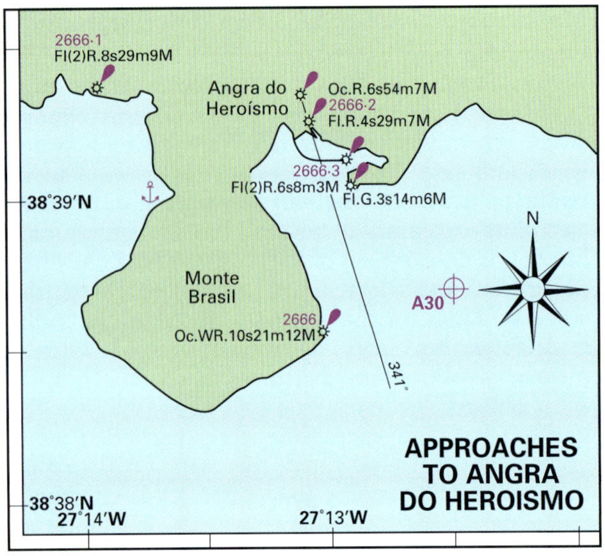

weekdays, 0900–1200 Saturday). Angra was declared a UNESCO World Heritage Site in 1983 while restoration following the 1980 earthquake was still under way – the high proportion of bright terracotta roofs visible from Monte Brasil indicate buildings which sustained damage – and remains a most attractive city with considerable atmosphere. The west end of the marina is overlooked by the handsome 15th century *Alfandega* building and the magnificent 18th century *Misericordia* church, both now restored. Between them, a handsome double stairway sweeps around an artificial waterfall and descends to the ancient *Cais Alfandega*. Below the harbour wall and south of the fountain a modern, glass-panelled building houses a restaurant, bar and the marina services block. Renovation work has started on some of the old, semi-derelict buildings which overlook the marina from the northeast, though the decision to site a massive, modern hotel/apartment building close east of them will be questioned by many people.

The city museum in the former monastery of São Francisco (open 0930–1200, 1400–1700 Tuesday to Friday, 1400–1700 weekends, closed Monday) is fascinating and well worth a visit, even though many of the captions are in Portuguese only. Two particularly enjoyable walks are up to the pyramid monument which overlooks the city from the north and out to Monte Brasil, the entrance to which is through the main gateway of the fort. Both offer splendid views over the city and harbour.

A local boat enters the marina at Angra do Heroísmo. The angular building on the left houses the marina offices, with a new apartment building taking shape behind

Approach and entrance

By day Monte Brasil, rising to over 200m, is easily identified from a considerable distance and approach is straightforward, though the marina entrance itself is narrow. Rubble, marked in 2010 by a very small pink buoy, extends some distance beyond the end of the marina mole, but 3·5m should be found in the centre.

By night If approaching from the west, Monte Brasil light will not be visible until bearing less than 057°. Both sides of the marina entrance are lit, and combined with the considerable ambient light from the city night entry would be perfectly feasible in settled conditions (though see the note re rubble, above). Alternatively follow the leading lights until Porto das Pipas mole is abeam to starboard, when a course of about 287° will lead to the anchorage. Do not venture inside the 8m contour in darkness.

Anchorage

In suitable weather it is possible to anchor off the prominently marked *clube náutico* in the western part of the harbour. Depths (over sand) shoal

The end of the long mole which shelters Marina d'Angra, with Monte Brasil in the background. The small red buoy marks rubble off its end

gradually, but until Baixa da Prainha, awash at HW springs, has been identified it would be unwise to venture into less than 6m, even in good daylight.

Three areas close to the shore of Monte Brasil form an underwater archaeological park, where anchoring is prohibited. These sites – of 19th-century wrecks and an anchor graveyard – should each be marked with a yellow buoy to which one is welcome to tie a tender for diving. Yachts are recommended to anchor inshore of a line between the light structure on the marina mole and the yellow-walled chapel on Monte Brasil (the higher of the two buildings). This clears the southernmost marine reserve – the remains of the wreck of the *Lidador* – while, as mentioned above, two yellow buoys mark the reserve which lies inshore of the anchorage area. Information on the sites, scuba excursions and equipment can be obtained from local dive shops.

Although no charge is made for anchoring, skippers of anchored yachts are asked to visit the marina office on arrival to check in with the authorities. Thereafter, dinghies can be left at the *Cais Alfandega* at the head of the marina – but take care on the ancient steps, which can be slippery. A long painter will be needed as lines must be taken up to the quay, some 5–6m above the water at low tide. Crews of anchored/moored yachts may also use the marina toilets and showers – see Facilities below.

There are currently no mooring buoys in the bay, nor plans to lay any.

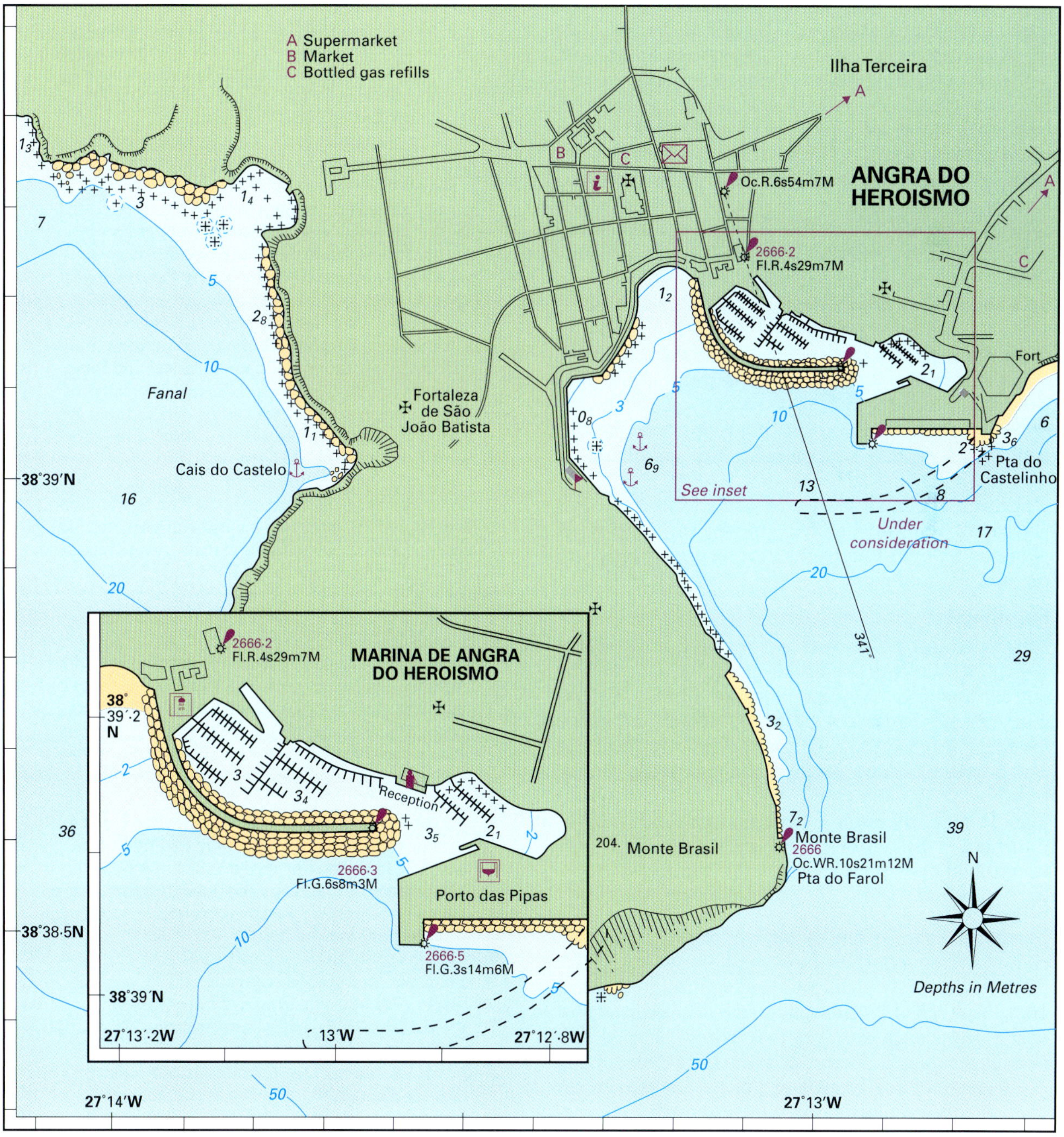

Marina d'Angra, Porto das Pipas mole and the coastline beyond, looking eastwards from the fortress of São João Batista

Berthing

On arrival, yachts should secure at the reception/fuel pontoon directly opposite the marina entrance to be allocated a berth. Alternatively, call on VHF Ch 09 or by mobile phone during the approach. At least 3·5m should be found in the entrance, at the reception pontoon and at the larger berths. All berths are alongside finger pontoons, with 25 berths reserved for visitors of over 10m though up to 50 visiting yachts have been squeezed in on occasion. The marina can take a few yachts of 18m LOA, though it would always be wise to check whether space is available before leaving one's previous port. Over 3·5m is carried at least half way up the harbour, though depths decrease to 1m at its head. If any swell is running it is worth requesting a spot in the western part of the harbour where the movement is least, though considerable motion sometimes pervades the entire marina – with an accompanying groaning and creaking of pontoons and rollers against the piles – and mooring line snubbers are highly recommended.

Security is particularly good – in addition to card-activated pontoon gates, the entire marina is overseen by CCTV cameras and security guards are on duty day and night.

Formalities

All formalities are carried out in the marina office, which overlooks the reception pontoon opposite the marina entrance. Marina manager Roldão Duarte and his staff could not be more helpful and speak excellent English. The handsome modern building also houses Customs, Immigration and police offices, but these are seldom manned. Check-in is carried out quickly and efficiently by the marina staff and the information passed on to the authorities, who may occasionally visit a yacht if they think it necessary.

Charges

Marina d'Angra is one of the Portos dos Açores SA chain, and shares their basic price structure. As of 2011 yachts of 10–12m LOA paid €12.22 per night and those of 12–15m paid €18.50, inclusive of everything except showers (see below). For further details see page 27 and www.marinasazores.com, the website of the branch of Portos dos Açores SA concerned with marina operation (though note that different charges apply to yachts owned by residents and by non-residents).

Facilities

Boatyard Not as such, though there is a secure gated area of hardstanding with 24-hour security at the east end of the Porto das Pipas mole (which is high enough to provide reasonable shelter from south winds), where both local and foreign-owned yachts were laid up ashore in May 2010. A full range of services are planned, but in the meantime consult either the marina office or Pedro Parreira of Flores & Parreira (see Chandlery, below) who can arrange welding, as well as repairs to GRP and aluminium.

Travel-lift 50-tonne capacity hoist on the Porto das Pipas mole, with about 3m depth at the dock. Organise via the marina office. Should a yacht be too large, or wide, for the travel-lift a mobile crane can be brought in from the docks at Praia da Vitória.

Diving services, engineers & electronics Can be arranged via the marina office or consult Pedro Perreira of Flores & Parreira (see Chandlery, below. The machine shop operated by Gil Sousa e Filhos Lda at Zona das Combustiveis 6 ✆ /*Fax* 295 213629, is highly recommended by MAYS in Horta.

Chandlery Both of Angra's chandleries operate from premises some distance from the harbour and marina.

Flores & Parreira ✆ 295 401280, 912 355308 *Email* geral@floresparreira.com (at Atalaia, Ribeirinha, 9700-416 Angra do Heroísmo, a few miles to the east of the city) is primarily an agricultural supplier, but with a growing marine side run by Pedro Parreira, who speaks fluent English. The company handles boat and engine sales (as a Yanmar agent) and also stocks International Paints (including antifouling), anodes, hardware including nylon and bronze plumbing, general chandlery, rope and Portuguese charts of local waters. Items not in stock can be ordered from the major catalogues. Open 0900–1200, 1330–1800 weekdays, 0900–1200 Saturday.

Maré d'Angra, also known as Fastomar, ✆ 917 385636, has its main premises at Rue Basilio Simões, Lot 40, No 20 in the city's industrial park, and stock general chandlery including hardware and electronics.

Water At all marina berths.

Showers The services block at the west end of the marina houses immaculate showers, sinks and toilets, accessible 0830–1200 and 1300–2000. There is a large jacuzzi, and even a babycare room complete with bath. Showers – which may also be used by the crews of yachts at anchor – cost €1.76, including soap and a towel, and are paid for on the spot. With six ladies' showers and 11 for men there should seldom be a queue.

Launderette In the shower block, with two washing machines and one dryer, though one more of each may be added. The machines are operated by tokens, available from shower reception during office hours, in 2010 costing €4.08 to wash a load and the same to dry. An iron and ironing board are available on request.

Electricity At all marina berths.

Fuel Pumps for both diesel and petrol at the east end of the reception pontoon, operational 0900–1200, 1400–1900 from 15 May to 15 September, 0900–1200, 1300–1600 at other times. As of 2010 fuel still had to be paid for in cash.

Bottled gas Camping Gaz cylinders can be exchanged at 124/126 Rua da Sé (opposite the cathedral), which advertises its hours as 1100–1200, 1630–1730

weekdays only, but in practice seldom appears to open at all. Alternatively cylinders of most types, including Camping Gaz, can be refilled (with butane only) at Frederico A Vasconcelos Lda (FAV) on Rua João Vaz Corte Real, about 10 minutes' walk from the marina, open 0900–1200, 1300–1700 weekdays only. Allow at least two days.

Weather forecast Three-day forecasts (in Portuguese) plus synoptic charts are posted daily outside the marina office.

Clube náutico The *Angra Iate Clube*, an offshoot club of the older *Clube Náutico da Angra*, has premises on the quay at Porto das Pipas. It is principally involved in racing, but is said to be friendly and welcome visitors. As of 2010 the older *Clube Náutico da Angra* on the west side of the bay was seldom open.

Banks Many in the city, plus cash dispensers seemingly on every corner.

Shops/provisioning Small supermarket opposite the Cathedral, the larger Guarita supermarket on Rua da Guarita about 10 minutes' walk northeast of the marina, plus a huge Modelo hypermarket about 10 minutes beyond that – worth the walk/taxi fare if stocking up for a long passage. A wide variety of other shops are to be found, as befits the Azores' second largest city.

Produce market Thriving fish and produce market beyond the cathedral.

Cafés, restaurants & hotels The Aquaemotion bar/restaurant in the marina services block is unexpectedly good (though not particularly cheap) and open 1200–2400 daily from April until December, or for more traditional dining try the Hotel Beira Mar besides the *Alfandega* building. These are the tip of the iceberg, however, with a range to suit all pockets. The same diversity appies to residential accommodation.

Medical services Hospital in the city, plus doctors, dentists and opticians.

Communications

Post office The main post office on Rua da Palha is open 0830–1830 weekdays and 0900–1230 Saturdays.

Mailing address Letters for yachts in transit can be sent c/o: Marina d'Angra, Porto das Pipas, 9700–154 Angra do Heroísmo, Terceira, Açores, Portugal.

Telephones Public telephone outside the marina services block, with cards on sale in the office, plus many others throughout the city.

Internet access Free Wi-Fi in and around the marina, with two Skype-enabled computers and printers in the services (not the administration) block, at €1 for 30 minutes, printing charged extra. Also in the *Biblioteca Pública* (public library), housed in the impressive Pálacio Bettencourt just behind the cathedral (open 0900–1900 weekdays, 0930–1200 Saturday and well worth a 'tourist' visit in its own right), and at the Cultural Centre on Rua Boa Vista, open 1000–2200 weekdays and 1400–2200 weekends.

Car hire Several companies have offices in the city – ask at the marina office.

Taxis The city's main taxi rank is on the town square only 100m from the marina.

Buses Services around the island – details from the tourist office. A free bus runs within the city limits, though most things are within walking distance. Ask at the marina office for times and routes.

Air services International and inter-island flights from the airport near Praia da Vitória, about 24km distant by road.

Cais do Castelo

38°39'N 27°13'·75W (anchorage)

Anchorage for easterly winds

When wind or swell from the eastern quadrant make the anchorage at Angra do Heroísmo uncomfortable, sheltered anchorage may be found under the cliffs west of Monte Brasil. Good holding in 5–10m has been reported at the mouth of the small inlet southwest of São João Baptista fort, near the distinctive white steps.

The bay and steps at Cais do Castelo, on the west side of Monte Brasil, seen from the northwest

São Mateus da Calheta

38°39'·33N 27°16'W (west molehead)

Lights
2666·7 **São Mateus** Iso.WR.6s11m10/7M
270°-R-296°-W-067°
White column, red bands 3m
Northeast mole Fl.G.3s5m3M
White post, green bands 3m
Southwest mole Fl(3)R.5s10m3M
White post, red bands 3·4m

Small fishing harbour

For many years protected only by a short southwest mole, the small fishing harbour at São Mateus has recently been improved by the addition of a new east mole, an inner spur near the end of the old southwest mole and new pontoons inside. Two ruined forts and an impressive church overlook the town, which has basic facilities including water on the quay, limited shopping and the usual restaurants and cafés.

An excellent reason to call at São Mateus, whether by sea or land, would be to visit the small whaling museum in the *Casa dos Botes* (part of the *Clube Naval de São Mateus*) just behind the quay. Two restored whaleboats occupy the ground floor, surrounded by harpoons and other equipment as well as photographs of the harbour during the 19th and 20th centuries, with more photographs and models upstairs. Entry is free, and while there are no formal opening hours it is generally open on Sunday morning.

Approach and anchorage

The enlarged harbour is clearly intended for local boats and it is uncertain how a yacht would be received should one enter, but there is space for a well-handled yacht of 12m or so to manoeuvre while assessing the situation – and the reception. It might be possible to lie alongside for an hour or two when things are quiet, and there is nothing to prevent the more adventurous anchoring off.

The prominent white church is visible from several miles off, dwarfing the surrounding village, but the rock-fringed coastline on either hand should be given an offing of at least 500m until the end of southwest mole bears between 330° and 000°. About 9m will be found in the entrance, shoaling rapidly to 3–4m, or choose a suitable spot outside in which to anchor in about 10m over sand and large boulders. The water is very clear.

São Mateus da Calheta, a small fishing harbour about 2M west of Angra do Heroísmo

Biscoitos

38°48'·05N 27°15'·59W

Lights
2669 **Biscoitos** Oc.6s13m9M
White column, two red bands 3m

Attractive north coast anchorage

In settled weather Biscoitos offers a pleasant daytime anchorage in 8–10m over rock. The mole was extended by 35m about ten years ago, apparently to increase its appeal as a swimming area, but though about 2m will be found at its head and 1m its root the bottom is rocky and it is not suitable for lying alongside. There is a slipway and steps near the root of the mole, as well as three ladders inside the angled head, at which one could land by dinghy. Nearby facilities are limited to a café/bar and swimmers' (ie. cold) showers, with shops in the village about 1km inland.

The anchorage is overlooked by a miniature three-cannon fort and a monument commemorating Biscoitos' place in Portuguese history when, in the run-up to the Miguelite rebellion of autumn 1828: 'it was through the Port of Biscoitos da Cruz that weapons and ammunition arrived from other islands in the Central Group, aiding the Royalist militias and troops who supported King Miguel'. With commendable honesty the caption (in English as well as Portuguese) continues: 'These weapons were neither great in number nor in a very good state, but they were enough to cause enormous commotion and dread among the Constitutional troops stationed in Angra'.

There are several other possible daytime anchorages east of Biscoitos which might be visited in calm southerly conditions, including Quatro Ribeiras and Vila Nova (Iso.6s10m9M, black and white column with red lantern 2m). However, none of the three can be recommended other than in very settled weather, being deep, poorly protected and fringed by rocky cliffs. All should offer excellent snorkelling and diving.

The fair-weather anchorage at Biscoitos on Terceira's north coast, looking northeast towards the small quay

Praia da Vitória

38°43'·58N 27°03'·06W (north breakwater head)

Waypoint
⊕A32 – 38°43'·5N 27°01'·7W (1M E of Praia da Vitória)

Tides
Predictions for Praia da Vitória are available via Admiralty *EasyTide* – see page 30
Time difference on Ponta Delgada: +0007
Mean spring range 1·4m
Mean neap range 0·6m

Plans
Admiralty *1957* (1:12,500)
Portuguese *46405* (1:10,000)
US *51064* (1:50,000 & 1:10,000)
Imray-Iolaire *E1* (1:20,000)

Lights
2662 **North breakwater** Fl.5s11m10M
White column, black bands with 'basket' top 9m
buoy **North breakwater obstruction**
Q(6)+LFl.10s3m6M
South cardinal buoy, ⯆ topmark
2662·8 **Sectored entrance light**
Fl(2)GWR.5s24m10M
255°-G-260°-W-270°-R-275° Post 7m
2662·5 **South breakwater** Fl.R.3s15m8M
White tower, three red bands 9m
Marina southeast mole Fl(3)G.10s
White post, green bands 2m
Marina southeast pontoon
Fl.G.2m White post, green bands 2m
Marina northwest mole
Fl(2)R.10s Red post 2m
Note The high level back-lighting from the town when coming from seawards can make the marina lights difficult to pick out
2663 **Fishing harbour mole** Fl.G.5s6m3M
White post, green bands 2·5m

Harbour communications
Harbourmaster ✆ 295 540500 *Fax* 295 540502
Email capitania.pvitoria@marinha.pt VHF 11, 16 (call *Capimar Vitória*) (0900–1230, 1400–1730)
Port Authority ✆ 295 540000 *Fax* 295 540019
Email aptg.sa@aptg.pt www.aptg.pt VHF 11, 14, 16 (0900–1200, 1300–1700)
Marina da Praia da Vitória ✆ 295 512082, 295 512121
Fax 295 512123 *Email* marina@cmpv.pt www.cmpv.pt (follow the Marina da Praia da Vitória link)
VHF Ch 09, 16 (1 June to 31 August: 0830–1930 weekdays, 0830–1200, 1300-1630 weekends; otherwise 0830–1730 weekdays, closed at weekends. The VHF may be answered by a security guard outside office hours)

Port limits
A rectangle extending 2·5M from Praia da Vitória north breakwater light – see Port limits, page 27.

Friendly marina and sheltered anchorage

Once an open bay, Praia da Vitória is now one of the best protected harbours in the Azores, with breakwaters extending from both north and south to enclose well over half a square mile of water. Following severe storm damage in 2002 both breakwaters have now been heavily reinforced and the southern part of the harbour developed as a commercial area for fishing and cargo handling.

The well-established marina in the northwest corner of the harbour has grown by stages. First a few pontoon berths were created inside the short mole which protected the old – and very shallow – fishing harbour, but it soon grew to its current 200 or so berths and has gained a deserved reputation for being friendly and welcoming with particularly good domestic facilities. It is a local initiative, owned and administered by the *Câmara Municipal da Praia da Vitória* (the town council).

Marina da Praia da Vitória is unique in the Azores in being surrounded by excellent sandy beachs – that to the east is a pepper-and-salt mixture of black and golden grains with a fine texture, unexpectedly clean and gently shelving, complete with small beach café, while to the west lies the town's main beach, its yellower tone indicating that local sand has been augmented by Saharan imports. Also nearby, though not so close as to be obtrusive, is Lajes International Airport, making the marina particularly handy for crew changes. One of the flight paths runs directly over the harbour, but there is still relatively little traffic and no commercial flights between midnight and 0800 – though the military are, of course, free to fly at any time.

An important settlement from early days, Praia da Vitória has some fine buildings including the 16th-century parish church and 17th-century town hall. Completion of a promenade opposite the marina has added to the town's charm and atmosphere, and there are several good restaurants. The marina office has a particularly good variety of tourist and general information – maps, bus timetables etc. – available for the asking. It is well worth walking up the switchback path to the statue of *Nossa Senhora Maria da Conceição* on the ridge north of the harbour which is lit at night, 'the colours changing on a somewhat variable schedule'. The path is in good repair and the views well repay the effort. For variety, follow the gently sloping road back down to the harbour (or vice versa).

Approach and harbour entrance

By day Quite clear. The pale concrete of the breakwaters shows up well from a distance, with the tall red and white banded tower on the south breakwater removing any possible doubt (that on the north breakwater is less conspicuous). The storm damage of 2002 left debris extending some distance from the end of the north breakwater, marked by a south cardinal buoy – do NOT cut inside it. The marina's solid southeast mole will be seen about 0·5M to the northwest, with no hazards between.

By night Bright shore lights, both from the town and around the US base in the northeast corner of the harbour, provide a handy beacon from several miles off. Both breakwaters are lit, as are the south cardinal buoy and the marina's southeast mole, both mentioned above. Entrance by night should therefore present no problems even in moderately heavy weather, though in such conditions it might be wise

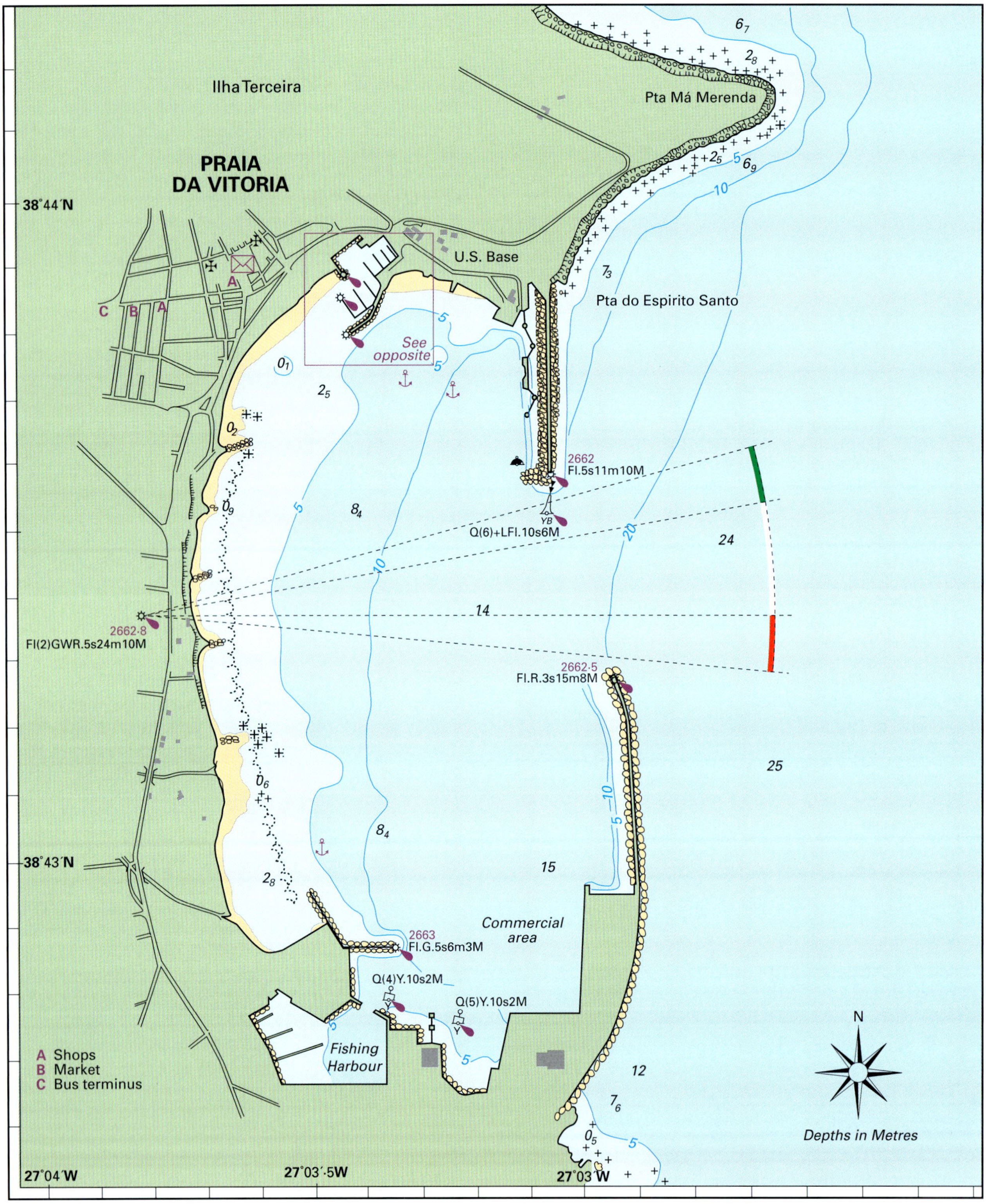

to anchor off the beach until daylight rather than continue directly to the marina reception pontoon.

Anchorage

In northerly or westerly winds good anchorage is to be found anywhere inside the northern arm of the breakwater over clean sand, but depths shoal suddenly well off the beach so a careful eye must be kept on the echo sounder. Holding is surprisingly patchy, and other than in very light winds the *Polícia Marítima* recommend that two anchors should be laid. A wreck (or other debris) liable to foul anchors has been reported at 38°43′·8N 27°03′·3W.

There is no charge for anchoring, but even so skippers should visit the marina office for clearance on arrival and departure. The crews of anchored yachts are allowed to use the marina's toilets, showers and laundry, and dinghies can either be left on the beach or secured between the outer marina pontoon and the protective mole.

Looking south over the wide bay at Praia da Vitória. Early in the season the lay-up area is almost full although the marina itself is relatively empty

A fishing boat heads in through the breakwaters, both repaired following serious damage. The south cardinal buoy marks rubble extending beyond the north breakwater

After a period during which anchoring in the northern part of the harbour was not permitted, apparently at the request of the nearby US military installation, restrictions have been relaxed other than when the tanker which delivers aviation fuel is in port (she berths close to the US Army base) when this anchorage is closed to all yachts.

At these time, or during strong southerly or southeasterly winds, equally protected though less convenient anchorage can be found in the southern part of the bay, provided care is taken not to impede fishing or cargo vessels. However, this is not officially sanctioned and yachts are likely to be told to move when conditions improve. There is a short pontoon in the corner of the fishing harbour where a dinghy might be left for limited periods, and a few shops in the small village almost hidden behind the new, port-related buildings to the south.

Marina entrance and berthing

On arrival, secure to the (clearly-labelled) reception berth at the outer end of the southwest pontoon to be assigned a berth, or contact the office on VHF Ch 09 or by mobile phone on entering the outer harbour. Deep-draught yachts should take particular care, as despite the marina entrance and reception area being dredged to 3·5m every spring, silting remains a problem and by late summer no more than 2·5m may be found at low water springs (the marina has its own small suction dredger which appears to work almost continuously). A string of yellow buoys cordons off the swimming beach on the northwest side of the entrance, including three larger ones directly opposite the reception area, but none are lit. Take particular care if approaching at night, when larger yachts may be better advised to anchor, moving to the reception pontoon in daylight.

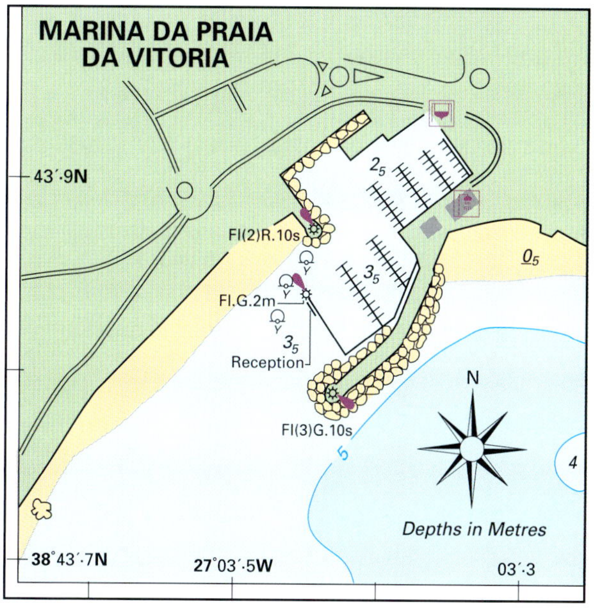

Marina da Praia da Vitória, seen from the statue of *Nossa Senhora Maria da Conceição* to the northeast

The outer two pontoons are reserved for visiting yachts, the inner with finger pontoons and the outer for larger and heavier yachts to lie alongside. The fingers are relatively short, making for considerable pontoon overhang, but fortunately remedial work to the bluffs southwest of the marina (which had become badly eroded) is said to have made reflected waves and currents much less of a problem than previously. Even so, manoeuvring a yacht into her berth on the northeast side of the inner pontoon tends to be a communal activity with plenty of fenders and lines in all directions.

There is no obvious size limit on the southwest pontoon, and several yachts of more than 15m have used the marina though it may be necessary to raft up at busy periods. This is particularly likely in mid to late June, when yachts ashore need to be relaunched before the start of the *festa* season – see Laying-up, below.

Security is provided by gates operated by magnetic cards, for which a deposit is payable – see under Charges, below. This also gives access to the services block. At first the door was left open during office hours, but swimmers from the nearby beach made use of the facilities gratis, bringing much sand with them. No incidents of theft or damage have been reported either ashore or afloat during the marina's entire existence.

Formalities

All formalities – for those at anchor as well as marina users – are carried out in the office near the root of the marina mole. Good English and French are spoken and Paulo, who has worked there since the marina accepted its first yachts in 2000, greets many skippers as returning friends. Both marina and staff receive consistent praise from visitors, 'very friendly and efficient', 'excellent and friendly little marina' and 'as always, most helpful and welcoming' being typical. The *Polícia Marítima* (maritime police), *Guarda Nacional Republicana* (*GNR*) and *Serviço de Estrangeiros e Fronteiras* (Immigration) have offices in the same building and receive copies of the computerised form, and non-EU citizens entering the Azores for the first time may be asked to step across the corridor get their passports stamped by the latter.

Departure clearance is also required, whether at anchor or in the marina, and yachts intending to leave over the weekend are requested to check out before 2000 on Friday.

Charges

Marina da Praia da Vitória offers the best value of any marina in the Azores – and possibly in the entire North Atlantic – by a considerable margin. As mentioned previously, it is owned and administered by the *Câmara Municipal da Praia da Vitória* (the town council) and is not part of the *Portos dos Açores SA* chain.

In 2011 the overnight fee for a visiting monohull of 10–12m LOA was €6.60 and that for 12–15m was €7.80, which included water, electricity, IVA (VAT, currently 16%) and a 4% 'residue' charge to pay for garbage disposal. Multihulls paid a 50% surcharge. Only showers, and of course laundry, are charged on an 'as used' basis. Considerable discounts are available for longer periods, and most winters see a small community of residents wintering afloat. Note, however, that no exemptions are made to the 18-month VAT limit (see page 27) whether afloat or ashore. For further details check the marina's website at www.cmpv.pt, then follow the Marina da Praia da Vitória link, in Portuguese only but relatively easy to follow.

A refundable deposit of €25.22 is charged for the magnetic card which gives access to the pontoons and services block.

Facilities

Boatyard No established yard, though the marina office can advise on whom to contact for various types of work. Among the companies which will carry out maintenance and repairs to GRP and aluminium are Flores & Parreira (see Chandlery, page 96), who also have a pressure washer. There is no restriction on DIY work or on owners and crew living aboard their boat while ashore in the lay-up area (below).

Laying-up The Marina da Praia da Vitória has become a popular place to lay-up ashore, a combination of its very favourable prices, excellent security record and proximity to a major airport. The main area of hardstanding is available from 1 September to 20 June only, however, and must be vacated by the latter because it is used for most of the city's *festas*. A small extension has been enclosed to allow a dozen or so boats to remain ashore during the summer, but once made the decision is irrevocable as access to the travel-lift dock will be blocked by tents and marquees until the end of August. Note, however, that no exemptions are made to the EU's 18-month VAT limit (see page 27) –

Dredging is ongoing at Marina da Praia da Vitória, as sand from the long beach tries to migrate into the harbour

the clock CANNOT be stopped while laid-up ashore as it can be in some countries.

Both lay-up areas have access to water and electricity, with security provided by wire fences and 24-hour surveillance. During the winter all yachts are placed on a northeast/southwest axis, the line of the strongest winds, but even so all sails should be removed and stowed below.

Travel-lift 35-tonne capacity hoist with plenty of yacht-sized props available for hire – in fact the care taken over shoring-up a newly lifted yacht is impressive. The lift dock is prone to silting, however, and deeper yachts may have to be lifted at high tide. At 5m beam the travel-lift is unable to handle multihulls, though the problem is under consideration (there is a wide slipway close to the travel-lift dock).

Diving services, engineer & electronics Can be arranged via the marina office or consult Pedro Perreira of Flores & Parreira (see Chandlery, page 96). The machine shop operated by Gil Sousa e Filhos Lda at Zona das Combustiveis 6, ✆ /*Fax* 295 213629, is highly recommended by MAYS in Horta.

Sail repairs In 2010 Chico Ferraz ✆ 966 302479 *Email* chicoferraz@yahoo.com included sail repairs, canvaswork and upholstery among other services.

Chandlery & charts Nothing closer than Angra – see page 96.

Water On the marina pontoons, where yachts at anchor are welcome to fill cans.

Showers Immaculate showers – and even a bathtub – in both the ladies and gents sections of the services block, which may also be used by those at anchor. In 2011 showers cost €1.52, which included soap and a towel. Access is by magnetic card (see Charges, above) with tokens available from the marina office.

Launderette Equally immaculate launderette, with three each washers and dryers, plus iron and ironing board, again open to those at anchor. In 2011 it cost €5.55 to wash and dry one machine load. Access is by magnetic card (see Charges, above) with tokens available from the marina office.

Electricity On the marina pontoons and included in the daily charge.

Fuel There is no fuel berth and apparently no plans for one. Small amounts can be collected by taxi from a filling station outside the town (the marina office can lend suitable cans, plus a cart for transport once back at the marina) otherwise the office can arrange for quantities of 200 litres (about 44 UK / 55 US gallons) or more to be delivered by road tanker to a point near the travel-lift dock. Twenty-four hours' notice is required, with no deliveries on Sunday.

Bottled gas Most cylinders, including Camping Gaz, can be refilled within two working days if left at the marina office. Only butane is available – no propane.

Weather forecast The marina office will provide a weather forecast on request, or one can print one's own using the computer and printer in the marina office.

Clube naval The *Clube Naval de Praia da Vitória* has premises up the road from the marina (the entrance is around the back), with a small café/bar and live music at weekends.

Banks Several in the town, all with cash dispensers.

Shops/provisioning Several small supermarkets in the town, plus vast Modelo and Guarita hypermarkets on the western fringes. Both will deliver significant purchases to the marina, or there is a frequent bus service which connects both stores and the marina.

Produce market Small but active produce market on Rua de Jesus.

Cafés, restaurants & hotels Several hotels and many restaurants and cafés at all price levels, some overlooking the bay. Small beach café just over the wall from the marina.

Medical services Hospital, plus doctors, dentists and pharmacies.

Communications

Post office On Praça Francisco Ornelas da Câmara (the main square), open 0830–1800 weekdays only.

Mailing address The marina will hold mail for visiting yachts: Marina de Praia da Vitória, 9760 Praia da Vitória, Terceira, Açores, Portugal.

Telephones Public telephone at the rear of the marina facilities, operated by coin or card (the latter available at the post office).

Internet access Free Wi-Fi throughout the marina (and often from the anchorage as well), plus three free computers in the services block (where there is also a book-swap). No printers, but the helpful office staff may be willing to print out the odd page on one of their computers.

Car hire Several of the companies based in Angra do Heroísmo have desks at Lajes airport, and will also deliver to the marina.

Taxis Taxi rank on the main square, or ask at the office for a taxi to be summoned by phone.

Buses Services around the island – details from the tourist office on Rua de Jesus. In 2010 the 20C bus ran from the marina to both supermarkets about every half hour – current schedule from the marina office.

Air services Direct flights to Lisbon, the US and Canada, as well as frequent inter-island flights, from Lajes airport some 3·5km away.

São Miguel

Between 37°42'N–37°55'N and 25°08'W–25°51'W

Introduction

At just over 750km² (65km by about 16km) São Miguel is the largest island in the Azores by a considerable margin and also has the largest population, at around 140,000. Its two areas of high ground to west and east are separated by a lower saddle which has long been cultivated, but the local name of '*A Ilha Verde*' (the Green Island) owes its origins as much to the dense natural woodland as to the acres of carefully tended crops and pasture. Many of those born and bred elsewhere in the Azores unhesitatingly choose São Miguel as their favourite island, both for its natural beauty and for the attractions of Ponta Delgada, the archipelago's commercial centre and largest city.

First settled about 1440 under the captaincy of Conçalho Velho, São Miguel must often have been visible on the northern horizon to the few people already living on Santa Maria. Landing was made on the beach at Povoação ('settlement') on the southeast coast, and the new island named in honour of São Miguel Arcánjel – Michael the Archangel. As in all the Azores dense natural forest inland encouraged villages along the coast, and even now probably three-quarters of São Miguel's towns are within 3km of the sea. In addition to Portuguese and Madeiran emigrants there were more than a smattering of French (commemorated in the parish of Bretanha on the northwest coast), transported convicts, and African and Moorish slaves.

The first capital was established at Vila Franca do Campo in the mid 15th century, probably because of the good anchorage behind its small off-lying island. By 1522 the town was thriving with some 5,000 inhabitants under the governorship of Rui Conçalves da Câmara, son of the *capitão donatório* of Madeira. However, eastern São Miguel was suffering a period of seismic activity, and in October that year an earthquake triggered a mudslide and avalanche which completely destroyed the town and killed many of its inhabitants. The government moved westwards, first to Lagoa and then to the slightly more protected bay at Ponta Delgada, which by 1546 had been granted full city status and become the island's new capital.

Even so Vila Franca do Campo figures the more prominently in history, suffering several pirate raids during the 16th and 17th centuries which prompted solid stone fortifications to be built. However, these proved insufficient when in July 1582 a French and Portuguese fleet was attacked just offshore by the forces of King Phillip II of Spain, by then ruler of mainland Portugal, with the town soon falling victim to the victorious Spaniards. Fifteen years later, while still under Spanish rule, the English Earl of Essex attacked one night at the head of 2,000 men. The inhabitants had sufficient warning to flee the town, but not to save it from being plundered and burned.

São Miguel was undoubtedly in need of its ports by this time, with wheat, sugar cane, wine and dairy products being exported. During the 17th and 18th centuries sweet potatoes, flax and oranges were added to the list, with the latter proving one of the

most profitable crops the island has ever known. The high stone walls which still dominate the northwestern part of the island date from the 'orange days', having been solidly built to protect the groves from both thieves and winter gales. Many of the domestic and religious buildings of those days have also survived, characterised by carved black ashlar, heavy ornate woodwork and the glazed tiles so loved by the Portuguese, while some of the older houses in Ponta Delgada still have their rooftop lookouts, possibly going back beyond the days of peaceful trade to the time when pirates and privateers were an ever-present threat.

São Miguel played its part in the 19th century struggles between the Absolutists and the Liberals, with the latter landing in the northeast of the island in 1831. Ponta Delgada was chosen as their port of embarkation for the mainland the following year, at the start of the campaign which led to the declaration of Dom Pedro IV as King of Portugal, and at least 3,500 Azoreans are thought to have joined the Liberal cause. Island life must usually have been much quieter, however, with agriculture, stockbreeding or fishing the occupations of the vast majority. Oranges for England and America remained a major export until disease struck in the 1880s, by which time tobacco, sugar beet, tea and pineapples had been introduced. The latter two, both highly labour-intensive crops, did particularly well in the mild climate and rich volcanic soil, and it is said that in 1878 two Chinese experts were engaged to teach the skills of tea picking and preparation to the local people. Even in São Miguel's benign climate pineapples have to be grown under glass, and as the old greenhouses fall into disrepair their cultivation may soon, sadly, become a thing of the past. Currently only the Arruda plantation at Fajã de Baixo, just outside Ponta Delgada, still welcomes visitors to see the fruit being grown. On-site sales include, in addition to the fruit themselves, pineapple-flavoured confectionery and a highly regarded liqueur – the latter a little sweet for many people's taste, but delicious on ice cream.

To describe São Miguel's two other major tourist attractions in such terms seems rather inappropriate, since both are natural features on the grand scale which owe little to man's intervention. Probably most famous is the Caldeira das Sete Cidades with its twin lakes, Lagoa Verde (Green Lake) and Lagoa Azul (Blue Lake). On a sunny day the view from Vista do Rei over the emerald and sapphire lakes is breathtaking. Legend has it that they were created by the tears of a princess and a shepherd boy who were forbidden to meet, their separate weeping forming the two lakes which cannot mix, in spite of a common junction now spanned by the road bridge. The more prosaic insist that either dissolved minerals or algae are the true cause.

For several centuries the village on the crater floor was inaccessible other than on foot, and doubtless generations lived their lives there without ever leaving it or seeing the sea. However, a narrow lane now plunges down the steep slopes to the east and exits through an impressively engineered cutting to the west, and the 19th century park full of azaleas, hydrangeas and exotic trees is a justifiably popular picnic spot with locals as well as visitors. Fortunately the *caldeira* is large enough to absorb a good many picnic parties and still stay hushed and peaceful, though its quietness must have been shattered during the First World War when the 3km expanse of Lagoa Azul is said to have been used for seaplane landings – surely a horribly difficult approach and takeoff.

São Miguel's second natural wonder, though this time showing a little more of man's influence, is the thermal springs of Vale das Furnas in the east. Approaching from Ponta Delgada by way of Vila Franca do Campo one first passes a large and attractive lake with a small Gothic church on its shores – most unexpected in this bastion of manueline and baroque. A track leads around the northern end of the lake to the famous 'natural kitchens' where complete meals are sealed into pots and buried in the hot earth for several hours to produce the local delicacy known as *cozido*, strongly flavoured with sulphur and something of an acquired taste. (The recipe for *poule au volcan* is said to begin with the words: 'Take a volcano...'.)

A few kilometres further up the valley, dotted around the village of Furnas, lie the more spectacular thermal springs and boiling mud pools, 22 in all and each said to have its own particular medicinal property, which attracted the health-conscious Victorians of the 19th century. In 1838 two English brothers, Joseph and Henry Bullar, wrote a book entitled *A Winter in the Azores and a Summer at the Springs of Furnas* (see Further Reading, page 403), but by then the area was already known as a health spa, soon to gain elegant bath houses and its own hospital. One of the first foreigners to discover Furnas was Thomas Hickling, the first American Consul to the Azores, who built his country home here in the late 18th century – his town house in Ponta Delgada is now the Hotel de São Pedro, itself worth visiting. It is said that he employed English gardeners to plan his grounds, now the celebrated Terra Nostra Park. As well as a naturally warmed swimming pool which is open to the public (iron deposits discolour the water and can stain pale swimsuits), for a nominal fee one can explore the winding paths of the park, almost tropical in its lushness and a haven for bird life as well as all varieties of exotic flowers and trees.

It is tempting to think of Ponta Delgada purely as a convenient base from which to explore the island of São Miguel, but this is perhaps not doing the old town justice. While lacking the relaxed atmosphere of Horta or the architectural distinction of Angra do Heroísmo, and already sporting the first high-rise buildings in the Azores, it is very much a thriving city and the busiest port in the archipelago. Work on the breakwater started in 1861, though it did not reach its present 1·5km length for over a century, but successive waves of building have covered up most traces of the old port. The latest – and, since the building of the breakwater itself, surely the most ambitious – has seen the construction of a new cruise ship terminal, the *Portas do Mar*, in the centre of the old harbour with a large new marina immediately to the west.

Further west again lies São Miguel's international airport, opened in 1969 to replace a small airstrip on the north coast in use since 1946 and enlarged several times since. Another source of pride is the island's university, which achieved full status in 1980 as the first Portuguese university outside the mainland. It is perhaps not a bad thing to be reminded that, behind the old world charm and courtesy prevalent in São Miguel as throughout the islands, Ponta Delgada is very definitely a thriving 21st-century city, with a life of its own and a particularly high proportion of well-educated young people.

Holidays and festivals

In addition to the national holidays listed on page 26, Ponta Delgada holds its official holiday on 1 April, Lagoa on 11 April, Ribeira Grande on 29 April, Povoação on 23 June, Vila Franca do Campo on 24 June and Nordest on 17 July. The Festival of *Espírito Santo* and Feast of *Senhor Santo Cristo* are celebrated about six weeks after Easter, with the Festival of St Peter following on 29 June.

Telecommunications

Mobile (cell) phone reception throughout the island is good. The country code for the Azores is 351, as it is for mainland Portugal, and the area code for São Miguel – which must be included even when dialling from within the island – is 296, shared with Santa Maria.

By 2011 free Wi-Fi was available at many locations in Ponta Delgada, and near the marina office in Vila Franca do Campo.

Websites

The internet appears to offer no website devoted to São Miguel as a whole, other than Wikipedia's www.en.wikipedia.org/wiki/Sâo_Miguel_Island. As of early 2011 neither had Ponta Delgada nor Vila Franca do Campo, though it is to be hoped that www.pontadelgadadigital.com will be reinstated in due course. The Clube Naval de Ponta Delgada has long maintained its own site at www.cnpdl.pt, in Portuguese only, but of more interest to yachtsmen will be www.boatsailservice.com, the attractive and well-designed website of Ponta Delgada's Boat & Sail Service (see page 111) in Portuguese, English, German and French. As well as outlining their own services it also carries information about Ponta Delgada, São Miguel and the Azores as a whole. In addition to these the island features on several of the general Azores sites listed on pages 24–5.

Approach

In daylight Pico da Vara (1,104m) to the east or the lesser Pico das Eguas (873m) to the west will be visible from many miles off if not obscured by cloud, which may itself reveal the island's presence. From the north or south São Miguel appears to lie in two parts – a long island of several linked peaks to the east, a gap, and a single lower island to the west. At some 25M off the serrated skyline of the lower hills in the centre of the island rises above the horizon.

The coastline is largely steep-to, with few off-lying dangers. However, many headlands are fringed by rocks and all should be given at least 500m clearance. Particular care should be taken in the vicinity of Baixa da Roida between Vila Franco do Campo and Caloura, Baixa da Negra about 0·5M south of the airport control tower, Ilhéu dos Mosteiros off the town of that name on the northwest coast, and Baixa do Morro bearing 065° from Rabo do Peixe and just under 2M distant. None of these hazards are lit. Currents set southerly around the ends of the island, and can sometimes produce a confused sea close to headlands.

Careful navigation is essential if on passage towards São Miguel from Terceira, particularly in poor weather, as the unmarked Banco Dom João de Castro shoal lies only 5M west of the direct course between the two. Although the shoal – the tip of a subterranean volcano – has broken the surface at least once during the last 500 years it is currently charted at 12m, confirmed in 1999 by the crew of a yacht who carried out several dives on the bank, but as there is ongoing seismic activity in the area depths could decrease at any time. They pinpointed the least depth to be at 38°13′·37N 26°36′·36W, and within 100m of this spot were off soundings. As one might expect, seas break heavily on the bank in strong winds.

Drinking fountain and seat combined, at Vila de Água de Pau on São Miguel's south coast

Navigation

Waypoints

- ⊕ A35 – 37°56'·6N 25°47'·7W (2M NNW of Pta da Bretanha)
- ⊕ A36 – 37°51'·7N 25°52'·6W (1M W of Pta da Ferraria)
- ⊕ A37 – 37°49'·2N 25°51'·6W (1M SW of Pta da Candelaria)
- ⊕ A38 – 37°42'·9N 25°41'·1W (1M S of Santa Clara)
- ⊕ A39 – 37°43'·9N 25°38'·9W (0·5M SE of Ponta Delgada)
- ⊕ A40 – 37°41'·9N 25°30'·6W (0·5M S of Pta da Galera)
- ⊕ A41 – 37°41'·9N 25°25'·2W (1M SSE of Vila Franca do Campo)
- ⊕ A42 – 37°43'·7N 25°09'·5W (1M SE of Fajã do Calhau)
- ⊕ A43 – 37°48'·5N 25°05'·5W (2M E of Pta Marquesas)
- ⊕ A44 – 37°52'·5N 25°06'·9W (2M NE of Pta da Ribeira)

Courses and distances

- ⊕ A35 – ⊕A37 via ⊕A36 = 9M, 218° & 162° / 342° & 038°
- ⊕ A37 – ⊕A39 via ⊕A38 = 12·5M, 127° & 060° / 240° & 307°
- ⊕ A38 – ⊕A31 (1M S of Ilhéus Fradinhos, Terceira) = 86M, 308° / 128°
- ⊕ A38 – ⊕A24 (1M ESE of Ilhéu do Topo, São Jorge) = 109M, 297° / 117°
- ⊕ A38 – ⊕A13 (0·5M E of Horta, Faial) = 149M, 288° & by eye / by eye & 108°
- ⊕ A39 – ⊕A41 via ⊕A40 = 11M, 107° & 090° / 270° & 287°
- ⊕ A39 – ⊕A45 (1M WNW of Pta do Lobaio, Santa Maria) = 48·5M, 154° / 334°
- ⊕ A39 – ⊕A50 (1M NE of Pta do Norte, Santa Maria) = 51·5M, 146° / 326°
- ⊕ A42 – ⊕A41 = 12·6M, 262° / 082°
- ⊕ A44 – ⊕A42 via ⊕A43 = 10M, 164° & 213° / 033° & 344°

Magnetic variation

9°20'W (2011), decreasing by 10'E annually.

Tidal Streams

Tidal streams run eastwards on the flood and westwards on the ebb at less than 1 knot, but may set up eddies around headlands particularly when meeting the southerly setting current.

Charts

Admiralty *1895* (1:100,000)
Portuguese *43103* (1:300,000), *46406* (1:100,000)
US *51081* (1:250,000)
Imray-Iolaire *E1* (1:750,000)

Lights

2655·6 **Bretanha** LFl.6s69m4M
Lantern on red post 1m
2655·4 **Mosteiros** Oc.R.3s9m6M
090°-vis-155° White column, red bands
2655 **Ponta da Ferraria**
Fl(3)20s106m27M 339°-vis-174°
Square white tower, red lantern, and building 18m
2654·2 **Airport control tower** Aero
Al.Fl.WG.10s83m28/23M 282°-vis-124° (occas)
2654 **Santa Clara**
LFl.5s26m15M 282°-vis-102°
Red metal framework tower 8m
2642 **Ponta Garça** LFl.WR.5s100m16/13M
240°-W-080°-R-100°
Round tower and building 14m
2640 **Ponta do Arnel**
Fl.5s65m25M 157°-vis-355°
Octagonal white tower and building 15m
2659 **Ponta do Cintrão**
Fl(2)10s117m14M 080°-vis-324°
Grey tower and building 14m

Coast Radio Station

São Miguel 37°45'N 25°29'W remotely controlled from Lisbon
VHF Ch 16, 26, 27, 28 (24 hours)

Radionaval/Maritime Rescue Coordination Centre

Ponta Delgada 37°44'N 25°40'W
DSC MF/VHF MMSI 002040100 (planned) ✆ 296 205277 (operations) 296 281777 (emergency) *Fax* 296 205239
Email mrcc.delgada@mail.telepac.pt
Email mrcc.delgada@marinha.pt
(This station does not accept public correspondence other than distress and safety traffic)
VHF Ch 11, 16 (24 hours)
Weather bulletins Ch 11 at 0830, 2000 (storm and bad weather warnings, synopsis and 24 hour forecast for waters within 20 miles of São Miguel and Santa Maria in Portuguese, repeated in English when possible)
Navigational warnings Ch 11 at 0830, 2000 (local warnings for São Miguel and Santa Maria in Portuguese, repeated in English when possible)

Exuberant wall art – one could not call this graffiti – near the harbour at Lagoa, east of Ponta Delgada

Harbours and anchorages

Ponta Delgada

37°44'·18N 25°39'·37W (breakwater head)

Waypoint

⊕ A39 – 37°43'·9N 25°38'·9W (0·5M SE of Ponta Delgada)

Tides

Ponta Delgada is the standard port for the Azores, with either Admiralty or Portuguese tide tables available – see Tides and tidal streams, page 30. MLWS is listed as 0·3m above datum, but heights are strongly affected by barometric pressure. Predictions for Ponta Delgada are also available via Admiralty *EasyTide* – see page 30

Mean spring range 1·4m

Mean neap range 0·7m

Plans

Admiralty *1895* (1:10,000)

Portuguese *46406* (1:10,000)

US *51082* (1:50,000 & 1:10,000)

Imray-Iolaire *E1* (1:10,000)

Lights

2654 **Santa Clara**
LFl.5s26m15M 282°-vis-102°
Red metal framework tower 8m

2647 **Breakwater** LFl.R.6s16m10M
White tower, red bands 7m

2648·5 **Clube Naval** Fl(2)GWR.5s24m10M
302°-G-306°-W-312°-R-317°
Lantern on terrace of Clube Naval 15m

2652 **Forte de São Brás** Fl(4)GWR.8s13m10M
259°-G-261°-W-263°-R-265°
Lantern on SE corner of fort 14m

2648 **Marina mole** Fl.G.3s12m10M
White tower, green bands 6m

2648·7 **Cruise ship terminal, east end**
Fl(2)R.5s2m3M White pillar, red bands 3m

2648·72 **Cruise ship terminal, west end**
Fl(3)G.15s2m3M White pillar, green bands 3m

2649·5 **Floating breakwater pontoon** Q(6)+LFl.15s3M
South cardinal pillar, ⧪ topmark 5m

2649·7 **Fishing harbour** Fl(4)R.15s2m3M
White pillar, red bands 3m

2645·5 **Pópulo cables**
Fl(2)R.8s8m9M (daylight range 1·7M) 349°-vis-031°
White post, red bands 4m. Marks submarine cables
Note Situated nearly 2M east of the harbour entrance

Harbour communications

Harbourmaster ✆ 296 205240 *Fax* 296 205259
Email capitania.pdelgada@marinha.pt VHF Ch 11, 16 (call *Capimar Delgada*) (0900–1200, 1400–1730)

Port Authority ✆ 296 285221 *Fax* 296 283390
Email apsm@apsm.pt www.apsm.pt VHF Ch 10, 16 (0900–1230, 1400–1730)

Ponta Delgada Marina (previously *Marina Pêro de Teive*)
✆ 296 281510 *Fax* 296 281311
Email marinapdl@apsm.pt www.marinasazores.com, VHF Ch 09, 16 (0900–1830 weekdays, 0900–1230, 1400–1730 weekends from 1 May to mid-September, otherwise 0900–1730 weekdays, closed weekends)

Port limits

A circle, radius 2M, centred on Ponta Delgada breakwater light – see Port limits, page 27.

Large 'double' marina inside commercial harbour

The capital of São Miguel and largest naval and commercial harbour in the Azores, Ponta Delgada is well protected behind its high 1,544m breakwater, though heavy swell can set into the harbour with winds from between east and south. Ponta Delgada is a favourite landfall in the islands for yachts coming from the UK or mainland Europe, and is a convenient place for crew changes. It also has the good storing-up facilities and is an excellent base from which to explore the beautiful and varied interior of São Miguel. The city itself is picturesque, with some fine churches and other buildings dating back to the 16th century. Maps and guides are available from the tourist office on Avenue Infante Dom Henrique.

The relatively small 'old' marina, known until recently as the *Marina de Pêro de Teive*, was completed in 1992 and soon filled up with local yachts, though visitors were always squeezed in somehow. By 2003 plans were in hand to build a second and much larger berthing area further west, combined with a purpose-built cruise ship terminal, the *Portas do Mar*, a project completed on schedule in July 2008. This increased marina berths four-fold to 670 in all – and at no time during the building work did the harbour lose its EU 'Blue Flag', held without a break since 1999. Although from the administrative angle the old and new berthing areas form a single marina, now known as Ponta Delgada Marina (or sometimes *Marina de Ponta Delgada*), for clarity and brevity they are referred to in this book as the west and east marinas.

Visiting yachts are generally berthed in the west marina which, in addition to many smaller berths, offers 100 finger berths for yachts of 10–15m, 25 berths for 15–18m, and 12 berths able to take 18m or more. All are alongside finger pontoons, which at the larger berths are anchored to individual piles, making them exceptionally sturdy. In addition long pontoons line the west side of the cruiseship terminal, providing alongside berthing for superyachts of up to 75m in length, in depths of around 10m. It will be a while before the marina fills up with local boats, but in the longer term at least 25% of berths are to be reserved for visitors.

The new west marina has not been without its problems, however. Completion of shoreside facilities such as showers lagged behind the marina itself and power failures were said to be frequent, though both problems are now things of the past. Not yet overcome are the problems of swell entering the marina during south and southeasterly winds … and seagulls. It seems that the former has much to do with the fact that the outer arm of the cruise ship pier is not solid but is formed of a series of arches, through which any swell can travel – it all but disappears when a ship is alongside. Wash from fishing boats who berth in the northwest corner of the harbours also entered the marina, though this has been largely cured by the positioning of a

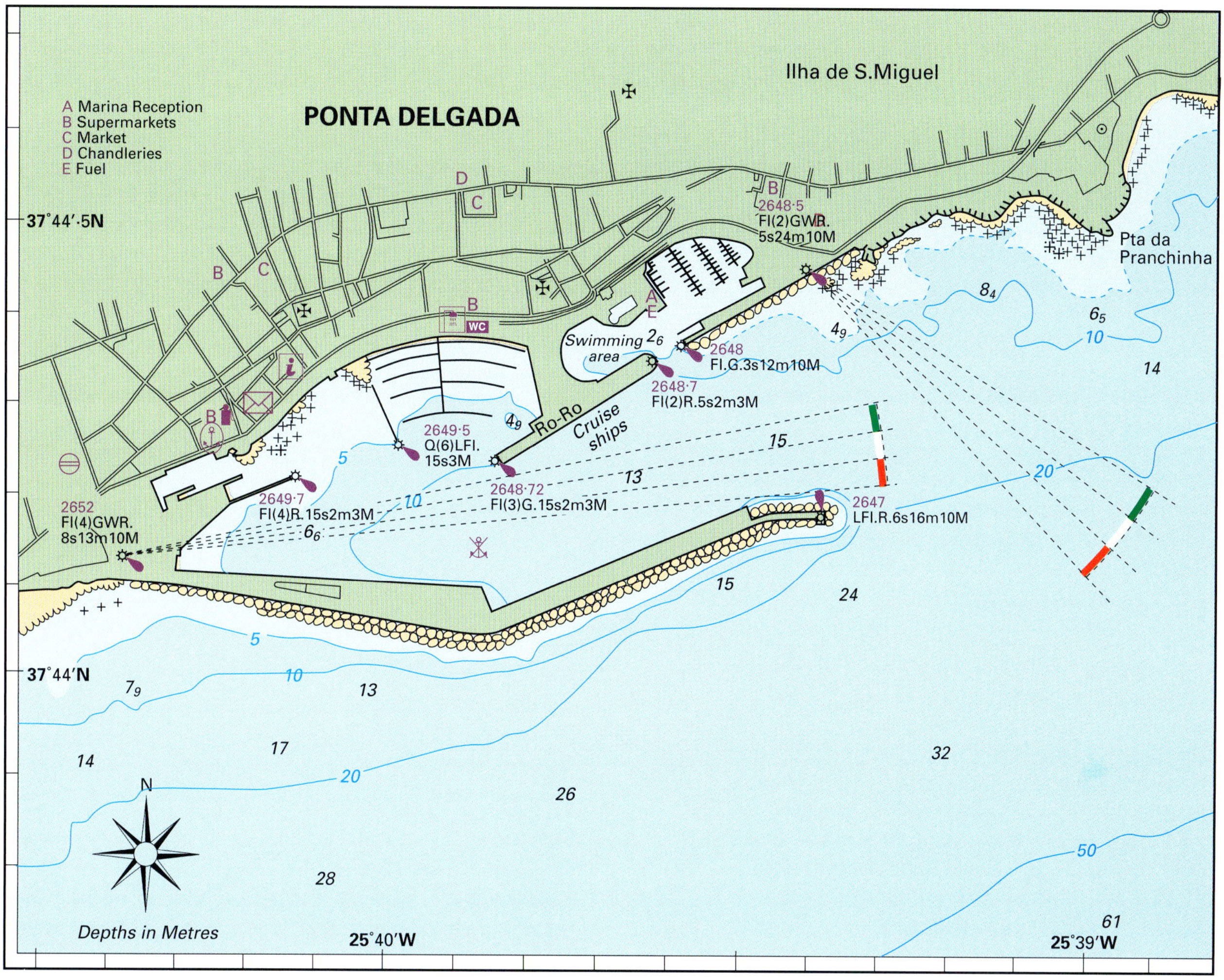

floating 'wave-break' pontoon between the two areas. A second pontoon to the south of the marina has been suggested, which would also protect it from scend during westerlies. Until these problems are remedied the west marina cannot be considered as a suitable place for overwintering. Longer term residents confirm that ripped out cleats and broken lines are common, and even in late May 2010 plenty of chaffing gear and stranded lines were to be seen.

The seagulls present a different problem. They apparently descended in their hundreds while the pontoons were empty – as many still are – and have proved hard to shift, coating walkways with smelly, slippery guano despite regular pressure hosing by staff. Various ideas have been tried, including a trained hawk (withdrawn because of fears that visitors would not welcome partially-devoured birds falling down their forehatches), sprinklers (though the logic of using water to drive away seagulls seems open to question) and various chemicals. The latest idea, red plastic netting suspended well above the

The large harbour at Ponta Delgada seen from a commercial aeroplane. The fishermen's area is in the foreground, with the new and old marina basins beyond. The interior of the harbour has changed beyond recognition since the first edition was researched in 1987

pontoons, is said to be working well. A final disadvantage, at least for some, is loud music drifting from the cafés and restaurants north and east of the marina. It is said to continue into the small hours at weekends, while concerts in the new auditorium on the 'stalk' of the cruise ship berth can go on until 0300.

To return to a more positive note, an extensive lido area has been created between the west and east marinas, providing access to a roped off sea swimming area (see plan). During summer 2010 the benefits of this form of exercise were in doubt, however, given that in dry weather a significant sewer overflow appeared to be discharging just west of the west marina. Alternatively there is a treated saltwater outdoor pool just behind the lido which, in 2010, cost €2.50 per day (with exit and re-entry permitted), with loungers and mats available for €1.60 per day plus a €1 returnable deposit on the latter.

Approach and entrance

By day Very simple, with no hazards. The grey stone breakwater may blend with the concrete esplanade behind if approaching on a bearing of less than 325°, but the red and white banded tower marking its eastern end is unmistakable. The breakwater extends both awash and underwater for a further 50–100m in line with the existing wall – exact depths are not known, but at least one yacht has grounded. If coming from the east, an outfall runs between 37°44′·5N 25°38′·9W (onshore) and 37°44′3N 25°38′W (offshore). The area may be crossed, but anchoring and fishing in the vicinity are forbidden.

The relatively narrow gap giving access to the marina reception berth lies almost opposite the end of the breakwater, the latter quite unmistakable with its row of flagpoles backed by white buildings surmounted by a squat observation tower complete with conical white roof. Rubble is said to lie some distance off the end of the marina mole and is sometimes, but not always, marked by a selection of small, green, unlit buoys. The swimming area opposite is cordoned off by a string of small red buoys, again unlit.

By night Ponta Delgada's city lights are by far the brightest on the coast, with a long row of street lights lining the esplanade behind the harbour. After the light at Santa Clara 1M west of Ponta Delgada, the first harbour light to be identified is likely to be that marking the end of the breakwater, with a range of at least 10M. Sectored lights have replaced both pairs of leading lights, with the white (safe) sector of the outer light spanning 306° to 312° while that of the inner light spans 261° to 263°. An incoming yacht might actually be safer in the red or green zones, and in any case will soon need to veer north to approach the reception quay. Both sides of the access gap are lit, though it would be wise to favour the port side in view of the rubble mentioned above.

All but the largest yachts are required to go to the reception berth on arrival – megayachts wishing to go direct to the west marina should make contact with the marina office prior to arrival for instructions.

Anchorage

Anchoring anywhere inside the harbour is strictly prohibited – in the event of engine failure, contact the marina via VHF or mobile phone for assistance. A towing launch is available if required.

Berthing

On arrival yachts should go to main reception quay directly opposite the gap giving access to the east marina, which had depths of 3·5m along its entire 60m length. If either depth or manoeuvring are likely to be difficult for a larger yacht, and contact is made before arrival, she will be directed straight to the west marina. This may be either to one of the large outer berths to or lie against the pontoons which fringe its east and southeast sides, where depths are a generous 10m.

If space is available, smaller visiting yachts may on request be berthed in the east marina, where manoeuvring room is relatively tight (if numbers

The unusual curved pontoons of Ponta Delgada's new west marina, looking almost due west. The high-rise building on the right is unique in the Azores and is highly visible from offshore

Looking northeast into the old marina from the cruise ship terminal, with a catamaran at the reception/fuel berth. The large area in the foreground is buoyed-off for swimming

permit, a crew member sent ahead to take lines can be useful). Depths range from about 3m in the entrance and the northern part of the basin to 8m or more along the wall. In contrast, space in the west marina is generous, with wide berths and plenty of turning space between the curved arms. Depths are said to be 3·5m or more at all but the smallest berths.

Security is excellent throughout, with pontoon access via card-operated gates (a single one for the west marina, a gate to each pontoon in the east), backed by both CCTV and round-the-clock security patrols.

Formalities

The marina reception office – where Pedro Santos has been welcoming visitors for the past 14 years – has been reorientated to overlook the reception/fuelling quay at the entrance to east marina (it used to be somewhat further north in the same range of buildings). The shared entrance also gives access to the offices of the *Guarda Nacional Republicana*, *Alfândega* (Customs) *Polícia Marítima*

Thomas Dargel of Boat & Sail Service has found the ideal way to commute between Ponta Delgada's two marina basins *Any Dargel*

and marina security, the latter two manned at all times.

The marina administration office overlooks the west marina and is situated almost opposite the single access gate, but this office has little direct contact with yachtsmen other than those in search of laundry tokens. Between 1 May and 15 September the reception office is open 0900–1830 weekdays, 0900–1230, 1400–1730 weekends, cutting back to 0900–1730 weekdays, closed weekends for the rest of the year. The administration office is open 0900–1230, 1400–1730 weekdays only throughout the year.

Even if arriving from within the Azores, in addition to marina reception the skipper must visit both the *Alfândega* and *Polícia Marítima* bearing ship's papers, passports and insurance documents. Non-EU nationals among the crew may also have to visit the latter to complete entry documentation.

On departure the marina office must be visited first to settle the bill (most major credit cards are accepted), and copies of the receipt presented at the other offices. There is no need to move the yacht herself back to the reception quay. If planning to visit any of the smaller islands it will be worth preserving the computer printout which one receives. This carries answers to all the standard questions, so avoiding potential language difficulties.

Charges

Ponta Delgada Marina is one of the *Portos dos Açores SA* chain, and shares their basic price structure. As of 2011 yachts of 10–12m LOA paid €12.22 per night and those of 12–15m paid €18.50, inclusive of everything except showers (see below). For further details see page 27 and/or www.marinasazores.com, the website of the branch of *Portos dos Açores SA* concerned with marina operation (though note that different charges apply to yachts owned by residents and by non-residents).

Facilities

Defying categorisation are Thomas and Any Dargel whose Boat & Sail Service ✆ 963 925707 *Fax* 296 281311 *Email* boatsailservice@gmx.net www.boatsailservice.com has been assisting visitors to Ponta Delgada since 1997. There seems to be little that they cannot handle – and if they cannot, they will know who can – in fluent English as well as their native German, plus French and Portuguese. Feedback received about Thomas and Any invariably heaps praise on their work in terms of both speed and quality.

Boat & Sail Service has long been established in the northwest corner of the east marina, just beyond the marina café, where Any handles sail repairs and general canvaswork while Thomas more often works in situ aboard yachts in both basins (a smart bicycle and trailer combination has proved ideal for commuting with tools and other heavy items). In early 2011 they were able to expand their previously somewhat cramped premises to allow more space for chandlery with a separate workshop behind. The shop is normally open 0900–1300 and 1430–1730 during the season, but if closed – because both Thomas and Any are working elsewhere – try contacting by mobile phone on the number above.

Further details of the services offered by Boat & Sail Service will be found below, to which should be added gas installation, plumbing, year-round *guardinage* and – should it be necessary – de-cockroaching.

Boatyard There are several yards where wooden and steel fishing boats are built and repaired, but no boatyard specifically for yachts. However several companies offer related services.

Boat & Sail Service (see above) specifically mention osmosis treatment, repairs to wood and GRP, and painting/antifouling among their services (they stock Epifanes and Coppercoat), but will tackle much more. Honorato Moreira Monteiro Lda, ☏ /*Fax* 296 385047 *Email* honoratomonteiro@hotmail.com 42 Rua da Boa Nova, 9500-296 Ponta Delgada (east of the old marina and one road inland) handle general repairs and maintenance. Tecnináutica ☏ /*Fax* 296 636401, 962 563233 *Email* tecninautica@gmail.com www.tecninautica.com on Rua Azores Park, Rosto do Cão – São Roque, 9500-795 Ponta Delgada, offers services including osmosis treatment, and GRP and gelcoat repair, and stocks Hempel paints.

Travel-lift The marina has a 25-tonne capacity lift, and shares the limited area of hardstanding on the east marina mole with the *Clube Naval de Ponta Delgada*. Arrangements should be made via the marina office.

Crane The *Clube Naval de Ponta Delgada* also have a 3-tonne crane suitable for removing engines etc., located on the east marina mole. Use is generally arranged directly with the *clube*, often by the person or company carrying out the work.

Diving services Tiago Augusto Garcia Domingues ☏ 916 886530, 919 137151 *Email* dominguessub@sapo.pt www.dominguessub.com has operated from a booth beside the east marina since 1999. Though mainly concerned with sport diving and cetacean-watching, the company can also handle underwater repairs or assessments. Diving in the marina is forbidden, so official permission should be sought.

Engineers Navel SA ☏ 296 205290 *Fax* 296 205299 *Email* commercial@navel.pt, a long-established firm with premises at Rua Engenheiro Avel Ferin Coutinho, Apt. 1841, 9501-809 Ponta Delgada (few hundred metres northwest of the root of the main breakwater) handles welding, machining and general engineering, and also sells a wide range of tools and hardware. Some English is spoken.

Walter Medeiros SA ☏ 296 302030, 913 461797, 916 635567 *Email* direccao@autowm.com www.waltermedeiros.com, Estrada Regional 77, Relva, 9500-655 Ponta Delgada (some distance west of the city, but they also have a mobile workshop) combines its main business of car sales and repairs with being an authorised service centre for Mercury, Cummins and Bosch.

Tecnináutica (see Boatyards, above), is an official Yamaha dealer, and also handles engine repairs plus work in stainless steel and aluminium. Varela & Ca Lda ☏ 296 301823, 918 792260 *Fax* 296 684470 *Email* volvo.penta@bensaude.pt at Rua dos Velados No.20, 9500–652 Ponta Delgada is an official Volvo dealer offering spares and maintenance.

AutoCentral Marine ☏ 967 313898 *Email* autocentral@hotmail.com, Armazém No.3, Clube Naval de Ponta Delgada offers repair and maintenance of yacht engines and transmissions; and finally MAP Açores (see Chandlery), is a Honda agent but does not appear to handle repairs.

Electrical work Thomas of Boat & Sail Service handles electrical installations and can trouble-shoot and repair those already in place. MAP Açores (see Chandlery, below) also offers electrical work.

Electronic sales and repair JB Electrónica Lda ☏ 296 283781, 919 006191 *Email* jbelectronica@sapo.pt at Rua do Perú No.73, 9500-340 Ponta Delgada (three blocks inland from the east marina), sells, installs and repairs most major international brands including Magellan, ICOM, Raymarine, Garmin, Simrad etc.

Auto & Marine ☏ 918 064525, 967 577576 *Email* automarine@live.com.pt based at the *Clube Naval de Ponta Delgada* offers general electronic repairs.

Sail repairs & canvaswork Any of Boat & Sail Service repairs sails (though she does not make them) and handles general canvaswork and boat upholstery. She has a good range of materials and fittings available.

Rigging Boat & Sail Service specialises in rigging and deck hardware, stocking Lewmar, Barton, Seldén, Profurl, Wichard, Furlex and Prorainer among others. They have a swage machine and hold stocks of rigging wire from 3mm to 16mm in diameter, plus yacht rope including exotics.

Liferaft servicing OREY Técnica Naval ☏ 296 929314 *Fax* 296 929315 *Email* azores.technica@orey.com www.orey-tecnica.pt are located at Caminho da Malaca, Portões Vermelhos – Armazém No.19, 9560 Rosário – Lagoa, a few miles east of Ponta Delgada. In addition to stocking RDF liferafts and Pains Wessex distress signals it is understood that they are licensed to service most liferaft makes. Arrange direct or via Boat & Sail Service.

Chandlery Ponta Delgada's largest chandlery is currently MAP Açores ☏ 296 285635 *Fax* 296 629244 *Email* map.pontadelgada@mail.telepac.pt www.mapazores.com. It has a branch overlooking the new marina (open 1000–1300, 1400–2000 daily) which is mainly given over to sport fishing equipment, but its main shop (open 0900–1230, 1400–1830 weekdays, 0900–1300 Saturday) remains at 51A Rua do Mercado, 9500-326 Ponta Delgada, three blocks inland from the west marina. Chandlery including International Paints, electronics, safety equipment and stainless steel fittings is held in stock, and items not on the shelves can be ordered from a range of catalogues. Good English is spoken.

Boat & Sail Service stock general chandlery and foul weather gear in addition to the rigging and deck hardware listed under Rigging, above. Again, anything not in stock can be ordered from catalogues, a process which usually takes three days or more. Tecnináutica (see Boatyards, above), stocks Hempel paints as well as general chandlery.

Charts Boat & Sail Service stock Imray charts and books covering nearby waters. MAP (see Chandlery above) hold stocks of both Portuguese and BA charts, the former of the Azores and the latter of popular destinations in mainland Europe. However, they are not formal chart agents so stocks will not be corrected to date.

Water At all berths in both marinas, including on the east marina mole and the west marina megayacht pontoon, with hoses provided.

Showers There is a new shower block behind the west marina, with 14 showers (four each in the ladies and gents areas, plus six rooms each containing a shower, basin and toilet, one specifically for disabled use). Rather than being charged as used, an additional fee of about €1.30 per crew member per day is added to the berthing fee, after which entry is by card at any time.

There is a second block at the east marina containing six showers, for which a similar charge is made.

Launderette Next to the shower block at the west marina (though serving both, as that at the east marina is now closed) and in 2010 equipped with just two washers and two dryers, though more may be installed. At that time it cost about €8 to wash and dry a load of laundry, using tokens obtainable from the marina administration office nearby (open 0900–1230, 1400–1730 weekdays only, so it may be necessary to plan ahead).

Electricity At all berths in both marinas, including on the east marina mole and the west marina megayacht pontoon. The standard is 220v 50Hz, but 380v is available at the larger berths.

Fuel Both diesel and petrol are available at the marina reception quay, and yachts are encouraged to fill up on arrival to avoid a return visit. A second diesel pump is to be installed to avoid queuing at busy times. After many years during which the pumps were administered by the *Clube Naval de Ponta Delgada* responsibility has now been transferred to the marina. During office hours (see Harbour Communications, above) fuel can be paid for by credit card, but although it is usually possible to refuel at other times only cash will be accepted. Megayachts can be refuelled in their berths by road tanker – enquire the marina administration office behind the west marina.

Bottled gas Camping Gaz exchanges are readily available, from hardware stores, MAP Açores (see Chandlery, above) and others. Boat & Sail Service can arrange for Calor Gas and other cylinders to be refilled (with Butane only) but allow at least two days.

Weather forecast Three-day forecast and synoptic chart posted daily outside the marina reception office.

Clube naval The *Clube Naval de Ponta Delgada* ✆ 296 308380 *Email* geral@cnpdl.pt www.cnpdl.pt occupies most of the large building at the root of the old marina mole and has long welcomed visiting yachtsmen. It has a pleasant bar and restaurant, and many of the members and officials speak some English.

Banks Many in the city, nearly all with cash dispensers. The latter will also be found at the root of the cruise ship pier, in the Solmar shopping centre and in the larger supermarkets.

Shops/provisioning There are several supermarkets within walking distance of the marinas, possibly the best stocked being Solmar in the shopping centre of that name, plus several large hypermarkets on the outskirts of the city. Most will deliver large orders to the marinas. The city also has many souvenir, clothing, pharmacy and other stores, as one would expect in the archipelago's largest city.

Produce market The large fruit and vegetable market, with fish market attached, lies three blocks inland from the waterfront on Rua do Mercado. A wide selection of good quality local produce is available, with the best variety early in the day.

Cafés, restaurants & hotels Numerous restaurants, cafés and snack bars to suit all tastes and pockets, plus hotels of all categories. Both marinas have pleasant cafés on site.

Medical services There is a hospital on the northern outskirts of the city, highly praised by a British yachtsman who used its services. The marina maintains a list of doctors, dentists and opticians.

Communications

Post office The main post office, open 0830–1830, is located in Rua Cons Dr L Bettencourt (off the seafront some distance west of the west marina). There is a smaller, nearer and more user-friendly one on Rua da Boa Nova, just east of the east marina. Stamps can be bought at any shop displaying the green *correio* sign.

Mailing address C/o Marina de Ponta Delgada, Avenida Infante Dom Henrique Ap.113, 9500 Ponta Delgada, São Miguel, Açores, Portugal.

Telephones Card-operated kiosks near the marina reception office (where cards may be bought), in the Solmar shopping centre and elsewhere.

Internet access Spoilt for choice! In addition to the free Wi-Fi provided by both sections of the marina, two Skype-enabled computers are to be installed for those berthed in the west (new) marina and one for those in the east (old) section, all linked to office printers. Use of the computers will be free, with a small charge for printing.

The west marina is overlooked by the *Baía dos Anjos* café which offers customers free Wi-Fi plus power sockets. Just across the Avenida Infante Dom Henrique is the Solmar shopping centre, where free Wi-Fi is available to allcomers with the username and password – currently solmar@ptwifi.pt and solmar – displayed on posters throughout the building. Chairs and benches are provided, but no tables (other than in the various cafés) and no power sockets. Using the same username and password it is said to be possible to access Wi-Fi throughout much of the west marina. Also in the Solmar centre is Publidecor ✆ 296 285995 *Email* publidecorservice@mail.telepac.pt http://publidecor.blogspot.com which offers Skype-enabled computers (at €1 for 30 minutes in early 2011), scanning, printing, writing to CD/DVD, photocopying, fax and a good deal more and is open 0900–2000 daily. Finally, the *Clube Naval de Ponta Delgada* makes its Wi-Fi available free to visiting yachtsmen, with power also available.

Car hire Numerous options, plus at least one company offering mopeds and bicycles.

Taxis In the city, or can be ordered via either marina office. There is a taxi rank on Praça Gonçalo Velho Cabral – the open square northwest of the west maria – with four others dotted around the city.

Buses Services run to most towns in São Miguel, though all services appear to start and finish in Ponta Delgada.

Air services The airport is situated some 4km west of the city and offers frequent inter-island flights, plus several to/from Lisbon each day and more limited links with other major European cities including London and Manchester – see Transportation, page 23.

Looking southwest across the small bay at Lagoa

Lagoa

37°44'·48N 23°34'·54W (molehead)

Lights
2646 **Lagoa** Fl.R.3s8m6M
White column, red bands 4m
2645·45 **Lagoa cables**
Fl(2)R.8s6m9M (daylight range 1·6M) 339°-vis-007°
White post, red bands 4m. Marks submarine cables

Small, scenic fishing harbour

About 4M east of Ponta Delgada and the site of one of São Miguel's oldest settlements, the mole at Lagoa was extended several years ago to create a small harbour where a few fishing boats lie afloat with others drawn up on the slipway. The surrounding shoreline is generally low, but the harbour is easily identified from seawards by the tall grey silo 0·5M to the west.

Several attractive swimming pools have been created among the rocks east of the harbour making Lagoa an interesting daytime anchorage in light conditions, but the area should be approached with care as depths have not been verified. The plans to build a small marina east of the fishing harbour, mentioned in the previous edition, appear to have been shelved.

A small *clube naútico* overlooks the harbour, as do several cafés and restaurants and a large fish market, while a post office, shops and a bank with cash dispenser will be found in the adjoining town. There is a regular bus service to/from Ponta Delgada.

Porto da Caloura

37°42'·81N 23°29'·73W (molehead)

Lights
2645 **Mole** F.4s6m9M
Square white column, red bands 3m
2645·4 **Ldg Lts on 333°** Oc.G.3s10/14m5M
White posts, red bands 2m

Not a port at all

Little more than a slipway protected by a short mole, where half a dozen brightly painted fishing boats are hauled ashore on rollers when not in use, Porto da Caloura is undeniably pretty but not in any way a port. It would be possible to anchor off, perhaps to use the natural swimming pool which lies among the rocks southwest of the harbour, but approach with extreme caution. There is a café and public toilets ashore, but nothing else at all.

The tiny inlet at Porto da Caloura. The red light on its striped base might be seen as optimism triumphing over reality

Vila Franca do Campo

37°42'·79N 25°25'·7W (breakwater head)

Waypoint
⊕ A41 – 37°41'·9N 25°25'·2W (1M SSE of Vila Franca do Campo)

Plans
Portuguese *47502* (1:7,500)
US *51081* (1:20,000)
Imray-Iolaire *E1* (1:15,000)

Lights
2645·2 **Marina east breakwater** Fl.G.4s11m9M
White tower, green bands 7m
Outer breakwater Fl.R.4s11m9M
White tower, red bands 9m
Note The light structure was toppled by storms shortly after it was erected, but was reinstated early in 2011

Harbour communications
Marina da Vila ✆/*Fax* 296 581488
Email marinaem@sapo.pt VHF Ch 09, 16 (0830–1230, 1330–1630 weekdays, closed weekends)

Quiet marina accessed via busy fishing harbour

A small town and off-lying islet (a miniature volcanic crater flooded by the sea) some 11M east of Ponta Delgada, Vila Franca do Campo was once the capital of São Miguel before being destroyed by a landslide in 1522. It is still relatively small and compact, with imposing churches around the attractive town square although sadly the picturesque old fishing quarter has largely disappeared under concrete. Its memory lives on, however, in the pervasive – though surprisingly pleasant – smell from the very old tuna canning factory which still operates nearby.

The tiny Ilhéu da Vila – which has protected status as a 'Natural Park' – contains as perfect a natural swimming pool as one is likely to find and should not be missed. No fishing of any kind is permitted near the island and permission is needed to take an engine-powered vessel through the narrow, shallow pass into the crater, but nothing in the regulations appears to prohibit entry under oars. Not surprisingly the island is very popular with local people (a ferry service runs from the old fishing harbour between June and September) so will be quietest if visited mid-week.

The construction of São Miguel's second marina on the east side of Vila Franca do Campo began in 2000 under the auspices of *Câmara Municipal da Vila Franca do Campo*, effectively the town council. Although the inner basin was largely complete by the following year and received its first yachts in August 2001, progress has remained slow. It is very much a local facility, with all 156 berths in the inner basin let long-term and not available to visiting yachts. The outer basin proved too exposed for berthing, and although occasionally visited by foreign yachts of up to 13m this is doubtless why no attempt has been made to publicise the marina or to attract foreign visitors.

Work on the second phase of development – a very substantial outer breakwater to protect and enlarge both the old fishing harbour and the marina's outer basin, began in late 2006 and was largely complete by early 2009. Even so, when visited more than a year later pontoons had yet to be installed to extend the marina southwards, and there was a strong implication that local fishermen were not in favour.

Approach

Approaching the area from the west, Ponta da Galera should be given a berth of 500m and a course of 088° then steered for Ilhéu da Vila in order to clear Baixa da Roida. There are several off-lying rocks to the south of the islet, but in good conditions when within 0·5M of the islet a course can be shaped to pass inside. The west wall of the new outer harbour follows the line of a long and extremely dangerous shoal which previously ran some 500m south-southeast from the shore. However, the wall covers only the northern part of the shoal, leaving the southern 250m or so exposed and unmarked, with one outlier rising from 13m to 1·6m or less. For that reason it would be wise to remain outside the 20m line until the end of the breakwater bears west of north before heading in.

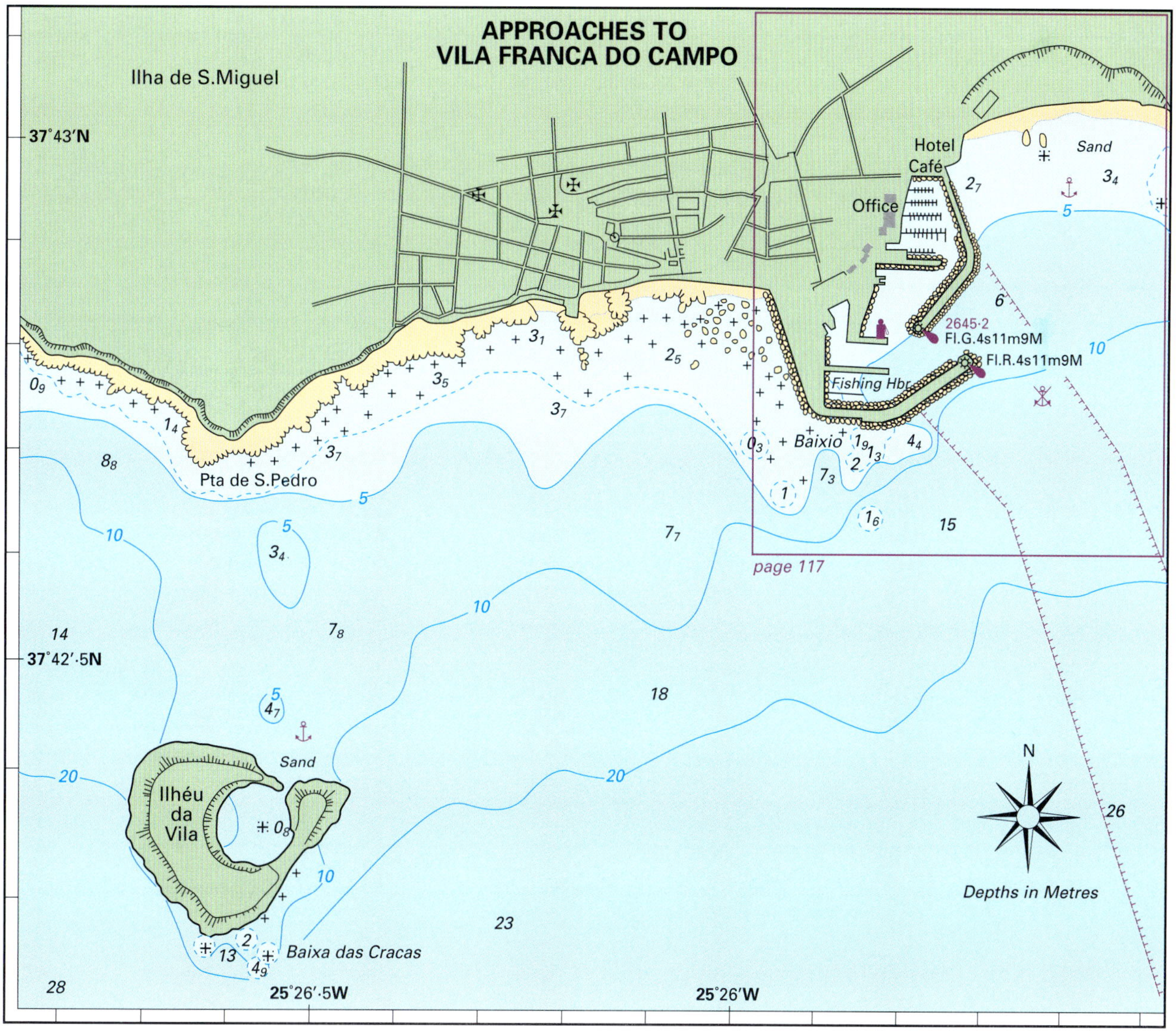

Fishing boats in the outer harbour at Vila Franca do Campo, with the harbour entrance beyond. The port hand light has been replaced since this photograph was taken

If coming from the east, an outfall runs just over 0·5M south-southeast from the bay close east of the marina, and fishing and anchoring in the vicinity are forbidden. Vessels are permitted to cross the area, however, and there are no other hazards. A long, arched, cream building – the Hotel Marina – lies directly behind the marina, while the beach close east is backed by a waterpark with slides and other structures.

Anchorages

In settled, daylight conditions delightful anchorage will be found northeast of Ilhéu da Vila, close off the entrance to the lagoon in 6–8m over sand. Note the various restrictions mentioned above.

Alternatively, the bay east of the marina offers protection from all directions other than south and southeast. Good holding will be found in about 5m over sand, avoiding the large rock in the centre of the beach and its varous offliers, none of which extend beyond the 3m line. Landing on the beach can be difficult even in calm conditions as it is steep and subject to rollers, but there are plenty of corners inside the harbour where a dinghy could be left without being in the way.

No charge is made in either location.

Entrance and berthing

Final approach to the dogleg entrance should be made from the southeast, a watch being kept for fishing boats leaving or approaching at speed. Once inside a sharp turn to starboard is required, through a gap no more than 30m in width, into the marina's outer basin. Here a good watch should be kept for smallcraft moorings, some no more than semi-submerged bottles and many with trailing lines attached.

Pontoons are due to be laid in this area, which has two shoreside fixing points ready to receive them and depths of 3·5m throughout. In 2010 it was said that 61 berths would be created, though only 13 would be able to take yachts of more than 10m. It was not known whether any of these would be reserved for visitors, or when the pontoons might actually materialise.

Looking south over Vila Franca do Campo, with the marina and fishing harbour on the left and Ilhéu da Vila to the right

The marina and fishing harbour at Vila Franca do Campo. Pontoons are planned for the central area, but it is not known when they are likely to be installed

Meanwhile it may be possible to lie alongside the north side of the short mole which divides the marina from the fishing harbour, at least for long enough to visit the marina office. The concrete appears relatively smooth and there are both bollards and steps. Do not be tempted to use the south side, however, as this is the fishermen's fuel berth, a fact easy to miss as the hoses are stored below steel trapdoors when not in use. Alternatively continue through a second gap into the inner basin, preferably making contact on VHF or mobile phone before doing so.

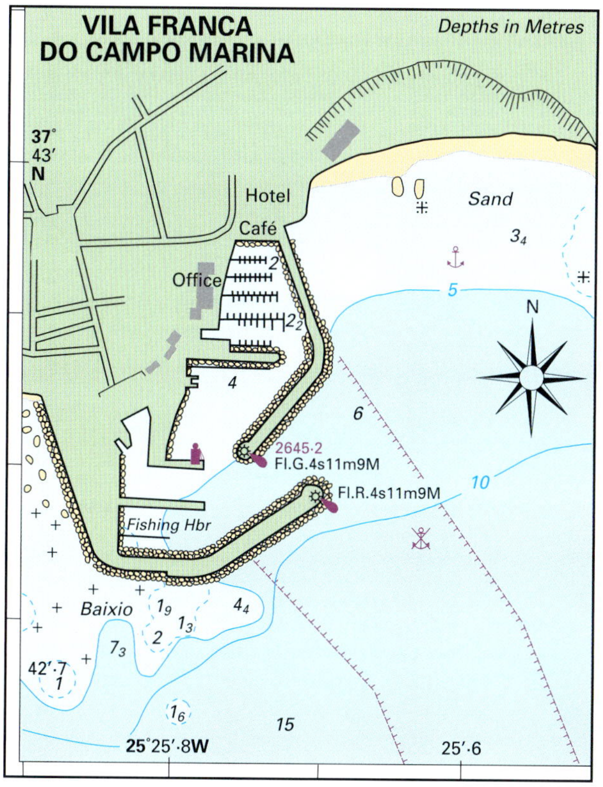

The inner basin contains 156 berths on five pontoons. Visiting yachts of up to 13m LOA have lain alongside finger pontoons in the southeast corner of the inner basin – presumably whilst the permanent residents were absent – but found a bare 2m at low water. Shelter is excellent, however, and it is difficult to think of a more protected spot in which to sit out storm-force winds ... always assuming space is available.

Security is provided by card-operated access gates – for which a deposit is required, see Charges below – CCTV and a permanent security presence.

Formalities

In view of the shortage of space it would be wise to contact the marina office by telephone, VHF or even email prior to arrival. In 2010 good English was spoken during office hours, but outside office hours and at weekends an arriving yacht is likely to be met by one of the security guards, who are generally helpful but speak almost no English.

Charges

As mentioned previously, Marina da Vila is owned by the *Câmara Municipal da Vila Franca do Campo* and is not part of the *Portos dos Açores SA* chain. In 2011 the overnight fee for a visiting monohull of 10–12m LOA was €16.45 and that for 12–15m was €24.60, which included water, electricity and IVA (VAT, currently 16%), with considerable discounts for longer periods. No price was quoted for multihulls, probably because there is currently no room for them. A refundable deposit of €52.78 is charged for the magnetic card which gives access to the pontoons.

Facilities

Boatyard/engineer Both run by a local man who speaks no English, so approach via the marina office.
Travel-lift A 75-tonne capacity hoist was delivered to the fishing harbour in 2009, and though primarily intended for fishing vessels (hence the size) can also be used for yachts. There is a reasonable area of concreted hardstanding, but props of suitable length and strength might prove a problem.
There is a wide slipway at the head of the fishing harbour where local smallcraft are winched ashore on rollers, a method which might also work for a modest multihull. In both cases consult the marina office.
Diving services Available – enquire at the marina office.
Chandlery A very limited amount is stocked by a fishing tackle shop opposite the tourist office on Rua Conego Sena Freitas.
Water At all marina berths, or from taps in the fishing harbour.
Showers In the same block as the marina office. Showers cost €2.33, including soap and a towel.
Launderette None at the marina or, apparently, anywhere in the town.
Electricity At all marina berths.
Fuel Available from pumps on the marina's southwest mole (ie. the one opposite the east mole) though well hidden in storage areas below steel trapdoors. Arrange via the marina office.
Clube naval The *Clube Naval de Vila Franca do Campo* has substantial premises on the west side of the inner basin, where dinghies are stored prior to launching on the adjacent slipway. It appears to be an active club, but without its own bar or restaurant.
Weather forecast Displayed outside the marina office.
Banks Several in the town, all with cash dispensers, plus a cash dispenser outside the marina office.
Shops/provisioning Sizeable and well-stocked supermarket on the Rua do Penedo, which leads west from near the Hotel Marina, plus a good range of other shops.
Produce market On Rua Teófilo de Braga (the main Ponta Delgada road).
Cafés, restaurants & hotels Several hotels and numerous cafés and restaurants, including one overlooking the marina's inner basin. The large Hotel Marina, right behind the inner basin, has a pleasant bar and restaurant – the entrance is at the east (beach) end of the building.
Medical services Hospital in the town.

Communications

Post office On the Rua Teófilo de Braga.
Telephones Public telephone at the south end of the marina office block, with others in the town.
Internet access Free Wi-Fi at the marina office, though it is not known how much of the marina itself is covered.
Car hire At least one company in the town, with many more in Ponta Delgada.
Taxis In the main square.
Buses To Ponta Delgada and elsewhere.
Ferries Regular summer foot ferry to Ilhéu da Vila, but nothing coastal.

Fishing boats line the apron at Ribeira Quente, with its southwest-trending breakwater visible in the background

Ribeira Quente

37°43'·98N 25°17'·93W (molehead)

Plans
Portuguese *47502* (1:5,000)

Lights
2641 **Breakwater** Fl.G.4s5m5M
White column, green bands 3m

Active fishing harbour

Ribeira Quente is very much a working harbour, but even so the (very) few yachts which have visited have generally been permitted to lie alongside the breakwater, at least while the larger fishing boats are at sea. It is also home port to several whale-watching RIBs. However space is limited – many of the smaller boats are brought ashore – and with little shelter from the southwest some swell is almost inevitable. Much of the harbour appears to carry 3m or more. There is a large travel-lift and a wide slipway.

The harbour has an attractive terraced backdrop, but there is little in the village other than a few small shops, restaurants and cafés.

Povoação

37°44'·68 25°14'·73W (east molehead)

Lights
2640·6 **West breakwater** Oc.R.4s6m3M
White column, red bands 5m
2640·65 **East mole** Oc.G.4s6m6M
White column, green bands 5m

Small, quiet harbour

About 10 years after completion, the small harbour at Povoção still appears to be little used even by local fishermen. The somewhat isolated town is thought to be the oldest settlement on the island – a date of 1432 is proudly displayed on a column in the attractive town square which gives onto a cobbled pedestrian area. Both town and harbour are noticeably tidy and well-kept.

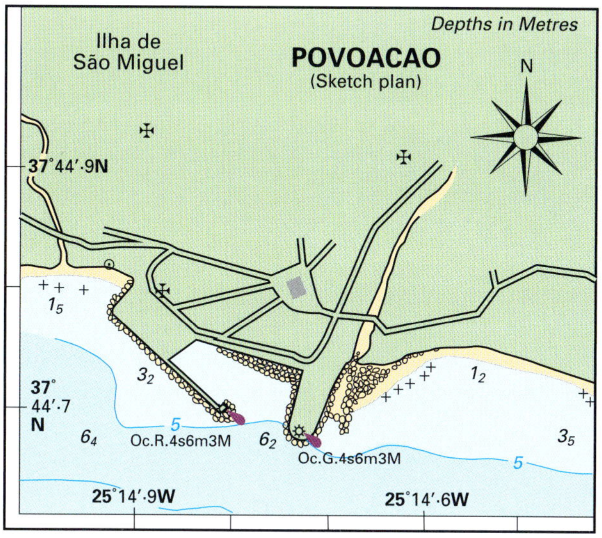

Approach and berthing

Straightforward, once the town has been identified – it lies in a valley with cultivated slopes on either side. The harbour itself, which is protected by substantial enclosing breakwaters, is backed by a long white hotel with a low tower at its eastern end. Close east of this is a large cream building (a sports hall).

In settled conditions it would be possible for a yacht to lie against the inside of the west breakwater, though good fendering would be necessary as some swell is almost guaranteed. There is one set of steps plus several ladders, and no shortage of bollards. Exact depths are not known, but there appears to be several metres at the wall.

Facilities and communications

No facilities at the harbour, not even water, though if desperate cans could be filled from the public tap at the east end of the bridge, beyond which there is a filling station. The town has several small supermarkets, a bank with cash dispenser and no shortage of cafés, restaurants and hotels. A post office will be found in the town centre and a card-operated telephone in the pedestrian area. A regular bus service connects Povoção with Vila Franca do Campo and Ponta Delgada.

Looking southeast over the small harbour at Povoação on São Miguel's southeast coast

Porto Formoso

37°49'·43N 25°25'·55W (east mole)

Plans
Portuguese *47502* (1:5,000)

Lights
2659·4 **Porto Formoso** Fl.4s6M
Lantern on building with red and white bands 3m
2659·5 **West mole** Fl.G.4s4m3M
White post, green bands
2659·6 **East mole** Fl.R.4s5m3M
White post, red bands

Possible anchorage off tiny harbour

A neat little semicircular harbour has been built in the tiny rock-fringed bay, possibly more to protect the beach behind than with any expectation of serving the needs of boats. It would be possible to anchor well off in very settled weather, protected from southeast through south to northwest, but extreme caution would be needed in the approach. There is a café/restaurant nearby, but the town is some distance inland.

The pretty bay of Porto Formoso on the north coast of São Miguel. It would be possible for a yacht to anchor off in very settled conditions

Rabo do Peixe

37°49'N 25°35'·11W (breakwater head)

Plans
Portuguese *47502* (1:5,000)

Lights
2657 **Rabo do Peixe** Iso.WR.5s59m5M
090°-R-120°-B-175°-R-190°-obscd-090°
Lantern on church tower 28m
2686·9 **Breakwater** Fl.R.5s10m6M
White column, red bands 2·6m

São Miguel's only north coast harbour

A wide bay giving protection from east through south to southwest, improved in 1999 by the construction of a new breakwater north of the old quay. In contrast to the sophistication of Ponta Delgada the town which overlooks it appears almost untouched by the 20th century, let alone the 21st.

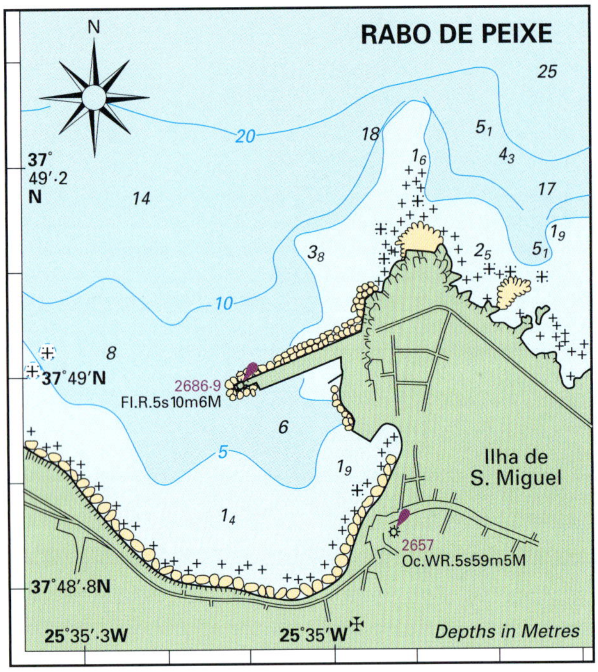

Approach, anchorage and berthing

Coming from the west an offing of 0·5M clears all dangers. From the east a course of no less than 250° should be maintained after rounding Ponta da Ribeirinha in order to avoid the 4·8m Baixa do Morro, 1·5M northeast of the anchorage. Final approach from either direction may be made on 135° on the prominent white church, diverging as necessary around the end of the breakwater. Night entry is not recommended.

Anchor in 6–7m over sand and rock, with the inner corner of the small quay bearing about 070° and the church bearing 120°. In settled conditions – and Rabo do Peixe should not be approached in anything else – it might be possible to lie alongside the breakwater for a limited period by agreement with the local fishermen (who, together with the town's children, might well regard a foreign yacht as something of a curiosity).

Facilities and communications

Travel-hoist at the root of the mole (though it would have to be a real emergency and the dock appears somewhat shallow), but no boatyard as such. There are taps near the fish market on the old inner quay and and shops, post office and banks (with cash dispensers) in the town.

Looking north towards the breakwater at Rabo de Peixe, São Miguel's only real north coast harbour

Porto das Capelas

37°50'·55N 25°41'·2W (quay)

Plans
Portuguese *47502* (1:5,000)

Lights
2656 **Morro de Capelas** Fl(2)R.12s114m8M
153°-vis-281° White post, red bands 7m

Attractive north coast anchorage

Not so much a 'port' as a narrow bay surrounded by sheer cliffs giving protection from east through south to west, but totally exposed to northerly winds and swell. The rocky headland to the east is penetrated by several long narrow inlets and would be fascinating dinghy territory, while the anchorage itself is exceptionally pretty with very clear water.

Approach and anchorage

If coming from the west, Ponta de São António should be given at least 800m clearance and Capelas quay and slipway approached on a bearing of no less than 175°. From the east, the anchorage will be completely hidden until around the Morro de Capelas, at least 200m clear. An isolated breaking rock (Calhau dos Burras) lies some 100m offshore in the southwest corner of the bay, but there are no other outliers. There is a light on the cliffs above the bay, but night entry is not recommended.

Anchor in 5–8m over sand and rock with the tiny quay and slipway bearing about 120°.

Facilities

There is a small town on the cliffs above the anchorage, with fresh water and fuel available by can, several small food stores, a bank and a post office.

Porto das Capelas – a misnomer, being no more than a natural bay – looking northeast

Santa Maria

Between 35°56′N–37°01′N and 25°01′W–25°11′W

Introduction

Santa Maria is the southernmost of the Azores group by almost a full degree, and other than the Ilhéus das Formigas is also the furthest east. It is one of the smaller islands, 17km long by up to 8km wide, with an area of 97km². About two-thirds of the 6,000 inhabitants live in or close to the capital, Vila do Porto. Like the other islands it is of volcanic origin, but is unique amongst the Azores in also having sedimentary rocks. The western plateau is formed of limestone rich in marine fossils, with useful deposits of red clay.

Santa Maria was the first of the Azores to be settled by the Portuguese, probably in 1427, when Gonçalo Velho Cabral landed on the beach at Praia do Lobos. Herds of pigs and goats were put ashore to ensure a ready food supply for the men who followed, and the native forest burned and felled to make way for cultivation. Scattered villages already existed throughout the island by February 1493, when Columbus anchored off the tiny village of Anjos (Angels) on the northwest coast whilst returning from his first voyage to enable his crew to attend Mass. Wisely, he allowed only half his men ashore where they were promptly imprisoned, probably either on suspicion of spying or because they were in the employ of the Spanish crown. After a quick appeal to higher authority in São Miguel Columbus returned to negotiate their release, and it would seem likely that he sailed round to anchor off Vila do Porto, already the island's capital. The islanders' suspicion of strangers was certainly justified, with repeated attacks from French, Turkish and Moorish pirates, who burnt crops and buildings and frequently made off with slaves. One church still preserves a slaver's iron whip dating back to the 16th century.

Although the island's major port from early in its history, the open bay at Vila do Porto did not gain any form of quay until 1874, when a short protective wall was built in the northwest corner of the harbour, now incorporated in the large reclaimed area. A whaling station, since abandoned, once thrived some 10km east at Ponta do Castelo.

One of the most formative events in Santa Maria's history occurred during the Second World War, when Britain invoked the ancient Treaty of Alliance – signed with Portugal in 1373 – to enable the Allies to build a large military airport. US forces arrived in 1944, completing an enormous sprawl of three runways, a hotel, cinema, sports facilities and dozens of smaller buildings the following year, and taking over a large part of the flat western plateau to do so. However, in exchange for the loss of some infertile heath and scrublands Santa Maria gained the largest civilian airport in the islands when it was handed over in 1947. While the other islands still had grass strips only capable of handling local flights Santa Maria served as the gateway to the Azores, but the prosperity it brought waned with the expansion of airports elsewhere, and until very recently there was little tourist development on Santa Maria itself. Now it is becoming a popular weekend destination for Azoreans living in São Miguel, who see the smaller island as a peaceful area in which to own a holiday home. Doubtless another attraction is Santa Maria's beaches, which are far superior to most of those on São Miguel, while its lower topography tends to result in less cloud, mist and rain than is typical of its northern sister.

Throughout the rural areas farming is still the major occupation, the steep volcanic slopes patterned with a chequerboard of tiny fields growing sweetcorn, wheat, bananas, vines and all the usual garden vegetables. Some of the old estates boast high walls and gateways surmounted with coats of arms carved from the soft volcanic rock, though the typical village architecture owes much to the Algarve region of southern Portugal from which many of the early settlers came. Most cottages are low and whitewashed, with an outside baking oven complete with tall round chimney and pointed conical cap. Everywhere rough lumps of pumice are piled into low stone walls. Eucalyptus and pine trees scent the air and wild flowers of all colours and varieties, both familiar and exotic, run rampant over walls and verges.

Navigation

Waypoints
⊕ A45 – 37°00'·4N 25°12'·1W (1M WNW of Pta do Lobaio)
⊕ A46 – 36°56'N 25°08'·9W (0·5M S of Vila do Porto)
⊕ A48 – 36°55'·1N 24°59'·9W (1M SE of Pta do Castelo)
⊕ A50 – 37°01'·4N 25°02'·4W (1M NE of Pta do Norte)

Courses and distances
⊕ A45 to ⊕A13 (0·5M E of Horta, Faial) = 187M, 300° & by eye / by eye & 120°
⊕ A45 to ⊕A39 (0·5M SE of Ponta Delgada, São Miguel) = 48·5M, 334° / 154°
⊕ A45 to ⊕A46 = 6·5M, by eye
⊕ A50 to ⊕A39 (0·5M SE of Ponta Delgada, São Miguel) = 51·5M, 326° / 146°
⊕ A50 to ⊕A46 = 14M, by eye

Magnetic variation
9°20'W (2011), decreasing by 10'E annually.

Tidal Streams
Tidal streams set northeast on the flood and southwest on the ebb, but are generally weak.

Charts
Admiralty *1959* (1:150,000)
Portuguese *43103* (1:300,000), *46407* (1:75,000)
US *51081* (1:250,000)
Imray-Iolaire *E1* (1:750,000)

Lights
2634 **Airport control tower**
Al.Fl.WG.10s116m25M 021°-vis-121° (occas)
2633 **Ponta do Norte** Fl(4)15s138m12M
White tower, red band 3m
2632 **Ponta do Castelo (Gonçalo Velho)**
Fl(3)13·5s113m25M Aeromaritime 181°-vis-089°
Square white tower and buildings 14m
2636 **Ponta de Malmerendo**
Fl(2)10s49m12M 282°-vis-091°
Red lantern on white building 6m

A rough road climbs almost to the top of Pico Alto rewarded – in clear weather – by stunning views of the island spread below. Even without a car or taxi the island is small enough to explore by local bus and on foot, with a good chance of a lift from a friendly Santa Marian, many of whom speak some English and all of whom are justifiably proud of their island.

Holidays and festivals

In addition to the national holidays listed on page 26, Santa Maria celebrates its official holiday on 15 August, with the August Tide Festival taking place from 22–25 August and the Harvest Festival in September. As throughout the Azores, the Festival of *Espírito Santo* is celebrated about six weeks after Easter.

Telecommunications

Mobile (cell) phone reception throughout the island is good. The country code for the Azores is 351, as it is for mainland Portugal, and the area code for Santa Maria – which must be included even when dialling from within the island – is 296, shared with São Miguel.

By 2011 free Wi-Fi was available in several locations in Vila do Porto, including the marina and the main square, as well as at the airport and in some of the smaller towns.

Websites

Although the internet appears to carry no website devoted to Santa Maria as a whole, that of the *Câmara Municipal de Vila do Porto* at www.cm-viladoporto.pt/ does have pages devoted to other parts of the island, in Portuguese only. Santa Maria is also covered by Wikipedia at www.en.wikipedia.org/wiki/Santa_Maria_Island, as well as featuring on several of the general Azores sites listed on pages 24–5.

Approach

Santa Maria can easily be seen in clear weather from the hills of São Miguel, though approaching at sea level from the north or south, the higher eastern part appears as a single cone until the lower plateau to the west rises above the horizon.

Steep cliffs form much of the coastline and there are few off-lying dangers. However, if making a landfall from the east care must be taken to avoid Baixa da Maia bearing 022° from Ponta do Castelo about 1M off, and Baixa do Sul bearing 234° from Ponta do Castelo about 0·5M off. Both are low, isolated breaking rocks, totally unmarked and unlit.

A monument to Portuguese maritime heroes in the Fortress de São Brás overlooking Vila do Porto

Harbours and anchorages

Vila do Porto

36°56'·63N 25°08'·92W (marina molehead)

Waypoint
⊕A46 – 36°56N 25°08'·9W (0·5M S of Vila do Porto)

Tides
Predictions for Vila do Porto are available via Admiralty *EasyTide* – see page 30
Time difference on Ponta Delgada: +0002
Mean spring range 1·4m
Mean neap range 0·7m

Plans
Admiralty *1959* (1:12,500)
Portuguese *46407* (1:7,500)
US *51081* (1:10,000)
Imray-Iolaire *E1* (1:10,000)

Lights
2636 **Ponta de Malmerendo**
Fl(2)10s49m12M 282°-vis-091°
Red lantern on white building 6m
2634·5 **Marvão** Fl.G.5s34m3M
010°-vis-190° White tower, green bands 3m
2635·3 **Breakwater** LFl.R.5s14m5M
White tower, red bands 8m
2634·7 **Clube Naval** Fl(2)GWR.8s24m10M
346°-G-351°-W-354°-R-359° Post 7m
2635 **Marina mole** Fl.G.3s8m3M
White post, green bands 2·5m

Harbour communications
Harbourmaster ✆ 296 882157 *Fax* 296 882772
Email capitania.vporto@marinha.pt VHF Ch 11, 16
(call *Capimar Viporto*) (0900–1230, 1400–1700)
Port Authority ✆ 296 882282 *Fax* 296 882766
Email portovdp@apsm.pt www.apsm.pt
VHF Ch 11, 12, 16 (0800–1200, 1400–1700)
Vila do Porto Marina ✆ 296 882782 *Fax* 296 882766
Email marinavdp@marinasazores.com
www.marinasazores.com VHF Ch 10, 16
(15 May to 15 September: 0800–1200, 1300–2000, closed Sunday; 16 September to 14 May: 0800–1200, 1300–1700, closed weekends)

Friendly marina offering excellent shelter

A breakwater some 350m in length was built in the mid 1980s across the western part of what had previously been an open anchorage, to increase protection and facilitate the landing of cargo. It affords good shelter to the western half of the bay, though swell from the south or southeast sets up considerable surge, and for many years visiting yachts had no option but to anchor.

In 2003 work to build a Ro-Ro ferry terminal began in the northwest of the harbour, and then in early 2007 construction started on Vila do Porto Marina, the fifth in the *Portos dos Açores SA* chain. This was effectively finished one year later, although some related facilities took several more years to appear. An excellent view of the marina is to be had via a webcam on www.climaat.angra.uac.pt – click on the weathercam at centre right – while the artistic will be happy to know that wall-painting is encouraged, with a great deal of virgin concrete still crying out to be decorated (brushes and paint are available at several shops in the town). Santa Maria has long been praised by the growing number of yachtsmen who visit the island, and the marina has likewise received the thumbs up.

The town is attractive if slightly ramshackle, with parts which are very old. White or pastel-washed houses under red tiles, their large windows picked out in darker colours, line the long cobbled main street which curves up a gently sloping spur away from the harbour. The curious may wonder why several of the large and once-elegant houses have been allowed to fall derelict, with shattered roofs and sagging balconies. It appears that their owners cannot be traced, having emigrated many years ago, and that although the island authorities would love to renovate them, possibly for commercial use, little can be done until title is established.

The typical Portuguese inlaid pavements feature a pattern of rope, fish, ships and shells, and there are several fine examples of ornately carved baroque and manueline architecture including the town hall buildings, formerly a Franciscan monastery, open to the public during office hours and well worth a visit. Excellent views over the harbour can be enjoyed from the 16th-century Forte de São Bras, the three-flue chimneys of which are said to represent the Father, Son and Holy Ghost.

Approach

By day Quite straightforward, with no off-lying dangers. The light grey concrete of the breakwater contrasts sharply with the dark cliffs behind. A bearing of 018° on the conspicuous white church tower on the skyline leads past the breakwater, which has 15m close off its end, but the north side of the wall should be given a wide berth as concrete rubble lies up to 30m from its base. There is a small wind farm on the skyline a short distance east of the harbour.

If a ship (including the inter-island ferry) is manoeuvring in the harbour a yacht may be asked to stand off for up to 30 minutes – a good reason to call the marina on VHF during the approach.

By night Perfectly feasible in good weather conditions, but perhaps best avoided for first-time entry by the less experienced, particularly in light of the narrow entrance to the marina itself (see below).

Anchorage

Anchoring is no longer permitted north of a line between Ponta Malmerendo to the west and Ponta do Marvão to the east – effectively ruling out the entire harbour. The only real alternative appears to be Baía da Praia (Praia Formosa) about three miles further east (see page 126).

Marina entrance and berthing

The gap which gives access to the marina is distinctly narrow, creating obvious scope for collision, and it would be wise to contact the marina before arrival to check that no one is about to depart. Larger or less manoeuvrable yachts should take particular care, as turning space is limited once inside – though

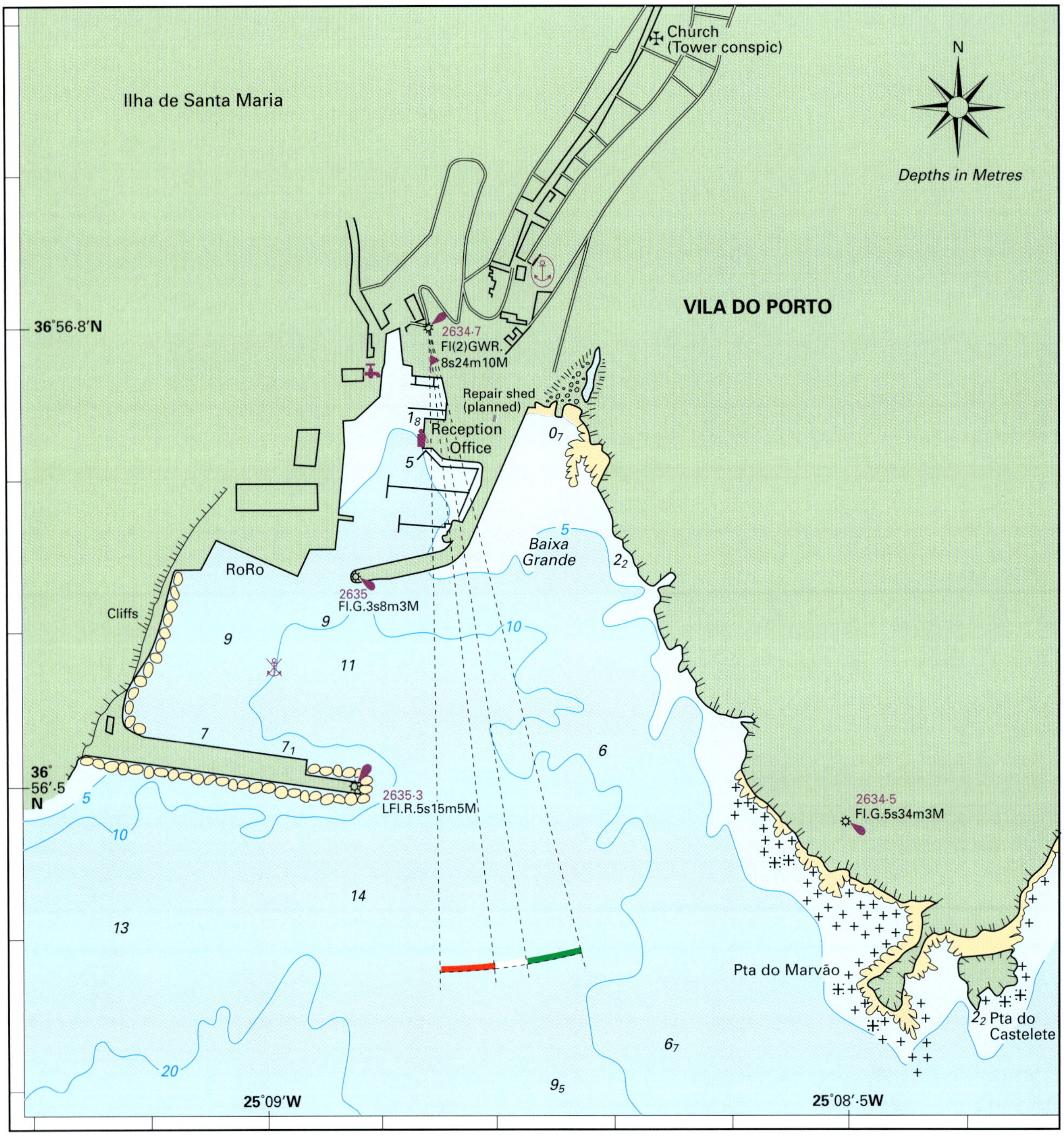

Approaching Vila do Porto, with the end of the marina mole just open of the breakwater *Mike Eastman*

Looking southwest over the new Vila do Porto Marina, still quite empty at the beginning of the season

not as limited as it appears, once past the two outer pontoons.

Protection is excellent and, like the main breakwater, the marina mole has proved itself equal to the challenge of winter storms and large seas. At least 5m should be found in the marina entrance, with 4m as far as the reception quay which doubles as fuel berth. Although the marina mole is lit, the opposing corner is not and first-time entrance after dark would be best avoided.

Many of the marina's 124 berths remained unused as of 2010, and it is likely to be some time before space becomes a problem. Visiting yachts are normally placed on the second (ie. longest) pontoon, the outer five fingers of which are reserved for larger yachts. The fingers are long and the bays unusually wide, but even so berthing can be tricky in cross winds. In office hours at least one of the marina staff will normally be on hand to assist. Although the marina can, in theory at least, accommodate at least one yacht of up to 32m, in practice it may be preferable on both sides to berth alongside the main breakwater if this is not required for commercial vessels. Contact well before arrival to discuss.

Formalities

The smart new marina office overlooks the reception/fuel pontoon, and as in all marina front offices throughout the Azores the staff, headed by Sr Armando Soares, are notably friendly and helpful with several speaking good English. The usual ship's papers plus crew passports will be required, as may proof of insurance. The offices of the *Guarda Nacional Republicana*, *Polícia Marítima*, *Serviço de Estrangeiros e Fronteiras* (Immigration) and *Alfândega* (Customs) are located in the same building, but the *Capitania* remains in the town (up the steep hill past the Forte de São Bras). The marina staff will advise on current requirements.

Note that it may not be possible to obtain formal outward clearance for a non-EU destination, as Santa Maria is not an official Schengen Agreement 'border post'. However EU-registered yachts departing for destinations within Europe (including the Madeira group, but not including the Canaries) should not encounter problems.

Charges

Vila do Porto Marina is one of the Portos dos Açores SA chain, and shares their basic price structure. As of 2011 yachts of 10–12m LOA paid €12.22 per night and those of 12–15m paid €18.50, inclusive of everything except showers (see below). For further details see page 27 and/or www.marinasazores.com, the website of the branch of Portos dos Açores SA concerned with marina operation (though note that different charges apply to yachts owned by residents and by non-residents).

Vila do Porto is one of the few Azorean harbours to collect 'lighthouse tax' – *Taxa de Farolagem e Balizagem* – which is payable at the Capitania rather than at the marina office. At just €2 for six months it is not too onerous, but it is worth keeping the receipt.

Facilities

Travel-lift A 75-tonne capacity hoist (in order to lift fishing boats as well as yachts) is anticipated by October 2011, and the previous month the dock (which was built for a smaller machine) was being enlarged to take it. There is generous hardstanding, and a 700 sq.m repair shed is planned for the northeast corner of the marina car park.

Boatyard None as such, though the repair shed mentioned above may attract a growing variety of skills. In the meantime Jorge Botelho handles small repairs and can be contacted via the marina office.

Engineers Paulo Chaves, who runs Nautipescas (next to the *clube naval*) can access most engineering services on Santa Maria and will work on boats in the marina.

Chandlery Nautipescas, ✆ 919 368481, 963 149058, next to the *clube naval*, stocks general chandlery as well as fishing equipment. Owner Paulo Chaves speaks English and will order from Ponta Delgada if necessary. Open 1000–1200, 1300–1800 weekdays, 1000–1300 Saturday during the summer (May to September).

Loja do Mar on the main street also offers a small amount of chandlery amongst the fishing tackle.

Water At all berths.

Showers For several years the marina relied on the *clube naval* for toilets and showers, not always with happy results. However by 2010 this had been rectified, with brand new toilets and (six) showers still in the *clube naval* building but with access by key. Showers cost €1.25 each, payable on departure.

Laundry Brand new launderette next to the showers, again with key access. In 2010 tokens for both washers and dryers cost just under €5, though it was fine to hang laundry out to dry on board.

Electricity At all berths.

Fuel A fuel berth is promised for the reception quay, but in the meantime yachts can take on diesel from the pump on the commercial quay opposite.

Bottled gas Camping Gaz exchanges, but no refills.

Weather forecast Available from the marina office on request.

Clube naval The *Clube Naval de Santa Maria* has premises beside the slipway at the head of the harbour with the offices and bar on the upper floor, the latter giving onto a large terrace. It has long been friendly and welcoming towards visiting yachtsmen, and some English is spoken. Shut on Mondays.

Banks Several in the town. Cash dispensers in the main street, including one inside the SolMar supermarket, but not at the harbour itself.

Shops/provisioning Several supermarkets, including a medium-sized SolMar supermarket on the main street, plus other shops.

Produce market Large (but underused) market behind the Hotel Praia de Lobos with a good meat section behind.

Cafés, restaurants & hotels Several hotels plus a growing number of restaurants and cafés, several of the latter run by returned emigrants who speak excellent English.

Medical services Hospital and pharmacy.

Communications

Post office with telephones Plus a phone inside the marina office building.

Internet access The marina has been praised for its fast and reliable Wi-Fi, available at all berths. There is also free Wi-Fi at the library (round the corner from the SolMar supermarket), at the Youth Centre (next to the Arriba Bar) in the main street and in the main square.

Car hire At least four companies, one of which also hires out motorbikes.

Taxis Taxi rank outside the town hall (a steep walk up from the harbour). Yet another island where a taxi tour (or car hire) is recommended as 'worth every penny'.

Buses To the airport and throughout the island. A bus comes down to the harbour every hour – ask at the marina office for current times.

Ferry Regular (but not daily) link with Ponta Delgada.

Air services Regular inter-island flights.

Baía da Praia (Praia Formosa)

36°57′·1N 25°06′·6W (ruined fort)

Waypoint

⊕A47 – 36°56′·5N 25°06′·4W (0·5M SSE of anchorage)

Lights

2632·1 **Formoso cables**
Fl(2)Y.8s8m9M (daylight range 1·7M) 000°-vis-040°
White post, red bands 4m. Marks submarine cables

Beach anchorage open to the south

A crescent-shaped bay almost 1·5M in length, situated 2·5M east of Vila do Porto and protected from northwest through north to east. Being entirely open to the south it provides a daytime anchorage only, with good swimming and a clean sandy beach against an attractive backdrop of cliffs and terraced vineyards. Anchoring (or fishing) in the centre of the bay is now prohibited due to submarine cables (see plan), though there is no restriction on passage through the area and it should still be possible to anchor on either side.

The extent of the beach itself varies from year to year, as the sand apparently disappears during the winter, only to reappear – sometimes! – in late spring. For much of the 21st century the beach has been narrow to virtually nonexistent, with the sea reaching almost to the road, but no one appears to know why. Feedback on this phenomenon would be appreciated.

Approach

From westwards, Ponta do Marvão may be rounded 200m off and a course of 102° steered for Ponta Malbusco before edging northwards into the bay itself. If approaching from the east care must be taken to avoid Pedrinha rock, which rises almost sheer from around 30m. The relevant Admiralty chart gives Pedrinha a least depth of 5·5m, though it has been reported to carry considerably less.

Anchorage

It is essential to avoid anchoring within the area through which the cables run, though this is not made easier by the fact that the light – a bank of LEDs rather than a conventional lens – is very

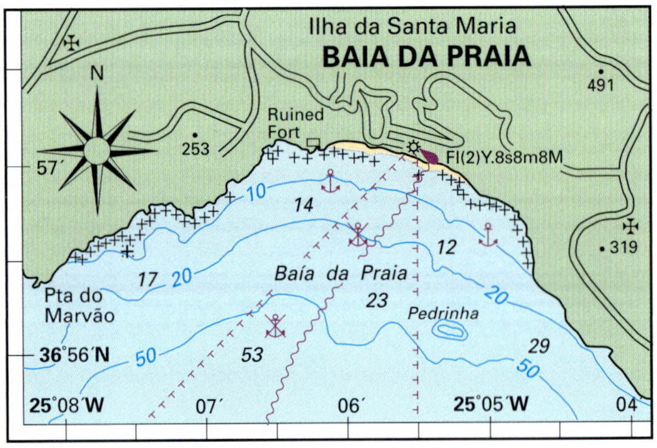

Crystal clear water characterises the Baía da Praia – also known as Praia Formosa or 'beautiful beach' – seen here from the northwest

difficult to identify. In fact it lies close east of a single Norfolk pine which grows on a small promontory near the centre of the beach. Fortunately the best anchorages are at either end of the beach – see plan – in 5m or so over sand. If opting for the western end, however, a wreck with depths of less than 1m lies at around the 4m line, making good light and a sharp lookout essential (the colourful fish which inhabit the wreck add to the snorkeling appeal).

Facilities

Cafés and a few small shops in the nearby village, but otherwise very little.

Baía de São Lourenço

36°59′·52N 25°03′·35W (front leading light)

Waypoint

⊕A49 – 36°59′·6N 25°02′·6W (0·5M ENE of anchorage)

Plans

Admiralty *1959* (1:12,500)
Portuguese *46407* (1:7,500)

Lights

2632·2 **Ponta do Espigão** Fl.6s206m12M
White column, red bands 6m
2632·3 **Ldg Lts on 273 3°** *Front* LFl.R.5s25m6M
White post, red bands, in front of white house with blue arches 6m
Rear, 64m from front, Oc.R.7·5s36m6M
Red lantern on white house with verandah 2m

Scenic beach anchorage open to the east

High surrounding cliffs (the semi-circular remains of a volcanic cone) give the 0·75M Baía de São Lourenço good protection from southeast through west to north, but leave it totally open to easterly winds or swell. Thus it should only be considered as an overnight anchorage in very settled weather. The beach is largely of sand with a small stone quay and concrete ramp among rocks at its northern end. In late 2010 bulldozers were working along the shoreline, possibly to reinforce the seawall and widen the road which it protects.

The Baía de São Lourenço provides one of the loveliest anchorages in the entire Azores, with cliffs terraced into a lacing of black lava walls and tiny green vineyards where the locally famous *vinho de cheiro* is produced. The island of São Lourenço (also known as Ilhéu do Romeiro) at the southeastern horn of the bay has some fine sea caves and many nesting birds. The water is exceptionally clear to considerable depths.

Approach

By day Islands fringe both ends of the bay, but there are no outliers. The leading marks (which are difficult to make out in daylight) lie just north of two distinctive, tall, thin trees.

By night The leading marks are lit and in offshore or light winds they could be followed from the vicinity of ⊕A49 into a suitable depth for anchoring.

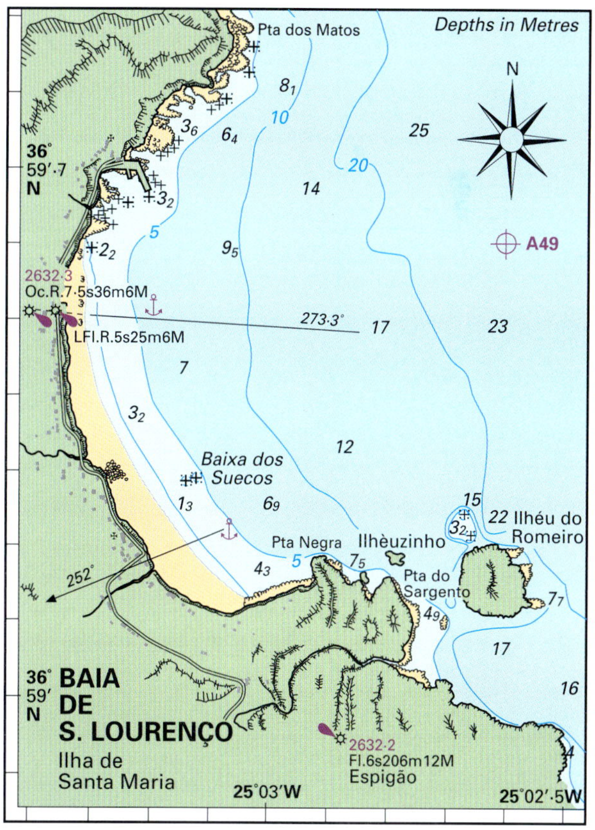

Looking northwest over the wide Baía de São Lourenço on Santa Maria's east coast

Anchorage

In 4–5m over sand opposite the leading marks, or in the southern corner of the bay with the unmistakable rising road bearing about 252°. The breaking Baixa dos Suecos – which extend further to seaward than indicated on Admiralty *1959* – lies about 200m offshore between the two suggested anchorages.

Facilities

Water tap on the quay and two summer restaurants, but no shops. The houses fringing the beach are mostly holiday homes.

Looking south along the beach at Baía de São Lourenço, with Ponta do Espigão and Ilhéu do Romeiro beyond

Baía dos Anjos

37°00'·32N 25°09'·52W (molehead)

Lights
2633·5 **Fábrica dos Anjos** Fl.4s12m10M
White column, red bands 6m
2633·7 **Ldg Lts on 173 4°** *Front* Fl.3s12m10M
Rear, 25m from front, LFl.6s20m10M
White posts, red bands 5m
Important Unsuitable for night approach

Attractive fair-weather anchorage

Columbus called here in 1493, but yachtsmen may prefer to visit by land. The tiny rock-fringed bay is protected from east through south to southwest, with a short concrete pier at its western end. An imaginative, semi-enclosed swimming area has been created, into which a small rowing dinghy (NO OUTBOARDS!) might be taken.

The village is also miniature and very peaceful, and the ancient chapel visited by Columbus's crew (though largely rebuilt in the 17th century) can still be seen. The doors are usually locked, but the key is held by the lady who lives next door.

Approach, anchorage and facilities

The red and white leading marks which lie behind the old quay are readily seen against the hillside and can be followed into 5–8m to anchor, probably over rock and large stones. Although lit, a night approach should not be attempted under any circumstances.

Most of the nearby houses are holiday homes and facilities are very limited. Water taps – and sinks – will be found in the barbecue area above the swimming pools and there is a summer café, but there are no shops for several miles.

Baía dos Anjos in northeast Santa Maria, Columbus's first European landfall in 1493 (see page 121)

Ilhéus das Formigas

37°16'·26N 24°46'·82W (lighthouse)

Introduction

The Ilhéus das Formigas – literally 'The Ants' – are reputed to have been the first of the Azorean islands to be sighted by the Portuguese, in 1426. They now form a Marine Reserve in which all forms of fishing, scuba diving, and the collection of shells, plants and geological specimens are forbidden and rubbish must not be dumped (which of course applies to the marine environment generally). The Reserve covers an area formed by two overlapping circles, both 5M in radius, centred on the Ilhéus das Formigas light and Dollabarat Shoal.

Approach

The Ilhéus das Formigas lie 34M from São Miguel and just over 20M from Santa Maria, bearing 147° and 040° respectively. A short chain of dark rocks no more than 11m in height, they mark the northwestern edge of a bank nearly 5·5M long and 2·5M wide, with average depths of 50–100m. A narrow shoal with breaking patches extends almost 0·5M south from the rocks themselves.

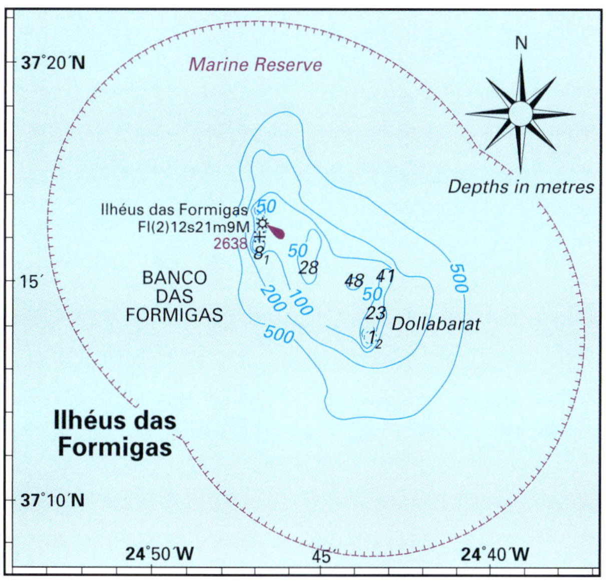

Navigation

Magnetic variation
9°20'W (2011), decreasing by 10'E annually.

Tidal Streams
Tidal streams set northeast on the flood and southwest on the ebb but – as is usual in what is effectively mid-ocean – are generally weak.

Charts
Admiralty *1959* (1:150,000)
Portuguese *43103* (1:300,000), *46407* (1:75,000)
US *51081* (1:250,000)
Imray-Iolaire *E1* (1:750,000)

Lights
2638 **Ilhéus das Formigas** Fl(2)12s21m12M
White conical tower with double lantern 19m, situated near the northern end of the visible rocks

The unmarked Dollabarat Shoal with a least charted depth of 3m (though reputed locally to be as little as 1·2m) bears 133° from the Ilhéus das Formigas at a distance of 3·5M, near the southeastern edge of the bank. Even moderate swells break on the shoal, and bad weather creates ferocious seas. The whole area should be given a wide berth when on passage.

Anchorage and landing

The bank is composed mainly of rock, with areas of pale sand, shell and coral debris. Yachts have occasionally anchored off in exceptionally calm weather, but should not be left unattended due to poor holding and unpredictable currents. Landing is reported to be possible on the east side of the rocks, from where there is access to the lighthouse.

Websites

Perhaps unsurprisingly there appears to be no website devoted solely to the Ilhéus das Formigas other than a very interesting page on Wikipedia at www.en.wikipedia.org/wiki/Formigas. They are also mentioned briefly on a few of the general Azores sites listed on pages 24–5.

The Ilhéus das Formigas seen from the southeast
Fernando Tempera

Spectacular cliffs bisected by a delicate waterfall, at Paúl do Mar on Madeira's southwest coast

II. The Madeira Group

Index to islands

The archipelago

The Madeira archipelago consists of the island of Madeira itself, together with Porto Santo, the Desertas and the Selvagens. Although by far the smallest group described in this book, with some of the islands little more than large rocks, there is a wide diversity of land forms and related weather patterns, closely reflected in the differing flora and fauna. More detailed descriptions will be found under each individual island heading.

Many thousands of tourists visit Madeira annually and it says much for the character of the archipelago that, other than in the main hotel area around Funchal, both the islands and their people have remained remarkably unspoilt by the influx. The tiny terraced fields are in the main well tended, the forests protected rather than exploited, and the Madeiran people friendly and welcoming towards visitors.

Suggested waypoints are listed on pages 143 and 149, and in Appendix II, page 400.

History

Like the Azores, the islands of the Madeira archipelago drifted on the edge of the known world for many centuries. Genoese explorers were probably aware of their existence by the middle of the 13th century, and they may even have been known to the Arabs hundreds of years earlier. Recorded history begins in 1418 when João Gonçalves Zarco and Tristão Vaz Teixeira, on passage to Africa as part of Henry the Navigator's grand design, were driven off course by a gale and eventually sought shelter under the lee of an unknown island. The direction of the gale is not recorded, but it seems likely that it was a northerly, or Porto Santo – 'Holy Port' – might have received a less complimentary name. A rapid passage back to

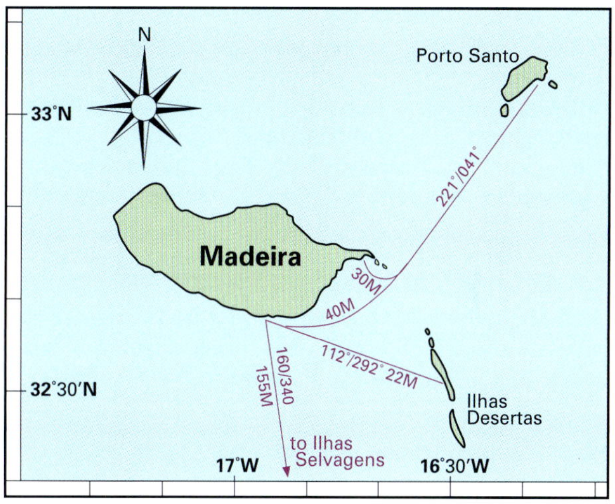

Courses and distances within the Madeira archipelago

Harbour	*Course / Reciprocal*	*Distance*
Porto Santo – Baía da Abra, Madeira	221° / 041° & by eye	29M
Porto Santo – Quinta do Lorde Marina, Madeira	221° / 041° & by eye	30M
Porto Santo – Funchal, Madeira	221° / 041° & by eye	40M
Quinta do Lorde Marina – Funchal, Madeira	by eye	13M
Quinta do Lorde Marina – Carga da Lapa, Ilhas Desertas	145° / 325° & by eye	17M
Funchal – Ponta do Sol (Marina do Lugar de Baixo), Madeira	by eye	11M
Funchal – Calheta, Madeira	by eye	16M
Funchal, Madeira – Carga da Lapa, Ilhas Desertas	112° / 292°	22M
Funchal, Madeira – Enseada das Cagarras, Selvagem Grande	160° / 340°	155M

Lisbon was followed by an equally hasty return, this time with orders to colonise the dry, uninhabited island before continuing to investigate the more mountainous one visible to the southwest. Porto Santo's first governor, who accompanied Zarco and Teixeira on their return, was Bartolomeu Perestrelo, a minor Portuguese nobleman chiefly remembered as father-in-law of Christopher Columbus.

Porto Santo had its share of ups and downs over the following centuries. Vines were established, together with vegetables and cereal crops, but rabbits introduced by the first settlers ate most of the natural vegetation down to the soil. Occasional pirate raids sent the inhabitants fleeing for safety to the heights of Pico do Facho, but the island's basic poverty was probably its best defence and also served to limit the population to a number which the land and surrounding seas could support. Life was not without excitement, including the wreck in 1724 of the Dutch treasure ship *Slot ter Hooge*, driven onto the north coast during a gale. Although much of her cargo of silver bars was recovered at the time, more finds have been made over recent years and are on display in the small museum in Vila Baleira on Porto Santo, as well as in the Quinta das Cruzes Museum in Funchal.

After centuries as a peaceful backwater, Porto Santo gained importance in 1960 with the opening of a large international airport – also a Reserve NATO Air Base – the first in the archipelago. Thousands of tourists arrived by air to transfer to the Madeira ferry, but within four years Madeira's own airport was complete and the traffic ceased. Porto Santo still receives long-haul flights when the runway at Madeira's Santa Catarina Airport is closed by strong crosswinds, and the occasional military exercise may take place, but the island is usually quiet and the pace of life slow. Having said that, the growth in the tourist industry even since the turn of the 21st century has been dramatic, with much of the long beach now backed by hotels and holiday developments, and a golf course in the northwest of the island. The authorities are to be commended, however, for ensuring that Vila Baleira retains its considerable charm – in fact the basic layout of the tiny capital can have changed little since Columbus lived there in 1480. Another thing which has not changed is the prevailing wind, and those who enjoy a touch of history in their cruising should take a leaf from Zarco and Teixeira's book and plan a landfall on Porto Santo before sailing on to Madeira. Even after five centuries of progress, the island of Porto Santo still lies over 20M dead to windward of its larger sister.

Madeira is famous for its mountain walks, but the mist can close in suddenly ...

Zarco and Teixeira landed on Madeira in July 1419, near where Machico now stands, claimed the island for Portugal, and returned the following year with the first permanent settlers. Within a few years sugar cane was introduced and quickly became an important export crop, followed in 1460 by vines from southern Europe. The sugar trade was responsible for attracting their most famous resident, Christopher Columbus, who lived in the islands for several years after marrying Perestrelo's daughter – though whether he met her in Lisbon or on his first visit to Madeira in the 1470s is not clear.

A vast amount of labour was needed to prepare the land for agriculture after the native woodland – the *madeira* from which the island gained its name – had been burned off, and to tend crops and build irrigation ditches. So in addition to immigration from the Portuguese mainland many slaves were brought from north and west Africa to work on the land, though little trace remains of them today. Funchal, with its relatively protected harbour, quickly grew in size and was granted city status in 1508, the cathedral being completed six years later in 1514.

Quiet prosperity and progress was interrupted by occasional setbacks, including an attack by French pirates in 1566 when Funchal was burned and many people killed, and the domination of the island by the Spanish between 1581 and 1640 following King Philip II of Spain's invasion and occupation of mainland Portugal. Many of the island's small protective forts were built at this time. After the restoration of the Portuguese monarchy British interest in the island, and particularly its unique wine, quickly returned, forging links which have only recently begun to weaken. Captain Cook visited Madeira twice around 1770, and in 1801 British troops were briefly stationed there to help protect it from the French. The defence force returned in 1807 during the Peninsula Wars and this time stayed for seven years, after which many of the soldiers chose to remain on the island to farm or grow vines. Unfortunately their prosperity was short-lived, with a succession of diseases attacking the vines in the 1850s coupled with a serious cholera epidemic, and then blight in the sugar crop in 1882.

However, Madeira's major modern industry was already becoming established with the beginnings of tourism, initially as a health resort for tuberculosis sufferers due to its clear air and mild but damp winter climate. During the First World War, in which Portugal joined the Allies, Funchal was twice attacked by German submarines – one of their victims still lies outside the harbour, ready to snag the anchors of unwary yachts. In 1921 the first aeroplane arrived in Madeira, a small seaplane which landed in Funchal harbour, but it was not until 1949 that a commercial seaplane service was established for passengers from Britain and northern Europe. However, less than a decade later two serious accidents brought flights to a halt, and for several years there were no air services to the islands until first Porto Santo and then Madeira gained airports in the early 1960s.

Since then tourism has grown at a pace which has threatened to drown more traditional ways of life, particularly the labour-intensive farming and viniculture. Sugar cane, although still grown, has become less important but Madeira wine is famous the world over with more than 13 million litres being produced annually, about half of which is fortified with brandy for export. In past years the barrels were transported in the holds of sailing ships which crossed the Atlantic before returning to Europe, the long, warm voyage giving the wine a distinctive flavour which is now produced artificially by gentle heating. Wine-tasting at an *armazem* is an essential part of any visit to Funchal, and the knowledge that bottles of Madeira taken back aboard have a proven history of travelling well under sail provides further incentive to buy.

Other industries are wicker and basketwork, made from locally grown osiers, and strikingly lovely embroidery. This last had long been made by the women of the island for their own use, but became a commercial concern around 1850 when an English lady, Mrs Phibbs, saw the opportunity for island women to supplement the family income while still remaining in their homes. Madeiran embroidery is said to have been on display at the Great Exhibition held in London in 1851. These small beginnings have led to a cottage industry employing women of all ages, some of whom one may still see on fine days in the villages outside Funchal, sitting on their doorsteps or by windows busily stitching away to produce what are probably Madeira's most original and genuine souvenirs.

Portugal's membership of the EU has brought some notable changes to Madeira, the two most obvious being the extended airport runway, a vast concrete apron supported by massive pillars rising up from the sea, and the dramatic new road system linking Caniçal in the east to Ribeira Brava, west of Funchal. However, while the *Via Rápida* network – see Road transport, on pages 135–6 – certainly makes life easier for the islanders, for the visitor in no particular hurry there is much to be said for getting off the beaten track. Madeira is full of contrasts, and it is worth making an effort to glimpse that older island known to the early settlers more than five centuries ago.

General information

Nationality and language

The Madeira archipelago is an autonomous region of Portugal, and therefore part of the European Union, with a governor resident in Funchal. Portuguese is spoken, but many Madeirans (particularly those concerned with the tourist trade) also understand Spanish, French, English or German.

Portuguese representation abroad

See page 21 of the Azores section.

Diplomatic representation in Madeira

The following are consulates – embassies are to be found in Lisbon:

UK: British Honorary Consulate, Rua da Alfandega 10, 3C, 9000-059 Funchal, Madeira ✆ 291 212860/7 http://ukinportugal.fco.gov.uk/en/help-for-british-nationals.
Open 0830–1330 weekdays; out of hours emergency assistance ✆ 213 924000.

USA: US Consular Agency, Rua da Alfândega, 10, 2°A/B, 9000-059 Funchal, Madeira ✆ 291 235636 *Email* ACAFunchal@eua.webside.pt
Open 0900–1300 weekdays. Closed on American and Portuguese Holidays.

Personal documentation

Passport and visa requirements are the same as for the Azores – see page 21.

Time

The Madeira group uses UT during the winter, as do both mainland Portugal and the UK, adding one hour (the equivalent to BST) during the summer. Changeover dates are normally the same as in the UK – i.e. the last weekends of March and October.

Money

Portugal, including Madeira, is part of the Eurozone. Most visitors rely on credit/debit cards, both for purchases and to withdraw cash – dispensers, often referred to as *Multibanco* – are to be found everywhere (except, currently, at Quinta do Lorde Marina) and accept all major cards. Most offer instructions in a choice of languages, including English.

Sterling, US dollars and other major currencies are readily exchangeable in banks, as are travellers cheques, but are less likely to be accepted by shops, hotels or restaurants. Banks normally open 0830–1500 weekdays only, though *Bureau de Change* offices may be open considerably longer hours, including all day Saturday.

Most restaurants, shops, car rental companies and other concerns welcome payment by credit card – principally Visa, MasterCard and American Express – but it is as well to confirm this in advance, particularly where fuel (for both yachts and vehicles) is concerned.

Shopping

As in most countries, town centre shopping is being eclipsed by out-of-town superstores – *hipermercado* in Portuguese – at least as far as foodstuffs are concerned. Otherwise, by far the best general shopping in the Madeira group is to be found in Funchal, which boasts a vast number of tourist-orientated shops as well as those to be found in any city of medium size. Most of the major Portuguese chains are represented in Madeira, including Pingo Doce, SA, Continente and Modelo with, as of late 2010, prices generally somewhat higher than in mainland Europe but a little lower than those found in the Canaries. The larger supermarkets provide almost everything that one might expect to find in their British or American equivalents, and plenty that one might not, though tinned meats, other than frankfurters, corned beef and luncheon meats, are seldom to be had. Alcohol, of which a wide choice is available, is considerably cheaper than in England.

Funchal's produce market remains superb, both visually and practically. Locally grown fruit and vegetables of all kinds are sold at very reasonable prices on the ground floor and in the gallery above, but not all vendors supply bags – or egg boxes. One local vegetable worth trying is the christophene, which resembles an oversized and sometimes spiky pear and has a consistency midway between cucumber and courgette. It can be eaten raw or cooked and will keep for at least six weeks, adding some crunch to the often rather bland ocean-crossing diet.

A brightly-painted fishing boat in Porto Moniz...

... on which the crew waste no time in salting down the catch

Surrounding the produce market are stalls selling fresh meat, with a large fish market to the rear of the building – worth a visit even if not intending to buy. A local delicacy is *espada* (scabbard fish), an evil-looking creature which lives at great depths and tastes delicious, with the added advantage of apparently having very few bones. For a few extra cêntimos the fish of one's choice will be gutted, cleaned and filleted, ready to be taken back aboard and sautéed gently in a little olive oil and garlic...

Some notes regarding ships' stores – principally fuel, bottled gas and chandlery – will be found on page 139.

Communications

Mail

All four operational marinas will hold mail for yachts whose arrival is anticipated. Addresses will be found in the Communications section of the relevant harbour details, and it is worth stressing that the word 'Portugal' should always be included. Mail from the UK usually takes about a week, longer from the USA.

Post office opening hours vary, but stamps (*selos*) can also be bought at newsagents and souvenir shops where the green *correio* sign is seen, or from vending machines, which list current rates but do not give change. There are two classes of mail, *correio azul* and *correio normal* – effectively express and fairly slow – with the former also noticeably more reliable.

Incoming packages

Much the same problems may occur as in the Azores – see page 22. Consult the marina office for advice.

Telephones

As in many countries, public telephones are seen as a lower priority with the widespread use of mobile (cell) phones. Even so, they are still to be found in most towns and details will be found under individual harbours. Not all, however, take coins, some requiring cards purchased from post offices, supermarkets and bars. Mobile phone coverage throughout both Madeira and Porto Santo is generally excellent, though there are 'holes' in some of Madeira's mountain valleys. Unsurprisingly, coverage fades as one heads offshore and does not extend to either the Ilhas Desertas or Ilhas Selvagens.

Calls to the United Kingdom begin with the prefix 0044, followed by the area code (without the initial zero) and number. Calls to the United States and Canada begin with the prefix 001 and the area code plus number. The US access code for AT&T, www.att.com, is 800 800 128.

The international dialling code for Portugal, including the Madeira, group is 351, and the area code for both Madeira and Porto Santo 291. This latter prefix must be included when dialling any landline number, even when calling from within the same island. Any telephone number not starting with this sequence can be assumed to be a mobile.

The costs incurred by using a mobile phone abroad are beyond the scope of this book, and individual phones may need 'unblocking' before they will work at all. If planning to spend some time in one country (remembering that the Azores and Madeira comprise a single entity in this context) it may be cheaper to buy a new phone or at least a new SIM card. The Portuguese have one of the highest rates of mobile phone – or *telemóvel* – ownership in Europe and nearly all shops will have at least one salesman fluent in English.

Fax

Although declining in use with the ubiquity of email, all four operational marinas will send and receive faxes for yachts – see individual harbours details. Many companies advertising photocopying also have a fax machine, as do most hotels.

Internet access

With email the communication method of choice for the majority of cruising sailors, free Wi-Fi is now available at or near all four operational marinas, either provided by the marina itself or by the locality – see photograph. In the latter case, however, power may not be available so reasonable battery life is essential. Cybercafés and other access points (public libraries, town halls or computer clubs) are also widespread.

Free Wi-Fi is available at many 'hotspots' throughout Madeira, a very progressive policy which other administrations would do well to follow

Electricity

Mains electricity is 220v 50Hz, as is standard throughout mainland Europe, and yachts from elsewhere should beware a probable difference in both volts and cycles. All Madeira's electricity (though not Porto Santo's) is generated by hydro-electric plants, making it so cheap that street lighting can be left on with impunity. Thus Madeiran towns often appear to be lit like beacons when seen from offshore at night.

Transportation

International and inter-island flights

Many airlines, both scheduled and charter, provide flights to Madeira from departure airports throughout Europe and North America. Schedules change frequently and the best deals will be found via the internet. Most flights are direct, though a few may be routed through Lisbon or Porto. Live arrivals and departure information is given in Portuguese and English on the *Aeroportos da Madeira* website at www.anam.pt/English-254.aspx. Most flights to/from Porto Santo take a detour via Funchal, but a few fly direct to the Portuguese mainland – there are currently no international flights from the island.

If planning crew changes it is worth bearing in mind that Madeira's Santa Catarina Airport is a long and expensive taxi-ride from Porto de Recreio da Calheta or even from Funchal, but much closer to Quinta do Lorde Marina and only a few kilometres from the anchorage at Machico. The airport on Porto Santo is near the town and harbour.

Ferries

Porto Santo Line's 112m car ferry *Lobo Marinho* provides a regular service between Funchal and the smaller island. She departs Funchal breakwater at 0800 daily except Tuesdays (when there is no service either way) and, during parts of the year, on Friday when there is an 1800 service instead; leaving Porto Santo at 1800, or 2230 on Fridays. The crossing takes just under 2½ hours and there is generally no need for foot passengers to book. Check the company's website www.portosantoline.pt for current schedules.

There are no regular services to the Ilhas Desertas or Ilhas Selvagens, though local vessels sometimes run day trips to the former in suitable weather and at least one company runs occasion voyages to the latter – see http://selvagens.seawatching.net.

A Spanish company, Armas Naviera, www.navieraarmas.com, runs a passenger and car ferry service from Portimão in the Algarve to Madeira, and thence to the Canaries (Lanzarote, Gran Canaria and Tenerife). The Portimão to Madeira service runs once a week, departing the mainland on Wednesday and Madeira on Tuesday, and takes just under 24 hours.

A great many cruise ships call at Funchal, but are unlikely to be of interest to yachtsmen except as a potential hazard.

Road transport

At least a dozen car hire agencies vie for custom in Madeira, most with offices at the airport and in Funchal, while those in Porto Santo are mainly located at the airport. Cars can also be delivered to, and collected from, a marina or other location for an additional fee. All car hire firms accept major credit cards and will require a card number to be left as 'deposit'. Either national or international driving licences are accepted, provided the former has been held for at least one year, and note that it is a legal

Vertiginous vineyards on the northwest coast of Madeira

requirement to carry one's passport and driving licence at all times when at the wheel. Most petrol stations (at least one in each town of any size) still have attendant service, but note that even in the 21st century some still do not accept credit cards.

There have been vast improvements to the road system in Madeira over the past 25 years, most notably the growth of the *Via Rápida* expressway system which now runs from Caniçal to Ribeira Brava, a succession of soaring concrete bridges and seemingly endless tunnels. If time is not important, however, far more will be seen by choosing the 'old' road, now mercifully relieved of fast through traffic, as it snakes its way around the valley sides – but do allow for the fact that, despite the lack of width and blind bends, most pedestrians and all dogs appear to take immortality for granted. Driving on Porto Santo is considerably easier, with roads generally wide, straight and fairly empty, but once again other users – whether on four legs or two – may act unpredictably on occasion.

Buses run throughout Madeira and are an excellent and economical way to see the interior. The eastern part of the island is covered by SAM (*Sociedade de Automóveis da Madeira*) and the western by Rodoeste, with websites at www.sam.pt and www.rodoeste.pt/horarios.html respectively. Neither website has an English version, but they are relatively simple to follow with route maps and downloadable timetables. Most buses run to and from Funchal, departing from a depot on the front a few minutes' walk east of the marina where timetables are on display. Roadside bus stops (marked *Paragem* or *Paragem de Autocarro*) do not usually display timetable or routes. On Porto Santo buses generally leave about once every hour from near the filling station on the southeast side of Vila Baleira, with a timetable on display nearby. The ferry's arrival and departure always merits its own bus, in 2010 charging €1 for the ride into the town. Coach tours to all the main places of interest in Madeira are readily available, mainly aimed at cruise ship and hotel guests and booked via hotel reception desks and travel agents.

Taxis in both islands are yellow with a broad blue stripe (the colours of the Madeiran flag) and are generally plentiful. Fares in Funchal and its environs are pre-set, but all taxis should be fitted with automatic tariff counters. Porto Santo's only taxi rank is in the town centre, though the arrival of the ferry is always well attended. All four operational marinas will phone for taxis on request.

Walking and hitchhiking

Madeira is famous for its mountain walks along the *levadas*, the island-wide irrigation and drainage system which provides paths through the otherwise untouched forests. Those intending to explore seriously on foot should buy a copy of *Landscapes of Madeira* by John and Pat Underwood in the *Sunflower Landscapes* series, now in its 10th edition, which gives details of routes and also of the small, cheap but clean and convenient rest-houses built by the *Direcção Regional de Turismo* near the summits of some of the highest peaks.

Further information

Madeira and Porto Santo are the subject of several general tourist guides readily available in the UK and elsewhere – see Further Reading, page 403. Once in the islands colourful leaflets and maps (including bus routes) can be obtained from the tourist offices in the larger towns – that in Funchal is situated at Avenida Arriaga 18, Funchal, with branches on Rua Dr Vieira da Castro in Porto Santo and at the airport.

The islands are well represented on the internet and the following sites (listed alphabetically) contain general information, some of which may be useful to the visiting yachtsman.

www.apram.pt – homepage of APRAM (the Madeiran Ports Administration), in Portuguese and English. Concerned mainly with commercial shipping (cargo and tourist) it nevertheless has some pages to interest yachtsmen

www.cm-funchal.pt – homepage of the Camâra Municipal (Town Hall) of Funchal, in Portuguese only

www.en.wikipedia.org/wiki/Madeira and **www.en.wikipedia.org/wiki/Porto_Santo_Island** – long and detailed even by Wikipedia standards, these sites probably offer the best background information on the islands and their history available on the web today

www.flytap.com – homepage of TAP (*Transportes Aéreos Portugueses*), Portugal's national airline. In Portuguese and English

www.gov-madeira.pt – homepage of the Regional Government of the archipelago, in Portuguese only

www.guia-madeira.net – an interesting site in Portuguese, Spanish, English, French, German and Italian with island history, folklore and gastronomy, in addition to the standard topics. Pity about the musical accompaniment...

www.hidrografico.pt – website of the Portuguese *Instituto Hidrográfico*, with details of charts, lights etc. In Portuguese only, but relatively easy to follow

www.madeiraguide.co.uk – a somewhat commercial site with links to tour operators, hire car firms etc., despite being independently run. In good, though not perfect, English

www.madeira-island.com – a commercial website with numerous links, but not the easiest of sites to navigate. Great photo gallery!

www.madeiraisland.com/english – laid out in headline style with 'read more' tags, this is not a visually impressive site. On digging deeper there's a great deal there, however, as each story links to others on the same topic. All are dated, apparently all prior to June 2008

www.madeiraislands.travel – the islands' official tourism website, in Portuguese, English, French, German and Spanish. Well-constructed and packed with useful and entertaining facts about the two major islands, from history and infrastructure down to 'stop press' news on which *levadas* (foot paths) are currently closed for maintenance. An excellent introduction to the islands

www.madeiraonline.com – a useful reference site containing lists of everything from doctors to someone who can fix your onboard computer, though not all are Madeira-based. Quite a few links appear to be broken. In English only

www.madeira-web.com – one of the Strawberry World series in Portuguese, English, German and Spanish. Particularly striking photographs backed by up-to-the-minute text

www.madeiraweb.info/ – after an unpromisingly commercial start, the eco-tourism link yields up pages on Madeira's five main nature reserves and rare plants

www.madeirawine.com – a complete guide to the island's most famous export, in Portuguese and English, including online sales. Well written and illustrated ... cheers!

www.meteo.pt – the website of Portugal's *Instituto de Meteorologia*, which provides immediate, five-day and 10-day weather forecasts (and much more besides) for six cities across the archipelago, in Portuguese and English. In early 2011 'Marine Meteorology' pages were under construction

www.netmadeira.com – a government-run site, in Portuguese only but quite easy to navigate. TV schedules, live web-cams and a list of duty pharmacies demonstrate its range

www.sata.pt – homepage of SATA (*Sociedade Açôreana da Transportes Aérios*) the Azores airline, which started small but now offers services to destinations including the US and Canada, the UK and many cities in mainland Europe. In Portuguese and English. See page 135 for further details

www.sra.pt/jarbot – website of Madeira's long-established Botanical Gardens, in Portuguese and English. Recommended (as is the Jardim Botânico itself)

www.travel-images.com – dozens of pictures of Madeira and Porto Santo (plus a couple of the Ilhas Selvagens), but with little accompanying text. All photographs are copyright, and while viewing is free downloading them is not

www.wikitravel.org/en/Madeira – everything you might ever need to know about travelling to or within the islands, with dozens of links. Finishes with a plea to add your knowledge and help it grow...

Updates to the book are available online at www.sunflowerbooks.co.uk. For those less keen to walk uphill it is often possible to get a bus to a viewpoint or place of interest and walk part or all of the way down. Hitchhiking does not seem to be common, though the chances of a lift may be better once off the beaten track.

Medical

The only immunisation required is against yellow fever if coming from certain Central American and African countries, though many people will also chose to keep vaccinations against tetanus and polio up-to-date. Funchal has a number of hospitals, including at least two with round-the-clock emergency departments, plus numerous clinics and health centres. There are also many well-stocked pharmacies as well as dentists and opticians, though wearers of glasses would be wise to carry a copy of their prescription (in addition to at least one reserve pair). Both Machico and Porto Santo have small hospitals, but serious medical emergencies are normally taken to Funchal.

Although in theory unnecessary, European citizens are well-advised to carry a European Health Insurance Card (EHIC), which entitles the holder to state-provided medical treatment in the country they are visiting. Application is straightforward – see www.ehic.org.uk for details – and there is no charge. In 2006 the EHIC replaced the E111, which is no longer valid. Otherwise, much of the advice in the Medical section referring to the Azores – see page 25 – holds good.

National holidays

These are much the same as in mainland Portugal, with a few regional differences:

1 January	New Year's Day
moveable	Carnival Tuesday (38 days before Easter)
moveable	Good Friday
25 April	National or Portugal Day
1 May	Labour Day
moveable	Corpus Christi
10 June	Portugal Day (Camões Day)
1 July	Madeira Day
15 August	Feast of the Assumption
5 October	Republic Day
1 November	All Saints' Day
1 December	Restoration of Independence Day
8 December	Immaculate Conception
25 December	Christmas Day
26 December	Boxing Day

In addition, each town or area celebrates its own municipal holiday, Porto Santo's on 24 June and Funchal's on 21 August. Almost everything except cafés and restaurants is likely to be shut, but there may be the bonus of a *festa* (festival) with processions or one of the ever-popular firework displays.

Sailing and navigation

Practicalities

Entry and regulations

All four functioning marinas are now official ports of entry. All formalities are handled by marina officials, who enter details on the port control authority's database. Requirements for EU and non-EU flagged vessels differ so far as the attendance of officials is concerned, and a non-EU flagged vessel should try to give its intended port of entry 24 hours notice of arrival. Skippers of yachts arriving from the Canaries – which are not part of the EU – have to complete an additional declaration of ship's stores and other items.

As in the Azores it is necessary to clear into and out of each island individually, obtaining outward clearance before leaving Porto Santo and going through the process again on reaching the larger island.

International Certificate of Competence

The same rules apply as in the Azores – see page 27 – though, as in the former, it is rarely inspected.

Port limits

Formal port limits, where various local byelaws apply, are in place around Funchal and may be extended to other harbours. Scuba diving is forbidden on security grounds, although swimming and snorkelling is generally permitted, and if wishing to scuba dive – perhaps to check the yacht's propeller or hull – it is essential to seek permission from the authorities first.

Cruising permits

If intending to visit either the Ilhas Desertas or the Ilhas Selvagens the skipper MUST obtain a permit before leaving Madeira. These are issued, without charge, by the National Parks Department from their office at the Botanical Gardens northeast of Funchal (well worth a visit in its own right). Although one can apply in person all four marina offices will handle the paperwork on request, in which case allow at least 48 hours, not including weekends, for the permit to be received.

Note that this is NOT a formality. Wardens guard both archipelagoes zealously, and those arriving without a valid permit are most unlikely to be allowed to land.

Laying up

There are three places in the Madeira group where a yacht might be laid up ashore – in the boatyard at Porto Santo, in the commercial yard at Caniçal and in the new facility under the airport runway at Água de Pena. Of these, currently only Caniçal can haul multihulls, though a marine railway is due to be installed at Porto Santo, hopefully for the 2012 season. Further information on each will be found under the individual harbour details.

A yacht could be laid up afloat at any time of year in either the Porto Santo or Quinta do Lorde marinas, both of which have good reputations for looking after yachts in their care. Ongoing problems with surge in the Porto de Recreio da Calheta mean that it cannot be recommended as a safe place to leave a yacht unattended during the winter, but it should be acceptable at other times or if crew are living aboard. There is no room to lay up in Funchal Marina.

Value Added Tax (*Imposto sobre o Valor Acrescentado*, or IVA)

Value Added Tax, commonly referred to as VAT, is known in Portuguese as *Imposto sobre o Valor Acrescentado* (IVA). Madeira enjoys a reduced rate, which on 1 January 2011 increased from 15% to 16% as against 23% in mainland Portugal. Food, water, electricity, pharmacy items, and – a little oddly – wine and restaurant meals are all taxed at a lower rate. Refer to the relevant section for the Azores (page 27) regarding documentation, time limits for which relief is available, etc.

'Long-stay' tax (*Imposto Unico de Circulação*)

Yachts which remain in Portuguese waters for more than 183 days in a calendar year, whether local or foreign-registered and afloat or ashore, may be liable to pay a tax known as *Imposto Unico de Circulação* (IUC) and calculated according to engine capacity. Refer to the relevant section for the Azores (page 28) for full details.

Lighthouse tax (*Taxa de Farolagem e Balizagem*)

In theory all yachts, including visitors, are liable to pay lighthouse tax. This is currently set at €2 for six months irrespective of the size of yacht, and is collected by the *Polícia Marítima*, usually from an office within the *Capitania*. In practice it does not appear to be actively collected in either Madeira or Porto Santo, but if it has been paid in mainland Portugal or the Azores it would be worth retaining the receipt.

Ships' stores

Diesel (*gasóleo*, pronounced *gas-OH-leo*) is available alongside in all four operational marinas, petrol (*gasolina*, pronounced *gas-ol-EE-na*) from all except Porto Santo. Elsewhere both must be transported by can from filling stations. Note that credit cards are not always accepted when buying fuel for either yachts or cars, and where they are an additional fee is often levied. If buying fuel at a filling station it is worth paying particular attention to pronunciation, as if the stress falls on the final vowels of *gasóleo* a Portuguese-speaker may well hear it as *gasolina*, with disastrous consequences. Confusion can also arise with paraffin or kerosene (*petróleo*, pronounced *petr-OH-leo*, though both *parafina* and *querosene* are likely to be understood) though less potentially dangerous than if the situation were reversed. Paraffin is available in two grades – poor quality from some filling stations (suitable for cleaning machinery but not for lamps or stoves) and a more expensive grade from chemists which burns well. Methylated spirits is *álcool metílico* (*AL-cool met-IL-ico*) and surgical spirits is *álcool etílico* (*AL-cool et-IL-ico*).

Butane gas is obtainable in both Porto Santo and Madeira, but in Camping Gaz rather than Calor Gas bottles. Calor Gas cylinders, as well as most American and Scandinavian bottles, can be refilled in Madeira (where it may take up to four days) but not in Porto Santo. Propane is not available, but no safety risk is incurred by refilling propane bottles with butane. At the time of going to press there were problems with refilling gas bottles throughout the Canary Islands, so some may wish to get them refilled in Madeira even if they are not completely empty.

There are two chandleries in Funchal (see page 163) and one in Machico (page 158), but stocks are inevitably limited and, due to transportation costs, prices are generally higher than in mainland Portugal. All three have catalogues from major manufacturers and suppliers and are willing to order in from Lisbon, often in as little as three working days. No duty is payable on spares or equipment ordered from within the EU, but importing parts from elsewhere (including the US) can be a lengthy process involving a variable import duty plus administrative and handling charges. In some cases it may prove not only faster, but also considerably cheaper, to pay the airfare of a friend or relative willing to act as 'courier' of the essential item.

Cruising

For many years the Madeira group was viewed by cruising yachtsmen as little more than a convenient stopover *en route* to either the Canaries or the Caribbean. Until Funchal Marina was built in the early 1980s there was nowhere that a yacht could shelter from poor weather, and within a very few years of opening the marina was so full of local craft that once again visiting yachts were forced to anchor outside. From the late 1980s yachts began to be welcomed into the large NATO-built harbour at Porto Santo, and for a number of years most yachtsmen who visited the larger island did so by ferry.

By 2011 the pendulum had swung back, with Quinta do Lorde Marina in the east and Porto de Recreio da Calheta in the west both welcoming cruisers for stays ranging from a day or two to a year or more. Outside the busy autumn season a few cruising yachts were still able to berth in Funchal, though the anchorage was much reduced – see page 162. Although confusion can arise in Portuguese-speaking countries where *ancondouro* means both anchoring and mooring, in the case of Funchal it is used in its normal UK sense.

The additional berthing may encourage some owners to arrive earlier and stay longer, but the vast majority will continue to visit between September and November. Unfortunately for them most rainfall occurs between October and February inclusive, peaking in November and December, with the mountains of Madeira receiving the lion's share and the much lower Porto Santo very little. Temperatures are mild throughout the year, averaging 24°C in summer and 16°C in winter, while water temperatures average 22°C in summer and 18°C in winter.

Barometric pressure and winds

The Madeira group lies on the northern fringe of the true trade winds, but at the southern extremity of the northerly Portuguese trade winds. Thus north to northeasterlies prevail for at least 60% of the year, and are slightly more likely in summer than in autumn and winter when the passage of depressions across the North Atlantic can produce strong west or southwesterly winds. The trades generally blow at 10–25 knots, although there is a fairly high incidence of calms throughout the whole year, and in most years true gales are rare.

The south coast of Madeira, however, and Funchal in particular, often experiences local weather conditions which bear no resemblance to those further out to sea. The high mountains which form the island's spine effectively block the north and northeasterly winds, often leaving the south coast calm at night with fresh onshore winds building up during the day from between southwest and southeast. These usually die by sunset but can leave an onshore swell running for the rest of the night.

The eastern end of the island is lower and narrower and thus experiences a truer wind – usually northwest in Machico where it funnels down the valley, and north in Baía da Abra due to a saddle in the narrow peninsula which runs out toward Ilhéu de Fora. Quinta do Lorde Marina lies in the windshadow of high cliffs and may frequently experience light breezes even when it is fresh to strong offshore.

Having said that, the winter of 2009–2010 was one of the worst ever recorded, in Madeira as well as northwest Africa and southwest Iberia. An experienced cruising couple who wintered in Quinta do Lorde marina aboard their heavy displacement 45-footer reported that: 'The polar front was apparently well south of its usual position, and we experienced extended periods of strong west or southwest winds, with low pressure systems tracking close to the island and sometimes even to the south. James Clarke's *Atlantic Pilot Atlas* indicates '2% gales' for February in the area of Madeira. Due to the island topography there are local acceleration zones, often with substantial wind shifts from the prevailing direction, so instrument readings need to be interpreted accordingly. Nevertheless, prolonged winds of between near and severe gale force (28–47 knots) were frequently recorded – often twice or more per week, and usually interrupted by winds of force 4–6 (11–27 knots).' February 2010 also saw some of the worst floods and landslides in Madeira's history, though neither Quinta do Lorde Marina nor Porto de Recreio da Calheta were directly affected. It should be stressed, however, that this weather remains very much the exception rather than the norm.

Visibility

Sea fog is almost unknown around the Madeira group, though it is frequently misty in the mountains and particularly on the high plateau of Paúl da Serra which occupies much of the western end of Madeira. Poor visibility at sea is most likely between July and September, when a dry, dusty, easterly wind known as *l'este* sometimes cuts visibility to within a few miles.

Weather forecasts

A Navtex station has been planned for Porto Santo for a decade or more (see page 143), but it was still not operational by early 2011. There is no other Navtex transmitter in the Madeira group.

Various websites carrying worldwide weather information are listed on page 9. In addition, three-day, five-day and ten-day general forecasts for Madeira and Porto Santo are available from Portugal's *Instituto de Meteorologia* at www.meteo.pt, in English as well as Portuguese.

In port, daily forecasts accompanied by synoptic charts are displayed at all four functioning marinas.

Magnetic variation

In 2011 magnetic variation varied from 5°45'W to 6°10'W throughout the archipelago, decreasing by about 8'E annually. Details for each island will be found in the text.

Tides and tidal streams

Volume 2 of the Admiralty Tide Tables: *The Atlantic and Indian Oceans including tidal stream predictions (NP 202)*, published annually, covers the Madeira group with Casablanca as standard port. Much the same information is available from the UK

Although native to South Africa, for many the Bird of Paradise flower (*Strelitzia reginae*) is synonymous with Madeira

Hydrographic Office's excellent *EasyTide* programme at http://easytide.ukho.gov.uk which gives daily tidal data for Porto Santo, Funchal, Porto da Cruz, Porto de Moniz and the Ilhas Selvagens.

Maximum mean spring range is no more than 2·2m and, while there is variation, high water can be reckoned to occur about three hours after high water Dover at springs and 3·5 hours after high water Dover at neaps. Tidal streams run northeast or east-northeast on the flood and reverse direction on the ebb, attaining 1·25 knots at springs and 0·5 knots at neaps.

Currents

Ocean currents flow south or southwest past the Madeira group at about 0·5 knots. However, an anticlockwise current runs inshore along the southwest coast of Madeira itself, meeting the main flow off Ponta de Cruz (close west of Funchal) and creating a clockwise eddy which may extend up to 4M offshore.

Navigational aids

Radio communications

Since the withdrawal of the very useful *NP289: Maritime Communications, United Kingdom and the Mediterranean* and *NP290: Maritime Communications, Caribbean* those wishing to carry details of all official radio communications in the Madeira archipelago now need to invest in three UKHO volumes – *NP281(1) Maritime Radio Stations*; *NP283(1) Maritime Safety Information Services* and *NP 286(1) Pilot Services, Vessel Traffic Services and Port Operations*.

Buoys and lights

All buoys and lights in the Madeira group follow the IALA A system, as used in western Europe. Whilst those on the major islands have a good operational record, maintenance of outlying lights – in particular those on the Ilhas Selvagens – is sometimes rendered difficult if not impossible by severe weather so that they may occasionally remain unlit for weeks at a time.

Note also that not every light listed in the text can be shown on the plans, in particular on the small-scale 'island' plans. Refer instead to the relevant – and preferably corrected – chart.

Charts

The most detailed charts of the Madeira archipelago are those published by the Portuguese Hydrographic Institute, www.hidrografico.pt, which covers the islands on eight sheets. These consist of a small-scale chart of the entire archipelago, two medium-scale charts again covering all the islands at a slightly larger scale, and fourteen approach and harbour plans on various scales.

British Admiralty charts, www.ukho.gov.uk, depict the archipelago on five sheets, comprising two small-scale charts (one including an inset of the Ilhas Selvagens) and six approach and harbour plans on various scales. The US National Geospatial-Intelligence Agency devotes three sheets to the islands. Though no longer available directly from the NGIA, they can be ordered online from approved suppliers. See page 396 for further details. Finally Imray Laurie Norie & Wilson Ltd's *Imray-Iolaire* series covers the archipelago on a single sheet, *E3*, at scale of 1:170,000, with four inset approach and harbour plans.

Some Portuguese, Admiralty and Imray charts are available from the Maré and Imersão chandleries in Funchal (see *Charts*, page 164), but stocks are generally limited to the Madeira group and adjacent waters and coverage of further afield would need to be ordered in.

See Appendix I, page 396, for chart lists.

Chart datum and satellite derived positions

Not all British Admiralty charts of the Madeira group are based on WGS84 Datum – e.g. positions taken from Admiralty *1831, Arquipélago da Madeira*, must be moved 0·22 minutes north and 0·25 minutes west to comply with both WGS84 and the plans in this guide. Other charts should be checked individually. For a fuller explanation see Horizontal chart datum on page 10 of the Passages section.

Caution and request

Any writer of pilot books takes a calculated risk when it comes to describing unfinished projects. The optimistic remarks regarding the Marina do Lugar de Baixo which appeared in the previous edition have proved to be unfounded, whereas those about Porto de Recreio da Calheta were substantially correct – just a small part of the information to be found in the interim supplements carried on the websites of both Imray Norie Laurie & Wilson Ltd, www.imray.com, and the RCC Pilotage Foundation, www.rccpf.org.uk.

The author and publisher are indebted to the hundreds of yachtsmen and women who have taken the trouble to send in corrections, comments and photographs for these supplements, either by email to ilnw@imray.com or by post to Imray Laurie Norie & Wilson Ltd, Wych House, The Broadway, St Ives, Cambs PE27 5BT. Even in these days of information overload there is nothing to compare with direct feedback from someone who is actually on the spot – thank you, and long may it continue!

Porto Santo

Between 32°60'N–33°08'N and 16°17'W–16°25'W

Introduction

Although discovered the year before Madeira and the only other inhabited island in the archipelago, Porto Santo has always been something of a poor relation due to its much smaller size and arid climate. Like Madeira it is of volcanic origin, and though much of the lower land consists of sandstones several of the higher peaks are unmistakably volcanic cones. It is barely 5% of the size of its sister island, with dimensions of around 11km by 6km giving it a land area of only 41km^2 – apparently much of that sandy beach.

Porto Santo is totally different from Madeira in both appearance and character and is well worth exploring. A taxi tour of the island, visiting the viewpoints at Portela overlooking the harbour, Pico do Castelo high in the centre, and Cabeco do Zimbralinho in the extreme southwest, plus the freshwater springs at Fonte de Areia (literally 'Fountain of Sand') perched halfway up the cliffs to the northwest, takes two hours or more. Alternatively, the energetic can walk and scramble over much of the island, with the views from the summits of Pico do Facho (506m) and Pico de Ana Ferreira (281m) said to be well worth the climb.

Vila Baleira is an attractive little town with a distinctly Mediterranean air of whitewash, palm trees and dust. Flower gardens lead from the old pier up to a tiny square overlooked by the venerable *câmara municipal* (town hall) and 15th-century church, with Columbus's reputed home on the island (now a small museum) up a narrow lane behind the latter. Like many Portuguese museums this is closed on Monday, but is open 1000–1230, 1400–1730 from Tuesday to Saturday, and 1000–1300 on Sunday.

However for many the biggest attraction of Porto Santo is its superb beach, the equal of anything the Caribbean has to offer except perhaps in the matter of water temperature. As Madeira itself has no beaches to speak of, and much cloudier weather due to its extra height, it is easy to see why so many Madeirans crowd off the ferry at weekends or own holiday homes on the island.

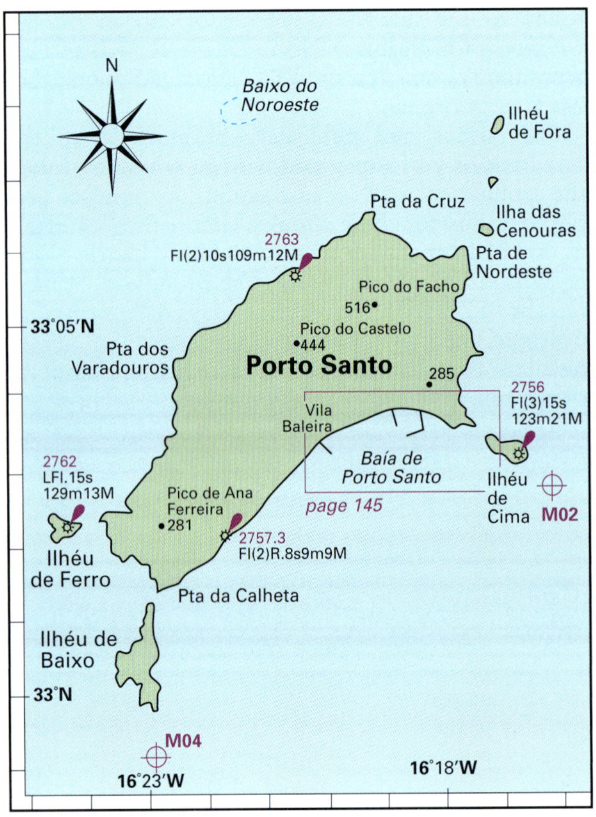

Telecommunications

Mobile (cell) phone reception throughout the island is good. The country code for the Madeira group is 351, as it is for mainland Portugal, and the area code for Porto Santo 291, which must be included even when dialling from within the island.

By 2011 free Wi-Fi was available in many places throughout the island including the marina, the main square and the airport.

Websites

By early 2011 a number of websites covered Porto Santo, mostly somewhat 'in passing', though it also features in most of those devoted to the archipelago as a whole – see page 137. Among the most informative single-island sites were www.portosanto.biz, subtitled 'a simple guide to Porto Santo Island', but user-friendly and well organised, in English only; www.porto-santo.com, one of the Strawberry World series of general tourist

Pristine sand near the west end of the Baía de Porto Santo

guides, with some striking photographs but limited text in English, German and Portuguese, and www.flickr.com/groups/portosantoisland on which anyone can post their photos taken in the island.

Porto Santo is perhaps best served by Wikipedia at www.en.wikipedia.org/wiki/Porto_Santo_Island, with the usual authoritative summary of history, geology, geography and economy plus a few photographs.

Approach

Porto Santo and its off-lying islets lie just over 21M northeast of Madeira itself, and appear from a distance to consist of several steep and isolated hills. Unlike Madeira, Porto Santo is very arid and there is little vegetation to be seen, though attempts are being made at reforestation.

The northwest, northeast and east coasts mostly consist of steep cliffs fringed by rocks within 0·5M of the shore, plus several small off-lying islands which are easily visible in daylight but are totally unlit and could be hazardous at night. In bad weather the Baixo do Noroeste, which lies about 5·5M northwest of Ponta da Cruz, breaks heavily and should also be avoided, but in fair weather its least depth of 9m will not concern a yacht. There is reputed to be good fishing over the bank.

If approaching from the northeast, as do the vast majority of yachts, Ilhéu de Cima with its powerful light may be rounded within 0·5M to bring the long sandy beach which forms the southeast coast of Porto Santo into view. When arriving from the northwest, Ilhéu de Ferro and Ilhéu de Baixo (unlit) can be left close to port before rounding up into the bay.

Submarines occasionally exercise in the waters between Porto Santo and Madeira.

Golden sands stretch for more than four miles (7km) along the south coast of Porto Santo. In contrast, its larger sister island has almost no natural beaches at all

Navigation

Waypoints

⊕ M01 – 33°09'N 16°15'·2W (2M NE of Ilhéu de Fora)
⊕ M02 – 33°02'·8N 16°16'·2W (0·5M SE of Ilhéu de Cima)
⊕ M03 – 33°02'·3N 16°26'·5W (1·5M W of Ilhéu de Ferro)
⊕ M04 – 32°59'·2N 16°22'·9W (0·5M S of Ilhéu de Baixo)
⊕ M05 – 33°03'·1N 16°19'·1W (0·4M SSW of Porto Santo harbour)

Courses and distances

⊕ M01 – ⊕ M02 = 6·5M, 188° / 008°
⊕ M02 – ⊕ M05 = 2·5M, 277° / 097°
⊕ M03 – ⊕ M04 = 4·5M, 136° / 316°
⊕ M04 – ⊕ M05 = 5·5M, 038° / 218°
⊕ M05 – ⊕ M06 (1M SE of Ilhéu de Fora, Madeira) = 42M, 342° / 162°

Magnetic variation

5°45'W (2011), decreasing by 9'E annually.

Tidal streams

Tidal streams run northeast on the flood and southwest on the ebb at 0·5 to 1·25 knots.

Charts

Admiralty *1831* (1:150,000)
Portuguese *36401* (1:50,000)
US *51261* (1:150,000)
Imray-Iolaire *E3* (1:170,000)

Lights

2756 **Ilhéu de Cima** Fl(3)15s123m21M
Aeromaritime 163°-vis-042°
Square white tower and building, red lantern 15m
2757·3 **Cabeço cables**
Fl(2)R.8s9m9M 308°-vis-328° Daytime range 3M
White post, red bands 4m. Marks submarine cables
2762 **Ilhéu de Ferro**
LFl.15s129m13M 302°-vis-318°, 338°-vis-036°
Round white tower and building, red lantern 14m
2763 **Ponta da Cruz (Costa Norte)**
Fl(2)10s109m12M 064°-vis-243°
White tower, red bands 4·5m

Coast Radio Station

Porto Santo 33°05'N 16°19'W, remotely controlled from Lisbon
VHF Ch 8, 16, 23 (24 hours)

Centro de Comunicações da Madeira (CENCOMARMADEIRA)

Porto Santo 33°04'N 16°21'W
VHF Ch 11, 16 (24 hours) ✆ 291 213110 *Fax* 291 228232 *Email* czmmadeira.com@marinha.pt
Weather bulletins Ch 11 at 1030, 1630 LT (storm and weather warnings, synopsis and 24 hour forecast for waters within 20M of Madeira and Porto Santo in Portuguese and English)
Navigational warnings Ch 11 at 1030, 1630 LT (local warnings for Madeira and Porto Santo in Portuguese, repeated in English whenever possible)

Navtex

A Navtex station has been planned for more than a decade, but as of 2011 had not begun broadcasting. It is understood that it will have the identification letters 'P' and 'M', and that transmissions in English (P) will be on the standard Navtex frequency of 518kHz at 0230, 0630, 1030, 1430, 1830, 2230, while those in Portuguese (M) will be on 490kHz at 0100, 0500, 0900, 1300, 1700, 2100. There is no other Navtex transmitter in the Madeira group.

Harbours and anchorages

Baía de Porto Santo

33°03'·49N 16°18'·86W (south breakwater head)

Waypoint

⊕ M05 – 33°03'·1N 16°19'·1W (0·4M SSW of harbour entrance)

Tides

Predictions for Porto Santo are available via Admiralty *EasyTide* – see page 141
Time difference on Funchal: +0020
Mean spring range 2·2m
Mean neap range 1·0m

Plans

Admiralty *1689* (1:20,000 & 1:7,500)
Portuguese *36401* (1:15,000 & 1:5,000)
Imray-Iolaire *E3* (1:25,000)

Lights

2757 **South breakwater** Fl.G.4s16m6M
White column, green bands 4m
2757·2 **West breakwater** Fl.R.4s12m7M
White column, red bands 4m
Ship's mooring buoys
Two buoys LFl.5s and two buoys Fl.2·5s
Large yellow and black steel buoys
Note Although still listed in official publications, all four buoys had been removed ashore by September 2010 and it was thought unlikely that they would be reinstated

Harbour communications

Harbourmaster ✆ 291 980070/1 *Fax* 291 980079
Email cp.portosanto@marinha.pt VHF Ch 11, 16 (call *Capimar Santo*) (0900–1230, 1400–1730, closed weekends)
Port Authority ✆ 291 980180 *Fax* 291 980181
www.portosdamadeira.com VHF Ch 11, 12, 16 (0900–1200, 1300–1700, closed weekends)
Porto Santo Marina ✆ 291 980080 *Fax* 291 983742
Email marinaportosanto@quintadolorde.pt VHF 09, 16 (0800–1200, 1400–1800 daily from mid-June to mid-November, otherwise closed at weekends). Website accessed via www.quintadolorde.pt

Ferry harbour, marina and moorings

The entire southeast coast of Porto Santo comprises a shallow bay some 3·5M in length, backed by a near-perfect golden sand beach and well sheltered from winds between west and northeast. Unfortunately use of this pleasant – though often rolly – anchorage is seriously discouraged (see Anchorage off the Beach, below) leaving yachts with little alternative than to enter the harbour, berthing either in the marina or on a mooring. The harbour entrance faces west, and swell from that quarter sets up a roll inside.

The harbour is used by the ferry to Madeira as well as commercial vessels, all of which berth on the south breakwater. There is also a small fishing fleet which uses the southern half of the west wall. The northern section of the wall, which overlooks the marina, displays the names of many of the yachts to have visited Porto Santo in recent years. Up to 850 yachts pass through the harbour annually.

Porto Santo harbour lies nearly a mile east of Vila Baleira – a hot walk or cycle ride, though just a few minutes by car.

Approach and entrance

By day Straightforward. In calm conditions both Ilhéu de Baixo and Ilhéu de Cima may be rounded at 400m or less (though ⊕M02 and ⊕M04 are positioned 0·5M offshore) and the gently shelving beach closed anywhere along its length. The concrete breakwaters enclosing the harbour will be seen near the eastern end of the bay. The 112m car ferry *Lobo Marinho* arrives at 1020 daily, other than Tuesday (no service) and Friday (either 1020 or 2130), departing at 1800 and 2230 respectively, so yachts should avoid entering and leaving the harbour at these times. There is a 3 knot speed limit throughout the marina, with 6 knots in the rest of the harbour.

Porto Santo's large harbour seen from hills to the northwest

By night Again straightforward, with powerful lights on both Ilhéu de Cima and Ilhéu de Ferro (though nothing on Ilhéu de Baixo). All three may be rounded within 0·5M. Much of the beach is backed by hotels and other brightly-lit developments, but there is a darker stretch to the east of Vila Baleira, between town and harbour. Both sides of the entrance are lit and there is considerable ambient light inside, though care must be taken to avoid moored yachts. The Madeira ferry runs a late schedule on Friday evenings – see previous paragraph.

Berthing

Porto Santo Marina is run by the same company as Madeira's Marina Quinta do Lorde (hence the shared website) and has expanded in recent years to offer 139 berths, including 42 for yachts up to 10·5m and 12 for yachts up to 15m. A few larger vessels (up to 30m) can berth alongside the concrete spur and the marina has once hosted a 40m megayacht – though not without considerable warning.

The reception berth is on the north side of the short concrete spur. Least depth alongside the reception pontoon is 3m, but a shallow spot has been reported about 15m off its end. Depths throughout the marina decrease from 3m on the outer pontoon to 2m or less further in, but are generally more than sufficient for the size of yacht in each area. If arriving out of hours and finding the reception berth full, choose any berth of suitable size and visit the office next morning. The marina lacks either security gates or a visible security presence outside office hours, presumably because they are considered unnecessary.

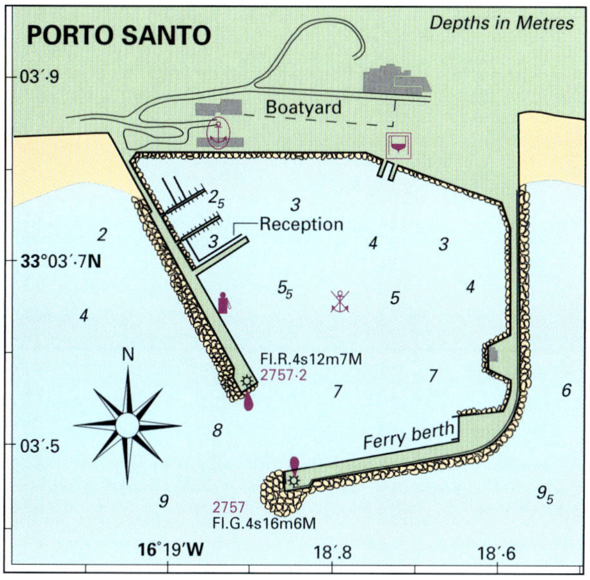

Yachts berthed in Porto Santo Marina. By September, when this photograph was taken, the island's low hills are dry and arid

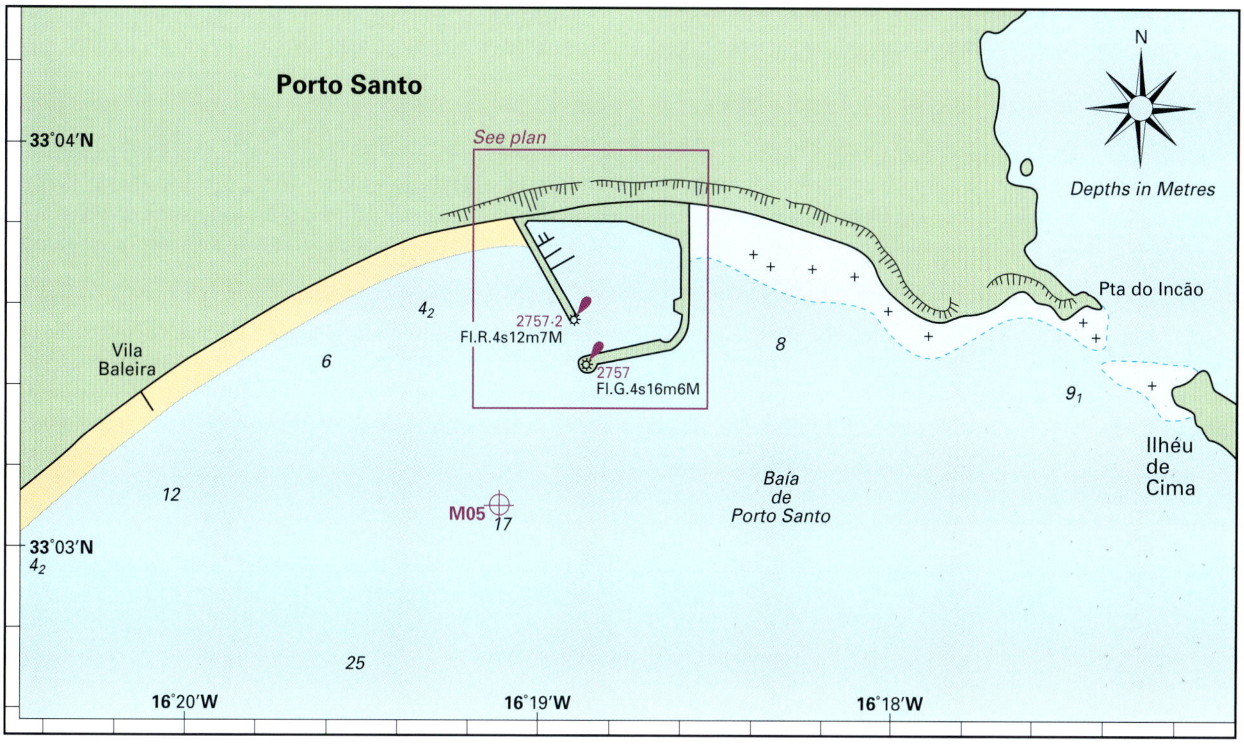

Harbour moorings

The marina administers around 35 conventional swinging moorings, each capable of holding 20 tonnes, though yachts are moved into marina if strong winds are forecast. The moorings are laid in four lines, with small yellow pick-up buoys to which a heavy rope is attached. Rather than attempting to bring this rope aboard it is suggested that two lines should be run through it, led to either side of the bow.

The old fore-and-aft moorings have now been removed, and despite the reference to 'anchoring' on the marina's website, note that this is not permitted anywhere inside the harbour. (The Portuguese word *ancondouro* covers both anchoring and mooring – very different things to English-speaking yachtsmen.)

Anchorage off the beach

For many years yachts have anchored off the beach in settled conditions, finding excellent holding in 8–10m over firm sand about 500m offshore, and an official 'small craft anchorage' was established close west of the harbour.

About six years ago the *Administração dos Portos da Região Autónoma da Madeira* (APRAM), based in Funchal, introduced a daily charge for anchoring within the port limits of Funchal, Caniçal or Porto Santo – for the latter effectively the entire length of the beach. Despite no facilities being provided, visiting yachts were expected to pay €27.50 if between 9m and 15m, or €41.50 if between 16m and 30m.

In early 2011 these charges were decreased to a more reasonable €5.80 for vessels of up to 15m and €7.60 for 16m to 30m, though it was stressed that this applied to non-commercial vessels only. Full details can be found on APRAM's website at www.portosdamadeira.com, though somewhat hidden on pages 8 and 9 of the Tariff Sheet (a downloadable PDF). Fees are payable at the harbour authority office.

If opting to anchor, note that northerly and northwesterly winds tend to whistle down Porto Santo's central valley in heavy gusts making a second anchor, both for security and to limit sheering, a wise precaution at these times. It is essential to show a light during the hours of darkness, even if well clear of the harbour entrance.

Porto Santo Marina, a welcome landfall for yachts after the passage from northern Europe or the Mediterranean

Formalities

Yachts are requested to call the marina on VHF Ch 09 on approach, and may be directed straight to a berth or mooring. Otherwise go alongside the reception pontoon (see plan) and visit the marina office, set well back beside the boatyard. The staff all speak English, and some also speak French and/or German. The usual documents will be needed (including proof of insurance) and the marina office normally retain the yacht's documents until departure. Once on the system the yacht's details are retained and should be accessible to all marinas throughout the Madeira group. Advance bookings are accepted.

It is also necessary to visit the *Guarda Nacional Republicana* (*GNR*) in their office close to the root of the mole, though not the *Polícia Marítima* or the *Serviço de Estrangeiros e Fronteiras* (Immigration service). Both will be forwarded a copy of the paperwork and may visit the yacht, though this appears to be the exception rather than the rule. The *GNR* office is open around the clock, and should be visited soon after arrival even if outside marina office hours.

If planning to depart directly for the Ilhas Desertas or Ilhas Selvagens it is necessary to obtain a permit from the National Parks Department in Funchal (see page 138). The marina staff can arrange this, but it may take up to 48 hours for it to come through.

Charges

In 2011 the daily charge for a marina berth for a yacht of 11–12m was €25.07, rising to €42.21 for yachts of 14–15m. This included water, electricity, showers, IVA (VAT) at 16% and a 10% 'TECM fee' to cover repair and maintenance of the marina facilities. Intermediate prices will be found on the marina's web pages. Use of a mooring (somewhat confusingly listed as 'Anchorage' on the website) cost €13.75 and €17.50 for the two lengths, again inclusive. Multihulls paid a 50% surcharge in all cases. Discounts were available for longer stays.

As in Quinta do Lorde Marina, members of various clubs including the Ocean Cruising Club, Cruising Association, RORC, TransOcean and Voiles Sans Frontières, as well as those taking part in the Atlantic Rally for Cruisers, are eligible for discounts of 20% or more. Reservations can be made by telephone, email or fax.

Facilities

Boatyard The largest boatyard in the archipelago, with fenced space for 80 monohulls of up to 15m LOA and 4·35m beam. 33°/16° Assistência Naútica SA (now under the same ownership as the marina) can handle repairs in GRP, wood and metal (including s/s) and has undercover space if required. DIY work is permitted, and owners can live aboard while ashore. Security is good, with CCTV and key-controlled entry. There is access to water and electricity and the yard has its own toilets and showers.

The hardstanding is clean though dusty, with boats normally laid up facing southwest as that is the 'dangerous wind' direction. However, with the prevailing wind from northeast, boats tend to gather a lot of grit below whilst ashore. Costs are comparable with mainland yards – see the marina website for details – and various packages are available.

Travel-lift 25-tonne capacity lift at the boatyard (max beam 4·35m, max draught 3·2m), with supports and ladders provided. Permission has been sought to install a marine railway for multihulls, hopefully for the 2012 season. A crane is available for lifting masts.

Engineering, electronic & radio repairs Can be organised via the marina office. There is a diesel mechanic at the boatyard with others throughout the island.

Sail repairs Can be organised via the marina office, though usually sent over to Madeira.

Rigging Order from Madeira via the marina office. There is no swage machine on Porto Santo.

Liferaft servicing No longer available on Porto Santo – liferafts are now sent over to Madeira for servicing.

Chandlery No chandlery as such, though the Casa Leao hardware store in Vila Baleira stocks stainless steel fastenings and household paint. Yacht paint, including antifouling, can be ordered from Madeira with no price surcharge, as can other chandlery items.

Water From taps on the pontoons and the marina spur, as well as in the boatyard compound. The island has two desalination plants and water quality is good.

Showers Near the root of the west breakwater and also in the boatyard. In November 2010 the marina showers were said to be without hot water at least once a week.

Laundry Although there are washers and dryers on site they are operated by an attendant rather than being self-service (so limited to office hours, though clothes are normally ready within 24 hours). This makes it pricey – nearly €21 per 5kg dry weight to wash and dry in early 2011.

Electricity Throughout the marina and in the boatyard. 220v 50Hz is standard, but 380v may be available at some larger berths. Yachts must normally provide their own cable and plug, plus adaptor if necessary. After ongoing problems with power surges, all pontoon sockets are now fitted with trip switches.

Fuel Diesel from the fuel berth on the southern section of the west breakwater, best visited near high tide. Call first at the GALP office near the root of the breakwater, open 0900–1200, 1400–1800 weekdays, 0900–1300 Saturday, closed Sunday. Payment must be made in cash. No petrol, which can be obtained from the filling station passed as one enters the town.

Bottled gas After problems in late 2010, by 2011 Camping Gaz swaps were once again readily available. There is no possibility of getting other bottles refilled on Porto Santo.

Weather forecast Posted daily in the window of the marina office.

Banks Several in the town, all with cash dispensers. No cash dispenser at the marina however.

Shops/provisioning Several supermarkets in the town, including a well-stocked Pingo Doce on the left as one approaches Vila Baleira from the harbour (open 0800–2200, entrance down the slope at the back), and Super Zarco a short way up the road opposite. Others include chemist, hardware and many souvenir shops.

Cafés, restaurants & hotels Café at the harbour, plus a wide variety of bars, restaurants and hotels in the town and throughout the island. For a short while a club/bar complex near the marina created nocturnal disturbance, but capping the volume and installing screens is said to have overcome the problem.

Medical services There is a small health centre, though serious cases are normally flown to Funchal (a Portuguese Air Force aeroplane or helicoper is on permanent standby).

Communications

Post office In a road leading off the town square, open 0900–1700 weekdays only.

Mailing address Porto Santo Marina, Porto do Porto Santo, 9400-080 Porto Santo, Madeira, Portugal.

Telephones Several around the harbour, requiring cards from the post office.

Internet access Free Wi-Fi outside the marina office, where seating and tables are provided (though limited to about eight people) and in the nearer parts of the marina. Despite an awning it can be difficult to see the screen when the sun is bright, and both laptops and users are exposed to the elements (including the all-pervading gritty dust) in periods of wind or rain.

Outside the marina, Wi-Fi is available in the pedestrianised main square in Vila Baleira, at the airport and elsewhere. About ten computers are available to all-comers in the undercroft of the *câmara municipal* (town hall) overlooking the town square, again without charge.

Car hire In the town, or can be arranged through the marina office for collection/return at the harbour. Scooters and bicycles are also available.

Taxis Available in the port area when the ferry is due, plus a taxi rank in the centre of the town. The office staff will phone for a taxi if requested.

Ferries Car ferry to Funchal, daily except Tuesday – see Ferries, page 135.

Air services Regular flights to Madeira and the European mainland – see Transportation, page 135.

The marina boatyard, where work can be carried out professionally or on a do-it-yourself basis *Sue Thatcher*

Madeira

Between 32°38'N–32°53'N and 16°39'W–17°16'W

Introduction

By far the largest island in the archipelago, Madeira – correctly called Madeira Grande – has a maximum length of 57km and maximum width of 22km, giving it an area of about 741km², a great deal of that mountainous. The volcanic peaks which form the island rise sharply out of very deep water, with depths of 2,000m less than 4M offshore, often continuing upwards from sea level as steep cliffs. However, unlike in the Azores, Canaries and Cape Verde islands there have been no eruptions since its discovery in the 15th century, and although many of the mountain tops reach above 1,500m there are no individual giants such as exist in the other groups. Its massive form largely dictates Madeira's climate, with generous rainfall on the north coast and in the highlands, while the south coast including Funchal normally lies in a rain shadow, protected from the northeasterly winds.

The natural forest vegetation was largely destroyed by the early settlers who burnt off the lower slopes for cultivation, but with its rich volcanic soil and mild climate an amazing variety of flowers, trees and shrubs thrive at different altitudes, with fruit, vines and sugar cane cultivated on laboriously constructed terraces. Over 200 species of birds have been identified on Madeira, about one-fifth of which breed locally, though land animals are less varied and almost entirely introduced by man. Even non-enthusiasts should make the effort to visit at least one of the many lovely public gardens, of which the *Jardim Botânico* (which also houses a small museum) is undoubtedly the best known.

Madeira has long had a thriving tourist industry largely centred on Funchal, which continues almost year-round. In addition, a growing proportion of the permanent population of about 260,000 are 'incomers', mainly from northern Europe. Even so, for two decades following the completion of Funchal's small marina in the early 1980s facilities for visiting yachts showed little sign of further improvement – misleadingly, many of the portos marked on the chart are little more than rough, stony beaches up which a few local fishing craft are dragged each evening.

The new millennium saw major changes, with Quinta do Lorde Marina near the eastern end of the island receiving its first yachts in 2002 and swiftly becoming established as the island's premier marina. In addition, two new yacht harbours were under construction on the southwest coast. Of these, while Marina do Lugar de Baixo, near Ponta do Sol, has been beset with problems and remains closed, Porto de Recreio da Calheta some miles further west

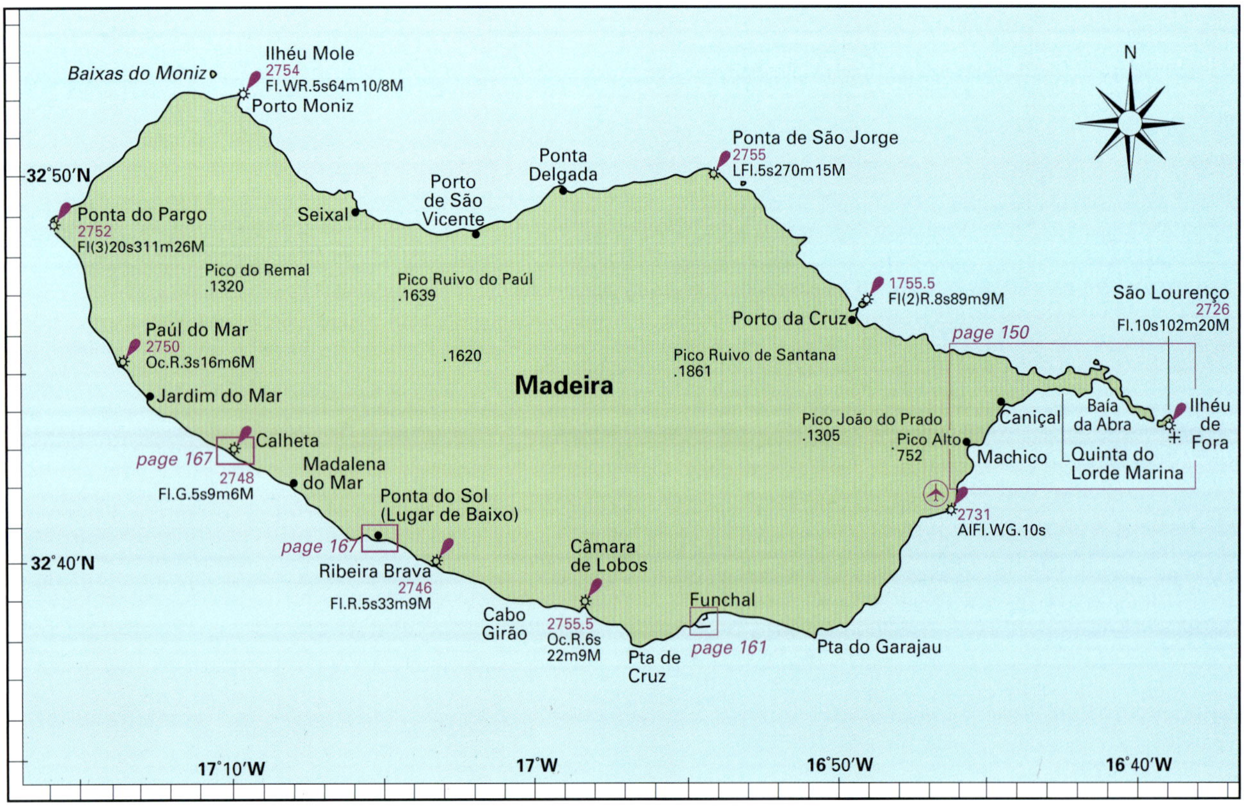

appears to be thriving, despite its somewhat isolated position.

In light of these developments, and breaking with previous editions, the island's harbours and anchorages are now taken in a clockwise direction, starting in the southeast where most yachts make their landfall.

Telecommunications

Mobile (cell) phone reception throughout the island is good. The country code for the Madeira group is 351, as it is for mainland Portugal, and the area code for Madeira 291, which must be included even when dialling from within the island.

By 2011 free Wi-Fi was available in many locations throughout the island, including all the marinas, Funchal's main square and the airport.

Websites

Nearly all websites relevant to Madeira cover the group as a whole – see page 137 for a comprehensive listing.

Approach

Madeira lies just over 21M southwest of Porto Santo and 10M northwest of the Ilhas Desertas. When seen from the north, the mountain chain which runs the length of island gives the skyline a serrated and somewhat forbidding appearance. Pico Ruivo de Santana, the summit of the chain at 1,861m and lying near the geographical centre of the island, can often be seen at up to 40M in clear weather. A great deal of the coast consists of high cliffs – those at Cabo Girão in the south drop almost sheer from 575m and are the second highest sea-cliffs in the world – with deep water generally to be found within 0·5M of the shore.

Exceptions to this are in the northwest of the island, where the Baixas do Moniz, a low group of unlit rocks, lie just under 1M offshore, and in the extreme east, where yachts rounding Ilhéu de Fora should allow a least offing of 0·5M to avoid the dangerous, unmarked Badajeira Rock, a breaking shoal which lies 800m southeast of the lighthouse. In heavier conditions this should be increased to a full mile – ⊕M06 – while in even moderate northeasterly winds overfalls may be encountered up to 7M northeast of Ponta São Lourenço, where depths shoal from around 160m to 80m.

Further west, in strong northeasterlies sudden windshifts of up to 180° can occur along the southeast coast between Santa Caterina airport and Ponta do Garajau. Yachts heading east under spinnaker in light southwesterlies have on occasion been backwinded and/or broached by unexpected northeasterly blasts, though approaching white horses will normally give some warning.

Navigation

Waypoints

⊕ M06 – 32°42'·9N 16°34'·6W (1M SE of Ilhéu de Fora, Madeira)
⊕ M07 – 32°37'·6N 16°50'·8W (0·5M S of Pta do Garajau)
⊕ M08 – 32°37'·4N 16°56'·5W (0·5M S of Pta da Cruz)
⊕ M09 – 32°48'·8N 17°16'·4W (0·5M W of Pta do Pargo)

Courses and distances

⊕ M05 (0·4M SSW of Porto Santo harbour) – ⊕ M06 = 42M, 342° / 162°
⊕ M06 – ⊕ M07 = 14M, by eye
⊕ M07 – ⊕ M08 = 5M, 268° / 088°
⊕ M08 – ⊕ M09 = 2·5M by eye
⊕ M08 – ⊕ M19 (0·5M SSW of Carga da Lapa, Ilha Deserta Grande) = 23M, 108° / 188°
⊕ M08 – ⊕ M20 (0·5M NE of Baixo do Nordeste, Selvagem Grande) = 158M, 159° / 339°

Magnetic variation

6°W (2011), decreasing by 8'E annually.

Tidal streams

Tidal streams generally run northeast on the flood and southwest on the ebb at 0·5 knot to 1·25 knots. However, they may occasionally attain 2 knots in the channel between Madeira and the Ilhas Desertas, raising steep seas in wind against tide conditions.

Charts

Admiralty *1831* (1:150,000)
Portuguese *33101* (1:350,000), *36201* (1:100,000)
US *51261* (1:150,000)
Imray-Iolaire *E3* (1:170,000)

Lights

2726 **São Lourenço (Ilhéu de Fora)**
Fl.10s102m20M 127°-vis-097°
White octagonal tower and building, red lantern 10m
2731 **Santa Catarina Airport**
Aero Al.Fl.WG.10s Control tower
2752 **Ponta do Pargo**
Fl(3)20s311m26M 336°-vis-226°
Square white tower and building, red lantern 14m
2754 **Porto do Moniz (Ilhéu Môle)** Fl.WR.5s64m10/8M
116°-R-127°-W-116° Hexagonal tower 3m
2755 **Ponta de São Jorge**
LFl.5s270m15M 085°-vis-300°
Round ribbed tower and building 14m

Coast Radio Stations

Pico da Cruz 32°39'N 16°56'W, remotely controlled from Lisbon
VHF Ch 16, 25, 27 (24 hours)
Ponta do Pargo 32°49'N 17°16'W, remotely controlled from Lisbon
VHF Ch 16, 24, 26 (24 hours)

Maritime Rescue Coordination Sub-Centre

Madeira (Funchal) 32°38'N 16°54'W (24 hours)
DSC – MF and VHF MMSI 002550100 (planned)
✆ 291 678140 (emergency), 291 213112 (operations)
Fax 291 228232 *Email* mrsc.funchal@marinha.pt
(This station does not accept public correspondence other than distress and safety traffic)

Harbours and anchorages

Baía de Abra

32°44′·67N 16°41′·63W (anchorage)

Waypoint

⊕ M10 – 32°44′·2N 16°41·5W (0·5M SSE of Baía da Abra)

Plans

Admiralty *1685* (1:30,118)
Portuguese *36402* (1:30,000)
Imray-Iolaire *E3* (1:30,000)

Lights

2726 **São Lourenço (Ilhéu de Fora)**
Fl.10s102m20M 127°-vis-097°
White octagonal tower and building, red lantern 10m

Attractive anchorage

Lying about 10M northeast of Machico and 2·5M northwest of Ponta da Barlavento in the extreme east of Madeira, Baía da Abra offers a remote and peaceful anchorage under high cliffs with a single building in sight ashore. The narrow neck of land running eastwards toward Ilhéu de Fora gives protection so long as the wind stays in the northerly quadrant, but the prevailing northeasterly whistles through a saddle in the ridge and may sometimes produce enough chop to make landing on the stony beach difficult, even by inflatable.

The area is popular with walkers – there is a large car park complete with ice-cream vans just over the hill to the west – and it is well worth taking the steep track up to the ridge to admire the contrasting views

Looking southeast over Baía da Abra towards Ponta de Barlavento and Ilhéu de Fora

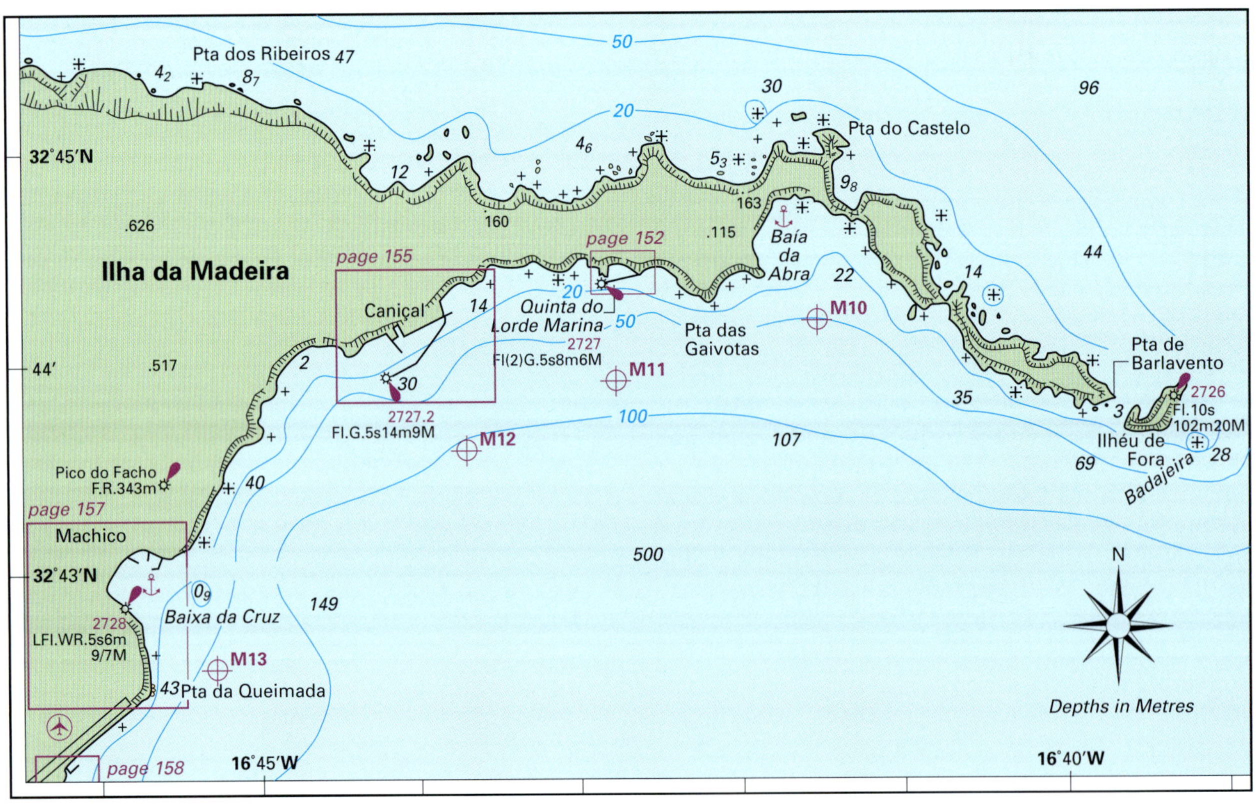

to north and south. The water is generally quite clear and the swimming and snorkelling good. The rocks and headlands to the east, including a spectacular natural archway, make for interesting exploration by dinghy.

Approach

By day Quite straightforward, though reasonable clearance should be given to Ponta das Gaivotas to the west, close to the new Quinta do Lorde Marina. If approaching from the east, a large natural arch will be seen before reaching the anchorage. A variety of structures have been moored in the outer part of the bay over the past decade, all seemingly connected with fish-farming research, but over the past few years these have been limited to eight circular fish cages marked by a number of unlit buoys. Fortunately the Baía da Abra is large and there is plenty of room to anchor inside these, but it would obviously be prudent to allow a generous berth on entry.

By night Not recommended, in view of both the moored structures and the total absence of lights either afloat or ashore.

Anchorage

Holding is good throughout most of the bay and the water crystal-clear. Beware, however, of the three old lorry chassis which lie at 32°44'·66N 16°41'·61W in about 13m, and pose an obvious threat to anchors. Anchoring in 10m or less should keep one clear, though a tripline might still be wise. Right under the steep cliffs to the east and northeast the ground is clear and the holding said to be excellent.

Baía da Abra, this time looking slightly north of west, is probably the best natural anchorage in Madeira

Quinta do Lorde Marina

32°44'·42N 16°42'·84W (south breakwater head)

Waypoint

⊕ M11 – 32°44'N 16°42'·8W (0·5M S of Quinta do Lorde Marina)

Plans

Admiralty *1685* (1:30,100), *1684* (1:7,500)
Portuguese *36402* (1:30,000)
Imray-Iolaire *E3* (1:20,000)

Lights

2727 **South breakwater** Fl(2)G.5s8m6M
Green and white banded column 6m
2727·5 **West mole** Fl(2)R.5s8m3M
Red and white banded column 6m

Harbour communications

Quinta do Lorde Marina ☏ 291 969607 *Fax* 291 960066
Email marina@quintadolorde.pt
www.quintadolorde.pt (in Portuguese, English and French), VHF Ch 09, 16 (office 0900–1800 daily; outdoor staff remaining on duty until 2100 from August to November inclusive)

Friendly and well-run marina

A 'new entry' in the previous edition of this book, the 267-berth Quinta do Lorde Marina is now the landfall of choice for most yachts visiting Madeira and almost invariably receives high praise. The staff in particular, headed by Director of Operations Cátia Carvalho, are consistently mentioned in feedback from cruising yachtsmen as being outstandingly efficient and helpful, with excellent English among other European languages. The marina can now accept yachts of up to 50m and 4·5m draught, though the majority of transients still appear to be in the 12m to 15m range.

A classic marina village development on an ambitious scale, although the marina itself was operational by August 2002 it was several years before its infrastructure – fuel, permanent office, showers, etc. – were completed. Eight years later, building work on the 'village' aspect was said to be effectively finished, though a good deal of superficial work still remained to be done. Once accessible – in late 2010 much of the village remained closed off behind metal barriers, giving a rather desolate impression – it should make an attractive backdrop complete with a church, village square and a variety of shops. The marina and its surroundings are noticeably well kept, and in 2010 Quinta do Lorde Marina received an EU 'Blue Flag' for the fourth consecutive year.

The area's only long-term disadvantage is its remoteness – about 13M from Funchal by sea, but nearer 30km (about half an hour) by road – though this is offset to a large extent by the regular bus service (see Facilites, below) and availability of taxis and hire cars.

Approach and entrance

By day The marina lies in the bay immediately west of Punta das Gaivotas. Its pale concrete breakwater

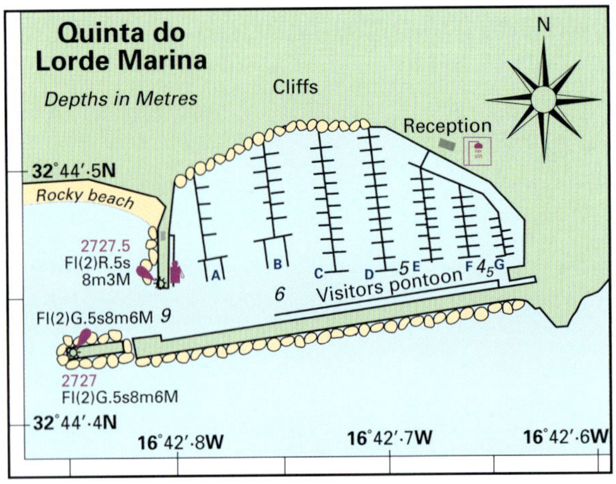

is 6m or more in height and is conspicuous against the dark volcanic cliffs behind. The approach from offshore is straightforward in reasonable weather, though there are various rocks and shoals fringing the coast on either side. A low neck of rubble extends from the south breakwater, terminating in a large concrete block on which the light is placed.

The entrance, which faces west, is narrow and requires a sharp turn to starboard not far from the cliff face. It would clearly be hazardous in strong onshore conditions – and even in light winds if a heavy southerly or southwesterly swell is running. Katabatic squalls have also been reported as 'falling off' the hills to the north, though these present no danger to yachts inside the marina. The centre of the entrance is reported to carry at least 9m, with more in the bay to the west, but the channel sides are much shallower. There is a 2 knot speed limit throughout the marina.

By night The marina entrance is narrow, but in reasonable conditions should present no difficulty. The small church on the cliff due north of the marina entrance is floodlit and (unlike many harbours) the entrance lights can be relied upon. Once inside there is no shortage of ambient light. The 150m pontoon directly inside the breakwater is reserved for very large yachts and visitors, and the western half is always cleared by the evening for overnight arrivals.

Berthing

Arriving yachts are requested to give notice of their arrival by VHF or phone, and will often be met by the marina RIB to be escorted through the entrance and directly to a berth. If arriving after dark, berth alongside the breakwater pontoon. Yachts of up to 25m are normally berthed alongside finger pontoons, with the possibility of accommodating vessels of up to 50m and 4·5m draught on the pontoon which parallels the inner part of the 315m south breakwater.

Quinta do Lorde Marina seen from near Ponta das Gaivotas ('point of the seagulls') to the east

Approaching the west-facing entrance to Quinta do Lorde Marina, with the marina's RIB leading the way *Simon Fraser*

Early in the marina's history surge was sometimes a problem, particularly in strong winds with any westerly component, though never to the point of making it untenable. The addition of tetrapods around the end of the breakwater, to reduce the energy of any surge rebounding inside the marina, appears to appears to have been successful and no recurrence has been reported in recent years.

Security is good, with access to the pontoons via card-operated gates. There is no charge for the card itself, though a €50 penalty is levied if it is lost or destroyed.

Formalities

Visit the marina office on the north side of the basin taking all the usual paperwork – registration documents, insurance, passports, etc. Office hours are 0900–1800 daily throughout the year and the staff speak fluent English, French and Spanish in addition to Portuguese. As noted previously, they enjoy an excellent reputation for efficiency and helpfulness, as do the outdoor staff, most of whom also speak English and/or French.

The marina is an official port of entry, collecting the necessary information and forwarding it to the relevant authorities. Non-EU flagged vessels should try to give 24 hours notice of arrival, so that the correct officials can be requested to attend for clearance.

If planning to depart directly for the Ilhas Desertas or Ilhas Selvagens it is necessary to obtain a permit from the National Parks Department in Funchal (see page 138). The marina staff are happy to arrange this, but allow at least 48 hours.

Charges

In 2011 the daily charge for a visiting yacht of 10–12m was €32.60, rising to €50.00 for yachts of 12–15m, which included water, electricity, showers and IVA (VAT) at 16%. Multihulls paid a 50% surcharge and discounts were available for longer stays.

As in Porto Santo Marina, members of various clubs including the Ocean Cruising Club, Cruising Association, RORC, TransOcean and Voiles Sans Frontières, as well as those taking part in the Atlantic Rally for Cruisers, are eligible for discounts of 20% or more. Reservations can be made by telephone, email or fax.

Facilities

Boatyard & travel-lift Quinta do Lorde's boatyard is situated about four miles away at Água de Pena, sheltered by the runway of Santa Catarina airport – see page 158. Multihulls can be hauled at the boatyard in Caniçal – arrange via the marina office. The marina offers a *guardinage* service for unattended yachts, including checking fenders and lines at least once a day and bilge and battery levels weekly or monthly.

Diving services Can be arranged via the marina office.

Engineers Work can be carried out on yachts while afloat, including engine removal etc. Arrange via the office.

Electronic & radio repairs The Maré chandlery in Funchal is agent for Raymarine and Simrad among other makes, and has technical expertise to match. Arrangements can be made via the office.

Sail repairs and rigging A local company handles sail repairs and rigging, and is said to offer a reliable and professional service (though unable to handle very heavy materials). Contact via the marina office.

Liferaft servicing Available at the Água de Pena boatyard (see above), to which liferafts are normally transported by road.

Chandlery A chandlery is planned for the Água de Pena boatyard (see above), with a smaller branch at the marina, hopefully by late summer 2011. Otherwise marina staff will help with sourcing individual items and Maré in Funchal will deliver.

Water Throughout the marina and included in the berthing charge.

Showers Excellent showers on the north side of the marina, with access via key pad.

Launderette Fully operational, but with only one washer and one dryer so queues can form at busy times. Although initial access is limited to office hours, once in progress there is no time limit and users shut the door behind them. In 2010 washing cost €7 per load and drying €2 per cycle, and the office kept a supply of the necessary coins. A full laundry and ironing service is also available – details from the office.

Electricity Throughout the marina and included in the berthing charge.

Fuel Diesel and petrol available from the fuel pontoon to port on entry during outdoor staff hours (see Harbour Communications). Payment can be made in cash or by card, though an additional 2·5% is charged for the latter.

Bottled gas Camping Gaz cylinders can be exchanged at the marina office, which will also arrange for other bottles to be refilled. The latter normally takes 24 hours but can take up to four working days. Read also page 191 if continuing to the Canaries.

Weather forecast Displayed outside the launderette (next to the marina office). GRIB files can be downloaded in the latter onto a USB stick.

Bank In Caniçal, about 4km along the coast. A cash dispenser is planned for Quinta do Lorde, either in the marina or the residential development, but is unlikely to be in place before 2012.

Shops/provisioning Shops, including a small *supermercado*, have been on the marina's wish list for some time, with a tentative opening date of December 2011. In the meantime fresh bread can be bought at the café (see below).

The marina runs a free minibus to/from Machico (where there are large Pingo Doce and SA supermarkets), sometimes continuing to Funchal. It usually departs around 1030 and 1400 and returns anything from 30 minutes to three hours later. Advance booking may be necessary as it is very popular. There is a branch of Modelo near the airport, while for major provisioning it may be worth visiting the large SA in São Martinho on the western outskirts of Funchal.

Cafés, restaurants & hotels The Lord's Club restaurant and the Captain's Bar café, both in the 'lighthouse' building at the east end of the marina, are open from 0900 until 2200 daily. There is currently no hotel on site, though a hotel and spa are planned for the Quinta do Lorde Resort.

Medical services Hospital in Machico, with simpler first aid facilities in the marina complex. Contact the office for assistance.

Communications

Post office In Caniçal, about 4km along the coast. Alternatively stamps can be bought at the marina office and mail left there for posting.

Mailing address C/o Quinta do Lorde Marina, Sítio da Piedade, 9200–044 Caniçal, Machico, Madeira, Portugal.

Telephones Public telephones have long been on the agenda, and should be installed by 2012.

Internet access Free Wi-Fi is now available thoughout the marina following the installation of boosters – previously visitors berthed some distance from the office generally had to take their laptops ashore to get a reliable signal. However, in busy periods there may still be problems with bandwidth if too many other users are downloading large files or talking on Skype.

Car hire The office staff can arrange car hire for collection and return at the marina. Online booking may be slightly cheaper but will probably entail collection/return either in Machico or at the airport.

Taxis Can be ordered by phone at the marina office.

Buses In addition to the marina minibus (see *shops/provisioning*, above), SAM (*Sociedade de Automóveis da Madeira*) service 113, which runs between Funchal and Baía da Abra, stops on the road near the east end of the development. Six or seven buses run on weekdays, fewer at weekends, the first departing for Funchal at 1020 and the last leaving the city at 1940. The trip takes around 90 minutes each way, using the old, scenic road and stopping frequently – an island tour in itself! A timetable can be downloaded from the company's website at www.sam.pt/, otherwise ask in the marina office.

Air services The large and spectacular airport is about 12km westward down the coast – no more than 20 minutes by road, thanks to the *Via Rápida* which runs west from Caniçal.

The attractive interior of Quinta do Lorde Marina. The office will be found in the cream building on the left

Caniçal

32°43′·96N 16°44′·12W (southeast breakwater head)

Waypoint
⊕ M12 – 32°43′·6N 16°43·7W (0·5M S of Caniçal)

Plans
Admiralty *1684* (1:7,500), *1685* (1:10,030)
Portuguese *36402* (1:30,000), *37501* (1:7,500)
Imray-Iolaire *E3* (1:30,000)

Lights
2727·7 **Southeast breakwater** Fl.G.5s14m9M
White column, green bands 4m
2727·75 **West breakwater** Fl.R.5s7m6M
White column, red bands 3m
buoys **Ship mooring buoys**
Four yellow buoys, one Fl(5)Y.10s4M, one Fl(4)Y.10s4M, and two Fl.Y.3s4M lie southeast of Caniçal centred on 32°44′·2N 16°43′·4W. They are used for mooring tankers four-square for pipeline transfer

Harbour communications
Harbourmaster ✆ 291 213110 *Fax* 291 228232
Email capiporto.funchal@telepac.pt VHF Ch 11, 16 (call *Capimar Funchal*) (0900–1200, 1400–1730)
Port Authority ✆ 291 208600 *Fax* 291 220196
www.portosdamadeira.com VHF Ch 08, 11, 16 (0800–2400)

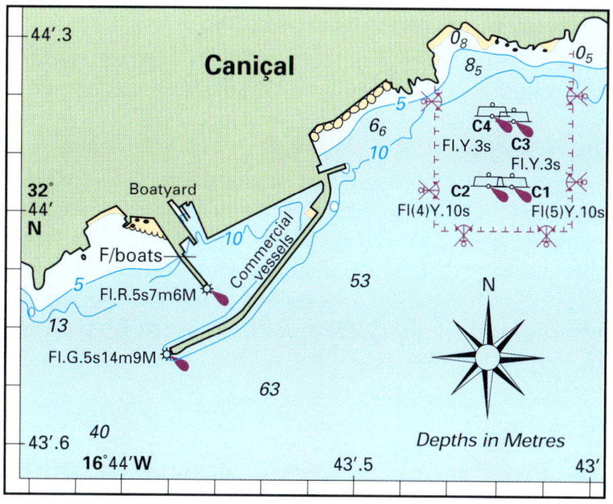

Commercial harbour with boatyard

Until 1981 the centre of Madeiran whaling, Caniçal is now the island's main commercial port, allowing Funchal to specialise in the lucrative cruise ship trade. Harbour works – including a 350m extension to the southeast breakwater – were completed late in 2006, providing three container berths, a quay for grain vessels and a RoRo facility. The port boasts its own *zona franca* (free trade zone) while the town is thriving if not particularly scenic. Hampered for many years by poor communications, the *Via Rápida* network has now reached Caniçal via a new, two-lane tunnel. There are floating pontoons for small fishing boats, but no space for yachts and casual visitors would not be welcome.

A *festa* takes place on the third Saturday in September, during which decorated fishing boats circle the harbour, one of which is chosen to carry the image of Nossa Senhora da Piedade, brought down from the chapel on the nearby hilltop. The following Sunday there is a second procession, after which the patron saint is returned to the chapel.

The *Museu da Baleia* (whaling museum), now located west of the town on Rua da Pedra d'Eira, is well worth a visit. Although by late 2010 it had still to reopen following its move, it is likely to retain the captioned engravings, models, audio-visual display and disused whale-boat which combine to tell the story first of killing and now of conservation. Visit the website at www.museudabaleia.org *Email* geral@museudabaleia.org or ✆ 291 961858, 291 961859.

The commercial harbour and large boatyard at Caniçal, looking northeast *Cátia Carvalho*

Approach, entrance and berthing

The only reason for a yacht to enter Caniçal would be to haul out at the boatyard, in which case a prior visit by land is advised. A confirmed booking would also be essential.

Approach and entry are straightforward, though there are various off-lying rocks and shoals along the coast on either side. It would be best to head in from the vicinity of ⊕M12, keeping a listening watch on VHF Ch 09 and 16 in case of ships manoeuvring. From offshore, the harbour is dominated by a block of enormous concrete silos with a small wind farm on the skyline to the east.

Anchorage

The best – indeed the only – anchorage is off the beach about 600m west of the entrance, near the *clube náutico*. The area is generally calm in summer and provides good anchorage in the right conditions. Dinghies can be left at the club and it may be possible to use the showers, etc. It is only a short walk into the town. The whaling museum lies a little way inland.

Facilities

Boatyard Large boatyard run by the fishermen's co-operative, with plenty of hardstanding. Though used mainly by multihulls since the new facility at Água de Pena came onstream, it does have the advantage that owners can live on board while ashore. DIY work is permitted, but bringing in other workers from outside is not. The yard is fenced off and guard dogs patrol at night, but security might still be an issue. The staff are said to be very competent, but little English is spoken and arrangements are best made via the office at Quinta do Lorde marina.

Travel-lift 200-tonne capacity hoist with three sets of slings – certainly the largest travel-lift in Madeira and very probably in all the Atlantic islands – owned by the fishermen's co-operative, plus a Syncrolift capable of handling vessels of up to 100m and of considerable beam.

Engineers Available at the boatyard, though help with translation might be required.

Chandlery There is no longer a chandlery in the port. The nearest is in Machico, though Maré in Funchal is much larger and will deliver.

Water & electricity In the boatyard.

Showers In the boatyard compound, but only open from 0800 to 1800 and said to be very basic.

Fuel By can from a filling station on the main road.

Bank On the main road, with cash dispenser.

Shops/provisioning Basic shops, though unusually well camouflaged.

Cafés, restaurants & hotels No shortage of the former, with several overlooking the harbour square, but little residential accommodation.

Medical services In Machico.

Communications

Post office On the main road.

Telephones In the town.

Taxis Surprisingly prolific.

Buses On the route of the 113 (see page 136).

Air services The airport is some 6km to the southwest.

Machico

32°43'·02N 16°45'·62W (east molehead)

Waypoint

⊕ M13 – 32°42·6N 16°45'·2W (0·5M SE of Machico)

Plans

Admiralty *1684* (1:7,500), *1685* (1:30,100)
Portuguese *36402* (1:30,000), *37501* (1:7,500)
Imray-Iolaire *E3* (1:7,500)

Lights

2728 **Machico (São Roque)**
LFl.WR.5s6m9/7M 230°-R-265°-W-230°
Red column, two white bands on red hut 4m
Note Not on the headland (Ponta da Queimada) but tucked well into the bay, hence the limited arc of visibility

2730 **East mole** Fl(3)G.8s6m6M
Rusty metal tripod, green lantern 2·5m

2730·2 **West mole** Fl(3)R.8s5m5M
White column, red bands 3·4m

Pico do Facho
F.R.343m TV mast 22m

Sandy bay with mole and smallcraft pontoons

Until relatively recently Machico was a small, somewhat remote community dependent largely on agriculture and fishing. However the opening of the massive and unlovely Hotel Dom Pedro Baía in the mid 1980s, followed some 20 years later by the extension of the *Via Rápida* (which crosses the upper valley on a massive bridge), has brought development to the area with a vengeance. A very old town, it was the landing place of João Gonçalves Zarco in 1419 and for a while the capital of the eastern part of Madeira under Tristão Vaz Teixeira, his fellow captain. Its 15th-century parish church is certainly the oldest in Madeira, and the tiny, triangular, whitewashed fort facing the beach and dated 1706 probably the smallest (it now houses the tourist office). Machico's other old fort, on the slopes east of the mole and dating back to 1708, is being converted into a hotel, though by late 2010 work had ground to a halt, apparently for financial reasons.

About 3M southwest of Quinta do Lorde Marina and 6M northeast of Funchal – or 10·5M by water – the bay offers good protection from southwest through west to northeast. Until recently just a wide, sandy bay with a short eastern mole fully occupied by fishing boats, in 2005 work started to extend the mole and lay smallcraft pontoons in its shelter. At the same time a swimming area was created to the west – the fine golden sand is said to have been imported from Morocco – cordoned off by a string of orange buoys and floats. The whole area lies almost directly under the flight path to/from Santa Caterina Airport, but the noise is seldom intrusive and there is little flying at night.

A medieval festival is held in the town during June, and a gastronomic festival in August.

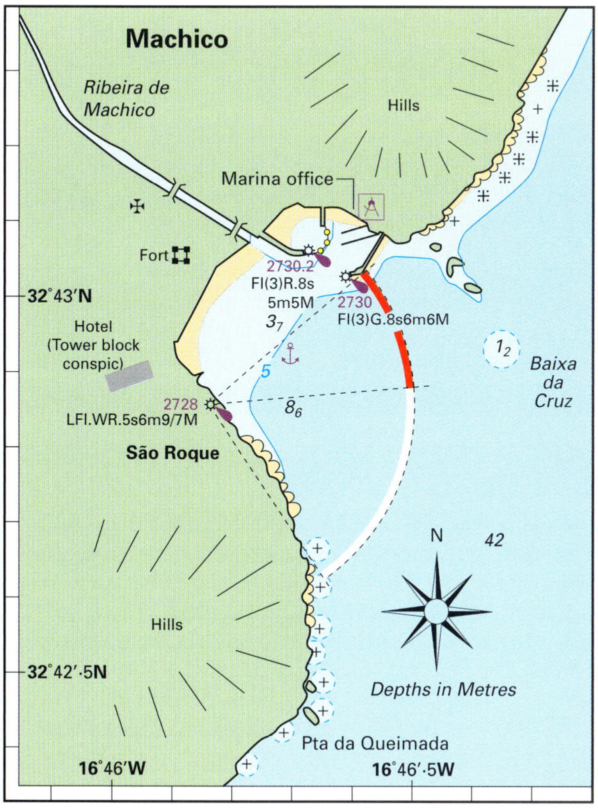

Approach

By day Ponta da Queimada to the south may be rounded in deep water with 200m clearance. However, if coming from the east generous allowance should be made for the outlying rocks which run at least 400m southeast from the northern headland. The outermost (Baixa da Cruz) is particularly treacherous, its 1m clearance precluding telltale breakers unless a considerable swell is running. Approach from the vicinity of ⊕M13 ensures adequate clearance.

Looking southwest across the bay at Machico with the airport's long runway in the distance

By night The white sector of the São Roque light leads clear of Baixa da Cruz, but the light may be difficult to identify against the many bright shore lights. A careful watch is required for unlit boats and mooring buoys.

Berthing

The two pontoons which constitute the *Porto do Recreio Machico* are fully occupied by local boats, mainly small runabouts plus a few yachts, and visitors are most unlikely to find space. In 2010 the only real choice was between anchoring (see below) and securing to the inside of the extended mole, generally three or four abreast. Surprisingly, there seemed to be no official objection to this, and neither was any charge made. Yachts generally use the outer part of the mole, which has depths of around 3m, but may sometimes lie further in, alongside fishing boats laid up out of season. It is important, however, not to block the fairway or obstruct the turning area, so this option is effectively limited to yachts of no more than 13m or so. There is a remarkable absence of movement in the shelter of the mole, even when boats on the pontoons are subject to noticeable surge.

Anchorage

Good holding in 7–10m over sand and gravel will be found throughout the bay, though the most sheltered area in the north and east has been taken over by the pontoons and swimming area. Winds are usually offshore, the prevailing northeasterlies being deflected down the broad valley which shelters the town, but even so an easterly swell often works around the end of Madeira and sets into the bay.

In winds from west or southwest a more protected anchorage would be found further south towards the São Roque light, while in very light conditions a stern anchor laid out to the southeast will cut down rolling by keeping the yacht's stern into any swell. The mole has four sets of steps at which to land by dinghy, though an inflatable might be best carried ashore up the slipway at its root.

Formalities

The *Porto do Recreio* office will be found at the northwest end of the block overlooking the pontoons, sharing a door (though not an office) with the *Guarda Nacional Republicana* (*GNR*) and *Polícia Marítima*. It is unlikely to be manned, in which case call at the nearby Nautileste chandlery. However, in 2010 the officials were said to take little interest in yachts berthed against the mole.

Machico is not an official port of entry, even coming from Porto Santo. Yachts – particularly those wearing non-EU ensigns – are occasionally visited by either the *Polícia Marítima* or the *Serviço de Estrangeiros e Fronteiras* (Immigration), so prior clearance at Quinta do Lorde Marina, Funchal or Porto de Recreio da Calheta would be wise.

Facilities

Chandlery Nautileste ✆ 291 965248 *Email* geral@nautileste.com www.nautileste.com is situated near the root of the east mole. In addition to fishing and dive equipment and some general chandlery they also have metalwork and GRP workshops.

Water On the pontoons but not the mole, though there is a press-button tap near the chandlery.

Showers Beach showers (ie. cold!) at the southwest end of the beach.

Electricity On the pontoons but not the mole.

Fuel By can from a filling station near the northwest corner of the beach.

Bottled gas Camping Gaz exchanges at Nautileste and elsewhere, but no refills.

Banks Several in the town, with cash dispensers.

Shops/provisioning Large Pingu Doce and SA supermarkets near the river about 0·5km inland, with a good range of other shops including hardware, pharmacies etc.

Produce market Back in operation after several years out of commission.

Cafés, restaurants & hotels Very pleasant café sandwiched between the chandlery and the harbour office, with plenty more throughout the town. Relatively few hotels other than the large Dom Pedro Baía at the southwest end of the beach.

Medical services Small health centre on the airport road, ✆ 291 969130. Serious medical emergencies are normally taken to Funchal.

Communications

Post office In the town, open 0900–1230, 1430–1830 Monday to Friday, closed Saturday.

Telephones Near the tourist office behind the beach and elsewhere.

Internet access Free Wi-Fi zone near the west end of the waterfront, both outside the large Forum building and inside its pleasant café.

Car hire At the airport.

Taxis No shortage.

Buses Regular service to Funchal etc.

Air services Santa Catarina Airport lies about 4km to the southwest.

The short moles and recently extended breakwater at Machico, seen from the southwest

Água de Pena (Santa Catarina)

32°42′·04N 16°46′·08W (southeast molehead)

Plans
Imray-Iolaire *E3* (1:5,000)

Lights
2730·5 **Southeast mole** Fl.R.5s8m3M
White post, red bands 3m
2730.55 **North (inner) spur** Fl.G.6s8m3M
White post, green bands 3m

Harbour communications
RepMarítima Estaleiro ✆ 291 969800 *Fax* 291 964639
VHF 09 (0900–1800 weekdays, 0900–1300 Saturday).
Fledgling website accessed via www.quintadolorde.pt

Boatyard

The tiny harbour at Água de Pena lies adjacent to, and (heading west) about a third of the way along, the runway of Madeira's Santa Catarina Airport. It shelters the lifeboats and firefighting vessels which are always on standby, and would be of no possible interest to yachts were it not for the RepMarítima Estaleiro (boatyard) which lies behind it. Owned and operated by the same company as the marinas at Quinta do Lorde and Porto Santo, it lifted out its first yacht in April 2010 and may well be unique in that its extensive hardstanding lies beneath the airport runway, though high enough for all but the largest yachts to be hauled with masts still in place. Proof of insurance is required when booking and security is excellent, with high, robust fencing and CCTV.

Approach, entrance and berthing

Yachts coming from Quinta do Lorde Marina are normally either escorted by the marina RIB, carry a member of the marina staff aboard, or both. Once identified beneath the airport columns the approach is straightforward, but the entrance itself is extremely narrow at just 25m. Depths are good, though larger yachts may need high water to enter the travel-lift alcove.

It is absolutely essential for all arrangements to be made in advance and for the yacht to be expected, as there is little area to lie alongside (the mole is generally occupied by a lifeboat and a small tug). It

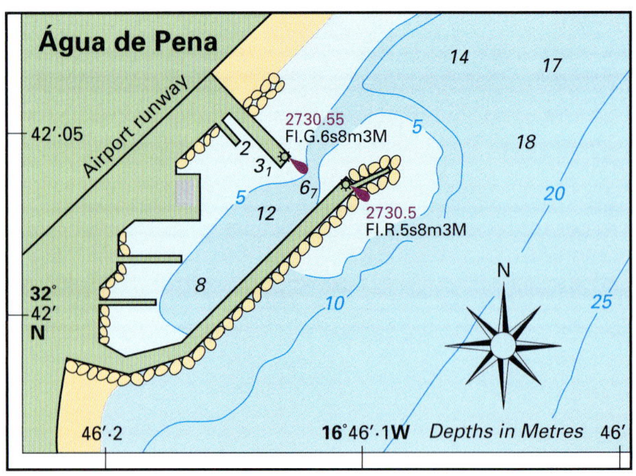

The entrance to the tiny harbour at Água de Pena can be difficult to make out, even when quite close to. The port hand light structure stands out well, however

A yacht in the travel-lift at RepMarítima Estaleiro, Água de Pena. All but the tallest masts will fit under the airport runway

will often be possible to enter the travel-lift dock immediately on arrival, for which warps and fenders should be prepared.

Facilities

Boatyard As mentioned previously, RepMarítima Estaleiro, ✆ 291 969800 *Fax* 291 964639, Água de Pena, 9200-226 Machico, is part of the Quinta do Lorde group. It it becoming popular as a place to lay-up, whether or not work is required, and all the usual services such as painting and *guardinage* (including a monthly hose-down) are available. Great care is shown during lifting and chocking-up, and the metal props – made on-site – are particularly substantial. DIY work is permitted, but owners cannot stay aboard overnight.

Travel-lift 30-tonne capacity, and able to lift up to 5·25m beam and about 20m LOA. Air height is said to be at least 70m.

Engineers Agents for Yanmar, but with a machine shop equipped to handle all kinds of mechanical repairs, plus stainless steel and other welding.

Electronic & radio repairs Can be arranged if required.

Liferaft servicing The only liferaft inspection centre in Madeira. Though currently certified for Plastimo and RFD only, this is to be expanded to include all other major brands.

Chandlery Due to open in late 2011.

Water, electricity and compressed air Provided at each lay-up slot.

Showers Brand new and gleaming!

Smallcraft harbours on the southeast coast of Madeira

Lights

2732 **Santa Cruz south wall** Fl.G.5s9m6M
White tower, green bands 5m

2732·2 **São Pedro east mole** Fl.R.4s6m3M
White post, red bands 3m

2732·25 **São Pedro north (inner) spur**
Fl.G.4s3m2M White block, green band 1m
(obscured other than from southeast)

Santa Cruz

32°41'·24N 16°47'·07W (molehead)

Situated at the southwest end of the Santa Catarina Airport runway, the single mole at Santa Cruz shelters a miniature harbour, apparently popular with local line fishermen despite appearing to carry no more than 1m at LW. It is of no possible interest to visiting yachts.

São Pedro

32°41'·05N 16°47'·59W (east molehead)

A small harbour behind an 80m mole and opening to the northeast, São Pedro is overlooked by an active *clube náutico* from which children are taught to sail dinghies, plus a hotel and restaurant complex. It houses an elderly lifeboat and an assortment of smallcraft on a single pontoon, but it is too small (and shallow) for cruising yachts. There is a small chandlery, stocking mainly dinghy fittings.

Porto Novo

32°39'·62N 16°48'·4W (west quay)

A port in name only, with a stony beach flanked by two small unlit quays and a rough boatyard for wooden fishing craft, the whole overflown – literally – by a vast concrete bridge, part of the *rapida* system. The quays are used by coasters loading cement and roadstone from the quaries close inland and there is no protection of any kind. All in all no place for a yacht.

Funchal

32°38'·51N 16°54'·41W (breakwater head)
32°38'·72N 16°54'·54W (marina mole, angle)

Waypoint
⊕ M14 – 32°38'·5N 16°53'·9W (0·5M ESE of Funchal)

Tides
Predictions for Funchal are available via Admiralty *EasyTide* – see page 141. Alternatively Portuguese tide tables are available for Funchal, with Casablanca as the standard port – see Tides and tidal streams, page 141.
MLWS is about 0·4m above datum and time difference on Casablanca: –0026
Mean spring range 2·0m
Mean neap range 0·8m

Plans
Admiralty *1685* (1:30,000 & 1:10,000)
Portuguese *36402* (1:30,000 & 1:10,000)
US *51263* (1:10,000 and 1:5,000)
Imray-Iolaire *E3* (1:10,000)

Lights
2738 **Breakwater**
Fl.R.5s14m8M 275°-vis-075°
Red and white banded column 6m
2739 **Marina south mole** F.G.9m2M
White tower, two green bands 7m
2739·2 **Marina west mole** F.R.10m3M
White column, three red bands 8m
Naval radio station F.R.137m Radio mast 20m
Pico da Silva F.R.1183m TV mast
2741·3 **Gorgulho cables** Fl(2)R.8s23m9M
330°-vis-025° Daylight range 1·7M
Lantern above white and red banded wall. Marks submarine cables
Note Situated west of Funchal, so of academic interest only

Harbour communications
Harbourmaster ✆ 291 213110 *Fax* 291 228232
Email capitania.funchal@marinha.pt
VHF Ch 11, 16 (call *Capimar Funchal*) (24 hours)
Port Authority (Administração dos Portos da Madeira – APRAM) ✆ 291 208600 *Fax* 291 220196
Email portosdamadeira@apram.pt
www.portosdamadeira.com
VHF Ch 08, 11, 16 (0800–2400 hours)
Funchal Marina ✆ 291 232717 *Fax* 291 225524
Email marinafunchal@sapo.pt
www.marinadofunchal.com (in Portuguese and English) VHF Ch 09, 16, (0900–1800, weekdays, 0900–1200 Saturday)

Port limits
Extend from Ponta do Garajau in the east to Ribeira do Socorridos in the west, and 3M out to sea – see Port limits, page 138.

Small marina inside large commercial harbour

Funchal is a busy commercial harbour and a favourite with the cruise lines, often having three or four ships alongside the breakwater at any time. They tend to arrive in the early morning and leave at dusk, a point worth remembering on approach. The harbour is well protected from the north and west by the high ground on which the city is built, and to the south by the 1,000m breakwater. However, it is fully open eastwards, allowing wind and swell from southeast or east to work straight inside.

The small marina tucked in to the west of the old Cais de Cidade gives total protection but throughout the autumn is packed with local boats, day-charter vessels and a few transient yachts, the latter rafting up six or eight abreast against the western part of the protective wall. Like that at Porto Santo, the inside of the marina wall has become a favourite place for crews to leave their yachts' names or portraits.

Although there have long been rumours that the marina would be extended, by 2011 this looked increasingly unlikely. The boatyard immediately to the west had closed and its small dock seemed likely to be filled in, while the area to the east – which has long been the site of a restaurant centred around a large ketch – was covered with several metres of unsightly stone and rubble, much of it cleared from the town's riverbeds following the floods of February 2010. Although there is a designated smallcraft anchorage area, by early 2011 much of it was buoyed-off while construction work took place – see Anchorage, page 162.

Having said that, there is much to be said for spending a few days in Funchal if at all possible. Much of the city is old and picturesque, and though the centre is usually thick with tourists patronising shops full of dubious souvenirs, 10 minutes' stroll in almost any direction will take one out of the commercial area and into the 'real' Funchal. One possibility is to ride up to Monte in the cable car – not cheap, but with an unsurpassed view – and then follow the narrow cobbled streets back down to the harbour. Take care though – a growing rumble means that one of the famous Funchal basket sledges is taking the same route, and they move at surprising speed.

Funchal is also an excellent base from which to explore the rest of the island by bus, coach or hire car. To discover and fully enjoy the many interesting buildings, museums and gardens in the city and beyond, anyone with more than a few days in Madeira would do well to buy a guidebook to supplement the free literature available from the tourist office on Avenida Arriaga.

Approach and entrance

By day Totally straightforward from all directions. Ponta do Garajau 3·5M to the east is extremely conspicuous, being topped by a huge statue of Christ with outstretched arms. The coast around the headland is a marine reserve, extending from Ponta da Oliveira (16°49'·8W) to Ponta do Lazareto (16°53'·3W) and out to the 50m depth contour or 600m offshore, whichever is further. Three unlit yellow buoys marked PNM (*Parque Natural da Madeira*) lie to the west of Ponta do Garajau. In theory vessels (other than fishing boats launched off the beach) are not supposed to pass through the area, but it is doubtful whether this would be enforced in the case of a yacht on passage. All forms of fishing, scuba diving, and the collection of shells,

Funchal harbour is a popular port of call for cruise ships, though few visiting yachts will manage to get a berth in the marina

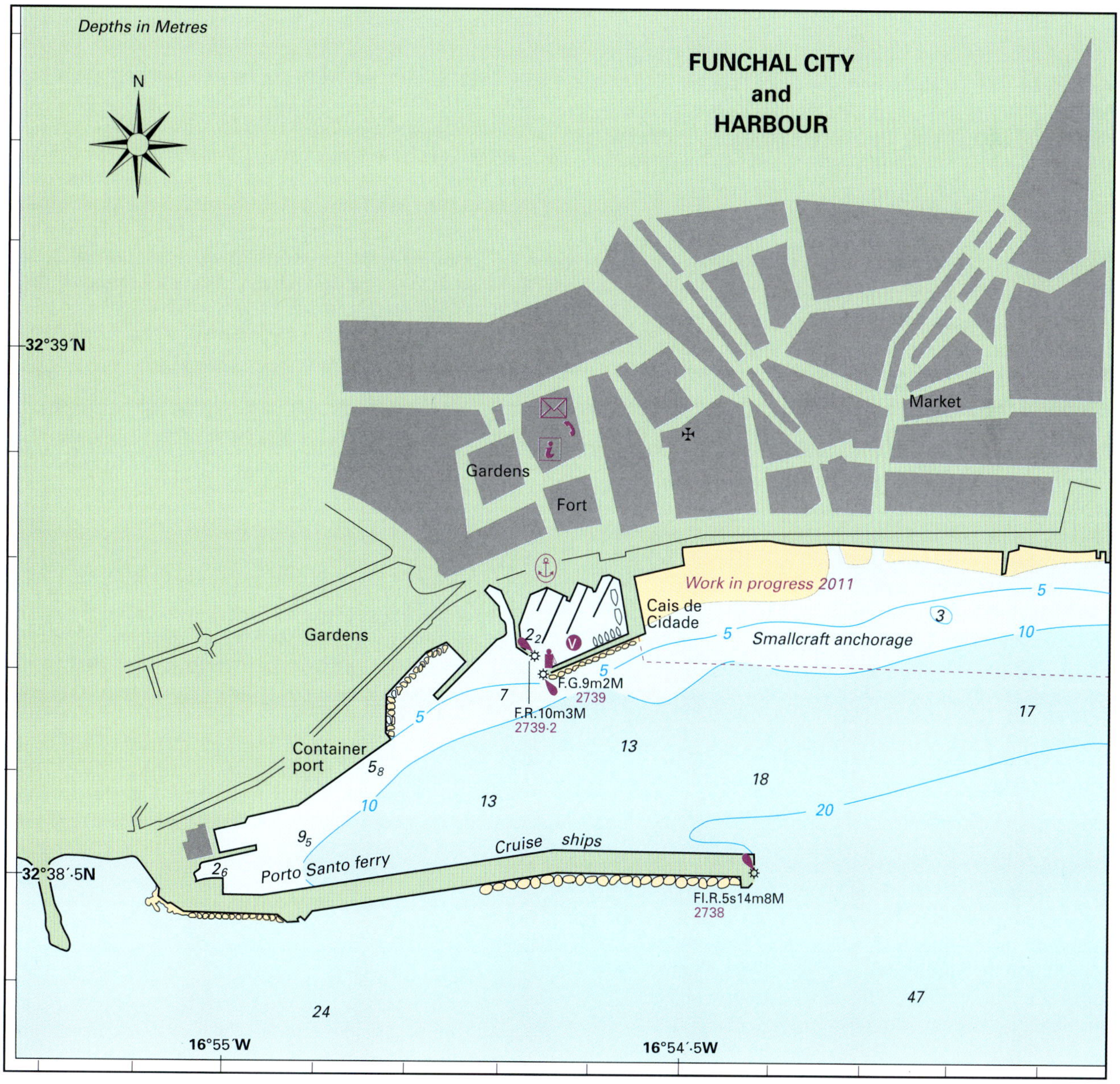

Looking southeast into Funchal Marina, with Ponta do Garajau on the skyline. Unfortunately the old Varadouro São Lázaro, seen in the foreground, has now closed, though vessels were given a few months to relaunch

plants or geological specimens are forbidden within this area.

Fewer yachts approach Funchal from the west, but this is also without hazards so long as the oil terminal at Praia Formosa (which is close inshore) is given reasonable clearance. Light and buoyage details for Praia Formosa are listed together with those for Câmara de Lobos on page 165. A tunny net is sometimes laid close southwest of the root of the main breakwater.

The breakwater should not be rounded too closely in case of large vessels leaving at speed. The marina entrance faces west – ie. into the harbour – and is distinctly narrow. There is an arrivals / fuel pontoon on the starboard hand just inside the entrance, under the windows of the small blue and white reception building.

By night The statue on Ponta do Garajau is floodlit and is quite unmistakable within a mile or two, whilst the city lights of Funchal are far brighter than any others on the island and most attractive from offshore. The breakwater is lit at its eastern end (though this can be difficult to pick out against the shore lights), plus there are tall floodlights at intervals along its length, but the inner cais is unlit other than by street lamps. The marina entrance is conventionally lit on either side.

Anchorage

With the area directly south of the marina occupied by moored tourist boats, most of them large day-trip catamarans, the only anchorage for visiting yachts lies outside the main harbour – see plan – in an exposed and frequently rolly position which becomes untenable in strong onshore winds.

Holding is patchy with areas of hard mud, soft mud and large stones. Once an anchor is well dug into the former it is unlikely to shift, but as the wind frequently blows onshore during the day it is essential to set it carefully. If laying a second anchor one should allow for several 180° wind shifts during each 24 hour period, taking care not to impede the swinging of those lying to a single anchor. Finally, tourist ferries and other charter boats sometimes pass through the anchorage at high speed, causing excessive wash and snubbing sufficient to break anchors out. Although it is possible to land on the shore, a dinghy will be safer left inside the marina itself – along with use of the showers and toilets a benefit for which there is no charge.

Over the years the smallcraft anchorage decreased in size as the beach was built up with imported sand, only for this to be covered in its turn by a thick layer of stone and rubble cleared from the town's riverbeds following the floods and landslides of February 2010. A year later further work had started, possibly to construct a retaining wall around the infill. Six yellow buoys, all Fl.Y.10s, were placed along the 5m contour, the easternmost at 16°54'·31W and the westernmost at 16°54'·54W. Interspersed with them lay a number of large, unlit, steel mooring buoys, apparently used by barges associated with the construction work. Although the outer part of the anchorage still appears to be usable, it would be unwise to approach in darkness and the smallcraft anchorage could be closed at any time.

About six years ago the *Administração dos Portos da Região Autónoma da Madeira* (APRAM) introduced a fee for anchoring within the port limits of Funchal – €27.50 per night for vessels of 9m to 15m, and €41.50 for 16m to 30m. In early 2011 these charges were decreased to a more reasonable €5.80 from vessels of up to 15m and €7.60 for 16m to 30m, though it was stressed that this applied to non-commercial vessels only. Collection was initially haphazard, but officials are now reported to visit anchored yachts several times a week. Full details will be found on APRAM's website at www.portosdamadeira.com, though somewhat hidden on pages 8 and 9 of the Tariff Sheet (a downloadable PDF).

Berthing

It would be most unwise to arrive at Funchal Marina without having previously made contact by phone or email to ensure that space is available – or more probably to join the informal waiting list, see below. The fuel/reception pontoon is immediately to starboard on entry, but is occupied by tourist catamarans for about 15 minutes each day between 1000 and 1030 and again around 1300 for transferring passengers. There are no bollards, just eyes projecting from each end, and one has to wonder if this is because the non-sailing passengers tripped over them!

Inside the marina four jetties with finger pontoons provide permanent berths for around 150 local craft, with more berthed stern-to inside the eastern part of the south wall. Visiting yachts lie alongside the western part of the south wall, sometimes up to eight abreast and often with the smallest trapped on the inside. Although it is claimed that up to 25

The small and crowded marina at Funchal seen from the northeast, with the container terminal and high-rise hotels behind

visiting yachts can be accommodated, half this number seems more likely. During busy periods, primarily the autumn, an informal 'waiting list' system operates, with yachts remaining in one of the island's other marinas until space becomes available.

After a period during which the harbour, and not least the marina, had a reputation for particularly dirty water, it has now achieved EU 'Blue Flag' status and major efforts are being made to keep it clean. Disposal bins are provided for used engine oil, and a repeated plea is made not to use marine toilets whilst berthed alongside. Even so, an occasional oil problem may be inevitable when the wrong combination of wind direction and vessels bunkering in the head of the harbour occurs.

Formalities

On arrival call at the small blue and white building overlooking the marina reception berth, where Immigration, the *Polícia Marítima* and the *Guarda Nacional Republicana* (*GNR*) will be found during office hours. Clearance – which is necessary even if only arriving from Porto Santo – averages less than ten minutes, though slightly longer for a yacht not registered in the EU.

The marina office is some distance away, in the centre of the range of buildings backing onto the road, and should be visited after inward clearance has been obtained and again before leaving the marina, particularly if planning to remain at anchor outside. The other three officials should also be revisited before final departure.

If departing for the Ilhas Desertas or Ilhas Selvagens it is necessary to obtain a permit from the National Parks Department in Funchal (see page 138). The marina staff can arrange this, but allow at least 48 hours.

Charges

There was no price increase between 2010 and 2011, with a 10–12m yacht paying €23.60 per night and a 12–15m yacht paying €38.92, both including water, electricity and IVA (VAT) at 16%, and with discounts available for longer stays. Multihulls – for which there is in any case very little room – paid double these amounts.

Advance bookings are accepted, but only for the very near future – in practice up to a week or so ahead. This allows the informal 'waiting list' to operate, without the marina having to hold berths empty for yachts which have been delayed on passage or diverted elsewhere.

Facilities

Boatyard The Varadouro São Lázaro west of the marina has now closed, leaving owners with a choice between the new yards at Água de Pena – see page 158 – and Linha Sextante Lda – see page 165.

Engineers A wide range of skills are available in the commercial harbour – enquire at the marina office.

Electronic & radio repairs The Maré chandlery (see below) is agent for Raymarine and Simrad among other makes, and has technical expertise to match.

Sail repairs A local company handles sail repairs and is said to offer a reliable and professional service. Enquire at the marina office.

Chandleries Imersão ✆ 291 234815 *Fax* 291 230589 *Email* imersao@imersao.com www.imersao.com has two small shops (open 1000–1300, 1430–1900 weekdays, 1000–1300 Saturday) in the marina complex stocking mainly sport-fishing equipment plus rope and some stainless steel fastenings and fittings.

Faria & Afonso Lda trading as Maré ✆ /*Fax* 291 236858 *Email* mare.madeira@gmail.com, open 0900–1230, 1500–1830 weekdays, 0900–1300 Saturday, have a small but well-stocked shop at 26 Rue Fontes, a small road on the other side of the Avenida do Mar opposite the marina. Stock includes electronics, yacht paints and general chandlery, plus pump spares and bottled gas fittings. Excellent English is spoken and they hold a good range of catalogues, with items not in stock generally obtainable from Lisbon in three working days.

Charts Imersão (see above) stock BA and Imray charts and publications as well as Portuguese charts, though stocks are generally limited to Madeiran waters and are not supplied corrected to date. Maré (see previous page) stock BA and Imray charts for Madeira and the Canaries, and are happy to order further afield on request.

Water Several taps on the marina wall, some of which are normally fitted with long hoses. Yachts at anchor can fill unlimited cans, but there is a small charge for coming alongside the reception pontoon to fill tanks.

Launderette Supervised launderette next to the ladies' showers, operational 0900–1300, 1400–1800 weekdays, 0900–1200 Saturday. Turnaround is usually a couple of hours, though up to 24 hours at busy periods, and in late 2010 10kg of laundry would be washed, dried and folded for €5. There are several other launderettes in the city, both supervised and DIY.

Electricity Numerous 220v 50Hz power points along the marina wall – provided one is within reach. Yachts must provide their own cable and plug, plus adaptor if necessary.

Fuel Diesel and petrol are available 0800–1730 daily on the reception pontoon. Payment must be made in cash. See Berthing, page 162, regarding the use of the pontoon by tourist catamarans.

Bottled gas The Maré chandlery (see above) is one of many in the city offering Camping Gaz exchanges. They can arrange for most other bottles to be refilled, but allow up to three working days.

Clube naval The *Clube Naval do Funchal* has premises on the waterfront about 3km west of the city at Quinta Calaça – but giving onto a beach without access by yacht. However it does have a pleasant swimming pool (open to all on payment of a small fee), plus bar and restaurant.

Funchal's colourful market is a magnet for local people as well as for tourists

Weather forecast Displayed daily outside the marina office, with copies available on request.

Banks Many in Funchal, nearly all with cash dispensers (though none in the marina complex itself).

Shops/provisioning Several well stocked and reasonably priced supermarkets within walking distance of the marina, including a large supermarket in the 'Marina Shopping Centre' opposite. If stocking for a longer period, try either the enormous Pingo Doce hypermarket on the road down to the lido (open long hours, including Sundays) or the equally large SA in São Martinho on the western outskirts of Funchal.

Almost all general shopping needs can be met, as might be expected in a large and thriving city catering for many thousand of tourists each year.

Produce market An excellent fruit, vegetable and fish market has been thriving in the eastern part of the city since its formal opening in 1940. The building – complete with central courtyard, large tiled panels and a tower topped with the city's coat of arms – merits a second look, while flower-sellers in traditional Madeiran costume throng the entrance. A case for the camera as well as the shopping bag!

Cafés, restaurants & hotels A vast number of all standards, prices and styles. A cluster of somewhat touristy restaurants will be found near the seafront east of the cable car terminal, but it may be necessary to range further afield to track down traditional Madeiran specialities.

Medical services Several hospitals, including at least two with 24 hour emergency departments, plus numerous clinics, health centres, dentists and opticians. Funchal Hospital ✆ 291 705730.

Communications

Post office The main post office, on Avenida Zarco, is open 0830–2000 weekdays, 0900–1300 Saturday. Stamps can also be bought from vending machines (in the tourist office on Avenida Arriaga amongst other places) which list current rates but do not give change.

Mailing address C/o Marina Funchal, 9000–055 Funchal, Madeira, Portugal. Mail will be held for yachts at anchor as well as those berthed in the marina itself.

Telephones Phone boxes in the marina complex, with cards available at the post office.

Internet access Free Wi-Fi is available on the wide paved area overlooking the marina buildings, in the city's main square and in a second public square one block east of the cathedral (where tables as well as seating are available). None offer any source of power. There are also various cybercafés throughout the city, most also offering printing, scanning, photocopying etc.

Car hire At least a dozen agencies in the city, or arrange via the marina office.

Taxis Taxi ranks on Avenida Arriaga and elsewhere, or order via the marina office.

Buses Cheap and reliable, though slightly complicated for out-of-town routes. Two different companies cover the island – see page 136 for details and websites.

Ferries Regular service to Porto Santo and beyond – see page 135.

Air services Santa Catarina Airport, with frequent international flights as well as inter-island hops to Porto Santo, is situated some 18km east of Funchal.

Linha Sextante boatyard

32°38'·66N 16°58'·23W (travel-lift molehead)

Waypoint

⊕ M15 – 32°38'·2N 17°58'·5W (0·5M SSW of Linha Sextante Lda boatyard)

New boatyard with 70-tonne hoist

In 2009 a new boatyard – Linha Sextante Lda, Estaleiro Naval dos Socorridos, Rua Pico da Torre, Bloco G4°A, Código Postal 9300-004, Câmara de Lobos; ✆ 962 485975, 964 556930 – opened about 0·25M east of Câmara de Lobos, sandwiched between a substantial seawall and an almost sheer cliff face with the main road passing some 100 feet above. Though intended primarily to serve the fishing fleet, yachts also use the yard and charges are reported to be reasonable. Boss Jorge Nunes Oliveira speaks reasonable English, but Sérgio Jesus from InoxLobos Lda (see below), who speaks the language fluently, will assist with translation if necessary.

The entrance faces just south of east and is extremely close to the rocky shoreline, and a southerly swell would make the area hazardous. Although the approach from due south is unimpeded, breaking shoals (which show up well on current Google satellite images) extend up to 100m offshore to the southwest. During the winter of 2010/11 a shingle bank built up close east of the entrance, though it is not known to what extent this affected depths in the hoist dock itself. Anyone considering hauling will need to visit the yard first to make an appointment, a good chance to examine the approach.

Security is good behind substantial gates, normally open from 0800 to 1800 weekdays and 0800 to 1300 on Saturday. DIY work is permitted and there is no objection to owners living aboard (toilets and showers are provided on site), but the very limited hardstanding makes it unsuitable as a place to haul other than for immediate work. Water and electricity are available throughout and the general impression is of a clean, well-kept, busy yard.

Linha Sextante boatyard west of Funchal. The sea here is benign, but with a southerly swell the approach would be hazardous

The unusually long travel-lift dock at the Linha Sextante boatyard is tucked right behind the breakwater and served by a 70-tonne hoist

Several concerns have premises on site, including InoxLobos Lda, *Email* inoxlobos@gmail.com, ✆ 965 754508, which handles all kinds of metalwork but specialises in stainless steel fabrication, and others handling carpentry, painting etc.

Câmara de Lobos

32°38'·88N 16°58'·5W (slipway)

Plans

Admiralty *1685* (1:30,000)
Portuguese *36403* (1:30,000 & 1:10,000)
US *51263* (1:10,000)

Lights

2741·5 **Formosa cables** Fl(2)R.8s6m9M
027°-vis-055° Daylight range 1·6M
White post, red bands 4m. Marks submarine cables
2743 **Praia de Vitória cement wharf**
Q(6)+LFl.15s12m9M White tower on jetty 10m
Duque d'Alba (east dolphin) Fl.R.2·4s
White structure, red lantern 2m
2744 **Câmara de Lobos** Oc.R.6s22m9M 304°-vis-099°
Red and white truncated column on white block 2m
Cabo Girão F.R.691m TV mast 42m
Note Three yellow buoys, one Q(4)Y.10s2M, one Q(5)Y.10s3M and one Fl.Y.3s2M form a triangle centred on 32°38'·4N and 16°58'·1W (between Praia de Vitória and Câmara de Lobos)

Picturesque inlet best visited by land

A very small and busy fishing harbour which lies 4M west of Funchal and 1M west of the oil terminal and prohibited anchorage off Praia Formosa, Câmara de Lobos is very scenic despite the inevitable construction work and well worth visiting – by land. The narrow bay is far too crowded with moored local boats to allow a yacht swinging room, with dozens of smaller craft hauled up on the stony beach to be launched as needed. It might be possible to lie briefly alongside the stone quay on the western side of the bay, but this too is in constant use by fishermen and it would be far better to leave the yacht elsewhere and enjoy the scenic coastal road.

All Madeiran fishing boats seem to be brightly painted, but none more so than in Câmara de Lobos where the crowded foreshore is a mass of primary colour, interspersed with the more muted tones of traditional wooden vessels under repair. Unlike many picturesque villages there is also plenty going on – a catch being landed, boats built or painted and nets repaired, whilst up the steep streets above the harbour the older women sit chatting on their doorsteps as they work on the intricate embroidery to be seen in the shops of Funchal. Sir Winston Churchill returned here several times to paint – as the tourist literature repeatedly informs you – while the modern visitor probably fills their digital memory card. Don't miss the little fishermen's chapel right beside the harbour, complete with 1587 gravestone and scenes from the life of St Antony which depict him apparently preaching to some *espada*!

Ribeira Brava

32°40'·07N 17°03'·8W (molehead)

Lights

2746 **Ribeira Brava** Fl.R.5s33m9M
Square red building 3m

2745 **Mole** Fl.R.5s6m6M
White tower, red bands 3·5m

Marine farm

A marine farm, marked by four yellow buoys with × topmarks, all Fl.Y.6s3M, lies about 0·6M to the southeast centred on 32°39'·6N 17°03'·3W.

Small harbour and possible anchorage

Ribeira Brava lies just under 9M west of Funchal, from which it is reached via a long tunnel. The area suffered badly in the floods of February 2009, and much of Ribeira Brava's former beach is now covered by rocks and rubble. However, the town itself survived relatively unscathed, and all the usual shops, banks, hotels and restaurants will be found close to the seafront road.

The small harbour at Ribeira Brava – accessed via a tunnel through the headland – looking south

Ribeira Brava's tiny harbour is reached via a tunnel through the headland to the east, but is too small to provide any real shelter from the usual afternoon onshore winds. The south arm – which suffered damage during the winter of 2010/11 – is sometimes used by a tourist ferry from Funchal, making it an unsafe spot to leave a dinghy, and the outer section has a low concrete overhang. There is reported to be good if deep holding over sand in the bay to the west, but rolling would be inevitable.

Marina do Lugar de Baixo

32°40'·7N 17°05'·55W (south breakwater head)

Waypoint

⊕ M16 – 32°40'·2N 17°'05·5W (0·5M S of Marina do Lugar de Baixo)

Lights

As of early 2011 there were no functioning lights at Marina do Lugar de Baixo and, despite inclusion in the current Portuguese *Lista de Luzes*, it seems unlikely that any will be reinstated while the marina remains inoperable.

Large marina which remains closed

Still under construction when the previous edition of this book appeared, the saga of Marina do Lugar de Baixo is sad in the extreme. It appears that it was originally to have been built some distance to the southwest at Ponta do Sol, but was then moved to the supposedly more sheltered Lugar de Baixo. This also proved too exposed, however, and even before completion serious damage had been caused to the south breakwater by winter gales and their associated swell. The marina has never formally opened and arguments – and the apportionment of blame – continue.

The root of the problem appears to be the relatively shallow depths which exist along that stretch of the coast. Unusually for Madeira, a mile southwest of the marina only 50m will be found and the seabed shoals smoothly to around 5m off the breakwater. This causes swell generated by winter storms to build to double its original height as it approaches the marina. This fact was not lost on local surfers, who bemoaned the destruction of one of their favourite waves and predicted – rightly – that it would overpower any breakwater built in its path. According to one experienced local yachtsman, 'Marina do Lugar de Baixo is located in one of the worst places on the island'.

Some hope was generated in September 2009 when the president of the regional government reopened the nearby swimming pool and restaurant, with the marina itself billed for reopening in April 2010. This reckoned without the exceptional weather suffered that winter, during which two further breaches were made in the south breakwater, and when visited in October 2010 the marina – and apparently the swimming pool – were firmly closed. However, work was taking place south of the breakwater to construct a wide defensive bank,

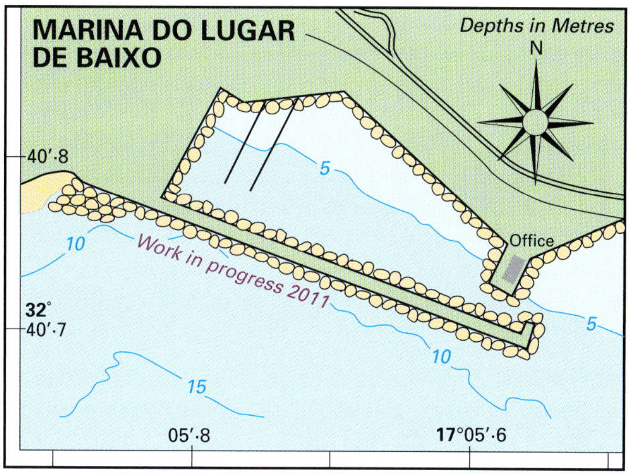

presumably intended to absorb the worst of the wave force and provide the marina with a second ring of armament. By early January rubble blocked the narrow marina entrance, and though this appeared to have occurred naturally it was soon consolidated into a causeway to allow vehicles access to the west end of the breakwater. Perhaps unsurprisingly, few details were forthcoming.

If and when Marina do Lugar de Baixo does finally open, its interior layout is unlikely to be markedly different from the original specification. This allowed for 349 berths, about 50 of them able to take yachts of more than 12m in depths of 3·5m or more. The marina office building on the east mole, empty since 2005 but not derelict, appears to need only a lick of paint and connection to the usual services to start functioning, with a restaurant on the floor above.

Ponta do Sol – the nearest town and accessed from Lugar de Baixo via one of Madeira's many tunnels – lies only 11M west of Funchal by water, making the area less remote than it at first appears. A pleasant village below towering cliffs, with a clean if stony swimming beach, it boasts a bank, shops, restaurants and hotel, medical services, post office and public telephones. Dating back to 1425, Ponta do Sol is one of the oldest settlements on Madeira and is also reputed to be one of the sunniest.

Rubble blocks the entrance to Marina do Lugar de Baixo, still out of commission nearly a decade after construction work started *Harald Sammer*

Porto de Recreio da Calheta

32°42′·99N 17°10′·3W (west breakwater head)

Waypoint
⊕ M17 – 32°42′·6N 17°10′·6W (0·5M SW of Porto de Recreio da Calheta)

Plans
Admiralty *1831* (1:150,000)
Portuguese *36403* (1:30,000)
Imray-Iolaire *E3* (1:6,250)

Lights
2748 **East breakwater head** Fl.G.5s9m6M
Green and white tower 4·5m
2748·2 **West breakwater head** Fl.R.5s9m6M
Red and white tower 4.5m
2748·4 **East breakwater root** Fl(2)G.5s7m2M
002°-vis-042°-obsc-075°-vis-125°
Green and white post on wall 1·5m
2748·6 **West breakwater elbow** Fl(2)R.5s7m2M
130°-vis-320° Red lantern on wall
2748·8 **East inner breakwater**
Fl(3)G.5s7m2M Green lantern on wall
Pico do Arco de Calheta F.R.887m TV mast 42m

Marine farm
A marine farm, marked by four yellow pillar buoys with bells and × topmarks, two Fl.Y.3s2M and two unlit, lies off Punta da Galé less than 1M west of the marina entrance, centred on 32°43′·2N 17°11′·3W.

Harbour communications
Porto de Recreio da Calheta ✆ 291 824003
Fax 291 824006
Email portoderecreiodacalheta@netmadeira.com
www.portoderecreiodacalheta.com (in Portuguese, English and French), VHF Ch 16, transferring to Ch 9 (0900–2300 daily)

Large new marina

Unlike its neighbour further east, the Porto de Recreio da Calheta – which opened to visitors in September 2004 – is thriving. Containing 339 berths for vessels of between 6m and 25m in depths of up to 3·5m, it continues to receive favourable comments from visiting yachts. Security is good, with CCTV and entry to the pontoons controlled via electronic gates.

Almost as soon as the marina opened constant movement in the basin was identified as a problem, and within a few years the entrance was re-modelled

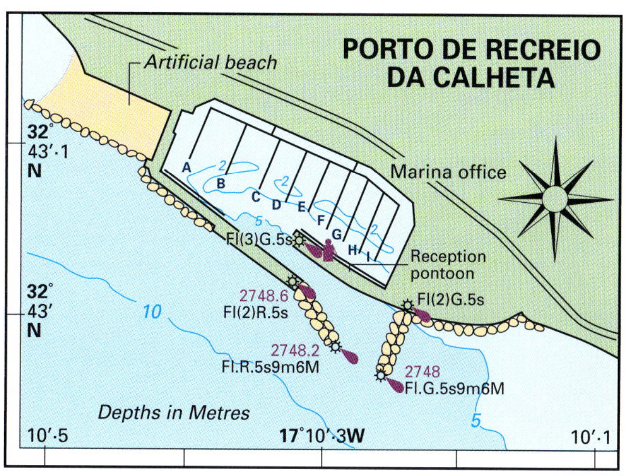

II. THE MADEIRA GROUP

and the outer moles added. Although much improved, surge inside the marina remains a problem, particularly at the western end where visitors are usually berthed. For that reason, Porto de Recreio da Calheta cannot be recommended as a safe place to leave a yacht unattended during the winter. The natural surge is said to be exacerbated by motorboats and jet skis, which frequently ignore the marina's 3 knot speed limit.

The marina lies beneath spectacular cliffs in what is claimed to be the sunniest part of Madeira, and a protected swimming area with large areas of golden sand (imported from Morocco) has been created just west of the marina. Although somewhat remote – 16M from Funchal by sea and considerably more by road – the old town of Calheta about 2km up the valley has a variety of shops, medical services, a post office and public telephones, while the parade of shops behind the marina includes a bank and a well-stocked supermarket. The marina itself has several flourishing restaurants, while the nearby Calheta Beach Hotel offers air-conditioned comfort and further dining possibilities.

On 24 June Calheta celebrates its annual *festa*, with religious processions and flower carpets.

Approach and entrance

Straightforward from offshore, although unpredictable squalls off the cliffs should be anticipated. The large white building behind the marina can be seen from some distance, with the pale grey breakwaters becoming obvious on closer approach. The entrance itself is narrow with a tight dog-leg, but though deeper draught yachts are advised to keep to the middle of the channel, particularly at low tide, it should present no problems in reasonable weather. Although well lit, first time entry at night is probably best avoided.

Yachts are requested to call up on VHF before arrival, not least to check that space is available. Porto de Recreio da Calheta is popular with local boatowners, and by late 2010 was almost full.

Berthing

A berth is often allocated via VHF, with visiting yachts usually directed to the western end of the basin, otherwise secure to the long pontoon inside the east mole in depths of 3m or more. To reach it, a U-turn to starboard is required immediately after passing the second pair of lights and, if the pontoon is full (it is often occupied by game fishing boats), a long-keeled yacht might have problems reversing back into clear water. An alternative on arrival is to secure to the inside the southwest breakwater just inside the entrance, where bollards and steps are provided. The long pontoon beyond is used by tourist ferries.

Formalities

Take all documentation to the marina office at the northeast corner of the basin, where several of the staff speak English.

Porto de Recreio da Calheta seen from cliffs to the northwest. The angled moles were added in an effort to prevent swell entering the marina *Harald Sammer*

The marina is an official port of entry, with all paperwork handled in the main office and forwarded as necessary. If planning to depart in the evening, formalities must be completed before the office staff leave at 1730.

Charges

There was no increase in the basic price between 2009 and 2011, though IVA (VAT) has risen twice, bringing overnight fees up to €24.20 for a visiting yacht of 10–12m and €32.26 for 12–15m. This includes IVA (VAT) at 16%, but not electricity or water, for which electronic cards must be bought. Multihulls pay a 70% surcharge, though a discount may be negotiated, and sizeable discounts are available for longer stays. The marina accepts bookings made by email or via the website.

Facilities

Travel-lift None, and no plans for one. There is a 1-tonne crane, but its jib is too low to handle the average mast.
Diving services Can be organised via the marina office.
Engineers, mechanics, electronic/radio repairs Enquire at the marina office.
Sail repairs and rigging A local company handles sail repairs and rigging, and is said to offer a reliable and professional service. Contact via the marina office.
Chandlery Two smallish chandleries in the same block as the marina office, both largely given over to fishing equipment but with limited stocks of paint, fittings and clothing. Otherwise Maré in Funchal will deliver.
Water At all berths.
Showers Next to the marina office.
Launderette There is no longer a launderette in the marina, though laundry left at the office will normally be returned dry within 24 hours. The laundry in the town does not allow DIY.
Electricity At all berths.
Fuel Fuel pontoon (petrol and diesel) just inside the east breakwater, open 0900–2300. Payment may be made by Visa, MasterCard or cash.
Bottled gas Nothing closer than Funchal, even for Camping Gaz exchanges.
Weather forecast Posted daily in the marina office.
Bank Beside the supermarket on the road behind the marina, plus a cash dispenser in the marina complex.
Shops/provisioning Small convenience store in the marina complex, plus a large (though not enormous) Pingo Doce supermarket on the road behind, no more than 250m away. Supermarket trolleys can be taken across to the marina (there are no steps to negotiate) provided they are returned.
Hotels, restaurants & cafés The Calheta Beach Hotel lies just west of the marina, with a choice of cafés and restaurants overlooking the basin itself.

Communications

Post office In the town.
Mailing address C/o Porto de Recreio da Calheta, Vila da Calheta, 9004-133 Calheta, Madeira, Portugal.
Telephones In the town, though it might be possible to use an office phone in an emergency.
Internet access Free Wi-Fi in the marina's terrace and restaurant area, though the signal is said to be unreliable at some of the remoter berths. At least one internet café in the town.
Car hire Available via both the travel agent next to the supermarket and the Calheta Beach Hotel.
Taxis Arrange via the marina office, though hiring a car may well prove cheaper.
Buses Infrequent buses to Funchal and elsewhere from a stop outside the hotel. A timetable may be available at the hotel, otherwise consult Rodoeste's timetable at www.rodoeste.pt/. Many more buses pass through Estrela, a steep 3km along the cliffs heading west.
Airport Calheta is a long way from the airport in terms of both time and distance. A taxi will cost at least €60, so if crew are leaving or arriving it may well prove cheaper to hire a car for the day.

Jardim do Mar

32°44'·25N 17°12'·78W (southwest beach)

Exposed beach anchorage

A stony beach backed by a high promenade with a slipway at its eastern end, Jardim do Mar has been suggested as a potential anchorage in settled weather. Most of the time, however, it would appear to have more appeal to surfers than to yachts. There is an artificial reef about 0·65M northwest of the town where fishing, anchoring and scuba diving are prohibited.

Paúl do Mar

32°45'·06N 17°13'·45W (molehead)

Lights
2750 **Paúl do Mar** Oc.R.3s16m6M
White post, red bands 13m

Small fishing harbour

The most westerly of the possible anchorages along Madeira's southwest coast, Paúl do Mar is an old fishing village where a paved slipway is protected by a short, angled mole, the whole backed by spectacular cliffs. It might be possible to lie alongside the mole for a short period with the agreement of local fishermen, the only alternative being to anchor southeast of the entrance – there is no space for a yacht to anchor inside the harbour. The small town has cafés, restaurants and a cash machine as well as basic shops.

Pretty little Paúl do Mar – also featured on page 130 – is the most westerly harbour on Madeira's south coast. Even so, a yacht would almost certainly have to anchor outside

Porto Moniz

32°51'·93N 17°09'·82W (breakwater head)

Waypoint
⊕ M18 – 32°51'·9N 17°09'·2W (0·5M E of Porto Moniz)

Tides
Predictions for Porto de Moniz are available via Admiralty *EasyTide* – see page 141

Plans
Portuguese *37501* (1:7,500)

Lights
2754 **Porto Moniz (Ilhéu Môle)** Fl.WR.5s64m10/8M 116°-R-127°-W-116° Hexagonal tower 3m
Note As of early 2011 the mole remained unlit

Fair-weather harbour in scenic surroundings

Porto Moniz lies in the extreme northwest of Madeira, and is a favourite tourist attraction due to the bathing pools created by concreting some of the western rocks together. A substantial 120m breakwater has recently been constructed on the southeast side of the headland, intended primarily for tourist ferries and fishing craft. However, it is seldom busy and at least one yacht has overnighted alongside, reporting it to be quite tenable despite the considerable northeasterly swell running outside (note, however, that this visit took place in June – winter conditions might be very different). At least 3m should be found near the breakwater end, shoaling towards the root. Although the quay is high – at least 5m above sea level – there are several sets of steps and plenty of bollards. Another possibility would be to anchor off and land by dinghy on the steps or slipway.

Facilities are limited, but include a tap at the fishmarket fronting the old quay at the head of the harbour and a cold (outdoor) shower next to the old slipway. Fuel is available by can from a filling station close to the west corner of the harbour. The village has a small supermarket, a bank with cash dispenser, several restaurants and hotels and numerous tourist shops.

There is a daily bus to/from Funchal – Rodoeste's 80 service, see www.rodoeste.pt/horas/80.pdf – an excellent way to visit the area if not intending to do so by yacht.

Smallcraft harbours on the north coast of Madeira

Seixal

32°49'·31N 17°06'·07W (molehead)

A 100m concrete mole, orientated approximately east/west, was built early this century to protect a smallcraft launching ramp, a black-sand beach and a few small fishing boats which appear to be stored ashore when not in use. Within a few years the *Clube Naval do Seixal* was also up and running, with premises overlooking the natural swimming pool to the west. Presumably it limits its activities to dinghies, as considerable surge enters the bay and depths are reported to be no more than 2m, shoaling further in. Although by early October 2010 the tall green and white banded column on the molehead was already listing visibly, by the following March it was reported to be lit, Fl.R.5s12m5M.

In very settled conditions it would be possible to anchor to the east and land either on the slipway or at the single set of steps, but it would be strictly a

The wide breakwater at Porto Moniz looking almost due north, with the dark bulk of Ilhéu Mole behind

The small bay at Seixal seen from hills to the south. Like the other small harbours on Madeira's exposed north coast most will prefer to visit by land

case for eyeball navigation as the area remains uncharted and nothing is known about the approach. The nearby village has basic facilities only.

Porto de São Vicente

32°48'·83N 17°02'W (west molehead)

A minuscule circular harbour fully exposed to the north, but nevertheless boasting its own *Clube Naval*. The narrow launching ramp must be unusable for much of the year, and by late 2010 the eastern arm was already half demolished despite having been built only a few years previously. Certainly no place for a visiting yacht.

Ponta Delgada

32°49'·68N 16°59'W (molehead)

A short breakwater on a northwest/southeast alignment was built a few years ago to provide protection for a few moored smallcraft, with a large swimming pool behind. There is no more than 2m depth and the rough inner face of the mole allows no possibility of lying alongside. Best visited by land.

A prominent white church with a richly decorated interior overlooks the harbour, a focus for the *arraiais* (religious festival) of *Senhor Bom Jesus*, held on the first weekend in September and one of the largest in the Madeiran calendar.

Porto da Cruz

32°46'·51N 16°49'·6W (dinghy harbour)

A port in name only, the tiny harbour and miniature slipway at Porto da Cruz are tucked in behind a high curved wall, opening onto a bay fully exposed to the northeast trades. The eroded strata on the seaward face of the promontory bear witness to the force of elements.

The village, with its ultra-modern church (unusual in Madeira) is quite unmistakeable, dominated by the sheer cliffs of massive Penha de Aguia (590m) to the west and with several rocky islets offshore. Running out towards them is a lower tongue of land, with a black sand beach to the northwest and an equally black stony beach and several rock-edged swimming pools to the southeast.

In calm or light southerly conditions it would be possible to anchor off either beach and land by dinghy at the steps inside the harbour, but the yacht should not be left unattended. Note, however, that cables run from a point close east of the harbour at 32°46'·25N 16°49'·5W. They are marked by a white post with red bands and lit both day and night, Fl(2)R.8s9m9M, over an arc from 188° to 216°. Anchorage within this area is prohibited.

The town has cafés, a few shops and a post office.

Ponta Delgada, midway along Madeira's north coast, seen from cliffs to the east

The tiny inner harbour at Porto da Cruz. Yachts occasionally anchor in the bay to the east when the weather is very settled

Ilhas Desertas

Between 32°24'N–32°36'N and 16°28'W–16°33'W

Introduction

The three islands which together comprise the Ilhas Desertas – Ilhéu Chão, Ilha Deserta Grande and Ilhéu Bugio – lie 10M south-southeast of the easterly tip of Madeira and form a low broken ridge nearly 12M long but less than 1M wide. Maximum elevation is 442m near the centre of Ilha Deserta Grande. All three islands are fringed by rocky cliffs and are largely steep-to, an offing of 0·5M being ample.

Once owned by a British family named Hinton, the islands later passed into the possession of the Madeiran government whose attempt to found a permanent settlement was frustrated by the lack of fresh water. In 1990 a Protected Area was established comprising the Ilhas Desertas and their off-lying rocks and islands, plus their surrounding waters to the 100m contour. Before departing Madeira or Porto Santo for the Ilhas Desertas the skipper MUST obtain a permit to land – see page 138. A warden is permanently stationed on the islands to protect the many breeding birds as well as the endangered monk seals (*Monachus monachus*), of which fewer than two dozen remain. The crew of a yacht will usually be met as they come ashore and no permit – no access!

All forms of fishing, scuba diving, and the collection of shells, plants or geological specimens are forbidden within the protected area. So are shooting and lighting fires, and wildlife – particularly birds – must not be disturbed. Rubbish must not be dumped (which of course applies to the marine environment generally).

Websites

The Islas Desertas do not run to their own website, though they are mentioned briefly on some of the sites devoted to the archipelago as a whole – see page 137. In 2011 a short but informative description, together with a few photographs, was to be found at www.en.wikipedia.org/wiki/ Desertas_Islands.

The Ilhas Desertas seen from eastern Madeira, with Isla Deserta Grande in the centre and Ilhéu Chão and Ilhéu Bugio on either side

Navigation

Magnetic variation
6°10'W (2011), decreasing by 8'E annually.

Tidal streams
Tidal streams around the Ilhas Desertas set northeast on the flood and southwest on the ebb at up to 2 knots at springs and 1 knot at neaps.

Charts
Admiralty *1831* (1:150,000)
Portuguese *36201* (1:100,000), *36406* (1:50,000)
US *51261* (1:150,000)
Imray-Iolaire *E3* (1:170,000)

Lights
2720 **Ilhéu Chão (Farilhão)**
LFl(2)15s111m13M 031°-vis-321°
Round tower and building 14m
2722 **Ilhéu Bugio (Ponta da Agulha)** Fl.4s71m13M
163°-vis-100° Hexagonal tower 8m

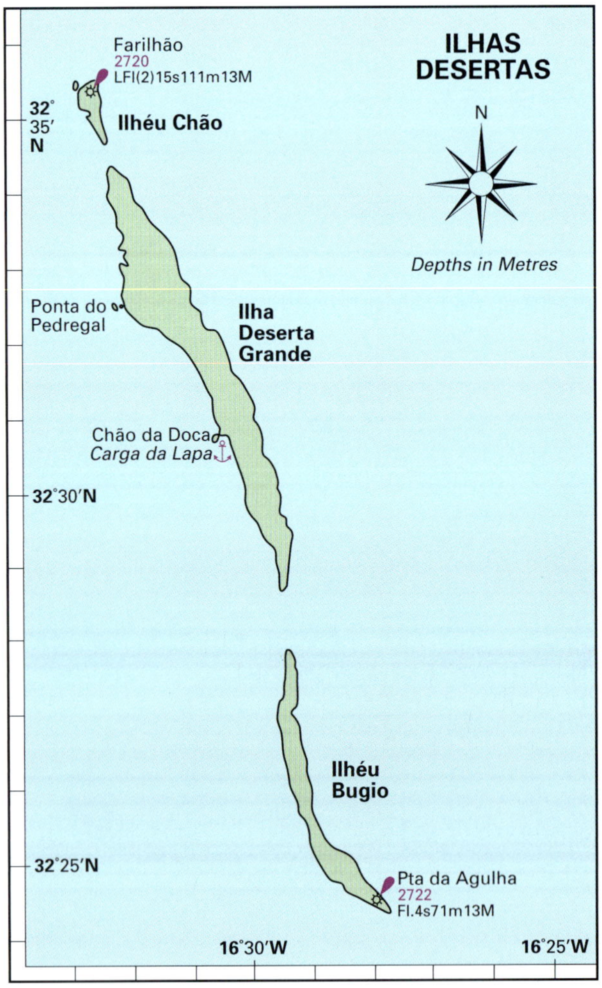

Carga da Lapa, Ilha Deserta Grande

32°30′·71N 16°30′·53W (anchorage)

Waypoints

⊕ M19 – 32°30′·2N 16°30′·7W (0·5M SSW of Carga da Lapa, Ilha Deserta Grande)

Courses and distances

⊕ M08 (0·5M S of Pta da Cruz, Madeira) – ⊕ M19 = 23M, 108° / 188°

⊕ M11 (0·5M S of Quinta do Lorde Marina) – ⊕ M19 = 17M, 143° / 323°

⊕ M14 (0·5M ESE of Funchal) – ⊕ M19 = 21M, 113° / 293°

⊕ M17 (0·5M SW of Porto de Recreio da Calheta) – ⊕ M19 = 36M, 110° / 290°

Plans

Portuguese *36406* (1:15,000)
Imray-Iolaire *E3* (1:25,000)

Tides

Time difference on Funchal: +0011
Mean spring range 2·0m
Mean neap range 0·8m

Small and scenic anchorage

Carga da Lapa – literally, *load of limpets*, but known locally as Baixa Doca – lies 21·5M from Funchal on a course of 112°, slightly north of the centre of the chain. The tiny bay is protected from north and east by Ilha Deserta Grande, and from northwest by Chão da Doca, a rocky islet and narrow spit of boulders, awash at high water, extending from a rock fall at the base of steep cliffs. Inside this runs a second reef with estimated depths of between 6m and awash. It is a favourite destination for tourist boats from Funchal and elsewhere, to the point that, in 2010, a visiting yachtsman described it as 'not deserted at all, but pretty crowded!'.

Looking down into the anchorage at Carga da Lapa from the northeast. Sadly, a landslip has since blocked access to the cliffs *Henry Adams*

A true deserted anchorage at the Ilhas Desertas, with Ilhéu Bugio visible in the distance *Harald Sammer*

Until a few years ago it was possible for the fit and energetic to gain access to the plateau almost 400m above via rough steps cut into the cliffs. Sadly the track was blocked by a landslip not far above the beach and is now considered too dangerous to attempt, making the excellent photograph below among the last of its kind. Shore access is now limited to a path of just a couple of hundred metres.

Approach

Chão da Doca is surrounded by off-lying rocks, including a group immediately to the south of the islet which are covered at high water and should be given a wide berth. The prevailing northeasterly wind may back to blow parallel to the coast in heavy gusts and no shelter will be found from the resultant swell until very close in. Final entry should be made from the south, where there is deep water close to the cliffs. The water is very clear.

Mooring and anchorage

With no shelter from between southeast and west there is an obvious need to keep a close eye on the weather, as the bay would rapidly become uncomfortable and possibly dangerous in deteriorating conditions. Even so, yachts regularly spend the night there in established northeasterlies, and the anchorage has been described as 'amazingly calm, despite the 25 knot northeasterlies with stronger gusts blowing outside'.

Several moorings have been laid, but reports suggest that they should not be relied upon and most prefer to anchor. The favoured technique is to approach the beach as close as one's nerve will allow, whilst leaving adequate room to swing. Alternatively, it may be possible to drop a bow anchor and take one or more stern lines ashore. Space is not quite as tight as one might expect – though note that the yacht in the photograph on the left is a 25ft Folkboat and not a 50-footer! – and about 15m will be found in the centre of the bay. Holding is patchy over large stones and sand, but as both are black one cannot 'eyeball' a good spot, despite the clarity of the water.

Ilhas Selvagens

Between 30°08'N–30°09'N and 15°51'W–15°52'W

Introduction

The Ilhas Selvagens (which translates as 'savage islands' and has nothing to do with salvage, the Portuguese for which is *salvamento*) consist of three small islands in two main groups nearly 10M apart, close to the direct course between Madeira and Tenerife. Lying nearly 160M from the former but less than 100M from the latter, Spain has recently been casting a covetous eye over the islands with a view to expanding its Exclusive Economic Zone, and in particular its fishing grounds. It appears that if the islands were to be reclassified as 'rocks' they would be deemed to be part of the nearest occupied landmass, and would thus become Spanish. However, Portugal shows no sign of wishing to relinquish its most remote remaining territory, possibly for the same reason. Largely due to the efforts of a Madeiran doctor, Paul Alexander (Alec) Zino, they have been a nature reserve and bird sanctuary since the early 1970s, and the surrounding waters inside the 200m contour have more recently been declared a marine reserve.

Selvagem Grande is the largest at about 2·5km^2. Steep cliffs rise to a small plateau with a saddle between two hills, Pico da Atalaia at 153m in the west and Pico dos Tornozelos at 136m further east. Although it looks barren and dry from a distance there is in fact some vegetation, largely eaten down by rabbits, and there are large breeding colonies of Madeiran petrels (*Pterodroma madeira*) known locally as *Friera*, and Cory's shearwaters (*Calonectris diomedea*) – see page 18. Without any natural predators they are remarkably unafraid of people, and in the past many eggs fell victim to fishermen who would sail down from Madeira to collect them. Further depredations were made in the late 19th century when no lady's hat was considered complete without a few feathers to finish it off – as it nearly did the resident bird population.

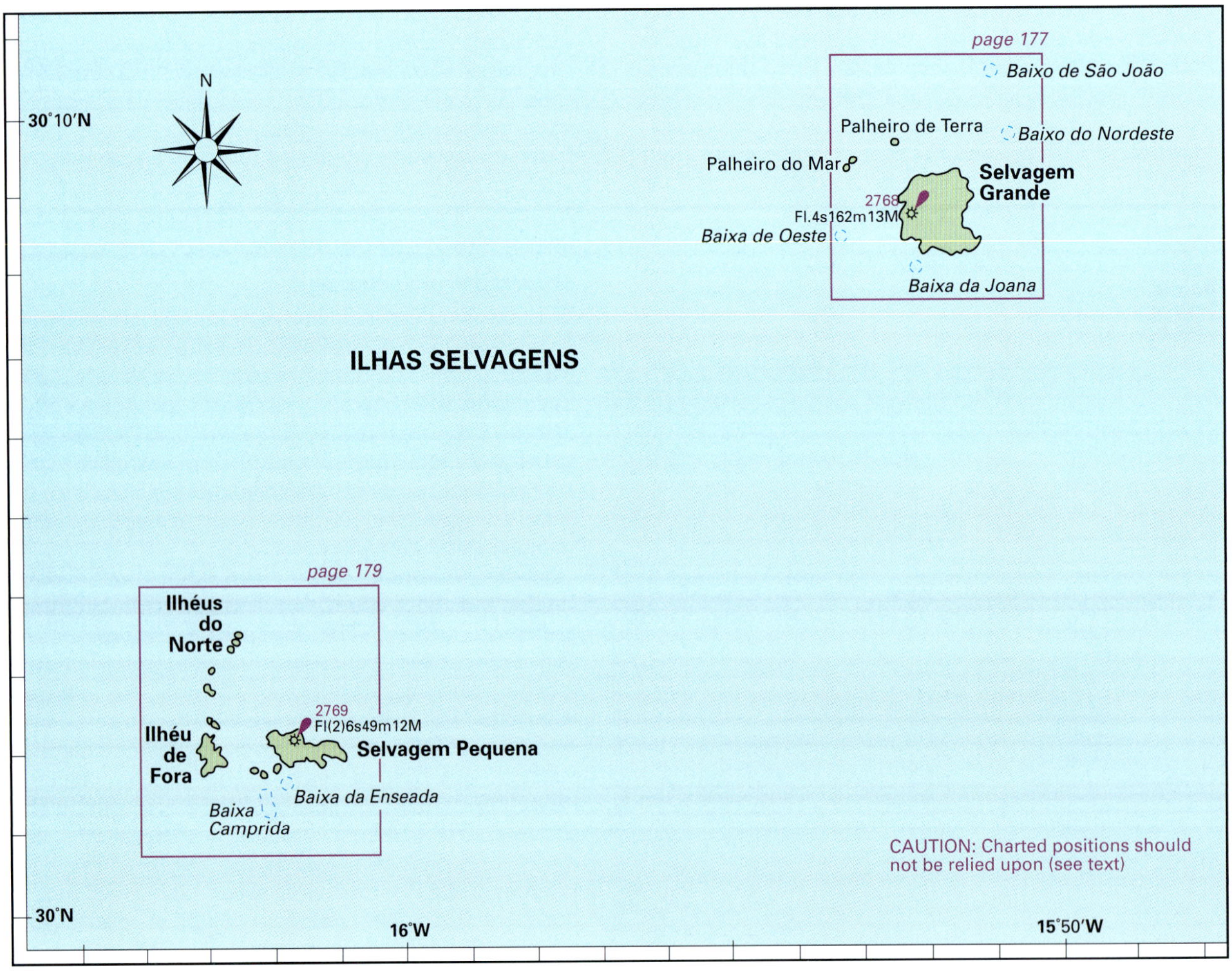

Navigation

Waypoints
⊕ M20 – 30°09'·9N 15°50'·1W (0·5M ENE of Baixo do Nordeste, Selvagem Grande)

Courses and distances
⊕ M08 (0·5M S of Pta da Cruz, Madeira) – ⊕M20 = 158M, 159° / 339°
⊕ M11 (0·5M S of Quinta do Lorde Marina) – ⊕M20 = 161M, 164° / 344°
⊕ M14 (0·5M ESE of Funchal) – ⊕M20 = 158M, 160° / 340°
⊕ M17 (0·5M SW of Porto de Recreio da Calheta) – ⊕M20 = 168M, 156° / 326°

Magnetic variation
6°10'W (2011), decreasing by 8'E annually.

Tides and tidal streams
Predictions for Ilhéu de Fora, west of Selvagem Pequena, are available via Admiralty *EasyTide* – see page 141. Tidal streams around Ilhas Selvagens set northeast on the flood and southwest on the ebb at 0·5 to 1·5 knots.

Charts
Admiralty *3133* (1:1,250,000 & 1:100,000)
Portuguese *33101* (1:350,000), *36407* (1:100,000)
US *51342* (1:103,640)

Lights
2768 **Selvagem Grande (Pico de Atalaya)**
Fl.4s162m13M White tower, red bands 10m
2769 **Selvagem Pequena (Pico do Veado)**
Fl(2)6s49m12M Concrete block 1m
Note Both lights are reported to be weaker than stated, and may not operate for extended periods following severe weather

CAUTION
On no account should either group be approached in darkness or poor visibility, when they should be allowed an offing of several miles. Both have extensive off-lying dangers, the hazards mentioned in the text being only the worst amongst many.

Not only are the lights unreliable, but the position of the entire group is believed to be inaccurate on many charts. Older charts were not based on WGS84 but on the islands' own (and unique) datum, with positions often expressed in degrees, minutes and seconds rather than the more usual decimal minutes.

After a period in the early 2000s when most charts, including electronic, gave the islands' correct position, early in 2010 a new error of 0·08M (148m) towards 192° appears to have been introduced across the board. This error will doubtless be corrected in due course, but it may not always be made clear when this has been done. Meanwhile, a correction of 0·079 minutes NORTH and 0·026 minutes EAST is required for positions on affected charts to comply with WGS84 (and the plans in these pages).

My thanks to Harald Sammer of yacht *Taniwani* for identifying and reporting this error.

Two wildlife wardens are permanently stationed on Selvagem Grande, and before departing Madeira or Porto Santo for the Ilhas Selvagens the skipper MUST obtain a permit – see page 138 – which the wardens will inspect on arrival. Anchoring is forbidden other than in authorised areas – effectively the two anchorages indicated on pages 177 and 179. In theory there is a third permitted anchorage at Fundeadouro das Galinhas, south of Selvagem Grande, but it is too exposed to be viable for a yacht. It appears that anchoring is no longer permitted at Enseada das Pedreiras on the east coast. There is reported to be excellent snorkelling in the very clear waters of Enseada das Cagarras, but all forms of fishing, scuba diving, and the collection of shells, plants or geological specimens are forbidden. So are shooting and lighting fires, and wildlife must not be disturbed or injured. Plants and animals must not be landed from visiting yachts, and prior authorisation must be obtained from the Regional Government before undertaking photography, filming or sound recording for commercial use. In addition to the wardens, two lighthouse keepers make up the permanent population, though visiting wildlife researchers and scientists sometimes swell the numbers.

A *cagarra* chick – more commonly known to British yachtsmen as a shearwater – in its burrow on Selvagem Grande, quite unworried by the camera. The entire archipelago has been a nature reserve since the early 1970s
Andy Scott

Selvagem Pequena and Ilhéu de Fora lie about 10M southwest of Selvagem Grande, separated from it by a deep, safe channel. Selvagem Pequena has an area of less than 0·25km² centred around 30°02'·1N 16°01'·6W, and is generally sandy and low-lying. Its most prominent feature is Pico do Veado in the extreme north – a single conical hill rising to 49m and topped by strange volcanic shapes.

Since 1998 Selvagem Pequena has also had two permanent wardens to watch over the wildlife and check the permits of visiting yachtsmen. The island is a main breeding area for white-faced storm petrels (*Pelagodroma marina*) – see page 19 – with an estimated population of some 250,000. Rather than build nests they excavate burrows into the sand, and for that reason visitors should stick to the shoreline or marked paths, one of which leads up to the wardens' hut, and NOT walk over the sandhills.

Even with the wardens' presence – and despite their radio link with their colleagues on Selvagem Grande – Selvagem Pequena is still about as far away from assistance as it is possible to get whilst still near land. The island has been variously described as 'desolate', 'spooky' and 'very lovely', doubtless depending as much upon the observer as on the island itself. Few places can be so totally at the mercy of changing weather conditions and free from the influence of man.

Ilhéu de Fora, about 1M west of Selvagem Pequena, is the southernmost and, at 17m, the highest of a long bank of small islets, rocks and breaking shoals extending about 2M on a north-south axis between 30°01′·7N and 30°03′·7N, and either side of 16°02′·8W. There are no outliers beyond 0·5M in any direction.

An interesting account of a visit to the Ilhas Selvagens by yacht in 1889 will be found in EF Knight's *The Cruise of the Alerte*.

Websites

Much fascinating information will be found at http://selvagens.seawatching.net/index.html, website of the Seawatching.net organisation, including visit reports, an extensive photo gallery and recorded bird sounds. Some information can also be gleaned from www.lanecc.edu/library/don/savage.htm and www. confluence.org/confluence.php?lat=30&lon=-16, and Wikipedia does its usual informative job at www.en.wikipedia.org/wiki/Savage_Islands. There are a few brief mentions on some of the sites devoted to the archipelago as a whole – see page 137 – but that appears to be it.

Approach

Numerous shoals, many both steep-to and unmarked, litter the area. Selvagem Grande's most dangerous outliers are the Baixa de São João, lying 1·3M off to the north-northeast with a charted depth of 2·6m that may be significantly lessened by an ocean swell without breaking; Baixo do Nordeste, just over a mile to the northeast with a charted depth of 4·5m; Baixa da Joana, 400m south of Selvagem Grande with less than 1·8m; and Baixa do Oeste, awash, 0·8M west of Ponta da Atalaia.

Selvagem Pequena is also fringed by rocks, reefs and islets, particularly to the west and east. Its most dangerous shoal is undoubtedly the Baixa Comprida, a long bank reaching more than 0·75M offshore to the southwest, with a breaking rock at its seaward end. Baixa da Enseada, also awash, lies about halfway between Baixa Comprida and Selvagem Pequena.

Selvagem Grande

Enseada das Cagarras

30°08′·44N 15°52′·2W (dinghy landing)

Tides
Time difference on Funchal: –0018
Mean spring range 2·2m
Mean neap range 1·0m

Plans
Portuguese *36407* (1:25,000)
US *51342* (1:20,625)

Remote and memorable mid-ocean anchorage

A small cove in the extreme southwest, sheltered from east through northeast to north but open from south to west and untenable in any swell. No more than four or five yachts can anchor at any one time.

Approach

Definitely a case for 'eyeball navigation' in good overhead light. From Madeira shape a course for ⊕M20, about 0·5M from Baixo do Nordeste and 1·6M from Selvagem Grande itself (see Courses and distances, above). Alter onto 201° to clear Ponta de Leste by at least 0·5M and maintain that distance offshore around the east and south coasts. Turn in towards the anchorage when Ponta da Atalaia bears due north, so avoiding Baixa da Joana and its associated shoals. Depart on a south or southwesterly course for the same reason.

Anchorage and mooring

Early arrivals can anchor in the centre of the cove in around 10m, latecomers being forced to stay in greater depths, though watch out for back-draughts which can push a boat inshore. The bottom consists largely of slabby rock with sand and gravel

Looking southwest across the Enseada das Cagarras, with the concrete landing ramp in the foreground. The peak of Selvagem Pequena can just be made out on the skyline at left *Andy Scott*

accumulations in the low spots, and anchors are said to hold by hooking the overlaps between slabs. A quick inspection with swimming goggles is recommended, no real hardship in the very clear water. A tripping line is essential, allowing the anchor to be pulled out at the same angle it went in.

A few years ago a large spherical ship's mooring buoy was laid for the use of the regular supply boat, to which yachts can otherwise moor. It is well out and somewhat exposed, and a small riding sail may be useful to keep the yacht clear of the metal buoy. Landing by dinghy at the rough slipway in the northeast corner of the bay is easiest at low tide when the uncovered rocks provide some shelter.

Crystal clear water in the Enseada das Cagarras, though a swell can be seen across the entrance *Andy Scott*

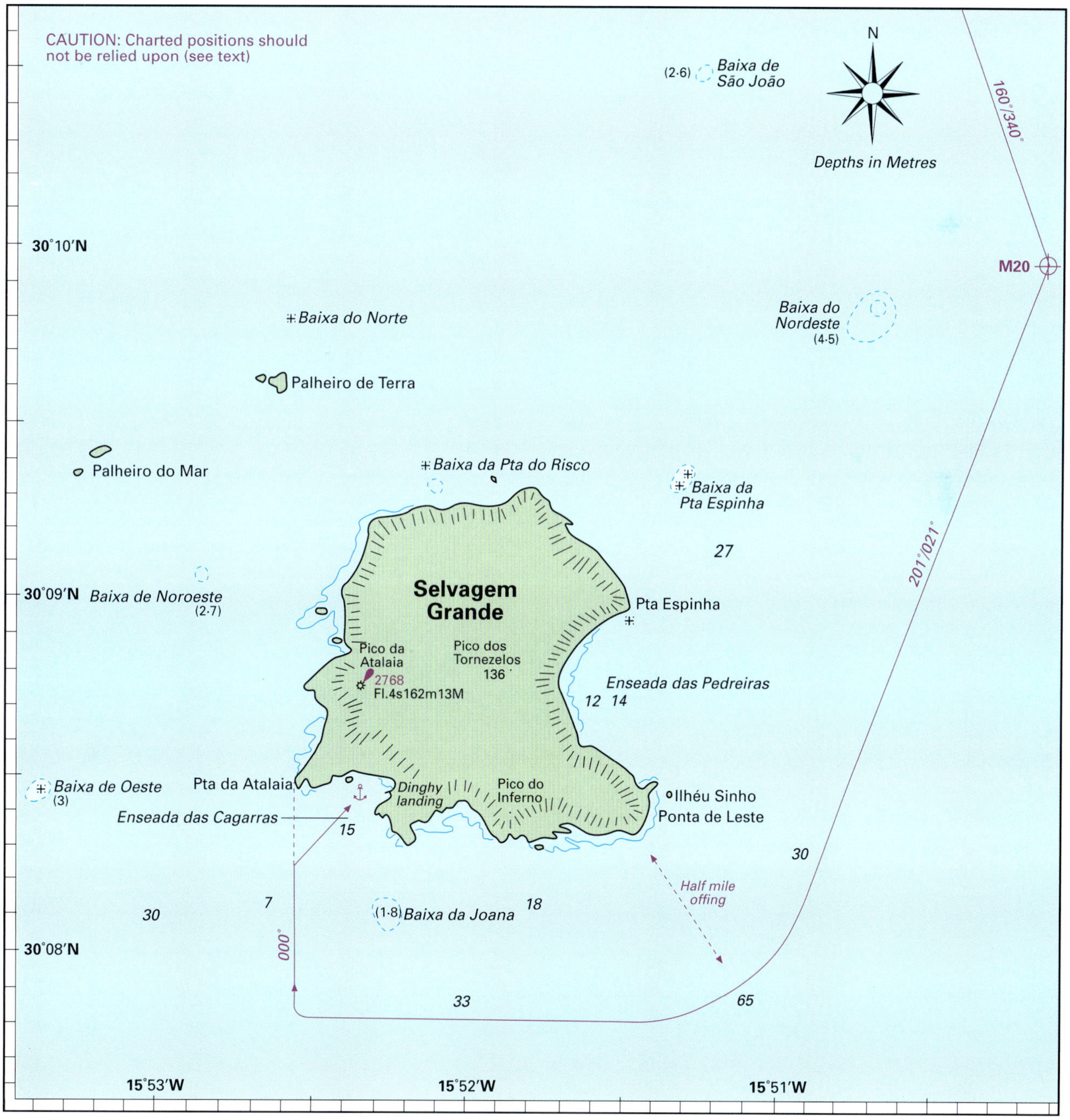

Lizards get their bearings on Selvagem Grande – for those facing northwest the next land is America *Andy Scott*

Formalities

Immediately on landing at Selvagem Grande yachtsmen are likely to be met by the wardens who will wish to check their permit. Provided this is in order permission to walk around the island is usually forthcoming, though only in the company of a warden – independent hiking is not permitted. Visiting yachtsmen have repeatedly commented on the friendliness and knowledge of the wardens and/or wildlife researchers, who in 2010 included two studying the resident *cagarras* (Cory's shearwaters) and another the many lizards and geckos. All were happy to talk about their specialities and answer questions, and the guided tour was rated 'excellent' – though someone had clearly planned ahead as T-shirts were on sale at the end!

Selvagem Pequena

Enseada do Selvagem Pequena

30°01'·9N 16°01'·5W (anchorage, approx)

Plans
Portuguese *36407* (1:25,000)
US *51342* (1:20,700)

Exposed, rarely-visited anchorage

A somewhat open anchorage off the southern shore of Selvagem Pequena, sheltered by reefs, rocks and the island itself from west through north to northeast. There is a drying rock in the northeast corner. Northeasterly swells tend to run around both ends of the island, making the anchorage and landing unusable except in near calms. It is occasionally used as an overnight stop by Madeiran fishermen working the banks around Ilhéu de Fora (which itself has no possible anchorages).

Approach

Selvagem Pequena can safely be approached from the northeast with no more than 500m offing until Pico do Veado bears 340°, and the anchorage approached on this bearing. On leaving, the course should not stray west of south for the first mile, in order to clear Baixa da Enseada and Baixa Comprida. Again, only to be tackled in good overhead light which, combined with the very clear water, should allow impending hazards to be seen.

Anchorage and landing

The 'approved' anchorage at 30°01'·48N 16°01'·3W (local datum) is nearly 0·5M south of the island, but most yachts will want to close in much further to anchor in about 12m over rock in very clear water. A tripping line is essential, but it would also be wise to inspect from in, or under, the water.

Approaching Salvagem Pequena from the southeast. Swell renders the anchorage untenable for much of the time *Andy Scott*

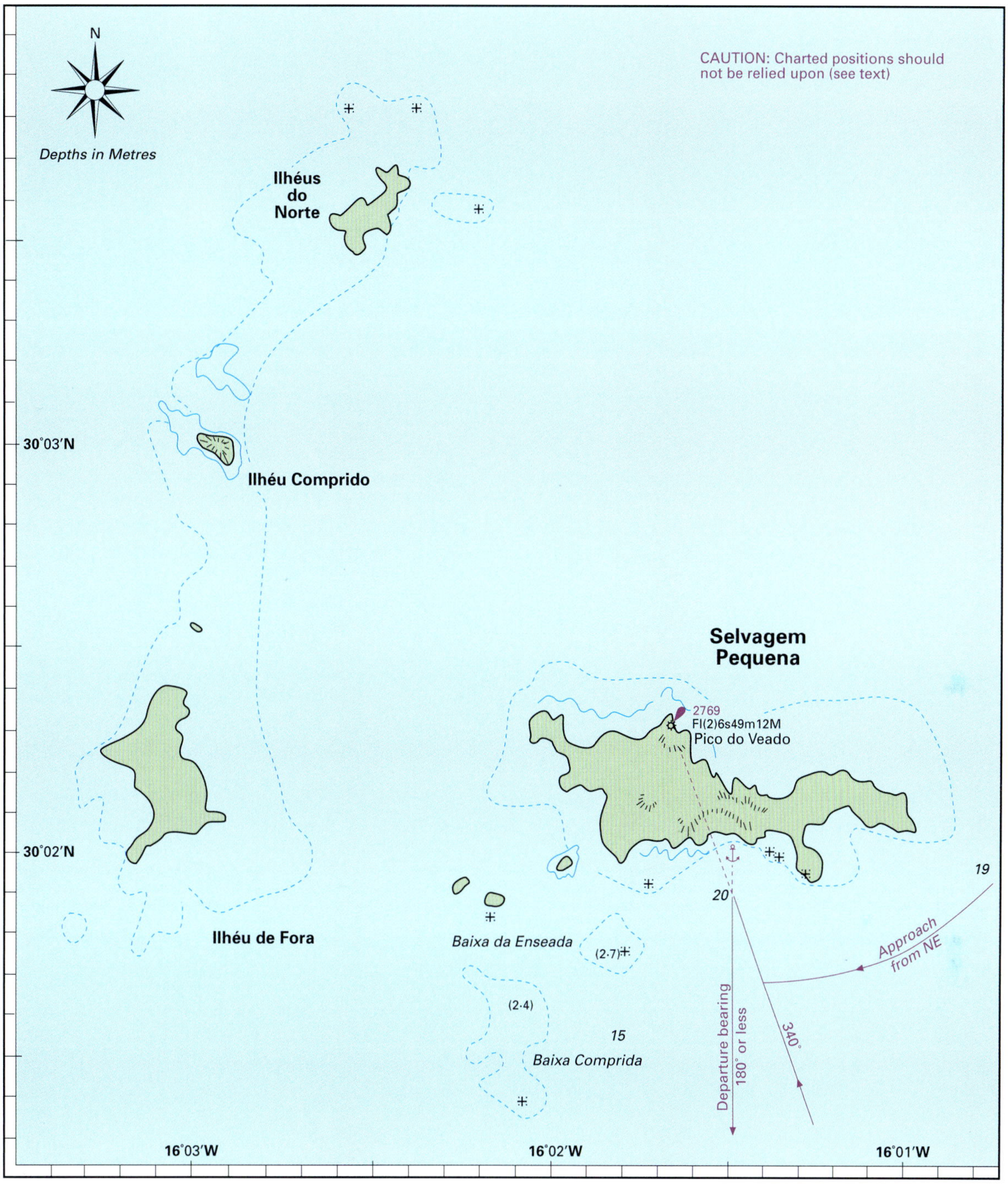

Landing can be difficult, and is usually easiest at low water on the eastern end of the island. There are many submerged rocks close inshore and use of an outboard motor would be unwise.

Few yachts will arrive without a prior visit to Selvagem Grande, where the wardens may offer to radio their colleagues on the smaller island to say that visitors are on their way. In this case a ride ashore may be forthcoming. Once ashore, note the point on page 175 regarding the breeding habits of the white-faced petrels and the need to avoid disturbing them or causing damage to their burrows.

Pico do Veado on Selvagem Pequena, with the hut used by the two resident wardens at far left *Andy Scott*

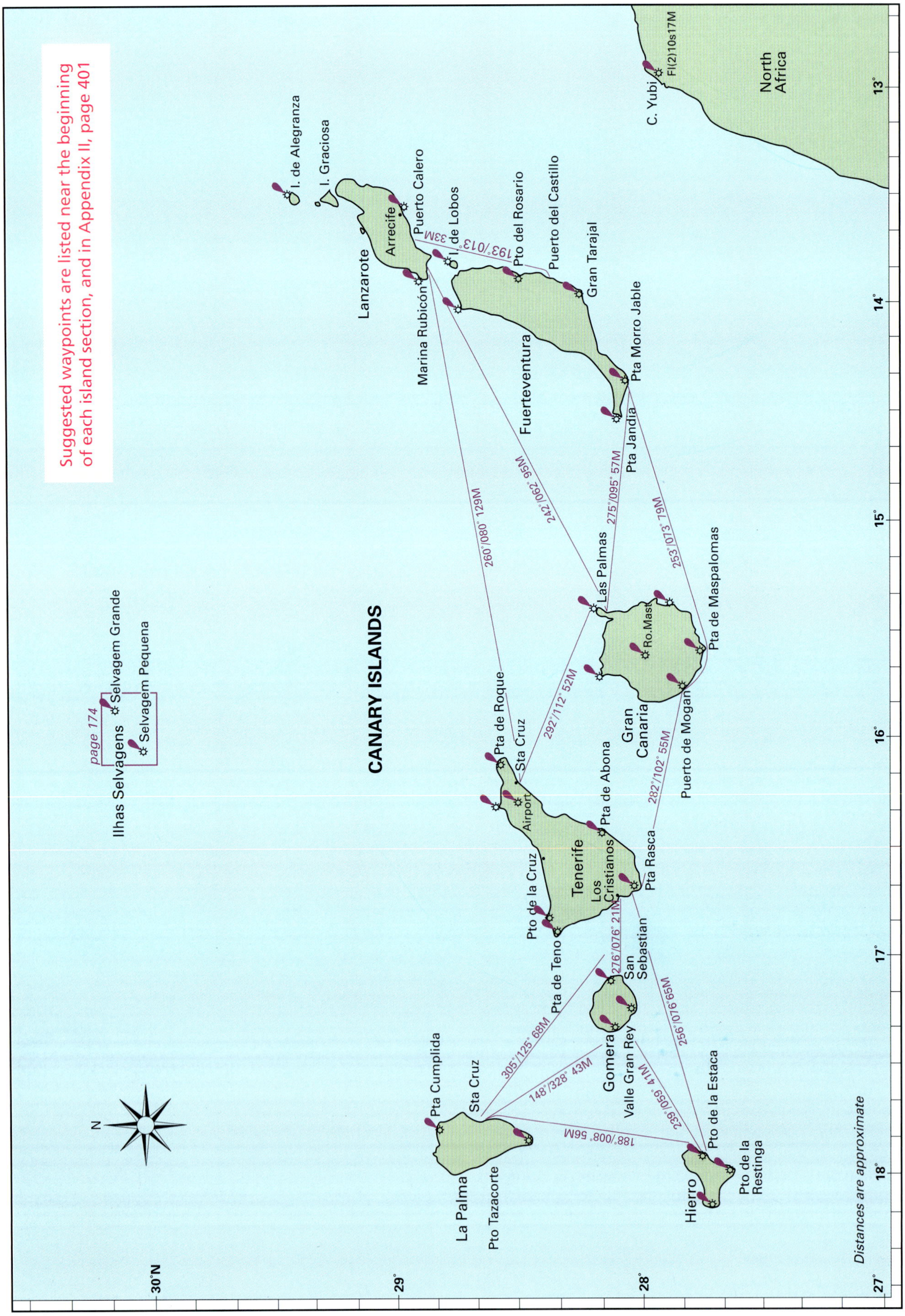
Suggested waypoints are listed near the beginning of each island section, and in Appendix II, page 401
CANARY ISLANDS
Ilhas Selvagens
page 174
Selvagem Grande
Selvagem Pequena
I. de Alegranza
I. Graciosa
Lanzarote
Arrecife
Puerto Calero
I. de Lobos
Marina Rubicón
193°/013° 33M
Pto del Rosario
Puerto del Castillo
Gran Tarajal
Fuerteventura
Pta Morro Jable
Pta Jandia
C. Yubi
Fl(2)10s17M
North Africa
260°/080° 129M
242°/062° 95M
275°/095° 57M
253°/073° 79M
Las Palmas
Ro.Masp
Pta de Maspalomas
Gran Canaria
Puerto de Mogan
292°/112° 52M
282°/102° 55M
Pta de Roque
Sta Cruz
Airport
Pta de Abona
Tenerife
Los Cristianos
Pta Rasca
Pto de la Cruz
Pta de Teno
276°/076° 21M
San Sebastian
256°/076° 65M
Gomera
Valle Gran Rey
239°/059° 41M
305°/125° 68M
148°/328° 43M
Pta Cumplida
Sta Cruz
La Palma
Pto Tazacorte
188°/008° 56M
Hierro
Pto de la Estaca
Pto de la Restinga
N
30°N
29°
28°
27°
18°
17°
16°
15°
14°
13°
Distances are approximate

III. The Canary Islands

Index of islands

The archipelago

The Canarian archipelago contains seven major islands together with many small islands and rocks, and lies off the North African coast between 27°39′N to 29°24′N and 13°25′W to 18°10′W. It has a total land area of around 7,300km^2. Fuerteventura is about 70M off Cabo Yubi in southern Morocco and the northern islands are some 250–270M from Madeira. The ancient sedimentary geological formations show that the islands were once part of the African continent, but their major features derive from more recent volcanic activity resulting in steep-sided shorelines with cliffs and water-eroded gorges – the last manifestation was an eruption in 1971 and the formation of a new crater, Volcán de Teneguia, at the southern tip of La Palma. Despite the evidence of water erosion there are few permanent surface streams, most of those being diverted to reservoirs and agriculture, and in the eastern islands natural water is scarce. These islands are largely dependent on irrigation for agriculture, with parts of Gran Canaria and Tenerife semi-desert and areas of Lanzarote and Fuerteventura totally barren. Temperatures in Santa Cruz de Tenerife range from the mid-30sC in August to the mid-20sC in January, though it is much colder at greater heights and El Teide is frequently capped with snow. The northeast trades predominate between April and October, tending to shift further south during the winter, and least rain falls between June and September.

The flora is a mix of southern European and African, and about a third of the flowering plants are indigenous. Coffee, dates, bananas, sugar, avocados, tobacco, grapes and other fruits and vegetables are

The peak of El Tiede, Tenerife, seen from the La Palma's central crater. The much lower La Gomera separates the two

grown and exported. For many the chief interest in the fauna lies in the birds, of which there are more than 200 species, many breeding in the archipelago and some unique to it – including the canary (named for the islands, rather than vice versa). Cattle and sheep are bred, goats roam the rougher areas, and closer to the ground there are lizards and the occasional hazard such as the scorpion.

Some revenue is generated from a small industry centred on silk, embroidery and linen work, but far more important is the tourist trade which, since the 1960s, has grown from tens of thousands into millions. In addition, between the archipelago and the African coast is – or was – one of the better fishing grounds of the world. The business of drying and salting *corbina*, canning tuna, processing cod, bream, mullet and other species grew to be of considerable value to the islands, assisted by the construction of massive breakwaters at many harbours. However, more recently a combination of over-fishing, reduced quotas and, some would say, competition for space from yachts, has seen a large reduction in the local fishing fleet.

The ever-increasing number of yachts, many of them based permanently in the islands, has led in many places to the construction of marinas and yacht harbours. These generally offer safe refuge in bad weather as well as travel-lifts, repair facilities and a secure place in which to leave a yacht should the owner need to return home for a month or two. However, the increase in the popularity of the Canaries amongst yachtsmen – as well as the fact that many berths in private marinas are sold together with the holiday apartments which surround them – has led to an inevitable shortage of space, particularly in the busy autumn season. Despite an increase of more than 45% between 2004 and 2010 (in the number of marinas, not of berths) it is still wise to plan well ahead, particularly in the high season. Unlike in the Azores, nearly all marinas are privately operated even when they lie inside commercial ports, and equally there are some spacious commercial and ferry harbours just crying out for a well-run marina – Morro Jable is a case in point. It will be interesting to follow progress over the coming decade.

History

The early inhabitants of all the islands have come to be called Guanches, although originally this was the name of the people of Tenerife only. Their origins appear to be Cro-Magnon, Berber and Semite though their practice of mummifying their dead, and the roots of their language, suggest an early Egyptian connection.

The islands were named 'Fortunate' by early visitors from Europe. Phoenician traders collected the purple dye *orchil* from the Canaries and Pliny the Elder (circa AD60) reported an expedition sent by King Juba II of Mauritania (Morocco) to the Fortunate Islands in 60BC. The troops discovered large dogs roaming the islands and brought two of them back to the king. The typical Canary dog is now much smaller but the name *Insulae Canium* – The Islands of Dogs – persists today as Islas Canarias.

Arabs landed on Gran Canaria in AD999 to trade, and French, Genoese and Portuguese navigators were well received by the inhabitants when they landed in the 13th and 14th centuries. They found that the local people existed comfortably, well supplied with the necessities of life. They had no knowledge of navigation and, with no boats, there was apparently no inter-island communication – though presumably this had not always been the case. They were primarily cave dwellers, using tools and weapons of wood and bone with obsidian cutting edges. Cooking utensils were of unfired clay, while clothing was made from goatskin and vegetable fibres. In the western islands long smooth poles were used for vaulting from rock to rock and over gullies when travelling on the mountainsides. Instead of yodelling, the Gomerans communicated across the valleys with a whistling language, and until recently whistlers and pole vaulters could still be found in La Palma and La Gomera.

It is recorded that a Genoese nobleman, Lancellotto Malocello, gave his name to Lanzarote (originally called Titerougatra) early in the 14th century when making a chart. Others say that a Norman Baron, Juan de Bethencourt, in the service of the Spanish Crown, after finally subduing the inhabitants in 1402 broke his lance and threw the pieces in the air crying the Norman equivalent of 'Lance broken!'

De Bethencourt and his lieutenant, Gadafier de la Salle, went on to conquer Fuerteventura in 1405 and later El Hierro. They made an attempt on La Gomera but met with stiff resistance from some of the chiefs and the island was not fully subdued for another eighty years. Gran Canaria, Tenerife and La Palma were even more difficult to conquer, in spite of the invaders' superior weapons, and the Spaniards suffered heavy losses before Fernandez de Lugo finally crushed the Guanche resistance at the battle of Acentejo on Tenerife on 25 December 1495. An early attempt was made to ship Canarians back to Spain as slaves, but Isabel la Catolica, Queen of Castile, took steps to see that they were returned to their islands and it appears that there has, over the years, been successful integration between Europeans and the original inhabitants.

In 1492 Christopher Columbus put into Las Palmas de Gran Canaria for repairs and, before setting off for the New World, attended Mass at San Sebastián de la Gomera in a church which still stands (albeit much modified). On future voyages he returned several times to the islands, particularly to San Sebastián de la Gomera, home of the beautiful widow Beatriz de Bobadilla whom he had met previously at the Spanish court.

The Canaries became a useful staging post for the Spaniards on their voyages between Europe and the Americas, though Lanzarote and Fuerteventura were frequently subject to attack by Arab pirates and

Terraces of bananas line the western slopes of La Palma

slavers. Dutch and English ships also raided the islands and Drake lost his flagship in one attack. Two centuries later, in 1797, Nelson led an attack on Santa Cruz de Tenerife but was repulsed, with 350 casualties and the loss of his arm.

In 1823 the archipelago was united to become a province of Spain, with Santa Cruz de Tenerife as the capital – much to the annoyance of the inhabitants of Gran Canaria. Thirty years later they were declared a free trade area, greatly increasing their prosperity. In 1927 the seven islands were split into two provinces – Tenerife, La Palma, El Hierro and La Gomera now comprise the western province, with Santa Cruz de Tenerife the capital and seat of local government; Gran Canaria, Fuerteventura and Lanzarote, together with the smaller islands such as Graciosa, form the eastern province, of which Las Palmas is the capital.

General Franco was military governor of the islands in 1936, at the time he planned and then led the nationalist revolt which sparked off the Spanish Civil War. In Tenerife, black bows were to be seen adorning the national flag following his death in 1975.

Deforestation and over-cultivation have altered the climate of the archipelago to such an extent that Fuerteventura has become a virtual desert, while the annual rainfall on Lanzarote is so low that farmers have to make cunning use of the dew for the cultivation of vines and fruit. It seldom rains in the southern parts of Tenerife and Gran Canaria, which accounts at least in part for the explosion of holiday developments in these areas. North of the mountains the climate is humid and well suited to the cultivation of bananas, vegetables and fruit.

'Canary-sack' or 'malmsey wine', first produced in Elizabethan times, was much sought after by British sailors and from that time onwards trade in wine and sugar developed between the UK and the Canaries, with several British companies involved in production and distribution. In the 19th century a fleet of fast schooners plied between Puerto de la Cruz on the north coast of Tenerife and south Devon carrying soft fruit, while other British firms began a trade in bananas which still continues – though in Britain the small but tasty Canarian banana is becoming difficult to find, having been crowded out by the large and somewhat pithy products of Central and South America. In an effort to diversify agriculture the production of exotic vegetables, cut flowers and pineapples is being encouraged.

Since the 1960s tourism has played an important part in the economy in both the construction and service sectors. After a slight decrease in the early 1990s it is now estimated that well over seven million people visit the islands each year, the majority from Britain, Germany, the Scandinavian countries and mainland Spain. Tenerife attracts the highest numbers, closely followed by Gran Canaria. The percentage of GNP derived from tourism is estimated at 65–70% and growing.

General information

Nationality and language

In constitutional terms the archipelago is an autonomous region of Spain, with its own parliament, consisting of the two provinces of Gran Canaria and Tenerife. Gran Canaria includes Lanzarote and Fuerteventura as well as its namesake; Tenerife constitutes the islands of Tenerife, La Gomera, La Palma and El Hierro. Mainland Spain is referred to as 'The Peninsula'. However, although Spanish territory the Canaries are not a part of the EU, sharing the somewhat anomalous status of the Channel Islands, Gibraltar, etc. The principal language is Spanish, with many younger Canarians and those around the ports and tourist resorts also speaking German, French or English.

Some care needs to be exercised to distinguish between La Palma the island and Las Palmas the capital of Gran Canaria, between Santa Cruz the capital of La Palma and Santa Cruz the capital of Tenerife, and regarding the use of the names Gran Canaria and Tenerife to describe the islands, the provinces or both. (In this book they can be assumed to refer only to the islands, unless stated otherwise.)

Spanish representation abroad

Spanish embassies and consulates

London (Embassy): 39 Chesham Place, London SW1X 8SB ✆ 020 7235 5555
Fax 020 7259 5392

London (Consulate): 20 Draycott Place, London SW3 2RZ ✆ 020 7589 8989
Fax 020 7581 7888 *Email* cog.londres@maec.es
www.conspalon.org

Manchester (Consulate): 1A Brook House, 70 Spring Gardens, Manchester M22 2BQ
✆ 0161 236 1233 *Fax* 0161 228 7467

Edinburgh (Consulate): 63 North Castle Street, Edinburgh EH2 3LJ ✆ 0131 220 1843
Fax 0131 226 4568

Washington DC (Embassy): 2375 Pennsylvania Avenue NW, Washington DC 20037, USA
✆ 202 728 2330 *Fax* 202 728 2302
Email cog.washington@mae.es www.spainemb.org

New York (Consulate): 150 East 58th Street, 30th Floor, New York, NY 10155, USA
✆ 212 355 4081 *Fax* 212 644 3751
Email cog.nuevayork@maec.es
www.maec.es/subwebs/consulados/nuevayork/en

Other Spanish embassies and consulates can be located via http://spain.embassyhomepage.com.

Spanish national tourist offices

London: 79 New Cavendish Street, London W1W 6XB ✆ 0207 486 8077
Fax 0207 486 8034 (0915–1330)
Email info.londres@tourspain.es www.spain.info

New York: 666 Fifth Avenue, New York, NY 10103-3599 ✆ 212 265 8822
Fax 212 265 8864

Diplomatic representation in the Canary Islands

The following are consulates – all embassies are located in Madrid.

UK (Gran Canaria): Edificio Cataluña, Calle Luis Morote 6, 35007 – Las Palmas de Gran Canaria
✆ 092 109356, 913 342194 *Fax* 928 267774
(open 0830–1330 weekdays)
Email LAPAL-Consular@fco.gov.uk
http://ukinspain.fco.gov.uk/en/

UK (Tenerife): Plaza Weyler 8, 38003 – Santa Cruz de Tenerife ✆ 902 109356, 913 342194
Fax 922 289903 (open 0830–1330 weekdays)
Email tenerife.enquiries@fco.gov.uk
http://ukinspain.fco.gov.uk/en/

Personal documentation

The same rules apply as in mainland Spain. Nationals of EU (and some other European) countries can travel using nothing more than a national identity card or passport. Visitors from elsewhere in the world require full passports and some – principally those from outside Europe, North America and Australasia – also need visas.

If wishing to stay in Spanish territory for more than 90 days it is necessary to apply for a *Tarjeta de Residencia* (resident's card) within a month of arrival. This is a lengthy process requiring yet more documentation, and it would be wise to apply to a Spanish Consulate before departure to find out what is involved.

It is a legal requirement to carry identity of some kind at all times whilst on Spanish territory, though this is seldom enforced.

Time

The Canaries use UT (as do the British Isles), with local daylight saving (+1 hour) from late March until late September.

Shopping in the market at Santa Cruz de la Palma

Money

Spain, including the Canaries, is part of the Eurozone (despite the Canaries themselves not being inside the EU). Most visitors rely on credit/debit cards, both for purchases and to withdraw cash – dispensers, locally referred to as *cajeros*, or *automáticos* – are widespread and accept all major cards. Many offer instructions in a choice of languages, including English.

Sterling, US dollars and other major currencies are readily exchangeable in banks, as are travellers cheques, but are less likely to be accepted by shops, hotels or restaurants. Banks normally open 0830–1400 weekdays only, though some also open 0900–1300 Saturdays from November to May inclusive.

Most restaurants, shops, car rental companies and other concerns welcome payment by credit card – principally Visa, MasterCard and American Express – but it is as well to confirm this in advance, particularly where fuel (for both yachts and vehicles) is concerned.

Shopping

A good range of food is easily obtainable in the larger supermarkets, though at somewhat higher prices than in mainland Europe (and, apparently, than in Madeira). Locally grown fruit and vegetables are often excellent in terms of both quality and value, with traditional markets in most of the larger towns and cities, and in some places the local fishermen sell a part of their catch straight from their boats at very reasonable prices. Wines and spirits are duty free and readily available – vines are cultivated on several islands and the local wines repay investigation. Most shops open 0900–1300, 1600–2000 weekdays, 0900–1300 Saturdays, though souvenir shops are often open for much longer periods.

The quality of fresh water varies from island to island, sometimes having an unpleasant chemical aroma though perfectly safe to drink. As a general rule the quality improves as one sails west. Every marina supplies water to all berths, but this may not be the case in other harbours when a few 5 or 10-litre carriers may be useful. Bottled mineral water can be obtained almost everywhere.

Regarding other items – clothes, toiletries, etc. – the range available generally reflects the size and antecedents of the place in question, be it a major city, a tourist resort or a modest fishing village. However, it is rare to find a bookshop stocking English-language paperbacks (though a growing number of marinas include book swaps amongst their facilities), so dedicated readers may wish to put a few aside for the coming passage – or invest in an eBook reader.

Some notes regarding ships' stores – principally fuel, bottled gas and chandlery – will be found on pages 190–1.

Communications

Mail

Most marinas are happy to receive mail for yachts either already with them or with berths pre-booked. They are naturally less keen to act as mail drops for yachts anchored off or of which they have never heard. If spending some time in one of the smaller harbours a café or restaurant may be willing to oblige. Use of the *poste restante* system should be avoided if possible as long delays can occur and mail will seldom be redirected. It is worth stressing that the word 'Spain' should always be included on the envelope, as should both the owner's and the boat's name (in that order).

Letters to the Canaries from the UK may take up to a fortnight, those back to the UK anything from a few days to several weeks (making email a much more reliable means of communication). Note also that private mail companies, licensed to print their own stamps, operate in some areas. Though often slightly cheaper, they have a poor reputation for reliability and should be avoided. Buy stamps from a post office – normally open 0930–1400 – to be certain of obtaining the real thing.

There is sometimes a choice of post boxes, though all are painted yellow. Those labelled *buzones* are for local mail, *península* is for mainland Spain while international post should go in the one marked *extranjero*.

Incoming packages

If ordering parts from outside the islands – or anticipating any other parcel – ensure that the package is clearly marked 'BOAT IN TRANSIT' and that a contact telephone number (possibly of a marina office) is prominently displayed. Where possible, passport details of the addressee should also be included in the paperwork. Failure to observe these precautions may result in the package being held up by Customs on arrival, sometimes without the addressee even being informed that it has reached the islands.

Small parcels are best sent from the UK via the Royal Mail's Airsure service, but the best way to import large shipments is said to be via a freight forwarder. The goods should be shipped to the airport only and a local agent organised in advance to clear them through Customs and deliver locally. The agent's details should be on the airway bill, and the goods MUST be addressed to the boat in transit, NOT to an individual, on ALL the paperwork. Global parcel delivery companies typically ship goods only as far as the airport, where they are handed over to a local delivery firm who may or may not be efficient.

A long-term Canaries resident advises: 'Items for boats in transit are exempt from import duty, provided they can be seen to leave with the boat. However, in many cases, especially when arriving by air, an application has to be made by a Customs agent or courier's Customs department before Airport Customs will accept this status. On production of the necessary paperwork the item will then be released. Unfortunately, couriers are often unaware of the special status of a boat in transit – or simply unwilling to handle the additional paperwork – so pay the duty and pass it on to the client on delivery. Weigh up the outlay, as it can sometimes cost no more to fly someone out with your package than to send it by courier. It is certainly more reliable, and infinitely faster! Finally, if a boat in transit needs to send an expensive part off the islands for repair and later receive it in the same place, it is always worth using the services of a Customs agent who can make sure all the paperwork is correct, the transport is as quick as possible, and the owner is not charged any import/export duty.'

Telephones

As in many countries, public telephones are seen as a lower priority with the widespread use of mobile (cell) phones. Even so, they are still to be found in most towns and details will be found under individual harbours. Not all, however, take coins, some requiring cards purchased from post offices, supermarkets and bars. Mobile (cell) phone coverage throughout the islands is generally excellent, with only a few 'holes' in the more mountainous western islands.

Calls to the United Kingdom begin with the prefix 0044, followed by the area code (without the initial zero) and number. Calls to the United States and Canada begin with the prefix 001 and the area code plus number. The US access code for AT&T (www.att.com) is 900 99 011.

The international dialling code for Spain, including the Canaries, is 34. If telephoning within the islands the area code – 928 for the three eastern islands, 922 further west – forms an integral part of the phone number (nine digits in all) even when calling from within the same island. Any telephone number not starting with one of these sequence can be assumed to be a mobile. Many telephone numbers are given in the text, otherwise Spanish Yellow Pages (*Paginas Amarillas*) can be consulted at www.paginasamarillas.es, in Spanish only.

The costs incurred by using a mobile phone abroad are beyond the scope of this book, and individual phones may need 'unblocking' before they will work at all. If planning to spend some time in one country it may be cheaper to buy a new phone or at least a new SIM card.

Fax

Although declining in use with the ubiquity of email, most marinas will send and receive faxes for yachts – see individual harbours details. Many companies advertising photocopying also have a fax machine, as do most hotels.

Internet access

Despite email being the communication method of choice for the vast majority of cruising sailors, Wi-Fi is still not available in many of the archipelago's marinas. However, nearly all have some source of Wi-Fi or other internet access point nearby, either paid for or requiring the purchase of coffee or beer. Mains power may not always be available, however, so reasonable battery life is essential. See individual harbours for details.

Electricity

Mains electricity is 220v 50Hz, as is standard throughout mainland Europe, and yachts from elsewhere should beware a probable difference in both volts and cycles. Several marinas also provide 380v to berths for larger yachts – see individual harbours for details.

Transportation and travel

International flights

Arrecife (Lanzarote), Rosario (Fuerteventura), Las Palmas (Gran Canaria), Reina Sofia (Tenerife South) and Santa Cruz de la Palma handle flights to and from Europe with a number of scheduled and charter airlines. Reina Sofia also handles New York flights.

Inter-island flights

Binter Canarias flights connect all seven islands, and though it is not always possible to travel direct, any journey can be made within a single day. On Tenerife most inter-island flights use Los Rodeos (Tenerife North), worth remembering if transferring to/from an international flight. Allow an hour or more if travelling between Los Rodeos and Reina Sofia by road.

Current timetables and fares will be found on Binter Canarias' user-friendly website (in Spanish, English and German) at www.bintercanarias.es.

Car ferry services

Frequent car ferries, provided by three major companies, link the larger islands. Schedules and fares vary according to the time of year and are best checked via the internet:

Líneas Fred Olsen SA, www.fredolsen.es (in Spanish and English), run conventional ferries and hydrofoil catamarans to all seven islands though not, strangely enough, linking the two eastern islands with the five to the west.

Trasmediterránea, www.trasmediterranea.es (in Spanish, Catalan, English, French and German), operate conventional ferries from Cádiz to Arrecife (Lanzarote), and onwards to all the islands other than La Gomera and El Hierro.

Naviera Armas, www.navieraarmas.com (in Spanish, English, French and Portuguese), run conventional ferries from Portimão and Huelva on the Iberian peninsula to Gran Canaria and Tenerife, and on many routes within the archipelago, linking each island to at least three others.

Foot passenger services

Smaller ferries link Lanzarote to Isla Graciosa and Tenerife to La Gomera:

Líneas Maritimas Romero www.lineas-romero.com run a regular service from Orzola at the northern tip of Lanzarote to Caleta del Sebo on La Graciosa (see page 204).

Líneas Fred Olsen SA (see previous page) have taken over the former *Garajonay Expres* route from Los Cristianos to San Sebastián de La Gomera, and on round the south coast of the island to Puerto de Santiago and Valle Gran Rey, using a small hydrofoil catamaran, the *Benchi Express.*

Road transport

There are bus services on all the islands – see individual harbours for details – and fares are generally cheap. Taxis are also reasonable by mainland European standards.

Car hire is readily available and reasonably priced, and a car is undoubtedly the best way to explore inland. Either national or international drivers licences are normally acceptable, provided the former has been held for at least one year. Major roads in all the islands are of a high standard, though the same cannot be said of some minor roads which occasionally turn into dirt tracks without warning. It is as well not to get caught in rough terrain after dark – and night falls swiftly just outside the tropics.

Most filling stations still have attendant service, and some do not accept payment by credit card.

Medical

The only immunisation required is against yellow fever if coming from certain Central American and African countries, though many people will also chose to keep vaccinations against tetanus and polio up to date. Other inoculations to consider – particularly for keen surfers and swimmers – are typhoid and hepatitis A and B.

There are reasonable medical facilities in the major towns and a clinic or lone doctor in all but the smallest, and many of those with medical training speak some English. Pharmacies abound, and usually appear to have good stocks of both non-prescription medicines and general items such as suntan creams and shampoo, often under familiar brand names. There are dentists and opticians in the larger towns, and wearers of glasses would be wise to carry a copy of their prescription (in addition to at least one reserve pair).

Consider taking out medical insurance, and if an EU citizen apply for a free EHIC (European Health Insurance Card) via www.ehic.org.uk. This covers the costs of medical treatment needed following illness or accident, though it may not be as comprehensive as would be the case in the UK and some contribution may be necessary. Neither does it cover the cost of repatriation, should that become necessary.

Needless to say, anyone with a chronic or recurring condition should take a good supply of medication with them even though, unlike its precursor the E111, the EHIC does cover the cost of treatment for a pre-existing condition. Every cruising yacht should, of course, carry a comprehensive first aid kit with instructions for its use.

Local people enjoy a *fiesta* in Sebastián de la Gomera
Andy Scott

National and regional holidays

1 January[1]	*Anõ Nuevo* (New Year's Day)
6 January[2]	*Epifanía/Día de los Reyes Magos* (Twelfth Night/Three Kings Day)
19 March[2]	*Día de San Juan* (St John's Day)
moveable[2]	*Jueves Santo* (Maundy Thursday)
moveable[1]	*Viernes Santo* (Good Friday)
1 May[1]	*Fiesta del Trabajo* (Labour Day)
30 May[1]	*Día de las Islas Canarias* (Canary Islands Day)
moveable[2]	Corpus Christi
25 July[2]	*Día de Santiago Apóstol* (St James's Day)
15 August[1]	*La Asuncíon de la Virgen* (Feast of the Assumption)
8 September[2]	*Día del Pino* (Pine Tree Day)
12 October[1]	*Día de la Hispanidad* (National Day)
1 November[1]	*Todos los Santos* (All Saints' Day)
6 December[2]	*Día de la Constitución* (Constitution Day)
8 December[1]	*La Inmaculada Concepcíon* (Feast of the Immaculate Conception)
25 December[1]	*Navidad* (Christmas Day)

[1] National
[2] Regional

In addition to the above, each town is also allowed two *fiesta* days of their own choosing – often the feast of a patron saint or commemorating a historical event.

Local festivals, and in particular Carnaval in February or March, can lead to serious congestion in marinas and anchorages. If planning to attend it is wise to arrive days or even weeks in advance.

Further information

There are many tourist guides dealing with the Canaries, a selection of which are listed under Further Reading, page 404. Colourful leaflets about each island, as well as the group as a whole, are also available either from the tourist offices in the larger cities or direct from the Spanish National Tourist Office (see Spanish representation abroad, above).

The Canary Islands are very well represented on the internet and the following sites (listed alphabetically) contain general information, some of which may be useful to the visiting yachtsman. Websites relating to each island are listed in the introduction to the relevant island, those to specific harbours throughout the text.

Note that most addresses use the Spanish form of the name (Canarias) rather than the English (Canaries).

www.aemet.es – homepage of the Spanish *Instituto Nacional de Meteorología*, in Spanish only but lends itself to auto-translation

www.armada.mde.es – website of Spain's 'Armada Española', of which their hydrographic office forms a part. Click on Science / Culture, followed by Hydrography – then Notices to Mariners to download weekly *Avisos a los Navegantes* or Paper Charts for the online chart catalogue. In Spanish, English and French

www.bintercanarias.com – user-friendly website of Binter Canarias SA, the Canaries' own inter-island airline based in Gran Canaria. See page 186 for more travel details

www.canariasfacil.com – a very useful portal and search engine providing factual information on all aspects of the Canary Islands, in a dozen languages including Russian, Chinese and Japanese...

www.canaryforum.com – a private site covering the four larger islands in varying detail

www.canaryphoto.com – a private site in five languages including English, created by Tenerife resident Peter Smola and featuring a carefully categorised selection of his stunning photos. (Also opens under www.canariasfotos.com)

www.dis.ulpgc.es/canarias – the University of Las Palmas de Gran Canaria's website has pages about all the islands, each in a different style. Only the Gran Canaria section has an English translation but the others respond well to auto-translation

www.ecoturismocanarias.com – website of Acantur, the Canarian Association for Rural Tourism, with information on all seven islands in Spanish, English, French and German

www.elcoleccionistadeinstantes.com – a gallery of stunning photographs, but sadly without captions

www.en.wikipedia.org/wiki/Canary_Islands – Wikipedia does its usual outstanding job, with vast amounts of background material relating to the history, geography and human resources of all seven main islands and several of the smaller islets

www.fredolsen.es – website of Líneas Fred Olsen SA, which runs ferries through the islands though not linking east to west. See page 186 for more travel details

www.iac.es – homepage of the Instituto de Astrofísica de Canarias, in Spanish and English. Particularly interesting pages cover the astrophysical observatories of El Teide on Tenerife and La Caldera de Taburiente on La Palma

www.iac.es/weather – clearly an offshoot of the above site, but with no obvious link from it. Weather data gathered from the two observatories, plus satellite images, interpretation etc., but tending toward the theoretical rather than the practical

www.maps.google.com – maps and satellite images of much of the world, with particularly good coverage of the Canaries. Although every image is labelled with the current year's date, this is somewhat misleading as many photos are at least two to three years years old

www.nautica7.com – a well-constructed website claiming to offer 'information on fields ranging from the Spanish legal sector to professionals in our archipelago, ports and marinas, yacht clubs, fraternities, fishing contests, races, plus a variety of topics of general interest'. And it does, too, though some of the harbour information is either out of date or planned rather than actually in place. The *Páginas Azules* featured on the homepage and listing everything from *Alquiler de Embarcaciónes* to *Webs Náuticas de interés* (though not, strangely, in alphabetical order) are particularly useful

www.navieraarmas.com – user-friendly website of Naviera Armas, the Canaries' most wide-ranging ferry company, in Spanish, English, French and Portuguese. See page 186 for more travel details

www.palmasport.es – official website of the Port of Las Palmas, responsible for the larger commercial ports in the three eastern islands as well as the Muelle Deportivo de Las Palmas (Las Palmas Marina)

www.puertosdecanarias.com – an offshoot of the Government of the Canary Islands' Department of Public Works, Housing and Water Works, and formerly carrying practical information and aerial photos relevant to the 12 harbours administered by the Department. By 2011 much of this information had been removed and many of the links were broken, but hopefully this situation is temporary

www.puertosdetenerife.org – well-constructed website of the Port Authority of Santa Cruz de Tenerife, responsibile for the larger commercial ports in the four western islands (though nearly all the marinas inside them are run by other concerns). Unfortunately the former complete list of lights and buoyage has been cut back and now covers major lights only – the very ones least subject to change. In Spanish and English

www.red2000.com – yet another tourist site in Spanish, English and German, a small part of the 'All about Spain' site. Slightly superficial, but some excellent photographs and pleasantly fast to download

www.trasmediterranea.es – the website of Trasmediterránea, in Spanish, Catalan, English, French and German, with details of ferry services from peninsula Spain and between the larger islands. See page 186 for more travel details

www.turismodecanarias.com/canary-islands-spain – website of Promotur, in eight languages including English, with some unexpected and interesting links. And who could argue with their statement that the Canaries are '...the best cruise destination' even if they didn't have yachts in mind?

Sailing and navigation

Practicalities

Entry and regulations

On arrival from abroad (other than from mainland Spain), clearance must be obtained from the Immigration and port authorities – if berthed in a marina the staff will normally give guidance – after which it is not necessary to clear in and out when moving between harbours or islands. Nevertheless marina staff will expect to see passports as well as ship's papers, and generally require proof of insurance.

Outward clearance is not compulsory – and in a few harbours is very difficult to obtain – but it is worth some effort to get formal clearance before departing the Canaries as it is likely to be required at the port of arrival, be it in the Cape Verdes, Brazil or the Caribbean. Neither La Gomera nor El Hierro are official 'border posts', but clearance can previously be obtained in either Tenerife (in which case the skipper may have to visit either Santa Cruz or Los Cristianos) or Santa Cruz de la Palma.

Booking berths in Puertos de Canarias harbours

Puertos de Canarias ✆ 928 455885 Fax 928 306391
Email laspalmas@puertosdecanarias.es,
sancruz.tenerife@puertosdecanarias.es or
lp.explotacion@puertosdecanarias.com
www.puertosdecanarias.com is responsible for many of the archipelago's smaller harbours, including any provision for yachts which they may contain. As of early 2011 the only true marina in their control was Gran Tarajal (Fuerteventura), but berthing (either on pontoons or alongside the quay) was also available in Caleta del Sebo (Isla Graciosa, Lanzarote), Corralejo and Morro Jable (Fuerteventura), Puerto de Arguineguín (Gran Canaria), Puerto de las Nieves (Tenerife), Puerto de Santiago and Puerto de Vueltas (La Gomera) and Puerto de la Restinga (El Hierro). It is the first of these which is likely to cause the greatest aggravation, with few visitors' berths, an idyllic location in which new arrivals tend to linger, and an anchorage which is itself subject to prior booking – see page 202.

The system is time-consuming, to put it mildly. A mooring application request is completed either online or on paper (copies are available from the harbour office at Caleta del Sebo, among other places), and then emailed or faxed to the *Puertos de Canarias* offices in Las Palmas de Gran Canaria. *Puertos de Canarias* should then notify the harbour officials at the relevant harbour to reserve a suitable berth, to be paid for on arrival. It appears that no confirmation is sent to the skipper that his request has been received and has gone through – or equally that it has not, should no space be available for the dates requested. This inevitably results in berths being reserved for yachts which never show up, yachts with 'booked' berths arriving to find no space, and the crews of non-booked yachts being understandably annoyed to be denied access to berths which are clearly empty.

If booking by fax it is necessary to append copies of crew passports, ship's papers and current insurance documents, though no mention is made of these when booking online. Should confirmation be received, the following words may be useful: *atraque de costado* – alongside berth; *atraque de punta* – bows-to berth; *fondeo medios propios* – lying to one's own anchor.

Shelter from heavy weather

There has long been a legal requirement throughout the Canaries for all harbours and marinas to provide shelter for a boat at risk from the weather, however full they may already be. This obligation generally appears to be honoured, though the vessel will probably be requested to leave as soon as conditions have moderated. However, there appears to be no formal definition of 'heavy weather', presumably leaving a decision to the discretion of harbour staff who may themselves not be sailors – or be willing to take the size and crew strength of an individual yacht into consideration.

Laying up

The number of harbours where a yacht might be laid up ashore, at least for a limited period, has increased dramatically over the past few years. The most obvious choices are: Puerto Calero or Marina Rubicón in Lanzarote; Pasito Blanco, Puerto de Arguineguín, Puerto Rico or Puerto de Mogán in Gran Canaria; Santa Cruz (Varaderos Anaga), Puerto Radazul or Los Cristianos in Tenerife; Puerto Tazacorte in La Palma and Puerto de la Restinga on the south coast of El Hierro. All have powerful travel-lifts and a reasonable amount of hardstanding but they vary greatly in the level of facilities and security available – and in cost. Refer to the text for further information.

There is even more choice if wishing to lay-up afloat, at least for a month or two, though space is likely to present the greatest problem and not all marinas accept advance bookings. Currently the choice would probably comprise: Puerto Calero or Marina Rubicón in Lanzarote); Gran Tarajal in Fuerteventura; Las Palmas, Pasito Blanco, Puerto Rico or Puerto de Mogán in Gran Canaria; Marina Santa Cruz, Marina Tenerife, Puerto Radazul, Puerto Deportivo La Galera, Marina San Miguel or Marina del Sur in Tenerife; San Sebastián de la Gomera; and Marina La Palma or Puerto Tazacorte in La Palma. Again costs and facilities vary and further information will be found in the text.

Problems with corrosion have occasionally been reported in the eastern islands. One yachtsman noticed that 316 stainless steel began rusting whilst berthed in Fuerteventura, and local people told him that this was due to open quarry mining of phosphor in Morocco. Dust enters the atmosphere, combines with moisture, and falls on the eastern Canaries as phosphoric acid. However, it can be removed by gentle rubbing, or more severe patches with oxalic acid.

Long-term visits: vessels registered in the EU

Under Spanish law, if a foreign – including EU-registered – yacht spends more than 180 days (cumulative, not consecutive) in any 365-day period in a Spanish harbour with her owner living aboard, the latter may be considered to be a resident '*de hecho*' (meaning 'in fact', as opposed to 'by law', as would be the case with a person who officially holds residency). Should this occur he (or she) will become subject to local taxes and other legislation. If his boat is of more than 9m LOA he will be obliged to import it at a cost of 13% of its value and then to pay 11% registration tax. Until recently the law also required the boat's registration to be changed to Spanish, with all that implied, but changes were under discussion at the time of writing. Anyone who might be affected by the above would be wise to seek professional advice.

It appears that the legal ways to avoid this highly undesirable scenario are either to move the yacht from time to time, thus preserving the 'right of innocent passage' or, if the boat is to be laid up while the owner leaves Spanish territory, to retain evidence of leaving and re-entering the country (aeroplane boarding cards should be acceptable).

In practice this law has rarely been applied in the Canaries, and then only to vessels belonging to those who, by any normal definition, are indeed long-term residents. Thus, while it is worth bearing in mind if laying up (see above) it is clearly not of major concern to most cruising yachtsmen. The law regarding commercial – including charter – vessels, while different, is outside the scope of this book.

Long-term visits: vessels registered outside the EU

Vessels registered outside the EU may only remain in Spanish waters for up to 183 days in any 365 day period. If an owner wishes to leave his boat unattended beyond this time he can employ a Customs agent to apply for a voluntary seal – a '*precinto voluntario*' – which allows the boat to exist 'outside time'. The boat cannot be moved while under seal – a small document taped to a window – but she can be accessed for service work or for living aboard for short periods by the owner. The agent's fee for sealing and unsealing the boat will normally be around €140.

IGIC (*Impuesto General Indirecto Canario*)

The Canary islands lie outside the EU, so VAT is not applicable. However a sales tax of 5% known as IGIC – *Impuesto General Indirecto Canario* – is applied to most bills, including marina fees. While not usually included in the quoted price, it has been added to all fees quoted in the following pages in order to simplify price comparison between harbours.

Recreational Vessel Tax (*Tasa de Embarcación de Recreo*)

From 1 August 2008 until 31 December 2010 Spanish yacht harbours and marinas under the jurisdiction of the state port authority or *Puertos de la Autoridad Portuaria* – normally those inside commercial ports, whether the marina was privately or state run – were obliged to charge recreational vessels a *Tasa de Embarcación de Recreo* of €0.06 per m^2 per day.

On 1 January 2011 this figure was reduced, albeit in a somewhat complex manner. Visiting sailing yachts of 12m LOA or less now pay only €0.02 per m^2 per day, while those of more than 12m LOA pay €0.05 per m^2 per day. Yachts on long-term visits (ie. marina-based for six months or more) pay €0.01 per m^2 per day and €0.04 per m^2 per day respectively. Motor boats pay similar sums, but with the cut-off length set at 9m LOA rather than 12m.

Navigational Aid tax (*Tasa de Ayuda a la Navegación*)

All vessels of more than 12m LOA which visit Spanish waters, including the Canaries, are liable to pay €4.24 per m^2 per year (just over €0.01 per m^2 per day) towards the upkeep of maritime aids.

In theory, 20% of this (€0.85 per m^2) is payable on entering one's first Spanish harbour with a further 20% due at 30-day intervals until, on the 121st day, the final instalment is paid. It is clearly essential to keep all receipts. In practice it is such a nightmare to apply that many marinas ignore it altogether, while others charge by the day – literally – and since all marinas charge per night, *Tasa de Ayuda a la Navegación* will be calculated for one more period than the berthing fee.

Ships' stores

Fuel can be obtained at nearly all marinas, though often during limited hours which may not include weekends – see individual harbour details. In a few cases payment must be made in cash, even though a card is accepted for the marina fees. Occasionally a pump will be found on a fishing harbour wall, but yachts cannot always buy diesel from supplies ear-marked for fishermen, which is taxed at a lower rate. When they can, cash will nearly always be needed.

Diesel is *gasoil*, petrol is *gasolina*, refined paraffin or kerosene is *parafina*, while lower grade paraffin (which is suitable for cleaning machinery but will carbon-up many lamps and stoves) is often referred to as *petróleo*. Both grades of paraffin are available at filling stations and hardware stores, though methylated spirits (*alcohol metalido* or *desnaturalizado*) and surgical spirits (*alcohol de 90°*) are more likely to be found at a chemist or pharmacy.

After many years with a shortage of good chandleries, there has been a dramatic improvement recently. The widest range will be found in Las Palmas de Gran Canaria or Santa Cruz de Tenerife, but there are also excellent chandleries at Puerto Calero and Marina Rubicón in Lanzarote and at

Puerto de Arguineguín, Puerto Rico and Puerto de Mogán in Gran Canaria. Nearly all the larger chandleries have at least one English-speaking employee, and most are willing to order from abroad if an item is not held in stock. Even where no large-scale chandlery yet exists, items such as yacht paint are often available from *ferreterías* (hardware stores).

Bottled gas

Previously included under the heading of Ships' stores, the current situation concerning bottled gas deserves a little more prominence.

Until mid-2009 the Disa plant on each island could refill a wide variety of cylinders, but in August the company introduced restrictions on refilling foreign cylinders – including standard 4·5kg Calor Gas – although Camping Gaz exchanges were unaffected. At the same time Disa's own unwieldy 13kg bottles were phased out and replaced by lightweight 6kg 'nu-b' butane canisters.

After several years of consultation, by August 2011 Disa were equipping their plants on all seven islands with a variety of propane adaptors to enable many foreign cylinders to be refilled. Final decisions had yet to be made as this book went to press, but G7/9, G8 and Jumbo adaptors seemed probable. These would enable most American cylinders to be refilled, as well as propane Calor Gas and those from Spain, France, Germany, Holland and Scandinavia.

Propane adaptors have been given priority on the basis that yachts continuing across the Atlantic should already be equipped for propane (butane is seldom available in the Caribbean except in exchangeable Camping Gaz bottles). A propane system will, of course, require the appropriate regulator, a topic outside the scope of this book. (At present the three western islands have only butane available but, although not ideal, filling propane bottles with butane is not dangerous.)

As of 2011 the situation regarding butane refills was less certain. Butane cylinders, including standard 4·5kg Calor Gas, could be recharged at the Disa plants on Lanzarote and Fuerteventura, but the situation elsewhere remained unclear. For current information regarding butane availability in all the islands contact reservas@puertocalero.com. Any skipper contemplating a long stay in the Canaries might consider adapting to the 6kg Disa cylinders mentioned above. These can be obtained against a deposit and returned on another island. Regulators are available from hardware stores.

As always, it is important that all cylinders are in good condition and, if they are of the type which carries a date tag, less than ten years old. There have also been occasional reports of repainted bottles being turned down for refilling, though varnishing appears to be okay.

Those wishing to research the whole subject before departure are recommended to visit the Calor Gas website at www.calor.co.uk, that of Southampton Calor Gas Centre at www.socal.co.uk (click the 'Marine' and 'Toolbox' tabs), and Will Hayward Engineering at www.gasboat.net. The latter's brochure, downloadable as a pdf, includes useful background and legal information in addition to showcasing the company's products. Disa's own website (in Spanish only) will be found at www.disagrupo.es.

Cruising

Since Columbus first crossed the Atlantic, leaving from San Sebastián de Gomera, the islands have been a favourite jumping-off point. With the prevailing northeast trade winds it used to be said that the easiest route back to Europe from the Canaries was via the Caribbean, and most would still agree. However, the number of yachts visiting the Canaries and returning to Spain either direct or via Madeira is steadily increasing and many European charter firms now operate in the area. The archipelago has become a popular cruising ground in its own right and, unlike the Mediterranean, it is possible to cruise there all year round. Situated as they are around 28°N, washed by the Canaries Current and lying in the northeast trades, the average monthly temperature seldom varies more than 5° either side of 25°C. Water temperatures throughout the year range from about 19°–22°C.

The seven major islands are spread over a distance of 240M in an east-west line. When sailing between islands it is generally possible to leave and to arrive in daylight – advisable when visiting for the first time, as harbour lights are often inconspicuous against the many hotels and apartment blocks.

The coastline is generally steep-to and, with a few exceptions, dangers do not extend for more than 0·5M offshore. Extra care must, however, be exercised when approaching the shore in a few areas and entering some harbours, as detailed in the text.

Particularly Sensitive Sea Areas (PSSA) / Traffic lanes

On 1 December 2006 large areas of Canarian coastal waters were designated 'Particularly Sensitive Sea Areas' (PSSAs) recognised by the International Maritime Organisation. This is in addition to the sizeable areas already set aside by the

The *Parque Natural del Archipiélago Chinijo* covers much of northern Lanzarote and its offlying islands

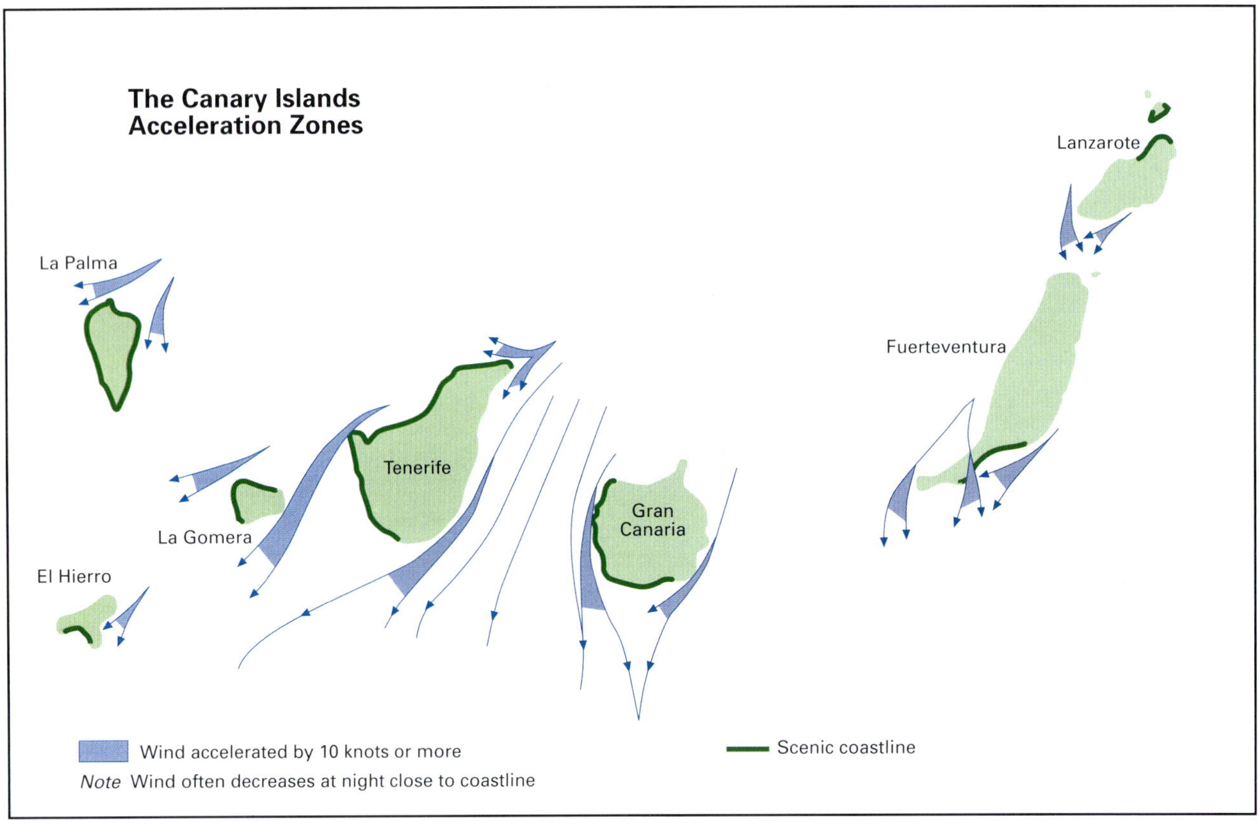

Spanish Government as Marine Reserves. At the same time, Traffic Lanes have been established between Fuerteventura and Gran Canaria, and between Gran Canaria and Tenerife. Full details of all of these will be found on current editions of BA *1869* and *1870*.

Anchoring and berthing

The nature of the bottom varies, but usually consists of sand and/or round volcanic stones and boulders. Serious ground tackle should be carried, preferably with a variety of anchors including a traditional fisherman with a tripline to the crown. The main bower needs to be on the heavy side and equipped with at least 50m of chain and the same length of warp, or preferably a full 100m of chain. Additionally, three 50m lines should be available for running ashore to rocks or wall, plus a 10m length of chain for use when rocks or stones are particularly sharp. Chafing gear will also be needed from time to time and a leadline is useful when anchoring, to test the bottom by feel.

Many commercial harbours have strict 'no anchoring' rules, details of which will be found in the text, but other than in the *Parque Natural del Archipiélago Chinijo* surrounding Isla Graciosa and the northern part of Lanzarote, and the *Reserva Marina Mar de las Calmas* on the south coast of El Hierro – see pages 203 and 319 respectively – anchoring is generally permitted elsewhere, often without charge.

Surge from the Atlantic swell works its way inside many harbours, making mooring to a wall an art to be acquired by practice. Chafe of warps and fenders can be severe and in some cases it is necessary to lay out a kedge amidships to haul clear of the wall. In addition, many harbour walls have an overhang which can cause damage to rigging and stanchions and/or alcoves into which fenders can slip, making a fender board useful. Climbing the wall can be difficult at low water and, if a kedge is used to haul clear, it is often easier to get ashore by dinghy.

Illegal immigrants

(Mentioned here because of the hazard posed by their abandoned and derelict vessels.)

Illegal immigrants arriving by boat from Africa have long been a problem in the Canaries, but fortunately the authorities have not responded by clamping down on cruising yachts. Previously *cayucos* full of immigrants, often in a sinking condition, generally made landfall in Fuerteventura but more recently Gran Canaria and Tenerife have become the landfalls of choice. Many *cayucos* depart from Mauritania, hiding themselves among the inshore fleet before departure. Despite Spanish spotter planes off the African coast and *Guardia Civil* vessels patrolling the waters between Africa and the Canaries, many boats slip through. About half of these are detected en route and intercepted on landing by the *Salvamento Marítimo*. The passage typically takes four days, though up to a fortnight is not unknown – often with fatal consequences. Abandoned *cayucos* are often reported adrift by Las Palmas NAVTEX station, and at around 15m LOA they, as well as those still manned but unlit, constitute a serious hazard after dark. Being almost entirely of wood, derelicts often float for a long time even when swamped.

Barometric pressure and winds

The northeast trades predominate throughout the Canaries and are associated with high pressure established over the Azores. The height and distribution of the islands causes the wind to funnel between them, which in turn produces zones in which the wind strength can increase from 5 knots to 25 knots in a distance of 200m. The acceleration zones off both the northwest and southwest coasts of Gran Canaria are amongst the worst. The plan showing these acceleration zones should be studied carefully. It is best to reef and reduce to a small headsail area before entering a zone, as warning is minimal. That said, in an acceleration zone the seas are usually moderate so that, if prepared, an exhilarating sail can be expected.

On a few occasions, usually in the winter months, an Atlantic low pressure system may move southwards to cross close north of the Canaries, replacing the Azores high pressure. When this occurs the barometer will fall rapidly from the normal ±1025mb. A fall of 10mb or more heralds winds of at least 35 knots from anywhere from south through southwest to northwest. Before the breakwaters were built, fishing boats were hauled out and yachts were advised to seek shelter in bays on the north sides of the islands. Although the situation has now improved greatly, a high proportion of harbours and marinas are open to the south and others have had breakwaters and walls breached in storm conditions – generally the swell is far more destructive than the wind. Local opinion holds that southerly gales have increased in both frequency and severity over the past two decades, causing increased damage to property both ashore and afloat.

A barometer rising to 1030mb or more indicates high pressure over the Sahara and a strong easterly can be expected. Seas are then steep and uncomfortable, and a *sirocco* should be anticipated.

Visibility

Visibility is normally good throughout the Canaries and once landfall has been made at least one island will nearly always be in sight. However, visibility can be reduced to 0·5M when a strong easterly *sirocco* brings a reddish haze of fine sand from the Sahara, and in these conditions – known locally as a *calima* – navigators will be glad to rely on GPS, radar or both.

Sources of further information

Further statistics are available from a number of sources – the British Admiralty *Routeing Charts, North Atlantic Ocean*, the US National Geospacial-Intelligence Agency *Pilot Charts of the North Atlantic Ocean*, James Clarke's *Atlantic Pilot Atlas*, now in its 5th edition (see Further Reading, page 403) and Imray Laurie Norie & Wilson Ltd's *Chart 100, North Atlantic Ocean Passage Chart*.

Weather forecasts

The Canaries are covered by Navtex transmissions from Las Palmas in English as well as Spanish (see page 237). It is recommend that Spanish speakers listen to both broadcasts, as it is reported that there is sometimes mis-translation into English (backing / veering is the commonest) while the Engish text can be missing detail, have different pressure data, or even omit parts of the Spanish synopsis.

Various websites carrying worldwide weather information are listed on page 9. In addition, general forecasts are available from Spain's *Instituto Nacional de Meteorología* at www.aemet.es, in Spanish only. If within VHF range of Tenerife, a weather bulletin in Spanish and English can be heard

Courses and distances within the Canaries

Harbour	*Course / Reciprocal*	*Distance*
Arrecife, Lanzarote - Puerto de Rosaria, Fuerteventura	209° / 029°	33M
Playa Blanca, Lanzarote - Santa Cruz de Tenerife	260° / 080°	129M
Playa Blanca, Lanzarote - Puerto de las Palmas, Gran Canaria	242° / 062°	95M
Morro Jable, Fuerteventura - Puerto de las Palmas, Gran Canaria	275° / 095°	57M
Morro Jable, Fuerteventura - Puerto de Mogán, Gran Canaria	253° / 073° & by eye	79M
Puerto de las Palmas, Gran Canaria - Santa Cruz de Tenerife	292° / 112° & by eye	52M
Puerto de Mogán, Gran Canaria - Los Cristianos, Tenerife	282° / 102° & by eye	55M
Los Cristianos, Tenerife - Santa Cruz de la Palma	305° / 125°	68M
Los Cristianos, Tenerife - San Sebastián de Gomera	276° / 096°	21M
Los Cristianos, Tenerife - Puerto de la Estaca, Hierro	256° / 076°	65M
Valle Gran Rey, Gomera - Santa Cruz de la Palma	328° / 148° & by eye	43M
Valle Gran Rey, Gomera - Puerto de la Estaca, Hierro	239° / 059°	41M
Santa Cruz de la Palma - Puerto de la Estaca, Hierro	188° / 008° & by eye	56M

at four-hourly intervals on Ch 74 – see page 264. All the other islands except El Hierro transmit similar bulletins but in Spanish only.

In port, daily forecasts (normally comprising a synoptic chart and text in Spanish, English or both) are displayed outside most marina or harbour office – see individual harbours for details.

Magnetic variation

Variation throughout the Canary Islands decreases by about 1°45′ from west to east, in 2011 averaging 5°40′ and decreasing by 8′E annually. Admiralty charts *1869* and *1870* mention local magnetic anomalies between Lanzarote and Fuerteventura and near La Palma.

Tides and tidal streams

Volume 2 of the Admiralty Tide Tables: *The Atlantic and Indian Oceans including tidal stream predictions (NP 202)*, published annually, covers the Canaries, with Casablanca as standard port. However, many more yachtsmen will turn to the internet and the UK Hydrographic Office's excellent *EasyTide* programme at http://easytide.ukho.gov.uk, which gives daily tidal data for the main commercial harbour on each island.

Maximum mean spring range varies from 2·2m in Lanzarote and Fuerteventura to 1·8m in La Palma, with mean neap range decreasing from 1·1m to 0·7m over the same area. Tidal streams are slight and can in general be ignored. However, it has been reported that the southwest-going stream may occasionally set down the east coast of La Gomera at up to 4 knots – see island information.

Currents

The Canary Current is associated with the northeast trades and sets through the islands in a southwesterly direction at around 0·5 knots, increasing to 2 knots at times in the summer. A strong southerly gale can cancel or even reverse this current.

Marine farms are a common feature around the Canaries, generally consisting of a number of circular cages and marked by four or more yellow pillar buoys. These lie below the spectacular cliffs just north of Puerto de Los Gigantes

Navigational aids

Radio communications

Since the withdrawal of the very useful *NP289 – Maritime Communications, United Kingdom and the Mediterranean*, those wishing to carry details of all official radio communications in the Canary Islands now need to invest in three volumes – *NP281(1) – Maritime Radio Stations*; *NP283(1) Maritime Safety Information Services* and *NP 286(1) Pilot Services, Vessel Traffic Services and Port Operations*.

Buoys and lights

The few navigational buoys and many lights in the Canaries adhere to the IALA A system, based on the direction of the main flood tide, as used throughout mainland Europe.

All major lights have good operational records (though the same cannot be said of all harbour lights, and even less so for the buoys marking marine farms). However, news of alterations to lights and other navigational marks, whether planned or arising from defects, can take months to percolate through the reporting system and the navigator should be aware that marks may not appear as described – or at all.

Note that not every light listed in the text can be shown on the plans, in particular on the small-scale 'island' plans. Refer instead to the relevant – and preferably corrected – chart.

Charts

By far the most detailed charts of the Canary Islands are the 28 sheets produced by the Spanish *Instituto Hidrográfico de la Marina*, based in Cádiz. These comprise five small-scale island charts and 23 sheets of larger-scale plans. There are currently two official agents for Spanish hydrographic publications in the Canaries – JL Gándara y Cía SA in Las Palmas (see page 244) and the *Centro Geofísico de Canarias* in Santa Cruz de Tenerife (see page 268). Náutica Chinijo in Lanzarote (see page 215) hope to become the third. Most chandleries either stock some Spanish charts or are willing to order as necessary, and it may soon be possible to buy online via the *Armada Española* website at www.armada.mde.es. Spanish charts are not normally supplied corrected.

British Admiralty charts (www.ukho.gov.uk) cover the archipelago on six sheets, with two small-scale plans and 12 approach and harbour plans. Suisca SL in Las Palmas (see page 244), hold the only official agency in the islands, though again most chandleries hold a limited stock. Imray Laurie Norie & Wilson Ltd are also official agents and will mail Admiralty charts worldwide. Note that while Admiralty charts obtained from an official agent should be supplied corrected to the date of despatch, those bought from other sources are unlikely to be.

The US National Geospatial-Intelligence Agency devotes five sheets to the islands. Though no longer available directly from the NGIA, they can be ordered online from approved suppliers. See page 396 for further details.

Finally, Imray Norie Laurie & Wilson Ltd's *Imray-Iolaire* series covers the archipelago on a single sheet, *E2*, at scale of 1:600,000, with 10 inset approach and harbour plans. Official distributors for Imray charts and pilots in the Canaries are Rolnautic and Sunshine Maritime in Gran Canaria, and Blancomar Nautica SL and Nordest in Tenerife (see pages 244, 259 and 268 respectively). However, many other chandleries stock Imray charts of the Canaries, the Cape Verde islands and the Caribbean, or they can be ordered online at www.imray.com.

See Appendix I, page 398, for chart lists.

Chart datum and satellite derived positions

All current editions of British Admiralty charts of the Canaries are based on WGS84 Datum, allowing satellite derived positions to be plotted directly onto them without further correction. For a fuller explanation see Horizontal chart datum on page 10 of the Passages section.

Bougainvillea cascades from archways in a pedestrian street in Puerto Mogan, Gran Canaria

Guides, pilots etc.

The archipelago is covered in the British Admiralty *Africa Pilot (NP 1)* and in the US National Geospacial-Intelligence Agency's *Sailing Directions for the West Coast of Europe and North West Africa (Pub 143)*, both of which are of course written with very much larger vessels in mind. In addition, the 6th edition of *The Atlantic Crossing Guide* covers the islands briefly, with additional harbour details for Puerto de las Palmas (Gran Canaria) and Marina Santa Cruz (Tenerife). They are also mentioned – even more briefly – in Rod Heikell and Andy O'Grady's *Ocean Passages and Landfalls*, and in *World Cruising Routes* and *World Cruising Destinations* by Jimmy Cornell.

The 5th edition of the *Canary Islands Cruising Guide* was published by World Cruising Club (www.worldcruising.com) in 2006 and it is understood that the 6th edition is due out during 2011. Primarily intended for those taking part in the ARC rally (which World Cruising also runs), it is particularly strong on repair and other facilities, and companies providing services to cruising yachts.

Caution and request

Facilities for the tourist trade, marine and shore-based, are being developed quickly. New tourist complexes, new high-rise hotels, new lights, new breakwaters and new marinas – six since the 4th edition of this book was published in 2004, bringing the total up to 20 – spring up rapidly. Although development appears to be slowing down, it would take little investment to radically improve facilities in a few under-used harbours, while one new one was visibly in build and a number of 'projects' were mentioned to the author during the course of her research. Works in progress frequently remain unlit, posing a hazard to those approaching after dark, while changes are often slow to be reported through the official channels. Thus even a brand new chart, fully corrected, should not be assumed to be fully up to date in all respects.

Where changes come to the notice of the author and/or publisher they are normally incorporated in the interim supplements carried on the websites of both Imray Norie Laurie & Wilson Ltd (www.imray.com) and the RCC Pilotage Foundation (www.rccpf.org.uk). The author and publisher are therefore indebted to the hundreds of yachtsmen and women who have taken the trouble to send in corrections, comments and photographs for these supplements, either by email to ilnw@imray.com or by post to Imray Laurie Norie & Wilson Ltd, Wych House, The Broadway, St Ives, Cambs PE27 5BT. Even in these days of information overload there is nothing to compare with direct feedback from someone who is actually on the spot – thank you, and long may it continue!

Isla Alegranza
Pta Delgada
2772
Fl.3s16m12M
page 201
Isla de
Montaña Clara
Ponta de
Pedro Barba
C02
C03
Roque
del Este
(Unlit)
29°15′N
Isla
Graciosa
2773·6 Q.Fl.
Pta Fariones
Orzola
Caleta del Sebo
Mirador
30
C04
Pta del Palo
Caves
608.
Pta de Mujeres
2773·8
Fl(2+1)R.8·5s9m5M
La Isleta
.670
.292
Lanzarote
.36
.322
.234
Montañas del Fuego
de
Timanfaya
29°N
.50
Costa Teguise
.59
Arrecife
2775
Fl.G.5s12m5M
page 211
.60
page 207
Puerto de los Mármoles
Puerto de Naos
Airport
Puerto
Calero
2780·5
Fl(3)G.9s4m8M
.60
page 213
Puerto del Carmen
2781
Fl(3)G.14s13m8M
Playa
Quemada
2782
Fl(3)30s
54m17M
Playa
Blanca
Pta Pechiguera
Marina
Rubicón
Fl(4)G.15s
3m5M
page 216
Pta Papagayo
C10
C08
Estrecho de la Bocayna
Pta Martiño
2786
Fl(2)15s28m14M
28°45′N
Isla de Lobos
N
Depths in Metres
Fuerteventura
13°45′W
13°30′W

Lanzarote

Between 28°50'N–29°14'N and 13°25'W–13°53'W

Introduction

Low-lying compared with the other Canary islands, with a multitude of smooth volcanic cones and a large area of dramatic black lava plains, Lanzarote has a charm all its own. It is about 60km long and 20km wide, and rainfall is so low that it cannot provide even for the 140,000 permanent population. New desalination plants are continuously being installed to cater for the booming tourist trade. Even so, serious efforts are made at cultivation, with carefully tended fields of cactus, tomatoes, onions and other vegetables. Viniculture is also successful, mainly in the centre of the island, and a range of highly drinkable wines – from dry to very sweet – is available.

Lanzarote itself is probably best explored by car with the boat securely moored in Puerto de Naos, Puerto Calero or Marina Rubicón. *Montaña del Fuego* (Fire Mountain) in Lanzarote's extraordinary *Parque Nacional Timanfaya* can be ascended on camel-back as well as by more conventional methods, and from the summit there is a unique view of volcanic cones and craters with an enormous sea of multicoloured and grotesquely shaped lava. The eruptions that produced these craters, covering the most fertile farming region and pushing the coastline 8km to the west, started in 1730 and continued for six years. In the Islote de Hilario restaurant on the side of the mountain meat is roasted over a fumarole and twigs burst into flame when dropped into one of the smaller vent holes.

On the northeast coast is Cueva de los Verdes, a lava pipe 7km long with dramatic concealed lighting, while the nearby Jameos del Agua, a short section of pipe open at both ends, was a refuge for the inhabitants from Arab slavers and during the later volcanic eruptions. A unique species of blind crab exists in a shallow pool in the cave, the rest of which has been converted into a spectacular night club and concert hall. If exploring by car it is worth visiting the seven attractions run by the *Centros de Arte, Cultura y Turismo*. Although dotted around the island, a multi-entrance ticket is available. Further information from the tourist centre in Puerto del Carmen or their website at www.centrosturisticos.com.

A ferry from Orzola takes visitors across to the peaceful island of Graciosa. Alternatively one can view the island, together with uninhabited Isla Alegranza and Isla de Montaña Clara, from César Manrique's spectacular lookout, the *Mirador del Río*.

Telecommunications

Mobile (cell) phone reception is good throughout Lanzarote and Isla Graciosa. The country code for the Canaries is 34, as it is for mainland Spain, and the area code for Lanzarote – which must be included even when dialling from within the island – is 928, shared with Fuerteventura and Gran Canaria.

By 2011 free Wi-Fi was available in both marinas, with cybercafés and pay-to-use internet access elsewhere, including Isla Graciosa.

Roque del Este seen over the newly extended breakwater at Orzola

Navigation

Waypoints

⊕ C01 – 29°29'N 13°30'·6W (4M N of Isla Alegranza)
⊕ C02 – 29°17'·1N 13°27'·7W (1M NE of Isla Graciosa)
⊕ C03 – 29°15'·6N 13°27'·9W (0·5M SE of Pta de Pedro Barba, Isla Graciosa)
⊕ C04 – 29°12'·5N 13°24'·3W (1M E of Pta del Palo)
⊕ C05 – 28°57'·5N 13°31'·3W (0·5M SE of Puerto de los Mármoles)
⊕ C06 – 28°56'·7N 13°32'·8W (0·5M SSE of Puerto de Arrecife)
⊕ C07 – 28°54'·4N 13°42'·4W (0·5M S of Puerto Calero)
⊕ C08 – 28°49'·8N 13°47'·2W (0·5M S of Pta Papagayo)
⊕ C09 – 28°51'·1N 13°49'·6W (0·5M SW of Marina Rubicon)
⊕ C10 – 28°50'·3N 13°52'·4W (0·5M S of Pta Pechiguera)

Courses and distances

⊕ C04 – ⊕ C05 = 17M, by eye
⊕ C06 – ⊕ C07 = 8·8M, by eye
⊕ C07 – ⊕ C08 = 6·3M, by eye
⊕ C08 – ⊕ C10 = 4·6M, 276° / 096°
⊕ C09 – ⊕ C12 (1M NE of Corralejo, Fuerteventura) = 6M, 190° / 010°
⊕ C10 – ⊕ C22 (0·5M SE of Las Palmas, Gran Canaria) = 92M, 242° / 062°
⊕ C10 – ⊕ C37 (0·5M SE of Santa Cruz de Tenerife) = 127·5M, 259° / 079°

Magnetic variation

4°50'W (2011), decreasing by 8'E annually. Local magnetic anomalies have been reported south of Lanzarote – see Admiralty chart *1870*.

Tidal Streams

Generally insignificant – see Tides and tidal streams, page 194. Details of range, etc. will be found under the combined information preceding Puertos de los Mármoles, Naos and Arrecife.

Charts

Admiralty 1870 (1:300,000)
Spanish *60A* (1:200,000), *600*, *601*, *605* (1:60,000)
US *51380* (1:263,900)
Imray-Iolaire *E2* (1:600,000)

Lights

2772 **Punta Delgada (Isla Alegranza)** Fl.3s16m12M 135°-vis-045° Dark grey conical tower and building, white lantern 15m
2773·6 **Punta Fariones** Q.14m4M Black over white tower 8m
2773·8 **Punta de Mujeres** Fl(2+1)R.8·5s9m5M White tower, blue bands 6m
2775 **Puerto de los Mármoles** Fl.G.5s12m5M Green tower 3m
2780 **Puerto de Arrecife breakwater** Q(6)+LFl.15s10m3M South cardinal tower 6m
2780·5 **La Tiñosa (Puerto del Carmen)** Fl(3)G.9s4m8M Green tower
2781 **Puerto Calero** Fl(3)G.14s13m8M Octagonal stainless steel tower 4m
2781·5 **Marina Rubicón** Fl(4)G.15s3m5M Green post 3m
2782 **Punta Pechiguera** Fl(3)30s54m17M White tower 50m

Coast Radio Stations

Arrecife 29°13'N 13°28'·7W, remotely controlled from Tenerife
VHF Ch 16, 25, 72 (24 hours)

Yaiza 28°55'·1N 13°47'W, remotely controlled from Tenerife
VHF Ch 03, 16, 74 (24 hours)
DSC VHF MMSI 002241025, 29°08'N 13°31'W, remotely controlled from Tenerife

Weather and navigation broadcasts

VHF 29°06'·7N 13°31'·3W, remotely controlled from Tenerife
Weather bulletins Ch 25 at 0833, 1333, 2033 (forecast in Spanish for coastal waters)
Navigational warnings Ch 25 at 0833, 2033 (in Spanish for coastal waters)

Websites

Lanzarote is particularly well served by the internet and, like the island itself, many of its sites appear to be carefully constructed and well run. The following contain general information about Lanzarote, some of which may be useful to the visiting yachtsman. Websites relating to specific harbours are listed under Harbour Communications, those covering all or most of the Canary Islands on page 188 of the Introduction.

www.en.wikipedia.org/wiki/Lanzarote – all the usual in-depth wikipedia information without the spin which one comes to expect from 'local' websites

www.cabildodelanzarote.com – the official site of the island council, carrying local news and current affairs. In Spanish only but translates well

www.centrosturisticos.com – website of Lanzarote's *Centros de Arte, Cultura y Turismo* which runs seven very different attractions, from the Montaña del Fuego to the Jardín de Cactus. (See also Introduction, above)

www.cesarmanrique.com – all about the artist and sculptor whose benign influence can be seen throughout the island

www.discoverlanzarote.com – an English language guide to the island. Easy to navigate and with some potentially useful information, if slightly superficial

www.lanzarotedigital.com – rather similar to www.cabildodelanzarote.com but stronger on current news. Practical information includes emergency telephone numbers, ferry timetables, etc.

www.lanzaroteguidebook.com/ – far more comprehensive than it appears at first glance, with background articles as well as news and events, one could spend a lot of time on this site

www.lanzaroteisland.com – an attractive site containing a smattering of history and culture, plus some nice photographs. In English only

www.lanzarotetourist.com/ – a bit of everything (history, gastronomy, beaches, etc.) plus a useful Attractions Reviews section with photos, opinions, opening times and contact details

www.turismolanzarote.com – the official website of the Lanzarote Tourist Board. Interesting and very well constructed in Spanish, English, German and French (look under Languages at top right)

The Fuerteventura ferry backs into her berth at Playa Blanca

Approach and navigation

If coming from the north, a yacht will sail down the coasts of both Lanzarote and Fuerteventura in the most practical direction – from north to south. To sail northwards is to go against the prevailing wind, the swell and the Canaries Current, a much tougher proposition. The northerly winds, which may reach 15–20 knots at midday (and sometimes more than that in August) are accelerated around the southern point of the island – see the chart of acceleration zones on page 192. Whitecaps will be visible, so reef before entering the zone. These winds generally decrease at night.

The *sirocco* – a strong, hot wind, gusting easterly from the African coast – can blow when the barometer is high, and creates steep seas and poor visibility due to its load of fine Saharan sand. If the barometer falls rapidly a southerly gale is imminent, and unless berthed in Caleta del Sebo, Puerto de Naos, Puerto Calero or Marina Rubicón it would be best to put to sea. While there are several fair-weather anchorages on the south and west coasts of the island, none are to be recommended along the east coast and only the four harbours already mentioned can be considered comparatively secure in bad weather.

Coming from the north, Caleta del Sebo on Isla Graciosa is a most pleasant landfall. At night, the light at Punta Delgada on Isla Alegranza may be raised first (though note that it is obscured from southeast through the entire westerly quadrant and right around to northeast). Roque del Este, 6·25M northeast of Punta del Palo at 29°16′·6N 13°20′·3W, is unlit and presents a hazard for night approach, though in daylight it becomes a useful landmark. When visiting Lanzarote from the west or south Marina Rubicón may well be the first port of call, though if the northeast trades are blowing the passage further up the coast may be unpleasant.

Although much of the eastern shore of Lanzarote descends almost vertically to 100m or more, there are several shallow banks – generally lava flows – which extend up to 0·5M offshore and are easily overlooked if relying on Admiralty chart *1870*. Off Orzola in the northeast depths of 3m have been reported, south of Arrecife a large shallow area extends off the old port, and off Punta Papagayo in the southeast a breaking reef extends some 500m beyond the headland.

Three large, unlit mooring buoys lie about 0·5M offshore southeast of the airport, at approximately 28°56′N 13°36′W. In addition, several marine farms were in place in early 2011, centred on 28°55′N 13°41′·5W, 28°53′·5N 13°44′·2W and 28°51′·2N 13°51′·1W.

Harbours and anchorages

Isla Alegranza

Between 29°23′N–29°25′N and 13°29′W–13°32′W

Waypoint

⊕C01 – 29°29′N 13°30′·6W (4M N of Isla Alegranza)

Plans

Spanish *600A* (1:25,000)

Lights

2772 **Punta Delgada** Fl.3s16m12M135°-vis-045°
Dark grey conical tower and building, white lantern 15m

The original deserted island

The east and south coasts of Isla Alegranza are part of the much larger *Parque Natural del Archipiélago Chinijo*, a marine reserve where fishing, scuba diving and anchoring all require prior permission (see page 203). Fortunately the designated anchorage – in Bahía El Veril west of Punta Trabuco – is also the best, though only feasible in very settled weather. There is a cave to the west of the bay which can be explored by dinghy.

The island is normally uninhabited, though a derelict house is visible together with the remains of some old stone buildings. There are no facilities of any kind.

Isla Graciosa

Between 29°13′N–29°17′·5N and 13°27′W–13°33′W

Waypoint

⊕ C02 – 29°17′·1N 13°27′·7W (1M NE of Isla Graciosa)
⊕ C03 – 29°15′·6N 13°27′·9W (0·5M SE of Pta de Pedro Barba, Isla Graciosa)

Plans

Spanish *600A* (1:25,000)
Imray-Iolaire *E2* (1:50,000)

Peaceful island which repays advance planning

Isla Graciosa is about 6·5km long and 3km wide. It is flat and sandy with four low volcanic cones, the largest 265m high, no made-up roads, and a small population living in Caleta del Sebo and Pedro Barba. So long as development can pass it by, Isla Graciosa will remain one of the most appealing spots in the entire Canaries. 'When you land' a Lanzarotean said, 'you can take off your shoes and forget the world.' Landing, however, was until recently at the dictate of the weather and in unsuitable conditions the island may best be admired from the spectacular Mirador del Río, designed by much respected local artist and sculptor César Manrique, who until his death in 1992 exercised a benevolent and effective control over the design of buildings on Lanzarote as artistic adviser to the island council. From a viewpoint on the edge of a vertical precipice at the northern point of Lanzarote you can look down from nearly 500m across the narrow Estrecho del Río, a passage favoured by migrating pilot whales.

The northeast trade winds funnel through the strait, while in winds from south of east strong katabatic gusts from the cliffs should be anticipated.

Looking over the Estrecho del Río towards Isla Graciosa, with Isla de Montaña Clara and Isla Alegranza beyond. The photograph was taken from near the *Mirador del Río*

In these conditions shelter will be found in the harbour at Caleta del Sebo (La Sociedad on most charts), or in the bay at Playa Francesa further west, though in both cases restrictions apply – see Berthing and Anchorage, both below). A marine reserve, the *Parque Natural del Archipiélago Chinijo*, surrounds much of Isla Alegranza, Isla de Montaña Clara, Isla Graciosa and the northern part of Lanzarote. Fishing, scuba diving and anchoring are all restricted inside the reserve and prior permission must be obtained (see page 203).

Punta Fariones, which forms the northeast 'corner' of Lanzarote

Caleta del Sebo

29°13'·6N 13°30'·09W (east breakwater head)

Plans
Spanish *600A* (1:25,000)

Lights
2773·6 **Punta Fariones**
Q.14m4M Black over white tower 8m
2773 **East breakwater**
Fl.G.5s3M Metal sculpture 2m
2773·5 **South breakwater**
Fl.R.5s3M Metal sculpture 2m

Harbour Communications
Harbour office ✆ /*Fax* 928 842104,
Email lg_juan@yahoo.es, hb_juan@hotmail.com
(0745–1415 weekdays only)

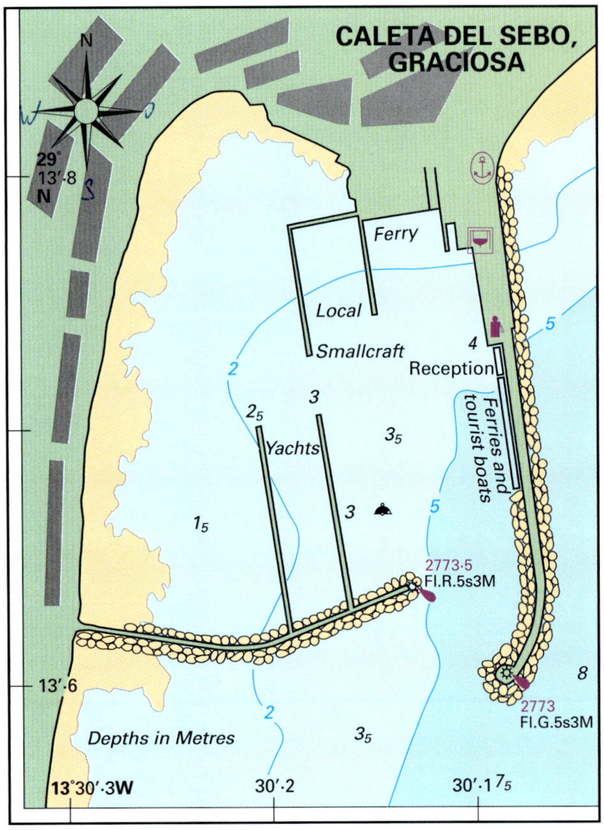

Small harbour lacking pontoon space

Although officially referred to either as La Sociedad or Puerto de La Graciosa, the village and its small harbour are known locally as Caleta del Sebo. It lies in the narrowest part of the strait, opposite a headland on which is a square grey tower, clearly visible for several miles and from which the island's power supply is routed.

Despite some new building, mostly of holiday apartments, Caleta del Sebo has retained its slightly detached 'holiday' atmosphere (not dissimilar to that of Porto Santo, Isles des Saintes or even the Scillies) and, with the necessary pre-planning, makes an excellent landfall assuming that no urgent repairs or services are required. It is particularly enjoyed by boat children, who can amuse themselves unhampered by either restrictions or significant traffic. For adults, a stroll ashore should take in the tiny town square surrounded by well-tended gardens, and the delightful little church with its nautically themed carvings and furniture.

Perhaps inevitably, the harbour has become a victim of its own popularity and suffers from chronic overcrowding, which is not always handled sympathetically. The pontoons are largely occupied by local smallcraft and permanently moored yachts, not all of which are owned by Canarian residents.

Caleta del Sebo seen from the *Mirador del Río*

Spaces are sometimes visible, but arriving yachts who attempt to use them are generally met by security guards, well provided with truncheons and handcuffs but not with foreign languages, who nevertheless make it very clear that they are not allowed to berth.

Neither is moving into the anchorage always simple as, in order to remain there, written permission must be applied for well in advance – see Anchorage, below.

For a full explanation of the berthing system see Booking berths in *Puertos de Canarias* harbours, page 189, but in the case of Caleta del Sebo the net result is empty berths being held for yachts which may never arrive, and angry and frustrated cruisers who do not understand why they have been told to leave. (Of course some of the empty berths may belong to legitimate, paid-up, long-term residents, who have a right to find their berth unoccupied on their return.)

Entrance

Both breakwaters at La Sociedad were extended about 10 years ago and good water is to be found off their ends. The entrance may be difficult to pick out if approaching from the east – the dark rubble breakwaters merge, with a spit of rocks (Punta Corrales) running out beyond. Look for the angular, rusty sculptures, one vaguely reminiscent of a child's swing, on the ends of both breakwaters. Though relatively narrow, the entrance, once identified, presents no particular problems in daylight – other than the possibility of a fishing boat or the Orzola ferry leaving at speed.

Entry in darkness is feasible though not recommended, but beware the mooring for the reserve ferry inside the entrance to port.

The northern end of the pontoon inside the east breakwater is designated a 'reception berth' – among other things it is handy for the port office – but in practice is usually occupied by fishing or tourist boats, though it might be possible to raft alongside until daylight

Berthing

Nearly all the 120 yacht berths on the two pontoons west of the entrance are occupied by local boats, long-term liveaboards or foreign-owned boats left there for long periods, leaving only two dozen or so spaces for yachts in transit (itself a term open to flexible interpretation). As a result and as stated above, in the busy months of October to December inclusive it is most unlikely that a berth will be available unless it has been pre-booked (see Formalities, below). The two northern pontoons are occupied by fishing boats and other local craft.

All the yacht berths have substantial finger pontoons, the majority of those to the east capable of taking yachts of up to 15m LOA in depths of 2·5m or more. Manoeuvring space between the two pontoons is limited.

Anchorage

As mentioned previously, much of Isla Graciosa lies within the *Parque Natural del Archipiélago Chinijo*, and anchoring is now limited to Playa Francesca. Bahía Cocina and Bahía del Salado are both reserved for diving. Playa Francesa is protected by an extensive reef to the east and Punta Marrajos to the west. Best holding is to be found in the western or central part – to the east are stones covered by a thin layer of sand. The bay is large enough for at least two dozen yachts and the water is very clear, but take care on landing, particularly near low water, as there are submerged rocks off the beach. It is a popular swimming beach where propulsion is limited to oars and paddles, but this does not

The west breakwater and yacht pontoons at Caleta del Sebo. Note the single buoy in the foreground, a potential hazard if arriving in darkness

prevent a profusion of jetskis, waterskiers and inflatable towing rings slightly further offshore. There are no facilities whatsoever, not even a road, though a footpath leads through the scrub towards Caleta del Sebo.

While it is entirely reasonable to restrict anchoring, along with fishing and scuba diving, the system is not administered in a particularly yacht-friendly manner. An application form must first be obtained from the *Servicio de Medio Ambiente*, a part of the *Cabildo de Lanzarote*, either from their main office in Arrecife, by email on

Playa Francesca, Isla Graciosa's only legal anchorage
Andy Scott

Footsteps in the sand at Caleta del Sebo on Isla Graciosa, Lanzarote's own 'holiday island'

medioambiente3@cabildodelanzarote.com, ✆ 928 810100 ext. 2283 (in Spanish only), *Fax* 928 805877, or from the small office on the breakwater at Caleta del Sebo. The form requires definite arrival and departure dates (a maximum of 10 days are permitted) together with details of the yacht and her crew and, unless already in Caleta del Sebo, must be returned to the main office in Arrecife, along with copies of passports and the boat's papers. Perhaps the least yacht-friendly aspect is that this must be done **a minimum** of 10 working days before the specified arrival date. There is no charge either for the permission or for anchoring itself.

Having said that, it appears that checking and enforcement of the permit system is sporadic. At least once during the autumn of 2010 all yachts without the necessary paperwork were ordered to leave, but more frequently a patrol boat was seen to pass by without stopping. When, in November, a strong southeasterly made the Playa Francesca anchorage untenable, more than a dozen yachts were to be seen sheltering off Playa del Rojo, west of La Punta on the southern shore of the Estrecho del Río. Although within the *Parque Natural* and not a designated anchorage, either the authorities decided to be lenient or were reluctant to leave the harbour themselves, as the yachts remained unmolested until the winds died down.

Formalities

As already stated, it is necessary to pre-book a berth – see Booking berths in *Puertos de Canarias* harbours, page 189 – but it would be wise to copy the same details to *Oficial de Puerto* Juan Pedro Hernández. Even with a berth reserved, the over-zealous and occasionally aggressive security guards may prove difficult outside port office hours, though some command of Spanish will certainly help. It has been suggested that the real purpose of the security guards – who are on duty around the clock in a community where crime is negligible – is to apprehend illegal immigrants arriving by boat from Africa (see Illegal immigrants, page 192). Although one would have thought the difference between a yacht crewed by northern Europeans and a *cayuco* overloaded with desperate Africans would be obvious, there may well be a grain of truth in this.

In contrast to the security guards Sr Hernández, who has been in post for 18 years, is very pleasant and speaks reasonable English. Visit him in his white and blue office at the root of the east (main) breakwater bearing the usual ship's papers, passports and evidence of insurance. He is frequently out of his office during the somewhat unusual – 0745 to 1415 – opening hours, but will usually be found there at the beginning and end of the day.

There are no Immigration officials on Isla Graciosa, and if non-EU and intending to stay more than a few days it may be wise to take the ferry to Lanzarote and visit Arrecife to complete formalities.

Charges

The berthing fee is calculated on a length x beam basis and in 2010 was set at €0.19 per m^2. This included water and tax, and was expected to increase by about 2% each year. There is no charge for anchoring.

Facilities

Travel-lift 64-tonne hoist operated by the *Cofradía de Pescadores* (fishermen's confederation). Although not really tuned to handling yachts, help would almost certainly be forthcoming in an emergency.

Chandlery None as such, though the FerroBox *ferretería* stocks tools, paint and limited chandlery.

Water Available on the eastern pontoon only, and from upward-facing spigots which appear to require a hose connection even to fill a can.

Showers Shower and toilet block next to the port office, and thus a longish walk from the yacht pontoons.

Electricity Wiring and sockets were installed on the pontoons when new, but have never been connected up.

Fuel A pair of diesel pumps next to the crane on the east breakwater serve the needs of the whole island, as well as of visiting yachts. Hours are limited to 1100–1300, 1600–1800 weekdays only (though service outside these hours can often be obtained by enquiry at La Caletilla restaurant), and payment must be made in cash.

Rubbish bins At the root of the south breakwater, with recycling bins dotted around the village.

Bank Open 1100–1300 weekdays only, with a single cash dispenser **inside** the building.

Shops/provisioning Three small supermarkets, plus a greengrocer, bakery, butcher etc. – more than adequate for day to day needs

Cafés, restaurants & hotels Several hotels and guesthouses plus a variety of restaurants and cafés, mostly near the harbour.

Medical services A small pharmacy, open 1000–1400 Monday to Saturday, and two doctors, one of whom speaks English. Serious problems are transferred to Lanzarote.

Communications

Post office In the village. Hours are irregular and are normally posted on the door.

Telephones Many throughout the village, with phone cards available at supermarkets and bars.

Internet access At Rosa's Net, two blocks back from the harbour on Calle Noray, offers Wi-Fi at €1.50 for 15 minutes, €2 for 30 minutes and €3 per hour (2010), whether using one's own computer or one of the four terminals provided. Photocopy and fax services were also available.

Taxis Three or four, mostly off-road vehicles.

Bicycles Available for hire – no car hire.

Ferries Líneas Maritimas Romero ✆ 902 401666 *Email* info@lineas-romero.com, www.lineas-romero.com run seven or eight passenger ferries each day to/from Orzola, where a bus makes the connection to Arrecife. During the summer two of them cruise around Isla Graciosa, visiting Playa Francesa at about 1300 to unload passengers onto the beach, re-embarking them for the return to Caleta del Sebo at about 1800.

Orzola

29°13′·6N 13°27′·15W (breakwater head)

Plans

Spanish *600A* (1:25,000)

Small ferry and fishing harbour

After many years during which the tiny harbour at Orzola (pronounced *Orh'so'lah*) was fully open to the prevailing northeast trades, in 2008 work finally started on a long breakwater. This follows the line of the reefs in a northwesterly semicircle, finishing with a straight section running northwest to close slightly with the mainland shore. The outer parts are awash at high tide, but nevertheless it provides much improved protection for the short quay from which the ferry departs for Caleta del Sebo on Isla Graciosa. Two north cardinal beacons mark the outer parts of the breakwater.

In calm conditions a visit by sea could be interesting, though it might be wise to recce by land or dinghy first. There appears to be room for a yacht of moderate size to anchor east of the quay, being certain not to impede the ferry, but depths have not been verified and extreme caution would be needed.

The north end of Orzola breakwater at high tide

Much of the harbour's inner part is taken up with local smallcraft on moorings. On no account should the area be approached at night or in less than very settled weather.

Anchorage

A highly experienced cruising couple (doubtless equipped with serious ground tackle) report finding good protection from strong southwesterlies in the small bay to the northwest of the village at about 29°13′·7N 13°27′·7W in good holding over sand. However, they add that as soon as the wind moderated a heavy swell set in from the northeast, necessitating a hurried departure.

Punta de Mujeres

29°08′·62N 13°26′·81W (headland, SE angle)

Lights

2773·8 **Punta de Mujeres** Fl(2+1)R.8·5s9m5M
White tower, blue bands 6m

Anchorage sheltered from the west

Punta de Mujures is a tourist development area, though on a relatively small scale, now almost linked to Arrieta by ribbon-development along the shore. It is the closest feasible anchorage to Jameos del Agua and Cueva de los Verdes, about 3km along the road to the northeast, and although wide open to the south and east offers a chance to visit these attractions in settled westerly conditions, rare though they may be.

The main part of the village occupies a square peninsula with a small quay on its southern corner, southwest of which there are extensive sand patches, still largely free of moorings. The smaller bay to the northeast has a greater density of local smallcraft moorings – possibly because it offers better shelter – and a rocky bottom. Restaurants and a few small shops will be found in the village, which has yet to be overtaken by tourism.

The inner harbour at Orzola, looking north

In westerly winds the anchorage at Punta de Mujures is more promising than this photograph would suggest

In weather permitting of a visit by yacht, it should be possible to land a dinghy either on the beach or at the steps and ramp by the short quay, though the latter can only be accessed at half-tide and above.

Arrieta

29°07'·71N 13°27'·76W (lop-sided quay, head)

Lights

2774 **Arrieta** Fl.R.2s9m5M
White tower, blue bands 7m

Anchorage in open bay

A pleasant little fishing village with surprisingly limited tourist development, Arrieta is nevertheless developing a reputation with visitors. Situated at the north end of the Rada de Arrieta, a bay some 2M across with no outlying dangers on approach, it is worth a visit in daylight in calm conditions. In a strong northeast or east wind the swell breaks along the length of the bay.

This unusual red and blue house with its double-pitched roof provides a distinctive landmark just north of Arrieta

On entering the bay the town can be seen to the north. A small stone quay lies near the north end of the town, with an unusual red and blue house with a double-pitched roof (Arrieta's distinctive feature) on its own separate peninsula close northeast. At the southern end of the town is a wooden jetty terminating in a strange, lopsided stone quay – apparently a swimming platform – with underwater projections, south of which is a sand and stone beach. Anchor either close south of the quay (if moored smallcraft permit), or off the beach to the south in 5m or so, both over sand and stones

Do not confuse Arrieta with Punta de Mujeres, a mile further north.

Costa Teguise

28°59'·75N 13°29'·14W (south molehead)

Tourist development offering possible shelter

Costa Teguise is a massive tourist development, the network of holiday villas a maze from which escape is difficult. If the trades are from northwest or north, the bay with its very solid breakwater appears a sheltered haven compared with the waves breaking on the reef off Orzola. However, when the wind comes east of north, sailboarders flip in rollers that break right across the entrance.

The low white buildings of Costa Teguise are visible from well offshore. On closer approach the reef off the north head of the bay extends up to 500m offshore and must be given a generous berth – the northern of the two rough, lava-block breakwaters curves southeast from near its root. The hotels and major buildings are on the southern arm of the bay, from which the main breakwater extends to the northeast. Two pillars, conspicuous on the breakwater head, are the artistic work of César Manrique, totem poles of rusty artefacts welded one on the other. A course of 310° for the breakwater should find sufficient water for an approach but do so with caution, a lookout and an eye to the echo sounder. Do not be misled by the very shallow harbour to the north – make certain you are heading for the totem poles.

Though obviously built primarily to provide shelter for a long and crowded bathing beach, the breakwater is more substantial than many of its ilk, with a solid top and sheer inner wall with bollards and ladders. It might well be possible to lie alongside – check first by dinghy. Otherwise anchor in 3m or so near the head of the breakwater. Local smallcraft lie on running moorings in its angle, and the rest of the bay is shallow. The usual tourist facilities of restaurants, cafés, shops and ice creams will be found in abundance ashore.

Puertos de los Mármoles, Naos and Arrecife

Waypoints

⊕ C05 – 28°57′·5N 13°31′·3W (0·5M SE of Puertos de los Mármoles)

⊕ C06 – 28°56′·7N 13°32′·8W (0·5M SSE of Puerto de Arrecife)

Combined harbour information

Lanzarote's three primary harbours – each with its separate entrance – occupy some 3km of coastline with no obvious demarcation ashore. Much of the more general information is therefore common to all.

Tides

Standard port for the Canary Islands is Casablanca, with Arrecife a secondary port. MLWS is about 0·4m above datum and time difference on Casablanca: –0053. Predictions for Puertos de Arrecife are also available via Admiralty *EasyTide* – see page 194

Mean spring range 2·2m
Mean neap range 1·1m

Plans

Admiralty *886* (1:75,000 & 1:12,500)
Spanish *6010* (1:10,000)

Lights

2775 **Puerto de los Mármoles breakwater**
Fl.G.5s12m5M Green tower 3m

2777 **Puerto de Naos breakwater**
Fl.R.5s11m3M Red tower 4m
Note Temporarily withdrawn in July 2011, presumably until the work shown below is complete

2780 **Puerto de Arrecife breakwater**
Q(6)+LFl.15s10m3M
South cardinal tower 6m

Harbour Communications

Port Authority ✆ 928 598301, 598305 *Fax* 928 598303
Email arrecife@palmasport.es (24 hours)

Three ports adjacent to Lanzarote's capital

The three harbours are very different. None normally offers the chance to berth rather than anchor, but whichever is chosen it is worth visiting the Castillo de San José, opposite the end of Puerto de Naos breakwater, for its panoramic views.

Puerto de los Mármoles (pronounced *Pwerto de los Mahr'moh'less*) is a busy commercial harbour serving container and cruise ships, with no place for yachts other than a possible anchorage in the bays on either side.

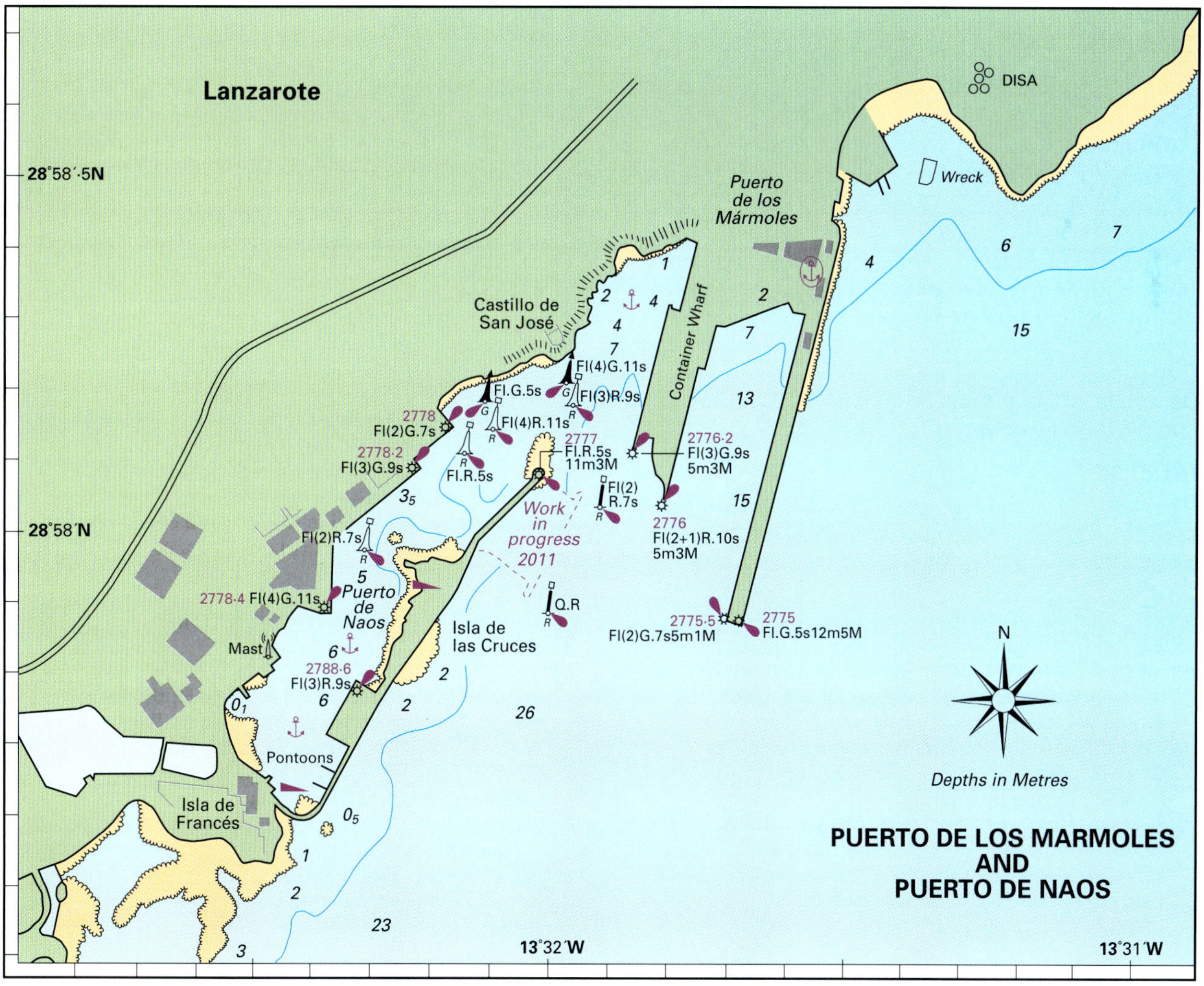

Puerto de Naos (pronounced *Pwerto de Nowse*) offers shelter in all conditions but is best entered for the first time in daylight. Once inside it is extremely secure, if currently somewhat unprepossessing. By late 2013 the new, 400-berth Marina Lanzarote should be operational – see page 210 – backed up by facilities which will add significantly to those detailed below.

Puerto de Arrecife (pronounced *Pwerto de Arressifay*) is the most convenient and pleasant of the three in settled trade wind weather, but is open to wind or swell from the southwest – see plan page 211.

Approach

The surrounding coastline is low-lying with rounded volcanic cones inland. The airport 5km west of Arrecife is busy with traffic from Europe and the other Canary islands, and white and green hotels and holiday villas, limited to four storeys by the influence of the island's late artist and advisor César Manrique, are mushrooming along the coast. The high-rise Arrecife Gran Hotel (marked on Admiralty chart *886*), built before the planning regulations came into force, is a conspicuous landmark and, after some years of dereliction has now been renovated and reopened. Non-residents are welcome to visit the restaurant and bar on the top floor from which there are stunning views, but note that the restaurant, which occupies the harbour side of the building, is only open between 1300 and 1530 and again from 2000.

Formalities

Clearance is handled by the *Policía Nacional* in their office in the *Edificio Autoridad Porturia* (Port Authority Building) building near the root of the Los Marmoles breakwater (a long, hot walk if anchored in Arrecife or even Naos, but lacking any convenient dinghy landing point). Skippers should report with ship's papers and, if this is the port of entry to the Canaries, attempt to get passports stamped (particularly important in the case of non-EU crew members or those who will be flying home).

Facilities

Facilities are certain to both change and improve with the opening of the new Marina Lanzarote – see pages 209–10.

Boatyards A large boatyard with three slipways has long been established on Isla de las Cruces, halfway along the Puerto de Naos breakwater, but it is not really tuned to yachts. It will be closed prior to work starting on the new marina, but a boatyard is among the promised facilities, hopefully by late 2013.

Travel-lift 100-tonne capacity hoist at the Isla de las Cruces shipyard, as well as a marine railway capable of handling large multihulls.

Engineers Several workshops on Calle Augustin de la Hoz Betancort (one road north of Puerto de Naos), including a well-stocked Volvo Penta agent. The Rio Centre (see below) is a service agent for Mariner, Mercury and Yanmar.

Electronic & radio repairs Electronica Naval ✆ 928 802535 *Email* elecnaval@canariastelecom.com at Calle Agustin de la Hoz 7 (the road immediately north of Puerto de Naos, or call in Navalectric Lanzarote ✆ 659 822118 *Email* yottitek@yahoo.com from Puerto Calero.

Sail repairs Aquatex Sails ✆ /*Fax* 928 592351, 616 283034 *Email* aquatexlanz@hotmail.com are in Costa Teguise (see page 206) about 7km northeast along the coast. There are also two sailmakers at Puerto Calero.

Chandlery Efectos Navales Duarte ✆ 928 811117, 800346 *Fax* 928 802108 on Calle Agustin de la Hoz (one road north of Puerto de Naos) carries a wide stock of serious chandlery including rope, paint, stainless steel shackles, etc., plus general hardware. The Rio Centre, opposite, is also part of the Duarte operation selling smallcraft (including inflatables) and outboards. Duque Hnos SL, next door to Efectos Navales Duarte, carries generators, outboards, hardware, tools, etc. The *Cofradía de Pescadores*, a little further along towards the fishing wharf, sells mainly hardware and practical items.

InoxNaval Lanzarote ✆ 928 814620, *Fax* 928 803017 just round the corner at Calle Puerto Naos 3, specialise in stainless steel and other metalwork, and are agent for Jotun paints.

Charts Efectos Navales Duarte can supply Admiralty charts to order, but delivery may take some time.

Water On the pontoons in Puerto de Naos.

Electricity On the pontoons in Puerto de Naos.

Fuel No alongside fuel available to yachts, though small amounts can be collected by can from a filling station. Strangely, cans brought by hand-trolley are sometimes refused, whereas those transported by car are generally filled without question.

Bottled gas Camping Gaz bottles can be exchanged at several hardware stores in the city, but as of 2011 the situation regarding refilling other cylinders remained uncertain – see page 191.

Club náutico The *Real Club Náutico de Arrecife* www.realclubnauticoarrecife.com at Avenida Rafael González 1 combines a social programme with sailing activities.

Banks Throughout the town, all with cash dispensers.

Shops/provisioning Good choice of supermarkets and other shops, as might be expected of the island's capital.

Produce market Vegetable market just west of the large church marked on Admiralty chart *886*.

Cafés, restaurants & hotels Wide choice around the harbour and town.

Medical services Hospital in the city, and clinic (where English is spoken) at Puerto del Carmen.

Communications

Post office Overlooking Puerto de Arrecife.

Telephones At all three harbours.

Internet access In late 2010 free Wi-Fi (and power) were available in the Gran Hotel at Arrecife, though it would plainly be tactful to buy a drink. Pay-to-use Wi-Fi is available at Redes Servicios Informática, Calle Coronel Bens 17, open 0900–1330, 1700–2000 weekdays, 0900–1300 Saturday.

Car hire, taxis and buses In the town, plus a a taxi rank opposite the root of Puerto de Arrecife breakwater.

Ferries To Fuerteventura and Gran Canaria.

Air services European and inter-island flights from the airport 5km west of the city.

Puerto de los Mármoles

28°57'·85N 13°31'·69W (breakwater head)

Waypoint

⊕ C05 – 28°57'·5N 13°31'·3W (0·5M SE of Puertos de los Mármoles)

Lights

2775 **Breakwater** Fl.G.5s12m5M
Green tower 3m
2775·5 **Breakwater, southwest corner**
Fl(2)G.7s5m1M Green post 3m
2776 **Container wharf, southeast corner**
Fl(2+1)R.10s5m3M Red post, green band 3m
2776·2 **Container wharf, southwest corner**
Fl(3)G.9s5m3M Green post 3m

Busy commercial port

Puerto de los Mármoles is the northeasternmost harbour of the complex and shares its outer entrance with that of Puerto de Naos. It is the main commercial port for the island. The area between the main breakwater and the container wharf, the latter widened during 2005, is heavily used by commercial traffic which berths along the inner sides of both walls. Yachts should avoid this area, and take particular care if passing across its mouth. However, the west side of the container wharf appears to be little used, and creates a sheltered if somewhat gritty anchorage in the prevailing northeasterlies.

Approach

See under combined harbour information. If approaching from the southwest or south, steer for the town and then, keeping more than half a mile offshore to avoid the reefs off Arrecife, steer northeast for Mármoles breakwater head. If approaching from the northeast, again keep half a mile offshore until the breakwater is identified. A group of tanks for the Disa and desalination plants will be seen on a point to the northeast.

Anchorage

As noted above, the area between the container wharf and the Castillo de San José offers anchorage in 4–7m over sand, mud and stones, with good protection

Yachts find calm anchorage northwest of the container wharf at Puerto de los Mármoles

from all directions other than south-southwest. It is not particularly scenic and can be gritty in strong winds, but is convenient for the city, with several places to land by dinghy in Puerto de Naos.

Alternatively, less sheltered anchorage can be found in the small bay to the northeast of the main breakwater. A pair of rails runs into the water at a shallow angle from a small mole at the head of the bay, so care should be taken if intending to anchor. Chose a spot south or southwest of the stranded and broken hulk of the steamer *Telemon* (of which only the stern now breaks surface) in 5m over sand and stones.

Formalities and facilities

See under combined harbour information.

Puerto de Naos

Lights

2775 **Puerto de los Mármoles breakwater**
Fl.G.5s12m5M Green tower 3m
2776·2 **Container wharf, southwest corner**
Fl(3)G.9s5m3M Green post 3m
2777 **Puerto de Naos breakwater**
Fl.R.5s11m3M Red tower 4m
Note Temporarily withdrawn in July 2011, presumably until the work shown on page 207 is complete
buoy **Port hand buoy** Q.R.3M Red buoy, ■ topmark
Marks the SE extent of reclamation work outside the breakwater

Entrance channel

buoy **Port hand buoy** Fl(2)R.7s1M
Red pillar buoy, ■ topmark 3m
Marks the NE extent of reclamation work – see overleaf
buoy **Port hand buoy** Fl(3)R.9s Red pillar buoy 4m
buoy **Starboard hand buoy** Fl(4)G.11s
Green pillar buoy 4m
buoy **Starboard hand buoy** Fl.G.5s Green pillar buoy 4m
buoy **Port hand buoy** Fl(4)R.11s Red pillar buoy 4m
2778 **Fishermen's wharf, northeast corner**
Fl(2)G.7s8m Green tower 4m
buoy **Port hand buoy** Fl.R.5s Red pillar buoy 4m
2778·2 **Fishermen's wharf, angle**
Fl(3)G.9s8m Green tower 4m
buoy **Port hand buoy** Fl(2)R.7s Red buoy, ■ topmark 3m
(marks a shoal off the end of the shipyard)
2778·4 **Fishermen's wharf, south corner**
Fl(4)G.11s8m Green tower 4m
2778·6 **Shipyard wharf, north corner**
Fl(3)R.9s8m Red tower 4m

Safe but scruffy fishing harbour

Puerto de Naos is a secure harbour in all weathers and the home of the local fishing fleet with all its attendant noise and smells – one well-travelled skipper aptly summed it up as 'very safe but grotty'. However, it is very crowded, with many unlit vessels and floating lines, and if arriving after dark it may be better to anchor west of Puerto de los Mármoles, as described above, and continue into Puerto de Naos in daylight.

In early 2011 a considerable area was being reclaimed southeast of the breakwater, understood to be earmarked for a cruise ship berth, and other work was taking place on the Isla de Frances.

Just as this book went to press it was confirmed that the concession to create a large, full-service

III. THE CANARY ISLANDS

Looking southwest into Puerto de Naos from the Castillo de San José in late 2010, with land reclamation in progress on the left

marina in Puerto de Naos – to be called Marina Lanzarote – had been awarded to the group responsible for Puerto Calero and Marina La Palma. Full details were not yet available, but preliminary plans show it occupying the entire inner length of the breakwater from Isla de las Cruces southwards.

Approach

See under combined harbour information. Approaching from the southwest or south, steer for the town and then, keeping more than half a mile offshore to avoid the reefs off Arrecife, steer northeast for the entrance between Mármoles and Naos breakwaters. From the northeast, again keeping half a mile offshore, Mármoles breakwater can be identified by the tanks of the Disa plant to the northeast.

Entrance

A dangerous spit of rocks runs north from Puerto de Naos breakwater head and it is essential to keep in the channel. Steer for the southwest corner of Mármoles container wharf, keeping east of the two red pillar buoys which mark the land reclamation mentioned above. The first pair of channel buoys will be seen ahead, beneath Castillo de San José. From a distance they appear very close together, but open out on closer approach. The second pair lie about 200m to the west – favour the north side of the channel to clear the spit. Continue southwest, keeping close to the fishermen's wharf, often masked by a mass of colourful fishing trawlers rafted four or five abreast. Two port hand buoys indicate the south side of the channel, the second marking a rocky shoal which runs out beyond the Isla de las Cruces mole.

Anchorage

Anchoring is likely to be either forbidden or severely restricted once work begins on the new marina – treat the information which follows with caution.

The anchorage is extremely crowded, both with long-term liveaboard yachts and semi-derelict hulks. Much of the bottom is foul with old chains, etc. (a problem compounded by a number of moorings laid for local boats) and a tripline is strongly recommended.

North of the Isla de las Cruces mole holding is good over sand and stones, but there is considerable disturbance from fishing boats departing and returning at all hours. Moorings limit the space available to a narrow strip just inside the line of the port hand buoys – on no account impede the channel itself, as it is needed to allow turning room for the large trawlers which berth against the harbour wall opposite. Depths do not exceed 5m and are much less in some areas. South of a line between the southwest corner of the mole and the mast of the School of Fishing opposite the holding is poorer. Even so, in early 2011 the whole southern end of the harbour was crowded with anchored yachts. Depths are in the 5–6m range.

Dinghies can usually be left at the southern end of the fishermen's wharf, where there is a substantial ladder. This area is sometimes used to berth pilot boats, however, and care must be taken not to impede them. Both dinghy and outboard should be securely padlocked.

Berthing

Current: As of early 2011 there were two short pontoons in the southern corner of the harbour, which were most unlikely to have space for a visiting yacht, particularly in the autumn. Berthing is bow or stern-to, with buoys and lazy lines provided, the latter making a careful watch for submerged lines necessary if approaching the area. The berthing master's office is nearby, open 1000–1400 Monday to Saturday.

Future: Preliminary plans for Marina Lanzarote look most impressive. Thirteen pontoons will provide berthing for around 400 yachts, many of them of significant size, with the harbour dredged as necessary.

The breakwater is to be widened to provide space for a range of ancillary services, including a large boatyard at the northern end. This is to be equipped with two travel-lifts, the smaller of 80–100 tonne capacity and the larger for vessels of up to 720 tonnes. The latter will also take large multihulls. From the south corner of the marina a pedestrian walkway will cross the corner of the harbour, significantly decreasing the distance into Arrecife – a thoughtful feature, even though the widened breakwater will doubtless be lined with shops, cafés and restaurants.

A completion date of late summer 2013 has been set, with the new facility fully operational for that autumn's seasonal migrants. Progress can be followed on the Puerto Calero website at www.puertocalero.com or on www.marinalanzarote.com.

Formalities and facilities

See under combined harbour information.

Puerto de Arrecife

28°57'·14N 13°33'·01W (breakwater head)

Waypoint

⊕ C06 – 28°56'·7N 13°32'·8W (0·5M SSE of Puerto de Arrecife)

Lights

2780 **Breakwater** Q(6)+LFl.15s10m3M
South cardinal tower 6m

buoy **La Lagarta Bank**
Fl(3)10s3M East cardinal buoy 4m

Large, clean open harbour

With Puerto de los Mármoles the commercial and Puerto de Naos the fishing port for the island, the old Puerto de Arrecife has become almost redundant. However, with the trade wind blowing the harbour is attractive and secure, and the water clean enough for swimming. Berthing alongside the breakwater – a favourite spot with local fishermen – is forbidden.

Looking southeast over Puerto de Arrecife from the top (restaurant) floor of the Arrecife Gran Hotel (see plan below)

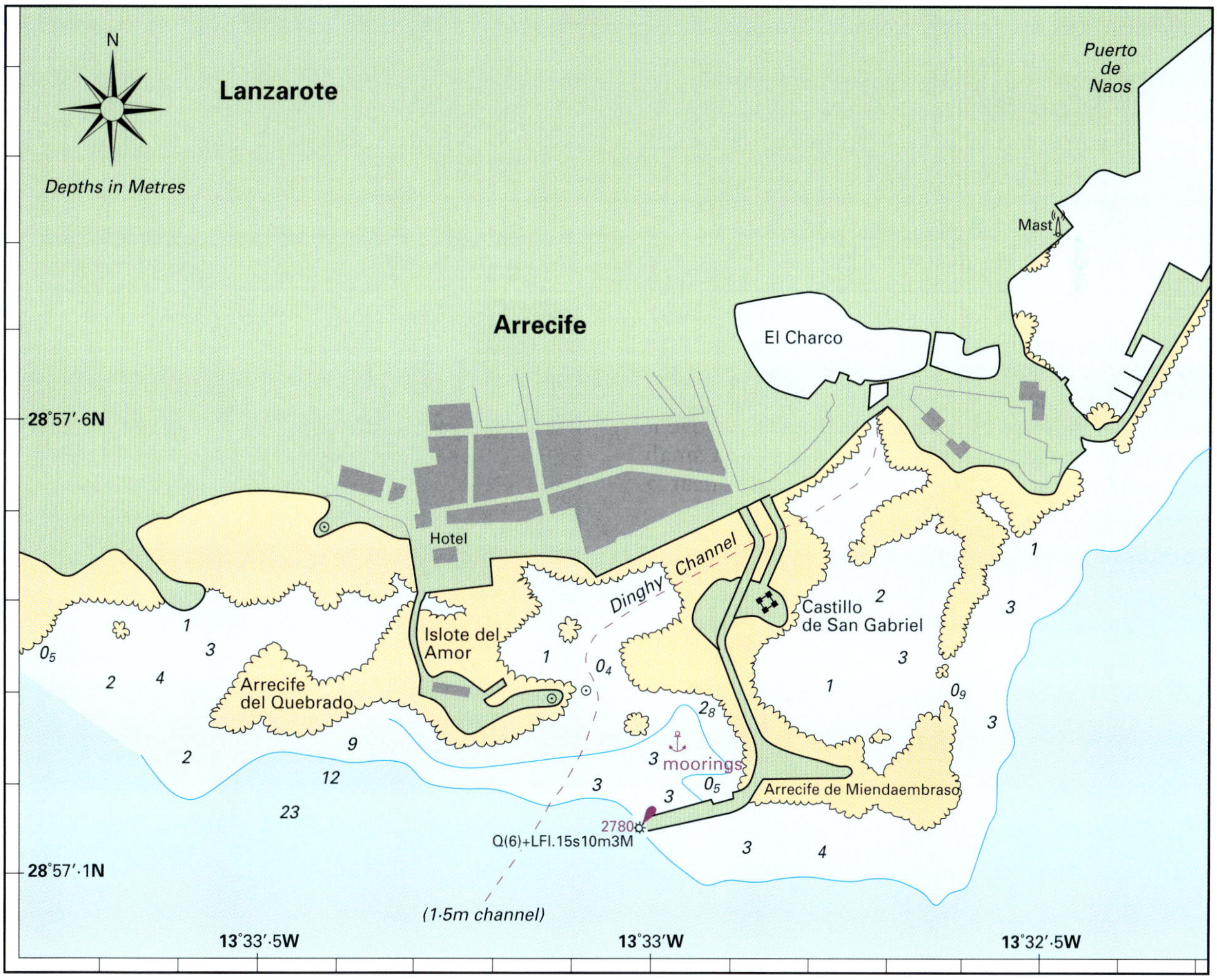

III. THE CANARY ISLANDS

Approach and entrance

See under combined harbour information. From any direction, keeping one mile offshore, steer a course until the western end of the town bears due north. The most dangerous trap is the Arrecife de Miendaembraso, which stretches about 500m east from the curve of the breakwater. To the west of the inner mole lies Islote del Amor, itself surrounded by a reef which extends 0·25M westward as the Arrecife del Quebrado. There has long been an anchorage area for laid-up fishing vessels south of the Arrecife de Miendaembraso, its southern edge marked by two unlit yellow buoys, though in recent years it has had few tenants.

Arrecife literally means 'reef', though if entry is made relatively close around the end of the main breakwater all should be avoided.

Anchorage

Much of Puerto de Arrecife is shallow, effectively limiting the yacht anchorage to the southeast corner where 3m is to be found over stones. Holding is poor over rock, and with little protection from the prevailing northeast wind yachts have frequently had trouble persuading their anchors to hold. Perhaps for this reason, some years ago the *Real Club Náutico de Arrecife* laid a number of concrete blocks with eyebolts, to which it is possible to dive and attach a line. Their condition is now said to be somewhat variable, and it would be wise to check the eyebolt for both thickness and sharp edges, or possibly to pass a shackle around it with the line attached. In late 2010 three of the blocks sported plastic bottles serving as pick-up buoys, but these were understood to be private.

After several years' closure while the Castillo de San Gabriel was undergoing restoration, the breakwater is now open again. There are several sets of steps near its southern tip where a dinghy can be left, or alternatively is is possible to take a dinghy through the pass – marked by a single leaning pole which must be left very close to starboard – to the shallow inner harbour, a very wet experience when the trade winds are blowing. At half tide or above it is possible to continue as far as El Charco, a small lake in the centre of the city conveniently near a large supermarket.

Formalities and facilities

See under combined harbour information.

Puerto del Carmen

28°55'·2N 13°40'·57W (breakwater elbow)

Plans
Spanish *605* (1:12,500)

Lights
2780·5 **La Tiñosa (breakwater spur)**
Fl(3)G.9s4m8M Green tower 3m
Breakwater angle Q(6)+LFl.15s3m5M

Marine farm
A marine farm, marked by four yellow pillar buoys with × topmarks, all Fl.Y.5s5M, lies southwest of Puerto del Carmen, centred on 28°55'N 13°41'·5W.

Small harbour for locals only

An attractive harbour backed by extensive low-rise development at the southern end of Lanzarote's largest tourist development, Puerto del Carmen is a popular spot for an evening stroll. Unsurprisingly, its hinterland includes a wide choice of cafés, bars and restaurants.

Despite the breakwater being almost doubled in length a few years ago to increase space within the harbour, it remains packed with excursion boats, ferries and local smallcraft. In late 2010 work was taking place at the entrance where a short opposing mole was under construction.

There is no provision for visiting yachts, though it would be possible to anchor off in settled weather. The approach from the south is straightforward, with depths shoaling rapidly as the land is closed. The original Puerto del Carmen, a tiny and very shallow harbour with a single quay, lies about 0·5M further east.

The small harbour of Puerto del Carmen, looking southwest into the evening sun

Puerto Calero

28°54'·92N 13°42'·42W (breakwater head)

Waypoint
⌖C07 – 28°54'·4N 13°42'·4W (0·5M S of Puerto Calero)

Plans
Spanish *605* (1:12,500)

Lights
2781 **South breakwater** Fl(3)G.14s13m8M
Octagonal stainless steel tower 4m
Port hand buoy Fl(2)R.8s3M Red can buoy
North mole Fl.R.15s3m3M
Set into the wall and very inconspicuous

Marine farm
A marine farm, marked by four yellow pillar buoys with × topmarks, all Fl.Y.5s5M, lies southwest of Puerto Calero, centred on on 28°53'·5N 13°44'·2W.

Harbour Communications
Puerto Calero ✆ 928 511285 *Fax* 928 514568
Email reservas@puertocalero.com
www.puertocalero.com (0800–2000 Monday to Saturday, 0900–2000 Sunday) VHF Ch 09, 16 (24 hours)

Well-run marina with pleasant atmosphere

Puerto Calero is a privately-run marina which has enjoyed an excellent reputation ever since it opened in 1989. Ten years later it almost doubled in size, and in 2006 a further 18 mega-yacht berths were created near the entrance. It now contains 450 berths for yachts of up to 50m, around 150 of them reserved for visitors and at least two dozen able to take those in the 25–50m LOA range.

The marina, which is very well run and spotlessly clean, has received an EU 'Blue Flag' each year for more than a decade and is part of a development designed by Luis Ibañez, a colleague of César Manrique. The bollards and manhole covers are of polished brass, the ladders of stainless steel and many of the buildings marble. Security is excellent, with outdoor staff on duty around the clock, and it would be a secure place to leave a yacht unattended for any length of time. The entrance is partially open to the west but is protected to some extent by the curve of the coast towards Punta Gorda and Punta Papagayo.

Approach, entrance and berthing

The grey octagonal tower on the south breakwater forms a useful landmark, though since the latter was extended in the late 1990s it no longer stands at the tip. On closing the coast towards the entrance the bottom shelves very steeply from 200m to 20m in less than 500m, and in a southerly swell seas could doubtless build up, but in normal conditions entrance is straightforward by day or night.

After many years during which the reception quay was to starboard on entering, in April 2011 this was changed, with arriving yachts berthing on the end of the spur opposite the tower. However, incoming yachts are requested to make contact by telephone or VHF before arrival and may then be directed straight into a berth. CCTV cameras are also being installed to monitor arriving and departing traffic, so someone should always be on hand to greet an arriving yacht and take their lines. Depths are ample (in the 10m range).

Formalities

Visit the marina office on the top floor of the tall building overlooking the 'main square' (see plan) as soon as convenient with the usual paperwork, including proof of insurance. Non-EU crew arriving in the Canaries must get passports stamped, which

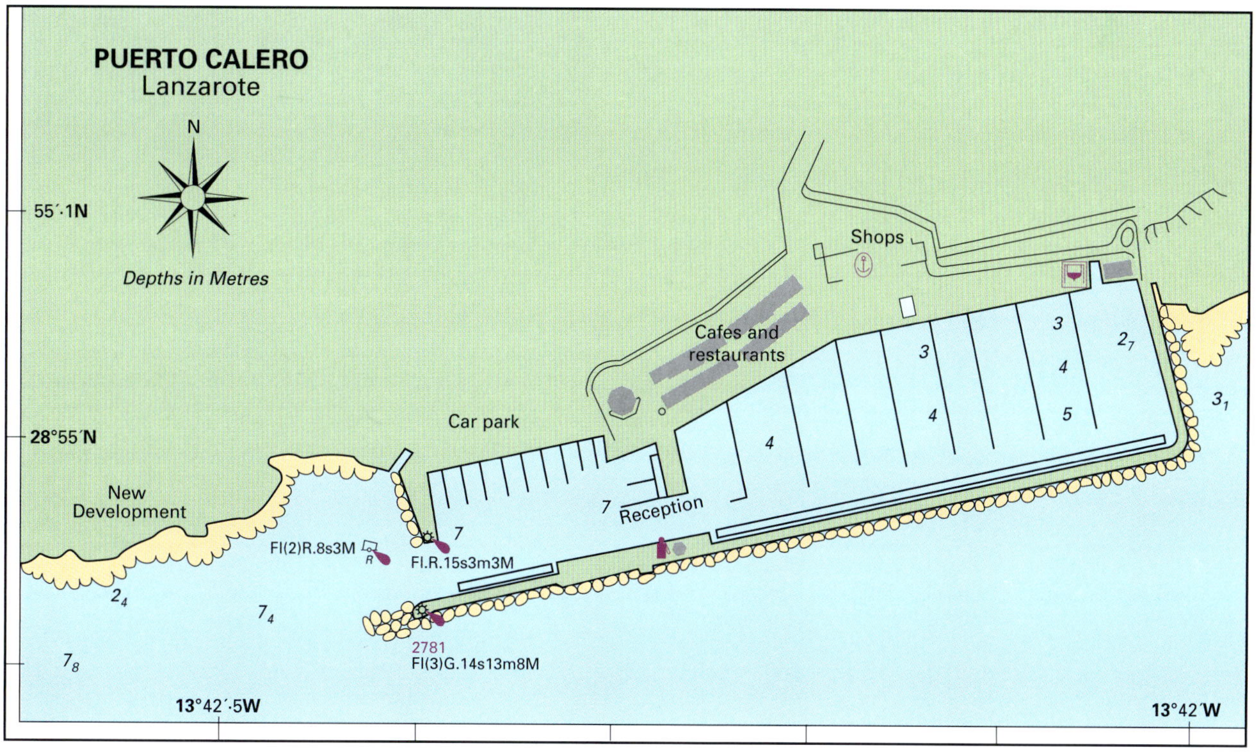

Puerto Calero seen from the southwest *Puerto Calero*

can either be arranged via the marina office (allow 48 hours) or carried out on the spot at Puerto de los Marmoles (see page 208). The very helpful office staff all speak English, with several other European languages also available.

Charges

In 2011 the overnight berthing fee for a monohull of 10–12m was €23.25, or €30.14 for 13–14m, including water, electricity and 5% tax (at berths for yachts of more than 25m electricity is metered and charged in addition). A 10–12m multihull paid €30.14, while one of 13m paid €41.33. Considerable discounts were available for stays of 30, 90 or 180 days.

Facilities

Boatyard In addition to the usual boatyard tasks Varadero Puerto Calero ✆ 928 510158 *Fax* 928 510763 *Email* varadero@puertocalero.com, open 0800–1300 and 1500–1800 weekdays, closed weekends, provides workshop space to a number of individual enterprises, most of which feature below. Yard manager is Sergio (Queco) Morales, but initial contact is likely to be made with Lucy who is extremely helpful in fluent English, German and Spanish and is happy to translate if necessary.

Hardstanding in the gated area is limited, effectively ruling out long-term layup, but DIY work by the owner and crew is permitted, and there is no objection to owners living aboard whilst their yacht is ashore.

Olivier Youf (see Sail repairs, below) has specialised in servicing Amel yachts since 1981. Fellow Frenchman Jean-Michel Alliot, ✆ 616 286574, who like his compatriot also speaks fluent English and Spanish, has also received praise for being able to do 'virtually any repair on a boat'.

Looking west through Puerto Calero's new entrance

Travel-lift 90-tonne hoist in the boatyard.

Engineers Wes Lunday of Catlanza ✆ 629 145294 *Email* wes@catlanza.com www.catlanza.com combines ownership of a large day-trip catamaran with a thriving engineering business. His boatyard workshop offers full machining and welding services in stainless, aluminium, titanium and copper-nickel (aka cupronickel) as well as exopy and carbon-fibre work. American himself, and with French and Polish employees, language is seldom a problem.

Electronics Navalectric Lanzarote ✆ 659 822118 *Email* yottitek@yahoo.com, located in the Galería Comercial Náutica is run by English engineer Jan Hayward. The company handles Raymarine, Simrad and various makes of watermaker, as well as installation and repair of yacht electrical systems.

Sail repairs There are two sailmakers in the boatyard area, though neither find it economically feasible to make sails from scratch: John Beamish (✆ 636 488403 *Fax* 928 510763 *Email* veleria@puertocalero.com) and Olivier Youf (✆ /*Fax* 928 515901 *Email* olivier_youf@yahoo.fr).

John, from the UK, will handle repairs ranging from sails in Kevlar and other exotics to putting a new zip into an elderly canvas cover (or will make a replacement from scratch). He can match most materials in terms of weight and colour.

In addition to servicing Amel yachts (see Boatyard, above) Frenchman Olivier Youf – who also speaks English and Spanish – specialises in work on Incidences Sails, as used by most large multihulls, as well as producing the splicing, nets and webbing such vessels require. If time allows he also does canvaswork including making sprayhood and biminis.

There is a North Sails shop on the Paseo de la Moda, but it sells sportswear and general clothing with not a sail in sight!

Rigging Lanzarote Yacht Services, based in the boatyard, is run by Clive Strickett who also carries out general work on yachts. Wes Lunday (see Engineers, above) has a swage machine in his workshop capable of handling wire between 2·5mm and 12mm diameter.

Liferaft servicing Varadero Puerto Calero can arrange for most major makes to be serviced by a reliable company, which will collect and return liferafts to yachts in the marina. Turnaround normally takes about a week.

Chandlery Náutica Chinijo ✆ 928 849681, 606 349329 *Fax* 928 849681 *Email* nauticachinijo@gmail.com is an independent company run by Jorge Toledo, who speaks good English and clearly understands the needs of yachtsmen. Its wide selection includes Harken, Plastimo, Ronstan, Sika, Spinlock and Vetus among others. Items not in stock can be ordered from mainland Europe, taking 48 hours by air freight (at a price) or two to three weeks by ship. It is located at the back of the Galería Comercial Náutica and open 0900–1400, 1500–1900 weekdays, 0900–1400 Saturday.

The classic schooner *Windrose of Amsterdam* backs into Puerto Calero to lie alongside the south breakwater

The nearby Distrimar meets the needs of sport fishermen, and there is said to be a good general hardware store in Tías, about 10km along the road towards the airport.

Charts Náutica Chinijo (see above) stock Imray charts of the Canaries and Caribbean, and hope to become official agents for the Spanish *Instituto Hidrográfico de la Marina*.

Water To all berths.

Showers Two blocks, one behind the administration building and the other near the breakwater's right-angle bend, a total of seven showers for men and five for women. Well maintained and open 24 hours a day.

Launderette Located at the back of the main building (also accessible via the Galería Comercial Náutica), with two washers and one dryer. For a full laundry service call Smartie Pants Launderette and Dry Cleaners ✆ 928 512440.

Electricity 220v throughout the marina, with 3-phase 380v also available at some larger berths.

Fuel Diesel and petrol at the pontoon below the tower (the old reception berth), open office hours.

Bottled gas Camping Gaz bottles can be exchanged in the marina complex, but as of 2011 the situation regarding refilling other cylinders remained uncertain – see page 191.

Weather forecast Four-day forecast posted daily at the marina office and in the Galería Comercial Náutica.

Bank No bank as such, but two cash dispensers in the commercial and restaurant area.

Shops/provisioning Small but quite well-stocked supermarket, open 0800–2000 daily, on the ground floor of the building which also houses the marina's administrative offices. While fine for day-to-day living (with many familiar brands for homesick Brits) it would not be equal to storing ship for a long passage.

The Hiperdino Supermercado on the main Arrecife road (ask for directions in the marina office) is recommended, as is the EuroSpar about 7km away. Frozen items and meat (vacuum packed on request) together with a good selection of fruit and vegetables will be found at Congelados Roper, near the airport.

Cafés, restaurants & hotels Two hotels and a wide choice of cafés and restaurants, most with views over the marina.

Medical services An English-speaking doctor is available and there is a clinic (where English is spoken) at Puerto del Carmen, with a hospital, dentists, opticians, etc. in Arrecife.

Communications

Post office In Puerto del Carmen. Stamps are available in the supermarket, with a post box outside.

Mailing address Puerto Calero Marina, Edif. Antiguo Varadero 2°, 35571 Urb. Puerto Calero – Yaiza, Lanzarote, Islas Canarias, Spain.

Telephones Several on the shore side of the complex, but not on the breakwater.

Internet access Wi-Fi throughout the marina. Reception is sometimes poor in the more remote berths, a problem which is being addressed. A 30-hour account is included in the berthing fee, and can be renewed without charge at the marina office.

Car hire Rental company in the marina complex, with many more at the airport.

Taxis Taxi rank in the marina complex.

Buses Bus stop at the exit roundabout.

Air services European and inter-island flights from Lanzarote airport, about 14km by road.

Playa Quemada

28°54′·3N 13°44′·1W (anchorage)

Anchorage open to east through southwest

The small fishing village of Puerto Quemada lies about 1·6M west of Puerto Calero. It is occasionally visited by cruising yachts, but there is no pier or breakwater, and local boats are hauled out on the stony beach. The coastline of cliffs west of the village provides shelter from southwest though north to east.

A marine farm, marked by four yellow buoys with × topmarks, all Fl.Y.5s5M, lies south of Playa Quemada centred on 28°53′·N 13°44′·2W.

Punta Papagayo to Punta del Aguila

28°50′·3N 13°47′·3W to 28°51′·3N 13°48′·7W

Waypoint

⊕C08 – 28°49′·8N 13°47′·2W (0·5M S of Pta Papagayo)

Plans

Spanish *601A* (1:25,000)

Open beach anchorages

In settled conditions this stretch of coast offers several possible anchorages sheltered from easterly winds by Punta Papagayo, with sandy beaches off which one can anchor to make a dinghy landing or, with an eye on the barometer, spend a peaceful night. All call for careful eyeball navigation. If staying overnight, remain at least 200m offshore due to the possibility of swell setting in.

The beaches, reached by a dirt track from Playa Blanca, are popular with tourists and the more secluded are frequented by naturists. Since being designated a *Parque Natural*, to which cars are charged admission, the area has apparently become even more popular.

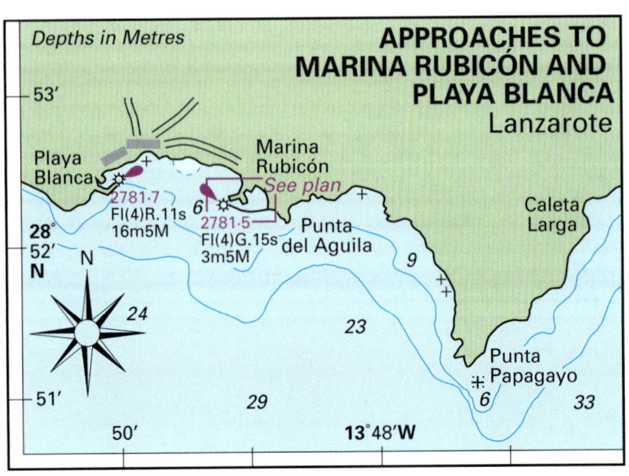

Marina Rubicón

28°51′·46N 13°49′·18W (breakwater head)

Waypoint

⊕C09 – 28°51′·1N 13°49′·6W (0·5M SW of Marina Rubicon)

Plans

Spanish *601A* (1:25,000)
Imray-Iolaire *E2* (1:25,000)

Lights

2781·5 **Breakwater head**
Fl(4)G.15s3m5M Green post 3m
2781·55 **North mole, outer**
Fl(4)R.15s1m5M Red post 2m
2781·6 **Breakwater spur**
Fl.G.5s1M Green lantern on breakwater wall 1m (obscured from seaward by the breakwater)
2781·65 **North mole, inner**
Fl.R.5s1m1M Grey post, red lantern 2m
Interior pontoon Fl.G.2s Post 6m
Note All lights other than that on the breakwater head are obscured from seaward

Harbour Communications

Marina Rubicón ✆ 928 519012 *Fax* 928 519035
Email info@marinarubicon.com
www.marinarubicon.com (0900–2000 from August to November inclusive, otherwise 0900–1800, both daily), VHF Ch 09 (24 hours)

Large marina close to tourist resort and beaches

Marina Rubicón celebrates its tenth anniversary in 2013, though much of the surrounding housing and other surrounding developments are considerably newer. Approximately half the 500-odd berths are reserved for visiting yachts of up to 70m LOA, making Marina Rubicón one of the few harbours in the Canaries where space is nearly always available. However, its large size leaves those in outer berths with a long walk round to the marina office – either bicycles or a dinghy would ease this problem – but this is offset by the unusual range of (free) facilities on offer, from a church to a good-sized swimming pool.

Both the marina and the surrounding area are well maintained, and several skippers have reported leaving their yachts afloat there while they returned

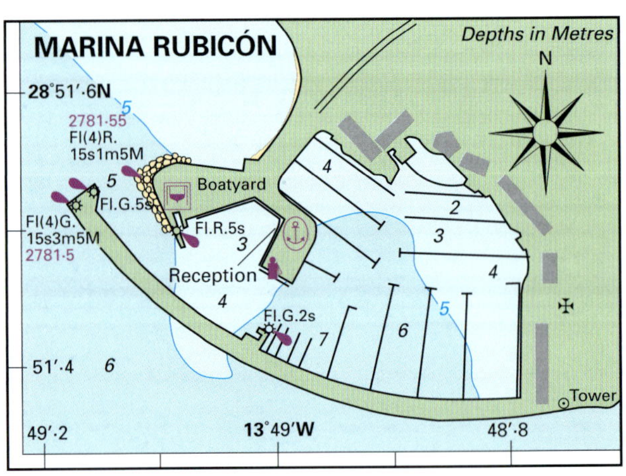

Looking southeast over Marina Rubicón, with Punta Papagayo in the distance

to northern Europe or the US. All appear to have been well satisfied. The many bars, restaurants and nightclubs close to the waterfront inevitably generate some noise, but excessive disturbance is quickly stamped on by the management. Of course the upside is an excellent choice when tired of dining aboard! Finally, note that the extreme end of the main breakwater is a designated helicopter landing pad – keep well clear if in use.

Approach and entrance

The entrance to Marina Rubicón lies about 2M northwest of Punta Papagayo, facing Playa Blanca across a wide bay. The tall lighthouse of Punta Pechiguera 3M to the west makes a distinctive landmark when approaching from that direction, with the isolated cone of Montaña Roja (194m) behind. In sunshine, the long pale grey breakwater shows clearly against the reddish-brown hills behind, though the sprawl of white buildings now extends well to the east.

The once prominent Castillo de las Coloradas on Punta del Aguila, which dates from the 1740s and is identified by name on Admiralty chart *886*, lies within a few metres of the root of the breakwater. However, it has quite literally been overtaken by events and is now difficult to pick out against the buildings behind. Inland the level plain known as the Rubicón stretches north some 8km towards the 'Fire Mountains'.

Depths shoal gradually towards the shore, with about 5m in the northwest-facing entrance. Various buoys lie further north – the usual yellow string off the beach to indicate a swimming area, a channel for jetskis leaving the beach, plus an assortment of small buoys apparently laid by the local sailing school.

If approaching after dark the marina lights can be difficult to pick out against the almost continuous string of shore lights, though the long, dark sweep of the breakwater may help and, in late 2010, a line of prominent green lights lay northwest of the entrance. Once identified with certainty, night entry should present no problems. None of the buoys mentioned above are lit, so a careful watch will need to be maintained until safely inside.

Anchorage

There is space for a few yachts to anchor in 3–4m over sand northeast of the entrance channel in settled northerly weather, keeping clear of the jetski channel markers and sailing school buoys. Further in, a continuous line of yellow buoys connected by a floating cord defines a swimming area off the beach.

A riding light would be advisable and considerable rolling can be expected, generated by ferries departing and approaching Puerto de Playa Blanca. While short-term anchorage is normally permitted, particularly if waiting to enter the marina (in which case contact the marina on VHF Ch 09), long-term anchorage is not encouraged.

Arrival and berthing

The reception area is to port on arrival, in the basin to the west of the dark tower (clearly intended to resemble a lighthouse). The pontoon south of the 'main square' is now a fuel berth, though recent arrivals may be directed there. The main reception pontoon is in the bay immediately to the west (see plan). Day tourist boats occasionally use part of it, generally berthing at the southernmost end which is, in any case, most open to swell. In westerly winds there can be a good deal of movement throughout

The inner entrance at Marina Rubicón lies between a 'lighthouse' and a 'mast'. The pontoon area immediately below the tower is used by tourist boats; the reception area for yachts is out of shot to the left, close to the inner angle (see plan page 216

the reception area, but staff are reported to be competent and helpful, particularly in gusty conditions when problems are most likely and if pre-warned on VHF Ch 09.

As mentioned previously, due to its generous size Marina Rubicón is seldom full, although prior booking is preferred. Many of the berths are of good size (185 able to take yachts of 10–13m, 125 for those in the 13–22m, while a further 60 take yachts of 22–70m), doubtless due to its comparatively recent construction. Berths for smaller boats – in this context up to 13m or so – are in depths of around 3m, though up to 7m is available at the larger berths. Neither is there any of the cramping typical of older marinas, and manoeuvring space between pontoons is generous. All berths are against robust fingers of generous length.

In spite of the entrance being relatively narrow, a heavy northwesterly swell can result in considerable movement of yachts in the southern part of the marina, where the larger berths make the most of the greater depths, but more protection is to be if had tucked around the corner to the north and east.

Formalities and charges

Report to the marina office, on the square near the 'lighthouse', with the usual paperwork, including evidence of insurance. The staff are friendly and helpful, and speak at least six European languages.

In 2011 the overnight berthing fee for a monohull of 10–13m was €23.63, or €34.13 for 13–15m, including water, electricity and tax at 5%. Discounts were available for stays of 15, 30, 90 or 180 days if paid in advance. Multihulls were charged €0.44 per m^2, again inclusive.

Facilities

Boatyard The boatyard is run by the marina as a separate division. Yard manager is Augusto Escolar Escuder, ✆ 660 556349, though initial contact is likely to be made with Cecilia on ✆ 928 519012 ext. 3 *Email* varadero@marinarubicon.com. Cecilia, whose office is immediately to the right on entering the yard area, is Dutch but also speaks fluent English, German, French and Spanish, and is happy to translate if required. Office hours are 0900–1330, 1430–1800 weekdays only.

There is plenty of hardstanding and no shortage of solidly-constructed adjustable cradles, making long stays ashore feasible, the only caveat being that the area is somewhat exposed to the south and west. DIY work is permitted, and owners are welcome to live aboard while their boat is ashore. The boatyard even has its own toilets and showers (reported by one cruising skipper to be 'even nicer than those in the marina'), and a key is provided for the gate, which is locked at night.

Boatyard staff can handle all normal repairs and maintenance, and there are metal fabrication workshops, engineers and electronics experts onsite. Standards are reported to be high and costs reasonable.

Travel-lift 90-tonne hoist plus trailer-type yacht transporter, both capable of handling up to 7·4m beam.

Diving services Enquire at the boatyard or at the marina office. There is a PADI diving school near the boatyard for those wishing to gain a formal qualification.

Engineers, electronics & radio repairs Enquire at the boatyard.

Sail repairs Straightforward repairs to canvaswork and sails can be carried out in the boatyard, but new items cannot be built from scratch.

Chandlery MarineStore Rubicón ✆ 928 519990 *Email* rubicon@marinestore.co.uk www.marinestore.co.uk is situated at the entrance to the boatyard, open 1000–1800 daily. The only non-UK branch of the MarineStore chain, stocks are comprehensive and include international brands such as Musto, Marlow Ropes, Plastimo XM, Unipart Marine and Dubarry and range from anchors to varnish and beyond. Items not in stock can be sourced from MarineStores in the UK and shipped in by air or sea.

Charts MarineStore Rubicón stocks Imray books and charts for the Canaries and Atlantic waters.

Water To all berths.

Showers Four or five shower blocks dotted around the marina, so convenient to all berths, plus those in the boatyard area as mentioned above.

Launderette Located in the centre of the marina complex and containing two washers and two tumble dryers. Tokens are available from the marina office.

Electricity 220v throughout the marina, with 3-phase 380v also available at berths intended for yachts of 18m or more.

Fuel Diesel and petrol at the pontoon south of the 'square', available 0700–1900 daily.

Bottled gas Camping Gaz exchanges at the fuel berth, but as of 2011 the situation regarding refilling other cylinders remained uncertain – see page 191.

Weather forecast Posted daily at the marina office.

Banks Cash dispenser at Banca March near the entrance to the marina complex, but for full banking facilities it is necessary to go into Playa Blanca.

Shops/provisioning There is a HiperDino supermarket on the road leading out of the marina, open 0830–2200 daily, with others in Playa Blanca. Alternatively leave the marina heading east along the paved coastal way towards the Centro Commercial El Pueblo, where there is a branch of Congelados Roper which, despite its name, stocks fruit, veg, fish, meat and groceries. The walk takes about 20 minutes, but it is reported to be well worth the effort and the pathway fine for a trolley.

Cafés, restaurants & hotels Several hotels on site with dozens more in Playa Blanca, plus a tempting variety of cafés, bars and restaurants in the surrounding development.

Medical services A health centre in the marina complex, open 24 hours and with multilingual doctors, plus dentists, etc. in Playa Blanca.

Communications

Post office In Playa Blanca.

Mailing address Puerto Deportivo Rubicón SA, Urbanización Castillo del Águila, Calle Berrugo 2, 35580 – Playa Blanca, Lanzarote, Islas Canarias, Spain.

Telephones Five public phones dotted around the marina complex.

Internet access Free Wi-Fi throughout the marina. Also available – often without charge – in many of the bars, restaurants, etc. in Playa Blanca.

Car hire Cabrera Medina has offices in the marina complex.

Taxis The marina office will telephone for a taxi on request.

Buses A shuttle bus runs into Playa Blanca, from which services run to Arrecife and elsewhere.

Ferries From Playa Blanca to Fuerteventura.

Air services European and inter-island flights from Lanzarote airport, some 30km away by road.

Puerto de Playa Blanca

28°51'·57N 13°49'·94W (breakwater head)

Plans
Spanish *601A* (1:25,000)

Lights
2781·7 **Breakwater**
Fl(4)R.11s16m5M Brick tower 7m
Dolphins Each of the four dolphins which lie between the pontoons and the ferry channel carries a single blue flashing light, similar to those on British emergency vehicles

Harbour Communications
Harbour office ✆ /*Fax* 928 517540 VHF Ch 08, 09

Ferry and smallcraft harbour

With the advent of Marina Rubicón a mile or so across the bay, Puerto de Playa Blanca (pronounced *Pwerto de Ply'a Blanca*) no longer accepts visiting yachts – mainly because there is absolutely nowhere for them to berth. The five short pontoons are packed tight with local boats – a mixture of speedboats and small fishing craft – while the southern part of the harbour handles the car ferries which provide an almost continuous service across the Estrecho de la Bocayna to Corralejo, Fuerteventura. Ambitious plans drawn up in the mid-1990s to extend the harbour appear to have been dropped, presumably following the construction of Marina Rubicón.

The tourist conurbation which backs the harbour has expanded markedly over the past two decades, and now stretches almost solidly to Punta Pechiguera.

Anchorage

There is no possibility of anchoring in the harbour itself, but in settled northerly weather good anchorage can be found a little further east – though well clear of the entrance in order to allow ample room for the ferries to make their turn. A continuous line of yellow buoys connected by a floating cord defines a swimming area off the beach. A riding light would be advisable and considerable rolling can be expected, generated by the departing and approaching ferries.

The coastline between Marina Rubicón and Puerto de Playa Blanca, with the growing holiday resort laid out behind

III. THE CANARY ISLANDS

N
Depths in Metres
28°45′N
28°30′N
28°15′N
28°N
14°30′W
14°15′W
14°W
Estrecho de la Bocayna
2786
Fl(2)15s
28m14M
C13
C12
Pta Martiño
Isla de
Lobos
page 223
C11
30
2792
Fl.8s34m14M
Pta Tóston
Corralejo
El Cotillo
.530
.688
.684
.510
.624
page 225
Puerto del
Rosario
Pta Gavioto
2793·5
Fl.5s47m20M
Fuerteventura
.723
.707
Puerto del
Castillo
page 227
Puerto de la Torre
Playa de Pozo Negro
Playa de Jacomar
Pta las Borriquillas
.690
Las Playitas
Gran Tarajal
Pta Lantailla
C16
2795
Fl(2+1)18s195m21M
Ginijinamar
Playa de la Lajita
page 229
Tarajelejo
30
Punta de los Mollinos
Pta Pesebre
2791
Oc(2)6s10m10M
.806
Puertito
de la Luz
.682
Morro
Jable
Pta Jandia
2790
Fl.4s32m22M
C20
page 233
Morro Jable
C18
2796·5
Fl(2)10s61m20M

Fuerteventura

Between 28°03'N–28°45'N and 13°49'W–14°30'W

Introduction

Barren and bare, with some of the best beaches of the whole archipelago, Fuerteventura (pronounced *fwert'eh-ventoor'ah*) is the second largest island at 1,725km². It is also the most sparsely populated, the majority of its 100,000 or so inhabitants living around Puerto del Rosario (Port of the Rosary), formerly known as Puerto de los Cabras (Port of Goats). The attractiveness of this island lies in the desert-like appearance of its curious empty valleys and immense sandy beaches. A series of hills rising to 800m forms the Jandia peninsula, the southernmost and highest part of the island, and it was here that Bernard Moitessier fell in love with the tranquil views of the dunes, brought as dust by the *sirocco*. It is possible to explore much of the island by Tiadhe-line buses – consult their user-friendly website at www.maxoratabus.com/tiadhe/ for timetables and routes.

Websites

The following sites contain general information about Fuerteventura, some of which may be useful to the visiting yachtsman. Websites relating to specific harbours are listed under Harbour communications, those covering all or most of the Canary Islands on page 188 of the introduction.

www.en.wikipedia.org/wiki/Fuerteventura – all the usual in-depth wikipedia information without the spin which one comes to expect from 'local' websites

www.cabildofuer.es – the official site of the island council, carrying local news and current affairs. In Spanish only but translates well

www.canaryventura.com – a private site in six languages including English, compiled by a British woman after five visits to the island. Quirky and becoming slightly dated, but a fresh take and blessedly free from advertisements

www.fuerteventura.com – a particularly good tourist site in Spanish, English and Italian, easy to navigate and packed with useful information. Includes a slide show facility

www.fuerteventurainfo.com/ – another general tourist site, but more comprehensive than most on the island's history and natural environment, and with a well populated What to Do section

www.fuerteventuraturismo.com – the excellent Fuerteventura Tourist Board site, in Spanish, English, German and Italian, with a wide range of practical information, photos and links. Puts many of its fellows to shame

www.fuerteventura.ws – Fuerteventura's very own weather website, with links, though orientated towards the beach-bound more than the sailor

www.sunnyfuerteventura.com – a general tourist site with the usual photos and maps, including some useful suggestions for routes if exploring by car

The islanders are mainly occupied in the constant struggle to cultivate the dry land – and increasingly to cultivate the tourists which the dry climate and endless beaches attract. However, most resorts differ from those on its two western neighbours, being attractively designed and landscaped.

Fuerteventura lags somewhat behind the other islands so far as visiting yachts are concerned, the only harbours boasting anything like marina status being Puerto del Castillo and Gran Tarajal, though the former has little space for visitors and the latter still lacks many facilities normally considered essential. Corralejo in the north and Morro Jable in the south have very limited berthing for visitors and the capital, Puerto del Rosario, does not cater for yachts, though a marina is said to be under consideration. As with the majority of the other islands, the west coast is unfriendly and has little to offer the yachtsman save unease.

Fuerteventura is reported to be the destination of choice for many smugglers of illegal immigrants, which may explain the armed security guards to be seen around some of the island's harbours. However, a yacht – provided she and her crew have the correct papers – is unlikely to attract much official interest.

Telecommunications

Mobile (cell) phone reception is good in most parts of Fuerteventura, though it has not been tested inland. The country code for the Canaries is 34, as it is for mainland Spain, and the area code for Fuerteventura – which must be included even when dialling from within the island – is 928, shared with Lanzarote and Gran Canaria.

By 2011 Wi-Fi was available in all the larger towns, either free on a pay-to-use basis.

Approach and navigation

The general remarks regarding navigation around Lanzarote also apply to Fuerteventura.

In strong northerly winds the north coast of Fuerteventura becomes a dangerous lee shore. When there is a large ground swell running between Isla de Lobos and Fuerteventura, do not attempt this passage or enter Corralejo because of numerous rocks and the rapidly shelving depths – however, in suitable weather it can offer a pleasant sail with good fishing.

Puerto del Castillo offers a secure berth in bad weather, but again entry should not be attempted in strong onshore winds. Wind acceleration zones exist along the south coast of the island, one lying between 2M and 12M west of Gran Tarajal and another 3M west of Morro Jable – see plan page 192. The two may sometimes combine.

Navigation

Waypoints
⊕ C11 – 28°44'·9N 14°02'·4W (2M NW of Pta Tostón)
⊕ C12 – 28°45'·2N 13°50'·8W (1M NE of Corralejo)
⊕ C13 – 28°47'N 13°48'·5W (1M NNE of Isla de Lobos)
⊕ C14 – 28°29'·2N 13°50'·8W (0·5M SE of Puerto del Rosario)
⊕ C15 – 28°23'N 13°51'·4W (0·5M S of Puerto del Castillo / Caleta de Fustes)
⊕ C16 – 28°12'·9N 13°56'·2W (1M SE of Pta Lantailla)
⊕ C17 – 28°11'·9N 14°01'·2W (0·5M SSE of Gran Tarajal)
⊕ C18 – 28°01'·7N 14°19'·9W (1M S of Pta de Morro Jable)
⊕ C19 – 28°02'·8N 14°22'·4W (0·5M SW of Morro Jable entrance)
⊕ C20 – 28°01'·2N 14°32'W (3M SSW of Pta Jandia)

Courses and distances
⊕ C11 – ⊕ C22 (0·5M SE of Las Palmas, Gran Canaria) = 81·5M, 242° / 062°
⊕ C11 – ⊕ C37 (0·5M SE of Santa Cruz de Tenerife) = 118M, 261° / 081°
⊕ C12 – ⊕ C09 (0·5M SW of Marina Rubicon) = 6M, 010° / 190°
⊕ C13 – ⊕ C14 = 18M, by eye
⊕ C14 – ⊕ C16 = 17·5M, by eye
⊕ C16 – ⊕ C18 = 24M, 242° / 062°
⊕ C18 – ⊕ C20 = 10·7M, 267° / 087°
⊕ C20 – ⊕ C22 (0·5M SE of Las Palmas, Gran Canaria) = 46M, 277° / 097°
⊕ C20 – ⊕ C37 (0·5M SE of Santa Cruz de Tenerife) = 94M, 286° / 106°

Magnetic variation
5°W (2011), decreasing by 8'E annually. Local magnetic anomalies have been reported to the north of Fuerteventura – see Admiralty chart *1870*.

Tidal Streams
Generally insignificant – see Tides and tidal streams, page 194. Details of range etc. will be found under Puerto del Rosario.

Charts
Admiralty *1870* (1:300,000)
Spanish *60A*, *60B* (1:200,000), *505* (1:50,000), *507* (1:55,000), *604*, *605* (1:60,000)
US *51380* (1:263,900)
Imray-Iolaire *E2* (1:600,000)

Lights
2792 **Punta Tostón (Punta Ballena)**
Fl.8s34m14M White tower, red bands 30m
2786 **Punta Martiño (Isla de Lobos)**
Fl(2)15s28m14M 083°-vis-353°
Yellow tower and building, white lantern 6m
2793·5 **Punta Gavioto (Puerto del Rosario)**
Fl.5s47m20M Reserve light 9M White tower 43m
2795 **Punta Lantailla** Fl(2+1)18s195m21M
Stone tower on building 12m
Note Obscured when bearing less than 228°
2796·5 **Morro Jable** Fl(2)10s61m20M White tower 59m
2790 **Punta Jandia** Fl.4s32m22M 276°-vis-190°
Dark masonry tower on building on low spit 19m
2791 **Punta Pesebre** Oc(2)6s10m10M
Grey and white truncated tower 5m

Coast Radio Station
Fuerteventura 28°24'·4N 14°02'·7W, remotely controlled from Tenerife
VHF Ch 06, 16, 22 (24 hours)
DSC VHF MMSI 002241025, 28°33'N 13°55'W, remotely controlled from Tenerife

Weather and navigation broadcasts
VHF 28°30'·6N 13°55'W, remotely controlled from Tenerife
Weather bulletins Ch 22 at 0833, 1333, 2033 (forecast in Spanish for coastal waters)
Navigational warnings Ch 22 at 0833, 2033 (in Spanish for coastal waters)

Harbours and anchorages

El Cotillo

28°40'·84N 14°00'·74W (molehead island)

Lights
2792 **Punta Tóston (Punta Ballena)**
Fl.8s34m14M White tower, red bands 30m

Tiny harbour best visited by land

A tiny harbour formed by the construction of a high breakwater between the shore and a small islet, El Cotillo is home to a few moored smallcraft. Though totally unsuitable for yachts, in the right conditions it would be possible to anchor off and explore by dinghy.

The only real point of interest ashore is the old watchtower complete with wooden drawbridge – there are few facilities in the nearby village beyond a few bars and restaurants. If intent on visiting, it would be far preferable to do so by land.

Corralejo

28°44'·43N 13°51'·64W (breakwater head)

Waypoint
⊕ C12 – 28°45'·2N 13°50'·8W (1M NE of Corralejo)

Plans
Spanish *601A* (1:25,000)
US *51343* (1:50,000)

Lights
2786 **Punta Martiño (Isla de Lobos)**
Fl(2)15s28m14M 083°-vis-353°
Yellow tower and building, white lantern 6m
2793 **Breakwater**
Fl.G.3s8m4M Green column 5m
Note A tall green and white banded column with a triangular top is situated on the ferry quay, and could be confused with the breakwater light structure

Harbour Communications
Harbour office ✆ /*Fax* 928 866524 VHF Ch 09, 16 (0730–2100 daily)

Ferry and fishing harbour

Corralejo (pronounced *Corrale'ho*) is a former fishing harbour now dominated by the frequent car ferries plying across the Estrecho de la Bocayna to Playa Blanca on Lanzarote. As there are excellent sandy beaches with a diving club and sailboarding, the once small village has expanded as a tourist centre and the development behind the port can make the entrance difficult to identify on approach. Two large windfarm-type windmills are prominent on the shore west of the harbour.

There are reefs and shallows on both sides and entry can be exciting, but with good navigation and a reliable engine it is safe in most conditions. However, when the wind is from northeast it funnels

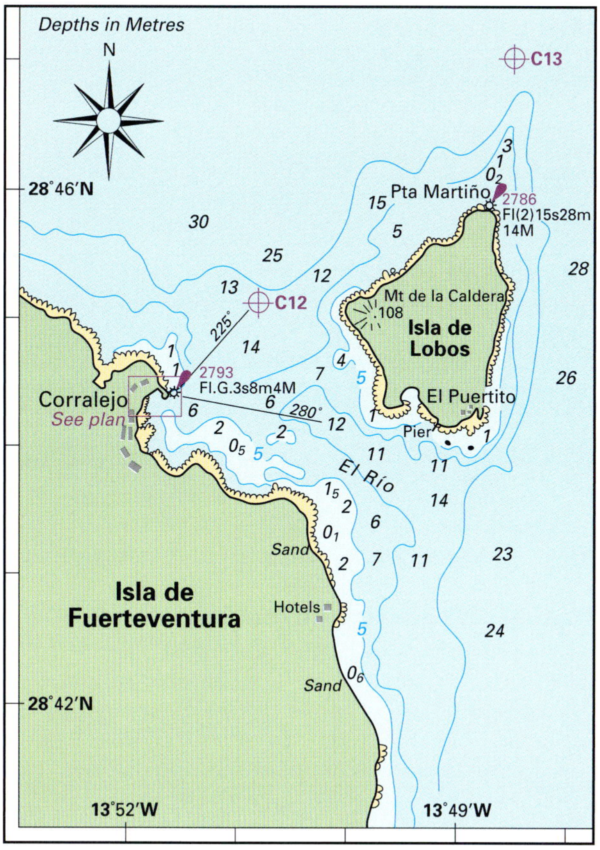

through El Río between Isla de Lobos and Fuerteventura. If any swell has developed in the Estrecho de la Bocayna it would be unwise to attempt to enter Corralejo or to pass through El Río.

In early 2011 it was stated that a large new government-funded marina was planned for the harbour, providing at least 600 berths, but although initial contracts have apparently been awarded no schedule has yet been set.

Approach

From north The reefs which extend north of the harbour also curve somewhat east, hence the placing of ⊕C12. From this position turn onto a course of 225° until the light tower on the end of the breakwater has been positively identified. Do not allow any drift westwards but head for a point 200m east of the breakwater before turning to enter the harbour. The breakwater head can then be passed fairly close-to, keeping a watch for manoeuvring ferries.

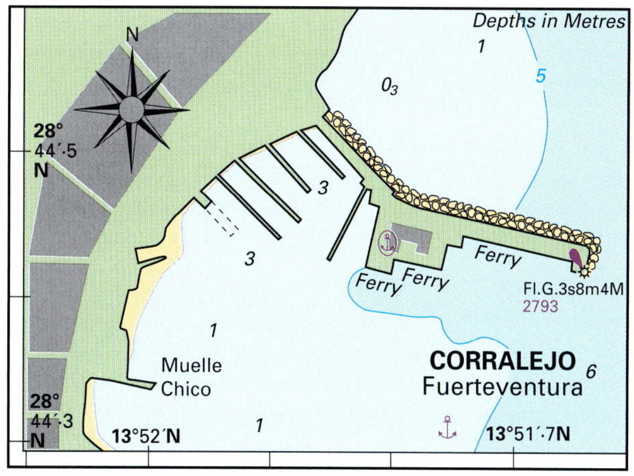

From south Approaching El Río, the strait between Corralejo and Isla de Lobos, the coast of Fuerteventura resembles a low desert. Several large apartment blocks have joined the two conspicuous hotels at the southern entrance to the strait. With the hotels abaft the beam, if the strait is passable, steer for the south of Isla de Lobos.

South of Montaña de la Caldera (107m) the island is low-lying with the fishing hamlet of El Puertito on the southern tip. Just west of this group of houses is a small stone pier. Keeping the pier bearing due north to avoid rocks to the east, approach it to within 300m and then turn onto a course of 280°. Rollers breaking on the shallows on both sides can be unnerving and the entrance to Corralejo may be difficult to identify from this distance. This bearing, however, if adhered to carefully avoids all dangers. If unable to identify the stone pier on Lobos, leave the island to port and approach Corralejo from the north.

Entrance and berthing

Final entrance is straightforward, after which is may be necessary to circle several times while assessing the situation. Four pontoons run out directly from the shore, with a fifth angled southwest from the breakwater, containing a total of around 115 berths. However, despite 12 berths on the new pontoon nominally being reserved for yachts in transit, in practice nearly all are permanently occupied – once again, the definition of 'transit' appears to be loosely applied.

Looking west down the breakwater at Corralejo towards the ferry berth, with the town beyond

Unless a slot has been pre-booked – see Booking berths in *Puertos de Canarias* harbours, page 189 – a larger yacht is unlikely to find space during the high season (though the chances for one around the 10m mark are reported to be considerably better). A short-term possibility would be to secure to the west side of the ferry quay whilst visiting the harbour office for instructions.

Anchorage

Anchor in 5–6m southeast of the breakwater, leaving ample room for manoeuvring ferries. Official policy appears to fluctuate, but it appears that a yacht is most likely to remain undisturbed if a marina berth has been requested but is unavailable. Much of the harbour bed is said to be foul with rope and ground tackle, making a tripline a sensible precaution. A small charge is made for anchoring.

Formalities and charges

The skipper should visit the harbour office (next to the post box on the ferry quay) bearing the usual ship's papers and passports. Although advertised hours are 0730–2100 daily the office is frequently left empty during an extended lunch break. Very little English is spoken.

The berthing fee is calculated on a length x beam basis and in 2010 was set at €0.24 per m². This included water, electricity and tax, and in the past had increased by about 2% each year.

Facilities

Travel-lift 20-tonne hoist operated by the *Cofradía de Pescadores* (fishermen's confederation) with an area of hardstanding to the northwest of the harbour, but no boatyard as such.
Water On the pontoons.
Launderette Conveniently close to the breakwater, but closing at 1500.
Electricity On the pontoons, though again not always turned on.
Fuel By can from a filling station inland from Muelle Chico.
Banks Several in the town, with cash dispensers.
Shops/provisioning Supermarkets and other shops in the town.
Cafés & restaurants Many, some overlooking the harbour and its small sandy beach.
Medical services Two medical centres, one with German doctors who speak some English.

Communications

Post office In the town.
Telephones At the ferry terminal and elsewhere.
Internet access At the Rincha Cabra bar near the Plaza and elsewhere.
Car hire & taxis In the town.
Buses Bus station on the northern edge of the town, with services to El Cortillo as well as Puerto del Rosario and beyond.
Ferries Car ferries several times daily across El Estrecho de la Bocayna to Playa Blanca on Lanzarote, and foot passenger ferries to El Puertito on Isla de Lobos.

Isla de Lobos

Between 28°44'N–28°46'N and 12°48'·5W–12°50'W
28°44'·33N 13°49'·53W (bar to lagoon entrance)

Waypoint
⊕C13 – 28°47'N 13°48'·5W (1M NNE of Isla de Lobos)

Plans
Spanish *601A* (1:25,000)
US *51343* (1:50,000)

Lights
2786 **Punta Martiño**
Fl(2)15s28m14M 083°-vis-353°
Yellow tower and building, white lantern 6m

Marine farm
A marine farm, marked by four yellow pillar buoys with × topmarks, all Fl.Y.3M, lies east of Isla de Lobos, centred on 28°44'·5N 13°48'·1W.

Natural park and marine reserve

The word *lobo* normally means 'wolf', but as *lobo marino* it is also the name given to the fur seal. However Seal Island, northeast of Fuerteventura, is sadly no longer a home for these animals which presumably have been hunted out of existence. The island, which is separated from Fuerteventura by the narrow channel of El Río, is part of a protected area, the *Parque Natural de las Dunas*. It remains largely unspoilt, wildlife abounds and the surrounding waters offer excellent diving and snorkelling, with many colourful reef fish. Roughly triangular, the highest point is Montaña de la Caldera (107m) near the western apex but much of the rest is low-lying, including Punta Martiño in the extreme north.

The single village of El Puertito on the southern shore of the island boasts a restaurant but little else – nearly all visitors return to the mainland at the end of the day. Close west of the village is the stone pier used by the ferries, and further west again a shallow lagoon guarded by a bar which dries 1·2m at springs. The beach inside offers totally protected swimming and has occasionally been used by multihulls for scrubbing, though technically all boating in the lagoon is prohibited and the only permitted entry to the island is via the stone pier. In settled north conditions it is possible to anchor off the lagoon in good holding 7–8m over sand and rock and experience only slight swell.

Puerto Ventura and Puerto de las Lajas

28°36'·36N 13°49'·49W & 28°32'·3N 13°50'·3W

Two misnomers

The names 'Puerto Ventura' and 'Puerto de las Lajas' on large-scale maps are all that remains of two ambitious plans which have come to nothing.

Work started in the early 1990s on a large and upmarket tourist development complete with marina, to be called Puerto Ventura, but the project

Looking northeast across El Río to Isla de Lobos

was soon abandoned. It says a good deal for the quality of the original work that much of the east breakwater still survives, albeit derelict and partially submerged, and a number of smallcraft lie on moorings in its shelter. A few houses overlook the bay and a dirt track connects with the island's main coastal road, but little else remains.

It is understood that work never even started at Puerto de las Lajas, a tiny village where a few small fishing boats are either hauled up the beach or lie on moorings close off the stony beach. It might be possible to anchor off in settled weather, though there is little obvious reason to do so.

Puerto del Rosario

28°29′·46N 13°51′·3W (breakwater head)

Waypoint

⊕C14 – 28°29′·2N 13°50′·8W
(0·5M SE of Puerto del Rosario)

Tides

Standard port for the Canary Islands is Casablanca, with Puerto del Rosario a secondary port. MLWS is about 0·4m above datum and time difference on Casablanca: –0056. Predictions for Puerto del Rosario are also available via Admiralty *EasyTide* – see page 194
Mean spring range 2·2m
Mean neap range 1·1m

Plans

Admiralty 1870 (1:75,000 & 1:7,500)
Spanish *6030* (1:5,000)
US *51343* (1:50,000 & 1:10,000)
Imray-Iolaire *E2* (1:10,000)

Lights

2793·5 **Punta Gavioto (Puerto del Rosario)**
Fl.5s47m20M White tower 43m
2794·05 **Breakwater, southeast corner**
Fl(3)10s12m3M East cardinal pillar, ♦ topmark 2m
2794 **Breakwater end**
Fl.G.5s13m5M Green tower 10m
2794·1 **West mole extension, south end**
Fl(2+1)R.10s6m3M Red pillar, green band 3m
2794·2 **West mole, north (old) end**
Fl(2)R.7s6m4M Red column 4m
2794·22 **South RoRo ramp**
Fl(2)G.7s5m1M Green column 3m
2794·15 **Beach protection mole**
Fl.R.5s5m3M Red column 3m

Harbour Communications

Port Authority ✆ 928 860200, 860201 *Fax* 928 860203
Email ptorosario@palmasport.es (0700–1400 weekdays only) VHF Ch 12, 16 (24 hours)

Recently enlarged commercial harbour

Rosario is the capital of Fuerteventura with an active commercial and tourist life, and Puerto del Rosario (pronounced *Pwerto del Rosah'rio*) is the main commercial port of the island. Container ships and ferries from Arrecife and Las Palmas berth on the inner side of the eastern breakwater, which has doubled in size over recent years, while cruise ships use the north-south spur on the west side of the harbour. There is no space for visiting yachts to lie alongside, but the extended breakwaters have created a reasonably sheltered anchorage southwest of the harbour.

In late 2010 there was mention of a marina being created in the harbour, but if this ever materialises it is unlikely to be for several years.

Approach and anchorage

The town is easy to identify on the low coastline, with four large grey silos on the breakwater and no outlying dangers in the approach. Allow good clearance for ship movements when closing the breakwater end.

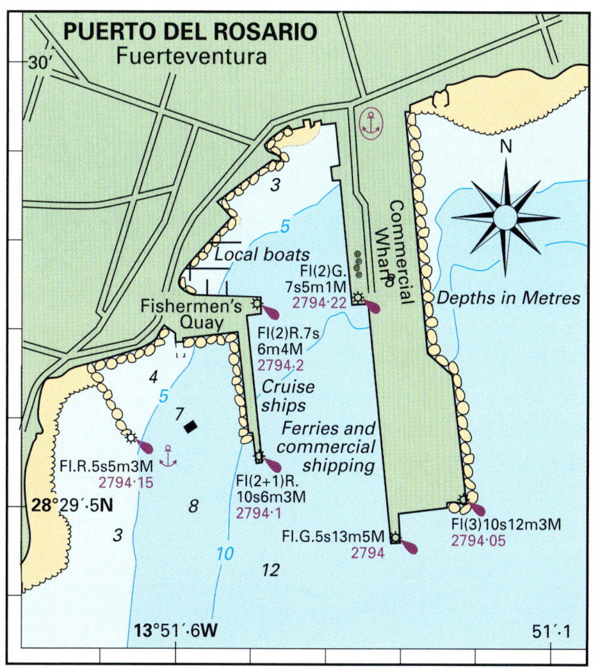

Although Puerto del Rosario offers no chance for a visiting yacht to lie alongside, good shelter will normally be found between the cruise ship quay and the beach propection mole

In northeasterly winds the area between the cruise ship quay and the beach protection mole remains well sheltered and offers good holding over sand in 6–7m. There appears to be no official objection to this, or to dinghies being left on the (artificially created) sandy beach to the west, but it is obviously essential to avoid the large float which lies in the centre of the area. Alternatively, the cream building on the quay to the north is occupied by the Centro Náutico Insular, who have a slipway where a dinghy might be left in greater safety.

Formalities

The port authority office will be found in the large grey and white building just outside the port gates. It also houses the Immigration department, which should be visited with the ship's papers if this is the yacht's port of entry to the Canaries (though the officials are largely uninterested in yachts, being much more concerned with illegal immigrants). No charge is made for anchoring outside the harbour.

Facilities

Travel-lift 30-tonne hoist near the fishing quay, but no real boatyard.

Engineers, electronics & radio repairs All the skills necessary to service the fishing fleet, but most workshops are outside the port area. Delfin Servicios Nauticos, ✆ 928 530699, have premises on Calle Almirante Colon and elsewhere, and handle engineering and electrical work as well as repairs and fabrications in steel and aluminium.

Chandleries Several, of which the largest is Deportes Chacón Náutical SL with premises in the west of the city on Calle León y Castillo and Calle Antonio Espinosa ✆ 928 533185 *Email* nauticachacon@gruponautico.com www.gruponautico.com. The two branches hold a good range of general chandlery, electronics, inflatables and outboard engines. Somewhat smaller is Duque Hnos SL, ✆ 928 851194, on Calle Alfonso XIII northeast of the city. Ferretería Fuerteventura, also on Calle León y Castillo, is the city's largest hardware store.

Water On the fishing quay, or possibly from the Centro Náutico Insular.

Fuel Petrol and diesel pumps near the fishing quay, serving cars as well as boats.

Bottled gas Camping Gaz or Disa bottles can be exchanged at several hardware stores in the city, but as of 2011 the situation regarding refilling other cylinders remained uncertain – see page 191.

Banks In the city, all with cash dispensers.

Shops/provisioning Supermarkets and other shops, including an enormous hypermarket in the industrial zone northeast of the town.

Produce market Near the root of the southwest mole, but relatively small.

Restaurants & hotels Wide choice to suit all tastes and pockets.

Medical services Hospital south of the town, plus a clinic near the church.

Communications

Post office On Calle Primero de Mayo, two roads inland from the harbour.

Telephones Opposite the dock gates and elsewhere.

Internet access As of March 2011 free Wi-Fi was available throughout much of the city, including the public parks and along the waterfront. The free service is distinctly slow, with faster speeds accessed for a small fee.

Car hire & taxis In the town.

Buses Bus station the north end of the main square, with services throughout the island.

Ferries Car ferries to Lanzarote and Gran Canaria.

Air services European and inter-island flights from the airport about 5km south of Rosario.

Puerto del Castillo (Caleta de Fustes)

28°23′·49N 13°51′·37W (breakwater head)

Waypoint

⊕C15 – 28°23′N 13°51′·4W (0·5M S of Puerto del Castillo/ Caleta de Fustes)

Lights

2794·5 **Breakwater** Fl(2)G.12s9m5M
White tower, pale green band 5m

buoy **South cardinal**
Q(6)+LFl.15s5M Yellow spherical buoy

buoy **Starboard hand buoy**
Fl(3)G.9s1M Green pillar buoy, ▲ topmark

buoy **Port hand buoy**
Fl.R.5s3M Red can buoy, ■ topmark

Note All three buoys are listed as 'pillars' in official publications, but this is incorrect – the above were observed by the author in November 2010 and had reportedly remained unchanged for at least four years. All three lights are reported to be unreliable and of reduced range. Two smaller spherical red buoys could also be seen, both apparently unlit, as well as various others marking windsurfing and jet-ski areas

Harbour Communications

Marina ✆ 928 163514 *Fax* 928 163999
Email marcan@abaforum.es VHF Ch 09 (0900–1400, 1600–1900 weekdays only)

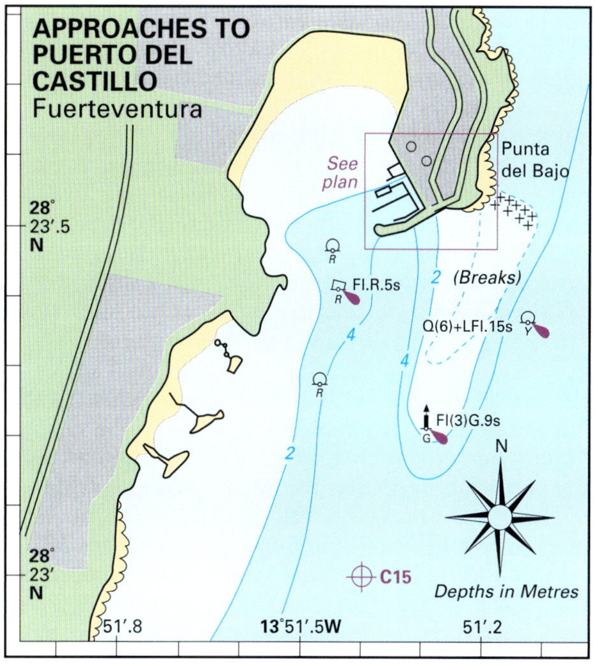

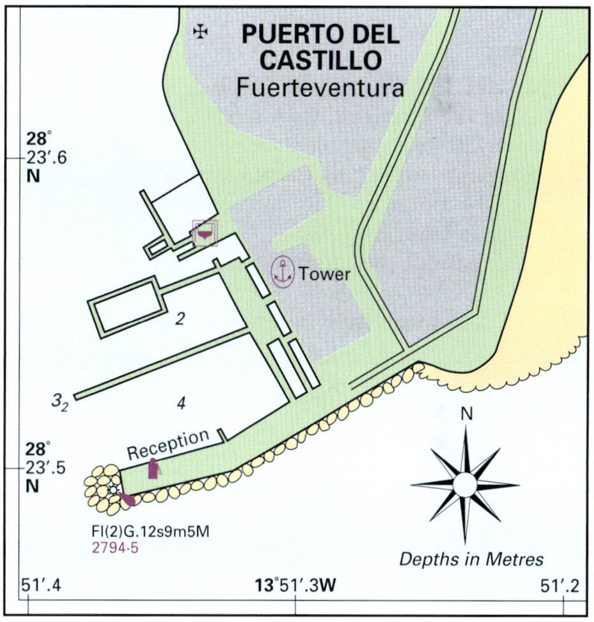

Small marina with little space for visitors

Puerto del Castillo (pronounced *Pwerto del Casti'yoh*) – sometimes referred to by its older name, Caleta de Fustes (*Caleta de Foostess*) – is a small marina built as a part of a predominantly German holiday development. Outlying and inshore reefs and sandbanks make entry distinctly hazardous unless an exact course is followed, and this is not a harbour to be entered for the first time at night. Once inside protection from the prevailing northeasterlies is good, but it essential to check first that space will be available.

Approach and entrance

For at least 4M either side of Puerto del Castillo the coast edges a low plain backed by a range of rounded volcanic hills. The old castle from which the town derives its name still stands, but it is inconspicuous against the holiday villas and the harbour is best identified by a tall round tower of rough brown volcanic rock with a domed roof, near the root of the breakwater. A dangerous reef which has claimed several yachts stretches southeast from

Looking northeast across the entrance to Puerto del Castillo. Arrows draw attention to the undersized buoys which mark the entrance

Punta del Bajo and considerably further south than the breakwater, enclosing a shallow sandy bay which opens to the south, its limits indicated by the three 'official' buoys described above as well as others apparently laid by local concerns.

Approaching from any direction, keep at a good half mile offshore until able to approach ⊕C15 on a bearing of at least 270°. From there the green and white light tower on the breakwater end (not the brown domed tower on the shore) bears slightly east of north and the starboard hand pillar (no more than 1m in height) should be visible fine on the starboard bow. Although the latter appears to lie well south of the end of the shoal it is actually placed close to the 2m line – on **no account** attempt to cut the corner. Others buoys mark windsurf and jet-ski areas, and the potential for confusion is plainly considerable.

There are shoals on the west side of the bay, marked by one lit red can buoy and, as of late 2010, two smaller red buoys, and yachts should not stray from the channel. There is claimed to be at least 3m in the entrance, but even so it would be wise to enter slowly under power with an eye on the depth sounder.

Berthing

Puerto del Castillo is the probably the smallest marina in the Canaries, with fewer than 100 berths, of which 20 are supposedly reserved for visitors – though some appear to be making very long visits indeed. Maximum size, limited by draught as much as length, is 16m.

Berths cannot be reserved, but telephoning to check for space before leaving one's previous harbour, and then again via mobile phone or VHF at least 30 minutes before arrival, appears to offer the best chance of success.

The reception and fuel berth, with a stated 4m, is immediately to starboard on rounding the breakwater head, or one may be directed straight into a berth (if the former, beware the fendering of elderly black tyres). Security is good, with gates to the pontoons. Keys (which also give access to the showers) are available from the marina office on payment of a €25 returnable deposit.

Formalities and charges

The marina office has moved several times over the years and is currently located near the root of the breakwater from which it gives access to the two pontoons used by yachts and sport-fishing boats. Some English is spoken. Charges are relatively high at more than €35 per night including tax for a yacht of 13m, but discounts are normally available for longer periods.

Facilities

Travel-lift 12-tonne capacity hoist with limited hardstanding, but only basic boatyard facilities.
Water At all berths.
Showers Behind the restaurant near the root of the mole. Access is by key (see Berthing, above).
Launderette In the resort, a short walk from the marina.
Electricity At all berths.
Fuel From the fuelling berth near the end of the breakwater which also serves vehicles. Nominally open 0800–1300 and 1600–1930 but hours are said to be irregular.
Weather forecast Posted daily outside at the marina office.
Banks In the resort, all with cash dispensers.
Shops/provisioning Close to the tower, with a supermarket about 1km from the harbour.
Produce market Weekly produce market in the resort on Saturday mornings.
Cafés & restaurants Many in the holiday resort, including a restaurant overlooking the marina.
Medical services Medical centre in the resort.

Communications

Post office In the resort.
Mailing address Muelle Deportivo El Castillo, Caleta de Fustes – 35610 Antigua, Fuerteventura, Islas Canarias, Spain.
Telephones Outside the old marina office in the base of the brown tower.
Internet access In the reception area of the nearby Barcelo Hotel on a pay-to-use basis, and elsewhere.
Car hire & taxis Readily available.
Buses Along the main road (about 2km away) to Rosario and elsewhere.
Air services Airport about 6km up the coast.

Anchorages on the east coast of Fuerteventura

Between Puerto del Castillo and Punta Lantailla lie a number of beach-backed coves which can be used in calm weather or light northerlies. Working southwards they include the misnamed Puerto de la Torre (28°21'·8N 13°52'·3W) with its Guanche ruins, just south of Punta del Muellito; Playa de Pozo Negro (28°19'·4N 13°53'·7W), protected to the north by Punta del Viento; and Playa de Jacomar (28°16'·4N 13°54'·3W), tucked behind Punta las Borriquillas and some 2·5M north of Punta Lantailla. This latter anchorage – which has little ashore beyond a small group of fishermen's houses – has shoals in the approach and needs to be closed carefully and in good light. Holding is patchy over small boulders and rocks.

Las Playitas

28°13'·65N 13°59'·05W (molehead)

Anchorage sheltered from west to northeast

Lying 2M west of Punta Lantailla, Las Playitas (also called 'El Poris de Las Playas') occupies a steep-sided valley which offers some protection even in a moderate northeasterly, and provides good anchorage in 3m or more over sand. The lack of a sandy beach – unusual in Fuerteventura – may be providing some protection from overdevelopment, as much still remains of the pleasant fishing village which has stood there for decades. A short stone mole with steps lies at the east end of the bay, but facilities once ashore are limited to a small supermarket and several fish restaurants.

Gran Tarajal

28°12′·32N 14°01′·44W (breakwater head)

Waypoint
⊕C17 – 28°11′·9N 14°01′·2W (0·5M SSE of Gran Tarajal)

Plans
Spanish *6030* (1:5,000)

Lights
2796 **Southeast breakwater**
Fl(3)G.7s8m5M Green tower 7m
2796·1 **West breakwater**
Fl(3)R.7s8m5M Red metal tower 7m

Marine farm
A marine farm, marked by four yellow pillar buoys with × topmarks, all Fl.Y.3M, lies east of Gran Tarajal, centred on 28°12′·5N 13°59′·2W.

Harbour Communications
Port authority / Marina ✆ 928 162151, 164101
Fax 928 164045
Marina VHF Ch 09 (0800–1400 weekdays only)

Fuerteventura's most welcoming harbour

In the early 1990s a substantial breakwater was built to the west of the single mole at Gran Tarajal (pronounced *Gran Tah'ra'hal*) to form a large and well protected, though relatively shallow, harbour for fishing craft, ferries and small freighters. Two pontoons occupied by local smallcraft were installed near its head. About 10 years later a curved inner mole was added to shelter the travel-lift dock, a single pontoon used by small fishing boats, and a small boatyard, and plans were announced to further improve the harbour by adding an angled arm to the end of the old east mole. Work started in 2006 and was completed the following year, since when further yacht pontoons have been added and services provided, albeit in a somewhat ad hoc manner. Sleepy and quiet, even in November, it remains a harbour with yacht pontoons rather than a true marina.

The surrounding area also remains relatively undeveloped – at least by Canarian standards – and although some might consider Gran Tarajal's attractions limited it has retained its 'village' atmosphere and offers a real glimpse of how the island must have been before the tourist boom took off.

Approach

Punta Lantailla lighthouse is set high on a point with cliffs running 2M west to Las Playitas. 1·5M beyond Las Playitas is another high point topped by a white building and mast. Gran Tarajal lies 1M further west in a wide valley with a low coastline. Approach and entry are straightforward, though beware of floating lines and plastic bottle 'moorings' close south of the inner (fishermen's) mole.

Berthing

Short-term visitors are normally berthed on one of the two eastern pontoons, with boats anticipating longer-term stays bows-to the south or west walls. Local smallcraft occupy the remaining pontoons. All yacht berths are alongside finger pontoons, with up to 16m LOA against the south part of the breakwater and 12m against the western angle.

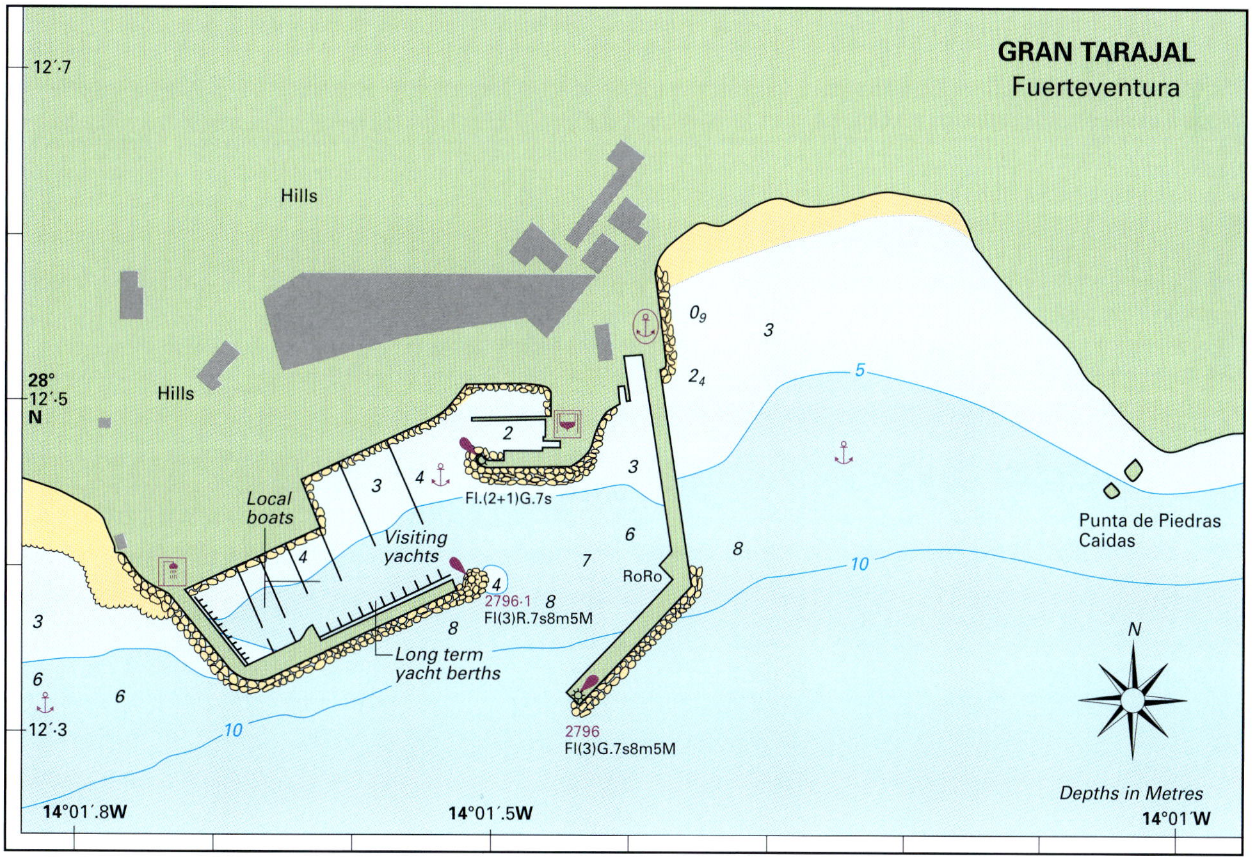

A yacht rounds the west breakwater at Gran Tarajal, with the outer arm of the east breakwater beyond. Together they give good protection to those within

In normal conditions the two easternmost pontoons are reported to be good, though swell can work into the harbour in southeasterlies and set yachts rolling. They are also the most convenient for the town, and offer plenty of space to manoeuvre. They are less suitable for long-term berthing, however, particularly if the yacht will be left unattended, and suffered storm damage in February 2010. In these conditions the breakwater berths are to be preferred, particlarly the ones against the western wall – winter gales can cause waves to break over the breakwater's south wall, depositing not just water but the occsional head-sized rock on the yachts below.

There is no formal reception area, and unless waved into a berth by one of security guards (some of whom speak English), arriving skippers should make their own choice and confirm it with the Port Captain afterwards. There are currently said to be 247 berths in total and even in the high season, when other harbours are full to capacity, Gran Tarajal is likely to have space for a visiting yacht. Having said that, it could do no harm to pre-book a berth via the authorities in Las Palmas – see Booking berths in *Puertos de Canarias* harbours, page 189.

Security appears to be good. Although the pontoon gates usually remain open there are round-the-clock patrols – although not entirely for the benefit of yacht owners. As mentioned on page 192, the authorities are aware that many illegal immigrants hope Fuerteventura will provide them with a back door to the EU and Gran Tarajal has, in the past, been a favourite landing point.

Anchoring

Anchoring is prohibited inside the harbour, and the inner part of the bay to the east is cordoned off for swimmers (marked by a line of small yellow buoys). The bay shelves gently and holding is reported to be good over sand, though the area is sometimes affected by ground swell.

Formalities

Confusingly, the building at the northwest corner of the harbour which is prominently labelled *Oficina* is seldom used, the Port Captain generally being found in a small, pale blue, tiled building at the root of the main (east) breakwater. Office hours are 0800–1400 weekdays only, but he appears to work alone and is often out and about. Many yachtsmen have commented (approvingly) as to the relaxed way in which the formalities are handled in Gran Tarajal, but the skipper should nevertheless visit the Port Captain as soon as feasible after arrival, bearing the usual ship's papers and crew passports.

Out of hours, and when the Port Captain is on holiday, the formalities are dealt with by the security guards, but they generally appear unwilling to handle payments.

A panoramic photo of Gran Tarajal, looking from due east almost round to west. The apparent curvature in the foreground is due to distortion in the camera lens

Charges

The berthing fee is calculated on a length x beam basis and in 2010 was set at €0.24 per m^2. This included water, electricity and tax, and in the past had increased by about 2% each year.

Facilities

Travel-lift A 70-tonne capacity lift is operated by the *Cofradía de Pescadores* (fishermen's confederation), inside the curve of the inner mole. Depth in the hoist dock and hardstanding and props once ashore are all limited, however.
Sail repairs Fuerte Velas, ✆ 928 161027, the only sailmaker/repairer on Fuerteventura, is based at Tarajalejo about five miles down the coast to the southwest.
Chandlery A branch of Duque Hnos SL (which has its main shop in Puerto del Rosario) lies on the road behind the harbour. Though mainly serving the fishing fleet, it also has some yacht chandlery on display and other items can be ordered on request. Comercial Langenbacher SL has premises on Calle Betancuria and stocks limited chandlery as well as general hardware.
Water On the pontoons.
Showers Near the root of the breakwater. It is normally kept locked though a key may be available from the Port Captain.
Electricity On the pontoons. There have been reports of electrical connections incorrectly wired as regards polarity (i.e. live and neutral reversed) so check before connecting sensitive items.
Fuel Rather surprisingly, there is no fuel available in either the fishing harbour or the marina. Small quantities can be collected by can from a filling station on Calle San Diego, about 10 minutes' walk from the harbour.
Banks In the town, with cash dispensers.
Shops/provisioning Several good supermarkets in the town, including a HiperDino on the large main square, but all some distance from the harbour. Bakery just outside the harbour gates.
Cafés, restaurants & hotels Bar/restaurant at the northwest end of the harbour with many more in the town, though apparently no hotel.
Medical services Health centre in the northern part of the town.

Communications

Post office & telephones In the town.
Internet access Good free Wi-Fi in the small public square overlooking the beach and at the nearby Casa de Cultura, plus several internet cafés in the town.
Taxis Available in the town.
Buses Regular bus service throughout the island, including to the airport.
Ferries Regular service to Las Palmas, Gran Canaria.

Anchorages on the southeast coast of Fuerteventura

From Gran Tarajal the coast runs west for 10M before turning southwest at the Península de Jandia, the highest portion of Fuerteventura with Pico de la Zara at 806m. It is a scenic coast to explore, with lovely white sand beaches and several anchorages sheltered from the prevailing winds, though further west the accelerated wind blows from the north across the low neck of land leading to the peninsula.

Possibilities for daylight stops in settled weather include Ginijinamar (28°12'·1N 14°04'·4W), a small bay with 3–5m over sand and a restaurant ashore, though landing can be difficult as the beach is steep; Tarajalejo (28°11'·5N 14°07'·1W), where there is a rough quay at the east end of a black sand beach and facilities include fresh water, supermarkets, a post office, telephones, restaurants and hotels; and Playa de la Lajita (28°11'N 14°09'·1W) also with a beach restaurant.

From Playa de Matas Blancas the coast – named Playa de Sotavento, 'The Leeward Strand' – swings southwest, and beaches backed by dunes of sand blown across from Africa run down to Punta de Morro Jable (occasionally referred to as Punta del Matorral). The only anchorage along this stretch to offer even vestigal shelter from the prevailing northeasterlies is off the growing tourist resort of Punta de los Mollinos (28°10'N 14°13'·2W), though it would be comfortable only in very settled weather and is not recommended for an overnight stop.

Morro Jable

28°02'·97N 14°21'·9W (breakwater head)

Waypoints
⊕C18 – 28°01'·7N 14°19'·9W
(1M S of Pta de Morro Jable)
⊕C19 – 28°02'·8N 14°22'·4W
(0·5M SW of Morro Jable entrance)

Plans
Imray-Iolaire *E2* (sketch plan)

Lights
2796·5 **Morro Jable**
Fl(2)10s61m20M White tower 59m
2797 **Breakwater**
Fl.G.5s7m4M Green metal tower 5m
Note In November 2010 this was reported to be Fl(4)G.10s
Northwest mole, angle Red metal tower 5m
Note Although characteristics have still to published officially, in November 2010 it was reported to be Fl(4)R.10s
Northwest mole, head Red metal tower 5m
Note Reported to be unlit as of November 2010
2797·2 **North inner quay**
Fl.R.4s4m3M Red column 3m

Marine farms
Two marine farms lie northeast of Morro Jable, one centred on 28°06'·6N 14°27'·5W and marked by four yellow pillar buoys with × topmarks, all Fl(5)Y.20s3M; the other centred on 28°03'·5N 14°29'·3W and marked by four yellow pillar buoys with × topmarks, all Fl(4)Y.15s3M.

Harbour Communications
Harbour authority ✆ */Fax* 928 540374 (0900–1900 weekdays) VHF Ch 09 (24 hours)

Large, under-developed ferry harbour

Morro (a headland) and *jable* (a croze or cooper's gouge) is said to explain the name, which is pronounced *Morr'oh Hab'lay*. A large tourist development, La Cebada, has been established on the point to the east and it is now difficult to tell where that ends and the old fishing village of Morro Jable begins.

Protection inside the harbour was greatly improved in the late 1990s by the construction of a short, angled, northwest mole, but despite elevation to the status of '*puerto deportivo*' (sports harbour) very little progress has been made since then. Evidence of the authorities' general lack of concern may also be seen in the confused situation regarding the harbour's lights, where changes made on the ground typically do not appear in the official Spanish *Faros y Señales de Neibla* for years, if ever.

A few berths at the end of the westernmost of the three eastern pontoons are reserved for visiting yachts

Approach and entrance

From the west, pass at least 3M south of Punta Jandia to clear shallows and disturbed water southwest of the point. Holiday apartments are conspicuous on the elevated ground east of the harbour and on close approach the breakwater will

Morro Jable seen from the northwest, with an inter-island ferry alongside the breakwater and the remaining two 'old' pontoons in the foreground. Visiting yachts berth on the more distant pontoon at centre left

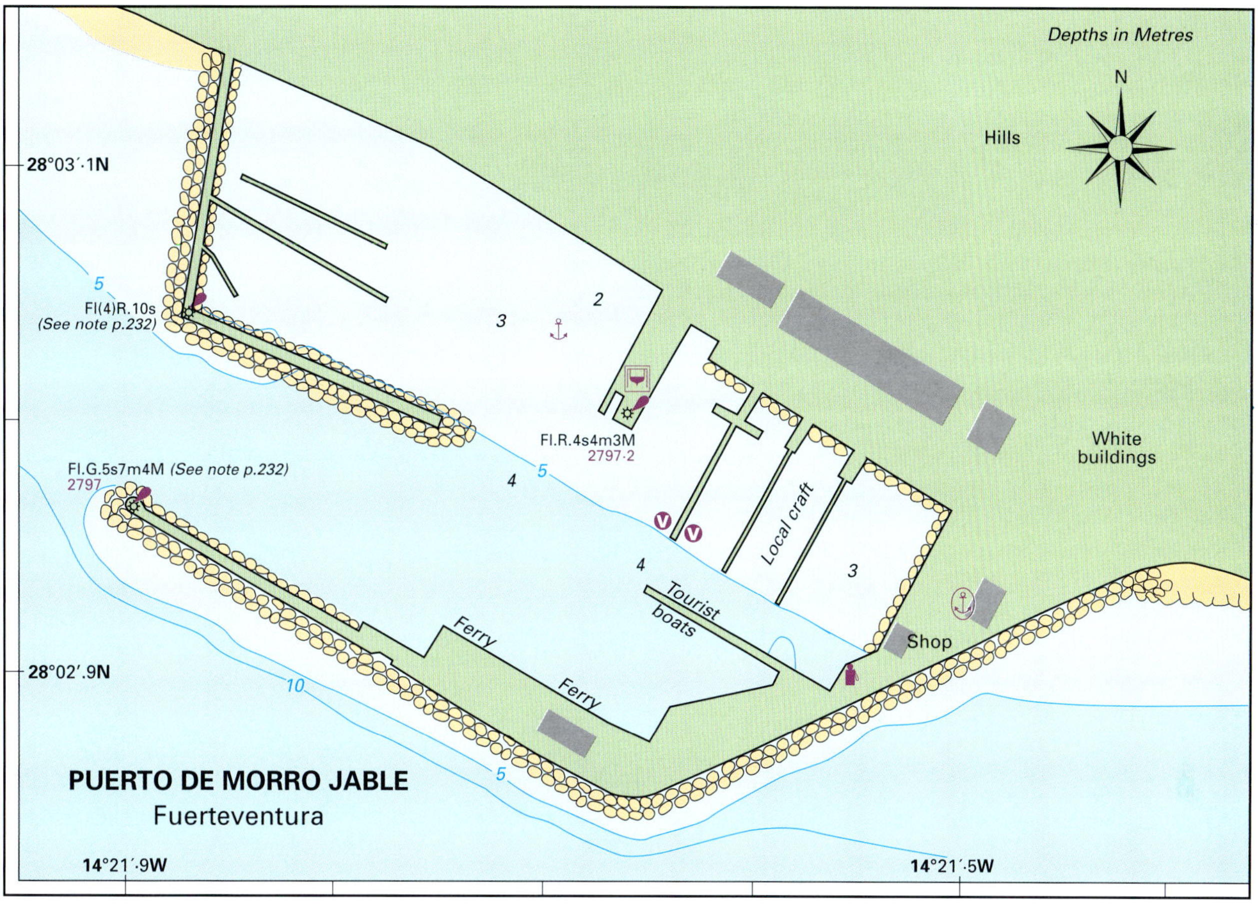

be seen below them. From the east, Punta de Morro Jable appears as a wide sandy beach stretching northeast, with a tall white lighthouse on the point. On rounding Punta de Morro Jable the breakwater will be seen at the west end of the holiday development. Entry, between the breakwater and the northwest mole, is straightforward.

At times – particularly when the mountains are covered by a cloud mantle – sudden, vicious gusts can blow down from the hills to the north without warning. These have been reported to reach Force 10 (50 knots), albeit briefly, and one should be prepared for them when entering or leaving the harbour.

The tall white lighthouse marking the low sandy promontory 1·5M east of Puerto de Morro Jable could have been taken from a child's drawing
Tom Hammon

Berthing

Three pontoons were established in the shelter of the northwest mole soon after it was completed, but maintenance has been poor and by 2010 one was no longer attached to the breakwater, one had largely disappeared with only a short section remaining, and although the third remained in place it still lacked facilities such as water and electricity. Yachts which secure there are likely to be checked by the security guards who patrol the entire port (largely to watch for illegal immigrants) and the skipper requested to visit the harbour office.

A maximum of six or eight yachts are permitted to berth on the end of the westernmost of the three pontoons in the east part of the harbour, the inner section, along with the two eastern pontoons, being fully occupied by local craft and fishing boats. Although well sheltered from the usual northeasterlies, should the wind shift to the south or east these berths catch the very worst of the resulting surge. In theory berths should be booked in advance – see Booking berths in *Puertos de Canarias* harbours, page 189 – but in practice this does not always seem to guarantee space and luck appears to play a major role. Due to the chronic shortage of space visits of more than a few days are discouraged.

The single pontoon to the southeast is used by the ubiquitous tourist catamarans. The breakwater is also unusable – in addition to regular car ferries and jetfoils there is an overhang which will catch stanchions and fenders on a rising tide.

Anchorage

Yachts of modest draught may be able to anchor between the travel-hoist dock and the western pontoons. Holding is poor however, and the bottom very foul with cables and chains, making a tripline a wise precaution. Note the previous warning regarding sudden strong gusts, a phenomenon which can also occur in the early hours of the morning. There have been occasional reports of thefts from anchored yachts, most often of dinghies and outboards and sometimes while the crew were asleep aboard.

Formalities and charges

The port captain's office is on the ground floor of the ferry terminal at the root of the main breakwater. Although nominally open 0900–1900 weekdays only, there is only one official in attendance and he is frequently elsewhere.

The berthing fee is calculated on a length x beam basis and in 2010 was set at €0.24 per m^2. This included tax, plus water and electricity on the few berths where it is available.

Facilities

Boatyard Operated by the *Cofradia de Pescadores*, with limited facilities but good security.
Travel-lift 70-tonne capacity hoist, with adequate hardstanding but a shortage of props – consult the *Cofradia de Pescadores.*
Engineers & electronics Nautica Puerto Jandia (see Chandlery, below) advertise these services, but their work has not been independently verified.
Chandlery Nautica Puerto Jandia SL ✆ 928 540512 *Email* nauticapuertojandia@telefonica.net has a small chandlery shop opposite the main gates stocking general chandlery including outboards, electronics and related spares, and larger premises on Avenida del Salada in the tourist centre, mainly devoted to promoting land and waterborne 'excursions'. Comercial Langenbacher SL also has premises in the town centre, at Calle Senador Velázquez Cabrera, where stocks include limited chandlery as well as general hardware.
Water On the pontoons at the east end of the harbour, but still no supply to the one remaining attached pontoon in the northwest corner.
Showers No showers, though toilets are available in the ferry terminal.
Fuel There is a filling station, which also serves vehicles, at the head of the harbour. The wall is high and although there are several large bollards there are no ladders, so if crew numbers permit it would be preferable to send a shore party on ahead. In theory sales are limited to fishing boats only, though several yachts have refuelled there without problem in the past few years. Payment must be made in cash.
Banks In Morro Jable, with cash dispensers.
Shops/provisioning Surprisingly well-stocked minimarket next to the fuel pumps on the main breakwater, as well as good general shopping in the tourist resort.
Cafés & restaurants Two in or close to the harbour, with many more in the tourist resort.
Medical services Medical centre in the tourist resort and hospital outside the town.

Communications

Post office In Morro Jable.
Telephones At the ferry terminal.
Internet access No Wi-Fi at or near the harbour, though there is understood to be at least one cybercafé in the resort area.
Car hire In Morro Jable.
Taxis On the quay to coincide with ferries, otherwise in the town.
Buses Bus stop at the ferry terminal, timed to coincide with the latter's schedule.
Ferries Jetfoil and car ferries to Gran Canaria and Tenerife.

Puertito de la Luz, Punta Jandia

28°04'·23N 14°30'·04W (anchorage)

Waypoint
⊕C20 – 28°03'·2N 14°31'·2W (1M SW of Pta Jandia)

Lights
2790 **Punta Jandia**
Fl.4s32m22M 276°-vis-190°
Dark masonry tower on building on low spit 19m

Open 'passage' anchorage

Punta Jandia (pronounced *Punta Handee'ah*) is a long narrow spit of volcanic material. Shoals extend some 3M south-southwest from its tip and the associated disturbed water and whirlpools should be given a wide berth. To the east of the spit a wide, shallow bay off the village of Puertito de la Luz (pronounced *Pwertitoh de la Loose*) makes a useful anchorage in light offshore conditions, whether arriving late from the west or intending to depart at first light. However, it is not suitable for use in stronger winds from any direction as heavy swell works around the island.

At night, a course of 310° for a point on the spit 0·5M northeast of the light will, with soundings, lead to an anchorage in 12m over sand with the lighthouse bearing 270° and the lights of the village due north. Even in settled weather the anchorage is prone to ground swell, but holding is in general good though there are a few patches of rock. In daylight the disturbance can be reduced by closer approach to the village and anchorage in 4–5m. The bottom changes to stones inshore, but the water is clear enough to choose a patch of sand for the anchor. The village has a couple of bar/restaurants, but little else.

Gran Canaria

Between 27°44′N–28°11′N and 15°22′W–15°50′W

Introduction

The third largest of the Canary islands, with an area of 1,500km^2 and a population of some 850,000 (of whom at least half live in the capital, Las Palmas), the 'Gran' prefix was added in honour of the Guanches' valiant defence of the island. Circular and almost cone shaped, the mountains culminate in the 1,950m Pico de las Nieves.

Gran Canaria has been referred to as a continent in miniature due to its great variety of landscapes, a major feature being the steep ravined *barrancos* or dry river beds. The north of the island is green and cultivated but the hot, dry south is only suitable for cacti, goats and sun-worshippers. In the extreme northeast the low-lying peninsula of La Isleta provides shelter for Puerto de las Palmas, the busiest commercial harbour in the Canaries, and its thriving yacht marina.

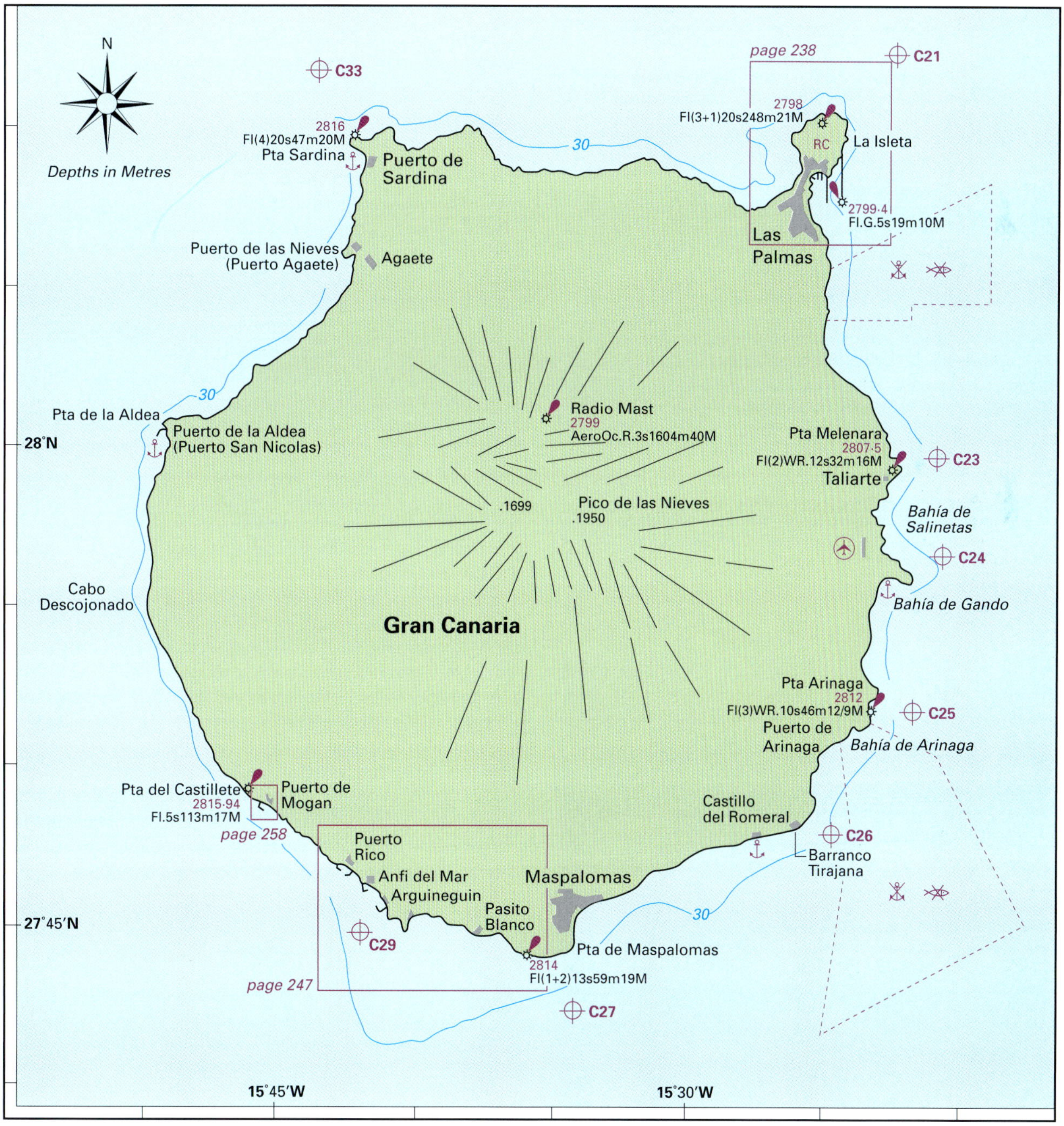

Websites

One would expect the second island in the Canaries – in terms of both size and population – to be well served by the internet, but until recently this has not been the case. The following sites contain general information about the island, some of which may be useful to the visiting yachtsman. Websites relating to specific harbours are listed under Harbour communications, those covering all or most of the Canary Islands on page 188 of the introduction.

www.en.wikipedia.org/wiki/Gran_Canaria – all the usual in-depth wikipedia information without the spin which one comes to expect from 'local' websites

www.grancanaria.com – dual website of the Gran Canaria Tourist Board (on the left of the homepage) and the island council (on the right). The former in eight languages with photos, short video clips and even iPhone Apps

www.grancanariainfo.co.uk – a general tourist site, but more comprehensive than most on the island's history and natural environment, and with a comprehensive To Do section

www.gran-canaria-info.com – a site which appears to be intended as much for those working in the tourist business as for visitors, and noticeably slow to open new pages, but covering a wide range of subjects if one is prepared to dig a little

www.laspalmasgrancanaria.com – the slightly old-fashioned website of Gran Canaria's capital city, with few links and almost no photographs but a useful source of addresses and phone numbers – always assuming these have been kept current

www.palmasport.es – official website of the Port of Las Palmas, responsible for the larger commercial ports in the three eastern islands as well as the Muelle Deportivo de Las Palmas (Las Palmas Marina)

www.spain-grancanaria.com – one of the Strawberry World sites, in English, Spanish, German and Portuguese. Fast and easy to navigate, with all the usual tourist information. The Images tab brings up a host of island webcams

www.vinest.net/wineareas/canarias.htm – the Gran Canaria page of Vinest, a 'unique network that promotes the interplay of small European wine areas', complete with details of island *bodegas* which can be visited

The cultivated terraces and dramatic cliffs of northwest Gran Canaria could hardly be in greater contrast to the flat, over-developed tourist areas fringing the Playas de las Meloneras and del Inglés in the south

For nearly a decade rumours have circulated that the number of yacht berths in Gran Canaria is to increase by some 2,500, with new marinas planned for Melenara and San Agustín on the east coast and Puerto Tauro and Puerto Aldea to the west. However, it seems that little credence can be given to these and, as of 2011, no major construction work was in evidence and the pressure on those marina berths available continued to increase.

Telecommunications

Mobile (cell) phone reception is excellent around the coast of Gran Canaria, though holes may exist inland. The country code for the Canaries is 34, as it is for mainland Spain, and the area code for Gran Canaria – which must be included even when dialling from within the island – is 928, shared with Lanzarote and Fuerteventura.

By 2011 Wi-Fi was available at the marinas at Las Palmas, Pasito Blanco and Mogan, but not in Puerto Rico. All the larger towns, including Puerto Rico, had at least one cybercafé.

Approach and navigation

There are no particular hazards except when approaching from the east at night, when part of the white sector of Maspalomas light lies across the land. When approaching from this direction the light should bear no less than 120°. It is advisable to keep 2M off, in soundings of more than 20m, to clear the shallows round the point. Further up the east coast, in the vicinity of Punta Melenara and Punta de Gando, shoals lie up to 0·5M offshore.

Winds blow from northeast for most of the year, with a protected area in the south created by the high mountains. In this wind shadow, between Punta de Maspalomas and Puerto de Mogán, there is often a more westerly belt of thermal wind up to 4M from the shore, surrounded by light southerly breezes. However, it is not possible to predict changes of wind direction which may reverse during the course of a day.

Beware of the accelerated winds along much of the coastline – see page 192. Particularly dangerous is the area around Punta Arinaga in the southeast, where the wind also funnels down a valley and mini waterspouts have been reported. The acceleration zones off both the southwest and northwest coasts can also be particularly bad, and there may be strong down-draughts off the high land between Puerto Rico and Punta Sardina. Be sure to reef on first sighting white horses, and always reef when approaching an acceleration zone in darkness, even though wind strength often decreases at night.

Navigation

Waypoints

⊕ C21 – 28°12'·3N 15°22'·3W (2·5M NE of La Isleta)
⊕ C22 – 28°06'·9N 15°23'·9W (0·5M SE of Las Palmas)
⊕ C23 – 27°59'·7N 15°20'·8W (1M NE of Pta Melenara)
⊕ C24 – 27°56'·6N 15°20'·6W (1M NE of Pta de Gando)
⊕ C25 – 27°51'·7N 15°21'·7W (1M E of Pta Arinaga)
⊕ C26 – 27°47'·9N 15°24'·6W (1M SE of Pta de Tenefé)
⊕ C27 – 27°42'·3N 15°34'W (2M S of Pta de Maspalomas)
⊕ C28 – 27°44'·3N 15°37'W (0·5M SSE of Puerto de Pasito Blanco)
⊕ C29 – 27°44'·8N 15°42'W (1M SW of Puerto de Arguineguín)
⊕ C30 – 27°46'·4N 15°43'W (0·5M SW of Puerto Rico)
⊕ C31 – 27°48'·5N 15°46'·2W (0·5M SW of Puerto de Mogán)
⊕ C32 – 28°05'·6N 15°43'·2W (0·5M SW of Puerto de las Nieves)
⊕ C33 – 28°11'·8N 15°43'·6W (2M NNW of Pta Sardina)

Courses and distances

⊕ C21 – ⊕C37 (0·5M SE of Santa Cruz de Tenerife) = 48M, 288° / 108°
⊕ C22 – ⊕C10 (0·5M S of Pta Pechiguera, Lanzarote) = 92M, 062° / 242°
⊕ C22 – ⊕C11 (2M NW of Pta Tostón, Fuerteventura) = 81·5M, 062° / 242°
⊕ C22 – ⊕C20 (3M SSW of Pta Jandia, Fuerteventura) = 46M, 097° / 277°
⊕ C22 – ⊕C24 via ⊕C23 = 11M, 159° & 177° / 357° & 339°
⊕ C24 – ⊕C25 = 5M, 191° / 011°
⊕ C25 – ⊕C27 via ⊕C26 = 14·5M, 214° & 236° / 056° & 034°
⊕ C27 – ⊕C29 = 7·5M, 289° / 109°
⊕ C29 – ⊕C31 = 5·5M, 315° / 135°
⊕ C31 – ⊕C37 (0·5M SE of Santa Cruz de Tenerife) = 46M, 2M 312°/ 132° + 44M 328° / 148°
⊕ C31 – ⊕C40 (1M SSE of Pta Montaña Roja, Tenerife) = 42·5M, 287° / 107°

Magnetic variation

5°40'W (2011), decreasing by 8'E annually.

Tidal Streams

Generally insignificant – see Tides and tidal streams, page 194. Details of range, etc. will be found under Puerto de las Palmas.

Charts

Admiralty *1869* (1:300,000)
Spanish *60B*, *61A* (1:200,000), *610*, *611* (1:60,000), *D210* (1:100,000)
US *51260* (1:300,000)
Imray-Iolaire *E2* (1:600,000)

Lights

2798 **La Isleta**
Fl(3+1)20s248m21M Aeromarine
White tower, yellow band, and building 10m
Note Shows fixed between flashes within 6M
2799 **Radio Atlantico**
Aero Oc.R.3s1604m40M Radio mast 55m
2807·5 **Punta Melenara**
Fl(2)WR.12s32m12M 270°-W-152°-R-270°
White tower 17m
2812 **Punta Arinaga** Fl(3)WR.10s46m16M
012°-R-052°-W-172°-R-212°-W 012°
White tower, red bands 13m
2814 **Punta de Maspalomas (Punta Morro Colchas)**
Fl(1+2)13s59m19M 251·5°-vis-093°
Conical grey tower, white lantern 56m
2815·94 **Punta del Castillete** Fl.5s113m17M
Square yellow tower with stair and gallery 20m
2816 **Punta Sardina** Fl(4)20s47m20M
White tower, red bands 23m

Coast Radio Station

Las Palmas 27°57'·5N 15°33'·5W, remotely controlled from Tenerife
VHF Ch 16, 26, 74 (24 hours)
DSC VHF MMSI 002241025, 27°58'N 15°33'W, remotely controlled from Tenerife

Weather and navigation broadcasts

VHF 27°58'·8N 15°33'·5W, remotely controlled from Tenerife
Weather bulletins Ch 26 at 0833, 1333, 2033 (forecast in Spanish for coastal waters)
Navigational warnings Ch 26 at 0833, 2033 (in Spanish for coastal waters)

Maritime Rescue Coordination Centre

DSC VHF MMSI 002240995, 28°09'N 15°25'W
✆ 928 467757, 467955 *Fax* 928 467760
Email laspalma@sasemar.es VHF Ch 10, 16 (24 hours)
(This station does not accept public correspondence other than distress and safety traffic)

Navtex

Identification letters 'I' and 'A'. The Canaries fall within NAVAREA 11. Transmissions in English (I) are on the standard Navtex frequency of 518kHz, those in Spanish (A) are on 490kHz. Las Palmas 'I' transmits weather bulletins for the coastal waters of the Canaries at 0920, 1320, 1720 and navigational warnings for the same area at 0120, 0520, 0920, 1320, 1720, 2110. Las Palmas 'A' transmits the same information in Spanish at 0800, 1200, 1600 and 0000, 0400, 0800, 1200, 1600, 2000.

ARC yachts in Las Palmas marina – correctly the *Muelle Deportivo de Las Palmas* – in November 2010

Harbours and anchorages

Las Palmas de Gran Canaria

28°07′·28N 15°24′·28W (Dique Reina Sofía, head)
28°07′·69N 15°25′·39W (marina northeast molehead)

Waypoints
⊕C21 – 28°12′·9N 15°25′·2W (2M N of La Isleta)
⊕C22 – 28°06′·9N 15°23′·9W (0·5M SE of Las Palmas)

Tides
Standard port for the Canary Islands is Casablanca, with Puerto de las Palmas a secondary port. MLWS is about 0·4m above datum and time difference on Casablanca: –0100. Predictions for Puerto de las Palmas are also available via Admiralty *EasyTide* – see page 194
Mean spring range 2·1m
Mean neap range 1·0m

Plans
Admiralty *1856* (1:75,000 & 1:12,500)
Spanish *6100* (1:12,500), *D210* (1:10,000)
US *51344* (1:30,000 & 1:10,000)
Imray-Iolaire *E2* (1:20,000)

Lights
2798 **La Isleta** Fl(3+1)20s248m21M
White tower, yellow band, and building 10m
Note Shows fixed between flashes within 6M
2799·2 **Roque del Palo** Q(3)10s11m6M
East cardinal post, ♦ topmark 6m
2799·4 **Dique Reina Sofía, head** Fl.G.5s19m10M
Green tower, white bands 8m Racon *C* 360° 12M
2799·5 **Dique Reina Sofía, outer angle**
Q(3)5s12m8M 150°-vis-360° East cardinal post 1m
Note Various other lights exist along the 2·1M length of the Dique Reina Sofia
2799·6 **Dique Reina Sofía, inner angle** Q(2)G.6s7m4M
335·5°-vis-181·5° Green tower 4m
2800·2 **Dique de Léon y Castillo, east side**
Fl.R.5s7m5M Red tower 4m
2801·2 **Dique de Léon y Castillo, southwest head**
Fl(3)G.12s19m7M 291°-vis-182°
Octagonal stone tower, white bands 9m
2807·36 **Marina northeast mole, head**
Fl(2+1)R.15s9m3M Red column, green band 6m
2807·37 **Marina west mole, head**
Fl(2)R.7s7m3M Red post 5m
2807·35 **Marina north mole, angle**
Fl(3)10s4m3M 160°-vis-320°
East cardinal post, ♦ topmark 4m
buoy **Red pillar buoy** Fl.R.4s
Red pillar buoy, green band, ■ topmark
2801·85 **Real Club Náutico mole, angle**
Fl(3)5s7m1M 180°-vis–090°
East cardinal tower, ♦ topmark 4m
2801·9 **Real Club Náutico molehead**
Fl(4)R.10s7m3M Red pyramid 4m
2802 **Muelle del Arsenal, southeast corner**
Fl(2+1)G.14·5s5m1M Red post, green band 3m
Note Many other lights exist in both the Puerto Exterior and the Puerto Interior

Harbour Communications
Port Authority ✆ 928 300400, 300480 *Fax* 928 300422
Email palmasport@palmasport.es www.palmasport.es
VHF Ch 10, 12, 16 (24 hours)
Muelle Deportivo de Las Palmas (marina) ✆ 928 234960
Fax 928 232378 *Email* marina@palmasport.es
VHF Ch 11, 16 (0900–1400, 1600–1900 weekdays, 0900–1400 weekends)

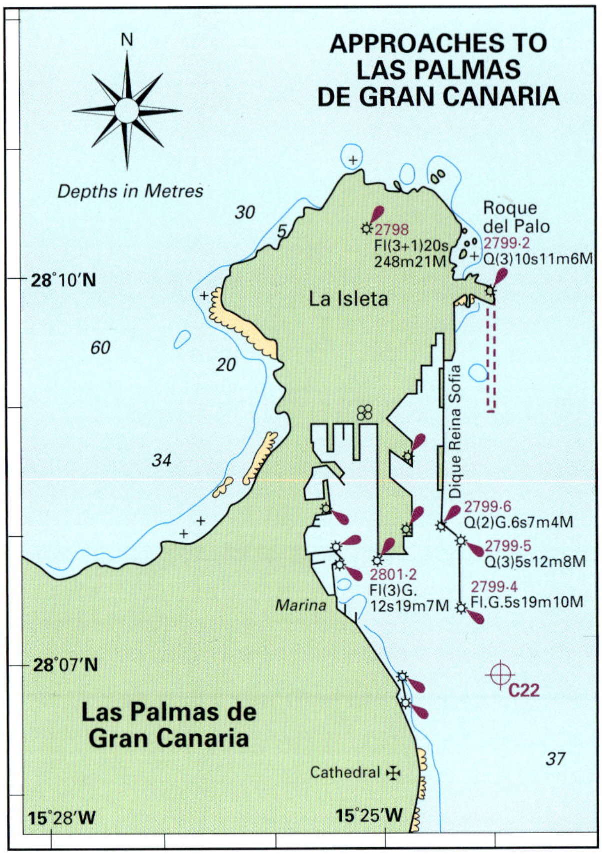

The Canaries' largest marina

For many years Puerto de las Palmas – previously known as Puerto de la Luz – had a reputation as a dirty, oily port, subject to almost continuous wash from passing commercial craft and best avoided by yachts. However, over the past few decades this has changed – possibly being chosen as the departure port for the Atlantic Rally for Cruisers (ARC) has opened official eyes to the benefits of visiting yachts – and its appeal has increased markedly.

Work first started in 1882 to turn a poorly protected bay into the largest – and busiest – commercial port in the Canaries, and appears seldom to have stopped since. In particular, work on the Dique Reina Sofia has enabled the port's bunkering facilities, formerly blamed for the frequent occurrences of black oily scum, to be moved eastward from the Dique de Léon y Castillo, and the oil nuisance now appears to be largely a thing of the past. Then the problem of wash created by high-speed ferries passing close to the marina, apparently with scant regard for speed limits, was largely overcome with the addition of an angled arm to the marina's north mole. More recently the Dique Reina Sofia has been extended even further south and work started on land reclamation at its root.

With some 1,250 berths the marina – correctly called the *Muelle Deportivo de Las Palmas* – is seldom full other than in the weeks prior to the Atlantic Rally for Cruisers in late November. While space for participating yachts is pre-booked by the organisers, those not associated with the event are unlikely to find berths available for four to six weeks

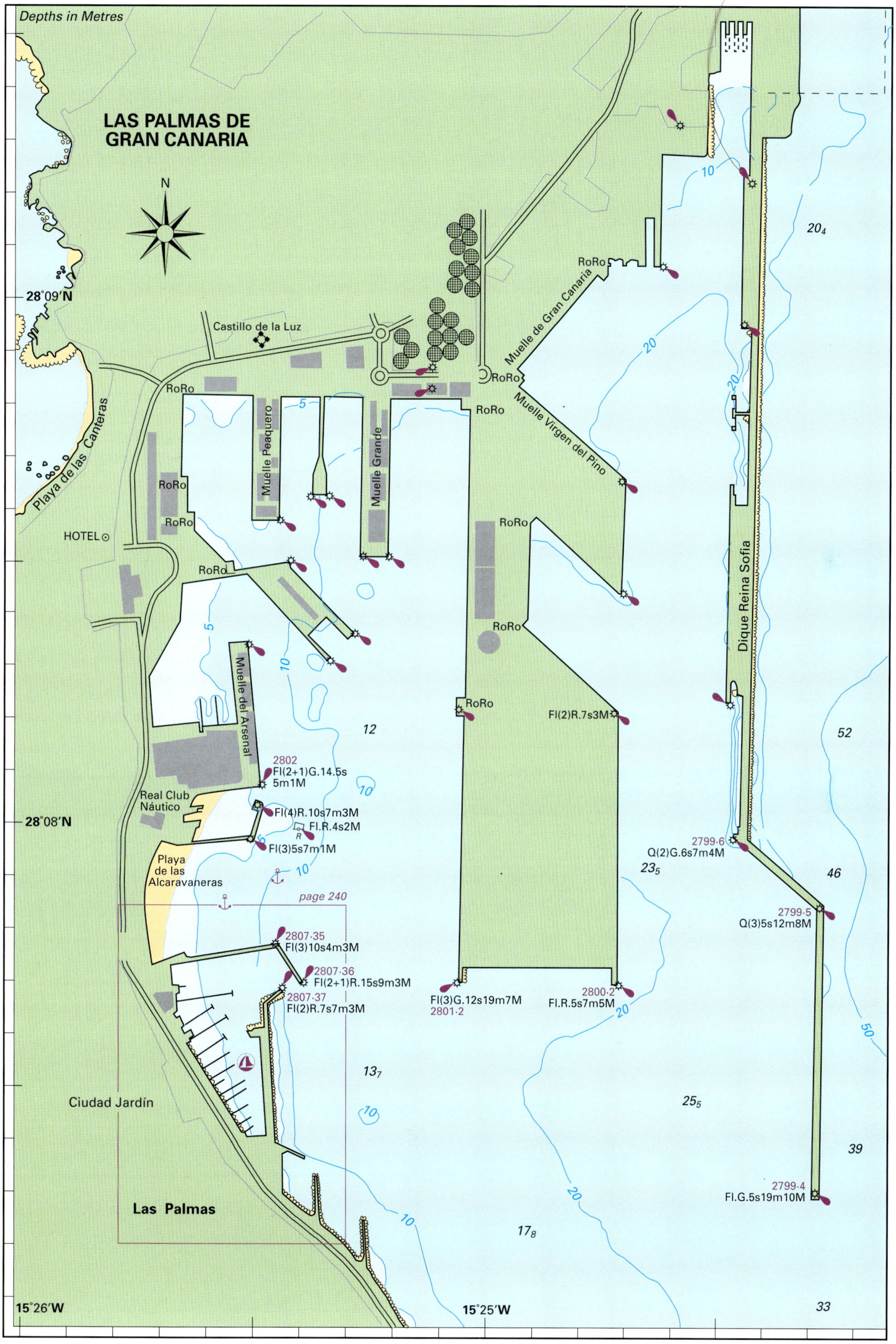

III. THE CANARY ISLANDS

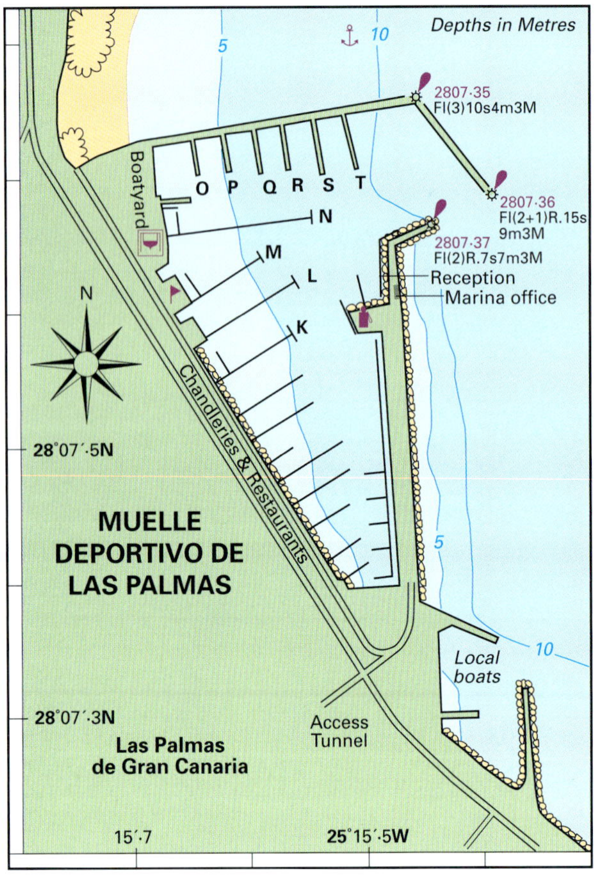

before the start, and those already berthed in the marina may be asked to leave. Space in the anchorage is also likely to be at a premium.

The marina has two access points from the city – a south (main) entrance via a tunnel for vehicles and pedestrian steps, and a ramp at the north end which opens about 0730 and closes at 2200, or sometimes earlier. If berthed in the northern part of the marina the detour via the southern entrance is in the order of 1·5km. And even experienced navigators may experience problems finding their way into the marina complex by car, as it is not possible to turn off the Avenida Alcalde José Ramirez Bethencourt (the busy dual-carriageway which divides the marina from the town). If intending to hire it may be worth checking out the approach on foot first.

Places of interest in the town include the *Casa de Colón* (Columbus house and museum) at Calle Colón 1, ✆ 928 312386, the *Museo Canario* (Canarian history) at Calle Doctor Chil 25, ✆ 928 315600, and the new *Museo Elder* (science and technology) on Parque Santa Catalina, ✆ 928 011282. The city has its own website at www.promocionlaspalmas.com and a tourist office on Parque de Santa Catalina, about 2km north of the marina. Excellent views down over the city and harbour can be had from the bluff behind the aptly named *Ciudad Jardin* (garden city) area, though parts of the hillside appear to be somewhat rough and are perhaps best not visited alone with an expensive camera around one's neck.

Approach and entrance

La Isleta is a peninsula 3km across, the northern half a high conical mound (230m) with steep cliffs, the

Looking northwest across the *Muelle Deportivo de Las Palmas*, with the (crowded) anchorage at top right
Puerto de Las Palmas

southern half falling away to Puerto de La Palmas and the low neck joining it to the mainland. The city and its suburbs appear from seaward as one continuous line of buildings, rising up to the south on the slopes of Cordillera de San Francisco.

From the north keeping 1M off La Isleta in order to clear Roque del Palo and the land reclamation to its south and east, as well as the various wrecks and hulks which lie outside the Dique Reina Sofia (the outer breakwater), make for ⊕C22 before turning west so as to pass well south of the breakwater head.

From the south the cathedral marks the south end of Las Palmas proper and the port will lie below La Isleta. Three yellow pillar buoys lie up to a mile offshore, but need not concern a yacht. A little further north, straddling 28°06'·8N, a 400m mole has been constructed a few hundred metres offshore, marked at its southeast end by an cardinal pillar buoy with ⧫ topmark, Fl(3)5s5M, and at its north end by a square red tower, Q.R.5M. Its purpose is not clear, and though it would appear possible to pass between it and the shore this would not be wise.

The marina entrance can be surprisingly difficult to pick out on approach, with the opening not becoming obvious until quite close in. Once located the entrance is straightforward, and the marina itself secure in virtually all weather conditions. If entering the marina at night, one passes between two **RED** lights – one a port hand light for the marina, the other a port hand light for traffic continuing north into the commercial and ferry harbour.

Berthing

A reception pontoon has been installed on the port hand once in the marina proper (the section which faces north in the entrance is the lifeboat berth) but this can become congested and it is wise to make contact by VHF or mobile phone before entering. If there is no chance of rafting up on the reception pontoon secure instead at the fuel berth. At least 3·5m should be found in both places.

Six pontoons extend south from the north mole and visiting yachts of medium size are normally berthed on one of the four outer ones (Q to T). All berths are bow or stern-to, with a buoy and lazy line provided. A combination of a beam wind and a manoeuvre unfamiliar to many northern European yachtsmen can lead to problems, and it is worth deploying all available fenders around vulnerable areas such as self-steering gears. Fortunately there is reasonable space between the pontoons and assistance is available if required. Large yachts – the marina can accept five of up to 45m – are likely to be assigned a stern-to slot south of the fuel berth. Again, docking may be a problem as the prevailing wind blows parallel to the quay wall and thus beam-on to a manoeuvring yacht, but more crew may be available to retrieve and handle the buoy and lazy line. Beware old lines left attached to some of the buoys, which could foul a propeller.

Security has been a problem in the past, with intruders of two-legged, four-legged and six-legged species. The first seems to have been addressed by moving the main pontoon entry gates to halfway down the ramps, with side panels and spikes above. There is also a substantial police presence in the marina area, particularly prior to the ARC departure, and finally no less than 22 CCTV cameras were installed early in 2011. This may partly be the result of several thefts from ARC yachts in November 2008, often while the owners were asleep below. While security inside the marina has clearly improved, in December 2010 a British yacht reported an attempted theft in the anchorage, so sadly the problem may merely have shifted north.

No problems with intruders of the four-legged variety – rats – have been reported for several years, although they certainly exist in the marina. Fitting rat-stoppers to shorelines (old funnels, or large plastic plates drilled through the centre work well) can do no harm, and yachts continuing westward may be glad of them in some Caribbean harbours. Six-legged pests of the insect variety remain widespread, however, and though cockroach powder on the lines may help, they have many other ways of coming aboard, primarily in food packaging.

The view from the southern apex of the *Muelle Deportivo*, at 1,250 berths the largest marina in the Canary Islands

Anchorage

Anchoring is permitted north of the marina though a fee is payable – see Charges, overleaf – and visits from the port police and Customs (*aduana*) are said to be common. Holding is relatively good over mud, sand and shale, though a patch of rock has been reported close to the buoyed-off swimming area in 5–6m. The bottom is foul in some areas, making a tripline advisable. The anchorage is bounded on its northern side by the private marina of the *Real Club Náutico de Gran Canaria*. A gap must be left clear to the south of the RCN marina mole to allow access to and from the beach – the Playa de las Alcaravaneras. This has been built up with imported sand and is popular with city residents, but although claimed to be both clean and safe, water quality may be suspect.

There is an ongoing problem with swell – created both by northeasterly winds refracting around the two outer breakwaters to set up a southeasterly swell in the anchorage, and by wash from passing

Yachts moored stern-to outside the *Muelle Deportivo's* north mole

vessels – but while this movement may sometimes make life uncomfortable it is seldom untenable.

Late autumn gales are relatively common, and precautions (such as laying additional anchors) should be taken if the yacht is to be left unattended. In late 2010 more than a dozen yachts lay to a bower anchor and stern line to the breakwater, but this may prove unsustainable if the wind veers further east than normal.

Dinghies can be left inside the marina, at the southern end of the reception pontoon or on a pontoon at the south end of the marina. Alternatively, some choose to leave them on the north side of the marina mole close to the end of the security fence, in which case a long painter is needed. In all cases outboards need to be well secured (also a wise precaution on a dinghy left astern).

Yachts from the anchorage can visit pontoon T (the easternmost on the north mole) to take on water, for which a charge is made, or collect it by can from there or from the reception or fuel pontoons for nothing. Crews may use the marina showers and toilets, and there are also public toilets on the beach though they are reported to be closed on Sundays.

Formalities

The marina office, where Customs and other formalities are also handled, overlooks the reception pontoon just north of the fuel berth. The staff are helpful with good English, though queues can form in the run-up to ARC. Ships' papers and crew passports are normally held until departure, though crew members who will be leaving the islands by air will need to recover their passports and take them to the *Policía Nacional* office in the main *Edificio Autoridad Portuaria* (Port Authority Building) near the root of the main breakwater for stamping. The skippers of yachts at anchor also need to visit the marina office, taking the same paperwork with them.

It is wise to reserve a berth by email at least a week, or preferably two weeks, in advance, for which no deposit is required. This is unlikely to be possible in the weeks prior to the ARC, however, as much of the marina is reserved by the organisers for participating yachts. No reservation is required if intending to anchor.

Charges

The berthing fee is calculated on a length x beam basis and in 2010 was set at €0.20 per m² per night, including 5% tax but not water and electricity, which cost €1.10 per night plus a small connection fee. Anchoring cost €0.05 per m² per night, again including 5% tax. In addition all yachts, whether in the marina or at anchor, paid Navigational Aid tax – *Tasa de Ayuda a la Navegación* – at just over €0.01 per m² per day – see page 190.

All payment must be made in advance, and discounts are available for longer periods. All credit cards in the Visa family are accepted, but not American Express.

Facilities

Puerto de las Palmas has some of the best facilities in the entire Canaries, and though not all concerns are familiar with the needs of yachts, almost anything can be done once the correct person is located. Although the listing below includes contact details, personnel at many companies based outside the marina area speak little English, and non-Spanish speakers would be well advised to enlist the help of Jon Crouch Yacht Services (see Engineers, below). Note also that engineers and electricians outside the marina deal primarily with commercial ships and fishing boats, so yachts take third place.

Boatyard At the time of writing the marina boatyard (*varadero*) was closed while new owners were sought. No date had been set for reopening, which may not take place until 2012.

Travel-lift Out of commission until the boatyard reopens, but previously able to lift up to 60 tonnes and 6m beam. The *Real Club Náutico de Gran Canaria* has its own travel-lift for the use of members, where one might receive assistance in an emergency.

Diving services Ocean Shore Canarias (see Chandlery, below) has a diver licensed by the marina to carry out hull cleaning, anode replacement, photographic inspection, etc.

Engineers There are numerous engineers in the commercial harbour and the city, not all of whom speak English. If in doubt, contact Jon Crouch of Jon Crouch Yacht Services ✆ 609 388355 *Email* joncrouchyachtservices@hotmail.co.uk, an ex-Royal Marine and liveaboard with wide experience of solving mechanical, electrical and charging problems. If a job is outside his field he will advise on where best to take it.

Otherwise, and alphabetically, try: *Alternators and starter motors* – Zurelectrica SL ✆928 482111 *Email* tma@zurelectica.com Atalya 24, Urb. Ind Lomo Blanco, Las Torres; *Electric motor repairs* – Antonio Brito ✆928 465768 Calle Prof Lozano 21, El Sebadal; *Evinrude/Johnson dealer* – Delmar ✆928 463027 *Email* delmarnautica@tlelfonica.net Calle Dr Juan Domingo Perez 75, El Sebadal; *Fabrication* – Mecanizados Atlántiko ✆928 002083

Email mecanizadosatlántiko@hotmail.es Calle Sao Paulo, El Sebadal; *Hydraulics* – Caloplax SL ✆928 466655 *Email* caloplax@infonegocio.com Calle São Paulo, El Sebadal; *Seals, bearings, fan belts and windlass gearboxes* – Rodamientos Gallardo SL ✆928 465000 Calle Mendoza, El Sebadal; *Volvo Penta, Perkins, Mitsubishi, Jabsco* – Potencia Marina SL, based in the marina complex (see Chandlery, below) with good English spoken; *Watermakers and calorifiers* – Rolnautic, based in the marina complex (see Chandlery, below) with good English spoken; *Welding and fabrication in s/s and aluminium* – Gallarta Inoxidables ✆ 928 460603, 461648, 460905 *Email* gallartainox@terra.es at Calle Sao Paolo 46; *Welding, including aluminium* – Tecnavin SL ✆ 928 465454 *Email* talleres@tecnavinsl@telefonica.net Avda de los Consignatarios s/n, Puerto de la Luz; *Yamaha* – Fueraborda SL ✆ 928 270674, 928 465549 *Email* yamaha@step.es at Inés Chemida 69; *Yanmar* – Navales Cazorla SL ✆ /*Fax* 928 721175, 660 403512 *Email* yanmargrancanaria@casorla.net and rep.navales.cazorla@hotmail.com www.tallercazorla.net on Calle Castille y Leon (behind the beach north of the marina), with its main workshop at Puerto de Pasito Blanco – see page 249.

Electronic & radio repairs Again there are many possibilities, most of whom speak some English. For specific makes and services try: *Apelco, Autohelm, Garmin, Globalstar, Icom* – Tesa Nautica SA ✆ 928 223707 *Email* tena@gtc-tesa.com at Albareda 53; *Electrolysis control* – Tech Tronic Nautica ✆ 928 787744, 646 675836 *Email* techtronic@terra.es at Calle Torna Golosa 28; *Furuno, JCR, Sailor* – Nautical ✆ 928 474020 *Email* nautical@nautical.es at Esplanada del Pantalan de Cory in the port area; *Garmin, Magellan, Plastimo, solar panels* – Potencia Marina SL (see Chandlery, below); *Garmin, solar panels* – Lopacan Electronica SL ✆ 928 290658 *Email* malorenzo@worldonline.es at Calle Alemania 66; *Icom, JRC, Koden, Skanti, Neco, Navitron* – Electronica Naval Bridgecom ✆ 928 224022 *Email* bridgecom@terra.es at Albareda 60; *JRC, Koden, Simrad, Sperry* – Radio Pesca SA ✆ 928 463308 *Email* laspalmas@radiopesca.es www.radiopesca.es on the Muelle Pesquero in the port area; *McMurdo EPIRBs, Skanti* – Radio Marítima Atlantico ✆ 928 467666 at Calle Juan Rejon 129; *Plath, Yaesu* – Etel ✆ 928 463697 at Calle Profesor Lozano 17–2; *Raymarine, Mastervolt* – Rodritol (see Refrigeration, below); *Sailor, Simrad, Skanti* – Ecomarin ✆ 928 488310, 650 198735 *Email* comercial@aeenergias.com at La Naval 79.

Refrigeration Rodritol ✆ 928 461384, 928 460090 *Fax* 928 462594 *Email* rodritol@rodritol.com www.rodritol.com at Calle Pinillos Izquierdo in the outer port area, handle refrigeration problems and are agents for Frigoboat, Vetus and Jabsco pumps.

In the marina itself Jean-Marie, ✆ 695 595458, a French liveaboard who speaks good English, is recommended locally.

Sailmaker/repairs Velas Linton ✆ /*Fax* 928 291934, 606 555928 *Email* prendergast@wanadoo.es at Alfredo Calderon 37, makes and repair sails, handles general canvaswork, and is agent for Profurl and other roller-reefing gears, which they will also repair. Several endorsements for the work of Charlie Linton (who is British) have been received over the past few years.

Alisios Sailing Centre SL ✆ 928 233171 *Fax* 928 243275 *Email* alisios-sailing@terra.es (open 0900–1430, 1630–1900) has premises opposite the *Club Marítimo Varadero*. Sails of all kinds can be repaired, or created from scratch using computer cutting.

Rigging Alisios Sailing Centre (see above), have rigging wire and terminals of all sizes and a swage machine up to 16mm, together with the necessary skills to deploy them. Other possibilities are Nauti-Sport ✆ 928 240830 *Email* nautisport@telefonica.net at Calle Barcelona 3 and Ocean Products Española (see Liferaft servicing, below).

Liferaft servicing Three companies in Gran Canaria, each specialising in different makes. Allow at least two weeks although turnaround is often quicker. *Avon, RFA, Zodiac* – Tonogami Canarias SL ✆ 928 463747 *Fax* 928 470402 *Email* info@tonogamicanarias.es www.tonogamicararias.es at Calle Dr Juan Dominguez Perez 44 reported to be expensive; *Plastimo* – Inprecasa ✆ 928 469422, 617 447144 *Email* inprecasa@inprecasa.com www.inprecasa.com which has premises in El Sebadal north of the commercial harbour as well as in Tenerife; *RFD, Viking* – Ocean Products Espanola SA ✆ 928 706672, 706755 *Fax* 928 706724 *Email* info@oceanproducts.es www.oceanproducts.es based near the airport but willing to collect and deliver.

Chandlery After years of having to search the city for chandleries, six shops selling chandlery of various types now front the west side of the marina. Even so, all may run out of popular items prior to the departure of the ARC in November, particularly those required by the event's safety regulations. In late 2010, from south to north these companies comprised:

Puerto Marina Terraza (which also owns the adjacent café) ✆ 928 234449, open 1000–1400, 1600–1900 weekdays, 1000–1400 Saturday, selling mainly fishing gear but also anodes, paint, and limited chandlery;

Marmare,✆928 296352, selling mainly clothes, shoes and a little 'fancy' chandlery in addition to the charts detailed below;

Potencia Marina ✆ 928 463647, 928 471044 *Email* mail@potenciamarina.com www.potenciamarina.es, open 0800–1900 weekdays, 0800–1200 Saturday, with English, French, German and Eastern European languages spoken, selling practical chandlery (pumps, batteries etc.) in addition to its main specialisation in engineering and electrical work;

Rolnautic ✆ 928 296811 *Email* rolnautic@rolnautic.com www.rolnautic.com, open 0900–1300, 1600–1930 weekdays, 0930–1300 Saturday, with English, German and Scandinavian languages spoken, which carries a wide range of general chandlery and will order from mainland Europe as necessary. Expect to queue at busy periods such as pre-ARC, when a deli-type ticketing system is used;

Alisios Sailing Centre SL (see Sailmaker/repairs, above) which also stocks rope and deck hardware;

Ocean Shore Canarias ✆ 928 248091, 616 902599 *Email* correo@oceanshoresl.com, open 0900–1300, 1600–2000 weekdays, 0900–1300 Saturday. Primarily a Bénéteau dealer, with spares etc., some general chandlery is also stocked. Fluent French is spoken, though little English.

Finally, one of the largest chandleries in theCanaries – with some of the best prices but no Englishspoken – is King Hogar ✆ 928 467304 *Email* info@kinghogar.com www.anidia.com at Calle Dr Juan Dominguez Pérez 10 in El Sebadal, north of commercial harbour.

Charts Suisca SL ✆ 928 220000 *Fax* 928 227866 *Email* laspalmas@suiscasl.com www.suiscasl.com at Avenida de Los Consignatorios 7, is the only Admiralty chart agent in the Canaries, though Rolnautic (see Chandlery, page 243) also stocks some. JL Gándara y Cía SA ✆ 928 466675, 465366 *Fax* 928 463368 *Email* laspalmas@gandara-sa.com www.gandara-sa.com on the Esplanada Dársena del Castillo, are agents for the Spanish Hydrographic Office.

Official Imray distributor is Rolnautic, though the much smaller Marmare (see Chandlery, above, for both) also stocks a good range of Imray charts and guides for the Canaries and the Caribbean, as well as BA Caribbean Leisure Folios. Not surprisingly, prices are somewhat high.

Water To all berths, but has on occasion been reported as tasting unpleasant.

Showers Three shower blocks, two built into the wall on the west side of the marina and the third situated in the block behind the fuel berth, all with card entry systems. The men's showers have been criticised for standing water and a lack of hooks, though the ladies' are somewhat better.

Launderette Built into the wall on the west side of the marina and about halfway along. Open 0900–2100, with four washers (€8) and three dryers (€0·50). A service wash can be arranged via the manager of the Texaco fuel dock.

Electricity 220v at all berths, with 380v at the large yacht berths south of the fuel dock.

Fuel Diesel, petrol and a variety of oils at the Texaco fuel berth near marina reception, open 0800–2000 Monday to Saturday, 0900–1300 Sundays and holidays (though closed on the Sunday prior to the ARC departure while a party is held).

Bottled gas Camping Gas exchanges are available at the Texado fuel dock or in the city, but as of 2011 the situation regarding refilling other cylinders remained uncertain – see page 191.

The Disa plant, open 0900–1300, is some distance south of the city (leave the GC-1 motorway at Junction 12, signposted for Salinetas). A preliminary recce would be wise, after which it will be necessary to hire a car as it is illegal for taxis to transport gas bottles.

Weather forecast Posted daily at the marina office, with copies also on display next to the minimarket and opposite the boatyard.

Club náutico The *Real Club Náutico de Gran Canaria* ✆ 928 234566 *Email* rcngc@rcngc.com www.rcngc.com (in English as well as Spanish) has large premises north of the marina, recently augmented by a small, private marina which does not accept visitors. Even so, temporary membership may be offered to visitors from recognised clubs, including use of the large outdoor swimming pool, gym, library, computer room and Wi-Fi.

The *Club Maritimo Varadero de Gran Canaria* overlooks the northern part of the marina ✆ 928 249919. *Email* administration@clubmaritimovaradero.es www.clubmaritimovaradero.es. Visiting yachtsmen can become temporary members on payment of around €20 per week.

Banks Many throughout the city, plus hundreds of cash dispensers but, strangely enough, no cash machine in the marina itself. The nearest is across the road from the main entrance.

Shops/provisioning Two minimarkets in the marina complex, one at the southwest corner of the marina, open 0800–2200 daily, and the other behind the fuel berth, open 0800–2000 Monday to Saturday, 0900–1300 Sundays and holidays (though closed on the Sunday prior to the ARC departure while a party is held). Both stock bread, fruit and other perishables, as well as other day-to-day needs.

The closest real supermarket is the Hiperdino on Calle Manuel Gonzalez Martin (leave the marina via the ramp at the northern end, cross the main road at the second set of traffic lights and continue west for three blocks). (More than €60 and delivery is free.)

For major storing it may be worth visiting Carrefour in Centro Comercial Las Arenas at the far end of Las Canteras beach, a pleasant 3km walk north from the marina (or catch the No.17 bus at the stop just to the south of the steps near the tunnel). They charge €5 to deliver, about the same as a taxi. Alternatively, about 10km south of the city, near the junction of the GC1 and GC3, is the new El Mirador shopping centre with a variety of shops including a good supermarket. For upmarket shopping, visit El Corte Inglés on Avenida Mesa y Lopez in the city centre just north of the marina. Almost everything is said to be available in its supermarket ... at a price.

Produce market Two – one on Calle Nestor de la Torre in the old part of the city, the other on Calle Albareda near the commercial harbour, with a fish market behind. The former is highly recommended but only open from 0800–1400 weekdays. Some of the stallholders speak English and at least one (on the top floor) will deliver to the marina.

Cafés, restaurants & hotels A growing choice of cafés and restaurants are to be found in the marina complex. Particularly recommended is the Embarcadero Restaurant, in the same building as the *Club Marítimo Varadero*, which serves excellent food and is open to all. Further afield, the city abounds with restaurants and hotels at all levels.

Medical services Two main hospitals in the city, as well as many health centres and clinics. The one on the narrow road past the entrance to Hiperdino is said to provide free treatment to EU citizens on production of an EHIC (European Health Insurance Card) and passport.

Communications

Post office Several in the city, including one on the 6th floor of the El Corte Ingles supermarket (with stamps available from the tobacconist on the ground floor).

Mailing address Oficina del Puerto, Calle Joaquín Blanco Torrent s/n, 35005 – Las Palmas de Gran Canaria, Islas Canarias, Spain.

Telephones Several around in the marina area, including on the fuel dock.

Internet access Wi-Fi finally became functional throughout the marina in early 2011. At the time of writing it remains free, though a password must be obtained from the office, but a small daily charge may be introduced. Most of the cafés which line the west side of the marina offer free Wi-Fi to customers, and there are several cybercafés in the city.

Car hire Numerous companies in the city and at the airport.

Taxis Readily available.

Buses Fast services to all parts of the island.

Ferries Regular ferries to/from all the islands other than La Gomera, as well as Madeira and the Iberian peninsula.

Air services The airport, which handles inter-island and European flights, is 19km south of the harbour.

Taliarte

27°59'·32N 15°22'·13W (breakwater head)

Waypoint
⊕C23 – 27°59'·7N 15°20'·8W (1M NE of Pta Melenara)

Lights
2807·5 **Punta Melenara** Fl(2)WR.12s32m12M
270°-W-152°-R-270° White tower 17m
Breakwater Fl.G.5s11m3M
White tower, green bands 4m
West mole (unlit as of November 2010)
White tower, red bands 3m

Marine farm
A marine farm, marked by four yellow pillar buoys with × topmarks, all Fl.Y.3M, lies south of Taliarte, centred on 27°58'·8N 15°22'·3W. It extends some 550m north/south and 400m east/west.

Harbour Communications
Port Captain ✆ 928 372144

Research centre and fishing harbour

Taliarte (pronounced *Taliart'eh*) is home to the Canary Institute of Marine Sciences (*Instituto Canario de Ciencias Marinas* or *ICCM*) as well as various commercial companies engaged in marine research. Located just south of Punta Melenara, it remains primarily a fishing harbour occupied by smallcraft on moorings and four short pontoons, all protected by a high concrete wall which gives good protection. A short west mole runs out from the shore opposite the breakwater head and the entrance faces southwest towards Punta de Salinetas.

There are no facilities for visiting yachts, though it might be possible to lie alongside the breakwater for a short period, or to anchor just outside in 7–10m. The *Cofradía de Pescadores* (fishermen's confederation) operates a 50-tonne capacity travel-lift which is sometimes used by local yachts, but transport would be necessary as there are no facilities on site.

The small fishing harbour at Taliarte, looking a little north of west

Puerto de Salinetas

27°58'·52N 15°22'·59W (breakwater head)

Plans
Admiralty *1856* (1:75,000 & 1:15,00)

Lights
Breakwater, extreme SW
Fl.G.4s15m3M Metal post 13m
Note Two pairs of leading lights mark the approach, operating only when required

Marine farms
Two marine farms lie off Puerto de Salinetas, one to the northeast centred on 27°58'·7N 15°22'·2W and marked by four yellow pillar buoys with × topmarks, all Fl.Y.3M, and one to the southeast centred on 27°57'·7N 15°22'·5W and marked by four yellow pillar buoys with × topmarks, all Fl.Y.5M.

Commercial quay

Despite being no more than a single mole alongside which commercial ships discharge, Puerto de Salinetas is said to handle more than a million tonnes of cargo a year. An industrial complex stands on the headland to the north.

The single quay which comprises Puerto de Salinetas

Bahía de Gando

27°55'·9N 15°21'·5W (Punta de Gando)

Waypoint
⊕C24 – 27°56'·6N 15°20'·6W (1M NE of Punta de Gando)

Lights
2810·5 **Peninsula de Gando**
Oc.R.5s 225°-vis-260°

Marine farm
A marine farm, marked by four yellow pillar buoys with × topmarks, all Fl.Y.5s3M, lies in the Bahía de Gando centred on 27°53'·9N 15°22'·7W.

Military area close to airport

This previously useful anchorage, well sheltered from the prevailing winds (though very strong gusts may be encountered around the headland), has for some years been a military area where anchoring is prohibited – and likely to be enforced by heavily armed military police. It lies very close to the island's airport and there is at least one pipeline in the northern part of the bay, its end marked by an unlit buoy.

Care must be taken when on passage past the headland to avoid Baja de Gando, lying 0·5M offshore and with a least depth of 0·2m.

Bahía de Arinaga

27°51'·3N 15°23'·66W (molehead)

Waypoint
⊕C25 – 27°51'·7N 15°21'·7W (1M E of Pta Arinaga)

Lights
2812 **Punta Arinaga** Fl(3)WR.10s46m16M
012°-R-052°-W-172°-R-212°-W 012°
White tower, red bands 13m

Possible short-term anchorage

Technically, both anchoring and fishing are prohibited in the area south of Punta Arinaga (pronounced *By'eeah de Arinah'gah*). However, it is quite possible that temporary anchorage could be found in 4–5m close south or west of the short mole without anyone appearing to object. There are restaurants and shops ashore.

Puerto de Arinaga

27°50'·53N 15°23'·97W (breakwater head)

Lights
2812·3 **Puerto de Arinaga, Breakwater**
Fl.G.5s5M Green column 8m
2812·4 **Breakwater angle**
Fl(3)5s3M East cardinal post, ♦ topmark, 3m

Commercial harbour closed to visitors

In 2004 work started on a commercial harbour less than a mile south of Punta Arinaga. Effectively finished by October 2006 – by which time it was said to have absorbed more than €8 million of EU funds despite the Canaries being located outside the EU's physical area – Puerto de Arinaga (pronounced *Pwerto de Arinah'gah*) is now admitted to be something of a white elephant. It had apparently been intended that a good proportion of the shipping currently using Las Palmas would be diverted to the new harbour, but as of early 2011 this had not happened, perhaps partly due to the poor roads and general lack of infrastructure.

The harbour comprises a southeast-running breakwater some 800m in length with a 400m right-angled head, the inner quayside and Ro-Ro ferry berth protected by 10m concrete walls. It is open to the south, though some shelter is offered by Punta Gaviota. Guards man the port gates and unauthorised access from landward is prohibited.

Yachts have occasionally made use of its shelter for overnight anchorage, taking care to keep well out of the way of possible shipping movements. Holding is said to be good in about 15m over sand and rock. A brief stop appears to be tolerated and, with no facilities whatsoever, there seems little point in tarrying. A large windfarm lies close southwest of the harbour.

Puerto de Arinaga from the southeast

Barranco Tirajana

27°47'·96N 15°26'·03W (southeast molehead)

Waypoint
⊕C26 – 27°47'·9N 15°24'·6W (1M SE of Pta de Tenefé)

Lights
2812·5 **Molehead** Q(6)+LFl.15s7m5M
South cardinal post, ▼ topmark 4m
buoy **Outfall buoy** Q(6)+LFl.15s3M
South cardinal buoy, ▼ topmark

Not a harbour at all...

Although from a distance the hooked mole appears to contain a harbour, in fact it merely provides cooling water for the adjacent power station.

Castillo del Romeral

27°47'·68N 15°27'·83W (molehead)

Lights
Breakwater
Green light on white column
Note As of November 2010 the characteristics remained unlisted

Marine farm
Two marine farms lie southwest of Castillo del Romeral, one centred on 27°46'·4N 15°28'·4W (though extending from 27°46'·1N to 27°46'·6N and 15°28'·1W to 15°28'·6W) and marked by four yellow pillar buoys with × topmarks, all Fl(4)Y.10s3M; the other centred on 27°46'N 15°30'W and marked by four yellow pillar buoys with × topmarks, all Fl(5)Y.15s3M.

Small, very basic, fishing harbour

Simple even by Canarian standards, the single hooked breakwater at Castillo del Romeral some 1·5M west of Punta de Tenefé shelters a few small fishing boats and local smallcraft from the prevailing northeasterlies. Improvements have long been on the cards, but as of late 2010 had yet to materialise. Some protection would be found if wishing to anchor, though depths and quality of holding are not known. The town and close northeast has grown considerably in recent years, with the usual range of shops, cafés and restaurants following close behind.

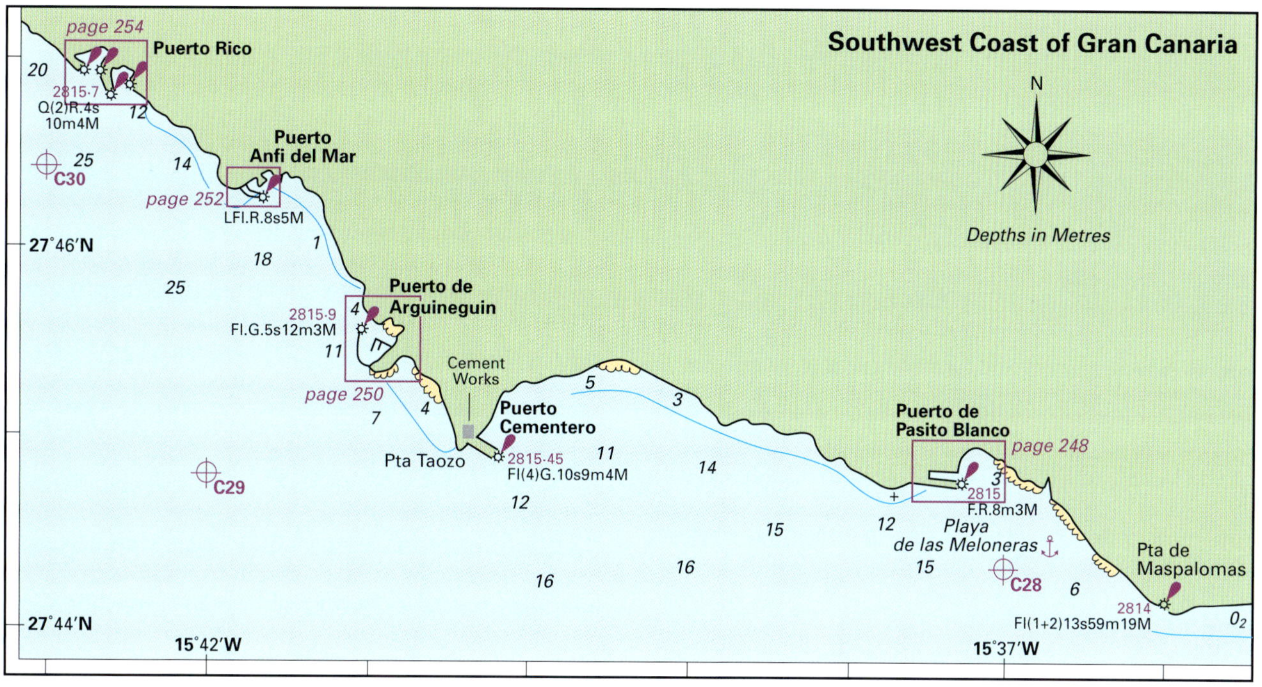

Playa de las Meloneras

27°44′·6N 15°36′·8W & 27°44′·8N 15°36′·2W (anchorages)

Lights

2814 **Punta de Maspalomas (Punta Morro Colchas)**
Fl(1+2)13s59m19M 251·5°-vis-093°
Conical grey tower, white lantern 56m

Anchorage off a sandy beach

A sandy beach protected to the east by Punta de Maspalomas and less than 1M southeast of Puerto de Pasito Blanco, Playa de las Meloneras (pronounced *Ply'a de las Melonerass*) offers daytime anchorage in 5m over sand – work in carefully as parts of the beach have off-lying rocks. For some reason this beach usually seems to escape the worst of the swell, though there can be enough surf to make landing by dinghy difficult. More shelter may be found in the bay close east of the entrance to Puerto de Pasito Blanco in 4–5m over sand, particularly in any hint of a westerly swell. Dinghies may be taken into the marina and left at the fuel berth for short periods while visiting the minimarket. There is no charge for anchoring.

Looking north across the entrance to the reception and fuel berths at Puerto de Pasito Blanco

Puerto de Pasito Blanco

27°44′·74N 15°37′·27W (breakwater head)

Waypoint

⊕C28 – 27°44′·3N 15°37′W (0·5M SSE of Puerto de Pasito Blanco)

Plans

Spanish *D210* (1:10,000)

Lights

2814 **Punta de Maspalomas (Punta Morro Colchas)**
Fl(1+2)13s 59m19M 251·5°-vis-093°
Conical grey tower, white lantern 56m
2815 **Breakwater**
F.R.8m3M Red metal post 3m
2815·2 **Breakwater spur**
Q(2)R.4s3m3M Red metal post 3m
2815·22 **Reception mole**
Fl.G.3s3m3M Green metal post 3m

Harbour Communications

Clube de Yates Pasito Blanco ✆ 928 142194
Fax 928 142546 *Email* info@pasitoblanco.com
www.pasitoblanco.com (0800–1800 weekdays, 0900–1300 Saturday) VHF Ch 12 (24 hours)

Small, secure, private marina

Pasito Blanco, run by *El Club de Yates de Pasito Blanco*, is a secluded and secure marina in peaceful if rather isolated surroundings, surrounded by privately-owned (not hotel or timeshare) bungalows and houses, no two the same and apparently nearly all second homes of people from Las Palmas or mainland Spain. Though very much a private concern, visiting yachts are made welcome if space is available, though longer visits are preferred to short – it is an excellent place to leave a boat while returning home or travelling elsewhere. Prior booking is essential, as is a hire car or other transport. The marina is generally secure from bad weather, although damage has occasionally been suffered in

III. THE CANARY ISLANDS

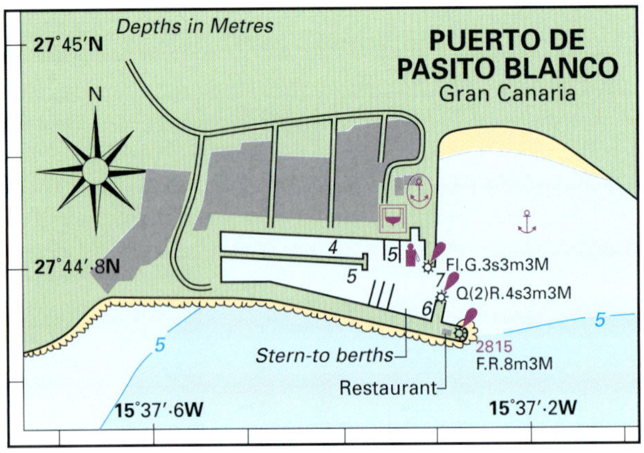

major storms. In 2010 it received the EU 'Blue Flag', awarded to marinas with a particularly good record for water quality and general cleanliness – among the many other facilities there is a pump-out station for holding tanks. The local birdlife certainly seems to approve, with terns diving for fish in the marina and a hoopoe seen ashore.

Pasito Blanco has a particularly good website, in Spanish, English and German, which features – among such useful information as berthing and boatyard rates – an interesting sequence of aerial photographs showing its development since 1974. Maintenance standards have always been so high, however, that it is very hard indeed to believe that Pasito Blanco is one of the oldest marinas in the Canaries.

Approach

Punta de Maspalomas, the 'Point of More Pigeons', is the southernmost point of Gran Canaria. Large flocks of holidaymakers have replaced the pigeons east of the point which is largely made up of impressive sand dunes, much used in the past as a desert film set.

The lighthouse is conspicuous on the western side of the point. If approaching Pasito Blanco from the east keep well offshore to avoid shallows on the point and, when the lighthouse is abeam to starboard, the breakwater will be seen 1·5M up the coast.

Approaching from the west, the cement works on Punta Taozo near Arguineguín are unmistakable. Pasito Blanco lies 3M beyond.

Entrance and berthing

The entrance faces east, and should be approached on a northerly heading to avoid inshore dangers. On entry the reception berth will be seen to starboard by the travel-lift and fuel berth. Outside office hours secure to the reception berth and await instructions. The boatyard gate is locked overnight, confining night time arrivals to that area.

There are 388 berths in total, of which 10% are reserved for yachts in transit. The vast majority are for craft of under 8m or so, but there is space for about 60 boats in the 10–13m range on pontoons, and 14 for larger vessels near the end of the breakwater. One or two yachts of up to 40m LOA and 4·5m draught can be accommodated, and

Puerto de Pasito Blanco looking slightly north of west. Yachts may find good anchorage off the beach outside the marina's east mole *Puerto de Pasito Blanco*

certainly depth would not be a limiting factor with 7m in entrance, 6m at the larger berths and 5m at the yacht pontoons. All berths are bow or stern-to with pick-up lines.

As mentioned previously, although space is occasionally found for a couple of days at short notice, most foreign yachts stay – sometimes laid up ashore – for several months, in which case prior booking, preferably well in advance, is essential. (Emails typically receive immediate replies in excellent English, not the case in all Canarian marinas.)

Security throughout the entire 'gated community' is excellent, from the manned barrier at the single entrance to the round-the-clock security patrols by polite, smartly uniformed guards who appear to be more than usually alert.

Brief details of the anchorage east of the harbour will be found under Playa de las Meloneras, page 247.

Formalities

Visit the marina office at the rear of the boatyard, taking ship's papers, passports and evidence of insurance. There are normally two or three people in the office, at least one of whom speaks English.

Charges

Berthing fees are calculated on a length x beam basis. In 2011 this was set at €0.38 per m^2 including tax at 5%, but not including water and electricity, which are metered. Discounts are available for longer stays if booked in advance. A 50% deposit is required when booking, but will be refunded if plans change.

Facilities

Boatyard Fair-sized, very tidy boatyard where DIY work and living aboard are permitted (though apartments are available to rent if carrying out major work) and expert help is available if required. Current prices for all boatyard services will be found on the marina's website, together with details of five companies or individuals offering a range of services including general repairs and maintenance, osmosis treatment and painting/antifouling.

Travel-lift 64-tonne capacity hoist. Boats are shored up using wooden 'box' props, but plenty of them.

Diving services A diver is available for both emergency work and hull clearning – enquire at the marina office.

Engineers Rep. Navales Cazorla SL ✆ /*Fax* 928 721175, 660 403512 *Email* rep.navales.cazorla@hotmail.com www.tallercazorla.net has its workshop in the boatyard area (in addition to premises in Las Palmas) and is run by two brothers, one a transatlantic skipper who speaks some English. The company will handle most engineering problems including gearbox, transmission, steering system etc.

Jorge Ramos ✆ 928 142368, *Fax* 928 141206, *Email* Jorgeramosnav@hotmail.com also works from the boatyard, handling both engineering and general repair/maintenance tasks.

Sail repairs Alisios Sailing Center SL is located in Las Palmas, but do work at Pasito Blanco when required.

Chandlery Not on site, but transport may be available to Náutica Motoracer in Puerto de Arguineguín. Alternatively the office staff will contact retailers in Las Palmas.

Water To all berths.

Showers Two well-kept shower blocks.

Electricity 220v throughout the marina, with 380v available at the larger berths.

Launderette Next to the marina office, with two washers but no dryers.

Fuel Next to the reception berth, available 0800–1800 daily.

Bottled gas Camping Gaz exchanges are available at the marina office, but as of 2011 the situation regarding refilling other cylinders remained uncertain – see page 191.

Weather forecast Posted daily at the marina office.

Banks No bank or cash dispenser at the marina.

Shops/provisioning Small but well-stocked minimarket just outside the boatyard gates, sufficient to supply daily needs but not to stock-up for a long trip. Free transport is provided to the supermarkets in Arguineguín.

Cafés & restaurants After many years with no onsite catering at all, in early 2011 the La Punta Yacht Club – complete with restaurant, sunbeds and enclosed swimming area – opened at the end of the main breakwater.

Communications

Post office No, though there is a post box outside the minimarket.

Mailing address Club de Yates Pasito Blanco, Ctra GC - 500, Puerto Deportivo Pasito Blanco, Edif. Oficinas, 35106 San Bartolomé de Tirajana, Gran Canaria, Islas Canarias, Spain.

Telephone Outside the boatyard gates.

Internet access Wi-Fi is available throughout the marina on a pay-to-use basis.

Car hire Can be arranged through the marina office

Buses Frequent service along the main road to Playa del Inglés/San Agustín and beyond.

The La Punta Yacht Club, aptly described as the marina's 'chill-out area', opened in early 2011
Puerto de Pasito Blanco

Puerto Cementero, Punta Taozo

27°44′·89N 15°40′·14W (breakwater head)

Plans
Spanish *6100* (1:12,500)

Lights
2815·45 **Breakwater** Fl(4)G.10s9m4M
Metal structure 4m
2815·4 **Inner mole** Q(2)R.6s11m6M
White column, red bands 5m

Commercial harbour

Just what it sounds like – a commercial harbour serving a cement works, and no place for yachts. The dusty grey buildings, silos and chimneys are conspicuous from all directions and quite unmistakable.

Puerto de Arguineguín

27°45′·52N 15°41′·19W (breakwater head)

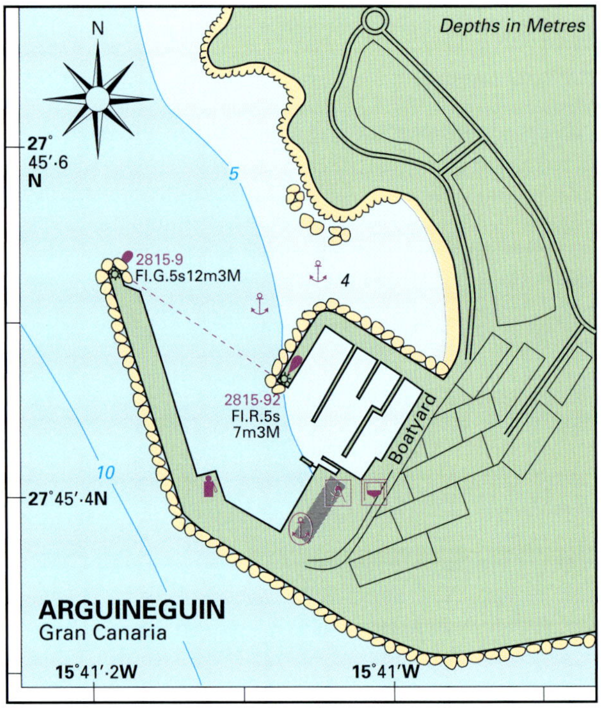

Waypoint

⊕C29 – 27°44′·8N 15°42′W (1M SW of Puerto de Arguineguín)

Plans
Spanish *6100* (1:12,500), *D210* (1:10,000)

Lights
2815·9 **Breakwater** Fl.G.5s12m3M
Green tower, white band 5m
2815·92 **Inner Mole** Fl.R.5s7m3M
Red tower, white band 5m

Harbour Communications
Port Captain ✆ 928 3736441 VHF Ch 10, 16 (0800–1500 weekdays only)

Anchorage off fishing harbour

A small but busy fishing harbour which still retains some vestige of its original character, Puerto de Arguineguín (pronounced *Pwerto de Arg'in'egg'in*) has changed remarkably little over the past two decades. Plans for a marina in the bay north east of the harbour were drawn up in the 1990s, and though yet to materialise are apparently revisited from time to time.

In contrast to the many tourist resorts on the southwest coast of Gran Canaria, Arguineguín retains a range of 'high street' style shops aimed at – and priced for – local people rather than tourists.

Approach and entrance

The cement works on Punta Taozo are very conspicuous from offshore, with Puerto de Arguineguín lying 0·5M to the northwest. The mountainous region of Gran Canaria extends to the west, with the coast running northwest from Arguineguín to Punta de la Aldea lined with high cliffs split in places by steep-sided valleys. The long

Puerto de Arguineguín seen from the northwest. Lying in the wind shadow of Gran Canaria, a sea breeze often blows onshore during the day

The inner harbour at Puerto de Arguineguín, with the travel-lift at left and the boatyard at right

breakwater runs out to the northwest with a shorter, L-shaped quay opposite. Although the harbour is no longer used by ferries there is a fair amount of fishing boat traffic – enter cautiously, keeping a watchful eye out for buoys marking fish traps.

Berthing

The three pontoons on the east side of the harbour are fully occupied by local smallcraft. A few yachts are normally permitted to raft up on the outer section of the breakwater, but lengthy stays are not encouraged. There is often considerable surge in the harbour, and it may well prove more comfortable to anchor.

Anchorage

In normal conditions it is possible to anchor north of the inner mole in about 4m over rock. A patch of sand large enough for two or three boats has been reported as surrounding the western anchor symbol on the harbour plan. This gives much better holding than the surrounding rock, where holding is poor. Up to six yachts can also lie stern-to the inner mole, with an anchor out to the northwest and a sternline ashore, which has the advantage of holding the bow into any swell. Should this become serious, however, it will be necessary to vacate the anchorage and even in windless and apparently flat conditions quite a bit of surge can be anticipated. There are a few mooring buoys in the anchorage area, but all are private.

A reef with only 0·8m at LWS extends some 40m northeastwards from the mole almost opposite the root of the outer pontoon, and the southern quarter of the beach is also rocky at low tide. The entire length of the beach is roped off with the usual string of yellow buoys.

Dinghies can be left on the short pontoon close south of the travel-hoist dock. This is watched over by security guards who may wish to see the passports of those coming and going.

Formalities

The harbour is among those run by *Puertos de Canarias* – see Booking berths in *Puertos de Canarias* harbours, page 189 – but in practice this does not always seem to guarantee space and luck appears to play a major role. The harbour office is at the southwest corner of the large building on the quay, which also houses the *Cofradía de Pescadores* offices and restaurant as well as the Náutica Motoracer chandlery (see Facilities, below).

The harbourmaster is pleasant and speaks some English, and in late 2010 did not require visiting skippers to present ship's papers and passports at his office. His jurisdiction ends at a line between the end of the breakwater and the end of the inner mole, outside which the *Guardia Civil* have sway.

Charges

If space to lie alongside is available it is a bargain, Arguineguín levying some of the lowest fees in the entire Canaries. It is calculated on a length x beam basis and in 2010 was set at €0.15 per m^2, including 5% tax and water, if available. There is no charge for anchoring.

Facilities

Boatyard Run by the *Cofradía de Pescadores* (fishermen's confederation), though see also Náutica Motoracer, below. Both DIY and owners living aboard are permitted by the *Cofradía*, though the latter is discouraged by Náutica Motoracer, who have seven allocated slots in the yard and will organise and oversee hauling if they are to carry out the work while ashore. The chandlery side of the business is agent for Hempel Paints, and topside spraying is among the services on offer.

In 2010 a 12m yacht was charged just over €170 for lifting, one week ashore and relaunching, which included 5% tax. Round-the-clock security is provided, but no toilets or showers.

Travel-lift Capacity 70 tonnes.

Engineers & electronics Náutica Motoracer are Yamaha dealers and agents for Mercury. They can organise engineering, welding in stainless steel and aluminium (contracting out to a local machine shop if necessary), and also have electronics experts available.

Sail repairs Náutica Motoracer handle sail repairs and general canvaswork.

Chandlery Náutica Motoracer ✆ 928 736419 *Fax* 928 736782, 646 896028 *Email* info@automotoracer.com www.automotoracer.com (open 0900–1400,

III. THE CANARY ISLANDS

1600–1900 weekdays, 1100–1400 Saturday) will be found at the north end of the large building which also houses the harbour authority and *Cofradía de Pescadores* offices, with workshops below and chandlery above.

It is a family-run business owned and managed by Barrie Simpson, a motorcycle enthusiast who originally intended to meet the needs of fellow bikers, plus quadbike, speedboat and jetski enthusiasts. The company remit has since broadened to include boats of all types, but the practical slant remains, including in the chandlery on offer – which includes a useful range of safety equipment, small electronics, Hempel paint, etc.

Water Taps on the breakwater and inner mole.

Showers No showers in the entire harbour area, though there are public toilets in the large building on the quay.

Launderette In the town.

Fuel Fuel pumps have been installed near the root of the main breakwater, apparently happy to serve yachts as well as fishing boats. Payment must be made in cash.

Bottled gas Camping Gaz exchanges at the hardware store in town.

Banks Several, with cash dispensers.

Shops/provisioning Several large supermarkets and a good range of other shops.

Produce market Open air market on Tuesdays.

Restaurants & hotels Many nearby.

Medical services Medical centre in the northwest of the town.

Communications

Post office In the town.

Telephones On the quay and in the town.

Internet access There is believed to be at least one cybercafé in the town.

Car hire & taxis Readily available.

Buses Bus service along the coast between Puerto Rico and Maspalomas/San Agustín, and on to Las Palmas.

Puerto Anfi del Mar

27°46'·19N 15°41'·76W (molehead)

Plans
Spanish *D210* (1:10,000)

Lights
Southwest mole
LFl.R.8s5M Wooden post 4m
Southwest inner mole
F.R.3M Wooden post 4m
Artificial island, south corner
Iso.G.2s3M Green post

Harbour Communications
Marina Anfi del Mar ☎ */Fax* 928 150120, 639 021202
Email marina@anfi.es VHF Ch 09 (0900–2000 daily)

Immaculate marina, but very small

During the 1990s a new timeshare resort was built against a spectacular sandstone cliff almost equidistant between Puerto de Arguineguín and Puerto Rico. Although labelled Patalavaca on some older maps and occasionally referred to by local people as Puerto de la Balita (Punta de la Balita lies just to the west), to visitors it is known as Anfi del Mar.

A southwestern breakwater and a short inner mole shelter a small but beautifully-kept marina surrounded by landscaped grounds, with a wide beach of imported white sand close by to the northeast. The entrance faces southeast and the breakwater would appear to give good protection other than from strong southeasterlies. Although most of the 93 berths are reserved for owners of timeshare apartments, space for a short-term visitor may sometimes be available but advance reservation is essential – see Formalities, opposite. The harbourmaster's description of the marina as '*muy tranquillo*' seems entirely accurate.

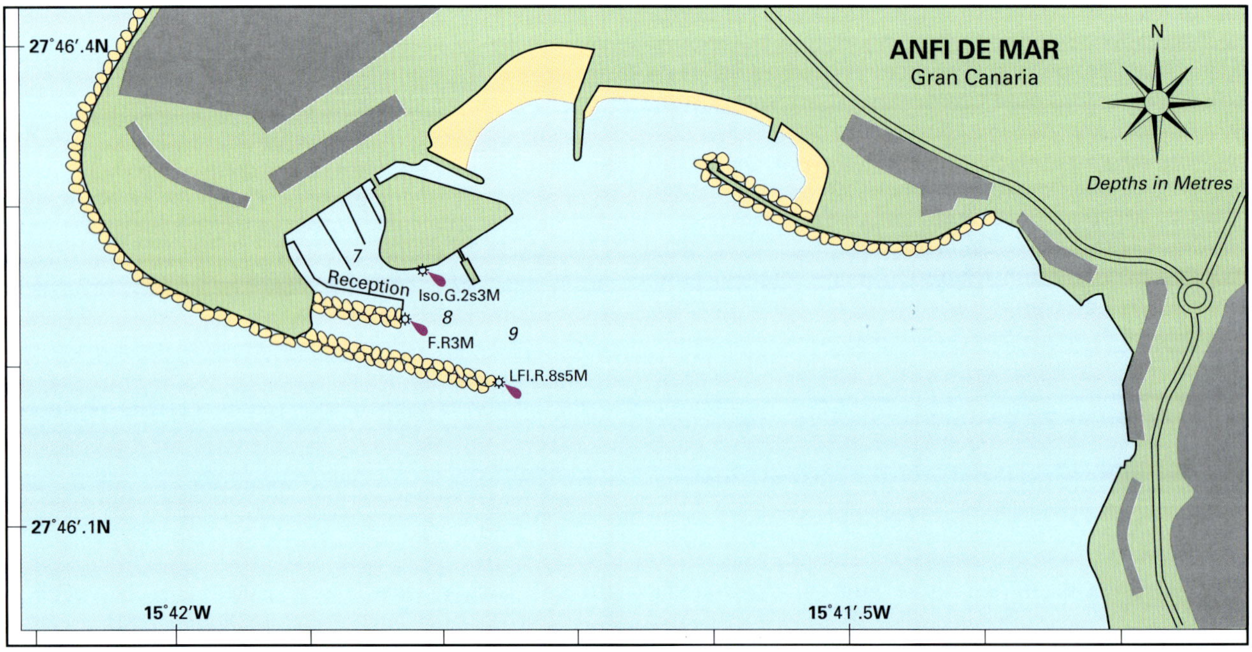

Looking southeast over the well-kept resort complex at Puerto Anfi del Mar

Approach

As with Puerto de Arguineguín, the most unmistakeable landmark in the vicinity is the cement works on Punta Taozo a mile or so south, though the high-rise buildings of Anfi del Mar itself, backed by even taller orange cliffs, would be hard to miss. The approach is straightforward.

Entrance and berthing

On rounding the breakwater the 'island', with its angled pontoon, will be seen ahead. Ignoring this, secure to the pontoon which parallels the inner port hand mole – as the marina should not be entered without prior contact, the harbourmaster is likely to be on hand to greet new arrivals. About 9m should be found in the entrance, with 7–8m at the reception berth. The entire marina is notably well-kept and security is excellent.

Anchorage

The usual line of yellow floats closes off the entire beach area, but reasonable holding over sand and rock in about 6m is to be found a little further south. Shelter is good in most conditions, though the area would become untenable in southerly or southeasterly winds. The anchorage is under the jurisdiction of the local *Guardia Civil* rather than the resort, but they are said to take little interest and as of 2010 there was no charge.

Dinghies may be left for short periods at the 'island' pontoon – perhaps while visiting the supermarket or a restaurant – but this is a concession which should not be abused.

Formalities and charges

Visit the marina office at the root of the inner breakwater. When visited in late 2010 the harbourmaster was pleasant and helpful, and spoke good English. The overnight berthing fee in 2011 for a monohull of 10–12m was €20–81, or €27.50 for 12–15m, including water, electricity and 5% tax.

Facilities

Boatyard No boatyard facilities in place or anticipated.
Water On the pontoons.
Electricity On the pontoons.
Fuel No fuel available.
Banks Not as such, but several cash dispensers in the resort, including one next to the supermarket.
Shops/provisioning Well stocked (though expensive) supermarket on the ground floor of the resort building overlooking the marina. More varied (and cheaper) shopping in Puerto de Arguineguín.
Cafés & restaurants Many in the resort complex.

Communications

Telephones Near the supermarket.
Car hire & taxis Can be arranged via the reception desk.
Buses Bus service along the main road – a steep walk up from the marina – to Puerto Rico, Maspalomas/San Agustín etc.

Most of Puerto Anfi del Mar's 93 berths are occupied on a long-term basis, but space may sometimes be available for a visiting yacht

III. THE CANARY ISLANDS

Puerto Rico

27°46'·8N 15°42'·67W (Yacht harbour west breakwater head)

Waypoint

⊕C30 – 27°46'·4N 15°43'W (0·5M SW of Puerto Rico)

Plans

Spanish *D210* (1:10,000)

Lights

Yacht harbour (to east)

2815·7 **West breakwater**
Q(2)R.4s10m4M Red tower 4m

2815·6 **East mole**
F.G.10m4M Green tower 3m

Smallcraft harbour (to west)

2815·82 **West mole**
F.R.10m5M Red tower 4m

2815·8 **East mole**
Fl.G.3s5m4M Green tower 4m

Harbour Communications

Puerto Deportivo Puerto Rico ✆ 928 561141, 561143
Fax 928 561632 *Email* pricomarina@puertoricosa.com
www.puertoricosa.com/en/puerto VHF Ch 08, 16
(0800–0700 daily – the office is only closed during the changeover period)

Large double harbour in tourist resort

Puerto Rico (pronounced *Pwerto Reeko*) is effectively two separate harbours lying side-by-side but not interconnected. The western – Puerto de Escala – is reserved for tourist ferries and local smallcraft, while both resident and visiting yachts berth to the east in Puerto Base. The town of Puerto Rico is a thriving holiday resort popular with tourists from northern Europe, and both parts of the harbour are owned by the same company. They clearly got it right first time, as other than improved facilities and some additional berths, little has changed in Puerto Base since the first edition of this book was researched in 1987. Though pleasantly quiet during the week, loud music continuing into the small hours has been reported at weekends.

Approach

The most unmistakable landmark is the cement works on Punta Taozo 2·5M to the south. On close approach, the walls of the valley in which Puerto Rico lies are seen to be covered with white apartment blocks. These extend southeast of the port and one must close the shore to identify the marina entrance.

Entrance and berthing

A 200m breakwater running southeast separates the western (smallcraft) harbour and bathing beach from the yacht marina to the east. Once identified, the red tower on the end of the breakwater can be closed, but must not be confused with the similar tower on the western harbour molehead. The entrance to the eastern harbour, Puerto Base, opens to the southeast, with the reception/fuel berth immediately to port on entry.

Puerto Base now contains 534 berths, including 68 for yachts of 10–12m, 70 for 12–15m and 21 able to

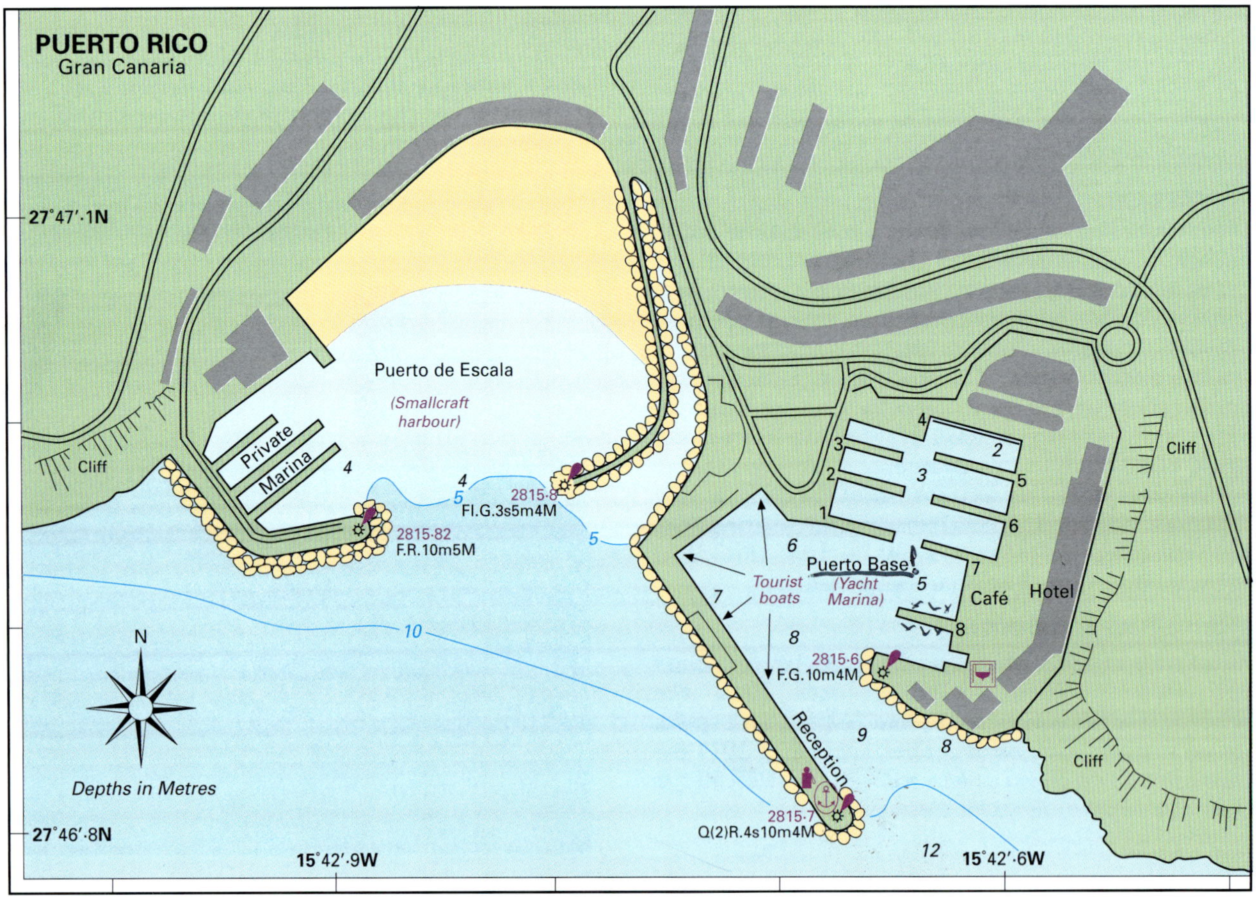

The double harbour at Puerto Rico seen from the northwest

take more than 15m LOA. It may be possible for a single yacht of up to 25m to lie alongside the breakwater, but this is mainly occupied by tourist boats and contact with the office several weeks in advance of arrival is essential. Space can generally be found for a yacht of more moderate size, other than in the weeks preceding the ARC departure, but booking three or four weeks before arrival is preferred. The system changes in November, when bookings are only taken up to five days in advance. No deposit is required.

Berthing is all bow or stern-to with pick-up lines, and if wind and swell are strong from the southern quadrant conditions – and particularly berthing itself – can become challenging. Visiting yachts are normally berthed on Pontoon 8, close to the boatyard but quite a long walk from almost everything else. There are no security gates to the pontoons, though the area is patrolled by the usual uniformed guards.

Formalities and charges

Ship's papers, passports and evidence of insurance should be taken to the harbour office, most conveniently done while still at the reception berth. It is claimed to manned at all times other than during the 0700–0800 'change over' period. The staff are helpful and several speak good English.

The berthing fee is calculated on a length x beam basis and in 2010 was set at €0.46 per m^2. This included tax at 5%, but not water and electricity which are both metered. Discounts are available for longer stays. Visitors who hire cars must also pay for parking.

Facilities

Boatyard Good-sized, secure yard, though the large undercover work area no longer exists. Time ashore should be arranged via the marina office, but most services are provided by small onsite companies or

Looking northeast across the yacht harbour at Puerto Rico, with the boatyard and travel-lift at far right

The interior of Puerto Rico's yacht harbour looking a little south of west

individuals. The anonymous GRP workshop next to Seilas (see Chandlery, below) is recommended locally. In late 2010 Washington Servicios Náuticos, ✆ 615 484705, handled GRP repairs, osmosis treatment and painting, and Alejandro Artiles García ✆ 696 227544 *Email* alejandroartilesg@hotmail.com offered general maintenance services, but it would best to ask around locally.

The entrance to Puerto Rico's eastern or yacht harbour, with Punta de la Balita beyond and Puerto de Arguineguín and the towers of Puerto Cementero just visible in the distance

Travel-lift Capacity 35 tonnes, with props and a ladder provided and a pressure washer available for hire. Arrange via the marina office.

Engineers & electronics Ask at Seilas (see Chandlery, below). Albert Strik ✆ 659 405888 *Email* albert@infomogan.com advertises his services for refrigeration and air conditioning.

Sailmaker/repairs In November 2010 a lady sailmaker had recently taken premises in the boatyard area, but it was not possible to obtain further details.

Liferaft servicing Can be arranged via Seilas (see Chandlery, below), who can also arrange for EPIRBs to be checked and certified.

Chandlery Although not long established when visited in late 2010, Seilas ✆ /*Fax* 928 561769 *Email* enrique@seilas.es, mai_ly@seilas.es www.seilas.es, (open 0830–1800 weekdays, 1000–1300 Saturday) shows great promise. Owners Enrique and Mai Ly (who grew up in Norway) both speak excellent English as well as Scandinavian languages, Dutch and some German. In addition to being island agents for Harken and Spinlock they pack a surprisingly wide range of other chandlery into a small space and are very happy to order anything not to hand (air freight from mainland Europe normally takes 48 hours or less, but does not come cheap). If moving on to another harbour in Gran Canaria they are willing to deliver by road.

Charts Seilas stocks Imray books and charts.

Water On the pontoons.

Showers Four blocks around Puerto Base. Showers are free, but entry needs a key for which a deposit is required.

Launderettes Several in the tourist resort plus one in the boatyard.

Electricity 220v to all berths, with 380v in some areas.

Fuel Diesel and petrol from pumps near the end of the breakwater, available 0800–1645 daily.

Bottled gas Camping Gaz exchanges at Seilas, but currently no provision for getting cylinders refilled.
Weather forecast Posted daily at the harbour office.
Banks In the tourist resort, with several cash dispensers in the harbour area.
Shops/provisioning Supermarkets and general shopping in the tourist resport, though a wider choice will be found in Arguineguín.
Cafés, restaurants & hotels A wide choice, many overlooking the marina. Crews berthed on Pontoon 8 may find the nearby café particularly convenient.
Medical services The British Medical Clinic (✆ 928 560016) and Centro Médico Vulcano (✆ 928 560428, 549 281543) both have English-speaking staff and a wide range of services.

Communications

Post office In the tourist complex.
Mailing address Torre de Control, Puerto Deportivo Puerto Rico, Avda Juan Diaz Rodrigues s/n, Mogán 35130, Gran Canaria, Islas Canarias, Spain.
Telephones Dotted around the marina complex.
Internet access There is no Wi-Fi in or around the marina, though there are several cybercafés in the tourist resort, some of which offer Wi-Fi as an alternative to their own computers.
Car hire & taxis Readily available.
Buses Bus service along the coast in both directions.
Ferries Tourist ferries from the west mole of the smallcraft harbour (a fair walk from the marina) to Puerto de Arguineguín and Puerto de Mogán.

The coast between Puerto Rico and Puerto de Mogán

At present there are no particularly inviting stopping places between Puerto Rico and Puerto de Mogán, but this may change. Sailing northwest from Puerto Rico one passes a large swimming area at Playa de los Amadores, enclosed between curved arms and with the ubiquitous line of yellow buoys lying about two-thirds of the way towards the mouth. Yachts occasionally anchor in the entrance while the crew swim, but a longer stay would not be popular.

Northwest of Playa de los Amadores lies the wide Playa de Tauro, backed by a development of the same name under the auspices of the Anfi Group who also own Anfi del Mar. Although far from finished in late 2010 it will, according to company publicity, eventually include a 500-berth marina as well as two golf courses and 'an extensive range of leisure facilities'.

Continuing past Playa de Tauro one passes Playa de los Frailes and then a second, nameless indentation. Neither of these have road access or offer much in the way of shelter. Finally, about 0·5M southeast of Puerto de Mogán lies Playa del Taurito, a holiday complex set slightly back from the seafront, which appears to make up for its narrow beach with generous man-made pools.

Puerto de Mogán

27°48'·94N 15°45'·81W (breakwater head)

Waypoint

⊕C31 – 27°48'·5N 15°46'·2W (0·5M SW of Puerto de Mogán)

Plans

Spanish *6100* (1:12,500), *D210* (1:10,000)

Lights

2815·94 **Punta del Castillete** Fl.5s113m17M
Square yellow tower with stair and gallery 20m
2815·96 **Breakwater** Fl(3)R.8·5s12m3M
White truncated pyramid, three red bands 6m
2815·98 **Reception mole** Fl(2)G.7s2m4M
White truncated pyramid, three green bands 2m
buoy **Outfall** Fl(4)Y.1M Yellow buoy

Harbour Communications

Puerto de Mogán ✆ 928 565151, 565668
Fax 928 565024 *Email* servicios@puertomogan.es (0800–1500 weekdays only) VHF Ch 12 (0800–2100 daily)

Attractive, long-established marina

Puerto de Mogán (pronounced *Pwerto de Moh'ganne*) is one of the older – and therefore better-known – marinas in the Canaries, celebrating its 25th anniversary in 2011. The surrounding marina village, nicknamed 'Little Venice', has matured into an attractive, shady area through which to stroll. The many bars and restaurants overlooking the marina add much to the atmosphere while, reportedly, creating very little night-time noise. In other ways the marina is showing its age, in the bow or stern-to mooring system (there are no finger pontoons) and, in particular, in the showers and toilets which are lacking in number and, often, cleanliness. Sadly but predictably, this has a direct effect on the water quality both in the marina and in the swimming area close to the marina entrance.

Despite this, Puerto de Mogán remains very popular and its 216 berths are usually fully occupied. It is advisable to book at least four weeks in advance, though even then a berth may not be available in the high season. If a berth can be secured, Puerto de Mogán – Mogán village lies about 8km inland – is a secure marina in which to leave a yacht, whether to explore the island by car or to return home for a period. It offers protection from all normal weather conditions, though southerly winter gales have caused severe damage to the breakwater several times over the past decades. The inner section of the harbour is set aside for local fishing boats, while a small breakwater to the east protects a horseshoe-shaped bathing beach, with a row of small buoys outside.

Approach

Puerto de Mogán lies in one of the many steep-sided valleys which fissure the high cliffs between Arguineguín and Punta de Aldea. However, with low green-roofed buildings behind a high breakwater it can be difficult to to identify until close to. Approaching from the south, Puerto Rico will be

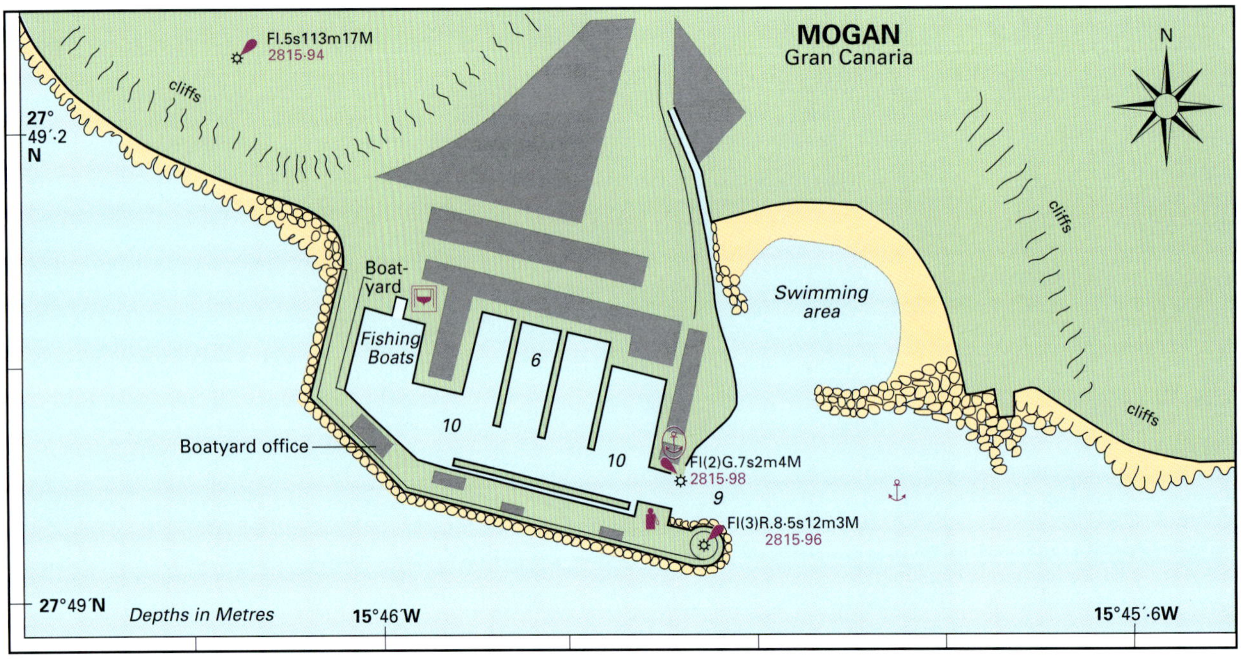

passed 3·5M northeast of the conspicuous cement works on Punta Taozo, with Puerto de Mogán 3M further up the coast.

From the northwest, where the shoreline is steep-to, a close approach can be made to the coast which can then be followed until the breakwater is located. Under sail, with the northeast trades blowing at 25 knots or so between Tenerife and Gran Canaria, the wind will be found to follow the coast with the calm of a wind shadow close inshore. To hold the wind keep 2M offshore until within sight of Puerto de Mogán, at which stage a head wind may well be encountered as the trade wind sweeps around the south coast of the island. The acceleration zone approximately 5M northwest of Mogán is considered to be one of the worst in the islands – see page 192.

Entrance and berthing

The marina opens to the east. Arriving at the breakwater head, turn to port and secure to the reception berth on the starboard hand outside the port office building. Large fenders will be required. The berth is also used by the many ferries and tourist boats which frequent the marina, so be prepared to move at short notice.

The staff are helpful and assist in berthing, either bow to the wall or to pontoons (there are no finger pontoons – a point to be borne in mind by the less agile). On approaching an allocated berth one is handed the bight of two light lines attached to the wall or pontoon. By walking aft hand over hand one retrieves the after mooring lines which lie on the bottom (gloves are advisable). The pontoon lining the south breakwater is said to be reserved for visitors – a flexible term as some appear to have been there for many years – but in practice visiting yachts tend to be dotted around as space permits.

Puerto de Mogán suffered a spate of thefts a number of years ago, after which CCTV was installed. Together with round-the-clock security patrols this appears to have combated the problem, and the pontoons still lack the usual security gates.

Anchorage

It is possible to anchor outside the entrance in 7–10m over good holding, but there is no protection from the south and it would be unwise to leave the yacht unattended for any length of time. It can also be untenably rolly, not least due to the passing tourist ferries and fishing boats. However, shelter is good in normal, northeasterly conditions, while local winds tend to blow along the coast and die at night.

Dinghies can be left in the marina for short periods, at the root of a pontoon or elsewhere so long as they do not cause an obstruction. They should **not** be left at the reception berth or at the outer end of any of the pontoons where they impede larger craft manoeuvring and from which they are likely to be removed. There is no charge either for anchoring or for leaving a dinghy as described above. Crews of anchored yachts can use the showers and toilets on payment of a small deposit.

Formalities

An outside stairway leads to the marina office, open 0800–1500 weekdays only. Although the staff are helpful, in late 2010 only one person spoke English. The ship's papers and passports will be required, plus evidence of insurance. It is advisable to book at least four weeks in advance – more if the shedule permits – but a deposit is no longer required.

Charges

The berthing fee is calculated on a length x beam basis and in 2010 was set at €0.46 per m^2. This included tax at 5%, but not water and electricity which are both metered and for which deposits must be paid. Discounts are available for longer stays.

Looking almost due west into Puerto de Mogán. The very clear water shows why yachts intending to anchor should stay well off the swimming area's eastern mole

Facilities

Boatyard Run by the *Cofradía de Pescadores de Mogán* (the fishermen's confederation) ✆ /*Fax* 928 565483, 565128 *Email* cofradia.mogan@canarias.org from their office on the breakwater (see plan), open 0800–1400, 1600–1800 weekdays, 0800–1400 Saturday. The officials are helpful, and reasonable English is spoken. Both DIY and living aboard are permitted, the latter possibly a good idea as the boatyard has little security. Water and electricity are available and metered.

Various boatbuilders advertise their services, including Mike Platzer ✆ 928 170551, 628 104890 *Email* mjplatzer@yahoo.de who specialises mainly in woodwork; Peter Hobbisiefken, ✆ 679 385106, a stainless steel specialist; and Nardo y Monica Reparaciones Navales, ✆ 607 806862, who handle GRP repairs as well as painting and antifouling.

Travel-lift 65-tonne capacity and up to 22m LOA x 6m beam, with very reasonable prices for such a well-known venue. Other than in an emergency it is necessary to book at least a week ahead.

Engineers Consult Sunshine Maritime (see *Chandlery* below).

Electronic & radio repairs Sunshine Maritime (see Chandlery below), Náutica Santana, ✆ /*Fax* 928 756641 ✆ 639 330237 and Columbus Navigation, ✆ 607 182530.

Sail repairs & rigging Sunshine Maritime (see *Chandlery* below) and Tatel Sails, ✆ /*Fax* 928 569165 *Email* tatelsails@ctv.es.

Liferaft servicing Can be organised by Sunshine Maritime (see *Chandlery* below).

Chandlery Mike and Mayla have been running Sunshine Maritime ✆ /*Fax* 928 565474 *Email* admin@sunshinemaritime.com www.sunshinemaritime.com (open 1000–1800 weekdays, 1000–1300 Saturday) since 1994, and have recently moved to Calle Rivera del Carmen 13 (about five minutes' walk inland from the marina). As well as stocking general chandlery they specialise in watermakers, water filters and fuel filters, and offer services including *guardinage* and general repairs. With all the major catalogues to hand, they are happy to order from mainland Europe if required.

The *ferretería* a few doors away stocks a good range of tools and other hardware.

Charts Sunshine Maritime are an official distributor of Imray charts and guides for the North Atlantic and the Caribbean, and also stock a range of British Admiralty charts and publications.

Water On the pontoons.

Showers Not up to the standard of the rest of the complex, with only four (elderly) showers and four toilets serving the entire marina – and then not always as clean as one might wish. Access to the showers requires a key, obtainable on payment of a small deposit. Crews of anchored yachts can use the showers on the same basis.

Launderette On the Calle Rivera del Carmen (see Chandlery, above). In 2010 it cost €9 to wash and dry a 7kg load, which normally took 24 hours (DIY is not permitted). Some English is spoken.

Electricity On the pontoons.

Fuel On the main breakwater opposite the reception pontoon (open 0900–1300, 1500–1800 Monday to Saturday, 0900–1400 Sunday).

Bottled gas Camping Gaz exchanges at the hardware store mentioned above, but as of 2011 the situation regarding refilling other cylinders remained uncertain – see page 191.

III. THE CANARY ISLANDS

The very distinctive lighthouse on Punta del Castillete, overlooking Puerto de Mogán

Fishing boats, yachts and a yellow 'glass-bottomed' boat all make use of the boatyard at Puerto de Mogán, which is operated by the local *Cofradía de Pescadores de Mogán*

Weather forecast Posted daily in the entrance to the marina office.

Bank On the village square a short distance inland from the harbour, plus cash dispensers in the marina complex.

Shops/provisioning Well stocked supermarket in the marina complex and more in the village, plus a larger one in Mogán, some distance up the valley. The Friday market around the harbour offers fresh produce as well as tourist souvenirs.

Cafés & restaurants Dozens in the marina complex, including a restaurant built around the light tower on the breakwater head, with more in the town.

Medical services European Medical Centre ✆ 928 565090, 565365, where English and other languages are spoken.

Communications

Post office Not as such, though stamps are available and mail left at the marina office will be collected when the post is delivered.

Mailing address Torre de Control, 35140 – Puerto de Mogán, Gran Canaria, Islas Canarias, Spain.

Telephones In the marina complex.

Internet access Wi-Fi is claimed to be available throughout the marina – at a charge of €5 per day, €25 per week – though reception is reported to be somewhat unreliable. Many of the bars surrounding the harbour offer free wife to patrons.

Car hire Via the hotel directly north of the marina control tower.

Taxis Readily available.

Buses Anti-clockwise around the coast to Las Palmas, including an express service which is claimed to take only 90 minutes.

Ferries Tourist ferries to Puerto Rico and beyond.

Anchorages on the west coast of Gran Canaria

North of Puerto de Mogán towards Cabo Descojonado the coast is largely steep-to, cleft by narrow, ravine-like river valleys (*barrancos*) some of which give onto small beaches (*playas*) off which anchorage is possible in settled weather. These include Barranco del Parchel (27°49'·8N 15°46'·8W), Barranco de las Secos (27°51'·1N 15°48'W), Playa de Tasárte (27°52'·2N 15°48'W), Playa del Agua Palmito (27°53'·6N 15°49'·1W) at the mouth of the Barranco de las Lanias, where there is a fresh water spring, and Playa del Asno (27°54'·3N 15°49'·8W). All have deep water close inshore and are in the lee of the wind acceleration zone.

North of Cabo Descojonado it is advisable to keep well offshore in all but the most settled conditions. Buoys marking shellfish and other pots may be encountered all along this coast, sometimes several miles offshore in considerable depths of water.

Puerto de la Aldea (Puerto San Nicolas)

28°00'·34N 15°49'·15W

Lights
Breakwater
Fl.R.5s5M Red tower 4m

Anchorage off small harbour

Punta de la Aldea (pronounced *Al'day'ah*) lies some 14M north of Puerto de Mogán by sea, though a great deal further by road, and is lower than the cliffs to the south. The town of San Nicolas is 4km inland up the Aldea valley, with the pretty village of Puerto de la Aldea in the bay south of the headland. Facilites are limited to a few bars, shops and restaurants, with more shops and a filling station in San Nicolas.

Limited shelter is provided by the short breakwater, which runs southwards parallel to the stony beach, but much of the interior space is occupied by moored smallcraft. Holding is reported good either off the beach or inside the end of the breakwater in about 5m, though a second anchor might be wise in view of the limited swinging room. There are some rocky patches close to the beach, visible at low water.

The small and simple harbour at Puerto de la Aldea, seen from a little north of east

A local yacht makes her way into Puerto de las Nieves, between a Ro-Ro ferry and the line of floats which mark the swimming beach

Puerto de las Nieves (Puerto Agaete)

28°05'·87N 15°42'·68W (breakwater head)

Waypoint
⊕C32 – 28°05'·6N 15°43'·2W (0·5M SW of Puerto de las Nieves)

Plans
Spanish *D210* (1:10,000)

Lights
2815·99 **Breakwater**
Fl(2)R.9s13m12M Red column 10m
Roque Partido (Baja de la Marina)
Fl(3)G.5M White post, green bands 5m
Note Stands in the water outside the rocks which it marks
2815·995 **Breakwater spur**
Fl(3)R.7m3M Red column 5M
Note Obscured from seaward by the breakwater

Harbour Communications
Port Captain ✆ 928 554227 VHF Ch 10

Gran Canaria's west coast ferry harbour

Previously a small fishing harbour with a short quay and few facilities, the breakwater at Puerto de las Nieves (pronounced *Pwerto de las Nee'evess*), also referred to as Puerto Agaete (*Pwerto A'gay'tay*) was extended in the early 1990s to provide the ubiquitous Ro-Ro ferry berth and give much improved protection. Even by Canarian standards the breakwater is notably wide and high, particularly after being augmented by several off-loading ramps to accommodate the enormous catamaran ferries. Three tall blue and white banded posts with triangular tops support floodlights on the quay.

The coastal scenery is spectacular with high cliffs and rock formations, though sadly the much-photographed *Dedo del Dios* (God's Finger) just south of the village fell during a storm in late 2005. Not surprisingly, Puerto de las Nieves is developing as a tourist resort, though most visitors appear to be from Las Palmas or perhaps mainland Spain. The town of Agaete lies about 2km inland, framed by an attractive valley.

Approach and entry

The pale grey breakwater is easily seen from offshore, and there are no hazards in the approach – other than the frequent ferries and hydrofoil catamarans. Lack of space forces the ferries to depart going astern, whereas the catamarans turn outside the harbour and reverse in, enabling them to leave the harbour at considerable speed. The entrance is wide with good depth, and the rocks to the east marked by a green and white striped post.

Berthing

Plans drawn up more than ten years ago to enlarge the harbour by means of a second breakwater knuckle south of the current one appear to have been shelved, and there is very little room for

Puerto de las Nieves seen from cliffs to the southeast. It is the main ferry port for departures to Santa Cruz de Tenerife

visitors. Space should be booked in advance (see Formalities and charges, below), after which the authorities are said to allow up to three yachts to raft up alongside the rough wall overnight. A fender board is advised if 'inside boat'. The three pontoons in the northwest corner are fully occupied by local boats, though it may occasionally be possible to find space if a regular occupant is absent.

Anchorage

There is good water off the end of the breakwater, with the green and white post marking Roque Partido (breaking) opposite. Anchor between Roque Partido and the short inner mole in 5–6m over black sand and stones, taking care to remain well clear of the ferry berth. Holding is poor and following repeated rockfalls much of the bottom is foul, and a fisherman-type anchor is probably the best choice. The swimming beach is delineated by posts joined by strings of easily-seen floats.

There are several sets of steps at which to land, in addition to the beach and a slipway next to the travel-lift dock, but the three pontoons are protected by security gates.

Formalities and charges

Puerto de las Nieves is one of those harbours for which a berth should be booked in advance – see Booking berths in *Puertos de Canarias* harbours, page 189. On arrival visit the harbour authorities at their office in the ferry terminal. The berthing fee is calculated on a length x beam basis and in 2010 was set at €0.24 per m^2, including tax and water if available.

Facilities

Travel-lift 70-tonne capacity backed by ample hardstanding.

Chandlery A small and rather anonymous *ferretería*, which sells some chandlery, exists one street back from the harbour.

Water & electricity On the pontoons only.

Banks No bank closer than Agaete, but a cash dispenser in the entrance to the Laguete Restaurant (which overlooks the harbour) and another a few streets away.

Shops/provisioning Two small supermarkets plus other shops.

Cafés & restaurants Numerous, with a particular reputation for local fish dishes.

Communications

Telephones On the quay and in the village.

Bus service Regular service to Las Palmas and elsewhere.

Ferries Frequent ferry service to Santa Cruz de Tenerife.

Puerto de Sardina

28°09'·14N 15°41'·86W (SE molehead)

Waypoint

⊕C33 – 28°11'·8N 15°43'·6W (2M NNW of Pta Sardina)

Lights

2816 **Punta Sardina** Fl(4)20s47m20M
White tower, red bands 23m

Pretty bay with little shelter

Tucked into an indented and largely unspoilt bay about a mile southeast of Punta Sardina and overshadowed by spectacular sandy cliffs, tiny Puerto de Sardina has much less to offer than Puerto de las Nieves. The short quay, extended about 10 years ago, was damaged in storms in early 2010 and it is no longer possible to lie alongside.

Anchor instead off the sandy beach in 5–6m clear of the many fish pots, rocks and swimmers – the bay is very popular with divers. There are steps in the harbour at which to land, close to the crane with which small local fishing boats are lifted out when not in use.

Facilities are limited. There are a couple of small restaurants beside the harbour where it might be possible to get a water carrier filled (as well as enjoy a very good seafood lunch), plus a few shops in the rapidly expanding village up the hill, but little else.

Tenerife

Between 28°00'N–28°35'N and 16°07'W–16°55'W

Introduction

Roughly triangular in shape, Tenerife (pronounced *Tenereef'eh*) is the largest island in the archipelago with an area of 2,050km², a population of around 900,000 and the highest mountain in Spain, El Teide, a gigantic volcanic cone, often snow-capped, rising to 3,717m.

The backbone of mountains runs east-west and causes a dramatic climatic difference between the north and south of the island. Winds carry moisture up the north face of the range, resulting in high rainfall and a humid, temperate climate, ideal for many varieties of fruit. The world-famous botanical gardens at the foot of the fertile Orotova valley, on the outskirts of Puerto de la Cruz, were established on the orders of Charles III of Spain (1716–1788) in an attempt to acclimatise tropical plants from the New World before onward shipment to Europe.

There are three major towns in the northern part of the island – the capital, Santa Cruz, which has wide tree-lined streets, art deco buildings and the best produce market in the Canaries; La Laguna, the old capital, which dates back to the 16th century and is typified by narrow streets, churches and monasteries; and Puerto de la Cruz, which has long been a major Spanish tourist town and in Victorian times was a favourite English wintering resort – a status which it is fast reclaiming. The southern part of the island, in particular the beaches of the southwest, rivals the Costa del Sol with its tourist resorts aimed at the package tour industry.

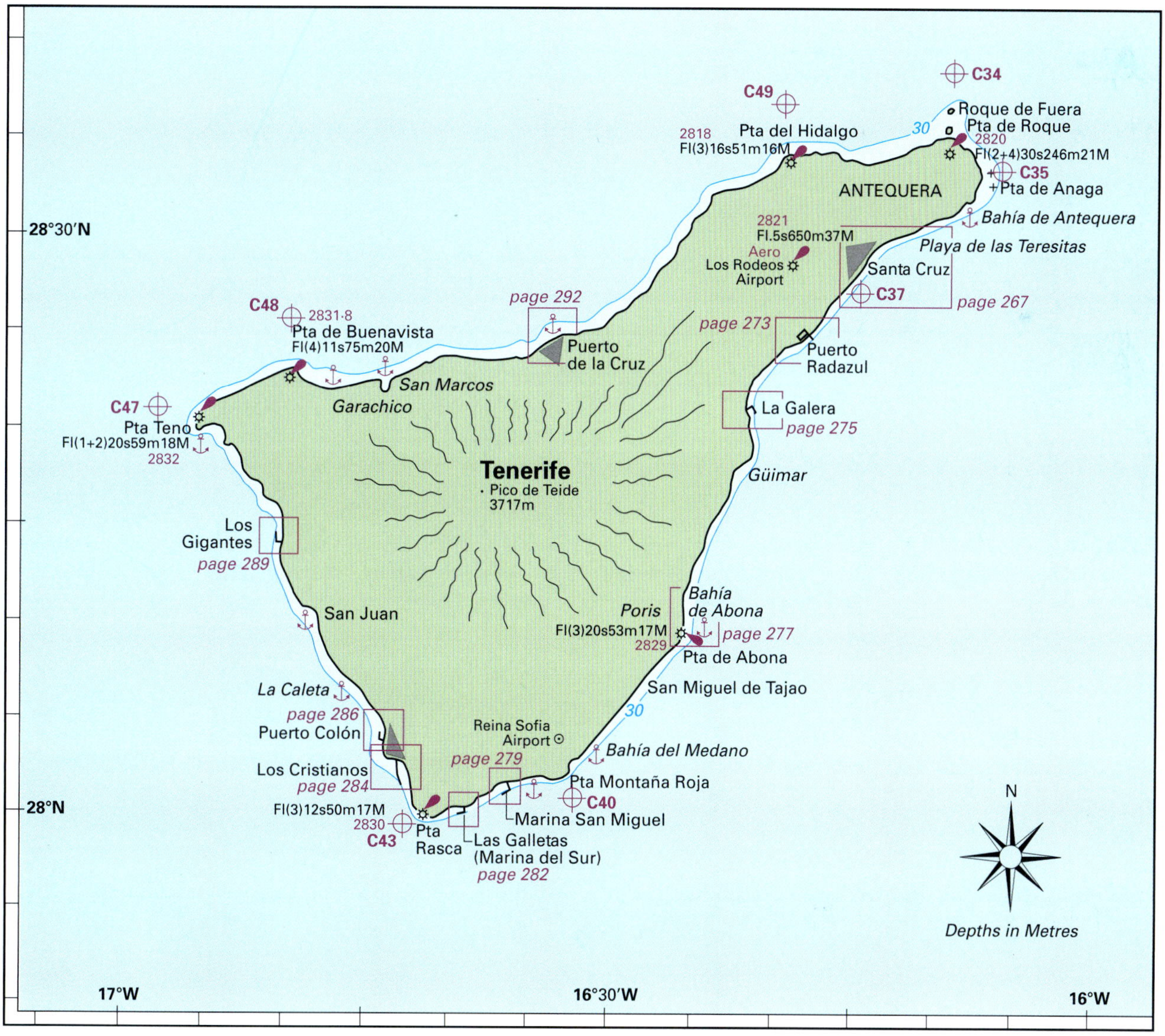

Navigation

Waypoints

⊕ C34 – 28°38'·3N 16°09'·3W (2M N of Roque de Fuera)
⊕ C35 – 28°33'·3N 16°06'W (1M E of Pta de Anaga)
⊕ C36 – 28°29'·2N 16°12'·3W (0·5M SE of Dársena Pesquera, Santa Cruz de Tenerife)
⊕ C37 – 28°27'N 16°14'·5W (0·5M SE of Dársena de los Llanos, Santa Cruz de Tenerife)
⊕ C38 – 28°23'·5N 16°19'·3W (0·5M SSE of Puerto Radazul)
⊕ C39 – 28°21'·2N 16°21'·5W (0·5M SE of Puerto Deportivo La Galera)
⊕ C40 – 28°00'·7N 16°32'·1W (1M SSE of Pta Montaña Roja)
⊕ C41 – 28°00'·6N 16°36'·6W (0·5M SSE of Marina San Miguel)
⊕ C42 – 27°59'·9N 16°39'·8W (0·5M SSW of Las Galletas / Marina del Sur)
⊕ C43 – 27°59'·4N 16°42'·7W (1M SW of Pta Rasca)
⊕ C44 – 28°02'·4N 16°43'·4W (0·5M SW of Los Cristianos)
⊕ C45 – 28°04'·6N 16°44'·8W (0·5M WSW of Puerto Colón)
⊕ C46 – 28°15'·3N 16°50'·9W (0·5M NW of Puerto de Los Gigantes)
⊕ C47 – 28°21'N 16°57'·7W (2M W of Pta de Teno)
⊕ C48 – 28°25'·6N 16°49'·8W (2M N of Pta de Buenavista)
⊕ C49 – 28°36'·8N 16°19'·3W (2M N of Pta del Hidalgo)

Courses and distances

⊕ C34 – ⊕ C37 = 16M, by eye
⊕ C34 – ⊕ C47 via ⊕ C49 & ⊕ C48 = 46M, 260°, 247° & 237° / 057°, 067° & 080
⊕ C37 – ⊕ C10 (0·5M S of Pta Pechiguera, Lanzarote) = 127·5M, 079° / 259°
⊕ C37 – ⊕ C11 (2M NW of Pta Tostón, Fuerteventura) = 118M, 081° / 261°
⊕ C37 – ⊕ C20 (3M SSW of Pta Jandia, Fuerteventura) = 94M, 106° / 286°
⊕ C37 – ⊕ C21 (2·5M NE of La Isleta, Gran Canaria) = 48M, 108° / 288°
⊕ C37 – ⊕ C31 (0·5M SW of Puerto de Mogán, Gran Canaria) = 46M, 44M 148° / 328° + 2M, 132° / 312°
⊕ C37 – ⊕ C40 = 31M, by eye
⊕ C40 – ⊕ C31 (0·5M SW of Puerto de Mogán, Gran Canaria) = 42·5M, 107° / 287°
⊕ C40 – ⊕ C43 = 9·5M, 262° / 082°
⊕ C43 – ⊕ C47 = 25·5M, 329° / 149°
⊕ C43 – ⊕ C51 (0·5M SE of San Sebastián, La Gomera) = 21·5M, 284° / 104°
⊕ C43 – ⊕ C63 (1M SE of Puerto de la Estaca, El Hierro) = 64M, 258° / 078°
⊕ C47 – ⊕ C51 (0·5M SE of San Sebastián, La Gomera) = 18M, 205° / 025°
⊕ C47 – ⊕ C58 (1M SE of Santa Cruz de la Palma) = 45·5M, 294° / 114°

Magnetic variation

6°W (2011), decreasing by 8'E annually.

Tidal Streams

Generally insignificant – see Tides and tidal streams, page 194. Details of range, etc. will be found under Santa Cruz de Tenerife.

Charts

Admiralty *1869* (1:300,000)
Spanish *61A* (1:200,000), *612*, *613*, *614* (1:60,000)
US *51260* (1:300,000)
Imray-Iolaire *E2* (1:600,000)

Lights

2820 **Punta de Roque (Punta de Anaga)**
Fl(2+4)30s246m21M Grey tower, white building and lantern 12m
2821 **Los Rodeos Airport**
Aero Fl.5s650m37M Metal tower 14m
2829 **Punta de Abona**
Fl(3)20s53m17M 214°-vis-040°
White tower, red bands 39m
2830 **Punta Rasca**
Fl(3)12s50m17M
White tower, three red bands 32m
2832 **Punta Teno**
Fl(1+2)20s59m18M
White tower, red bands 20m
2831·8 **Punta de Buenavista**
Fl(4)11s75m20M Square white tower 40m
2818 **Punta del Hidalgo**
Fl(3)16s51m16M Masonry tower 50m

Marine farms

Three marine farms, each marked by four yellow pillar buoys with × topmarks either Fl.Y.5s3M or Fl(4)Y.11s3M, lie off the northeast coast of Tenerife, centred on 28°30'·9N 16°09'·6W, 28°30'·6N 16°09'·7W and 28°22'·7N 16°21'W.

Coast Radio Station

Tenerife 28°18'·4N 16°30'·2W
VHF Ch 16, 27, 72 (24 hours)
DSC VHF MMSI 002241025 28°26'·3N 16°17'W
☎ 922 826324 *Fax* 922 826326
Email ccr.tenerife@abertistelecom.com

Maritime Rescue Coordination Centre

DSC VHF MMSI 002241007 28°29'N 16°14'W
☎ 922 597551, 597552 *Fax* 922 597331
Email tenerife@sasemar.es VHF Ch 16, 74 (24 hours)
(This station does not accept public correspondence other than distress and safety traffic)

Weather and navigation broadcasts

VHF 28°29'N 16°14'W
Weather bulletins Ch 74 at 0015, 0415, 0815, 1215, 1615, 2015 (gale warnings, synopsis and forecast for the channel between Gran Canaria and Tenerife, and the coasts of Tenerife, La Gomera, La Palma and El Hierro, in Spanish and English)
Navigational warnings Ch 74 on receipt (in Spanish and English)
VHF 28°26'·9N 16°22'·7W
Weather bulletins Ch 27 at 0833, 1333, 2033 (forecast in Spanish for coastal waters)
Navigational warnings Ch 27 at 0833, 2033 (in Spanish for coastal waters)

As with Gran Canaria, a characteristic feature of the island is the *barrancos* or dry river beds, and the beautiful Barranco del Infierno belies its name, 'Ravine of Hell'. With clear visibility the view of all the Canaries from the top of El Teide is quite outstanding – on windless days a cable car takes one to within a few hundred feet of the top, though the ascent is not advised for those with high blood pressure or heart problems.

Tenerife has several harbours suitable for yachts, though not all are likely to have room for visitors. However, with the yacht in a secure berth, visitors should not miss the opportunity to hire a car for two or three days to visit the Orotova valley, drive along the ridge of the mountain range and view El Teide with its extensive plain of raw lava to the south. The narrow winding road cut into the mountainside between Garachico and Buenavista and on to Masca and Santiago, with glimpses of the sea through swirling clouds down the steep and narrow ravines, will not easily be forgotten.

Websites

The following sites contain general information about Tenerife, some of which may be useful to the visiting yachtsman. Websites relating to specific harbours are listed under Harbour communications, those covering all or most of the Canary Islands on page 188 of the introduction.

www.cabtfe.es – the homepage of Tenerife's island council, in Spanish, English and German and far more welcoming than many of its kind

www.canaries-live.com – a Strawberry World site, fast and easy to navigate site in Spanish, English, German and Portuguese, offering all the usual tourist information if not in much depth

www.en.wikipedia.org/wiki/Tenerife – all the usual in-depth wikipedia information without the spin which one comes to expect from 'local' websites

www.ost.es/en – homepage of the Tenerife Symphony Orchestra, whose auditorium (see page 272) overlooks the entrance to the Dársena de los Llanos. In Spanish and English

www.puertosdetenerife.org – website of the Port Authority of Santa Cruz de Tenerife, responsibile for the larger commercial ports in the four western islands. In Spanish and English

www.tenerife-info.to – a general (but totally anonymous) guide to the island with good photos but limited detail. English only

www.tennews.com – billed as 'The Tenerife Guide Online, the latest information from Tenerife', it does pretty well what it says on the tin, with recent posts on which one is invited to comment

www.todotenerife.es/ – like www.cabtfe.es this site also represents the island council (in Spanish, English, German, Italian, French) but in a rather more traditional manner. The sections on General Information and Island Information are particularly interesting

www.webtenerifeuk.co.uk – the website of the Tenerife Tourism Corporation, this claims to be the official website for the promotion of Tenerife for tourism. And they do a good job – it's a bright cheerful site, well-illustrated and easy to navigate but with more depth than most

Telecommunications

Mobile (cell) phone reception is excellent throughout Tenerife. The country code for the Canaries is 34, as it is for mainland Spain, and the area code for Lanzarote – which must be included even when dialling from within the island – is 922, shared with La Gomera, La Palma and El Hierro.

Internet access is available in all the larger towns, most often at cafés which provide free Wi-Fi (and sometimes power sockets) for patrons. Somewhat surprisingly, among the island's nine marinas of any size, only Puerto Deportivo La Galera and Marina San Miguel offer free Wi-Fi to visiting yachts.

Approach and navigation

There are few hazards on approaching Tenerife other than on the north coast between Punta Teno and Punta de Anaga, much of which is fringed by off-lying rocks, and a 4m shoal, Bajo de La Mancha Blanca, about 0·4M off Punta de Anaga. However beware both the wind acceleration zones around the northeast, southeast and northwest limits of the island – see page 192 – and the strong down-draughts over the cliffs between Los Gigantes and Punta Teno at its northwestern tip. Reef before entering these areas.

Northeast and northwest winds are dominant on the east and west sides of the island respectively, reducing at night and often changing to an offshore breeze along the west coast between Punta Rasca and Punta Teno. Sailing north along the east coast is easier at night when the wind strength is much reduced.

The snow-capped peak of El Tiede dwarfs a ketch sailing up the channel between Tenerife and La Gomera
Nigel Mercier

Harbours and anchorages

Bahía de Antequera

28°32′N 16°07′·8W (quay)

Popular open anchorage

A pretty bay about 5M northeast of Santa Cruz, sheltered from northerly winds by Punta de Antequera but totally open to the south, Bahía de Antequera is a popular destination for the many small motorboats kept in Santa Cruz and San Andres. It offers good holding in 5m or more over sand, off a rocky beach with sand exposed at low water. There is a small quay on the east side of the bay from which it is possible to climb a path over the headland but nothing whatsoever ashore, not even a road.

Playa de las Teresitas (San Andrés)

28°30′·21N 16°11′·3W (breakwater south head)

Plans
Spanish *6120* (1:12,500)

Lights
buoy **San Andrés mole, northwest end**
Fl(3)10s3M East cardinal buoy, ♦ topmark, 3m
buoy **San Andrés mole, southeast end**
Fl(3)10s3M East cardinal buoy, ♦ topmark, 3m
Note The above mark a long mole running parallel to the shore, which provides protection for local smallcraft moorings

Anchorage with beach access

The town of San Andrés, fronted by the Playa de las Teresitas, lies some 4M north of Santa Cruz city centre. The golden sand beach – imported from the Sahara, complete with 'harmless' scorpions – is protected by a long mole running parallel to the shore about 150m off, creating a safe swimming area and space for several hundred moored smallcraft. The gaps at both ends are narrow and it would not be possible for a yacht to enter, but there is good holding outside in 10–15m and a dinghy can be taken through the southern opening.

Many claim that Playa de las Teresitas is the best beach on Tenerife, not least because, while popular with local people, it is remote from the main tourist centres. The small town of San Andrés has shops, a bank and a post office, and there are numerous restaurants and beach cafés. There is a tap on the quay and swimmer's (i.e. cold) shower on the beach.

The long detached mole at San Andrés shelters local smallcraft as well as the Playa de las Teresitas, possibly the best beach on Tenerife

Santa Cruz de Tenerife – Marina Tenerife and Marina Santa Cruz

Combined harbour information
Although the two marinas in Santa Cruz de Tenerife which accept visiting yachts are situated in separate harbours with entrances some 3M apart, there is no obvious demarcation ashore and much of the more general information is therefore common to both.

Tides
Standard port for the Canary Islands is Casablanca, with Santa Cruz a secondary port. MLWS is about 0·3m above datum and time difference on Casablanca: –0059. Predictions for Santa Cruz are also available via Admiralty *EasyTide* – see page 194
Mean spring range 1·9m
Mean neap range 0·8m

Plans
Admiralty *1858* (1:75,000), *1847* (1:12,500)
Spanish *6120* (1:12,500)
US *51341* (1:50,000 & 1:10,000)
Imray-Iolaire *E2* (1:17,500)

Lights
Full entrance and interior Lights for the Dársena Pesquera and Dársena de los Llanos are listed under those headings. Further Lights exist within the Dársena Este and Dársena Sur.

Dársena Pesquera (Marina Tenerife)
2826·5 **Southwest mole**
Fl.R.5s12m3M Red post 6m
2826 **Breakwater head**
Fl.G.5s10m3M Green column 5m

Dársena Este
2822·6 **Breakwater, northeast angle**
Q(6)+LFl.15s10m5M
South cardinal post, ▼ topmark 3m
2822·7 **Breakwater, southwest angle**
Q(6)+LFl.15s10m5M
South cardinal post, ▼ topmark 3m
2822·8 **Breakwater head**
Fl(2)G.7s12m9M Green tower 6m
Note Various other lights exist inside both Dársena Este and Dársena Sur

Dársena Sur (Dársena de Anaga)
2822 **Breakwater head**
Q(2)R.7s18m10M Red tower 5m

Dársena de los Llanos (Marina Santa Cruz)
2826·7 **Breakwater angle** Q(3)10s8m5M
East cardinal post, ♦ topmark 2m
2826·72 **Breakwater head** Fl(3)G.9s12m9M
Green tower 6m
2826·82 **Southwest mole** Fl(3)R.10s7m9M
Red post standing in the water
2827·49 **Palmetum** Q(6)+LFl.15s14m3M
South cardinal column, ▼ topmark 4m

Berthing in Tenerife's commercial port

Santa Cruz is an interesting city with attractive parks and is well worth visiting. It is by far the largest commercial port on Tenerife, its harbour effectively split into four behind separate breakwaters. The two marinas which accept visitors are situated in the northernmost and southernmost harbours, the Dársena Pesquera (pronounced *Dársena Peskehra*) and the Dársena de los Llanos (*Dársena de los Yan'oss*) respectively, with that of the *Real Club Náutico* inside the Dársena Sur. However, this latter is reserved exclusively for members and visitors are not made welcome, a situation which has not changed since the 1970s. A fourth, extremely small, marina known as Puerto Chico also exists in the Dársena Pesquera, but it does not normally have space for visitors.

For many years no real provision was made for yachts in Santa Cruz – they were tolerated in the Dársena Pesquera ('fishermen's harbour') but largely left to shift for themselves, rafting up to one of the rusting hulks or alongside the very oily wall. It was not until the early 1990s that six pontoons (since increased to thirteen) were laid just inside the entrance under the name Marina Tenerife. However, space was always short and a few years later it was announced that a new facility, the Marina del Atlantico (now renamed Marina Santa Cruz), was to be built in the northern part of the Dársena de los Llanos. For reasons rumoured to be 'political' this took some years to get off the ground, and having expanded from an initial 60 berths to around 300 by 2003 – and despite having a great deal of unused space – has changed remarkably little since. The shoreside infrastructure was even slower in putting in an appearance, though by 2010 the basics were at last in place. Both marinas are exceptionally well sheltered and provide secure berthing for yachts of all sizes.

Approach

From the northeast, the high backbone of the island extends right up to the northeast cape, Punta de Anaga. Keeping at least 1M offshore, the rocky peninsula of Punta de Antequera is passed, followed by Punta del Roquete. The village of Igueste lies on an inlet to the west of the point. One mile further southeast is Punta de los Organos, at the northern end of the Playa de la Teresitas.

A further mile down the coast will be seen the long breakwater of the Dársena Pesquera which opens to the southeast, followed by those of the Dársenas Este and Sur, and the Dársena de los Llanos. This last is almost a mile in length with a relatively narrow entrance facing south. Major land reclamation has taken place near the root of the Dársena Pesquera breakwater, but it is close enough in not to affect a yacht on passage.

Approaching from the south, after passing the lights and chimneys of Puerto Caballo and the small headland of Punta Maragallo backed by its extensive tank farm, the entrance to the Dársena de los Llanos will be seen about 0·5M ahead. The white and shining *Auditorio de Tenerife* (see page 272) which lies directly opposite the entrance to the basin is visible from at least 10M off on a clear day.

Entrance and formalities

See under individual harbour/marina information.

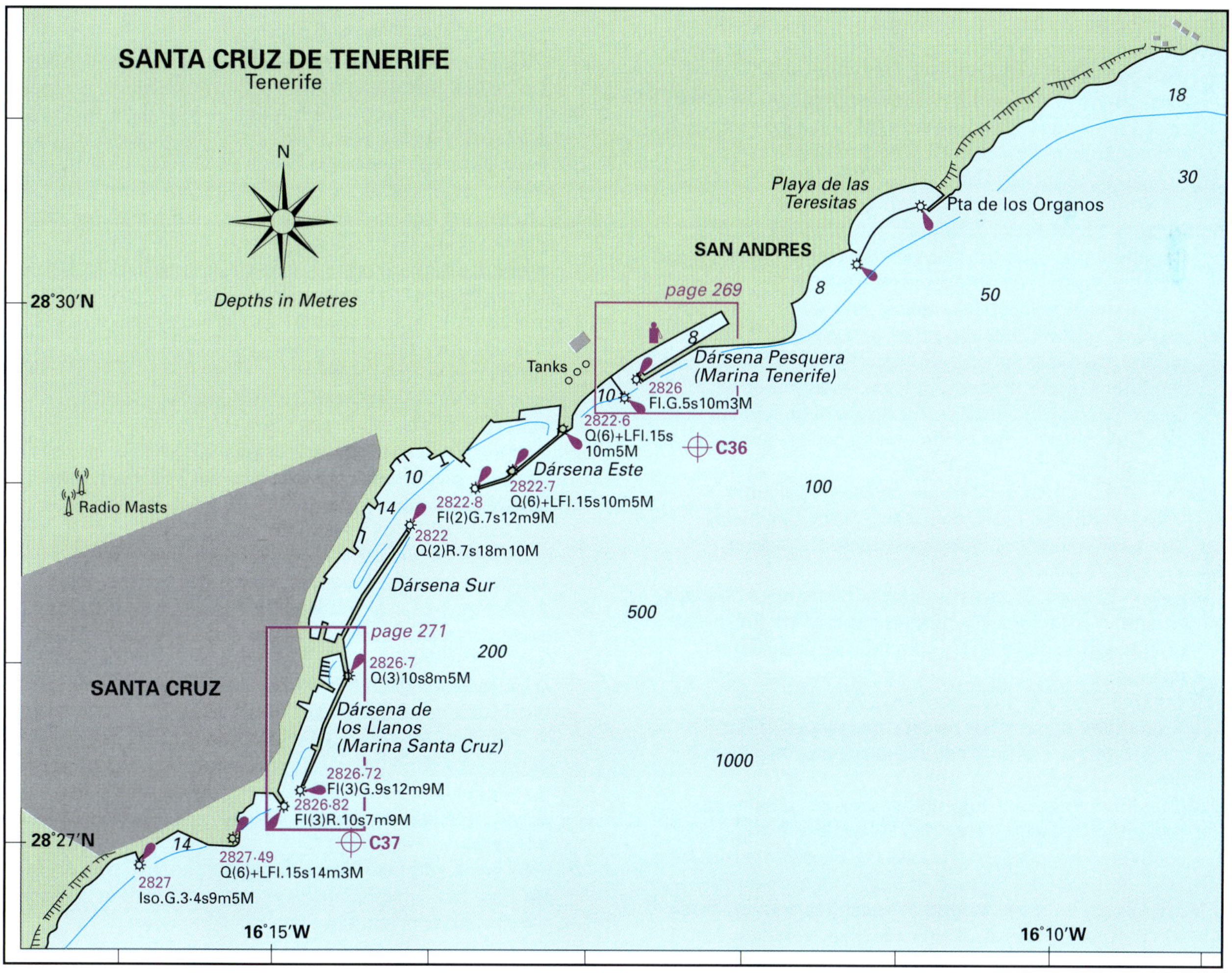

Facilities

Unlike in many harbours where individual companies have grown to meet different needs, Santa Cruz is home to four large concerns each offering a variety of services, many of which duplicate. Contact details for each follow, with only names mentioned in the text: Blancomar Nautica SL (formerly Sucesores Tomás Fernández Blanco) ✆ 922 275014 *Fax* 922 279769 *Email* blancomar@blancomanautica.es www.blancomarnautica.es at Calle Santiago, 109 (note that they do not keep standard Spanish hours, and instead of closing for a long lunch break shut for the day at 1630); Nautica y Deportes Tenerife ✆ 922 549840 *Fax* 922 591 287 *Email* nautica@nauticaydeportes.com www.nauticaydeportes.com (part of the same group as Varaderos Anaga and Marina Tenerife) near the head of the Dársena Pesquera and open 0900–1300, 1600–1900 weekdays, 1000–1300 Saturday; Nordest (which has amalgamated with Radar Canarias SL) ✆ 922 577322, 669 845552 *Fax* 922 577031 *Email* nordest@nordest-canarias.com www.nordest-canarias.com at Calle Benavides 91, San Cristobal De La Laguna; and Spinnaker Shop ✆ 922 243975 *Fax* 922 293830 *Email* info@spinnakershop.es www.spinnakershop.es at San Juan Bautista 32.

Boatyard It took a surprisingly long time for a yacht-friendly boatyard to become established at Santa Cruz, but Varaderos Anaga, ✆ 922 591313 *Fax* 922 591011 *Email* varaderosanaga@nauticaydeportes.com www.nauticaydeportes.com (part of the same group as Nautica y Deportes Tenerife and Marina Tenerife) has made good the omission. Situated in a sheltered position at the head of the Dársena Pesquera, with a dedicated waiting pontoon, they run a well-kept yard with plenty of hard-standing, some undercover work area, and no shortage of yacht-length props. Security via CCTC is good, and owners (who can do their own work) can live aboard with access to onsite water, electricity, toilets and showers. Office hours are 0900–1700 weekdays only, and good English and German are spoken. Prices are very reasonable and, though bookings must be confirmed in advance, two to three weeks' notice is normally sufficient.

A pressure washer is available and services include engineering, welding and other metalwork, GRP repairs, painting and antifouling. The yard has received consistent praise from visiting yachtsmen, both for their work and for the careful way in which yachts are lifted and moved. Prices are said to be very reasonable, particularly if paid in advance.

Travel-lift Currently a 70-tonne capacity travel-lift (maximum 23m LOA, 6m beam) at the boatyard, though a 300-tonne hoist is planned. A crane is available for mast removal.

Engineers Consult Varaderos Anaga. Blancomar Nautica, Nautica y Deportes Tenerife and Spinnaker Shop also offer engineering services, specialising in different makes.

Electronics Nordest and Blancomar Nautica, with the former handling nearly twenty international brands including Furlex, Lofrans, Aqua-Signal, Whale and Goïot.

Sail repairs Spinnaker Shop (sometimes referred to as Spinnaker Náutica), and Luis Gonzales, ✆ 922 219105, who can be contacted via Blancomar Nautica.

Rigging Nordest and Spinnaker Shop can both handle major rigging projects, and between them stock most of the leading brands of roller furling, winches, etc.

Liferaft servicing Nautica y Deportes Tenerife and Liferaft Services SL ✆ 922 620617 *Email* ebm@liferaft-services.com (in Santa Maria del Mar, about 9km south of the city) can organise servicing for most makes including Avon, Plastimo, Viking, etc. Plastimo is also handled by Inprecasa ✆ 922 650131, 617 442068 *Email* inprecasa@inprecasa.com www.inprecasa.com, which has premises at La Laguna about 10km northwest of Santa Cruz.

Chandlery Santa Cruz is, by Canarian standards, unusually well served in this respect. All four companies listed above stock general chandlery, as does La Marina ✆ 922 271246 *Fax* 922 591362 *Email* lamarina.sal@telefonica.net who have a city centre shop at Calle Celia Cruz (beyond the bus station), as well as premises near the head of the Dársena Pesquera. Hours at the latter are 0800–1300, 1500–1800 weekdays, 0800–1300 Saturday. Nearly all major international brands are represented by one or more of the above, and items not in stock can be ordered.

There is also a large and well-stocked hardware store across the street from the market (see opposite), but very little English is spoken so non-Spanish speakers had best either take the broken item or a picture of what they need.

Charts There is no longer an Admiralty chart agent in Tenerife. The Centro Geofísico de Canarias ✆ 922 287054, 243017 at Calle La Marina 20, is official agent for the Spanish Hydrographic Office, though they may also be available from the *Delegación del Instituto Geográfico Nacional* ✆ 922 287054, 287066 *Fax* 922 243027 at Avenida de Anaga 27 (the Port Office building). Blancomar Nautica SL and Nordest both stock Imray charts and publications.

Water On the pontoons at both marinas, and the quayside at Marina Santa Cruz.

Showers Next to the marina office in Marina Tenerife and at the rear of the office block at Marina Santa Cruz. After many years of complaints the latter were rebuilt a few years ago, with six showers each for men and women, although there is said to be a general lack of hot water until lunchtime or beyond.

Launderette At Marina Santa Cruz, though the two washers and single dryer are insufficient for the number of visiting yachts.

Electricity On the pontoons at both marinas and the quayside at Marina Santa Cruz.

Fuel From the Repsol filling station immediately east of Puerto Chico (itself opposite Marina Tenerife) in the Dársena Pesquera, open 0700–2030 daily. A pontoon and separate pumps serve the needs of yachts, but there is a single attendant who is also responsible for the vehicle side of the business, which can lead to delays. Access may be complicated by boats berthed on the east side of the easternmost pontoon in Puerto Chico, leaving yachts using the fuel berth with the choice of approaching upwind but with a very tight turn at the last moment, or coming in downwind.

Yachts in Marina Santa Cruz can arrange for delivery by road but minimum amounts are said to be very large. Enquire at the marina office, where the service needs to be booked at least two working days in advance.

Bottled gas Camping Gaz exchanges at hardware stores in the city, but as of 2011 the situation regarding refilling other cylinders remained uncertain – see page 191.

Weather forecast Posted daily at both marinas.
Banks Numerous, plus many cash dispensers (but none close to the Dársena Pesquera).
Shops/provisioning Excellent supermarkets and other shops in Santa Cruz. Closest to the marina is a Hiperdino in Calle San Francisco, with a larger one in Calle San Clemente. At the bus station on Avenida Tres de Mayo is an El Corte Ingles, with a large Carrefour a block away and a Mercadona nearby. All are withing walking distance of the marina. By car or taxi one can visit the large Carrefour on the first exit south, or the Al Campo and Lidl in the Centro Comercial on the way to La Laguna. For seriously deprived Brits there is the world's smallest M&S Simply Food just off the Plaza Espana close to Marina Santa Cruz.
Produce market The excellent Nuestra Senora de Africa market on Calle de San Sebastián (or cross the Barranco de Santos via the Puente Serador) is within walking distance of Marina Santa Cruz. There is a small supermarket in the basement.
Cafés, restaurants & hotels Many throughout the town. Marina Tenerife has an open-air café next to the office, while from Marina Santa Cruz the nearest cold beer will be found across the carpark at a café which also serves the ferry terminal.
Medical services Several hospitals in the city plus dentists, opticians etc.

Communications

Post office Several in Santa Cruz. The city's main post office is on the Plaza de España, directly opposite Marina Santa Cruz.
Mailing address Both marinas will hold mail for yachts: Puerto Deportivo Marina Tenerife, Dársena Pesquera, Vía Auxilliar s/n, 38180 Santa Cruz de Tenerife, Islas Canarias, Spain; and Marina Santa Cruz, Muelle de Enlace, Dársena de los Llanos s/n, 38001 Santa Cruz de Tenerife, Islas Canarias, Spain.
Telephones At the Marina Tenerife office, the main post office and elsewhere.
Internet access No service at either marina. Free Wi-Fi is a available on benches near the fountain opposite Marina Santa Cruz (but it is not secure, so beware hackers). The best password-protected service is currently to be found at the Café Bar Atlantico on Plaza Espana, free other than the cost of a beer, and there are many others. Hotspots are being set up around the city by FON (www.fon.com) with locations mapped on the city council's site at www.sctfe.es.
Car hire Several companies in Santa Cruz, with a wider choice (and apparently better prices) if picked up at Tenerife North Airport (Los Rodeos), which can be reached by bus from the city.
Taxis Many in the city, though it may be necessary to order by telephone from the Dársena Pesquera area.
Buses Frequent buses to the centre of Santa Cruz from a bus stop opposite the wholesale fish market close to the Dársena Pesquera. Island buses depart from the main bus station on Avenida Tres de Mayo to both the island's airports, Los Cristianos (for ferries to the western islands) and many other points.
Ferries Numerous ferries and jetfoils to all the surrounding islands.
Air services International flights use Reina Sofia Airport in the south of the island, whereas inter-island services are concentrated at Los Rodeos in the north – an important difference if transferring to/from an international flight. Allow a good hour if travelling between the two by road.

Marina Tenerife (Dársena Pesquera)

28°29'·57N 16°12'·66W (breakwater head)

Waypoint
⊕C36 – 28°29'·2N 16°12'·3W (0·5M SE of Dársena Pesquera)

Lights
2826·5 **Southwest mole**
Fl.R.5s12m3M Red post 6m
2826 **Breakwater head**
Fl.G.5s10m3M Green column 5m
2826·6 **Reclaimed area**
Q(6)+LFl.15s8m2M South cardinal post, ⯆ topmark
buoy **Reclaimed area**
Fl.Y.5s3M Spherical yellow buoy, × topmark
2826·2 **Entrance, southeast side**
Fl(2)G.7s4m1M
Green column standing in the water
(obscured from seaward by the breakwater)
2826·4 **Entrance, northwest side**
Fl(2)R.7s4m1M
Red column standing in the water
(obscured from seaward by the breakwater)

Harbour Communications
Port Authority ✆ 922 605472 *Fax* 922 605443
Email atraques@puertosdetenerife.org
www.puertosantacruzdetenerife.net VHF Ch 11 (24 hours)
Marina Tenerife ✆ 922 591247 *Fax* 922 591390
Email marinatenerife@nauticaydeportes.com
www.nauticaydeportes.com (0900–1300, 1500–1700 weekdays, 1000–1400 weekends) VHF Ch 09 (24 hours)

Quiet, secluded marina

Marina Tenerife is the smaller and longer-established of the city's two marinas, and has a very different atmosphere to that of the Marina Santa Cruz. It is much favoured by local people as a base for jet-skis and small speedboats (many of which are kept ashore and craned in when required), and can thus be somewhat noisy at weekends, but is a haven of peace and tranquillity during the week. Every effort is made to keep the somewhat sterile surroundings as attractive as possible, even to daily watering of the plant tubs.

Onsite facilities are relatively good and the atmosphere notably friendly. Security is excellent behind an electronically operated gate, with CCTV

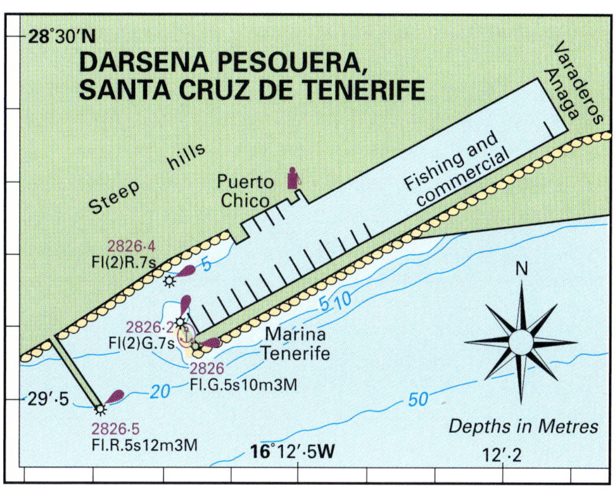

Looking northeast up Santa Cruz's Dársena Pesquera, with Marina Tenerife in the foreground. The Varaderos Anaga boatyard, which is owned by the same company, lies at the head of the long narrow basin *Marina Tenerife*

cameras also installed, and Marina Tenerife would be a good choice if wishing to leave a yacht unattended for several weeks – always assuming a berth is available. In theory about 20 of the 282 berths are reserved for visitors, but in practice some foreign yachts have been there so long they barely qualify as 'visitors' any more.

It can be a long, hot walk from the marina into Santa Cruz itself, though this can be reduced by crossing the harbour by dinghy to avoid walking round the length of the basin. There is a frequent bus service along the main road behind the harbour (every 10 minutes throughout much of the day). Alternatively there is almost unlimited secure parking.

Approach and entrance

See under combined information for outer approaches. Once in the vicinity the entrance to the Dársena Pesquera can be positively identified close north of a concrete silo, five oil tanks and two large buildings with red and blue roofs respectively, all close together at the northeast end of the city. The entrance to the basin is wide and unobstructed, and should not pose problems by day or night.

Berthing

Rounding the end of the breakwater elbow, Marina Tenerife will be seen to starboard. The pontoons to the southwest berth the smallest boats, with size increasing as one continues northwest. The furthest pontoon can accommodate yachts of up to 16m, all berths being alongside substantial finger pontoons. A floating barrier opposite the entrance shelters the marina from minor debris and oil pollution, though the marina has now expanded beyond this with several more smallcraft pontoons.

As mentioned above, the marina is very full and it is always necessary to make contact prior to arrival – apart from other considerations, there is no reception berth. Although the marina is home to yachts of up to 16m, the best chance of a visitors' berth is in the 11–12m size range.

Formalities and charges

The marina office is situated just inside the head of the breakwater next to the slipway and crane. Excellent English is spoken by the office staff but this may not be the case out of hours. Skippers of non-EU registered yachts, or those with non-EU crew, may also need to visit the Policía Nacional in their office in the Fred Olsen ferry terminal overlooking the Dársena Sur.

The berthing fee is calculated on a length x beam basis and in 2010 was set at €0.33 per m^2, which included water, electricity and tax at 5%. Both *Tasa de Embarcación de Recreo* (Recreational Vessel Tax) and *Tasa de Ayuda a la Navegación* (Navigational Aid tax) may also be payable – see page 190.

Facilities

See under combined information.

Puerto Chico

28°29′·76N 16°12′·55W (central pontoon)

Pontoons for local smallcraft

Puerto Chico ✆ 696 920631
Email pch@marinaalgomera.com which lies on the northwest side of the Dársena Pesquera, is mainly of interest for the fuel berth which lies just beyond its northeastern pontoon (which can make berthing an interesting exercise for less manoeuvrable yachts). A few of its 42 berths can take yachts of up to 12m, but space is seldom available for visitors.

Marina Santa Cruz (Dársena de los Llanos)

28°27′·34N 16°14′·82W (breakwater head)

Waypoint
⊕C37 – 28°27′N 16°14′·5W (Dársena de los Llanos)

Lights
2826·7 **Breakwater angle** Q(3)10s8m5M
East cardinal post, ◆ topmark 2m
2826·72 **Breakwater head** Fl(3)G.9s12m9M
Green tower 6m
2826·9 **Ldg Lts on 354°** *Front* Iso.1s7m3M
Rear, 75m from front, Fl.12m3M
White framework towers, red bands 5/11m
2826·82 **Southwest mole** Fl(3)R.10s7m9M
Red post standing in the water
2826·74 **Breakwater head spur** Fl(4)G.11s5m3M
Green post standing in the water 2m
2826·86 **Obstruction** Fl(4)R.11s7m3M
Red post standing in the water
2826·87 **Ro-Ro berth** Fl.R.5s5m1M
Red pyramid 2m
2826·78 **Breakwater interior spur**
Fl.G.5s5m1M Green pyramid tower 3m
2826·68 **Marina entrance, east side** Q.G.5m1M
Green post, white strut 2m
2826·67 **Marina entrance, west side, north corner**
Q.R.5m1M Red post, white strut 2m
2826·675 **Marina entrance, west side, south corner**
Q.R.5m1M Red post, white strut 2m
Note The above two lights, which are very close together, have identical characteristics. Should only one be working, and ambient light insufficient to see the mole itself, hug the main breakwater to ensure safe entrance

Harbour Communications
Port Authority ✆ 922 605472 *Fax* 922 605443
Email atraques@puertosdetenerife.org
www.puertosantacruzdetenerife.net
VHF Ch 11 (24 hours)
Marina Santa Cruz ✆ 922 292184 *Fax* 922 247933
Email reservas@marinasantacruz.com (0900–1330, 1530–1730 weekdays, 0900–1300 Saturday)
VHF Ch 09 (24 hours)

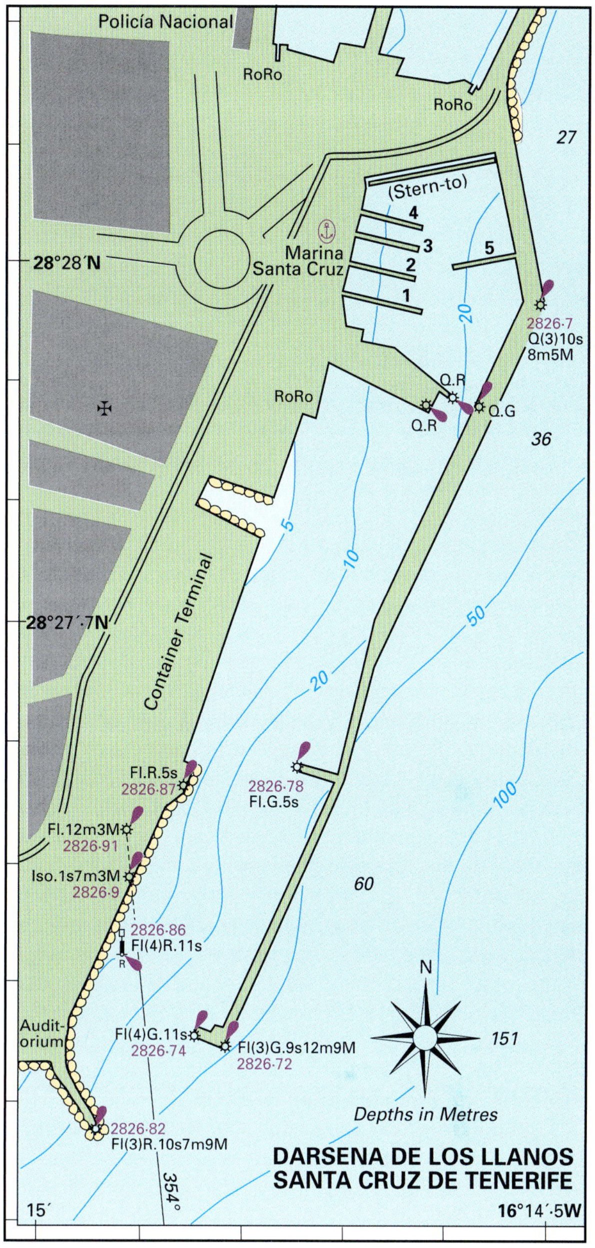

Large marina with space for visitors

A large-scale marina to be situated at the head of the Dársena de los Llanos was first announced back in 1994, when a plan was put forward for a grid pattern of pontoons radiating from a central island.

A yacht passes through the narrow entrance to Marina Santa Cruz, at the head of the Dársena de los Llanos

Marina Santa Cruz seen from the northeast. With so much space available it is surprising more pontoons have not been installed

Work started that year, and by 1995 a detached mole had been constructed to separate the marina from the commercial basin. The first pontoon was in position by November, and completion was anticipated for 1996. However, work slowed and then stopped altogether – 'political objections' were blamed – a situation which pertained until the end of the decade. Work did not resume until 2000, and then somewhat slowly, but by November 2003 the marina appeared effectively finished other than infilling of the narrow western entrance to connect the previously detached mole to the shore, and replacement of the extremely dilapidated services building. This was finally done in 2007, housing the marina office as well as much-improved showers, launderette, etc., though the planned chandlery and restaurant have yet to materialise. The number of berths has also grown, albeit slowly, and by mid-2010 Marina Santa Cruz was said to contain about 400 berths for vessels of up to 100m.

The harbour water can become very dirty, particularly in southerly winds when surge may also affect the marina, and may also be awash with detritus after heavy rain – presumably rubbish washed out of the storm drains. This includes plastic bags, logs, planks, stray ends of fishing net, etc., so if the water is brown instead of the usual dark green, keep a careful watch when manoeuvering.

The dramatic *Auditorio de Tenerife*, home to the city's symphony orchestra, forms a unique landmark at the south end of the Dársena de los Llanos

Approach and entrance

See under combined information for outer approaches. Once in the vicinity the lit leading marks may be used, though this is by no means essential for most yachts since the entire harbour carries a minimum of 5m other than in the entrance to the Barranco de Santos. The basin is nearly a mile long and used by a good deal of commercial shipping, including Ro-Ro ferries which berth on the mainland side. Should one have any difficulty identifying the entrance, look for the curved white superstructure of the Auditorium of Tenerife which stands at the root of the southwest mole.

Contact must be made on VHF Ch 12 with Santa Cruz Harbour Control at least five minutes prior to entering the Dársena de los Llanos (and again before leaving the marina basin on departure). On receiving permission from Santa Cruz Harbour Control to proceed, call Marina Santa Cruz on VHF Ch 09 for berthing instructions.

Access to and from the marina basin is via a narrow entrance next to the breakwater. It is easily seen by day and well lit at night, and with a reliable engine it would be possible to enter the Dársena de los Llanos and continue up to the marina by day or night in almost any weather conditions.

Berthing

The former reception berth to starboard on entry is no longer in use, and yachts will normally be directed to a berth either by VHF or visually. So far only 80 berths are occupied by local boats, and with apparently limitless space to raft-up there is no obvious reason why Marina Santa Cruz should ever have to turn a yacht away. Berths on the five pontoons are all against fingers, with those lining the north wall stern-on to a floating pontoon with a buoy provided for the bow. Seriously large yachts – and the marina accepts vessels up to 100m – are berthed against the quayside to the northeast.

Ongoing maintenance remains lacking, however, and by 2011 some of the pontoon fingers were in a poor state – in a few cases not even attached to the main pontoon. The rubber fendering which surrounds them is also becoming perished and leaves marks on topsides and fenders. As a final hazard, lines are occasionally strung between adjacent pontoons. Security gates are fitted to the pontoons, but it seem these are hardly ever closed.

Formalities

As mentioned previously, the marina office will be found in the new services block, near the root of pontoon No.2, and should be visited taking the usual ship's papers, passports and insurance documents. The front office staff are friendly and speak reasonable English, though the management are less helpful. Skippers of non-EU registered yachts, or those with non–EU crew, may also need to visit the *Policía Nacional* in their office in the Fred Olsen ferry terminal overlooking the Dársena Sur.

Charges

Berthing charges as Marina Santa Cruz are somewhat complicated. In the high season yachts are divided into bands, those of up to 48m² paying €18.14 per night, 48–54m² paying €20.41 and 54–75m² paying €28.35. In the low season this drops to €0.36 per m² for a pontoon berth or €0.29 if stern-to. Yachts of more than 20m pay extra for (metered) water and electricity, but otherwise the above prices include both these and tax at 5%. Discounts are available if booked and paid for in advance.

Both *Tasa de Embarcación de Recreo* (Recreational Vessel tax) and *Tasa de Ayuda a la Navegación* (Navigational Aid tax) may also be payable – see page 190.

Facilities

See under combined information.

Puerto Caballo (Puerto de la Hondura)

28°26′·92N 16°15′·87W (pierhead)

Plans
Spanish *6120* (1:12,500 & 1:5,000)

Lights
2827 **CEPSA oil refinery** Iso.G.3·4s9m5M
Green column in front of a black and white banded wall 6m

Note Four pairs of leading lights mark the harbour approach. A yellow pillar buoy with × topmark, Fl.Y.10s2M, is positioned close northeast of the harbour, together with two yellow can buoys, Fl.Y.4s3M and Fl.Y.3s4M respectively, to the southeast.

Commercial harbour closed to yachts

A commercial harbour used for loading oil tankers and other bulk cargoes, and unsuitable for yachts. A refinery with several chimneys backed by an extensive tank farm lies close north of the harbour.

Puerto Radazul

28°25′·03N 16°19′·44W (breakwater head)

Waypoint
⊕C38 – 28°23′·5N 16°19′·3W (0·5M SSE of Puerto Radazul)

Lights
2827·9 **Marina breakwater**
Fl(2)G.10s9m5M Green post 6m
2827·92 **Marina north mole**
Fl(2)R.7s3m3M Red post 2m
2827·925 **Club do Mar breakwater**
Q(6)+LFl.15s9m3M
South cardinal post, ▼ topmark 4m
(not associated with the marina – see next page)

Harbour Communications
Puerto Deportivo Radazul ☎ */Fax* 922 680933, 654 347059 *Email* puertodeportivoradazul@gmail.com
www.puertodeportivoradazul.com (0900–1700 weekdays, 1030–1300 Saturdays)
VHF Ch 09, 16 (0800–2000 daily)

Small, secure, private marina

Puerto Radazul (pronounced *Pwerto Rah'dah'sool*) is a private, family-owned marina with about 200 berths, the largest able to take one yacht of 22m. Many of these are owned by local residents, and though 54 are in theory reserved for visitors, most are rented on a long-term basis leaving only a few available for transients. It is therefore advisable to contact the marina office before arrival, by telephone if possible.

Entry should not be attempted in bad conditions, but with due warning of heavy weather it would provide a good refuge where a yacht could remain in safety. Small, clean and secure, it would also be a suitable place to leave a yacht unattended, either afloat or ashore. As space is not always available it is always wise to make contact in advance, even though reservations are not accepted (see Formalities and charges, overleaf).

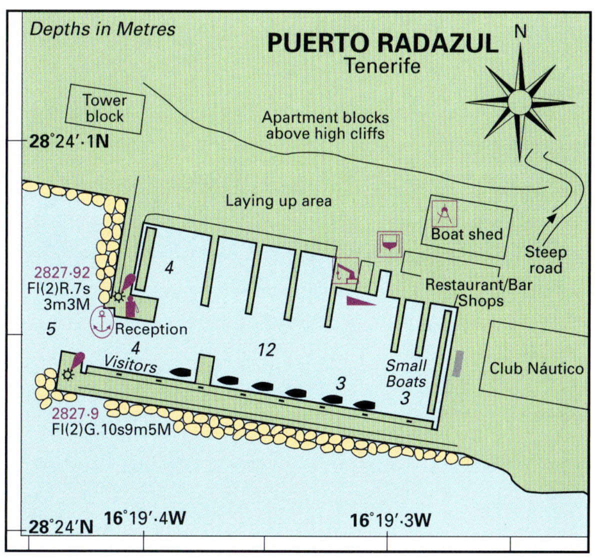

Approach and entrance

The marina lies 6M southwest of Santa Cruz and just south of Punta de Guadamojete. The power station a short distance to the southwest provides a useful landmark, its two tall grey chimneys often emitting a conspicuous plume of smoke. A group of tall apartment blocks line the zigzag road leading down to the marina, which is sited under a high cliff. The tallest block is at the base of the cliff behind the marina. A short, curved breakwater protects the Club do Mar close east of the marina but is not associated with it.

A swimming area, marked off by a string of small yellow buoys, lies off the beach close west of the entrance, which is west-facing and very narrow. There is a 2 knot speed limit in the approach. The end of the short north mole doubles as reception berth.

Berthing

Pontoons with fingers line the north side of the harbour, with stern-to moorings against the south breakwater and the north mole. Short-term visitors are normally berthed alongside the breakwater just inside the entrance, and this is the best place to go if arriving outside office hours. To avoid the inevitable surge and the small overhang on the wall, the helpful staff provide hauling-off lines led to a ground chain in the middle of the entrance. There are no gates, but round-the-clock patrols combined with the marina's quiet position appear to provide reliable security.

Formalities and charges

Visit the marina office on the north mole with the usual paperwork, including evidence of insurance. Good English is spoken.

The berthing fee is calculated on a length x beam basis and in 2010 was set at €0.41 per m^2. This included water, electricity and tax, and was not expected to increase significantly over the following few years. Discounts were available for longer stays and for paying in advance. Reservations are not accepted for marina berths, but are essential for the boatyard.

Facilities

Boatyard Owners normally do their own work, though the marina staff can advise on who best to call in for various jobs. It is permitted to live aboard a yacht while ashore.

Travel-lift Two, the larger rated at 60 tonnes, with no shortage of hardstanding.

Engineers Large workshop in the marina complex. Cris Motors SL, ✆ 922 681814 *Fax* 922 681734, are agents for Volvo Perkins and Yanmar as well as several makes of outboard.

Chandlery Cris Motors have a small chandlery. While wiling to order if necessary, it would almost certainly be simpler to visit one of the large chandleries in Santa Cruz de Tenerife.

Water At all berths.

Showers Near the office, with and several more let into the marina walls.

Electricity At all berths.

Fuel At the reception berth, open 0800–2000. Payment by credit card is accepted.

Weather forecast Available from the marina office on request.

Shops/provisioning Large supermarket in the commercial centre up the hill, open 1000–1330, 1700–2100 Monday to Saturday, plus pharmacy, etc.

Cafés, restaurants & hotels In the holiday complex behind the harbour, plus two restaurants on the quayside.

Communications

Mailing address Puerto Deportivo Radazul, Urb. Radazul s/n, El Rosario, 38109 – Santa Cruz de Tenerife, Islas Canarias, Spain.

Telephones Just behind the marina complex.

Internet access No Wi-Fi, though visitors can use a computer in the marina office for short periods.

Car hire & taxis Can be arranged through the marina office.

Buses Bus service to Santa Cruz and elsewhere from near the marina entrance.

The small, well-run marina at Puerto Radazul seen from cliffs to the northwest

Puerto Deportivo La Galera

28°21′·57N 16°21′·92W (breakwater head)

Waypoint

⊕C39 – 28°21′·2N 16°21′·5W (0·5M SE of Puerto Deportivo La Galera)

Lights

2827·93 **Breakwater head**
Fl(3)G.9s5m5M Green post 2m
Breakwater spur
Fl(3)G.9s3M Green post (synchronised with 2827·93)
2827·935 **Inner mole**
Fl(3)R.9s4m3M Red post 1m
Note Obscured from offshore by the breakwater

Harbour Communications

Puerto Deportivo La Galera ✆ /*Fax* 922 503282
✆ 922 500915
Email secretaria@puertodeportivolagalera.com
www.puertodeportivolagalera.com VHF Ch 09 (0900–1300, 1700–2000 weekdays, 1000–1400 Saturday)

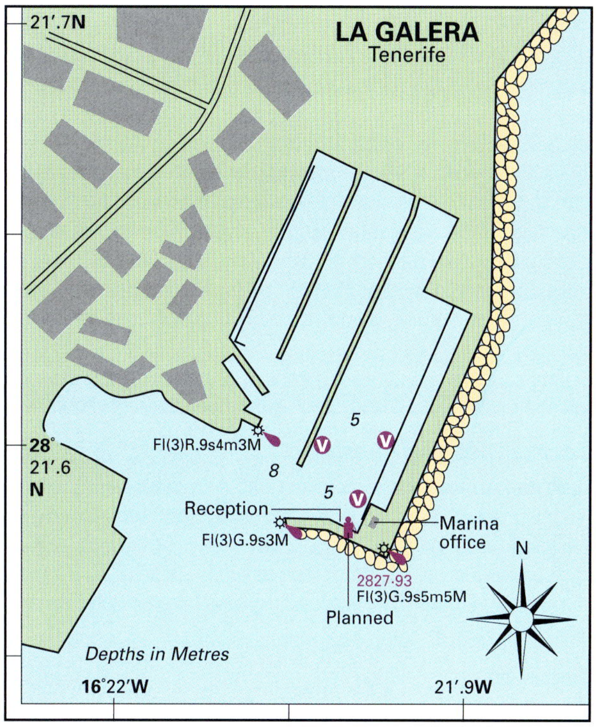

New *Club Náutico* marina

Since 2004 Puerto Deportivo La Galera has metamorphosed from a tiny harbour catering for small motorboats and jetskis, nearly all of which were lifted ashore when not in use, into a small but well-organised marina with 174 berths, though most are for craft of less than 10m. It is essential to make contact well before arrival, confirming a day or two in advance that a space will be available. It is owned by the local authority and operated by the *Club Náutico la Galera*, but although visiting yachts are welcomed into the marina their crew do not have access to the other club facilities, such as its tennis courts and large outdoor swimming pool. There is, however, a cordoned-off 'swimming channel' between the outermost pontoon and the wall, as well as several small beaches just outside the entrance.

The marina lies near the north end of the pleasant old town of Candelaria, a short description of which will be found overleaf.

Approach and entrance

The smoke plume from the power station a mile north of the harbour makes a good landmark as does, on closer approach, the church with its tall white tower and red roof a mile to the south. Two harbours front the town, separated by about 300m of dark sand beach, with Puerto Deportivo La Galera to the north and the old fishing harbour of Candelaria to the south. There are no hazards in the approach other than fishpot buoys, for which a good watch needs to be kept. The entrance itself is narrow, however, with little more than 20m between the breakwater head and the end of the central mole, though depths are generous at 8m or so. The small cove opposite is cordoned-off with the usual string of yellow buoys.

The sharp turn necessary to enter the marina brings the bow into and then through the prevailing wind, from which there is no shelter beyond that afforded by the breakwater itself – a manoeuvre perhaps best avoided by lightly-engined boats when the trades are blowing strongly.

Although the marina is lit, night entry is not recommended.

The new Puerto Depotivo La Galera, seen from just east of north. The tall white tower of Nuestra Señora de la Candelaria, visible just to the right of the entrance, makes a fine landmark

Berthing

The reception berth is immediately to starboard on entry, inside the breakwater head. The five visitors' berths – all bow or stern-to the breakwater and a couple able to take yachts of up to 15m – are adjacent, with a single alongside berth for up to 20m on the central pontoon. At least 5m will be found through this area, shoaling further into the marina. Although protected from serious waves, swell rebounding off the beach outside produces some surge, particularly around the reception and visitors' berths.

Security is excellent with a manned gate to the entire complex as well as round-the-clock patrols.

Formalities and charges

The marina office overlooks the reception berth, and when visited in late 2010 the welcome was friendly, helpful and in fluent English. The berthing fee is calculated on a length x beam basis and in 2011 was set at €0.43 per m^2, which included water, electricity and 5% tax.

Facilities

Boatyard Small boatyard for local craft only, with a 10-tonne crane but no travel-lift.
Engineers Can be arranged via the marina office.
Water At all berths.
Showers Still temporary as of late 2010, but a permanent shower block is planned.
Launderette In the commercial centre in town. Ask at the marina office for directions.
Electricity At all berths.
Fuel Diesel and petrol pumps are planned for the reception berth. In the meantime it may be possible to buy the former in the old fishing harbour.
Bottled gas Camping Gaz exchanges at the hardware store in town.
Weather forecast On the marina website, which may be printed out at the office on request.
Banks Several in the town, including one almost opposite the marina approach road, nearly all with cash dispensers.
Shops/provisioning Good food and other shopping in the town.
Produce market On Wednesday and Saturday – ask for details in the office.
Cafés, restaurants & hotels Many in Candelaria. The *Club Náutico*'s bar and restaurant are not open to visitors, but a waterside café is planned for the marina.
Medical services Health centre in the town, with all the resources of Santa Cruz to hand if necessary.

Communications

Post office In the town.
Mailing address Puerto Deportivo La Galera, Avda Generalísimo 22, 38530 Candelaria, Santa Cruz de Tenerife, Islas Canarias, Spain.
Internet access Free, password-protected Wi-Fi – ask at the marina office.
Car hire & taxis Available in the town.
Buses Regular services along the coast in both directions.
Air services About 45km to/from Reina Sofia Airport in the south of the island.

The small *club náutico* harbour at Puerto do Güimar (see opposite page) viewed from the north

Candelaria

28°21'·36N 16°22'·09W (breakwater head)

Lights
2827·96 **Breakwater angle** Q(3)10s8m3M
East cardinal post, ♦ topmark 2m
2827·94 **Breakwater head**
Fl(4)G.11s 8m5M Green post 3m
2827·98 **Inner mole**
Fl(4)R.11s 6m3M Red post 3m

Small fishing harbour

Candelaria (pronounced *Candelah'riah*) is an old town not yet seriously affected by tourism but nevertheless with many low-rise concrete apartments. A striking feature is the church of Nuestra Señora de la Candelaria at the southern end of the town, overlooking a paved square guarded by statues of Guanches, the ancient inhabitants of the islands. The church is a place of pilgrimage as it contains the beautifully decorated shrine of Our Lady of Candelaria, Patroness of the Canaries.

Although yachts occasionally visited the fishing harbour before Puerto Deportivo La Galera was built immediately to the north, should one attempt it now there is little doubt that it would swiftly be asked to leave.

The old fishing harbour of Candelaria, looking south-southeast

Puerto de Güimar

28°17'·66N 16°22'·36W (fishermen's pier head)
28°17'·18N 16°22'·83W (Club Náutico breakwater head)

Lights

Fishing harbour (to northeast)
2828 **Pier, head**
Fl.G.5s6m5M Green post 3m
2828·1 **Pier, root**
Fl.G.5s4m3M Green column 4m

Club Náutico harbour (to southwest)
2828·2 **Breakwater**
Fl(2)G.7s10m5M Green post 6m
2828·3 **Inner mole**
Fl(2)R.7s7m3M Red post 4m

Small, private marina

The town of Güimar lies 5km inland on the slopes of the central range, with a small fishing village surrounded by a good deal of newish low-rise development on the shore. Local fishing boats receive some shelter from a short pier with an angled end, which is also used to load local agricultural produce.

A short distance to the south is a large sports complex incorporating a *club náutico*, and facing it a small marina which does not accept visitors. Three pontoons provide berthing for an assortment of small motorboats and one or two sailing craft, but depths average less than 2m making it unsuitable for most cruising yachts even were they welcome.

Bahía de Abona

28°09'·96N 16°25'·72W (north quay)
28°09'·2N 16°25'·84W (south mole)

Lights
2829 **Punta de Abona**
Fl(3)20s53m17M 214°-vis-040°
White tower, red bands 39m

Double anchorage

The Bahía de Abona (pronounced *By'eeah de Abonah*) lies between Punta del Ternero to the north and Punta de Abona with its powerful light to the south. There is a choice of anchorages to suit wind direction – the northern corner, below the tourist village of Poris de Abona, is sheltered from the northwest while Ensenada (cove) del Pedregal in the southern corner provides safe anchorage in southerly winds. There has been talk of building a small yacht harbour below the village, but it looks increasingly unlikely to materialise.

Approach and entrance

Approaching from north or east the bay will open up to the west of the lighthouse. Punta del Ternero has a few outlying rocks and should be given reasonable clearance. Coming from the south, round Punta de Abona well offshore to avoid a patch of partly submerged rocks. In either case beware a spur of lava which extends into the centre of the bay from the west and which could be mistaken for a stone pier.

Anchorage

North Below the village of Poris de Abona will be seen a small stone quay with convenient bollards and 3–4m alongside, which might be usable in exceptionally flat conditions. Otherwise anchor off in 4–5m over sand and land at the ladder or steps. The area is popular with swimmers, for which a good watch must be kept. There are cafés and restaurants in the village and basic shopping needs can be met.

South In the right conditions the anchorage northwest of Punta de Abona is most appealing, lying off a beach of speckled sand fringed at either end by rocky outcrops. Anchor in 5m over sand off the eastern part of the beach – there are rocks further west – with the lighthouse just open of the short stone mole. Holding is excellent. Although it offers no facilities beyond a small café selling drinks and ice creams, it is worth wandering up the path to view the small, military-style village built around the church and square. The same cannot be said for the long tramp out to the lighthouse on the headland.

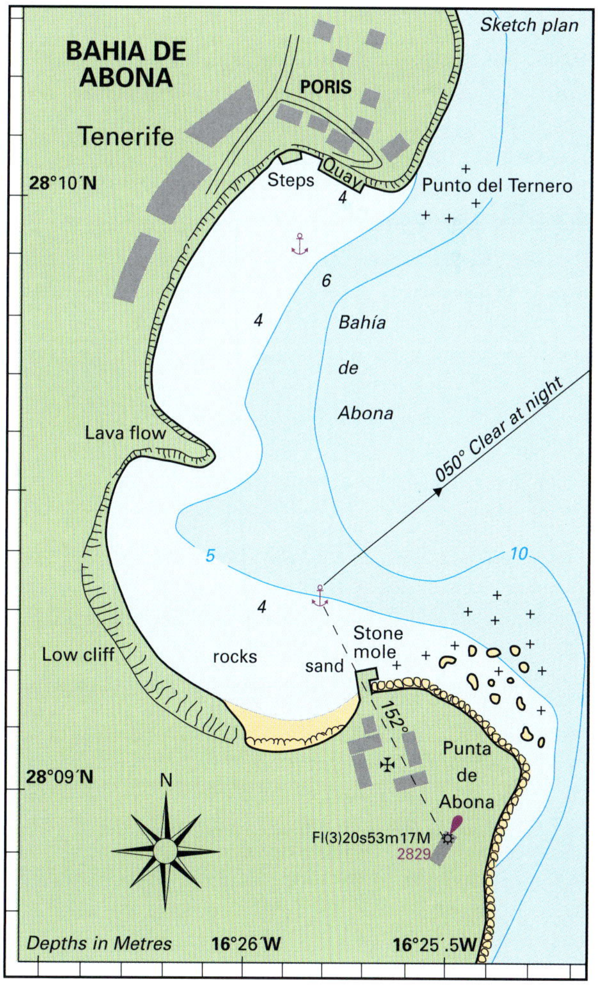

Puerto de San Miguel de Tajao

28°06′·52N 16°28′·2W (breakwater head)

Lights
2829·05 **Breakwater**
Fl(3)G.9s11m5M Green post 6m

Possible anchorage off small harbour

A small fishing harbour still relatively unaffected by tourism, Puerto de San Miguel de Tajao (pronounced *Pwerto de San Miggell de Tah'how*) lies behind a curved breakwater which opens to the southwest, the entrance partially closed by a short opposing mole. The harbour is packed full of moored smallcraft, with more drawn up on the black sand beach, and offers no feasible berth for a yacht. In settled weather it might be possible to anchor off but there appears little reason to do so.

Central Termica de Granadilla

28°05′·8N 16°29′·37W (molehead)

Lights
2829·3 **Molehead** Fl(3)10s8m3M
East cardinal post, ♦ topmark 4m
buoy **Outfall buoy** Fl.Y.5s3M
Yellow pillar buoy, × topmark

Not really a harbour...

Somewhat similar to Gran Canaria's Barranco Tirajana, although one or two smallcraft shelter inside the short hooked mole its main purpose is to provide cooling water for the adjacent power station. It is not open to yachts.

Anchorages around Punta Montaña Roja

Punta Montaña Roja (pronounced *Punta Montanya Roh'hah*) appears as a tall red pyramid, forming a small peninsula on the southeast coast of Tenerife. The island's main airport, the *Aeropuerto Transoceanico Reina Sofia*, lies on the plain north of the headland and aircraft can be seen taking off and landing. Southwest of Punta Montaña Roja the coast is low-lying as far as Punta Rasca, the most southerly point on Tenerife.

Bahía del Médano (28°02′·5N 16°32′·3W), a circular bay with a short unlit breakwater close northeast of Punta Montaña Roja, offers a pleasant anchorage in 3m over sand with some shelter from the north. However, while protection from the sea is good, the topology is such that any wind from the south or west makes it an extremely windy place – as evidenced by the number of kite surfers. There can be 20 to 30 knots in the bay yet virtual calm five miles further up the coast. The bottom shelves sharply across the mouth of the bay and it is essential that the anchor be properly set. The village of El Médano in the northern crook of the bay has restaurants, shops and other basic facilities.

Close west of Punta Montaña Roja lies Playa de las Tejitas (28°01′·7N 16°33′·3W), a comfortable anchorage in winds from north or northeast in 7–8m over sand. Several large yellow mooring buoys lie off the beach, only one of which is lit, Fl.Y.5s5M. Keep well clear as they are used by tankers bringing aviation fuel for the nearby airport. Two pairs of leading lights guide ships towards the buoys, but are only lit when a vessel is due.

About 2·5M west of Punta Montaña Roja will be found Los Abrigos (28°01′·7N 16°35′·6W), a once charming fishing village now given over mainly to tourism. A few fishing boats lie on trots secured to the quay, but are hauled out in bad weather. The quay itself bears a green pyramid tower, Fl(2)G.7s10m5M. The waterside area is famous for its fish restaurants, well worth a lunchtime stop by sea in calm weather – the holding is not particularly good – or an evening visit by road.

Marina San Miguel

28°01′·17N 16°36′·89W

Waypoint
⊕C41 – 28°00′·6N 16°36′·6W (0·5M SSE of Marina San Miguel)

Lights
2829·46 **Breakwater angle** Fl(3)10s10m3M
East cardinal beacon, ♦topmark 6m
2829·48 **Breakwater head**
Fl(3)G.9s11m5M Green column 6m
2829·47 **Inner mole**
Fl(3)R.9s6m3M Red column 6m
Note Twelve small buoys, some red and some yellow, of which three are lit, Fl.R, mark the channel into and inside the marina

Harbour Communications
Marina San Miguel ✆ 922 785124 *Fax* 922 785075
Email reservas@marinasanmiguel.com (0930–1400, 1430–1600 weekdays) www.marinasanmiguel.com
VHF Ch 09 and 610 777280 (24 hrs)

Large marina, a 'work in progress'

In the early 1990s work began on a large marina northwest of Punta Montaña Amarilla, in conjunction with the Amarilla Golf and Country Club development. However, the breakwater was severely damaged by a gale before it was finished, a pattern which was repeated several times over the following decade.

Work resumed in 2002, this time with greater success, and the marina finally opened in late August 2006. Only three of the planned eight pontoons were actually in place, providing around 60 berths, though a new pontoon was installed along the entire length of the main breakwater the following year, providing space for another 20 or so yachts. By July 2011 there were five pontoons, bringing the total berths to around 120. When pressed for a completion date, the very sensible response was that the marina would 'grow as the market demands'.

Owned and managed by the Tavio family, who include some serious sailors in their ranks, given time

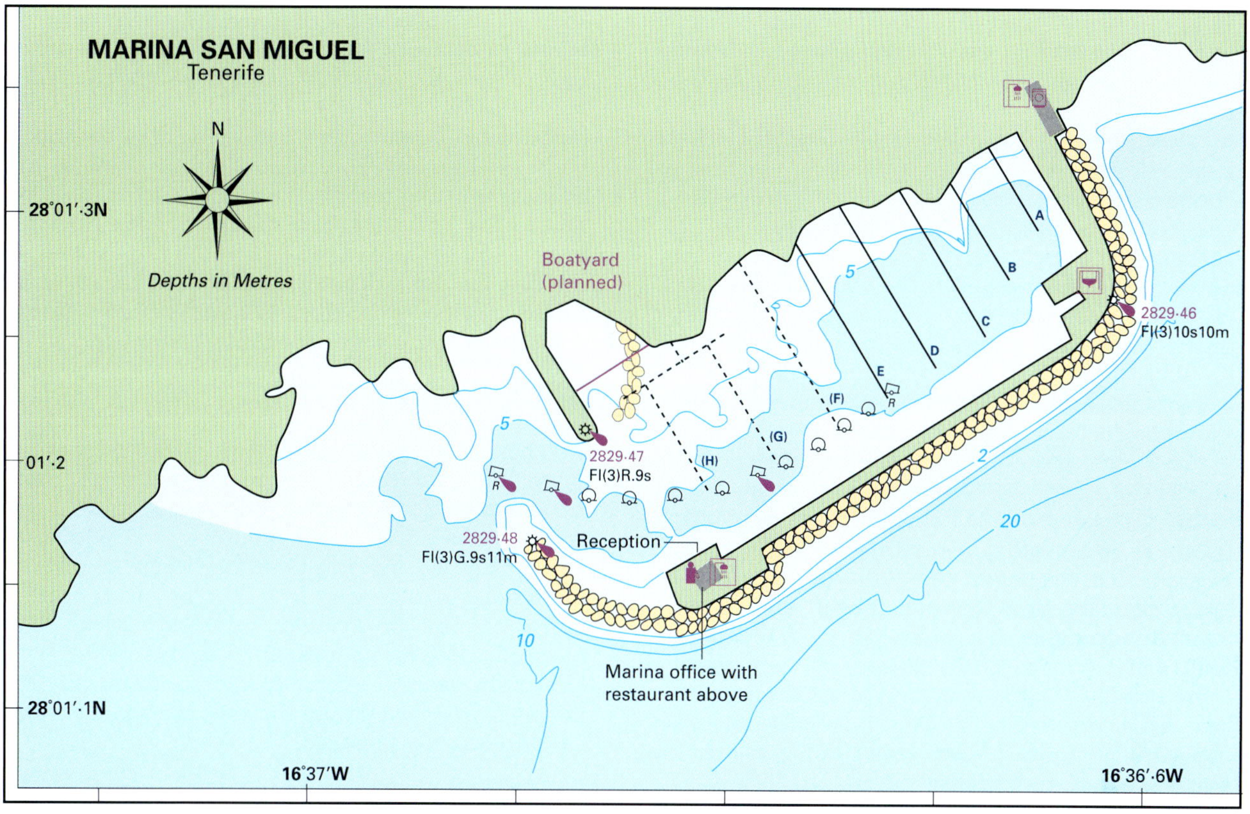

Looking southwest towards the entrance of Marina San Miguel. All the red and yellow buoys must be left to port on entry and a fair wind Marina San Miguel has the potential to rival the best marinas in the Canaries. It should eventually contain 344 berths for craft of up to 20m, a high proportion intended for visitors and most able to berth 12m or more. All berths – other than those alongside the breakwater – will be on finger pontoons, though currently some still use pick-up lines to buoys. Dredged spoil from the centre of the harbour is being used to infill an area to the northwest, earmarked for the planned boatyard. However, dredging is slow – the seabed is rock rather than sand, necessitating drilling (though not blasting) to achieve acceptable depths for the projected western pontoons. The plan on the previous page shows the 'natural' depths prior to this work.

The marina has a particularly impressive website, in Spanish, English, German and French, which includes unusual – and thoughtful – items ranging from a *Supermercado Virtual* (a full 'online shopping list' for delivery to your boat) to the local bus timetable. Both these highlight the marina's main disadvantage – it is backed by the Amarilla Golf and Country Club, which although offering some attractive landscaping and pleasant restaurants has little atmosphere. The busy Reina Sofia International Airport is less than 5km to the north-northeast, but nevertheless aircraft are heard as a rumble rather than a roar.

Approach and entrance

The entrance can be difficult to spot from offshore, though the circular blue tower near the end of the breakwater is distinctive. Low-rise development extends some distance in both directions, with one of the resort's several golf courses backing the marina itself.

A rocky ledge with depths of 5m or less lies opposite the end of the breakwater, parallel to and some 70m outside the line of the inner mole. It breaks in heavy onshore swell, and waves can break right across the entrance in strong southerlies. An inconspicuous red buoy – Fl.R., though first time night entry is not recommended – marks the shoal, with a string of eleven other buoys defining the channel into the marina. Final approach should be made on a bearing of about 023°. Rubble runs out some distance beyond the end of the breakwater, so the best line for a deep-draught yacht appears to be to swing wide, quite close to the first buoy, before completing the turn into the marina entrance.

Marina San Miguel's reception building – intended to resemble a ship's superstructure when seen from offshore – aids identification of the marina entrance *Nigel Mercier*

Berthing

It is essential to make contact prior to arrival, at which time the yacht may be directed straight to a berth, avoiding a stop at the reception berth. Take particular care if berthed on pontoon C, as the large steel tubes which attach the pontoon to its piles have sharp metal triangles at pontoon height which can put a hole in an unwary boat. Larger yachts usually berth on the breakwater pontoon, which has received praise for its substantial cleats.

Security gates are fitted to the pontoons but are normally left open during the day. There is the usual 24-hour security presence.

Formalities

After securing at the reception berth, visit the marina office at the head of the breakwater with ship's papers, passports and evidence of insurance, walking through a small tourist shop en route. The office staff are particularly friendly and helpful and several speak good English. Although office hours are relatively limited (0930–1400, 1430–1600 weekdays only), security staff will open the office at weekends if necessary to check in new arrivals.

Charges

The berthing fee is calculated on a length x beam basis and in 2011 was set at €0.45 per m^2, which included water, electricity and 5% tax. Discounts are available for longer stays if booked and paid for in advance.

Facilities

Boatyard The boatyard is currently situated part-way along the breakwater but is due to move to an infilled area just inside the north mole. Most services are available – enquire at the marina office. DIY work is permitted and owners are welcome to live aboard while the yacht is ashore.

Travel-lift Although a hoist bay was part of the original breakwater design, it remained empty until July 2011 when the 70-tonne hoist previously in the boatyard at Las Palmas was installed. A vast crane, capable of lifting almost any size, weight and beam, is also brought in as necessary.

Engineers, electronic & radio repairs Can be arranged via the marina office, or contact Club Yachting at Marina del Sur (see page 282).

Sail repairs Enquire at the marina office.

Chandlery A chandlery is planned for the head of the harbour, meanwhile contact Club Yachting at Marina del Sur (see page 282), who also handle rigging and general maintenance.

Water At all berths.
Showers Well-kept showers and toilets next to the marina office, with more in the services block at the head of the harbour.
Launderette At the head of the harbour, with two washers and two dryers all of which take €1 coins.
Electricity At all berths.
Fuel Diesel and petrol are available at the reception berth at all times.
Bottled gas Camping Gaz exchanges at the marina office, but as of 2011 the situation regarding refilling other cylinders remained uncertain – see page 191.
Weather forecast Displayed in the marina office and at the services block at the head of the harbour.
Banks Banks and cash dispensers in the resort, but both some distance from the marina.
Shops/provisioning Supermarkets and other shops in the resort, all well within walking distance – or patronise the *Supermercado Virtual* on the marina website, which offers a comprehensive choice of victuals to be delivered to your boat. Bread is made and sold at the café above the marina office.
Cafés, restaurants & hotels Outdoor café/restaurant on the upper floor of the marina reception building, a small 'beach bar' in the northeast corner, and many restaurants and hotels in the golf resort.
Medical services Medical centre and pharmacy in the resort.

Communications

Post office The nearest post office is in Las Galletas about 4km to the southwest by road.
Mailing address Marina San Miguel, Urb. Amarilla Golf – 38639 San Miguel de Abona, Tenerife, Islas Canarias, Spain.
Internet access Free Wi-Fi thoughout the marina. Best reception will be found close to the marina office, or on the restaurant terrace above. A computer (operated by coins or credit card) is provided in the services block at the head of the harbour.
Car hire Several companies have offices in the resort.
Taxis Can be ordered at the office for pick-up within the marina.
Buses Regular service from the resort. A timetable will be found on the marina website.
Air services Reina Sofia Airport is less than 5km to the northeast, about €15 by taxi.

Las Galletas (Marina del Sur)

28°00'·43N 16°39'·69W

Waypoint
⊕C42 – 27°59'·9N 16°39'·8W (0·5M SSW of Las Galletas / Marina del Sur)

Lights
2829·5 **Breakwater head**
Fl(4)G.7s4m3M Green post 2m

Harbour Communications
Marina del Sur ✆ 922 783620 *Fax* 922 783621
Email info@marinadelsur.es www.marinatenerife.com
0900–1400, 1600–1900 weekdays, 0900–1400 Saturday
VHF Ch 09 (24 hours)

Small new marina inside old harbour

Previously a rather crowded fishing harbour with little room for yachts, Las Galletas has, over the past few years, transformed itself into a medium-sized yacht harbour. Tucked behind the old curved breakwater, Marina del Sur (pronounced *Marina del Soor*) opened for business in August 2007 and now has five pontoons providing 196 berths, including 153 for yachts. Sixty-eight of these are able to take 12m or more, with two places for yachts of up to 20m LOA, though only seven places are reserved for visiting yachts of 12m or more.

Marina del Sur offers the major advantage, so far as most cruising yachtsmen are concerned, of backing straight on to the bustling Spanish town of Las Galletas. Although efforts have been made to promote the area as a tourist destination, the lack of appealling beaches keeps the numbers down and some vestige of the old atmosphere remains. The wild and dusty countryside outside the town also remains largely unspoilt.

Approach and entrance

The harbour of Las Galletas lies between Punta Rasca 2M to the west and the white apartment blocks of Costa del Silencio to the east. The dark

Looking northeast across Marina del Sur towards the town of Las Galletas

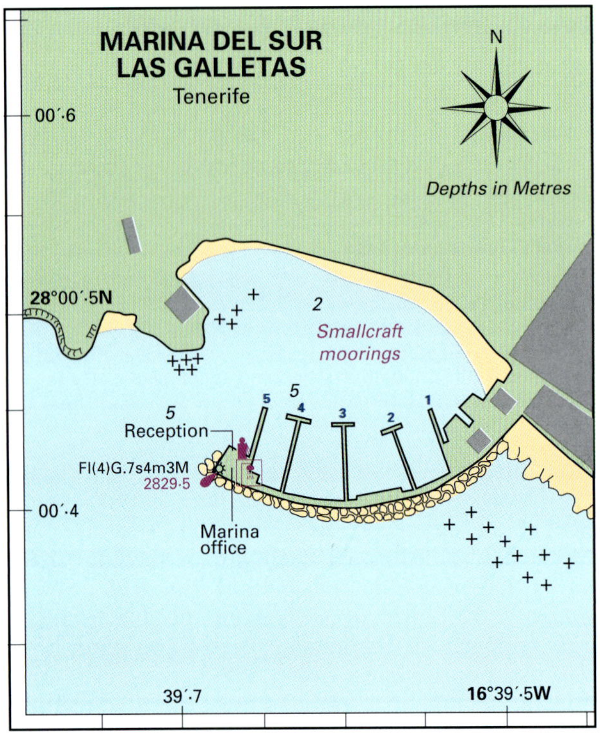

stone breakwater may be difficult to pick out against the shore behind, but the same cannot be said of the unusual – and rather pretty – blue and white building at its tip, which houses the marina office.

Approaching from the east, keep 0·5M offshore to avoid a reef stretching out from near the root of the breakwater. From any direction the final approach should be with the head of the breakwater bearing slightly east of north. Keep well to starboard on entry as a spit of rock runs out from the shore opposite. The marina's reception and fuel berth is immediately to starboard on entry. There is a 2 knot speed limit inside the harbour.

Marina del Sur's distinctive reception building, seen across several crowded pontoons *Alison Watkins*

Berthing

On arrival, secure to the reception berth below the office building, unless contact has already been made by VHF (recommended) and a berth already assigned. As stated above, there are now five pontoons in the harbour, numbered from the eastern end. The larger visitors' berths are on the western side of the central pontoon (No.3) at the outer end, with those few visiting yachts of less than 10m LOA berthed on the east side of the westernmost pontoon (No.5).

Mooring is stern-to with pickup lines (though no buoys), other than on pontoon No.4 which has fingers on both sides. Depths are generous with at least 5m in the pontoon area, but there is relatively little space between the ends of the pontoons – against which small motorboats are sometimes moored bow or stern-to – and the smallcraft moorings to the north.

Considerable surge enters the harbour in south or southwesterly winds, requiring multiple lines, springs, extra fenders, etc. Anyone considering leaving a boat unattended for any length of time should pay particular attention to this aspect, as well as taking precautions against chafe. Club Yachting – see Facilities, below – offer *guardinage* amongst their other services.

There are no gates to the pontoons, accessed off the breakwater which is accessible to all, but round-the-clock patrols are said to provide good security.

Anchorage

Anchoring is no longer possible inside the harbour, and all the moorings are private. Yachts occasionally anchor outside the entrance, but both protecting and holding are poor.

Formalities and charges

Visit the marina office on the first floor of the blue and white building, taking the usual ship's papers, passports and evidence of insurance. The staff are friendly and helpful, with English and French spoken.

In 2011 the overnight berthing fee for a monohull of 10–12m was €22.18, or €31.19 for 12–15m, both including 5% tax. Discounts were available for longer stays. Water and electricity were metered.

Facilities

Boatyard Small boatyard for local craft at the root of the breakwater.

Travel-lift Despite a hoist bay at the boatyard there is no travel-lift and no plans for one. An 8-tonne capacity crane lifts local craft ashore.

Diving services Ask at the marina office, or try one of the many SCUBA centres in the town.

Engineers, electronic & radio repairs Ask at the marina office, or consult Club Yachting, below.

Rigging, maintenance & chandlery Club Yachting (previously Club Sail), ✆ 676 496091, 618 383827 *Email* info@clubyachting.com www.clubyachting.com, have premises on pontoon No.2 and in the town. They have a small mobile chandlery, and items not in stock can generally be obtained within 48 hours and delivered to boats berthed in Marina del Sur or any of the other marinas in southern Tenerife. They also handle rigging (including mast replacement), GRP repairs, general maintenance and engine servicing – all this in addition to the company's main function as a sailing school and charter business. The staff are consistently helpful and knowledgeable and between them speak English, French, Spanish and Russian.

Water At all berths.

Showers Clean showers with plenty of hot water in the tower below the marina office. Access is by key, obtainable from the office.

Launderette In the town, a short walk away. Alternatively, laundry left at the office will be washed, dried and returned within 24 hours.

Electricity At all berths.

Fuel Diesel and petrol pumps on the quay outside the office, operational 0800–1800 daily. Although not permanently manned, if the *marineros* see a boat tying up one will come over. Check whether payment must be made in cash.

Bottled gas Camping Gaz exchanges at the *ferretería* (hardware store) in the town, but no refills available.

Weather forecast At the marina office.

Banks Banks with cash dispensers in the town.

Shops/provisioning Supermarkets and other shops in the town, all well within walking distance, including a good butcher and a greengrocer. Fish market at the root of the breakwater.

Cafés & restaurants Two restaurants on the breakwater overlooking the marina, both offering good food at reasonable prices, with many more in the town.

Medical services Medical centre in the northeast part of the town.

Communications

Post office In the northeast part of the town.

Mailing address Puerto Deportivo Pesquero Las Galletas, Torre do Control 2a Planta, CP 38631, Las Galletas – Arona, Tenerife, Las Canarias, Spain.

Telephones At the root of the breakwater and elsewhere.

Internet access No signal in the marina itself, but La Pantalan restaurant at the head of pontoon No.2 offers free Wi-Fi to customers, as does the Pink Parrot a little further east on the seafront.

Car hire Many companies at the airport.

Taxis In the town.

Buses Good bus service around the island, with a stop at the root of the breakwater and a major terminus just outside the town.

Air services Reina Sofia Airport is about 9km to the northeast, though considerably further by road.

Los Cristianos

28°02'·76N 16°43'·03W

Waypoint

⊕C44 – 28°02'·4N 16°43'·4W (0·5M SW of Los Cristianos)

Tides

Predictions for Los Cristianos are available via Admiralty *EasyTide* – see page 194

Plans

Spanish *6140* (1:3,500)

Lights

2831 **Breakwater**
Fl.R.5s12m5M Red column 6m

buoy **Starboard hand buoy**
Fl.G.5s3M Green pillar buoy, ▲ topmark

2831·01 **Breakwater spur**
Fl(2)R.7s6m3M Red post 4m

2831·1 **Inner mole**
Fl(2+1)G.21s5m2M Green column, red band 3m

Marine farms

Three marine farms lie southeast of Los Cristianos, centred on 28°01'·1N 16°42'·4W, 28°01'·8N 16°42'·6W and 28°01'·9N 16°42'·6W respectively. The first two are marked by four yellow pillar buoys and the latter by six yellow pillar buoys, all Fl.Y.5s.

Harbour Communications

Port Authority ✆ 922 790827, 791163
Fax 922 797863 VHF Ch 14, 16 (0800–1430 daily)

Cofradía de Pescadores ✆ 922 790014, 922 793912
Fax 922 751785 *Email* cploscristianos@gmail.com
0800–1500 weekdays, 0800–1300 Saturday

Ferry harbour with busy boatyard

Cristianos is primarily a passenger port, with conventional ferries and high-speed hydrofoils running regular services to La Gomera, La Palma and El Hierro. There are some fishing boats, the usual tourist catamarans, 'pirate' cruises, etc., and over the past decade it has also developed as a centre for whale-watching and is now home to many boats employed in the business. The harbour is sheltered by a 475m breakwater, facing which is a long sandy beach, centrepiece of the tourist conurbation and high-rise apartment blocks around which the town continues to grow.

For many years Los Cristianos was one of the most popular departure points for the Atlantic passage until, in the 1990s, the anchorage was closed to yachts. Pollution of the town's beaches was given as the main reason, though doubtless increasing ferry and hydrofoil traffic played its part. After two decades during which the situation remained ambivalent – in theory yachts were only allowed to anchor while waiting to be lifted at the boatyard, but in practice nobody seemed very concerned about moving them on – the authorities now enforce a strict no anchoring rule.

Approach and entrance

Seen from northwest through west to southwest, the 3-mile line of high-rise buildings is most conspicuous. At the extreme southern end is a single tower block with a distinctive dark vertical stripe. Further south there are cliffs and then a small development, Palm-Mar, followed by Punta Rasca, a low-lying point with a 50m light tower. Steer for the tower block until the harbour entrance opens to the north. In approaching from the south, the entrance will be obvious as soon as Punta Rasca is rounded. The southeasterly-facing entrance is wide and without hazards. The beach area is condoned off by a long string of yellow buoys.

Berthing

The only reason for a yacht to enter Los Cristianos is to be lifted ashore at the boatyard, in which case temporary berthing is permitted on the south side of the inner mole.

Anchorage

As stated above, no anchoring **AT ALL** is allowed inside the harbour. However, there are no restrictions on anchoring southeast of the entrance if conditions permit. In November 2010 several yachts also appeared to have found comfortable anchorage northwest of the harbour off the entrance to the swimming area.

In late 2010 about a dozen yachts lay on moorings in the harbour, a bone of contention with the authorities who were making strenuous efforts to have them removed.

Formalities and charges (boatyard)

The booking sequence is complex to say the least, possibly because while the *Cofradía de Pescadores* own and operate the travel-lifts, the *Capitanía Marítima* controls the boatyard. The office of the *Capitanía Marítima* ✆ 922 790827, 610 782996 (open 0900–1330 weekdays only), will be found on the first floor of the ferry terminal building; that of the *Cofradía de Pescadores Nuestra Señora de las Mercedes* (✆ 922 790014, open 0800–1500 weekdays, 0800–1300 Saturday), where limited English is spoken, at the root of the inner mole.

It is necessary to contact the *Capitanía Marítima* several weeks – or months – in advance, providing the following information IN SPANISH: LOA, beam, tonnes, official number, the approximate length of time to be spent ashore and evidence of third party insurance. The *Capitanía Marítima* will pass this information to the *Cofradía de Pescadores*, after which the skipper must arrange a suitable time for the lifting operation directly with the *Cofradía* and relay this information back to the *Capitanía* (it may be useful to note the name of the *Cofradía* official with whom the arrangement is made). As mentioned opposite, DIY work is not merely permitted but the norm, but it may no longer be possible to live aboard while the boat is ashore.

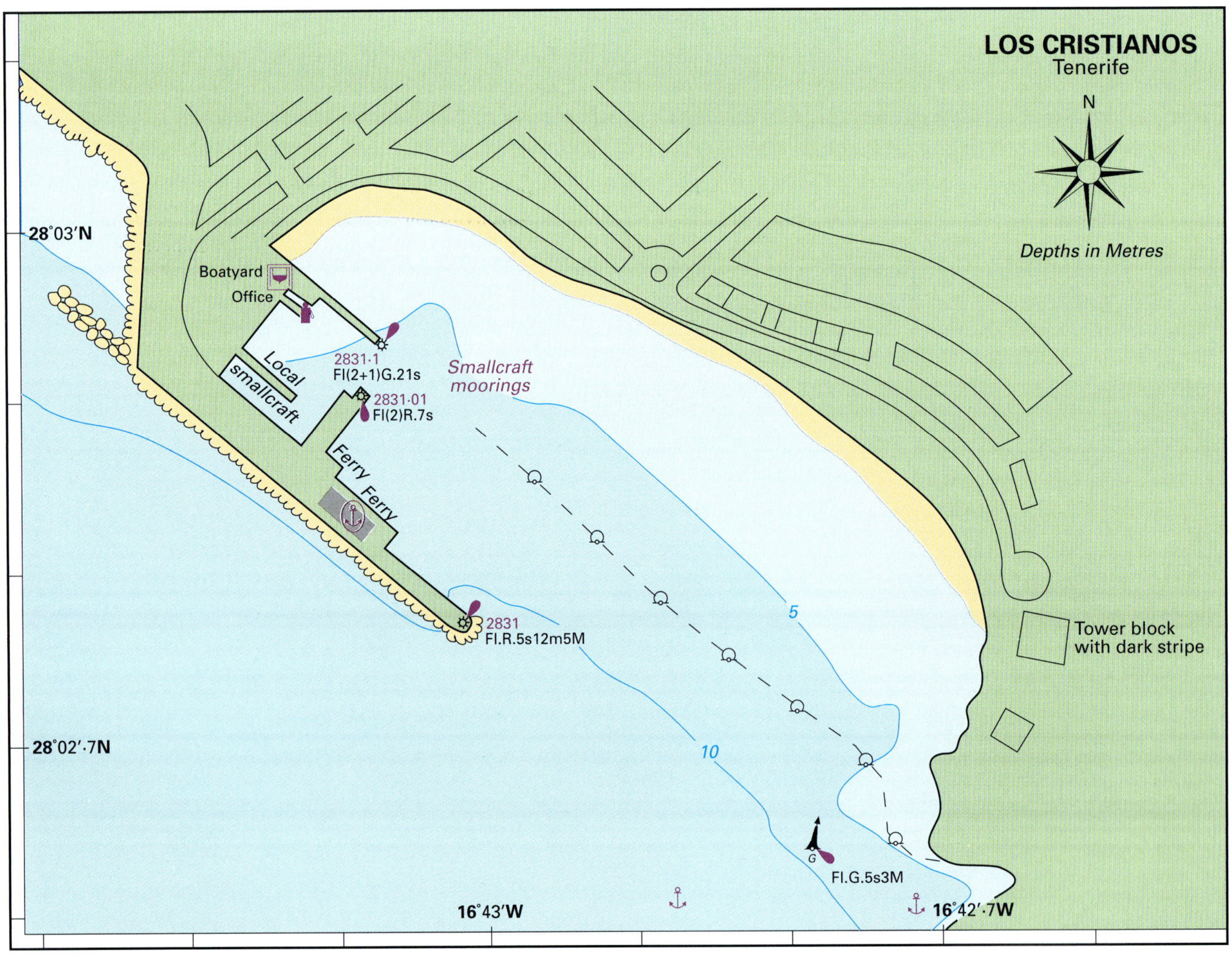

Entering the wide harbour at Los Cristianos, currently forbidden to yachts unless booked into the boatyard

Payment for the hoist, propping, pressure washing etc., as well as for water and electricity, is made to the *Cofradía de Pescadores*; payment for the hardstanding to the *Capitanía Marítima*. In 2010 this was done prior to relaunching, and while the *Cofradía* aspect was straightforward, payment to the *Capitanía* was more protracted. The sequence entailed visiting the *Capitanía* with the documentation to obtain a bill and banking document; taking this to the *Capitanía*'s branch of the La Caixa bank (situated on the main street leading towards the bus station) to pay the bill and obtain a receipt; and returning to the *Capitanía* with the receipt to obtain a stamped release note.

In 2010 lifting and launching a yacht of up to 13m cost €8.30 per m^2 each way, or €9.14 for 13–17m, both including 5% tax. A yacht of 12m LOA nominally paid €15 per day while ashore, though one skipper reported being charged considerable less than this.

Facilities

Boatyard Large boatyard with extensive concrete hardstanding, popular for hauling in preparation for the Atlantic passage. Although most work appears to be DIY, some skills are available – consult the manager for advice. In the past living aboard has been permitted, but in late 2010 it appeared this might be about to change so check the current situation before booking.

The security gates are locked at 2000, but even so thefts have been reported and all loose items should be either stowed away or padlocked.

Travel-lift Three travel-lifts, the largest rated at 110-tonnes. A mixture of wood and metal props are used and the whole operation is said to be extremely professional. A pressure washer is available.

Chandlery A small amount at the *Cofradía de Pescadores*, with wider stocks at two shops on Calle Dulce María Loinaz, two blocks behind boatyard. Larger of the two is Pesquera y Navales ✆ 922 797911 *Email* info@pesquerasynavales.com www.pesquerasynavales.com (open 0800–1300, 1600–1900 weekdays, 0800–1300 Saturday), with a good range of hardware, tools, batteries, antifouling and topside paint, hoses and pumps. Some English is spoken and items not in stock can be ordered. A few doors up the road is the smaller El Capitan ✆ 922 790852 *Email* elcapitan2010@live.it, open 0930–1330, 1600–2030, mainly supplying fishing needs.

Water In the boatyard.

Showers Very basic showers (and toilets) in the boatyard, otherwise swimmers' showers on the beach.

Launderette Several in the town.

Electricity In the boatyard.

Fuel Not on sale to yachts as of late 2010, a situation which is understood to be permanent.

Bottled gas Camping Gaz exchanges available, but no refills available.

Banks Several in the town, plus many cash dispensers.

Shops/provisioning Several good supermarkets nearby plus a wide variety of tourist shops, but no produce market. Fresh fish can sometimes be bought in the harbour area.

Cafés, restaurants & hotels Many around the harbour and town.

Medical services Clinic in the main street, conveniently located above a pharmacy.

Communications

Post office In the town.

Telephones On the ferry quay and in the town.

Internet access The Internet Center on Calle Juan XXIII (near the seafront a couple of blocks behind the boatyard), plus several others.

Car hire In the town.

Taxis On the quay, particularly when ferries are due.

Buses Frequent services to many destinations, including Reina Sofia Airport and Santa Cruz.

Ferries Conventional and hydrofoil services to San Sebastián de la Gomera, Santa Cruz de la Palma and Puerto de la Estaca, El Hierro.

Air services Reina Sofia Airport lies about 15km to the east, though rather more by road.

Puerto Colón

28°04'·81N 16°44'·27W

Waypoint

⊕C45 – 28°04'·6N 16°44'·8W (0·5M WSW of Puerto Colón)

Lights

2831·28 **Breakwater angle** Q(9)15s9m2M
West cardinal post, ⧗ topmark 2m

2831·2 **Breakwater head**
Fl(2)G.7s10m5M Green post 4m

2831·32 **East mole**
Fl(2)R.7s7m3M Red post 2m

Marine farms

Two marine farms lie northwest of Puerto Colon, one centred on 28°04'·7N 16°45'·3W and marked by four yellow pillar buoys with × topmarks, all Fl.Y.11s, the other centred on 28°05'N 16°45'·6W and marked by four yellow pillar buoys with × topmarks, all Fl(5)Y.13s3M.

Harbour Communications

Puerto Colón ✆ 922 714211, 714163
Fax 922 715550 *Email* puertocolon@terra.es
www.puertocolon.com (0900–1400, 1500–1800 weekdays, 0900–1400, 1600–1800 Saturday, 1000–1300, 1600–1800 Sunday) VHF Ch 09, 16

Private marina fronting tourist resort

The previous edition of this book effectively dismissed Puerto Colón, not least because of the unfriendly – even hostile – attitude which typically greeted potential visitors. Fortunately this no longer appears to prevail, although the harbour remains very crowded, mainly with day-charter catamarans, sportfishing boats and small runabouts. Most of the 355 berths were sold when the surrounding holiday development was created and the remaining ones were swiftly taken up by private yachts and commercial concerns. However, two berths are nominally available to visitors although it is essential to book in adance.

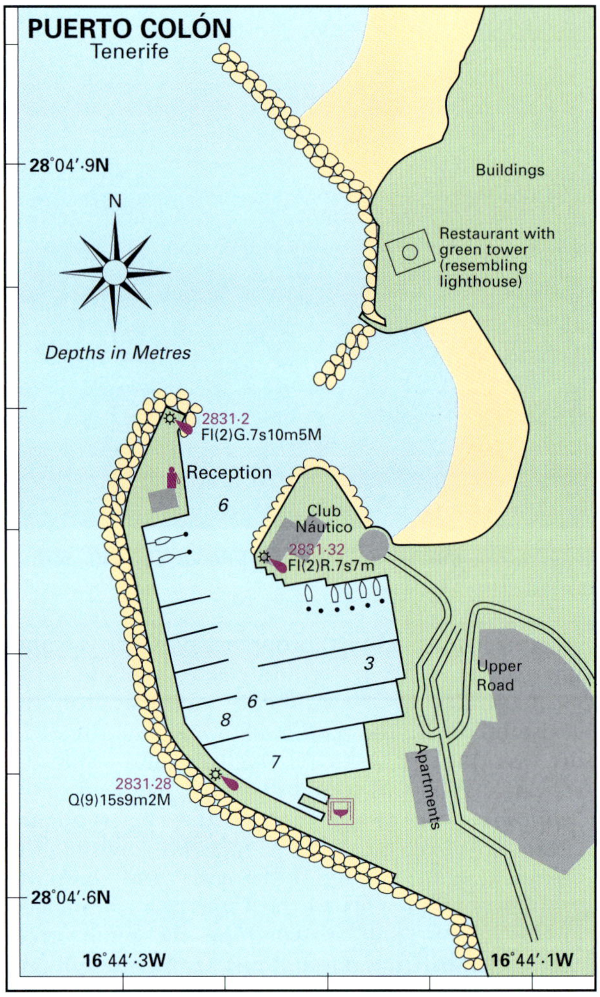

Looking southeast across Puerto Colón towards the high-rise hotels of Playa de las Americas

The well-sheltered entrance to Puerto Colón seen from the main breakwater. Although it may be sunny at sea level, Tenerife's higher areas are often covered by dark cloud

The marina is situated at the northern edge of the extensive – and still expanding – Playa de las Americas development, which has aptly been described as 'a real fish and chip town'. However, the breakwaters are well sited to provide shelter during southerly gales and it is a safe refuge in these conditions. The shoreline is low either side of the entrance which also reduces the danger of reflected swell in bad weather.

Approach, entrance and berthing

Keep 0·5M offshore until the entrance has been identified, as reefs extend along the low-lying coast. Once identified, approach the entrance on a course at right angles to the coast and turn to starboard to enter. Several beach-protection moles have been created north of the harbour entrance, but none are as substantial as the marina breakwater or carry buildings.

The reception (and fuel) berth is on the starboard side directly beneath the white control building, and though it has been reported to be almost untenable in a swell it would nevertheless be unwise to proceed further without permission. As stated previously, there is almost no chance of getting a berth without prior booking. Night entry should be avoided, not least because the breakwater lights are almost impossible to pick out against the background of shore lights. Depths are generous throughout the marina, with 6m in the entrance and 7–8m at reception.

Formalities and charges

Visit the marina office in the white 'control tower' taking the usual ship's papers, crew passports and insurance documents. Limited English is spoken. The berthing fee is calculated on a length x beam basis and in 2010 was set at €0.43 per m², including water, electricity and tax. Discounts are available for longer stays, in the unlikely event that a berth is available.

Facilities

Boatyard Secure and well-kept, but much of the (limited) space is taken up by day-charter catamarans and other commercial enterprises. DIY work is permitted and various services including engineering and GRP repairs are available.
Travel-lift Capacity 30-tonnes, plus slipway.
Water On the pontoons.
Showers Built into the breakwater itself.
Electricity On the pontoons.
Fuel At the reception berth 0800–1800 daily, and available to visitors as well as residents. Nevertheless it would be wise to make contact by VHF or mobile phone prior to arrival.
Banks Several in the nearby tourist complex, plus many cash dispensers.
Shops/provisioning A variety of shops surround the marina, plus several small supermarkets and many tourist shops in the Playa de las Americas development and a large Mercadona supermarket in the San Eugenio Commercial Centre up the hill.
Cafés, restaurants & hotels Literally hundreds, some overlooking the marina.
Medical services Health centre in the tourist complex.

Communications

Post office Near the seafront south of the marina.
Mailing address Puerto Deportivo Puerto Colón, Edificio Capitania, Playa de las Americas, 38660 Adeje – Tenerife Sur, Islas Canarias, Spain.
Telephones Dotted around the marina.
Internet access No Wi-Fi in the marina itself, but available at many nearby bars and restaurants.
Car hire & taxis Readily available.
Air services Reina Sofia Airport, about 17km to the east.

Anchorages northwest of Puerto Colón

A pair of bays northwest of Punta de las Gaviotas (Seagull Point) offer daytime anchorage 2M or so northwest of Puerto Colón. If approaching from the south stay outside the 20m line in order to clear the unmarked shoal of Baja de Adeje, off the headland immediately north of the small tourist development at La Caleta.

The southern of the two is the somewhat improbably named Spaghetti Bay (28°06'·4N 16°45'·8W), the southern part of which is backed by a white sand beach off which yachts can anchor in 7–8m over sand. Further in the seabed turns to rock, while the north part of the bay has large boulders likely to foul an anchor.

About half a mile to the northwest at 28°06'·7N 16°46'·2W is El Puertito, also known as El Pris, a tiny bay surrounded by high sand-coloured cliffs with a shallow reef on the northwest side of the entrance, easily seen in the clear water. There is a small village at the head of the bay, behind which is a church which forms a useful landmark. Best anchorage is to be found near the entrance to the bay in 5–6m over sand and rock. If staying overnight it is best to lay a second anchor to reduce swinging.

(With thanks to Club Yachting, see page 282.)

Puerto de San Juan

28°10′·69N 16°48′·85W

Lights
2831·38 **Breakwater**
Fl(3)R.10s12m2M Red column 3m

Marine farms
Two marine farms lie southeast of Puerto de San Juan, one centred on 28°07′·2N 16°47′·25W, marked by six yellow pillar buoys with × topmarks, all Fl.Y.5s3M, the other centred on 28°09′N 16°48′·3W, marked by four yellow pillar buoys with × topmarks, all Fl(4)Y.11s3M.

Harbour Communications
Port Captain ✆ 922 865434 VHF Ch 09, 16

Small, scenic fishing harbour

A small working fishing harbour tucked behind a high breakwater, about 8M up the coast from Playa de las Americas and 5M south of the Los Gigantes cliffs. There is little space for a yacht to enter, but unrestricted – though relatively unsheltered – anchorage outside. The beach inside the harbour is cordoned off by the usual string of yellow buoys, but it would be possible to land a dinghy on the wide slipway at the head of the harbour. The breakwater is popular with rod-and-line fishermen, particularly in the evenings – keep well clear!

Facilities include a 64-tonne travel-lift operated by the *Cofradía de Pescadores* (fishermen's confederation) and a small chandlery shop, Ferretería Naval Hernandez, a couple of streets back from the harbour. Water is available on the quay and by the slipway, and there are swimmers' showers near the harbour office. The village contains several small supermarkets and other shops, and numerous restaurants and cafés. At least one of the latter offers internet access.

Puerto de Santiago

28°14′·22N 16°50′·64W (northwest quay)

Small fishing village

An attractive fishing village – certainly not a port – less than a mile south of Los Gigantes, with an exposed bay where the fishermen crane their boats onto the wall in bad weather. It is a pleasant place to anchor off in settled weather but beware of rocks inshore.

Restaurants and tourist shops surround the bay, with more up the hill.

The entrance to Puerto de San Juan, looking slightly north of east. The bay at centre right offers good anchorage off the stony beach

Puerto de Los Gigantes

28°14'·94N 16°50'·52W (breakwater head)

Waypoint

⊕C46 – 28°15'·3N 16°50'·9W (0·5M NW of Puerto de Los Gigantes)

Lights

2831·4 **Breakwater angle** Q(9)15s10m4M
West cardinal tripod, ⧗ topmark 3m
2831·5 **Breakwater head** Fl.G.6s10m3M
Green column 3m
2831·6 **East mole** Fl.R.5s10m3M
Red and white diagonally striped tower and red tripod 5m
2831·65 **East mole spur** Fl(2)R.7s5m1M
Red tripod over red and white banded base 2m
2831·55 **Breakwater spur**
Fl(2)G.7s5m1M Green post 2m
2831·55 **Breakwater spur, angle**
Fl(3)G.9s5m1M Green post 2m
Note If approaching at night – not recommended unless familiar with the harbour – the angular shape of Puerto de Los Gigantes causes the entrance lights to appear reversed

Marine farm

Two marine farms lie northwest of Puerto de of Los Gigantes, each marked by four yellow pillar buoys with × topmarks, all Fl.Y.5s3M. They are situated close together, centred on 28°15'·6N 16°50'·6W and 28°15'·8N 16°50'·9W respectively.

Harbour Communications

Puerto Deportivo Los Gigantes ✆ 922 868343, 609 240078 *Email* padidivertenerife@hotmail.com
VHF Ch 09 (0900–1900 daily)

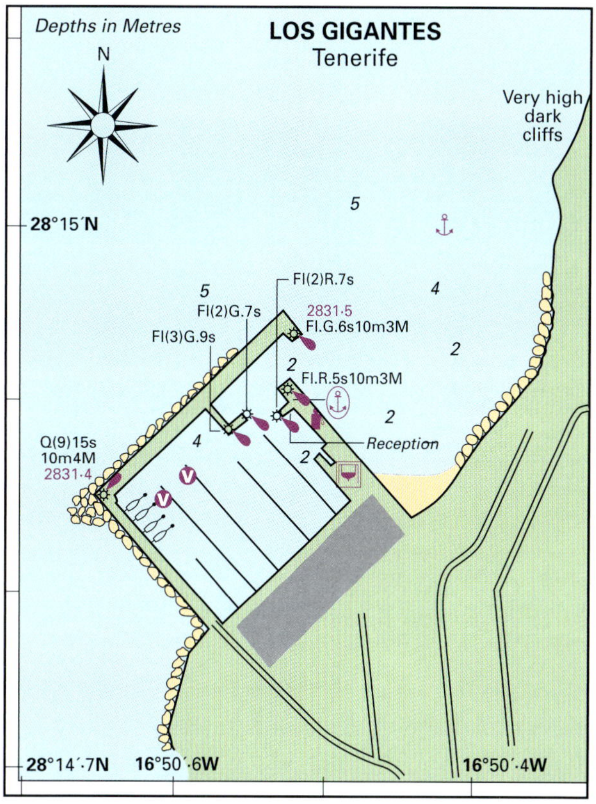

Marina with shallow entrance

Los Gigantes (pronounced *Los Hi'gantess*) is a rapidly expanding tourist town and the marina was constructed as part of the development (which probably accounts for the high proportion of small speedboats, mostly owned by local residents). Situated as it is at the southern extremity of enormous sheer cliffs which reflect incoming swell, the marina is very prone to surge. There are 362 berths for vessels of up to 20m, but only four or five are available for visitors and in practice there is frequently no room at all during the busy autumn season.

Caution

The harbour has an ongoing problem with silting of the approaches and entrance, and can become extremely dangerous at times. Entry should not be considered unless conditions are near-perfect and is said not to be viable for at least 50% of the time in winter. Conversely, once inside there is no guarantee of being able to depart. In late 2010 the entrance was said to carry no more than 1·8m at low water springs, which may be significantly reduced by surge. However, with a spring range of 1·9m this increased to 3·5m around the top of the tide.

When even an apparently insignificant swell is running from the north, northwest or west a yacht may encounter breaking waves BEFORE reaching the entrance – almost certainly the reason an 11m yacht was lost in the 1990s. Approaching early in the morning, it seems very possible that the shadow thrown by the cliffs, combined with the low height-of-eye of the helmsman, masked these breakers until she was beyond the point of no return.

Los Gigantes must therefore be approached with great caution and a close eye on the echo-sounder. Even then, if in any doubt at all, DO NOT ATTEMPT TO ENTER. The choice is either to free off and make the 17M downwind passage to San Sebastián de la Gomera, head back down the coast of Tenerife to Las Galletas or Marina San Miguel, or heave-to a few miles offshore in the hope that conditions may improve.

Approach and entrance

Punta Teno light lies about 8M northwest, situated on a low-lying spit backed by the northern end of the spectacular cliffs of Los Gigantes sweeping some 7M to the southeast. From any direction, it is not difficult to identify the town on a steeply rising promontory south of the cliffs. Buildings now rise in tiers at least halfway up the slope.

At a distance of 2M the marina wall can be made out under the cliff end, though the dog-leg entrance faces northeast in an endeavour to provide some shelter. There is a speed limit of 2 knots in the immediate approach.

Berthing

Call on VHF Ch 09 while still offshore, having made contact previously to confirm that a berth is likely to be available. The reception pontoon is located inside the short spur jutting out from the eastern quay, and

A speedboat makes the tight turn into Puerto de Los Gigantes, seen from the cliffs to the northeast. La Gomera, about 16M away, is very clear on the horizon

is shallow at low water. Visiting yachts are normally berthed on either side of the west outer finger of the third and fourth pontoons from entrance, though a larger yacht may be placed stern-to the breakwater in the western corner if a berth-holder is absent.

Formalities and charges

Visit the marina office on the end of the east mole bearing the usual ship's papers, passports and insurance certificate. In 2010 the overnight berthing fee for a monohull of 9–12m was €22.18, or €34.65 for 12–15m, which included water, electricity and tax.

Facilities

Boatyard Limited boatyard facilities, but specialists can be summoned if necessary.
Travel-lift Capacity 60 tonnes.
Water At all berths.
Showers Several shower blocks dotted around the marina.
Electricity At all berths.
Fuel Diesel and petrol pumps at the reception berth, operational 0900–1900.
Banks In the town, nearly all with cash dispensers.
Shops/provisioning A small supermarket fronts the marina, with others in the town.
Cafés, restaurants & hotels Many overlooking the harbour and throughout the resort.
Medical services In the town.

Communications

Post office In the town.
Mailing address Puerto Deportivo Los Gigantes, 38683 Santiago del Teide, Tenerife, Islas Canarias, Spain.
Internet access No Wi-Fi in the marina, but several nearby cafés offer the facility.
Telephones Near the root of the main breakwater and elsewhere.
Car hire & taxis In the resort.
Buses Anticlockwise around the island to Reina Sofia Airport and Santa Cruz, etc.

From this position near the breakwater's western angle the harbour entrance appears to be blocked – not the case, as can be seen from the photograph above. However the slalom-style bend is tight, and is shallow at low water – respect the caution on the previous page

Playa de Masca

28°17'·3N 16°51'·8W (anchorage)

Remote, unspoilt anchorage

In a natural bay surrounded by high cliffs, the anchorage at Masca is protected from north around to southeast but can suffer from overnight swell. Approaching from the southwest one notices a white beacon high up on the cliffs, with below it a pier in the north corner of the bay (used by tourist boats to pick up walkers) and a cluster of trees and bushes surrounding a small building. Anchor in 8m over sand and boulders, the latter making a trip-line a wise precaution.

(With thanks to Club Yachting, see page 282.)

Punta de Teno

28°30'·5N 16°55'·1W (anchorage)

Waypoint

⊕C47 – 28°21'N 16°57'·7W (2M W of Punta de Teno)

Lights

2832 **Punta Teno** Fl(1+2)20s59m18M
White tower, red bands 20m

Anchorage southeast of lighthouse

There is a possible anchorage – suitable for daylight and settled conditions only – in a small bay southeast of Punta Teno lighthouse in about 7m, protected from northeasterly winds but open to the south. Ashore there is a small fishing village and a road to the lighthouse on the promontory, but little else.

Anchorages on the northwest coast of Tenerife

There are a number of small fishing harbours along this unfriendly coast, a few of which offer potential anchorage in the right conditions. However, with a spectacular coast road running between the mountains and the sea there is much to be said for exploring this area by car, leaving the yacht secured in one of Tenerife's more sheltered harbours.

Garachico

28°22'·37N 16°46'·08W (quay)

Old harbour, with new taking shape

A small fishing harbour and tourist development, occasionally visited by yachts, Garachico was once a major port until destroyed by a volcanic eruption in 1705 with heavy loss of life. The town has been rebuilt on the lava flow. The harbour is not as suitable an anchorage as San Marcos 2M further east, and the few fishing boats are hauled up on the wall when not in use. A rocky islet, Roque de Garachico, is conspicuous offshore to the northeast.

Though possible to anchor off in very settled conditions, this is not a spot for the faint-hearted. There is at least one isolated breaking rock in the approach, very possibly more, while a low reef (said to be the semi-submerged remains of a breakwater) obstructs much of the entrance – very much a case for eyeball navigation. The tiny harbour consists of no more than a rough wall running along the east

The 'old' harbour at Garachico, seen here from a little west of south, would not be feasible in normal tradewind conditions but could provide interesting anchorage in light southerlies

Work on the new harbour at Playa las Aguas just east of Garachico, photographed from a little south of west in November 2010

side of a narrow inlet. Anchorage in the inlet is said to be possible, but would be very tight. Shops and restaurants will be found in the village.

In November 2010 work was in progress on a new harbour at Playa las Aguas, about half a mile east of Garachico, the root of the substantial new breakwater overlooked by the 17th century Ermita de San Roque. The work, for which a completion date of late 2011 was given, was marked by a single north cardinal buoy. Information available on site gave a rough idea of the planned internal layout, but no indication as to whether it would be occupied entirely by local fishing boats or whether any provision was to be made for yachts. Feedback would be appreciated.

San Marcos

28°22'·75N 16°43'·52W (quay)

Possible anchorage in settled southerlies

An attractive bay affording shelter in bad weather from the south and useable in light northeast winds, San Marcos lies 2M east of the conspicuous Roque de Garachico. Approach on a southeastly bearing, taking care to avoid the rocky reef which runs out from the northeast headland on which stands a large cream building with distinctive arcades. Anchor in the eastern part clear of the fishermen's wall and crane, in 4–5m over fine sand. Fishing boats are hauled out on the quay when not in use.

The bay is backed by a black sand beach on the eastern side and equally dark boulders to the southwest. A line of cafés and restaurants overlook it from the east, fronted by a road from which cars have been swept by northwesterly swells. There is a tap on the quay, but little else is available.

The bay at San Marcos offers good shelter in winds from the southern quadrant, but little will be found ashore other than restaurants.

Puerto de la Cruz

28°25'·19N 16°32'·98W (outer molehead)

Lights
2833 **Puerto de la Cruz**
Fl(2)7s30m16M Square tower 27m
2834 **Western (outer) mole**
Fl(3)G.9s7m4M Green column 3m
2835 **Eastern (inner) mole**
Fl(3)R.9s6m3M Red column 3m

Tiny harbour best visited by land

In the 18th century Puerto de la Cruz was the trading capital of the island, where fast schooners from Devon loaded soft fruit and through which much of the island's wine was exported. However, the problems caused by the prevailing onshore winds and seas gradually caused the port to lose its trade to the more sheltered Santa Cruz.

Following the tourist boom of the mid-20th century the old harbour entrance was closed off to create a bathing area, and though there is a small fishing harbour it is quite unsuitable for yachts. It might be possible to anchor off in very settled conditions, but there is no shelter from a northerly swell. The low 'breakwaters' either side of the town protect bathing beaches where one could doubtless land by dinghy.

Puerto de la Cruz was the first tourist resort on Tenerife and, though now overtaken in size by the Playa de las Américas/Los Cristianos sprawl along the southwest coast, still retains a measure of its charm and character. The Botanic Garden, established by King Charles III of Spain in the mid 18th century, is well worth a visit if exploring the area by road.

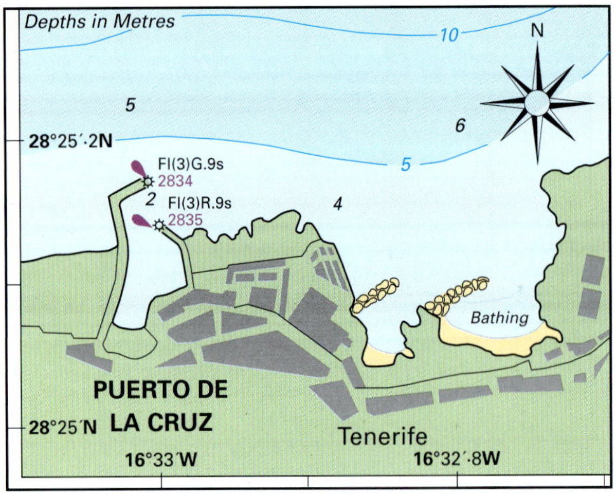

La Gomera

Between 28°01'N–28°13'N and 17°06'W–17°21'W

Introduction

La Gomera, with its 375km² and 23,000 population, resembles half a sphere with deep ravines, fertile green valleys with steeply terraced slopes, and dense, dark forests leading up to the almost central peak of Montaña Garajonay (1,487m) which is surrounded by the *Parque Nacional de Garajonay*. In common with the other western islands, much of La Gomera is extremely beautiful and it is worth making an effort to explore inland. An economical option is by bus – the route from San Sebastián to Valle Gran Rey and Puerto de Vueltas crosses the island in an almost continuous flow of hairpin bends through constantly changing scenery.

La Gomera was the last major island in the Canaries to have a functioning airport. Work started in 1993, but it soon came to a halt and the project remained unfinished until 1999. Even now La Gomera receives only inter-island flights, using small aeroplanes with limited seating capacity, and most visitors arrive by water – either by yacht or on the ferry from Tenerife.

Telecommunications

Mobile (cell) phone reception is good around each of La Gomera's three harbours, though walkers should note that holes may exist inland. The country code for the Canaries is 34, as it is for mainland Spain, and the area code for La Gomera – which must be included even when dialling from within the island – is 922, shared with Tenerife, La Palma and El Hierro.

By 2011 Wi-Fi was available at Marina La Gomera in San Sebastián, though not included in the price, with at least one cybercafé in the town.

Approach and navigation

Prepare well if sailing from Tenerife to La Gomera as strong winds are often encountered during the final third of the passage. Northern sector winds predominate around the island, and acceleration zones have been encountered off its northwestern tip.

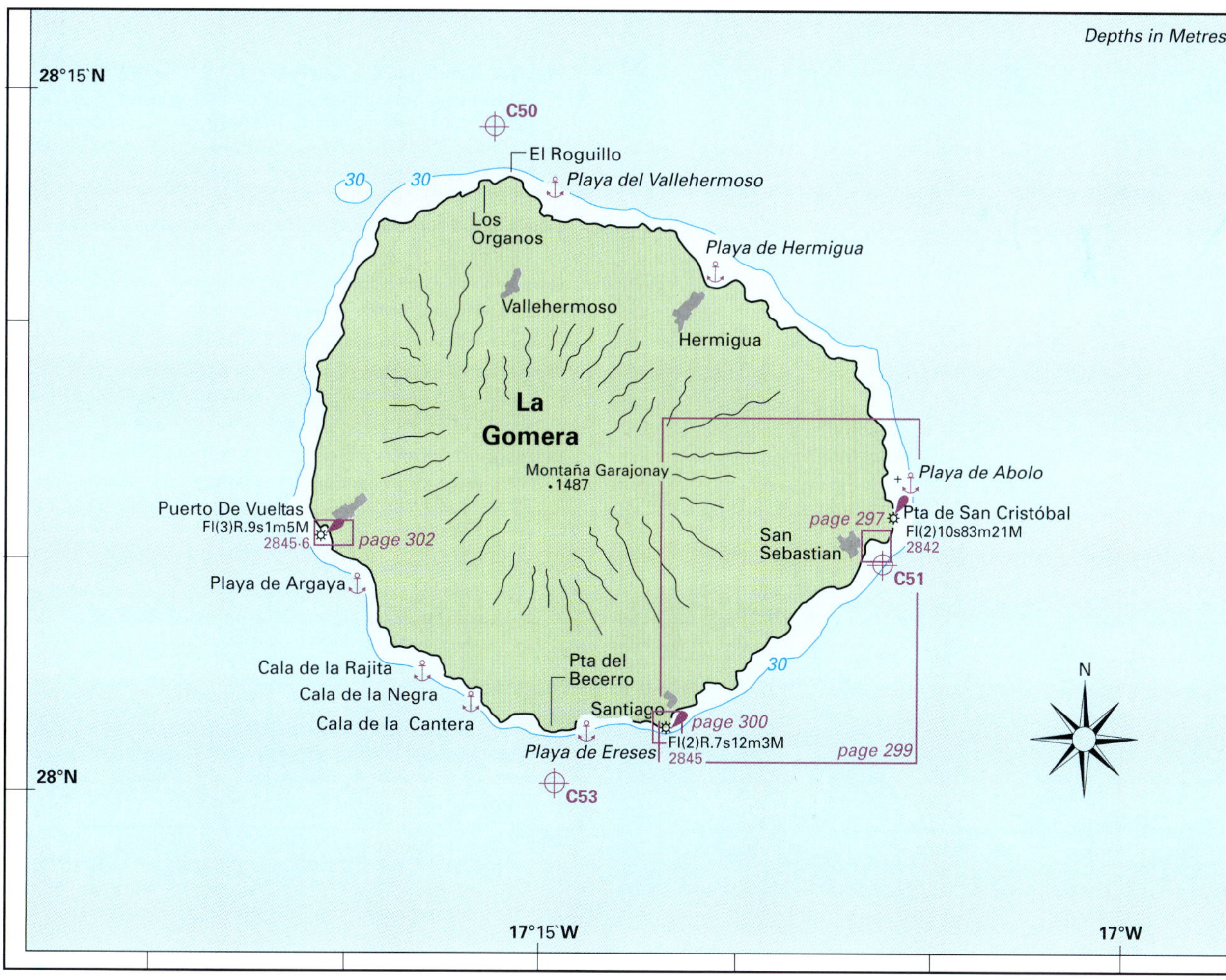

Navigation

Waypoints

⊕C50 – 28°14'·2N 17°16'·2W (2M N of El Roguillo)
⊕C51 – 28°04'·6N 17°06'·2W (0·5M SE of San Sebastián)
⊕C52 – 28°01'·3N 17°11'·4W (0·5M SE of Puerto de Santiago)
⊕C53 – 28°00'·2N 17°14'·6W (1M S of Pta del Becerro)
⊕C54 – 28°04'·3N 17°20'·3W (0·5M SW of Puerto de Vueltas)

Courses and distances

⊕C50 – ⊕C51 = 15M, by eye
⊕C50 – ⊕C54 = 12·5M, by eye
⊕C50 – ⊕C58 (1M SE of Santa Cruz de la Palma) = 36M, 315° / 135°
⊕C51 – ⊕C43 (1M SW of Pta de la Rasca, Tenerife) = 1·5M, 104° / 284°
⊕C51 – ⊕C47 (2M W of Pta de Teno, Tenerife) = 18M, 025° / 205°
⊕C51 – ⊕C53 = 8·5M, by eye
⊕C53 – ⊕C54 = 6·5M, by eye
⊕C53 – ⊕C63 (1M SE of Puerto de la Estaca, El Hierro) = 37M, 248° / 068°

Magnetic variation

6°15'W (2011), decreasing by 8'E annually.

Tidal Streams

It has been reported that the southwest-going tidal stream may occasionally set down the east coast of La Gomera at up to 4 knots. The reverse stream is much weaker, but even so a race forms off Punta de San Cristóbal when the northeasterly trades are blowing. Details of range, etc. will be found under San Sebastián.

Charts

Admiralty *1869* (1:300,000)
Spanish *61A*, *61B* (1:200,000), *617* (1:60,000)
US *51260* (1:300,000)
Imray-Iolaire *E2* (1:600,000)

Lights

2842 **Punta San Cristóbal** Fl(2)10s83m21M White tower, red band 15m
2845 **Puerto de Santiago** Fl(2)R.7s12m3M Red column 5m
2845·5 **Puerto de Vueltas (Valle Gran Rey)** Fl(3)R.9s1m5M Red column 1m

Coast Radio Station

Gomera 28°05'N 17°07'·1W, remotely controlled from Tenerife
VHF Ch 06, 16, 24 (24 hours)
DSC VHF MMSI 002241025, 28°06'N 17°06'W, remotely controlled from Tenerife

Weather and navigation broadcasts

VHF 28°05'·7N 17°06'·3W (remotely controlled from Tenerife)
Weather bulletins Ch 24 at 0833, 1333, 2033 (forecast in Spanish for coastal waters)
Navigational warnings Ch 24 at 0833, 2033 (in Spanish for coastal waters)

The shady courtyard of the Casa de Colón (Columbus House) in San Sebastián de la Gomera. The tourist office occupies one corner of the building

Websites

The following sites contain general information about La Gomera, some of which may be useful to the visiting yachtsman. Websites relating to specific harbours are listed under Harbour communications, those covering all or most of the Canary Islands on page 188 of the introduction.

www.cabildogomera.org – homepage of La Gomera's island council, in Spanish only but translates well

www.en.wikipedia.org/wiki/La_Gomera – all the usual in-depth wikipedia information without the spin which one comes to expect from 'local' websites

www.gomeralive.com – a commercial site, but not overtly so, with pretty pictures scattered amongst the practical information. In Spanish and English

www.gomera.info – website of La Paloma, which bills itself as La Gomera's only travel agency, in Spanish, English and German. Includes up-to-date bus and ferry timetables

www.gomera-island.com – an attractive tourist board website in Spanish, English and German, covering all the usual topics (but note that some of the information regarding the smaller harbours is distinctly misleading)

www.gomeraverde.com – not a 'green' site, as one might expect from the name, but local news in Spanish, not all of which translates fluently. Worth persevering with, however, if on the spot and keen to know what's happening and what's about to happen

www.m-e-e-r.de – the homepage of La Gomera's whale and dolphin research centre, in Spanish, English and German. Their *Whales and Dolphins of Gomera* recognition sheet would be worth printing out if there is no other cetacean guide aboard.

Harbours and anchorages

Anchorages on the northeast coast of La Gomera

Before breakwaters were built at the three main harbours, yachts were advised to move to the north of the island for shelter at the onset of a southerly gale. Though few would now willingly quit the shelter of Puerto de San Sebastián in these conditions, the option of lying in the shelter of the cliffs on the north coast of La Gomera should still be considered, particularly if the marina is already over-full. In northerly winds this coast should be approached with caution.

At 28°13′·06N 17°16′·55W, close to the northern tip of the island, are Los Organos – the Organ Pipes – a towering cliff face of basalt columns which can only be seen from seaward. They are worth inspecting in calm conditions, but be wary of strong down-draughts from the cliffs.

Playa del Vallehermoso

28°12′·3N 17°15′·1W (anchorage)

A rather uninspiring bay but useful in a strong southerly. A stony beach backed by a summer complex with pool, restaurant and swimmers' showers lies at the foot of a steep-sided valley. This leads up to the town of Vallehermoso about 3km inland, where supermarkets and other shops will be found. A small café functions during the winter when the waterside restaurant is closed, and a tap will be found at the west end of the small wooden footbridge, but there is little else.

The ruined Castillo del Mar (actually an old quay with a derrick for loading bananas) at the base of the cliff on the west side of the bay has now been renovated as a second summer restaurant.

The wide bay at Playa del Vallehermoso, looking northeast. Though untenable in normal tradewinds it offers good shelter from a southerly

Like Playa del Vallehermoso, Playa de Hermigua faces directly into the northeast trades. A brisk southwesterly was blowing when this photograph was taken, however, and other than a slight onshore swell it offered excellent shelter

Playa de Hermigua

28°11′N 17°10′·9W (anchorage)

Open to the northeast, but pleasant in calm weather and providing good shelter in a southerly, Playa de Hermigua is easy to identify from a distance – look for a row of multicoloured buildings set a few hundred metres back from the beach, and a valley running up to the village of Hermigua a mile or so inland. Best anchorage is to be found on the west side of the bay under a steep hillside covered with banana terraces, where there is reasonable holding in 8–10m over shingle and stones.

Unusually, there is no beach bar or café, though it appears there was once one at the east end of the beach where the remains of a jetty can be seen and a (rather dirty) seawater pool has been created among the rocks.

Playa de Abalo

28°06′·7N 17°06′·3W (anchorage)

A pretty bay 1·5M north of San Sebastián, facing east and therefore unlikely to be usable in winter. Beware Roca Bermeja (marked on Admiralty chart *1869*) off the headland at the north end of the bay which, despite rising steeply from about 25m to less than 2m at low water, remains unmarked.

The pretty village of Agulo lies amid spectacular scenery about a mile northwest of Playa de Hermigua
Nigel Mercier

San Sebastián de la Gomera

28°05'·01N 17°06'·53W (breakwater head)

Waypoint

⊕C51 – 28°04'·6N 17°06'·2W (0·5M SE of San Sebastián)

Tides

Standard port for the Canary Islands is Casablanca, with San Sebastián a secondary port. MLWS is about 0·3m above datum and time difference on Casablanca: –0106. Predictions for San Sebastián are also available via Admiralty *EasyTide* – see page 194

Mean spring range 2·0m
Mean neap range 0·7m

Plans

Admiralty *1858* (1:10,000)
Spanish *6150* (1:7,500)
Imray-Iolaire *E2* (1:10,000)

Lights

2842 **Punta San Cristóbal** Fl(2)10s83m21M
White tower, red band 15m
2844·68 **Roque la Hila** Fl(3)10s3M
East cardinal pyramid, ♦ topmark
2844·7 **Breakwater**
Fl.G.5s15m6M Green tower 7m
buoy **Port hand No.1**
Fl.R.5s3M Red pillar buoy
buoy **Port hand No.2**
Fl(2)R.7s Large red can buoy, ■ topmark
2844·65 **Marina west mole**
Fl(3)R.9s6m1M Slim red pyramid 3m
2844·6 **Marina east mole**
Fl(3)G.9s6m1M Slim green pyramid 3m

Harbour Communications

Port Authority ✆ 922 870357 *Fax* 922 141093
Email gomera@puertosdetenerife.org
Marina La Gomera ✆ 922 141769 *Fax* 922 871362
Email info@marinalagomera.es
www.marinalagomera.es (0900–1300, 1600–1900 weekdays, 0900–1300 Saturday) VHF Ch 09 (24 hours)

Friendly marina, great town and island

San Sebastián is the main harbour of La Gomera, with ferries running to Tenerife and El Hierro. Open to the southeast, it is easy to enter by day or night and provides a good base from which to explore the island. The town has strong links with Columbus, whose reputed house on Calle Real is now a museum and art gallery (open 1000–1300, 1530–1730 weekdays). The town hall (*Ayuntameinto*) was once the home of Columbus' friend (and possibly mistress) Beatriz de Bobadilla, and the *Iglesia Nostra Senhora de la Asunción* a little further up Calle Real was where Columbus and his crew said Mass before their departure. Also worth visiting is the *Museo Arqueológico de la Gomera* (open 1000–1800 weekdays, 1000–1400 weekends) housed in an old building next to the church.

The marina, which is owned by the same company as Marina Chico in Santa Cruz de Tenerife, has earned continuing praise since it opened in 1995–96. 'Quite the most pleasant marina in the Canaries' and 'without doubt the most helpful, well-run marina that I have come across in five years of cruising' are among the unsolicited comments received over the past decade. Prior to the opening of Marina La Palma it was almost unique in the Canaries in being adjacent to a medium-sized town in which local people go about their daily lives – neither a bustling city such as Las Palmas or Santa Cruz, nor a purpose-built development such as Puerto Calero or Puerto de Mogán. Maps of the town and of the island in general are available from the marina office.

The harbour at San Sebastián de la Gomera, seen from near the large statue of Christ on the hills to the southwest. The line of yellow buoys which mark the marina approach channel show up very well, as does El Tiede rising above the clouds on the horizon

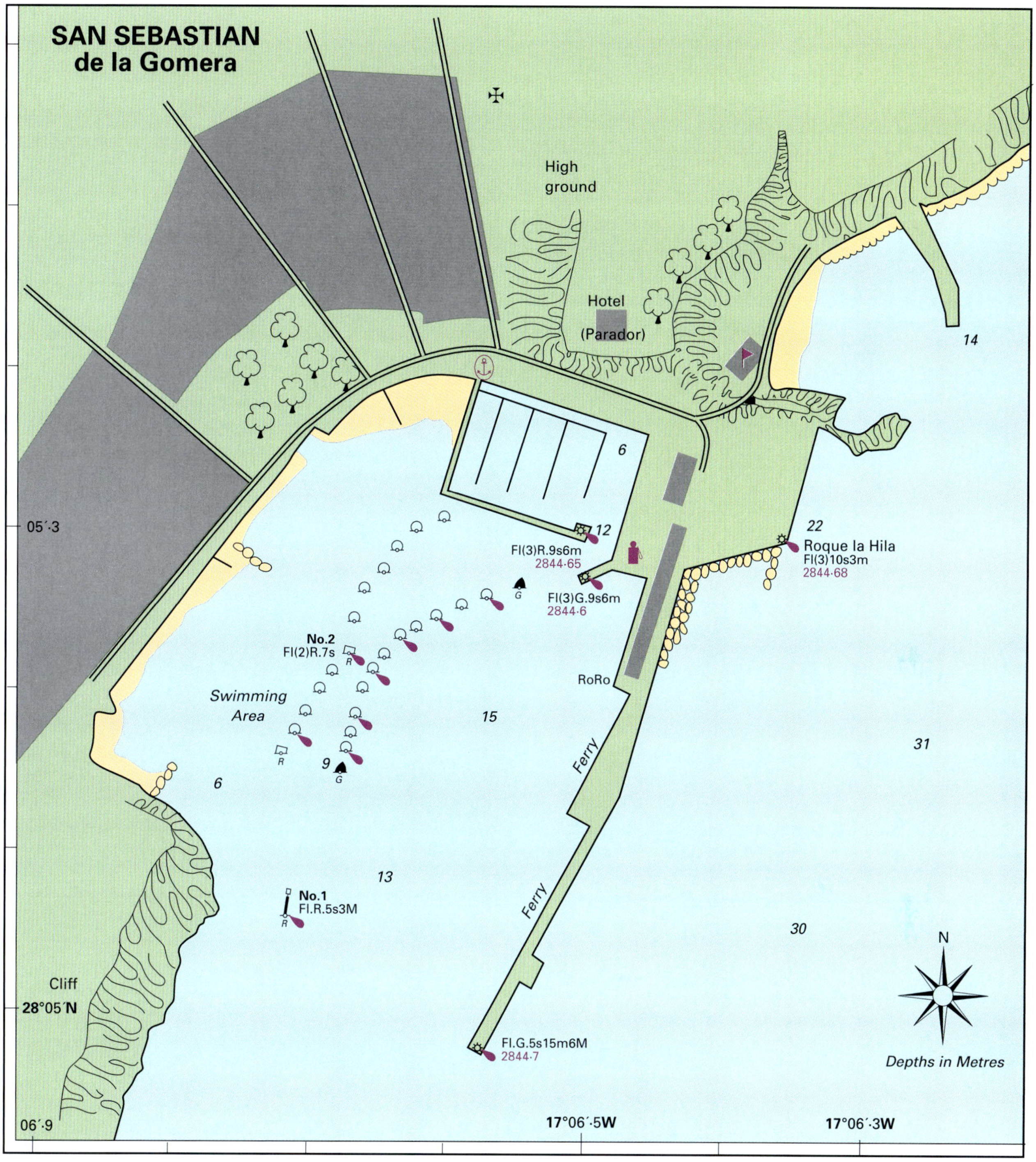

Inevitably the marina is often full between September and December, as well as in June when a sport-fishing championship brings thirty or more large motorboats to the island. Although it does not accept reservations, it would still be wise to get in contact several weeks in advance, reconfirming a few days before arrival. Fortunately, with at least 60 of the marina's 335 berths able to take yachts of 10–12m, and the same number for 12–15m, the chances of finding a berth available remain reasonably good. In many ways the marina is its own worst enemy, however – for too many yachts check in for a couple of days and end up staying a fortnight!

Harbour approach and entrance

From the northeast the radio mast makes a fine landmark – the lighthouse is less conspicuous and the breakwater and town are concealed by the headland. There are no outlying dangers, though a considerable tide rip can build up around Punta San Cristóbal. An area some 100m by 200m has recently been infilled east of the breakwater root, just south of Roque la Hila, and a short mole created north of the Roque to protect the small bathing beach, but both are well away from the harbour entrance.

From the south or east the town on the north side of the valley can be seen from some distance, and the breakwater will be raised on closer approach. Again there are no outlying dangers and a course can be set to clear the breakwater end. Keep a lookout for the hydrofoil and car ferry and remain well clear if either is entering or leaving.

Marina approach and entrance

After rounding the breakwater the buoyed channel leading to the marina will be seen ahead. This comprises two rows of yellow buoys – potentially confusing, as they are not unlike those used to cordon-off swimming areas – with small red and green buoys at the southern 'entrance'. Its purpose is to keep non-commercial craft clear of the large area which the ferries need for turning, so must not be ignored.

The channel begins north of the outer (lit) port hand buoy, curving north and then northeast towards the marina. Seven of the yellow buoys carry flashing lights – though not all were working in late 2010 – but neither of the 'entrance' buoys are lit. There is a somewhat larger (lit) port hand buoy about halfway up the channel, beyond which the yellow buoys to port are noticeably smaller and do not carry lights. The final green buoy, nearest the marina entrance, is also unlit. All in all, although arriving after dark should not present problems, a crew member posted forward with a powerful torch would certainly be reassuring.

The dogleg marina entrance is directly beyond the end of the buoyed channel, but skippers of larger yachts should be aware that it is relatively narrow – about 30m – and that the the small hydrofoil which takes foot passengers round the island to Puerto de Santiago and Puerto de Vueltas berths on the inside of the east mole, from which it reverses out.

Before leaving the marina, glance at the 'bus shelter' on the east mole. More than one or two passengers waiting indicates that the hydrofoil ferry, the *Benchi Express*, could arrive at any moment.

Looking south over the entrance to Marina La Gomera and the harbour beyond. A cruise ship and two ferries lie alongside the breakwater, with the smaller *Benchi Express* backing out of her berth alongside the marina's short east mole

Berthing

A member of staff (a *marinero*, not merely a security guard) is on duty at all times, though English may not be spoken outside office hours, and it is helpful to make advance contact by VHF or mobile phone. The fuel berth doubles as the reception area, though yachts are often directed straight to a berth.

The eastern part of the marina – which suffers from surge in southerly winds – contains the larger berths, most of which are reserved for visitors. All are alongside finger pontoons, including those stern to the east wall. If allocated a berth in the latter area, beware the shallow sloping ramp in the far corner. A few vessels in the 15–30m LOA range can lie alongside just north of the fuel berth, but are likely to have to raft up.

Security is good, with round-the-clock staffing and a card-activated gate to the entire marina area. This remains open until 2200 each evening after which the appropriate card is needed.

Anchorage

Anchoring in the harbour is not permitted at any time. If waiting for a berth in the marina and unwilling to raft up, in northeasterly winds good anchorage over sand can be found in one of the bays close southwest of the harbour. See Anchorages on the Southeast Coast of La Gomera, on pages 299–300.

Formalities

Visit the office at the northwest corner of the marina taking the usual ship's papers, passports and insurance documents. Marina manager José Navarro Fernandez has been in post for more than a decade, and both he and his staff have earned a reputation for being notably helpful and speaking excellent English.

Note that San Sebastián de la Gomera is not a frontier port, and one cannot obtain an exit stamp from the Canaries – and so from both Spain and the Schengen Area – which may be required on arrival in the next country. Obtain official clearance while still in Tenerife (for which it may be necessary for the skipper to visit Santa Cruz or Los Cristianos) or in Santa Cruz de la Palma.

Charges

The berthing fee is calculated on a length x beam basis and in 2011 remained at €0.42 per m^2, having not risen for several years. This included water, electricity and tax at 5%. Both *Tasa de Embarcación de Recreo* (Recreational Vessel tax) and *Tasa de Ayuda a la Navegación* (Navigational Aid tax) may also be payable – see page 190.

Facilities

Boatyard Not as such, though various individuals advertise their services for painting and general maintenance – consult the marina office.

Travel-lift No. Shallow-draught boats of up to 7m or so are brought ashore by fork-lift truck, but the nearest travel-lifts are at Puerto de Santiago on the south coast, Los Cristianos (Tenerife) and Puerto de la Restinga (El Hierro). See pages 301, 285 and 320 respectively.

Engineers Andy Altenhofer, who is German but speaks fluent English ☎ 638 766167
Email a.yachtservice@yahoo.de www.a-y-s.eu works from small premises on the east side of the marina. He and his team offer engine repairs, stainless steel welding and general services such as painting and antifouling and *guardinage*. Spares can usually be sourced within 48 hours, though it can take ten days to get parts from mainland Europe.
Diving services Andy Altenhofer (see above) includes diving and underwater repairs in his portfolio.
Sailmaker & repairs Butterfly-Service ☎ /*Fax* 922 872000, 626 386463 www.butterfly-service.com is run by Thomas Studer (German, but with fluent English and Spanish) from somewhat anonymous premises on Calle Virgen de Guadalupe (no fixed opening hours). Tom makes and repairs sails, does canvaswork including covers and awnings, and also tackles upholstery. Several yachtsmen have endorsed his work.
Rigging Andy Altenhofer (see Engineers, above) handles rigging with Norseman terminals but does not have a swage machine. Tom Studer at Butterfly-Service can arrange for swaged terminals to be made up in Santa Cruz de Tenerife and can set up rigging if required.
Chandlery Náutica y Pesca Océano Azul, ☎ /*Fax* 922 141502, on Avenida de Colón has a small amount of chandlery and yacht paint among its fishing equipment and general hardware. Little English is spoken.
In 2010 Butterfly-Service stocked limited chandlery (the premises are not large) but could order items from Nordest in Santa Cruz de Tenerife for delivery within 24 hours. Expansion was on the cards, however.
Water Good drinking water at all berths.
Showers Well-kept showers next to the marina office.
Laundry Washing left at the marina office before 0900 will be returned clean, dry and folded in the evening. Alternatively there is a launderette on Calle Real, beyond the church and post office.
Electricity On the pontoons.
Fuel Diesel and petrol available at the inner end of the reception berth, open 0830–1300 and 1600–1800.
Bottled gas Camping Gaz exchanges are readily available in the town, but as of 2011 the situation regarding refilling other cylinders remained uncertain – see page 191. Long-term visitors can obtain a Disa butane cylinder plus regulator and hose from the Cepsa garage or the mini-market opposite the marina. There is no deposit, although the marina office must provide a note to confirm the boat is berthed with them, and one is on trust to return the bottle before departure.
Club náutico The *Club Náutico de la Gomera* has premises on the Playa la Cueva close to the root of the main breakwater. Its bar and restaurant are open to visitors, but use of other facilities (including the swimming pool) requires temporary membership.
Weather forecast Posted daily at the harbour office.
Banks Several in the town, all with cash dispensers.
Shops/provisioning Several supermarkets and bakeries, plus a convenient mini-market near the root of the breakwater which is run by the marina and open even when other shops are closed for holidays.
The HiperTrebol supermarket at the western end of Avenida de Colón carries everything one might need when stocking up for a transatlantic passage, though prices are slightly higher than in Tenerife due to transport costs. There is a second large supermarket on Calle del Lamero to the west of the town.
Produce market Combined produce/fish market outside the HiperTrebol supermarket.
Cafés, restaurants & hotels Good selection, including the four-star *Parador Nacional* on the hill above the town.
Medical services Hospital just outside the town.

Communications

Post office Beyond the church on Calle Real.
Mailing address Marina la Gomera, Av. Fred Olsen s/n, 38800 San Sebastián de la Gomera, Islas Canarias, Spain.
Telephones In the square opposite the marina and elsewhere.
Internet access Secure Wi-Fi is now available from the mini-market, and in early 2011 cost €2 per day or €10.50 per week. It covers the visitors' berths at the east end of the marina. There are also several cybercafés, including Café Internet El @mbigú on the east side of the main square beyond the town hall.
Car hire & taxis In the ferry terminal on the breakwater, as well as in the town.
Buses Regular service throughout the island from the bus station next to the market. An interesting and relatively low-cost excursion would be to take the bus across the island to Puerto de Vueltas (Valle Gran Rey) and then catch the ferry back.
Ferries Ro-Ro ferries and large hydrofoils from Los Cristianos, sometimes continuing to El Hierro, plus the smaller *Benchi Express* which runs between Los Cristianos and Valle Gran Rey, calling at San Sebastián and Puerto de Santiago *en route*.
Air services Inter-island flights from the airport near Puerto de Santiago – but only four per day in early 2011.

Anchorages on the southeast coast of La Gomera

There are at least six fair-weather anchorages between San Sebastián and Puerto de Santiago – in addition to the three described below, Playa de la

Guancha (28°04′·4N 17°07′·7W), Playa de Suarez (28°02′·5N 17°01′W) and Playa del Medio (28°02′·2N 17°10′·8W) are also feasible in the right conditions offering some protection from the northeast and good holding in 8m or more over firm sand. None has much ashore other than dramatic cliffs and dry brown hillsides.

(With thanks to Club Yachting, see page 282, for additional input.)

Playa de El Cabrito

28°03′·7N 17°08′·5W (anchorage)

At the foot of a wide, wooded valley about 2M south of San Sebastián, Playa de El Cabrito ('goat beach') provides good holding in 6m over sand and stones, but any northwesterly swell is likely to work its way in. There is a small settlement ashore, which includes a quiet hotel where facilities are reserved for residents. Land on the beach or at the small jetty in the southwest corner, but be ready to leave at short notice should the wind veer.

Looking northwest into the secluded anchorage at Playa de El Cabrito, a few miles south of San Sebastián de la Gomera *Nigel Mercier*

Playa de la Roja (Playa de Oroja)

28°03′·3N 17°09′·1W (anchorage)

Just round the headland from Playa de El Cabrito, Playa de la Roja is marked at its southwest end by a distinctive exposed rock resembling a sharl's fin, known locally as the Rock of Heroes. There are a few smallcraft moorings off the dark sand beach and the bay is said to offer particularly good snorkelling, but again swell can be a problem.

Playa de Chinguarime

28°02′·3N 17°10′·5W (anchorage)

Just over a mile northeast of Puerto de Santiago and tucked in behind the protruding Punta Gaviota, Playa de Chinguarime offers protection both from the prevailing northeasterly winds and its associated swell. There are rocks in several places around the bay and a shallow reef in the northern corner, but the water is very clear making eyeball navigation straightforward. Anchor in 8–10m over sand.

Puerto de Santiago

28°01′·6N 17°11′·8W (breakwater head)

Waypoints

⊕C52 – 28°01′·3N 17°11′·4W (0·5M SE of Puerto de Santiago)
⊕C53 – 28°00′·2N 17°14′·6W (1M S of Pta del Becerro)

Lights

2845 **Breakwater**
Fl(2)R.7s12m3M Red column 5m
2844·9 **North (outer) mole**
Fl(2)G.7s8m5M Green column 3M
2845·2 **Northwest (inner) mole** Fl(2)G.7s1M
Green column standing in the water 1m

Harbour Communications
Port Captain ✆ 922 895275

Small ferry and fishing harbour

A small but pleasant fishing harbour facing onto a stony beach. Space for yachts is limited, and as the bay is open to southerly swell it would be wise to leave for better shelter if winds from this direction are forecast. Major damage to the breakwater occurred in January 1999, when it was breached by swells generated by a southerly gale, but it has since been rebuilt on an impressive scale and massively reinforced. The harbour office is situated at its root.

A 4-star hotel development occupies the clifftop to the east, with stunning views, swimming pools and a lift connecting it with the bottom of the cliff. The island's long-promised airport, finally completed in 1999, lies northwest of the town on the road to Valle Gran Rey and Puerto de Vueltas. However, planes are both small and very infrequent, so create minimal nuisance.

Approach and entrance

As with the other islands, the hills fall away to the south into a series of low promontories and bays.

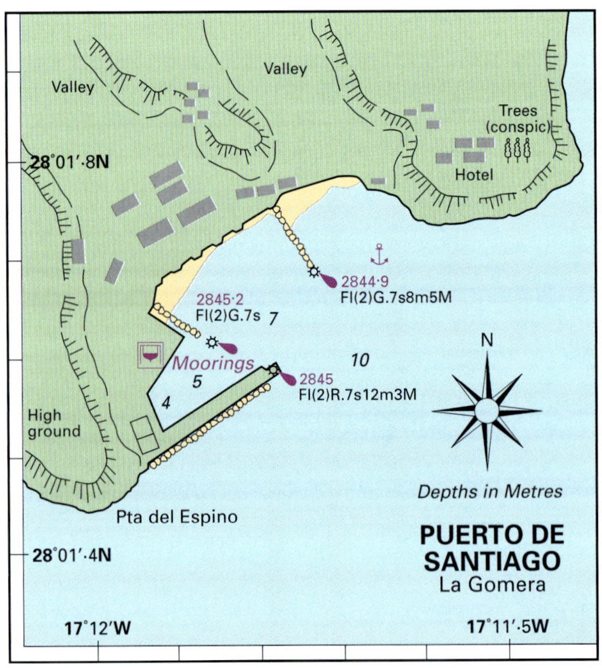

Approaching Puerto de Santiago from a little south of east *Nigel Mercier*

Approaching from the east a conspicuous pair of tall conical evergreens on the east head of the bay present an excellent landmark, as do the low-rise white hotel buildings. The trees can also be seen over the headland when approaching from the west. The harbour opens to the east, with the high breakwater wall running northeastwards from the western headland, and has no particular hazards in the approach.

Berthing and anchorage

In very calm conditions it might be possible to lie alongside the breakwater for a short period, well clear of the ferry berth (identifiable by some seating and a small booking office), though much of the inner length is normally occupied by fishing boats. Unusually, the quay is well provided with both bollards and ladders, having 11 and six respectively.

There is no possibility of anchoring within the harbour due to fishing boat moorings. However, in offshore winds secure, if somewhat rolly, anchorage can be found in 5–6m to the east of the short stone pier. Holding is good over sand and stones. Dinghies can be left on the beach or at the head of the harbour, where there are convenient steps (though a long painter will be needed if other users are not to be impeded).

Looking southwest across Baía de Santiago towards the harbour, with the angular Punta del Espino behind

Formalities

Visit the harbour office at the root of the breakwater with the usual ship's papers and passports, though it is doubtful if much notice will be taken of a yacht at anchor. No charge is made for anchoring.

Facilities

Boatyard Secure boatyard run by the *Cofradía de Pescadores* (fishermen's confederation). An economical place to work on a long-term DIY project, with owners permitted to live aboard, so long as materials and fittings are not needed in a hurry. The gates are open 0900–2000 weekdays, 0900–1400 weekends, but owners are understood to be given keys.

Travel-lift 64-tonne capacity, and with a new hoist dock which appears to have overcome the previous problems with turbulence, but few yacht-length props. Unless fluent in Spanish, lifting would most easily be organised via the marina office at San Sebastián but visit first to inspect – in 2010 the standards of lifting and shoring appeared questionable.

Water Good water from the a tap on the harbour wall or a hose in the boatyard.

Showers Basic showers in the harbour building.

Electricity In the boatyard.

Bottled gas Camping Gaz exchanges at the nearby filling station, but no refills.

Bank In the village, with cash dispenser.

Shops/provisioning Supermarket and other shops in the village, but no produce market despite the surrounding banana plantations.

Cafés, restaurants & hotels Several cafés and restaurants on the waterfront, serving excellent fresh seafood, plus the hotel on the hilltop.

Medical services Clinic 500m up the road towards Valle Gran Rey.

Communications

Post office Facing the square.

Telephones In the square and elsewhere.

Taxis Can be summoned by telephone.

Buses To San Sebastián and Valle Gran Rey. It may be necessary to walk up to the main road.

Ferries The *Benchi Express* hydrofoil catamaran calls at Puerto de Santiago six times each day carrying foot passengers between San Sebastián and Puerto de Vueltas.

Air services Inter-island flights from the nearby airport – two each day to Tenerife North and two to Las Palmas.

Anchorages on the southwest coast of La Gomera

Playa del Ereses

28°01'·4N 17°14'W (anchorage)

About 2M west of Puerto de Santiago, Playa del Ereses is a scenic open bay east of Punta del Becerro. Anchor in 12–16m over sand, but watch out for rocks.

Cala de la Cantera

28°02'·1N 17°16'·4W (anchorage)

About 3M west of Playa del Ereses lies Cala de la Cantera ('quarry creek'), where a disused tuna canning factory overlooks a small beach. Coming from the east one sees a large cave – the Cuevo del Obispo – and a natural rock arch. From the west first sight is of the disused factory and its associated stone pier at the southeast end of the beach. The bay sometimes suffers from swell, making it best to anchor in the centre in about 10m. If heading ashore by dinghy the beach is quite steep, and despite the poor condition of the pier it may offer the easiest shore access.

(With thanks to Club Yachting, see page 282, for additional input.)

Cala de la Negra and Cala de la Rajita

28°02'·8N 17°17'·5W & 28°03'N 17°17'·9W (anchorages)

Cala de la Negra and Cala de la Rajita share a double bay, the latter accessible by road and with a few houses set back from the beach, though the old fish cannery has largely been demolished. Both anchorages offer good holding in about 8m over firm, dark sand.

Puerto de Vueltas (Valle Gran Rey)

28°04'·68N 17°19'·85W (outer breakwater head)

Waypoint

⊕C54 – 28°04'·3N 17°20'·3W (0·5M SW of Puerto de Vueltas)

Lights

2845·6 **Outer breakwater, head**
Fl(3)R.9s1m5M Red column 1m
2845·7 **Outer breakwater, angle**
Q(9)15s3M West cardinal post, ⧗ topmark
2845·5 **Inner breakwater**
Fl(2+1)G.21s15m3M Green column, red band 2m

Harbour Communications
Port Captain ✆ 922 805476, 865434

Enlarged harbour but mostly unused

Puerto de Vueltas (pronounced *Pwerto de las Bweltass*), also referred to as Valle Gran Rey *Bye-eh Gran Ray*) after the impressive valley behind, is an old fishing harbour backed by high red cliffs which enjoys one of the most spectacular settings in all the islands. A great deal of work took place nearly ten years ago to enlarge the previously small harbour, with a long, angled breakwater built outside the old one. Completed by late 2005, the new wall appears to have withstood the elements well. However, the harbour remains little used, and although there is a Ro-Ro ferry ramp, currently the only regular ferry to call at Puerto de Vueltas carries foot passengers from San Sebastián and Puerto de Santiago.

In late 2010 it was suggested that a marina might be created in the inner harbour, though spurs would be needed at the end of both inner and outer breakwaters to provide adequate protection in southerly winds. Currently about half a dozen yachts can lie alongside the inner breakwater, with many more anchored in the bay to the southeast.

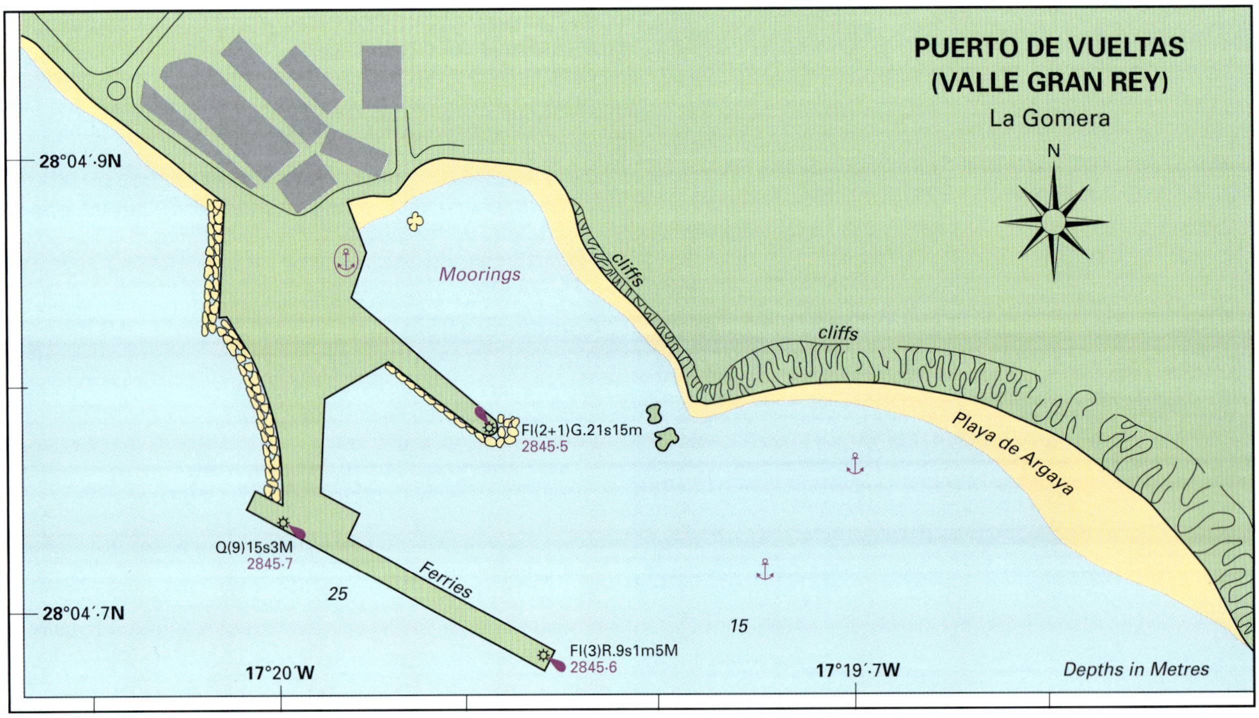

Yachts lie inside the inner breakwater at Puerto de Vueltas, sometimes referred to as Valle Gran Rey. Plans are afoot for a marina, or at least some pontoon berths, now that wall is no longer needed for the ferry

One of the main attractions of the area is the walk up (or down) the spectacular Valle Gran Rey ('valley of the great king'). Although the ascent is not steep – most of the gradient lies either side – one possibility would be to take a taxi a few kilometres inland and walk back down the well-maintained tourist path.

Approach and entrance

High cliffs line the west coast of La Gomera, but the harbour can be identified by the cluster of white houses rising up the valley and the long, pale grey breakwater.

From the south the conspicuous rock off Punta Iguala can be identified 2M southeast of the harbour, linked to the cliffs by a breaking reef. There are more outlying rocks just south of the entrance. Keeping 0·5M offshore, steer for the head of the breakwater when it bears northeast. From the northwest and west the final approach should be from a similar position as there are outlying rocks west of the breakwater root, though most have been incorporated into the outer arm.

Avoid cutting the end of the outer breakwater too closely, should that be the moment the ferry is revving up to depart.

Entrance and berthing

As of November 2010 six or seven visiting yachts were permitted to lie against the inside of the inner breakwater, possibly rafting to double or even treble that number in settled northeasterlies – always assuming that those on the inside do not wish to leave. No pontoon is provided and good fendering will be needed, but there are plenty of bollards and stainless steel ladders every 20m or so. Note that rubble projects about 7m inwards from the end of the inner breakwater, providing some protection from southerly swell while also adding challenge to the final approach for those berthed nearby.

A few yachts lie bows-to at the head of the inner harbour, but these appear to be long-term residents. Beyond them are several trots of smallcraft moored fore-and-aft. Currently no berthing (or anchoring) is allowed in the outer harbour, despite only a small part of the breakwater being used by the hydrofoil ferry.

Anchorage

In the usual autumn northeasterlies good anchorage can be found off Playa de Argaya, close southeast of the harbour, in 6–8m over sand (inside the 5m line the bottom is of rock and large stones). Strangely, while the beach at Playa de Argaya is composed of the usual dark volcanic sand, those who have dived to check their anchors maintain that from about the 5m line outwards the bottom sand is pale. Either way, holding is good and no charge is made.

Formalities and charges

Visit the harbour office with ship's papers and passports. Puerto de Vueltas is one of those harbours for which a berth should in theory be booked in advance – see Booking berths in *Puertos de Canarias* harbours, page 189. However the system appears to be flexible to say the least, and most yachts simply turn up. The berthing fee is calculated on a length x beam basis and in 2010 was set at €0.24 per m^2, including tax at 5%.

Facilities

Boatyard No boatyard, though in an emergency assistance might be forthcoming from the *Cofradía de Pescadores* (fishermen's confederation).

Metalwork There is reported to be a blacksmith's shop in the road opposite the bus station, equiped for welding stainless steel and for machining, turning and bending of stainless and other metals.

Water From a tap near the head of the harbour – the quality is usually excellent. For larger quantities the harbourmaster may be able to arrange a metered delivery from one of the manholes on the quay.

Showers Promised for well over a decade, but yet to materialise. There are patrons' toilets at the café mentioned below.

Fuel Available on the quay from a pump controlled by the *Cofradía de Pescadores*, 0900–1300, 1500–1900 Monday to Saturday. Small quantities by can from the filling station on the main road at La Calera, about 1·5km from the harbour.

Bank About 600m from the harbour, with cash dispenser.

Shops/provisioning Several small supermarkets and a hardware store in the harbour area, plus more shops in La Calera.

Cafés & restaurants Small café/bar at the head of the harbour, with restaurants and hotels along the seafront to the north.

Medical services Health centre on the main road, about 2km from the harbour.

Communications

Post office About 600m from the harbour on the inland road.

Telephone Near the head of the harbour.

Internet access No public Wi-Fi, but several cybercafés.

Car hire An agency just outside the harbour gates, and others in the town.

Taxis In La Calera, though taxis visit the harbour when the hydrofoil is due.

Buses To Puerto de Santiago, San Sebastián and elsewhere from a stop on the seafront about 300m from the harbour.

Ferries The *Benchi Express* small hydrofoil visits Puerto de Vueltas three times daily from Los Cristianos after calling at San Sebastián and Puerto de Santiago.

La Merica towers over Valle Gran Rey – the valley of the great king – just north of Puerto de Vueltas *Andy Scott*

La Palma

Between 28°27'N–28°51'N and 17°43'W–18°00'W

Introduction

La Palma, with a population of around 86,000 and an area of 517km², is a prosperous and strikingly beautiful island still largely unspoilt by the tourist invasion. It resembles an inverted cone in both outline and elevation, with steep coastal cliffs rising towards the world's largest volcanic crater, La Caldera de Taburiente. This chasm, 27km in circumference and 763m deep, is surrounded by the highest peaks on the island, including Roque de la Muchachos at 2,422m, and is clothed to the tree line by a huge pine forest. The entire area forms the *Parque Nacional de la Caldera de Taburiente*. The deep valley of the Taburiente/Angustias river runs out to the southwest, breaching the crater walls and reaching the sea at the old port of Tazacorte. The most recent volcanic activity occurred in 1971 when, with due warning and consequently no loss of life, a new volcano erupted at the southernmost tip of the island.

A theory has been advanced that it is only a matter of time before the entire western part of La Palma detaches itself from the rest and slides catastrophically into the Atlantic Ocean. While this may well be correct – it appears that pressure inside the mountain is building all the time – estimated dates vary from 2015 to 2515 or beyond and it is inconceivable that there would be no warning, so it would be a pity to avoid La Palma on this account. (In any case, the same predictions go on to describe tidal waves bringing doom and destruction around the entire Atlantic seaboard. Probably least affected will be yachts actually at sea... .)

La Palma is the greenest and most fertile of the Canary islands, with large cultivated areas of bananas, tomatoes, cucumbers and vines. The mountains are usually rimmed with clouds but the tops are often clear with excellent viewing, and an International Astrophysical Observatory has long been established on the northern rim of *La Caldera de Taburiente*. Together with other telescopes it includes the British Sir Isaac Newton reflector, controlled via satellite by observers in Edinburgh. A road runs around the crater's northern edge to serve the observatory – as well as a stunning viewpoint well worth the tortuous drive up – while another leads to La Cumbrecita, a breathtaking viewpoint on the southern rim.

There is ample rainfall in most seasons, with the direct benefit to yachtsmen that La Palma's tap water is some of the best in the Canaries. Over the years many thousands of vessels have filled their tanks at Santa Cruz in preparation for the Atlantic crossing.

The coastline is such that there are only two harbours suitable for yachts, both of which now contain marinas in which a yacht can safely be left while exploring the island by car. If car hire is a treat rather than a regular diversion, La Palma would be an excellent place to indulge.

Telecommunications

Mobile (cell) phone reception is excellent around Santa Cruz and Tazacorte, though holes may exist inland. The country code for the Canaries is 34, as it is for mainland Spain, and the area code for La Palma – which must be included even when dialling from within the island – is 922, shared with Tenerife, La Gomera and El Hierro.

Santa Cruz de la Palma is famous for its balconies, many enclosed by glass or festooned with flowers – or sometimes both

By 2011 Wi-Fi was available in both Marina La Palma in Santa Cruz and Puerto Tazacorte, as well as cybercafés in all the larger towns.

Approach and navigation

La Palma's great height – second only to Tenerife – makes it easy to identify from many miles off in reasonable visibility. The vast majority of yachts will approach from the north or east, and will encounter no off-lying hazards until close inshore. Northern sector winds predominate around La Palma and acceleration zones may be encountered off the northeast, northwest and southern tips of the island.

Websites

The following sites contain general information about La Palma, some of which may be useful to the visiting yachtsman. Websites relating to specific harbours are listed under Harbour communications, those covering all or most of the Canary Islands on page 188 of the introduction.

www.en.wikipedia.org/wiki/La_Palma – all the usual in-depth wikipedia information without the spin which one comes to expect from 'local' websites

www.ing.iac.es – homepage of the Isaac Newton Group of Telescopes, just some of those on the slopes above La Palma's spectacular Caldera de Taburiente

www.ing.iac.es/PR/lapalma – the Isaac Newton Group's well-researched guide to the island as a whole (but almost impossible to locate on the main site)

www.islabonita.es – the website of the *Asociación Turismo Rural Isla Bonita* in English, Spanish, German, French and Dutch, and much less brash than most tourist sites. Online booking for botanical walks, an 'astrotour', etc.

www.islalapalma.com – created by two emigrants to La Palma who plainly love their adopted home, this site carries general information in English, Dutch and German plus lots of excellent photos. Check out the refreshingly direct 'What NOT to expect' section

www.lapalmabiosfera.es – the island is a World Biosphere Reserve and is justly proud of it. This comprehensive website, in Spanish, English and German, explains why

www.lapalmaturismo.com – user-friendly website of the La Palma tourist office in Spanish, English and German, with some very useful links

Navigation

Waypoints

⊕ C55 – 28°53'·5N 17°55'W (2M N of Pta del Mudo)
⊕ C56 – 28°51'·8N 17°45'W (2M NE of Pta Cumplida)
⊕ C57 – 28°44'·6N 17°42'·3W (1M E of Pta Sancha)
⊕ C58 – 28°39'·8N 17°44'·8W (1M SE of Santa Cruz de la Palma)
⊕ C59 – 28°26'·2N 17°50'·5W (2M S of Pta Fuencaliente)
⊕ C60 – 28°38'·3N 17°57'·2W (0·5M WSW of Tazacorte)

Courses and distances

⊕ C55 – ⊕ C60 = 19M, by eye
⊕ C55 – ⊕ C56 = 9M, 101° / 281°
⊕ C56 – ⊕ C57 = 7·5M, 342° / 162°
⊕ C57 – ⊕ C58 = 5·5M, 205° / 025°
⊕ C58 – ⊕ C47 (2M W of Pta de Teno, Tenerife) = 45·5M, 114° / 294°
⊕ C58 – ⊕ C50 (2M N of El Roguillo, La Gomera) = 36M, 135° / 315°
⊕ C58 – ⊕ C59 = 15M, by eye
⊕ C59 – ⊕ C60 = 13·5M, by eye
⊕ C59 – ⊕ C62 (2M E of Pta Caleta, El Hierro) = 37·5M, 080° / 100°

Magnetic variation

6°25'W (2011), decreasing by 8'E annually. Local magnetic anomalies can increase variation by up to 2°15' southwest of La Palma – see Admiralty chart *1869*.

Tidal Streams

Generally insignificant – see Tides and tidal streams, page 194. Details of range, etc. will be found under Santa Cruz.

Charts

Admiralty *1869* (1:300,000)
Spanish *61B* (1:200,000), *616* (1:60,000)
US *51260* (1:300,000)
Imray-Iolaire *E2* (1:600,000)

Lights

2846 **Punta Cumplida** Fl.5s62m23M
104·5°-vis-337° Grey tower 34m
2848·45 **Santa Cruz breakwater**
Fl.G.5s16m5M Green tower 8m
2849·51 **Punta de Arenas Blancas (Punta Salamera)**
Oc(3)8s45m20M White futuristic tower 38m
2850 **Punta Fuencaliente**
Fl(3)18s35m14M 230·5°-vis-118·5°
White tower, two red bands 24m
Note The old light tower still stands nearby
2851 **Punta Lava** Fl(1+2)20s50m20M
Octagonal white tower, green lantern 48m

Coast Radio Station

La Palma 28°38'·9N 17°49'·6W, remotely controlled from Tenerife
VHF Ch 06, 16, 20 (24 hours)
DSC VHF MMSI 002241025, 28°39'N 17°50'W, remotely controlled from Tenerife

Weather and navigation broadcasts

VHF 28°39'N 17°49'·7W (remotely controlled from Tenerife)
Weather bulletins Ch 20 at 0833, 1333, 2033 (forecast in Spanish for coastal waters)
Navigational warnings Ch 20 at 0833, 2033 (in Spanish for coastal waters)

Santa Cruz de la Palma

28°40′·27N 17°45′·84W (breakwater head)

Waypoint

⊕C58 – 28°39′·8N 17°44′·8W
(1M SE of Santa Cruz de la Palma)

Tides

Standard port for the Canary Islands is Casablanca, with Santa Cruz a secondary port. MLWS is about 0·3m above datum and time difference on Casablanca: –0102. Predictions for Santa Cruz de la Palma are also available via Admiralty *EasyTide* – see page 194
Mean spring range 1·7m
Mean neap range 0·8m

Plans

Admiralty *1858* (1:75,000 & 1:10,000)
Spanish *6150* (1:7,500)
US *51344* (1:15,000)
Imray-Iolaire *E2* (1:12,500)

Lights

2848·45 **Breakwater**
Fl.G.5s16m5M Green tower 8m
buoy **Port hand 'A'** Fl.R.5s2M
Red pillar buoy, ▪ topmark
buoy **Port hand 'B'** Fl(2)R.7s2M
Red pillar buoy, ▪ topmark
buoy **Port hand 'C'** Fl(3)R.9s2M
Red pillar buoy, ▪ topmark
buoy **Port hand 'D'** Fl.R.5s2M
Red can buoy, ▪ topmark
2848·4 **Fishing harbour angle**
Fl(4)R.11s8m3M Red post 4m
2848·5 **Fishing harbour molehead**
Fl.R.5s8m3M Red post 4m
2849 **Container terminal** Fl(2+1)R.21s8m3M
Red column, green band 4m
2849·35 **Marina entrance, port side**
Fl(2)R.7s4m3M Red pyramid 5m
2849·3 **Marina entrance, starboard side**
Fl(2)G.7s4m3M Green pyramid 5m

Harbour Communications

Port authority ☏ 922 412121 *Fax* 922 420732
Email lapalma@puertosdetenerife.org
VHF Ch 16 (24 hours)
Marina la Palma ☏ 922 410 289, 608 223345
Fax 922 415973 *Email* info@marinalapalma.es
www.marinalapalma.es (0900–1300, 1700–1900 weekdays, 0900–1300 Saturday) VHF Ch 09, 16
Real Club Náutico de Santa Cruz de la Palma
☏ 922 411346, 667 774 350 www.rcnlapalma.com

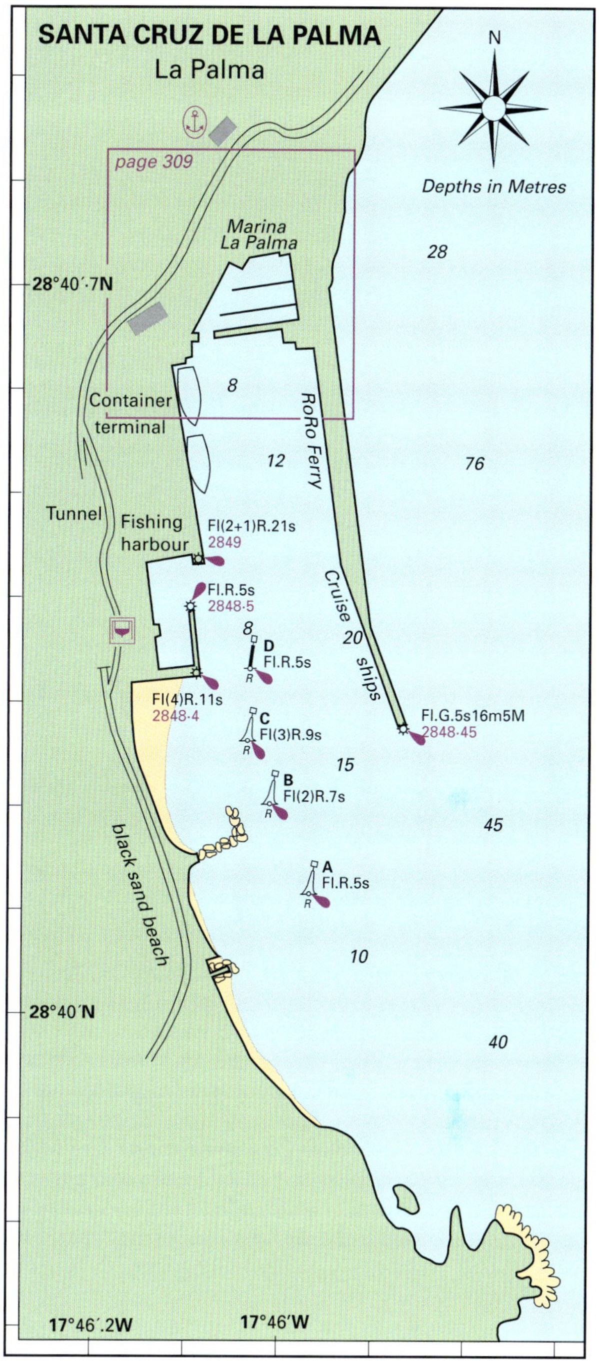

New marina adjacent to real Canarian town

Santa Cruz is one of the most attractive towns in the Canaries, though this may be hard to hard to believe on approach from the water, when from a distance one is presented with a facade of concrete apartment blocks. Below and behind them, however, much of the old city remains. Cobbled streets lined by original Canarian houses with ornately carved wooden balconies (which at one time contained the heads!) lead to shady squares, generally containing a café or two. There has been relatively little tourist development compared to most of the Canary islands, possibly because there are few sandy beaches, and the city has a busy, friendly atmosphere and good facilities for storing up.

Ferries, which berth on the breakwater, run to Tenerife, La Gomera and El Hierro, and Santa Cruz is also growing as a cruise ship destination. On the landward side of the harbour is a container terminal and next to it a small harbour, the Dársena Pesquera, intended for local fishing vessels and other smallcraft. Until very recently there was nowhere suitable for a visiting yacht to berth, a situation rectified by the construction of Marina La Palma behind a sheltering mole at the head of the commercial harbour. Initially the entrance was to be on the eastern side, moved to the west after construction had started, presumably to keep yachts well away from the commercial shipping on which the port depends. (In mid-2010 specific instructions for all vessels using the harbour, including yachts,

The commercial harbour at Santa Cruz de la Palma, seen from the cliffs to the southwest. The marina lies behind the grey mole with white uprights at the head of the harbour

were included in the Spanish hydrographic service's *Avisos a los Navegantes* and are summarised below under the heading Harbour bye-laws).

Responsibility for the marina's construction, maintenance and management was awarded as a joint venture to Puerto Calero SA of Lanzarote and the *Real Club Náutico de La Palma* for a term of 25 years, and by early November 2008 the marina was accepting visitors, although the shoreside infrastructure remained unfinished for another two years. The marina was formally opened in July 2010, by which time its offices, services and ancillary businesses such as shops and restaurants were housed in a curved building at the head of the harbour, apparently intended to become a new recreational area for the people of Santa Cruz.

The marina has not been without its problems, however, the chief of which is frequent surge. Major efforts have gone into combatting this, including the installation of an arched facing to the west wall of the marina basin (which has the unintended side-effect of making it even more difficult to pick out on the approach). Although claimed to be 90% successful, reports received over the winter of 2010/2011 imply that this is optimistic, with at least half mentioning surge as a serious issue. In November 2010 there was constant slight movement even when the water surface both inside and outside the marina mole appeared calm. A gentle swell appeared to be rolling in parallel to the west wall, catching yachts on the quarter or the side of the bow, and twisting them as it rolled along the hull. There was no consistency of movement, even between neighbouring boats of similar size and profile, and one yacht per double berth with lines to either side remained the norm. Strangely, the movement was no worse near the entrance than in the eastern corner of the marina. A barrier of some kind is now said to be under consideration.

The marina's other disadvantage is its immediate surroundings. While the town is lovely and the marina itself attractive enough, the area between the two – basically car and container parks – is not. There is also continuous underlying generator noise whenever a ferry or cruise ship is in, but that is common to many larger Canarian harbours.

Harbour approach and entrance

The island is mountainous and the fall-away to the southeast is less pronounced than on Gran Canaria and Tenerife. In most weather conditions the white buildings of Santa Cruz will be conspicuous at the foot of the mountains, which are often cloud covered, and aircraft will be seen coming into or leaving the airport a few miles to the south.

Santa Cruz is a large harbour by Canarian standards, with a wide entrance opening to the south and no natural hazards in the approach. A close watch needs to be kept for ferries and cruise ships, both in the approach and while proceeding up the harbour, as space is tight. Two ferries berth on the breakwater, turning to back into Ro-Ro berths in the process, with a smaller hydrofoil berthing against the marina mole. In addition there is a container berth on the west side of the harbour, and often a cruise ship or two for good measure.

According to the Harbour bye-laws below, contact must be made with the Traffic Control Centre on VHF Ch 06 while still two miles from the entrance, and no vessel is allowed to enter the harbour without authorisation. Once inside the harbour, yachts must follow a designated – though unmarked – route up its western side towards the marina entrance.

Harbour bye-laws

Summarised from the Spanish hydrographic service's *Avisos a los Navegantes* of Week 29, 2010, these state:

Communications: All communication with the Traffic Control Centre takes place on VHF Ch 06, and all vessels moving inside the harbour must maintain a listening watch.

Prior authorisation: No vessel, of whatever size, is allowed to enter, leave or move in the harbour without prior authorisation from the Traffic Control Centre – the former while two miles or more from the end of the main breakwater.

Speed limit: 4 knots.

Pleasure craft: Yachts must not enter the harbour or leave the marina without prior authorisation from the Traffic Control Centre, and must never impede commercial ships and fishing boats.

Prohibitions: Other than in an emergency, anchoring is prohibited within the harbour, as are sporting activities such as swimming, diving, waterski-ing and fishing.

Entrance and exit of yachts and smallcraft: After passing the end of the breakwater, yachts and smallcraft should continue across the harbour and not turn north for the marina entrance until close to buoy 'C' (see plan on page 307). When leaving the marina they should head for buoy 'B', and not turn east to cross the harbour until between buoys 'B' and 'A'.

Marina approach and entrance

The marina entrance is difficult to make out, even from quite close to, following the installation of the arched facing to its west wall – see photograph below. The small light structures on either side blend into the background, and should a ship be unloading at the container wharf it may partially mask the gap. Head for the west end of what may appear to be a solid barrier and the entrance will gradually become clear.

The marina staff request that yachts make contact before arrival, and in light of the possibility that a fixed barrier may actually be installed – see above – a call to the marina office on VHF Ch 09 (in addition to the Traffic Control Centre on VHF Ch 06), will in any case be reassuring.

The reception berth is directly ahead on entry, under the windows of the marina office, though yachts are often waved straight into a berth.

Berthing

The marina contains 180 berths for yachts of up to 18m, 55 of them able to take boats of 13–14m LOA and 34 capable of berthing more than 14m, all in wide bays between long finger pontoons. Each

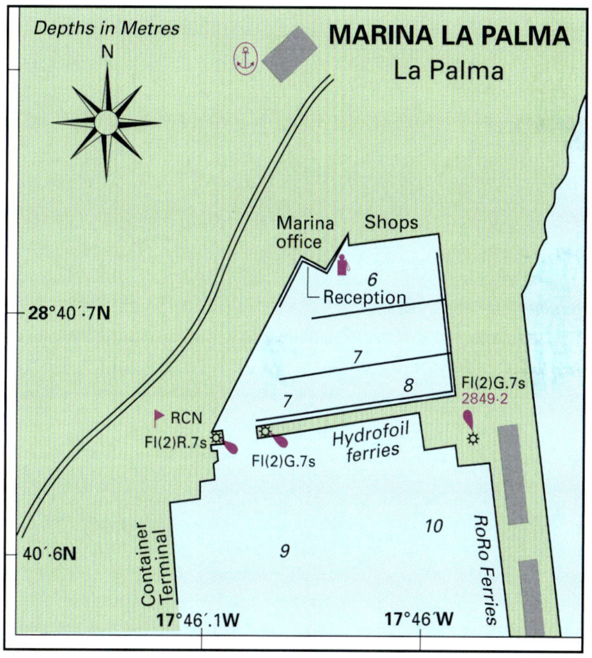

The entrance to Marina la Palma can be difficult to pick out, particularly since an arched facing was added to the west wall. In this photograph it is arrowed for clarity

hammerhead can berth 22m, while there is a single 25m slot in the northeast corner (though it must be interesting watching an incumbent arrive and leave). So far most of the larger berths remain empty, and in the long term at least 25% are to be reserved for visitors. Depths are generous, with at least 6m throughout the marina. The topic of swell has already been covered at length, but it does no harm to stress that multiple lines and fenders will give peace of mind both at night and while the boat is unattended, even if conditions are benign and they appear not to be needed.

Formalities

Visit the marina office with the usual passports, ship's papers and evidence of insurance. The staff are particularly friendly and helpful and speak excellent English and some French, and in late 2010 marina manager Guillermo Cabrera was also learning German.

If clearing of out of Spanish territory on departure it may be necessary to visit other offices to get the necessary exit stamp. The marina officials will advise, but it would be wise to check in advance – and to ascertain the relevant office hours – in order to avoid last-minute delays. If planning to visit El Hierro en route it is still necessary to obtain clearance in Santa Cruz as the former is not a frontier post – see page 317.

Charges

The berthing fee is calculated on a length x beam basis and in 2011 was set at €0.37 per m², which included water, electricity and tax at 5%. Increasing discounts were available for stays of 90, 180 and 365 days. Both *Tasa de Embarcación de Recreo* (Recreational Vessel tax) and *Tasa de Ayuda a la Navegación* (Navigational Aid tax) may also be payable – see page 190.

Facilities

Boatyard A small boatyard area is planned for behind the marina building, where smallcraft will be lifted out by a forklift truck, but it will not cater for yachts. There is a larger boatyard at the fishing harbour, and though only basic skills are available DIY work is permitted, as is living aboard while ashore. Security is rudimentary.

Travel-lift 70-tonne hoist in the fishermen's harbour, though in late 2010 the props appeared somewhat spindly, so careful supervision would be essential. Best arranged via the marina office, though it may also be necessary to visit the Port Authority building to collect the necessary paperwork. Payment is required in advance.

Engineers & electronics Ask at the marina office. Náutica El Chopo (see Chandlery, below) is distributor for Volvo Penta engines and can organise work on other makes.

Sail repairs Small repairs can be carried out locally – ask at the marina office – but larger jobs would need to be sent to La Gomera or Tenerife.

Chandlery Náutica El Chopo, ✆ 922 402256, open 1000–1330, 1600–2100 Monday to Saturday, has premises on the corridor which bisects the marina building. It mainly stocks fishing gear, but also line, fenders, paint and a few stainless steel fittings. There is a larger branch in Los Llanos – see page 313. In November 2010 only Spanish was spoken, but an English-speaking employee was being sought.

Water At all berths and ashore in the fishing harbour.

Showers Immaculate showers in the new services block, with access by electronic card.

Launderette Coin-operated washer-dryer in the services block.

Electricity At all berths and ashore in the fishing harbour.

Fuel Diesel and petrol pumps at the fuel berth near reception.

Bottled gas Camping Gaz exchanges in the town, but as of 2011 the situation regarding refilling other cylinders remained uncertain – see page 191.

Weather forecast At the marina office.

Club náutico Since the opening of the marina the *Real Club Náutico de Santa Cruz de la Palma* has become much more welcoming to the crews of yachts berthed in the marina. Use of the club's outdoor pool is free, and it may be possible to use the indoor pool, gym, jacuzzi and sauna for a small charge.

Banks Several in the city, all with cash dispensers, with the latter due for installation at the marina by early 2011.

Shops/provisioning Several good supermarkets able to supply all needs if storing up for the Atlantic passage, though perhaps without quite the variety of Las Palmas or Santa Cruz de Tenerife. The *Boutique del Pan* opposite the market is recommended for bread and cakes, and is open daily including Sunday.

Most of the shop and restaurant spaces in the marina complex were not yet occupied as of November 2010, though a good-sized Spar supermarket was due to open the following month.

Produce market The market on Avenida del Puente near the centre of the city has reopened after refurbishment and though relatively small is impressively clean. Open 0800–1400 Monday to Saturday.

Cafés, restaurants & hotels Wide choice at all price levels, including some delightful pavement cafés in the town. Several eating and drinking establishments overlook the marina, while the *Real Club Náutico* also has both a bar and a more formal restaurant.

Medical services Doctors in the town and a hospital (which looks more like a five-star hotel) on the slopes to the west.

Communications

Post office An imposing building overlooking the roundabout at the head of the harbour.

Mailing address Dársena de Embarcaciónes Menores del Puerto de Santa Cruz de la Palma, 38700 La Palma, Prov. de Santa Cruz de Tenerife, Islas Canarias, Spain.

Telephones Due to be installed in the marina complex, otherwise in the ferry terminal building and in the town.

Internet access Free Wi-Fi throughout the marina, with a computer available in the office if required.

Car hire At the ferry terminal on the breakwater and at the airport.

Taxis Available, but not in vast numbers.

Buses To the airport and throughout the island.

Ferries Regular service to La Gomera, Tenerife and El Hierro.

Air services European and inter-island flights from the airport about 7km south of Santa Cruz. One direct flight from the UK each week from May to December inclusive, otherwise via Tenerife.

Puerto Espíndola

28°48'·71N 17°45'·81W (mole hammerhead)

Lights
2847 **Breakwater**
Fl(3)R.9s7m3M Red post 2m

Tiny harbour on exposed coast

Not a port by any stretch of the imagination, Espindola (sometimes written as Spíndola) is a small village 2M south of Punta Cumplida with a hammerhead mole where local fishing boats are craned out onto the quay. After repeatedly losing contruction work to the elements, a southwestern arm was added to the quay a few years ago, but even so the small area of sheltered water is both too small and too shallow for most yachts, apart from being busy with local smallcraft.

Although it would be possible to anchor off in exceptionally calm weather it is generally preferable to visit by land, not least because the unexpectedly good road northwards from Santa Cruz offers some truly spectacular views. If intent on approaching by sea, be warned that there are several rocks in the approach and depths are not known.

A small ketch negotiates Marina Tazacorte's well-protected entrance, passing the reception berth to port and new pontoons for local boats to starboard. The marina reception building was due for completion by early summer 2011

Puerto Tazacorte

28°38'·46N 17°56'·63W (inner breakwater, west head)

Waypoint
⌖C60 – 28°38'·3N 17°57'·2W (0·5M WSW of Tazacorte)

Lights
buoy **Marks work on new outer breakwater**
Q.R.5M Red pillar buoy 3m
2853 **Outer breakwater**
Q(9)15s6m3M West cardinal post, ⧗ topmark 7m
2852 **Inner breakwater, west head**
Fl(2)R.7s16m5M Red post 2m
Inner breakwater, east head
Fl(2)R.7s5m5M Red post 2m
Note The above two lights are synchronised and have identical characteristics
2855 **East mole**
Fl(2)G.7s6m1M Green post 3m
2854 **Inner harbour, port side (marina reception)**
Fl(3)R.9s6m1M Red post 6m
Inner harbour, starboard side
Fl(3)G.9s4m1M Green post
2856 **Old harbour mole**
Q(9)15s3M West cardinal post 3m
Note Not associated with the main harbour – see below

Marine farm
Three marine farms, each marked by four yellow pillar buoys with × topmarks, either Fl(3)Y.9s3M, Fl(4)Y.11s3M or Fl(5)Y.13s3M, lie northwest of Puerto Tazacorte, centred on 28°39'·1N 17°57'·3W, 28°39'·2N 17°57'·8W and 28°39'·4N 17°57'W respectively.

Harbour Communications
Port Captain ✆ */Fax* 922 480807 (0800–1530 Monday to Saturday)
Puerto Tazacorte ✆ */Fax* 922 480386
Email informacion@puertotazacorte.com
www.puertotazacorte.com (0900–1300, 1500–1800 weekdays, 0800–1300 Saturday) VHF Ch 09, 16

New marina on La Palma's Atlantic coast

Puerto Tazacorte (pronounced *Pwerto Tassa-cort'eh*) lies halfway down the west coast of La Palma, about 0·5M south of the original harbour. The latter is now enjoying a new lease of life, its derelict breakwater rebuilt and enlarged to shelter a swimming area and a small, black-sand beach. The end of the restored breakwater is lit. Both harbours occupy the mouth of the steep-sided valley that originates in the Taburiente crater. There are cliffs to the north of the valley mouth, while to the south the coastline is lower with the land behind sloping gently up to the base of the central spinal range. Terraces of bananas line all but the steepest inclines.

Work to enlarge the main harbour started late in 1997 and the massive breakwater extension was officially opened in December 2002. It seems that no ferry company wished to run a regular service to the harbour, and in 2008 work started on converting the interior of the harbour from a mixture of somewhat ramshackle pontoons and local moorings into a modern, full-service marina. By late 2009 the first phase of the marina was making good progress, and by November the following year the interior was effectively finished. Work was still taking place at the end of the 'old' breakwater, with another arm taking shape to the west. At that time the new

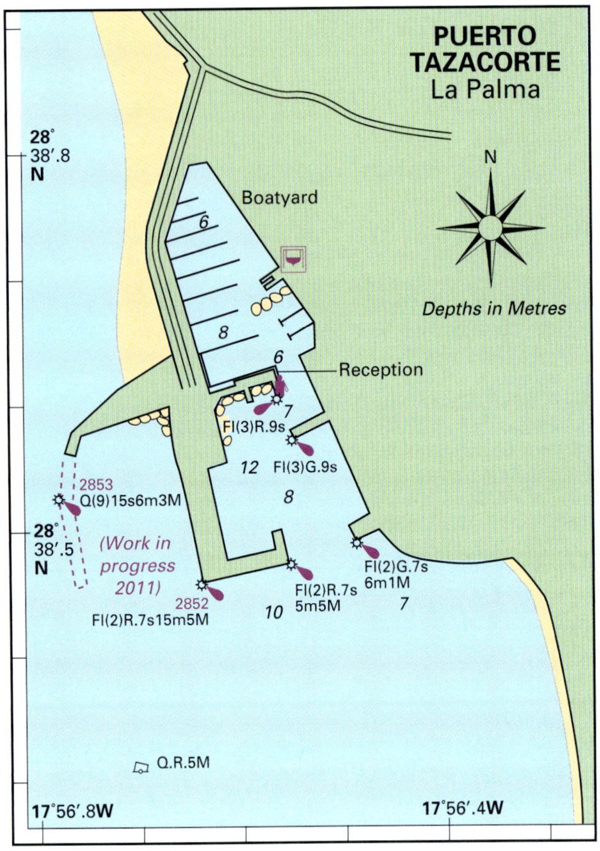

breakwater was unlit at its southern end, something which is certain to be rectified in due course.

In the inner harbour, nine pontoons run inwards from the breakwater with two more in the southeast corner of the harbour earmarked for local fishermen. Considerable infilling has taken place in the northeast to provide boatyard and dry storage space and, crucially, the inner entrance has been greatly improved by overlapping moles. While these make it narrower and something of a dog-leg, they should eliminate surge in all but the strongest southerly winds.

Several thoughtful touches are in evidence including a long, shaded parking area paralleling the west side of the basin (which also supplies welcome shade for those on foot), car and bicycle hire, serious recycling facilities and a holding-tank pump-out station near the travel-lift dock. Though somewhat remote – isolated even from the bright lights of Santa Cruz and with the local banana musuem listed among its attractions – Puerto Tazacorte would make a fine departure point for an Atlantic crossing, particularly for those who prefer to set off relaxed and well-rested.

Approach and entrance

There are outlying rocks at many points along the coast and it is advisable to keep at least a mile offshore while approaching Tazacorte until the harbour can be positively identified. The end of the old breakwater carries a large and unusual sculpture of a leaning figure, and unless the new outer breakwater is equally massive this should remain visible from offshore. Until work on both old and new breakwaters is complete it is plainly necessary to approach with caution, and if coming from the north do not turn landwards for the marina until well south of the entrance. Depths are good, and the double wall configuration offers protection from northwesterly winds and seas for some distance before the harbour is entered.

Berthing

The reception and fuel pontoon lines the outer face of the inner spur – see plan – directly overlooked by the marina office. A call on VHF Ch 09 before arrival is requested, and may allow a yacht to proceed directly to a berth.

As already mentioned, nine pontoons ran inwards from the breakwater, offering berthing for 341 boats of up to 14m, all alongside finger pontoons. Nearly 70 berths can take boats of 12m or more, and with relatively few locally-owned craft of any size it seems unlikely that the marina will experience overcrowding problems for several years. A second phase of development, which will see the harbour enlarged to offer berthing for yachts of up to 28m, is

The new marina at Puerto Tazacorte in November 2010, looking southwest. An outer breakwater was under construction, marked here by the towering crane

scheduled for completion by 2014 or earlier.

Security is provided by both electronics gates and CCTV, but one suspects that the threat is fairly minor to start with.

Anchorage

Anchoring is not permitted in any part of the harbour, though some protection from northeasterlies will be found in the bay to the southeast, where holding is good in about 7m over sand and stones. A dinghy could be taken into the inner harbour, perhaps landing at the slipway near the travel-lift bay – the pontoons are closed off by security gates.

Formalities

Visit the marina office overlooking the reception pontoon with the usual ship's papers, passports and insurance document. British yachtsmen may have feelings *of déjà vu* when greeted in perfect colloquial English by Janet Gómez León, who grew up in London after her parents emigrated when she was young, but returned to the island on her marriage. Other members of the staff are equally friendly and helpful, if slightly less fluent.

If departing the Canaries it may be necessary to visit the *Polícia Marítima* for an exit stamp, which is likely to be required on arrival in the next country. The marina office staff will advise.

Charges

The berthing fee is calculated on a length x beam basis and in 2010 was set at €0.37 per m^2. This included water and 5% tax, but not electricity which is metered. Discounts were available for stays of 30, 90 and 180 days.

Facilities

Boatyard Sharing space with the extensive dry-storage racks on the east side of the harbour, and with 24-hour security. Best suited to DIY work, but with some skills available locally. The marina plans a 'service area' with mechanical workshops, sail repair and chandlery.

Travel-lift 60-tonne capacity hoist operated by the *Cofradía de Pescadores* (fishermen's confederation), plus 125-tonne mobile crane. In 2010 charges for both the hoist and time ashore were very reasonable, but there was a (doubtless temporary) shortage of robust, yacht-length props.

Engineers & electronics Repairs available locally – ask at the marina office.

Sail repairs Planned, but not in place as of early 2011.

Chandlery A chandlery is planned for the marina – possibly a branch of Náutica El Chopo (which has premises at Los Llanos as well as Marina La Palma). Meanwhile it is necessary to travel some 8km to Los Llanos to visit either Náutica El Chopo ✆ /*Fax* 922 401033 *Email* elchopolapalma@hotmail.com or Nautic-Pesca Castillo ✆ /*Fax* 922 464217 *Email* nautical.castillo@telefonica.net.

Charts It is intended that a limited stock of charts will be on sale at marina reception.

Water At all pontoon berths, as well as in the boatyard.

Showers Smart cubicles with shower, wash basin and toilet in the services building. The water is heated by solar panels on the roof, so may be at its hottest later in the day!

Launderette Coin-operated machines in the services/office block.

Electricity At all pontoon berths.

Fuel At the reception pontoon in front of the marina office and available at all times. Most credit cards are accepted.

Bottled gas Camping Gaz exchanges in the Tazacorte, but as of 2011 the situation regarding refilling other cylinders remained uncertain – see page 191.

Weather forecast Internet forecast displayed at the marina office.

Banks In Tazacorte and Los Llanos, both with cash dispensers, plus the marina plans the latter for its reception area.

Shops/provisioning There is a small supermarket near the old north harbour, open 0800–2000 Monday to Saturday, with more shops in Tazacorte and Los Llanos (some of which offer a delivery service). A supermarket is planned for the harbour area.

Cafés & restaurants Pleasant outdoor café at the head of the harbour, with several more along the beach to the north and around the old harbour. A bar/restaurant is planned for the upper floor of the marina reception building (from which it will have an outstanding view).

Medical services Health centre in Tazacorte with a pharmacy en route.

Communications

Post office In Tazacorte, but well hidden behind the town hall. Open 0830–1430 weekdays, 0900–1300 Saturday.

Telephones At the marina office and elsewhere.

Mailing address Puerto Tazacorte s/n, 38779 – Tazacorte, Isla de La Palma, Islas Canarias, Spain.

Internet access Free Wi-Fi throughout the marina, plus at least one internet café in Tazacorte and more in Los Llanos. A 'business centre' is planned for the services building, with computers, printers, copiers and fax machines available.

Car hire & taxis Both readily available, and best arranged via the marina office.

Buses Regular service to Los Llanos and Santa Cruz from a bus stop on the beach road leading north from the harbour.

Air services European and inter-island flights from the airport near Santa Cruz.

Puerto Naos

28°35'·06N 17°54'·61W (beach)

Open beach anchorage

Another misnomer, and without the charm of Puerto Espindola on the northeast coast. A once small fishing village, south of the new lighthouse at Punta de Lava on the southwest coast, Puerto Naos now forms one of La Palma's mercifully few tourist resorts – and not a particularly pretty one. The open bay could offer a pleasant enough daytime anchorage in calm weather, perhaps for lunch and a quick swim, but it can seldom be really free from swell. Holding is reasonable over sand and rock, but jet skis and parasailing make the area less than peaceful.

El Hierro

Between 27°38′N–27°51′N and 17°53′W–18°10′W

Introduction

The smallest, most remote, tranquil and least spoilt of the main islands, El Hierro (pronounced *El Ee-err-oh*) has an area of 277km² and is populated by some 11,000 Herrenos. The coastline is steep and rocky, backed by hills running into a long semicircular ridge curving around the deep northwest bay of El Golfo, the submerged basin of an ancient crater. The central plateau, much of which is densely wooded, rises to 1,500m at Alto de Malpaso and the upland pastures are home to goats, cattle and a few horses. Numerous cones and lava flows are a constant reminder of the island's volcanic origins.

The capital, Valverde, is a pleasant town little affected by tourism, with a street plan said hardly to have changed since Columbus visited the island before his second Atlantic crossing. At 570m the air is cool compared to that at sea level.

For many centuries Punta Orchilla at the western tip of El Hierro was considered to be the limit of the known world, reinforced during the 15th century when the island was also noted as having zero magnetic variation. Perhaps for both these reasons Punta Orchilla was chosen in 1634 as a prime meridian – one of several at that time – a status it only relinquished in 1884 with the international recognition of Greenwich.

The breakwater at La Restinga has an Art Deco feel...
Liz Hammick

Navigation

Waypoints

⊕ C61 – 27°53′N 17°55′·8W (2M N of Pta Norte)
⊕ C62 – 27°48′·6N 17°50′·8W (2M E of Pta Caleta)
⊕ C63 – 27°46′·2N 17°53′·1W (1M SE of Puerto de la Estaca, El Hierro)
⊕ C64 – 27°37′·4N 17°58′·4W (1M SSE of Pta Restinga)
⊕ C65 – 27°42′·1N 18°10′·4W (1M SW of Pta de la Orchilla)

Courses and distances

⊕ C61 – ⊕ C62 = 6·3M, 135° / 315°
⊕ C62 – ⊕ C59 (1M S of Pta Fuencaliente, La Palma) = 37·5M, 000° / 180°
⊕ C62 – ⊕ C63 = 3·2M, 220° / 040°
⊕ C63 – ⊕ C43 (1M SW of Pta de la Rasca, Tenerife) = 64M, 078° / 258°
⊕ C63 – ⊕ C53 (1M S of Pta del Becerro, La Gomera) = 37M, 068° / 248°
⊕ C63 – ⊕ C64 = 10M, 208° / 028°
⊕ C64 – ⊕ C65 = 11·5M, 293° / 113°

Magnetic variation
6°35′W (2011), decreasing by 8′E annually.

Tidal Streams
Generally insignificant – see Tides and Tidal streams, page 194. Details of range, etc. will be found under Puerto de la Estaca.

Charts
Admiralty *1869* (1:300,000)
Spanish *61B* (1:200,000), *618* (1:60,000)
US *51260* (1:300,000)
Imray-Iolaire *E2* (1:600,000)

Lights
2838 **Puerto de la Estaca**
Fl.G.5s13m5M Green column 7m
2837 **Puerto de la Restinga**
Fl(2)G.7s14m1M Green column 1m
2836 **Punta de Orchilla** Fl.5s131m24M
Octagonal grey stone tower, grey and white building 25m

Coast Radio Station
El Hierro 27°47′·7N 75°56′·2W, remotely controlled from Tenerife
VHF Ch 16, 23, 74 (24 hours)
DSC VHF MMSI 002241025, 27°48′N 17°55′W, remotely controlled from Tenerife

Weather and navigation broadcasts
VHF 27°48′·4N 17°54′·9W (remotely controlled from Tenerife)
Weather bulletins Ch 23 at 0833, 1333, 2033 (forecast in Spanish for coastal waters)
Navigational warnings Ch 23 at 0833, 2033 (in Spanish for coastal waters)

Websites

The following sites contain general information about El Hierro, some of which may be useful to the visiting yachtsman. Websites relating to specific harbours are listed under Harbour communications, those covering all or most of the Canary Islands on page 188 of the introduction.

www.elhierro.com/index-en.php – a tourist site operated by the NetReservas travel agency (based in Lanzarote) and mainly concerned with booking accommodation, but also containing pages about the island's history and natural environment. Spanish, English and German

www.elhierro.es – website of the island's council, in Spanish, English, German and French (though not all pages appear to be translated). Useful maps and other information for hikers under the Tourist heading

www.elhierro.travel – the impressive and interesting website of the island council and Office of Tourism, in Spanish, English, German and Italian. Sections on geology, flora and fauna and other general interest subjects, as well as tourist information

www.elhierro.tv – website of El Hierro's own television station, with news and events in Spanish, English and German

www.en.wikipedia.org/wiki/El_Hierro – all the usual in-depth wikipedia information without the spin which one comes to expect from 'local' websites

http://folclorehierro.blogspot.com – El Hierro's island traditions appear to be going strong in the 21st century, if this website is anything to go by, as are the giant lizards...

www.hierroaventura.com – a company offering activities of all kinds and some useful links in the process, in seven languages including English.

Pillow lava lives up to its name in southern El Hierro
Liz Hammick

Telecommunications

Mobile (cell) phone reception is good throughout the more populated parts of El Hierro, though holes may exist in a few places. The country code for the Canaries is 34, as it is for mainland Spain, and the area code for El Hierro – which must be included even when dialling from within the island – is 922, shared with Tenerife, La Gomera and La Palma.

By 2011 Wi-Fi was available in the ferry terminal at Puerto de la Estaca and throughout the harbour in Puerto de la Restinga (at least in theory, though in practice it may be necessary to visit one of the waterfront cafés).

Approach and navigation

Northern sector winds predominate around El Hierro, with a protected area to the south of the island. Acceleration zones have been encountered off its northeast tip and have also been reported on the east coast between Punta de la Bonanza and Punta Restinga.

Approaching from north or northeast the coast appears low and ragged, with outlying rocks and hills rising steeply inland. The first houses seen will be those of Tamaduste with its swimming pool built among the rocks. A close look will show that the village is at the base of an old crater, half of which has been eroded by the sea. The island's airport lies a short distance to the south, by which time Valverde, the island's capital, can be seen on a ridge inland. If approaching at night its lights will be seen from 20M or more in good visibility.

Harbours and anchorages

Puerto de la Estaca

27°46'·83N 17°54'·06W (breakwater head)

Waypoints
⊕ C62 – 27°48'·6N 17°50'·8W (2M E of Pta Caleta)
⊕ C63 – 27°46'·2N 17°53'·1W (1M SE of Puerto de la Estaca, El Hierro)

Tides
Standard port for the Canary Islands is Casablanca, with Puerto de la Estaca a secondary port. MLWS is about 0·3m above datum and time difference on Casablanca: –0126. Predictions for Puerto de la Estaca are also available via Admiralty *EasyTide* – see page 194

Mean spring range 2·0m
Mean neap range 0·7m

Plans
Spanish *6150* (1:7,500)
Imray-Iolaire *E2* (1:7,500)

Lights
2838 **Breakwater**
Fl.G.5s13m5M Green column 7m
buoy **Port hand buoy** Fl.R.5s2M
Red pillar buoy, ■ topmark
2838·5 **Inner harbour entrance, starboard side**
Fl(2)G.7s4m3M Slim green pyramid 3m
2838·7 **Inner harbour entrance, port side**
Fl(2)R.7s4m3M Slim red pyramid 3m

Harbour Communications
Port Captain ✆ 922 550903 *Fax* 922 550160
Email controlhierro@puertosdetenerife.org
VHF Ch 14, 16 (0600–2200 daily)

Enlarged harbour still without pontoons

Puerto de la Estaca (pronounced *Pwerto de la Ehstacka*) is one of only two harbours on El Hierro and is used by the car ferries from Tenerife, La Palma and La Gomera. The stone breakwater was lengthened in 2005 and a smallcraft basin constructed in the northern part of the harbour – and then work stopped. The promised 120-berth marina, complete with travel-lift, restaurants and other amenities, has yet to materialise, despite the welcoming attitude of officials and the income it would undoubtedly bring to the island. In the meantime yachts lie alongside either the east wall or one of the moles. The design of the overlapping inner moles presumably reflects lessons learned from San Sebastián de la Gomera, though some movement is still inevitable in southerly winds.

Approach

See Approach and navigation, page 315. Keeping at least 0·5M offshore, Puerto de la Estaca breakwater will be sighted on rounding a bluff 2M south of the airfield, though the zigzag white wall of the road running down to the harbour may become visible before the breakwater itself.

Call the harbour authorities on VHF Ch 16 (likely to be transferred to Ch 14) while still in the vicinity of ⊕C63, as a yacht will be asked to delay her approach if a ferry is departing.

Entrance and berthing

Entering the outer harbour is straightforward, with shelter from northeasterly wind and seas as soon as one rounds the breakwater – having previously made contact with the harbour authorities, above. There is a slight dogleg to gain the inner basin, the gap about 35m wide at its narrowest point. Once inside there is limited room to manoeuvre, as much of the space is taken up by fore-and-aft moorings for local smallcraft, but it is claimed that yachts of up to 22m have berthed there. Depths are generous with a minimum of 6m throughout.

Visiting yachts can lie alongside either the east wall or one of the moles. Bollards are provided at 10m intervals, and there are three ladders and a set of steps on the east wall and a single ladder on the west mole (though rather close to the slipway). All three have surfaces of smooth concrete, but with overhanging upper parts and some recesses. Large fenders plus a robust fender board would clearly be useful.

Anchoring in the harbour is no longer permitted.

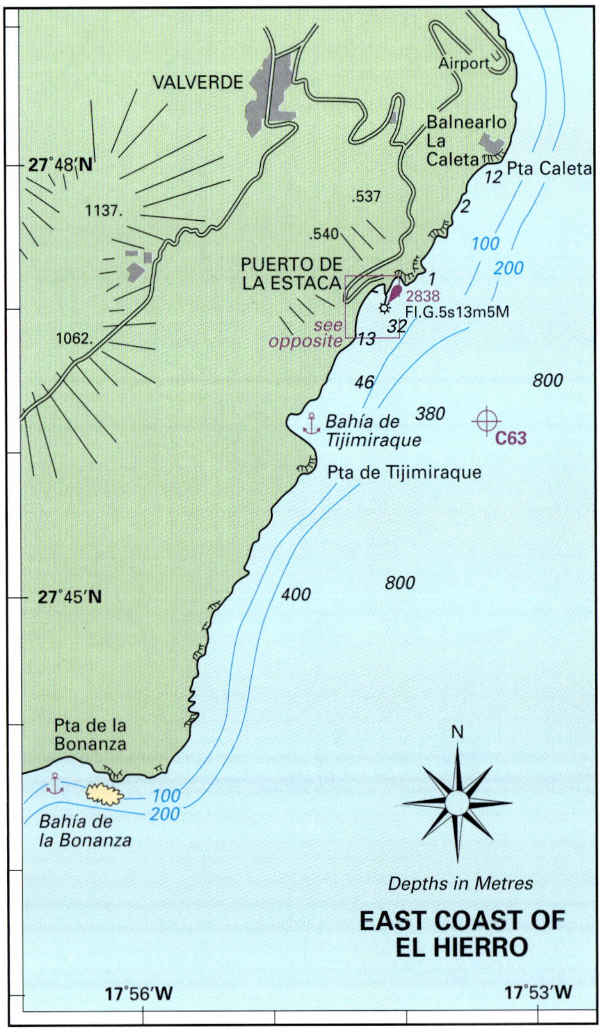

A ferry leaves Puerto de la Estaca, seen here from almost due north. Pontoons have long been promised for the enclosed area at the head of the harbour but by late 2011 they had still to materialise

Formalities

Visit the port authority office – marked *Polícia Portuaria* – on the ground floor of the ferry terminal building (at the north end, next to the Fred Olsen office) with the usual ship's papers and passports. Although normally open 0600–2200 it may be closed while a ferry is in and the officials are required elsewhere. They are clearly happy to see visiting yachts – not always the case in commercial harbours – and in late 2010 were extremely helpful and spoke good English.

Note that Puerto de la Estaca is not a frontier port, and one cannot obtain an exit stamp from the Canaries – and so from both Spain and the Schengen Area – which may be required on arrival in the next country. Obtain official clearance while still in Tenerife (for which it may be necessary for the skipper to visit Santa Cruz or Los Cristianos) or Santa Cruz de la Palma, after which a stop at El Hierro is not a problem.

Charges

The berthing fee is calculated on a length x beam basis and in 2010 was set at €0.37 per m^2, which included tax at 5%. Payment had to be made in cash – and the nearest cash dispenser is in Valverde. Water is charged separately (at €4 for 1,000 litres) but electricity is not available. Both *Tasa de Embarcación de Recreo* (Recreational Vessel tax) and *Tasa de Ayuda a la Navegación* (Navigational Aid tax) may also be payable – see page 190.

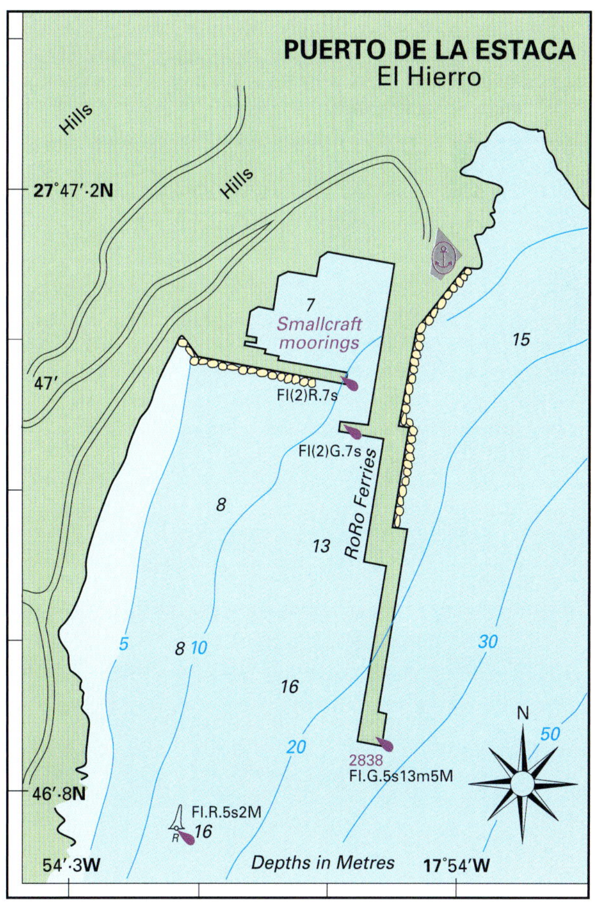

Looking west across the entrance to Puerto de la Estaca's inner harbour. The switchback hillside road is visible from well offshore

Facilities

Travel-lift A travel-lift is planned and the necessary dock exists at the root of the west mole, but it is not known when – or indeed if – the hoist itself will be provided. There is no shortage of hardstanding.

Engineers A range of skills are available on the island – enquire at the marina office – but spares would need to be ordered from Tenerife.

Chandlery There is a small chandlery at the boatyard in Puerto de la Restinga.

Water Metered water can be arranged (see Charges, above) but for smaller quantities there is a tap north of the terminal building where containers can be filled.

Showers At the head of the harbour, with a key from the harbour office. There are toilets in the ferry terminal, which may be closed out of hours.

Launderette No. (When asked this question the smiling harbour official pointed to a bucket...)

Electricity Not available at any of the yacht berths.

Fuel Quantities of 1,000 litres or more can be delivered by road tanker from the Disa plant south of the harbour – arrange via the harbour office. Smaller quantities must be collected by can from the filling station in Valverde.

Bottled gas Camping Gaz exchanges at the filling station in Valverde, but as of 2011 the situation regarding refilling other cylinders remained uncertain – see page 191.

Weather forecast Available at the harbour office

Banks In Valverde, with cash dispensers.

Shops/provisioning Small bar/grocery store on the road leading uphill from the harbour. Two supermarkets and other shops (including an excellent bakery) in Valverde. Both supermarkets are at the opposite end of the town to the Puerto de la Estaca road and close from 1300–1630 weekdays and from 1400 on Saturday. Alhough more than equal to everyday needs, Valverde would not be the best place to provision for an Atlantic crossing.

Produce market Saturday morning market in Valverde.

Cafés, restaurants & hotels Bar/restaurant in the ferry terminal and another a little way up the road. Several restaurants and hotels in Valverde and many throughout the rest of the island.

Medical services Hospital just outside Valverde.

Communications

Post office In Valverde, open 0800–1500 weekdays, 0900–1300 Saturday, with a postbox at the harbour.

Telephones In harbour area and ferry terminal building.

Internet access Free Wi-Fi around the harbour bar/restaurant, plus at least one internet café in Valverde.

Taxis & car hire In Valverde, or can be organised via the harbour office.

Buses A bus to Valverde leaves the harbour every hour between 0800 and 1700. From there it is possible to travel onwards to Frontera, Taibique and Puerto de la Restinga.

Ferries Regular service to/from Tenerife, La Gomera and La Palma.

Air services Inter-island flights from the small airport about 3km north of the harbour (though a great deal further by road).

Anchorages on the east coast of El Hierro

There are several possible anchorages south of Puerto de la Estaca. Bahía de Tijimiraque (27°46'·2N 17°54'·8W), nearly a mile south of the the harbour and just north of the headland of the same name, is a deeply indented bay formerly used as a refuge by local boats in strong southerlies. There is a small sandy beach.

A further 3M south lies Punta de la Bonanza, sheltering Bahía de la Bonanza (27°43'·7N 17°56'·6W) and the arched rock Roque de la Bonanza – 'Fair Weather Rock' – which is often surrounded by calm water in northerly conditions when there are breaking waves offshore. South from this headland runs a narrow strip of beach 2M long, backed by an impressive cliff and with the *Parador Nacional* at its southern end. Although a feasible fairweather anchorage this stretch is very deep – at least 30m close inshore over rock and stones.

Puerto de la Restinga

27°38'·32N 17°58'·92W

Waypoint

⊕C64 – 27°37'·4N 17°58'·4W (1M SSE of Pta Restinga)

Lights

2837 **South breakwater**
Fl(2)G.7s14m1M Green column 1m

2836·5 **West breakwater**
Fl(2)R.7s3M Red column 4m
Inner mole
Unfinished and unlit as of early 2011, but with a 1·5m post already in place

Harbour Communications

Harbour office ✆ /*Fax* 922 557081 VHF Ch 9 (0800–1400 weekdays only)

Much improved harbour

Puerto de la Restinga (pronounced *Pwerto de la Rest-ingah*) was originally constructed as a harbour of refuge for fishermen working off the inhospitable southwest coast of El Hierro. Its single, very solid, breakwater gave good protection from the easterly quadrant, but westerly winds – and, more importantly, seas – rolled straight into the harbour. In the late 1990s plans were drawn up to build a short mole southwards from a point just inside the harbour mouth, and to run two pontoons on a west-east axis in its shelter. In the event the reality proved even better, with a curved west breakwater completed during 2006 and two pontoons laid in the northeast corner of the harbour. At the same time the old south breakwater was massively reinforced and embellished. Work then paused before an inner mole was added in 2010 – to be followed, hopefully in 2011 or 2012, by a short spur run northwards from the end of the south breakwater. When work is complete the entrance will form a distinct dogleg about 40m in width.

The adjacent coastline is said to offer some of Europe's best diving and is home to several PADI centres, although the town itself has grown surprisingly little over the past decade or more. It lies at the east end of the *Reserva Marina Mar de las Calmas*, administered from offices near the root of the breakwater. The coastline is divided into three zones: Zone A is described as 'Integral Reserve' where everything other than passing through by boat is prohibited; in Zone B, 'Restricted Area', swimming and Scuba diving are also permitted; while in Zone C, 'Traditional Use', only anchoring, fishing from a boat, spearfishing and shellfish collecting are forbidden. The harbour lies in Zone C, with Zone B and then Zone A coming into force about 0·5M to the northwest. If planning to explore the coastline it would be wise to obtain current information from the above office.

Approach and entrance

A group of low volcanic cones and lava flows form the southern point of the island, and east of the harbour the swell breaks on a reef which runs out nearly half a mile from Punta Restinga. Approaching from that direction it is essential to keep well off the headland and not to steer for the end of the massive breakwater until it bears due north. The final approach from south or west should also be with the breakwater end bearing due north.

Enter with caution until work on the harbour is complete – as mentioned above, a spur running northwards from the end of the south breakwater is

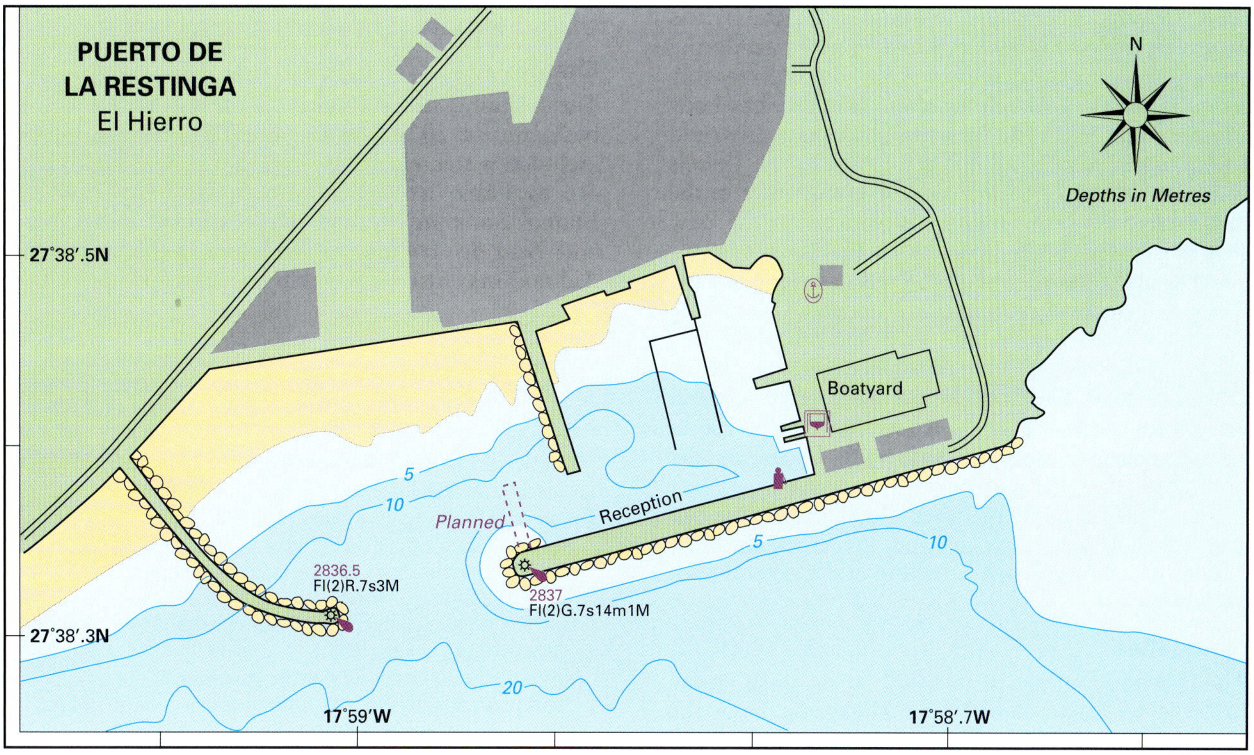

Puerto de la Restinga on the south coast of El Hierro, seen from the northeast

planned, hopefully for 2011 or 2012. Large concrete blocks are piled loosely along the outside of the breakwater, currently extending around its head and into the harbour to produce a slight reduction in the surge along the quay.

Berthing

The official reception berth is alongside the western part of the breakwater – the eastern end is home to a smart rescue vessel and other government-owned craft – but if space is available many skippers will prefer to go directly into a pontoon berth. If it is necessary to go alongside the wall good fendering will be necessary, together with long (preferably nylon) warps. Although the concrete edge has been smoothed opposite the bollards, chaffing gear would still be necessary for all but the shortest stay. Vessels of up to 35m have berthed on the breakwater in the past, but may find it more difficult once the new spur is in place.

Up to eight yachts of 14m or less can berth on the south end of the west pontoon, though two or three visitors may be allowed to lie against the north side of the 'joining piece' – the most sheltered spot in the entire harbour. This area should not be used without prior permission, however. About 8m will be found at the main pontoon berths, with 2–3m at the joining piece.

There are no gates or other obvious security, but *marineros* are on duty around the clock and the chance of crime in such a remote and peaceful spot appears small.

Formalities

The harbour office is located in a dark stone building set back slightly up a slight rise from the northeast corner of the harbour. In November 2010 the harbourmaster was pleasant and helpful, and plainly happy to welcome visiting yachts to his harbour, but spoke no languages other than Spanish.

Like Puerto de la Estaca, Puerto de la Restinga is not a frontier port and it is not possible to obtain an exit stamp from the Canaries – and so from both Spain and the Schengen Area – which may be required on arrival in the next country. Obtain official clearance while still in Tenerife (for which it may be necessary for the skipper to visit Santa Cruz or Los Cristianos) or Santa Cruz de la Palma, after which a stop at El Hierro is not a problem.

Charges

The berthing fee is calculated on a length x beam basis and in 2010 was set at €0.24 per m^2, which included water, electricity and tax at 5%. Discounts are available from longer periods. Both *Tasa de Embarcación de Recreo* (Recreational Vessel tax) and *Tasa de Ayuda a la Navegación* (Navigational Aid tax) may also be payable – see page 190.

Facilities

Boatyard Well-kept boatyard with good security and plenty of hardstanding, run by the *Cofradía de Pescadores* (fishermen's confederation). Welding, painting and other skills are available, and DIY work is allowed. Living aboard is permitted in the short-term, but not during long-term projects.

Travel-lift Capacity 70 tonnes. In 2010 charges for both the hoist and time ashore were very reasonable, but owners may wish to add some extra props if their boat is to be ashore for long.

Engineers Well accustomed to fishing boat diesels, but no yacht spares available.

Chandlery Small chandlery at the east end of the boatyard, mainly tuned to the needs of fishing boats.

Water Promised on the pontoons for March 2011 (the pipes were in evidence several months earlier), but no water on the breakwater other than a tap by the travel-lift dock.
Showers No showers and apparently no plans for any. However, several local hostelries will hire bathrooms to yachtsmen, including Casa Kai Marino, ✆ 922 557034, on Calle Juan Gutiérrez Monteverde (the road leading inland from the pontoon access quay.
Launderette In the town.
Electricity Also promised on the pontoons for March 2011, with all the wiring in place, but again no supply on the breakwater although available in the boatyard.
Fuel From the *Cofradía de Pescadores*. The fuelling point is near the crane in the southeast corner of the harbour. Payment must be made in cash.
Bottled gas No Camping Gaz exchanges closer than Valverde, and as of 2011 the situation regarding refilling other cylinders remained uncertain – see page 191.
Bank In the town, with cash dispenser.
Shops/provisioning Two small supermarkets, surprisingly well-stocked for their size, plus pharmacy and other shops. Fresh fish is available from the co-operative at the root of the breakwater, the best time (unusually) being late in the afternoon.
Produce market A travelling greengrocer selling good quality fruit and vegetables sets up his stall by on the north side of the harbour every Friday from 0830–1300.
Cafés, restaurants & hotels Several waterfront restaurants serving local seafood, at least one hotel, and several guest houses.
Medical services Health centre in the northwest part of the town, open weekdays only.

Communications

Post office Near the root of the pontoon access quay.
Telephones In the town.
Internet access In theory Wi-Fi is available throughout the harbour, but in practice it appears somewhat inconsistent. Most of the waterfront bars and cafés provide Wi-Fi for customers.
Car hire In Valverde but not locally.
Taxis Available – ask at the harbour office.
Buses After many years of a single return service to Valverde, departing at 0700 and returning at 1430, by 2010 there were said to be four buses each way every day.
Air services Small airport handling inter-island flights in the north of the island.

The boatyard at Puerto de la Restinga has a good reputation for careful lifting and reasonable prices

Visiting yachts of all nationalities enjoy the new facilities at Puerto de la Restinga. For some it will be their last harbour on the eastern side of the Atlantic Ocean

Looking northeast into Puerto de la Restinga from the end of the breakwater

Anchorages on the southwest coast of El Hierro

The southwest coast of the island has some fine sandy beaches, is generally steep-to and is known for its excellent diving and swimming. Hammerhead sharks are sometimes seen in the area – local advice is said to be 'if one gets too close, hit it on the nose!'.

Bahía de Naos (27°38'·7N 17°59'·9W) about a mile northwest of Puerto de la Restinga and previously recommended as a daytime anchorage now forms part of the Zone A mentioned on page 319. One can sail through it, but no more. The small unnamed bay backed by a sand and stone beach at 27°40'·7N 18°01'·8W is in Zone C, where anchoring remains prohibited, although with enough crew aboard one might stop for a swim in the very clear water while the boat drifts. There are submerged rocks to the southeast and a reef to the west, however.

Finally, a short stone mole will found about a mile southeast of Punta Orchilla at 27°42'·2N 18°08'W, with a ladder where it might be possible for the intrepid to land by dinghy. However, the mole itself is surrounded by shoals and the surrounding seabed offers poor holding over rock. A track leads up to the lighthouse and there is reputed to be a tap, but absolutely nothing else. For most it will be far preferable to head for the next destination, be it elsewhere in the Canaries or several thousand miles distant.

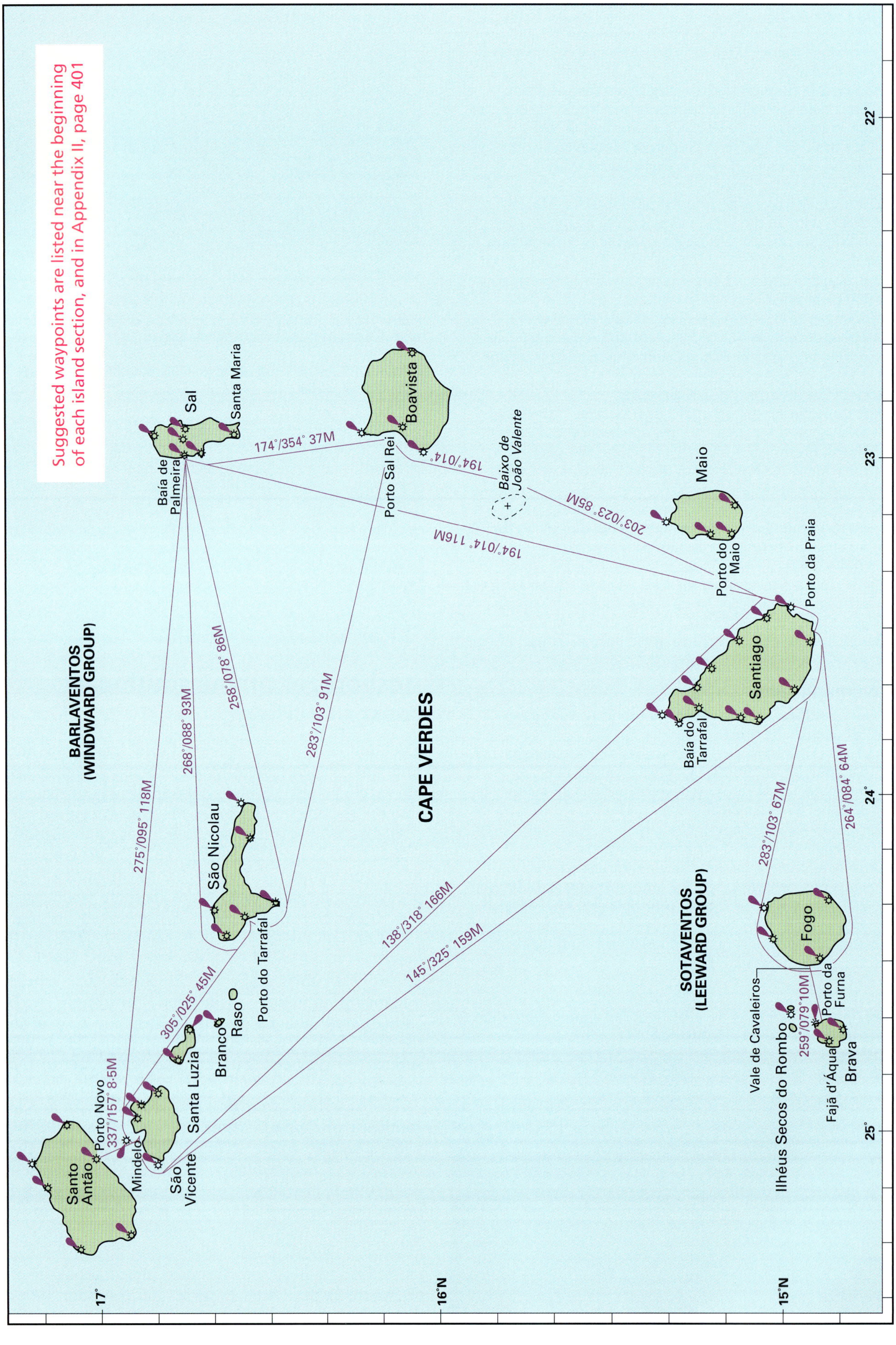
Suggested waypoints are listed near the beginning of each island section, and in Appendix II, page 401
BARLAVENTOS (WINDWARD GROUP)
SOTAVENTOS (LEEWARD GROUP)
CAPE VERDES
Santo Antão
Porto Novo
337°/157° 8·5M
Mindelo
São Vicente
Santa Luzia
Branco
Raso
305°/025° 45M
275°/095° 118M
São Nicolau
Porto do Tarrafal
268°/088° 93M
258°/078° 86M
Sal
Baía de Palmeira
Santa Maria
174°/354° 37M
Boavista
Porto Sal Rei
194°/014°
Baixo de João Valente
203°/023° 85M
283°/103° 91M
194°/014° 116M
Maio
Porto do Maio
Santiago
Porto da Praia
Baía do Tarrafal
138°/318° 166M
145°/325° 159M
283°/103° 67M
264°/084° 64M
Fogo
Porto da Furna
259°/079° 10M
Vale de Cavaleiros
Ilhéus Secos do Rombo
Fajã d'Água
Brava
17°
16°N
15°N
22°
23°
24°
25°

IV. The Cape Verdes

Index of islands

Barlaventos (Windward Group)

Sotaventos (Leeward Group)

The archipelago

The Cape Verde archipelago lies just over 800M southwest of the Canary islands and is separated from the West African coast by a channel some 325M wide. Its 4,033km^2 is made up of 10 larger and four smaller islands, which together form a rough horseshoe open to the west. Taken clockwise they are Santo Antão, São Vicente, Santa Luzia, Ilhéus Branco e Raso, São Nicolau, Sal and Boavista (the *Barlavento* or Windward group), and Maio, Santiago, Fogo, Brava and the Ilhéus Secos do Rombo (the *Sotavento* or Leeward group).

All are of volcanic origin and most are mountainous, with several classic craters. Only Ilha do Fogo has a volcano which is still active (most recently in 1995–6), but earthquakes and tremors sometimes occur throughout the Leeward group, particularly in Ilha Brava. The islands owe their existence to the major weakness in the earth's crust known as the Mid-Atlantic Ridge, and were never part of the African continent. Since their emergence some 120 million years ago new rock has steadily been formed along the Ridge, forcing the older rock outwards at up to 0·5cm per year, until they now lie over 1,200M east of the Ridge itself.

The islands have always been poor, not least due to lack of rainfall, deforestation and prolonged droughts over the past two centuries. Even so they are primarily agricultural, growing maize, fruit (chiefly bananas and oranges), sugar cane, sweet potatoes, beans and other subsistence vegetables and, in Ilha do Fogo, coffee and grapes. The fishing industry is also important, providing much-needed protein for local people as well as some exports, particularly of shellfish. Even so, at least 90% of food must be imported.

By far the largest source of income is foreign aid, much of the latter 'in kind' either in the form of subsidised staple foods such as flour, help with education or assistance with technological projects such as new harbours and airports. Europe is its most important trading partner, taking 60% of Cape Verdean exports and providing 80% of imports. Of these, 33% of exports and 38% of imports are with Portugal. On the plus side, between 2000 and 2009 GDP increased by an average of 7% per year, unemployment fell rapidly and in 2007 the Republic of Cape Verde became the 153rd member of the World Trade Organisation.

Much foreign currency is also received from the many Cape Verdeans who have emigrated, temporarily or permanently, but still support relatives at home – it is estimated that more Cape Verdeans live abroad than in the islands themselves. The greatest number of emigrants (more than 400,000) are in the USA, with around 150,000 in Portugal, 45,000 in Angola and 25,000 Senegal. Spain, Italy, France and Holland also have sizeable Cape Verdean populations.

Life expectancy in the islands has increased in recent years from 50 to more than 70 for men and nearly 78 for women, with infant mortality very low compared to much of Africa at about 20 per 1,000 live berths. Even so, population growth has levelled and few women choose to have more than four children. The average age is no more than 19, with an estimated 70% of the population under 30. A proud boast is that all young people have the opportunity to complete their secondary education – the literacy rate of nearly 85% overall and an impressive 99% of those under 25 far outshines that of most neighbouring countries – and many then go to Mindelo or Cidade da Praia to continue their education in subjects such as agriculture, languages or tourism. Even so, unemployment and downright poverty – particularly in the more remote country districts – are still major problems and likely to remain so for the foreseeable future. In contrast the cities, and particularly Mindelo, are growing fast. Most houses are built on bank mortgages, often with the owner doing his own work – even down to making breeze-blocks on site! An engineer is assigned to each building, checking structural progress for safety, and is then held responsible rather than the owner. This practical approach – typical of much Cape Verdean thinking – has resulted in a marked absence of the shanty towns so common in many parts of Africa and the Caribbean. The government is justly proud of its first place ranking in the United Nations' 'quality of life' index for West Africa.

The islands are visited by surprisingly few English-speaking yachtsmen (doubtless due in part to the popularity of the ARC leaving from the Canaries), the vast majority being French or Scandinavian, with a few Swiss and other Europeans. Until recently very little information was available regarding harbours and facilities, and it has taken a long time to shake off a residue of the difficult reputation gained in the first few years after independence in 1975. After a few years during which visiting yachts often cruised the islands calling at six or seven different islands, the construction of the archipelago's first marina at Mindelo on São Vicente has inevitably drawn in yachts which might otherwise have spent at least some time elsewhere. In 2010 one cruiser remarked that, of the skippers he had spoken to, most of those at anchor had made their landfall at Ilha do Sal and visited at least one other island (usually Boavista or São Nicolau) before reaching Mindelo. In contrast, most yachts berthed in the marina had made their landfall at São Vicente and did not plan to visit any other island.

Other than Mindelo the best harbours are Porto da Palmeira (Ilha do Sal), Porto do Tarrafal (São Nicolau) and Porto da Praia (Santiago), with the anchorages at Baía do Tarrafal (Santiago), Porto de Sal Rei (Boavista) and Fajã d'Agua (Brava) also very appealing. Most other harbours and anchorages are distinctly weather-dependent. As so often, the smaller the harbour the more enthusiastic the welcome and the safer it is likely to be in terms of theft – said to be a major problem only in Mindelo, Baía do Tarrafal and Porto da Praia, though the situation in the former has improved greatly over the past few years. In the less frequented anchorages it may be difficult to prevent curious locals (particularly children) from climbing aboard, so tempting items such as knives, fishing gear, etc. are best stowed out of sight. A large crew or big dog would probably dissuade boarders, but the best precaution throughout the archipelago is rigorously to observe the standard rules – never leave the yacht unlocked and never leave her unattended after dark.

Having said that, it should be stressed that the one yachtsman who experiences problems is far more likely to publicise the fact than are the 50 who do not, and that the vast majority of Cape Verdeans are friendly and hospitable towards strangers. Theft from yachts and youthful pickpockets ashore are an acknowledged problem, particularly if basic precautions are not taken, but violent crimes such as muggings are very rare.

Apart from the interest of visiting a fascinating and relatively little-known area, the practical advantages of breaking the transatlantic passage in the Cape Verdes are obvious. If en route to the Caribbean the distance to Barbados is cut to under 2,000M, compared with 2,700M from the Canaries or 2,900M from Madeira, and as the islands lie well within the trade wind belt a direct course can usually be steered. For the typical small cruising boat this may mean at least a week less spent at sea, with a passage of around 16–18 days as against 25 or more. Other yachts visiting the Cape Verdes are heading for Brazil – the shortest possible crossing in these latitudes is Ilha Brava to Fernando do Noroñha – with a few on their way to West Africa, most often Senegal or The Gambia.

History

In common with the majority of the Atlantic islands discovered by the fleets of Prince Henry the Navigator, the Cape Verde islands were already rumoured to exist before the arrival of the first Portuguese in the mid-15th century. There is some evidence that the Romans and Carthaginians were aware of their existence, while Arab seafarers may have visited in the 12th century. The year of their official discovery is in doubt, being placed anywhere between 1451 and 1460, and the truth is probably that they were explored and recorded piecemeal, as happened in the Azores. Almost certainly named after Cap Vert on the African mainland, they were also known to the Arabs as *el ras elkhader* – the green top – and were uninhabited when Diego Gomes and António da Nola sighted and named Ilha do Maio and Ilha de São Tiago (now Santiago), the island chosen by the first permanent settlers in 1462.

References to the islands over the next century are few, though by 1541 the capital city of Ribeira Grande, on Santiago, was sufficiently wealthy to attract the attention of attacking pirates. The period following King Philip II of Spain's invasion of mainland Portugal in 1581 brought even greater troubles, with an attack in 1583 by forces supporting the Prior of Crato, claimant to the Portuguese throne. Neither was the city spared by English and Dutch privateers, the traditional enemies of Spain. Sir Francis Drake sacked it in 1585, in 1592 a Dutch fleet attempted a less successful attack, and on visiting the islands the following year Sir Richard Hawkins's opinion was that 'It is wisedome to shunne the sight of them'. After a further attack on Ribeira Grande in 1712, this time by the French, in 1772 the site was abandoned in favour of the more easily defended hilltop position on which Cidade da Praia stands. (Ribeira Grande, now known as Cidade Velha or 'old city' though little more than a village, is well worth a visit whether by land or water – see page 383.)

As well as providing a base for Portuguese merchants trading with the African continent, many slaves were imported to work in the sugar plantations or to be resold further afield. However, even with free labour, agriculture was never more than marginally successful, and when Charles Darwin visited Porto da Praia in HMS *Beagle* in January 1832 he remarked on 'the novel aspect of an utterly sterile land'. This had not always been the case, however, and until the mid-18th century

The emigrants' memorial at Porto Novo, Santo Antão. It is thought that more Cape Verdeans live abroad than in the islands themselves

rainfall was regular if limited. Then in 1747 came the first of a series of droughts, exacerbated by the felling of trees for agriculture and overgrazing by goats. As Darwin pointed out, 'When the island was discovered the immediate neighbourhood of Porto Praya [sic] was clothed with trees, the reckless destruction of which has caused here, as at St Helena and some of the Canary Islands, almost entire sterility.' He also remarked on the 'impalpably fine dust, which ... falls in such quantities as to dirty everything on board, and to hurt people's eyes; vessels even have run on shore owing to the obscurity of the atmosphere.' Repeated droughts over the next two hundred years killed well over 100,000 people, with almost no assistance received from Portugal or any other source.

In the later 19th century the islands became a regular port of call for American whaling ships from New Bedford, and were known as a source of skilled crew who would work for little more than their keep. Not surprisingly many Cape Verdean seamen settled in America, founding the sizeable emigrant communities which exist in New England today. The further decline which followed the abolition of slavery in 1876 was alleviated to some extent by the growing importance of Porto Grande (now known as Mindelo), both as a bunkering station for steamships en route to the South Atlantic or Pacific, and as a centre of undersea cable-laying operations, with links to the African continent and the Americas. However, the opening of the Suez and Panama Canals, the demise of coal-burning ships in favour of oil, and later the introduction of radio communications, spelt the end of this short-lived period of relative prosperity.

For several centuries the islands were administered as a colony from mainland Portugal together with Portuguese Guinea (now Guinea-Bissau), an arrangement which was only terminated in 1878. After the split they remained as a colony until 1951 when their status was changed to that of an overseas province or territory. Full Portuguese citizenship was extended to all islanders in 1961, but in spite of this, local desire for independence in company with Guinea-Bissau grew steadily. Guerrilla warfare began on the mainland in the early 1960s, headed by the African Party for the Independence of Guinea and Cape Verde (PAIGC) and led by Amilcar Cabral, son of a Cape Verdean father and Guinean mother. In spite of this neither the PAIGC nor guerrilla fighting ever really took hold in the islands, and Cabral's assassination in 1973 increased the rift. When a new Portuguese government was installed after the Carnation Revolution in April 1974, independence was granted to Guinea-Bissau. Cape Verde chose to maintain a separate identity though still under the PAIGC banner, finally achieving independence from Portugal on 5 July 1975 as the Republic of Cape Verde.

The initial intention was for unification with Guinea-Bissau at some time in the future, but after a coup in that country in 1980 all references to a union were removed from the constitution and PAIGC was renamed PAICV (*Partido Africano da Independência de Cabo Verde*). For 10 years the Cape Verdes continued to be governed by the left-wing PAICV, with Amilcar Cabral the hero of many islanders. However, the easy-going Creole outlook fused with Marxist economic principles to produce an unusual but practical situation where state control actively encouraged private enterprise. Although the islands could have been of considerable strategic importance the PAICV wisely vetoed construction of foreign military bases, thus remaining on good terms with countries as diverse as the USA, Russia, Cuba and China – and at one stage said to be receiving aid from all four simultaneously.

Gradually other political parties were allowed to emerge, culminating in elections in 1991 in which the PAICV were defeated and the MPD (*Movimento Para a Democratia*), founded and led by Carlos Veiga, came to power with the PAICV forming the Opposition. A new national anthem and redesigned flag were adopted the following year. Ten years on the balance of political power changed again, with the PAICV narrowly beating the MPD in the election of February 2001. In 2006 the PAICV again won, followed by a third term in office from early 2011. More than half the population were registered to vote and the result was accepted unanimously. The Republic of the Cape Verdes is thus one of the very few African countries to have achieved truly stable democratic government, and to have done so peacefully and without bloodshed.

The Cape Verde islands have always had a foot in both Africa and Europe. Geographically and ethnically they clearly belong to the former, but centuries of European influence have left their mark in more than just the architecture and the political structure. The country currently has Special Partnership status with the EU, and membership has even been suggested as a goal for the long-term future.

Natural history

The waters surrounding the Cape Verde islands are particularly rich in cetaceans (whales and dolphins), while several of the islands have bird and plant species found nowhere else in the world.

Amongst the species recorded during a recent cetacean survey in Cape Verdean waters were pilot whales*, bottlenose dolphins*, Atlantic and pan-tropical spotted dolphins*, sei, bryde, sperm*, fin* and humpback whales. (Descriptions of those marked by an asterisk will be found on pages 19–20.) Sperm whales, though usually in depths of 500m or more, were found northwest of Ilha do Sal and between Boavista and São Nicolau, as were fin whales (which had not previously been reported in the area). Humpback whales are thought to calve in the lee of Ilha do Sal, Boavista and Ilha do Maio.

Ilha do Maio, together with Boavista, Sal and São Vicente, is a favourite laying area for several species of turtle. Although most laying takes place in summer when few yachts will be around, they do breed throughout the year. The slightly contradictory recommendations state that you should not disturb or approach turtles too closely while they are out of the water, but equally that you should note down the number on any tag spotted and report it to the natural history museum of your home country. A number of travel companies offer wildlife-centred holidays, alerting local people to the economic sense of protecting species which might otherwise be exploited for food or considered predators.

Cruisers with a particular interest in birds and plants should refer to Eraldo De Gioannini's long-established website at www.caboverde.com (see page 330), which contains 'Naturalist Pages' including a section entitled *Aves de Cabo Verde* detailing 48 local species of bird complete with pictures, and *Planta Endemicas e arvolres indigenas* covering some 60 plants. However, a dictionary may be necessary, as in both cases the text is in Portuguese only.

Perhaps not surprisingly, locusts are often found in the islands, though seldom in numbers which constitute a serious problem. They are assumed to come from West Africa, as though relatively poor fliers they can be carried by the wind for hundreds of miles. The last time serious swarms were seen was in 2004, when locusts spread throughout North Africa until controlled by pesticide and other means. In the Cape Verdes they are said to be a favourite snack with local cats, which enjoy both the thrill of the chase and the reward if successful – as well they might with insects which are larger than a British sparrow!

A locust at São Pedro, São Vicente
Chris Bates

General information

Nationality and language

The population, estimated at around 570,000 in 2010, is of mixed African and European (mainly Portuguese) descent. The national flag is predominantly blue, with white and red horizontal stripes and a circle of 10 gold stars to represent the 10 larger islands.

The native tongue of nearly all Cape Verdeans is Crioulo or Kriolu – a language with its origins in West Africa but owing much to Portuguese – but the latter is the official language and it is rare to encounter anyone who cannot speak it. For many years considered the language of the uneducated, as Cape Verdeans have come to place more value on their own culture Crioulo has lost its 'second-class' status. However, it remains almost entirely a spoken language, not least because of the major differences between the version spoken in the northern islands and that in the southern chain. See *Portuguese and Creole : Two Old Rivals* in Aisling Irwin and Colum Wilson's excellent *Cape Verde Islands* (Brandt Travel Guides) – see page 404 – for a far more detailed analysis.

Many older people, including shopkeepers and taxi drivers, have some command of French, while English is more likely to be spoken by the young. Many of the street vendors who speak fluent English are immigrants from the African mainland.

Cape Verdean representation abroad

Embassies and consulates

Washington DC (Embassy): 3415 Massachusetts Avenue NW, Washington DC 20007-1446 ✆ 202 965 6820 *Fax* 202 965 1207 *Email* ambacvus@sysnet.net cvesemedo@sysnet.net

Lisbon: Avenida do Restelo 33, 1400-314 – Lisbon, Portugal ✆ 21 301 5271 *Fax* 21 301 5308 *Email* emb.caboverde@mail.telepac.pt

Brussels: Rue Antonie Laborre 30, Brussels 1050, Belgium ✆ 643 6270, 646 9025 *Fax* 646 3385 *Email* emb.caboverde@skynet.be www.diplobel.org

In Western Europe there are also embassies in Paris, Berlin, The Hague, Rome, Luxembourg and Vienna and consulates in Madrid and Stockholm amongst other places. However, there is currently no diplomatic representation of any kind in the UK.

Diplomatic representation in the Cape Verde Islands

US: Rua Abílio Macedo 81, Cidade da Praia, Ilha de Santiago, República de Cabo Verde ✆ 261 5616 *Fax* 261 1355, open 0800–1700 weekdays. Consular Section: *Fax* 261 2551 *Email* praiaconsular@state.gov

UK: interests in the Cape Verdes are looked after by the British Embassy in Dakar, 20 rue du Dr Guillet, Boite Postale 6025, Dakar, Senegal ✆ (221) 823 7392/9971 *Fax* (221) 823 2766 *Email* britembe@orange.sn or dakar.visaenquiries@fco.gov.uk, http://ukinsenegal.fco.gov.uk

There is also an Honorary Consul in Mindelo, São Vicente ✆ 232 2830, 232 3512, 232 3123 *Fax* 232 1284.

Personal documentation

All foreigners need passports valid for at least six months and, unless spending every night aboard the yacht for the duration of their visit, most foreigners, including citizens of Europe, the USA and Canada, also need visas. Should one be required – and if arriving by air it almost certainly will be, even if going directly to a yacht – visitors from countries where there are Cape Verde embassies should in theory obtain their visa in advance. In practice visas are available at all legal points of arrival, by sea and air, for a fee (in 2010) of 2,500 Cape Verde Escudos (CVE), €25 or US$40. A duplicate passport photo may be required, and it would also be wise to carry a few spare copies of the information page of one's passport.

Hauling a small fishing boat ashore at Porto da Ponta do Sol, Santo Antão

A young Cape Verdean helps her mother pound maize as chickens roam around their feet and fishing nets are spread out in the foreground

Insist on a visa being issued if leaving by air or if planning to spend even a single night ashore – perhaps to go hiking in the mountains of São Nicolau or Santo Antão – even if Immigration officials say that it is not necessary. It is, and it is the hapless visitor who will suffer if an error is made. In theory visas are issued for 90 days, but officials sometimes issue them for shorter periods for no obvious reason, so state the duration required and check on the spot that it has been granted. (Strangely, while an individual staying ashore can only get a visa valid for 90 days, a yacht – and by extension those aboard her who do not need visas – can, apparently, remain indefinitely.)

As in many countries, the law requires visiting foreigners to carry identification at all times. However, it is accepted that passports are vulnerable to theft, particularly in the cities, so a photocopy of the visa and the 'information' page (on the same sheet of paper), will normally be accepted in lieu.

Finally, if irritated by all the paperwork bear in mind that the Cape Verde government has a serious problem with illegal immigrants, mainly from West Africa. Immigration officials are nearly always polite and many speak some English, but they are clearly trained to treat all arrivals – however poorly they fit the stereotype – in much the same way.

Time

The Cape Verde islands use UT –1 throughout the year.

Money

The Cape Verdean escudo (*escudo Caboverdiano*) has been tied to the Euro for more than a decade at the official exchange rate of CVE 110$265 to €1, though if using Euros to pay for goods or for services such as taxi fares, the 'local' rate of CVE 100$ to €1 will often be quoted. Although US dollars will often be accepted, an even higher 'penalty' may be imposed. When prices are written the ubiquitous dollar sign is, in theory, used to separate escudos and cents, though in practice the latter are rarely used.

Import and export of CV escudos is forbidden and it is therefore impossible to get currency through a home bank before departure, but once in the islands they can be withdrawn from cash dispensers by holders of internationally recognised cards including Visa, or exchanged for other currencies over the counter (when a passport will be required). If changing currency, give each note to the bank clerk individually to demonstrate that it is in good condition, to prevent a damaged note being substituted and politely 'refused'. Travellers' cheques will also be honoured, but commission may be charged.

Banking hours vary according to the size of the community served and are generally given in the text, though 0800–1500 appears to be fairly standard. There is no weekend opening, though some currency exchanges (*câmbios*) operate on Saturday morning and may remain open until 1700 or 1800 during the week. Note that many cash dispensers are installed inside the building so are only accessible during opening hours.

There is no limit on the import and export of foreign currency provided it is declared on arrival, though yachtsmen who are carrying considerable amounts of reserve cash aboard will probably prefer not to publicise the fact. In theory it is possible to change excess escudos back into other currency on departure, provided the original exchange receipt can be produced, but in practice not all banks hold a sufficient reserve to change large amounts.

Credit cards are proving relatively slow to catch on with companies in the Cape Verdes and many, including Marina Mindelo, pass on the fee charged by the card company to the customer. If intending to pay by card it is essential to check that it really can be accepted – despite a Visa sign being prominently displayed outside, the machine may be out of order or the power off. Having said that, many car hire firms, larger restaurants and better hotels now accept Visa, a trend which can only increase.

They don't come much fresher than this! Tuna for sale on the quay at Porto do Tarrafal, São Nicolau

Shopping

Shopping, and particularly the variety of foods available, varies markedly from island to island. By far the best choice is available in Mindelo (São Vicente) and Porto da Praia (Santiago) where there are busy produce markets in addition to surprisingly well-stocked supermarkets. In early 2010 meat of all kinds – fresh, frozen and chilled – was sold in the larger supermarkets of both cities, though this is said not always to be the case. UHT milk was readily available, as was alcohol of all kinds (though prices were high). In contrast, on some of the smaller islands local shops can barely meet day-to-day needs. In either case, all visiting yachts would be well advised to store up as fully as possible before arrival, not least because prices of most items are much higher than in Madeira or the Canaries.

Shops are usually open 0800–1200 and 1430–1800 Monday to Friday, 0800–1200 Saturday. Market hours are much the same, though the best choice is generally to be found early on. Although in theory market prices are set, a little good-humoured bargaining will sometimes produce results, particularly if buying in quantity. Market-bought fruit and vegetables are generally of a high standard, doubtless due to the fierce competition, though their shop-bought equivalents have often been chilled so will not keep. Although supermarkets usually provide bags, this is not the case in markets where strong bags – and egg boxes – are seldom available and, should they be provided, will generally be charged for.

Almost everything is shut on Sunday – with the exception of the ubiquitous 'Shell Select' convenience stores to be found at most (but not all) Shell filling stations. Prices are somewhat higher than in locally-owned establishments, but the Shell Select stores are air-conditioned, spotlessly clean and, like many of their brethren in the UK, carry an unexpectedly wide range of goods.

Alcohol of all descriptions is for sale almost everywhere, with Portuguese wine a particularly good buy. The locally-made Superbock lager goes down very well, though European brands are generally available if one is willing to pay. However, mixers are expensive and tonic, in particular, may be unobtainable. Cape Verdean rum – known as *grogue*, *aqua-dente* or *Sant' Anton* – is mainly produced in

If the Cape Verdes have a national dish it is *cachupa*, a tasty mix of maize, beans and meat or fish. Add a fried egg and *é perfeito*!

Santo Antão, where the sugar cane may be crushed in cattle or donkey mills with the 'ovens' (stills) nearby, and deserves to be treated with caution. *Ponche* – rum mixed with a honey syrup – is considerably less potent, or try *coupada* , which lies somewhere between the two.

A variety of local vendors work the more popular yacht anchorages and it is often possible to buy fish at very reasonable prices, less so prawns and crayfish. In other harbours fishermen may sell their catch on the beach. In both cases bargaining appears perfectly acceptable and bartering for fuel or other essentials may also be suggested.

Some notes regarding ships' stores – principally fuel, bottled gas and chandlery – will be found on pages 333–4.

Communications

Mail

The postal service is generally reliable (though very slow), as is *poste restante*. Letters for yachts sent c/o *Poste Restante* to post offices at the larger ports will normally be held for one month pending collection and then returned to the sender. Marina Mindelo – see page 361 – will hold mail for arriving yachts, though it would be wise to make email contact beforehand. Mail usually takes between one and three weeks from Europe, slightly less from the USA or Canada. Outgoing mail generally takes around two weeks to reach Europe or North America.

Note that post offices in smaller towns may be closed all day Saturday, as well as Sunday, and that post boxes for stamped mail appear to be unknown. Mail must therefore be handed in at the post office during working hours.

Telephones

International calls can be made from most post offices (marked *Correios* or CTT) as well as from CV Telecom offices and some shops (usually the cheapest option). Nearly all public telephones require phone cards, purchased at post offices and elsewhere, and most now accept international calls – or rather claim to, since a high proportion do not actually work. Calls to the United Kingdom begin with the prefix 044, followed by the area code (without the initial zero) plus number. Calls to the United States and Canada begin with the prefix 01 and the area code plus number.

The country code for the Republic of Cape Verde islands is 238, with no individual island or area codes. In July 2004 an extra digit was added to all phone and fax numbers, which now contain seven digits. If only six are given, add a 2 (for landlines) or 9 (for mobiles) between the country code (if required) and the listed number.

Mobile (cell) phone coverage via CVMovel is generally excellent (though expensive) throughout the islands, though there are the inevitable 'holes' in more remote areas. Do not rely on texting, however – this is said to work with some phones in some areas, while in others only voice calls can be made and received. The costs incurred by using a mobile phone abroad are beyond the scope of this book, and individual phones may need 'unblocking' before they will work at all. If planning to spend some time in the country it may be cheaper to buy a new phone or at least a new SIM card.

Fax

Although declining in use with the ubiquity of email, many post offices still have fax machines, as do most hotels. Marina Mindelo will also send and receive faxes, a service for which they naturally charge a fee.

Internet access

Internet access is becoming ever more widespread, either at cybercafés or using the free Wi-Fi provided in public areas such as some town squares and airports – see individual harbours for details. Take care, however. Not only is connectivity subject to frequent failure but it is demonstrably insecure. In late 2010 a cruising yachtsman's laptop was hacked into and infected by a virus, probably at a cybercafé in Ilha do Sal. The hard disk containing all his cruising photographs was corrupted and spurious emails sent to his entire contact list – though the latter being in Portuguese gave the lie as to their origin. A good firewall and antivirus program is clearly essential, and must be updated each time the computer is used.

Marina Mindelo offers password-protected Wi-Fi for visitors, charging by the quantity downloaded – see page 367 for details.

Electricity

Electrical current throughout the Cape Verdes is 220v 50Hz, as is standard in western Europe. The chances of plugging a yacht into mains current are slight other than in Marina Mindelo, though it might be possible to use power tools ashore in other places by arrangement with the *Capitão do Porto* or *clube náutico*.

Further information

There are now four travellers' guides which cover the Cape Verde islands in varying levels of detail – see Further Reading, page 404. Booklets and maps are also available on the larger islands, though generally via book and stationery shops rather than tourist offices.

The Cape Verdes have a growing presence on the internet and the following sites (listed alphabetically) contain general information, some of which may be useful to the visiting yachtsman. If carrying out a search, note that some addresses use the local form of the name, 'Cabo Verde', rather than the English, 'Cape Verde'.

http://allafrica.com – searchable site in English, carrying current news stories on all African countries including the Cape Verdes

www.archipelagocapeverde.com/ – website of Cape Verde Holidays, including the usual (slightly superficial) information about the islands' history and culture, plus brief details about each of the nine inhabited islands

www.asemana.publ.cv/ – fascinating newspaper-style site carrying a very wide variety of articles. Be sure to opt for the English version (unless you read Portuguese, of course) as the auto-translate option produces some fairly strange results

www.bcv.cv – the unexpectedly interesting website of the Banco de Cabo Verde. In Portuguese only, but translates well

www.bela-vista.net/cape-verde.htm – Italian site (with an English option) including impressive photo gallery and online bookshop. Also current ferry schedules and details of the ships which operate them, with links to individual transport companies. See opposite

www.boatcv.com – the website of Mindelo-based boatCV which, according to its home page 'supports and assists yachtsmen visiting Cape Verde'. The 'Navstuff' section, featuring local weather and tidal information, would be useful anywhere in the islands

www.caboverde.com – THE website for the islands, from which almost everything can be accessed. Italian webmaster Eraldo De Gioannini deserves a three star commendation, not only for building such an entertaining, user-friendly site but for keeping it up-to-date for more than a decade (I first visited it in December 2000). An excellent place to start any kind of research on the islands ... or download the recipes for *Cachupa Rica* or *Canja de Galinha* and get a culinary foretaste while listening to local musicians…

www.caboverdeexpress.com – website of Cabo Verde Express, a charter aviation company offering transfers, day excursions, etc. both between islands and to/from the African mainland. See opposite

www.capeverdeinfo.org.uk – primarily intended for people interested in the Cape Verdes as a holiday or property destination, but also carrying some general information

http://capeverde-islands.com – private site run since 1999 by John M Pinto, a Cape Verdean resident in New Bedford, Massachusetts. Hundreds of short video clips covering all aspects of Cape Verdean life, culture and history, plus dozens of useful links

www.capeverdetravel.com – homepage of Cape Verde Travel, the UK company used by the author to travel to and within the islands

www.cia.gov/library/publications – click on *The World Factbook* and select Cape Verde for a wealth of current information and statistics covering all aspects of Cape Verde life

http://cvfastferry.com – website of Cabo Verde Fast Ferry, which runs the 160-seater catamarans *Kriola* and *Liberdade* between Praia, Fogo and Brava. See opposite

www.dgmp.cv – the website of Cape Verde's *Direcção Geral da Marinha e Portos*, a government agency tasked with 'implementing and enforcing the government's policy for the sector of transport and shipping ... and to safeguard human life'. Contains, among other things, details of the islands' lighthouses

www.ecaboverde.com – thousands of photographs of the islands captioned in English, Portuguese, French, German or Italian

www.en.wikipedia.org/wiki/Cape_Verde – a particularly comprehensive site, even by Wikipedia standards, with dozens of links to individual topics as well as to each of the 10 islands. If only this site had existed when I started research on the first edition in 1987!

www.fco.gov.uk/ – website of Britain's Foreign & Commonwealth Office. Follow the Travel & Living Abroad link and select Cape Verde for official advice on visiting the islands. Note that in some instances (e.g. visas) the 'official' advice may be at variance with what happens on the ground

www.flyhalcyonair.com – website of Halcyonair Cape Verde Airways which runs scheduled inter-island flights to all seven islands with airports. See opposite

www.flytacv.com – website of TACV – *Transportes Aéroes de Cabo Verde* – the islands' oldest airline. Down for some (long overdue) maintenance at the time of going to press but due to be reinstated soon, hopefully including an online booking option. See opposite

www.google.co.uk/maps – although Google does not date its satellite images (©2011 refers only to the copyright) few of the Cabo Verde set appear to be more than two years old, and some much newer. The original 'overview'…

www.governo.cv – website of the government of the República de Cabo Verde

www.lonelyplanet.com/cape-verde – the islands are included in Lonely's Planet's *West Africa*, but chapters covering individual countries can be downloaded for a small fee. Meanwhile the web pages include an active forum, though some of the other information is distinctly out of date

www.marinamindelo.com – website of the archipelago's only marina, with current berthing rates, etc. See pages 364–7 for further details

www.mindelo.info – a French-language site (but translates easily) offering news about recent and forthcoming events in Mindelo and, to a lesser extent, the rest of the archipelago. Some excellent photographs

www.parlamento.cv – website of the *Assembleia Nacional de Cabo Verde*, the republic's parliament

www.sambaladevelopments.com – website of Sambala Developments in Santiago – see page 377 – but also featuring a number of short but interesting films covering the history, culture and natural history of Santiago island. Local musicians provide the background music

www-sul.stanford.edu/depts/ssrg/africa/capev.html – the Cape Verde pages of Stanford University, which describes it as 'an annotated guide to internet resources on Cape Verde for students, faculty, librarians, teachers, journalists, businesspeople and others'. And very useful it is too...

http://travel.state.gov/ – the US Department of State's Bureau of Consular Affairs. Select Cape Verde in the Country Information box to bring up their Country Specific Information on the islands, updated regularly

http://virtualcapeverde.net/news2/index.php – run by the Embassy of Cape Verde in Washington DC, with links to articles on all subjects relating to the islands

www.wtgonline.com/data/cpv/cpv.asp – the Cape Verde pages of Columbus Travel Media Ltd, with a wealth of practical detail though some of it a bit superficial

www.youtube.com – searching 'Cape Verde islands' brings up a range of commercial and non-commercial videos, including some spectacular footage of Fogo's volcanic eruption in 1995

Transportation

International flights

Amilcar Cabral Airport on Ilha do Sal in the northeast of the archipelago is the Republic's major international airport, handling flights to Lisbon, Paris, Amsterdam, Munich, Rome, New York, Boston and Johannesburg, amongst other destinations. The main carrier is TACV (*Transportes Aéroes de Cabo Verde*, www.flytacv.com) but it is also served by TAP-Air Portugal (www.flytap.com) and others companies, both scheduled and charter. International flights also land at Praia in Santiago, São Pedro in São Vicente and Rabil in Boavista. At the time of writing most flights from the UK were routed via mainland Europe, usually Lisbon, though Thomson (www.thomson.co.uk/flights) flew direct from Gatwick and Manchester to both Ilha do Sal and Boavista. Check the internet for current services. TACV also operates a weekly service from Boston and from Fortaleza in Brazil.

If flying with TACV it is **essential** to confirm the flight at least 48 hours before departure, but note that TACV offices, even at airports, are closed at the weekend. See individual harbours for opening times. It is also wise to check again the day before departure, as last-minute schedule changes are frequent and departure times are as likely to be brought forward as to be put back. Note also that a crewmember leaving by air will need to have a visa – see page 327.

Inter-island flights

There are small airfields on all the islands other than Santo Antão and Brava. However, inter-island flights are frequently booked up well in advance, and if planning a crew change it would undoubtedly be simplest to do so at Porto da Palmeira on Ilha do Sal. After holding a monopoly for many years, TACV is now receiving competition from scheduled services provided by Halcyonair Cape Verde Airways (www.flyhalcyonair.com) while Cabo Verde Express (www.caboverdeexpress.com) covers the charter market both inter-island and to the African mainland. At the time of writing none of these companies accepted online bookings. It is normally possible to buy tickets in person by Visa card, but do not rely on this. Allow enough time to queue at the airline desk, queue at the bank and queue again to buy the ticket ... time is cheap in the Cape Verde islands!

Check-in for inter-island flights is 90 minutes prior to departure, though in practice it may be wise to allow nearer two hours as standby passengers are occasionally given preference if a booked passenger is late to arrive. Inter-island flights seldom depart at the time specified – many are en route from another island, so any delays are cumulative – but every effort is made to ensure that passengers make their international connections, if necessary holding the long-haul flight until the inter-island flight arrives.

Ferries

The islands are served by a varying fleet of ferries, currently including the fast catamarans *Kriola* and *Liberdade* and the conventional ships *Sal Rei*, *Mar d'Canal*, *Tarrafal*, *Ribeira de Paúl* and *Barlavento* (her sistership, the *Sotavento*, sank in 2007).

The São Vicente – Santo Antão route, used by many yachtsmen who prefer to leave their boats safe in Mindelo, is normally serviced by the *Sal Rei* and *Mar d'Canal*, with the other three displacement ships linking the remaining islands other than Ilha do Fogo and Ilha Brava. In 2011 there were three return services between São Vicente and Santo Antão every weekday with fewer at weekends, and once- or twice-weekly services around the rest of the islands – schedules change from time to time and are best checked at the ferry offices on the *cais cabotagens* (ferry quays) in Mindelo and Praia. Departures are notoriously variable, not least because all ferries also carry cargo and the ship will be held until it arrives. After some fluctuation the cost of a single ticket between Mindelo and Porto Novo on Santo Antão appears to have stabilised at about CVE 550$ / €5 per person.

Cabo Verde Fast Ferry (http://cvfastferry.com) runs the Praia – Fogo – Brava route with a pair of modern 160-seater catamarans, *Kriola* and *Liberdade*. Departures are daily, with the current schedule available on the website. It is hoped soon to expand the service around the other islands. The company is based in Praia but it is normally possible to book online.

Road transport

The Cape Verdes are well worth exploring inland. Car hire, though generally available, is expensive compared to the Azores or Canaries and there may be a kilometre charge. It is worth inspecting the vehicle carefully before signing for it, and being seen to photograph it from all angles can do no harm. A British or American (i.e. not international) driving licence is accepted, and payment can generally be made by credit card.

In practice – and particularly given the state of the roads in the smaller islands – it is often simpler and

Everyone – and everything – travels by *aluguer* (literally 'to hire') in the Cape Verdes

more enjoyable to hire a taxi for the day, agreeing in advance on the number of passengers, approximate route, expected hours and fee. A tip can then be added if justified. The vehicles on offer range from the impeccable to the extremely dubious-looking, their drivers likewise. Rates are often set over common routes such as airport to town.

Buses seldom run to a formal schedule, but most of the islands have plentiful *aluguer* (literally 'to hire') pickup trucks and minibuses. These private-enterprise buses do not carry a destination board: simply ask the driver where he is headed, and if not lucky first time around you will almost certainly be directed to the right vehicle. Competition for passengers is such that no driver leaves until his vehicle is full – it then gets fuller, and fuller, and fuller en route. Fares are low and it helps to have the right change. On arrival, be sure to check what time the driver will be leaving for the return trip – asking him to write it down will avoid possible misunderstandings.

Walking and hitchhiking

There are some superb walks in the Cape Verde islands, notably in the mountains of Santiago, São Nicolau and Santo Antão, many described in detail in the excellent *Cape Verde Islands* by Aisling Irwin and Colum Wilson. A number of specialised walkers' maps are also available.

Finally, if offered a lift, be sure you have not flagged down an unmarked taxi or *aluguer* with a driver who will expect to be paid.

Medical

Other than in Ilhas Fogo and Brava it is probably best to avoid drinking local water, which in any case is somewhat chlorinated. The yacht's tanks should have been filled in Madeira or the western Canaries and, if possible, this water kept for the Atlantic crossing. Bottled water is available everywhere.

The climate is generally healthy though the usual 'tropical' problems (diarrhoea, infections, ulcers, etc.) can and do occur. Although malaria occasionally crops up in the mountains of Santiago in the 'wetter' autumn months, MASTA (the Medical Advisor Service for Travellers Abroad, www.masta.org) no longer advises visitors to take any form of preventative medication. Leprosy has been reported in Santo Antão and Fogo and tuberculosis throughout the archipelago, but neither are serious risks for the short-term visitor.

The southern islands suffered their first outbreak of Dengue Fever in late 2009, though only a handful of cases were reported in Ilha do Sal and none at all in São Vicente. Like malaria, Dengue Fever is spread by mosquitoes and cannot be transmitted from person to person. While the northern islands are normally dry all year, the southern chain has a 'damper' season from September to November, when the outbreak occurred. Although nearly 17,000 cases had been reported by mid-November, by late December it was effectively over. It seems the first cases were wrongly diagnosed as Swine Flu (about which there had been a worldwide scare a few months previously) and so given incorrect treatment, possibly allowing the disease to take hold.

Medical facilities in the Cape Verdes have improved radically over the past few decades, particularly in the major cities. However, the country does not have the infrastructure of Europe or North America and drugs in particular may be in short supply. Needless to say, anyone with a chronic or recurring condition should take a good supply of medication with them, and any yacht passing through the islands should carry a comprehensive first-aid kit put together with tropical areas in mind.

There are pharmacies in most towns and villages where non-prescription medicines and general items can be found, but outside the two major cities their stocks are likely to be limited. Prescription medicines, if available, will be expensive. Both dentists and opticians exist in the larger towns, and wearers of glasses would be wise to carry a copy of their prescription (in addition to at least one reserve pair).

A new road under construction in Tarrafal, Santiago. Chipped to shape and firmly hammered home, these blocks will stand decades of use despite being laid without foundations

Who needs a Playstation when you have friends and a skipping rope?

National holidays

1 January	New Year's Day
20 January	Heroes' Day
moveable	Ash Wednesday (46 days before Easter)
moveable	*Carnaval* (usually one week after Ash Wednesday)
1 May	Labour Day
moveable	Municipal Day (mid or late May)
5 July	Independence Day
15 August	Feast of the Assumption (*Nossa Senhora de Graça*)
12 September	National Day
1 November	All Saints' Day
25 December	Christmas Day

Although Good Friday is not an official holiday, the vast majority of Cape Verdeans are Roman Catholic and some shops may be closed. The same is true in Mindelo and some other towns during the run up to Lent, when *Carnaval* is in full swing.

Carnaval in Santa Maria, Ilha do Sal. Local people and tourists throng the streets to watch the parade go by

Sailing and navigation

Practicalities

Entry and regulations

Arrival: After a short period in the 1990s when entry regulations for yachts arriving in the Cape Verde islands appeared be becoming more relaxed, in July 1999 the law was changed. Since then it has been an offence to make landfall anywhere other than Palmeira (Ilha do Sal), Mindelo (São Vicente) or Porto da Praia (Santiago) – designated 'Official Sea Border Posts'. The republic's four international airports are designated 'Official Air Border Posts' so presumably it is now also possible to make initial clearance at Boavista, though few would choose to. Breaches can attract fines of up to CVE 5,000,000$ – more than €45,000.

Because entry formalities vary markedly from island to island, full details for each harbour are given in the text. Most commonly it will be necessary for the skipper to visit the *Delegação Marítima* (harbour office) where both the *Capitão do Porto* (port captain) and the *Polícia Marítima* (maritime police) are to be found. However, in Mindelo and Praia the first visit should be to the *Polícia de Fronteira* (effectively Immigration) while in Porto do Palmeira the *Polícia de Ordem Publica* (local police) stamp passports. Ship's papers, crew list and passports will always be required, while the *Polícia de Fronteira* may request an extra passport photo (always carry a few spares). A small fee is payable, normally on departure, in 2010 set at CVE 860$ (€8) or less.

Departure: Until 2011 final departure from the islands had to be made via one of the 'Official Border Posts' listed above, preventing yachts from legally visiting either Fogo or Brava unless they fancied the long beat back to Santiago. However, just as this book was going to press confirmation came through that the departure – though not the arrival – rules for private yachts had been relaxed, making it possible to clear out via Mindelo or Porto da Praia and then call in at one or more of the smaller islands before leaving territorial waters.

It is still necessary to visit the *Delegação Marítima* in Mindelo or Porto da Praia to retrieve the ship's papers and pay any dues, followed by the *Polícia de Fronteira* to get passports stamped, but one can now request a document from the former showing the next port (*próximo porto* or *porto seguinte*), and then leave for any other inhabited island, checking out with the local *Delegação Marítima* before final departure. It is of course possible that the rules will change yet again, making it prudent to check the current situation with the authorities on arrival.

See Personal documentation, page 327, regarding passport and visa requirements, particularly the necessity for crew leaving by air to obtain a visa in addition to the 'transit' entry stamp issued to those arriving and leaving by water.

Laying up

The only place where a yacht could be left unattended with any degree of confidence would be in Mindelo, São Vicente, either in Marina Mindelo – see page 361 – under the watchful eye of Kai Brosmann and his staff or possibly ashore at Lusonave, though the yard's future is uncertain.

Ships' stores

All kinds of ships' stores are very limited, including water which is in short supply in most of the islands. It must usually be carried from the tap, so plenty of five or 10-litre cans are essential – local children will probably be happy to help carry them in return for a few escudos. Only in Porto da Palmeira (Ilha do Sal), Porto do Tarrafal (São Nicolau), Mindelo (São Vicente) and Porto da Praia (Santiago) is there any possibility of filling tanks by hose, and only in Mindelo would it be simple. Other than in Ilha do Fogo and Ilha Brava water may be of doubtful quality, though bottled water is on sale almost everywhere.

Diesel and petrol (*gasóleo*, pronounced *gas-OH-lee-o*) and petrol (*gasolina*, pronounced *gas-oh-LEE-na*) can be found in most harbours, but again will probably need to be collected by can; only in Mindelo is it easy to take on fuel by hose, though it might be possible in Porto da Palmeira, Porto do Tarrafal or Porto da Praia – see under Facilities for each harbour. Paraffin or kerosene (*petróleo*, pronounced *petr-OH-leo*, though both *parafina* and *querosene* are likely to be understood) is generally sold by pharmacies but is expensive, and in 2010 was reported as difficult to obtain.

Camping Gaz uses the same fitting as in the UK and Europe, and exchanges are available in most towns (generally at the Shell filling station). Other cylinders can normally be refilled (with butane) by Enacol in Porto da Palmeira, Mindelo and Porto da Praia – see individual harbours for details. It would be wise to carry a selection of valve adaptors if relying on getting cylinders refilled, or possibly a few metres of rubber hose fitted with the necessary connector for the ship's bottles in the (reasonable) hope that the depôt will have a connector for their end.

Almost no yacht spares or other chandlery are available outside Mindelo, where boatCV's Ship Shop has stocks of commonly used items and can order if necessary – see page 366. More general items, including electrical goods, hose and some stainless-steel fittings, are readily available from hardware stores in the larger towns, as are a wide variety of tools.

Cruising

Although still viewed by most British yachtsmen as little more than a convenient stop en route to the Caribbean or Brazil – or perhaps a bolt hole in which to sort out problems – other nationalities are visiting the Cape Verde islands in ever-increasing numbers. It can only be a matter of time before this leads to improved facilities in islands beyond São Vicente, and before the authorities begin to realise that providing basic infrastructure for visiting yachtsmen – and easing the paperwork burden – can do nothing but good both for both the reputation and the economy of the Republic.

From the northern yachtsman's point of view they certainly have the weather in their favour – consistently high but not baking temperatures, combined with very limited rainfall. In Mindelo (São Vicente) this averages only 126mm annually, almost entirely during the months of August to November. Some higher areas may receive up to twice this amount, but droughts of several years' duration are common. Humidity averages about 70% and mid-day temperatures at sea level vary relatively little, from around 31°C in September to 26°C in January, dropping to the low 20s at night. However, it can feel surprisingly chilly at altitude – perhaps if walking in Santo Antão, Santiago or Fogo – when warm clothing will be appreciated.

The nine inhabited islands are spread over a distance of 145M in latitude and 155M in longitude, forming a neat horseshoe when viewed on the chart. Most passages between adjacent islands can be completed in daylight, while longer distances may entail night departure as no harbour other than Mindelo on São Vicente can safely be entered after dark – and even that should be avoided if possible.

Winds and swell

The Cape Verde islands lie squarely in the path of the northeast Trades with over 80% of winds coming from that direction, together with occasional northerlies or easterlies. According to published statistics speeds average around 10–12 knots with a 5% incidence of calms, while true wind speeds of 35 knots or more occur on average only four times a year and are unknown between July and January. However, in practice it generally appears to blow considerably harder than this, particularly in winter and spring, averaging nearer 18–20 knots between December and May and frequently reaching 25–30 knots. Gale or near-gale force winds appear to be much more common in the *Barlaventos* (the northern or 'windward' chain) than in the *Sotaventos* (the southern or 'leeward' chain).

This overall picture is further complicated by local land effects, the most obvious occurring in the channel between São Vicente and Santo Antão, a classic venturi (see page 362). In both groups, gusts funnelling down the ravines may create sudden squalls. One yacht reported 55 knot gusts in a true wind strength of 30 knots while sailing down the west coast of Santiago, and gusts of up to 35 knots may occur in mean winds of 10–15 knots. At sea, line squalls may be encountered. These heavy banks of cloud, usually lying on a north/south line and moving westwards at around 25 knots, are often preceded by gusts of up to gale force followed by heavy rain and sometimes thunder.

Wind strengths fall off towards the end of May, with light variables predominating from May to

Courses and distances within the Cape Verdes

Harbour	*Course / Reciprocal*	*Distance*
Palmeira, Ilha do Sal - Mindelo, São Vicente	275° / 095° & by eye	118M
Palmeira, Ilha do Sal - Tarrafal, São Nicolau (via north coast)	268° / 088° & by eye	93M
Palmeira, Ilha do Sal - Tarrafal, São Nicolau (via south coast)	258° / 078° & by eye	86M
Palmeira, Ilha do Sal - Porto da Praia, Santiago	194° / 014° & by eye	116M
Palmeira, Ilha do Sal - Porto de Sal Rei, Boavista	174° / 354° & by eye	37M
Porto de Sal Rei, Boavista - Tarrafal, São Nicolau	283° / 103° & by eye	91M
Porto de Sal Rei, Boavista - Porto da Praia, Santiago (avoiding Baixo de João Valente)	by eye & 194° + 203° 023° + 194° & by eye	85M
Tarrafal, São Nicolau - Mindelo, São Vicente	305° / 025° & by eye	45M
Mindelo, São Vicente - Porto Novo, Santo Antão	337° / 157°	8·5M
Mindelo, São Vicente - Porto da Praia, Santiago (via east coast)	138° / 318° & by eye	166M
Mindelo, São Vicente - Porto da Praia, Santiago (via west coast)	145° / 325° & by eye	159M
Porto da Praia, Santiago - Vale de Cavaleiros, Ilha do Fogo (via north coast)	283° / 103° & by eye	67M
Porto da Praia, Santiago - Vale de Cavaleiros, Ilha do Fogo (via south coast)	264° / 084° & by eye	64M
Vale de Cavaleiros, Ilha do Fogo - Porto da Furna, Ilha Brava	259° / 079°	10M

November interspersed with occasional periods of absolute calm, though these seldom last more than twenty-four hours. Southerly or southeasterly winds are common at this time of year, and though seldom exceeding 15 knots may occasionally become strong or even gale force, rising very suddenly with no visual or barometric warning. Local people take this danger very seriously indeed, and in a few harbours ships may move out overnight due to the danger of being trapped by a southerly gale. Both the pier at Santa Maria and the breakwater at Vale de Cavaleiros, Ilha do Fogo, were damaged by summer southerlies, and some years ago winds and swell from this direction put both a yacht and the inter-island ferry ashore at Ilha Brava. A heavy southeasterly swell may also cause problems at Porto de Sal Rei, Boavista, making it difficult to exit the bay.

Swell can arrive from almost any direction for no apparent reason. Local winds may be constant in strength and direction but storms further north (December to May) or south (June to November) can give rise to a nasty swell capable of running for several hundred miles. Almost any of the anchorages in the Cape Verdes may suffer, but those flanked by good beaches are usually most at risk – after all, something caused the beach to form in the first place!

In light of the above it has been suggested that the best time to cruise the islands is in late September or early October, when there is likely to be less wind and swell than a month or so later, so making some of the smaller anchorages much more inviting. While this may well be true, it would still be unwise to approach the Caribbean before the end of the hurricane season, which can extend into December.

Visibility

True fog is almost unknown in the Cape Verdes, though visibility may sometimes be cut drastically by dust haze carried from the interior of Africa by a hot, dry wind known as the *harmattan*, and if the northeast trades are (or have been) blowing at 17 knots or more such conditions should be expected. Most common between November and March, the effects of the *harmattan* can extend up to 600M from the mainland, usually cutting visibility to 5M or less (though a reduction to 0·5M is not unknown and 50m has been recorded). Indeed, more than one crew's first sight of the islands has been of surf.

Although GPS has eliminated the problem of accurate position fixing in such conditions, the possibility of collision with another vessel should not be overlooked. Neither should the fact that charting of the islands is still far from perfect – see Chart Datum and Satellite Derived Positions, below – and that many of the major lights are frequently unlit.

In *harmattan* conditions the horizon may appear quite firm with the overhead sky a clear blue, and without any external reference it is quite possible to remain unaware of the potential problem. In winds of more than 15 knots all yachts, and particularly those without radar, should approach the islands with extreme caution.

Sources of further information

Further statistics are available from a number of sources – the British Admiralty *Routeing Charts, North Atlantic Ocean*, the US National Geospacial-Intelligence Agency *Pilot Charts of the North Atlantic Ocean*, James Clarke's *Atlantic Pilot Atlas*, now in its 5th edition (see Further Reading, page 403) and Imray Laurie Norie & Wilson Ltd's *Chart 100, North Atlantic Ocean Passage Chart*.

Weather forecasts

Since 2006 the Cape Verde islands have been covered by Navtex transmissions from São Vicente in English as well as Portuguese – see page 360 – though these are reported to be of variable reliability.

Various websites carrying worldwide weather information are listed on page 9, and a forecast is normally posted in the office of Marina Mindelo.

Magnetic variation

Variation throughout the Cape Verdes decreases by about 1° from west to east, in 2011 averaging 10°40′W and decreasing by about 8′E annually.

Tides and tidal streams

Volume 2 of the Admiralty *Tide Tables: The Atlantic and Indian Oceans including tidal stream predictions (NP 202)*, published annually, covers the Cape Verde islands with Dakar, Senegal as standard port. However, many more yachtsmen will turn to the internet and the UK Hydrographic Office's excellent *EasyTide* programme at http://easytide.ukho.gov.uk, which gives daily tidal data for at least one harbour on every island other than Ilha do Fogo. Following a suggestion from the author, the island name is now included in cases where the harbour name alone (e.g. Tarrafal) is insufficient. Note, however, that for some unfathomable reason the Cape Verdes are indexed under the South Atlantic!

Tidal ranges are small, São Vicente having less than 1m at springs (0·4m above datum) and only 0·5m at neaps, and are given for each island. Tidal streams are also negligible offshore but can run strongly in the passages between islands, particularly in the Canal de São Vicente and the Canal de Santa Luzia where, combined with the ocean current, it may attain over 4 knots. A 2 knot east-going tidal stream has been reported to occur off the south coast of Santiago close west of Porto da Praia at mid-ebb.

Currents

The Cape Verdes lie in the path of the Canary Current, itself generated by the northeast trades, which sets southwest at up to 1·5 knots. It is heavily influenced by recent wind conditions and can be cancelled or even reversed by a southerly gale.

Navigational aids

Radio communications

Since the withdrawal of the very useful *NP289 – Maritime Communications, United Kingdom and the Mediterranean*, those wishing to carry details of all official radio communications in the Cape Verde islands now need to invest in three volumes – *NP281(1) – Maritime Radio Stations*; *NP283(1) Maritime Safety Information Services* and *NP 286(1) Pilot Services, Vessel Traffic Services and Port Operations*.

Buoys and lights

All lights and the few lit buoys in the Cape Verdes follow the IALA A system, as in Europe. It must be emphasised, however, that in the more than two decades since this guide was first published numerous yachtsmen and women have reported that many – possibly most – lights simply **DO NOT WORK.** Sadly, the marked improvement in the infrastructure as a whole over that time does not yet appear to have extended to navigational aids. In November 2010 a yacht making landfall from the north reported that Punta Leste (São Nicolau), Ilheu dos Passaros (São Vicente) and Punta da Tumba, (Santo Antão) were all dark. Her crew added: 'Perhaps it would be simpler to say that we didn't see any lights at all apart from the towns when navigating between the islands in darkness. It is well worth making every effort to arrive in daylight, including heaving-to if necessary.'

Some lights, even though working, may not exhibit their listed characteristics and even when this is intentional details of changes may take a year or more to appear in Admiralty *Notices to Mariners* – if they ever do. All in all, night sailing between the islands and especially landfalls after dark should be avoided if at all possible. If forced to do so, note that not every light listed in the text can be shown on the plans, in particular on the small-scale 'island' plans. Refer instead to the relevant Admiralty or local chart.

Charts

All charts of the Cape Verde islands should be used with caution, though a little more confidence can be placed in the current edition of Admiralty *367* (which covers the islands' three primary harbours and their approaches), the Portuguese *Instituto Hidrográfico*'s *66301*, *66302*, *67501* and *67503*, and those produced by the *Direcção Geral de Marinha e Portos* (Director General of Marine and Ports) in São Vicente. All other charts are based on surveys which predate electronic position fixing, including a few going back a century or more.

The first locally surveyed and printed Cape Verdean charts became available early in 2001 (previously all charts of the islands had been surveyed and printed by Portugal). The first three covered the islands' major harbours – *No 21: Porto da Palmeira, Ilha do Sal*; *No 41: Mindelo (Porto Grande), São Vicente*; and *No 71: Porto da Praia, Santiago*. A further two – *No 31: Porto do Tarrafal, São Nicolau*; and *No 11: Porto Novo, Santo Antão* – followed the next year, but since then work appears to have stopped. Neither are they easy to obtain – in theory they can be ordered from the Casa das Bandeiras ✆ 232 1391 *Fax* 232 1559 at Rua Governador Calheiros 14, Caixa Postal 16, São Vicente, República de Cabo Verde – see page 366. Having said that, attempts by the author to order from the UK met with no response whatsoever.

The Portuguese *Instituto Hidrográfico*'s *66301*, *66302*, *67501* and *67503* can be ordered online from J Garraio & Ca Lda in Lisbon (www.jgarraio.pt). If any other Portuguese charts are seen, avoid them – they will have been surveyed before the islands gained their independence in 1975 and are seriously out of date.

British Admiralty charts (www.ukho.gov.uk) cover the archipelago on three sheets, one small scale and covering all the islands, the other two containing between them three medium-scale island charts and 15 larger-scale plans of approaches, harbours and anchorages. However, a number of the harbour plans previously found on the non-metric *369* have been deleted from recent editions, and almost half of this chart now consists of blank space. An old copy (used with discretion) might be a useful addition to the portfolio if one can be found, though there is little on it which does not appear in this book. Even on the current edition of *369* several of the remaining plans – all based on very old surveys – are misleadingly inaccurate, particularly in terms of latitude and longitude (see below).

The US National Geospatial-Intelligence Agency devotes four sheets to the islands. Though no longer available directly from the NGIA, they can be ordered online from approved suppliers. See page 396 for further details. Finally, Imray Laurie Norie & Wilson Ltd's *Imray-Iolaire* series covers the archipelago on a single sheet, *E4*, with 10 inset harbour plans. The company (✆ 01480 462114 *Fax* 01480 496109 *Email* ilnw@imray.com www.imray.com) will mail both British Admiralty and their own charts worldwide, the former corrected to date of despatch.

See Appendix I, page 399, for chart lists.

Chart datum and satellite derived positions

None of the three British Admiralty charts of the Cape Verdes islands are yet based on WGS84 Datum – e.g. positions taken from Admiralty *366*, *Arquipélago de Cabo Verde* must be moved 0·1 minutes north and 0·4 minutes east to comply with both WGS84 and the plans in this guide. Metric chart *367* uses three different datum references for the islands of Sal, São Vicente and Santiago and their related harbour plans, while the venerable, non-metric, *369* pre-dates the whole concept of datum entirely and is, moreover, sometimes distinctly nebulous regarding both position and scale. For a fuller explanation see Horizontal chart datum on page 10 of the Passages section.

Guides, pilots, etc.

The archipelago is covered in the British Admiralty's *Africa Pilot (NP 1)*, and in the US National Geospacial-Intelligence Agency's *Sailing Directions for the West Coast of Europe and North West Africa (Pub 143)*, both of which are of course written with very much larger vessels in mind. In addition, the 6th edition of *The Atlantic Crossing Guide* includes brief passage planning notes, with additional harbour details for Mindelo, São Vicente. They are also mentioned – even more briefly – in Rod Heikell and Andy O'Grady's *Ocean Passages and Landfalls*, and in *World Cruising Routes* and *World Cruising Destinations* by Jimmy Cornell.

Two guides cover the Cape Verdes in some detail – *Kapverdische Inseln: Der Nautische Revierführer* by André Mégroz and Kai Brosmann, and Donald M Street's *Street's Guide to the Cape Verde Islands*. The full 200-page edition of the former is only available in German, though a 60-page 'light' version is also available in English, French and Italian and can be ordered online from www.segeln-kapverden.ch/. The latter, based on Don Street's visits to the islands over many years, was published in 2010 and can be ordered from various online retailers, including Seaworthy Publications (www.seaworthy.com). Neither of these books has been seen by this author.

Caution and request

Although tremendous progress has been made in the Cape Verde islands over the past 25 years, it is nevertheless essential to remember that they are not an outpost of Europe. They are very much a part of Africa, albeit a remarkably successful one in many ways, and the needs of visiting leisure sailors do not rate highly on the list of government priorities. Local people know their own waters, ships (unless visiting Mindelo or Praia) stay well clear, and search and rescue facilities are almost non-existent.

Charts may be dangerously inaccurate in some areas, the surveys on which they are based may in a few cases be more than a century old, and several years may elapse between changes in light characteristics, harbour developments, etc. taking place and appearing on new editions of charts – if they ever do. Even a brand new chart, fully corrected, should not be assumed to be fully up to date in all respects. See also the remarks regarding the frequent unreliability of lights.

Where changes come to the notice of the author and/or publisher they are normally incorporated in the interim supplements carried on the websites of both Imray Norie Laurie & Wilson Ltd (www.imray.com) and the RCC Pilotage Foundation (www.rccpf.org.uk). The author and publisher are therefore indebted to the hundreds of yachtsmen and women who have taken the trouble to send in corrections, comments and photographs for these supplements, either by email to ilnw@imray.com or by post to Imray Laurie Norie & Wilson Ltd, Wych House, The Broadway, St Ives, Cambs PE27 5BT. Even in these days of information overload there is nothing to compare with direct feedback from someone who is actually on the spot. Thank you, and long may it continue!

Ilha do Sal

Between 16°35'N–16°51'N and 22°53'W–23°W

Introduction

The most northeasterly of the Cape Verde islands, Ilha do Sal covers an area of some 216km². Much of this is low and flat, the highest point being Monte Grande (Monte Verhelho) at 407m. It is the oldest island in the archipelago at some 50 million years and arguably the least attractive, though there are some fine beaches at Santa Maria in the extreme south. Doubtless due to the latter it is amongst the most developed of the Cape Verdes, with the archipelago's largest airport – Amilcar Cabral International – near the centre of the island. By 2010 the population was estimated at around 26,000, nearly twice that of 10 years previously and more than four times that of 1980. Together with São Vicente and Santiago it is one of the three islands at which yachts may clear into the Republic of Cape Verde, and is obviously the most convenient at which to rendezvous with crew arriving by air or to wave off departing crew members.

In 2008 the wave of new development, nearly all intended for foreign buyers, was a noticeable feature particularly in the south of the island. By 2010 most building work had ground to a halt, leaving the eastern parts of Santa Maria resembling a wild west film set – flimsy frontages with nothing behind them, and entire blocks defined only by foundations. A few development companies had diversified, one such being Cabo Golf SA's imaginative *viveiro* project, which specialises in plants and garden design for hotels and other developments and is also working on grass species which require little water, primarily for use on golf courses.

Of the various marina village projects advertised in early 2010, only two appeared to still be afloat a year later – the Cotton Bay Marina and Golf Resort, and Murdeira Beach Marina Village – both on the southwest coast of the island between Porto da Palmeira and Baía de Santa Maria.

Plans for Cotton Bay Marina and Golf Resort (www.cottonbay-sal.com) were drawn up in 2007 and show a narrow doglegged entrance, planned for 16°37'·7N 22°55'·9W, leading to a marina containing 188 berths, more than half of them able to take yachts of 12m or more. Surrounding the marina are the usual houses and apartments, together with a small boatyard with travel-lift, fuel and other facilities. By early 2010 all the necessary permissions were in place but funds were still lacking, and a year later a completion date of 2014 was suggested (though that plainly depends on a worldwide economic recovery).

Inside the *viveiro* run by Cabo Golf SA, which supplies ornamental plants throughout Ilha do Sal as well as to their own developments. The Cotton Bay Marina and Golf Resort will be part of the same group

Navigation

Waypoints
⊕ CV01 – 16°55'·5N 22°55'·3W (4M N of Pta Norte)
⊕ CV02 – 16°51'·7N 23°01'·4W (3M NW of Pta Preta)
⊕ CV03 – 16°44'·8N 22°59'·9W (1M WSW of Porto de Palmeira)
⊕ CV04 – 16°34'·1N 22°55'·4W (1M S of Pta do Sinó)
⊕ CV05 – 16°44'·8N 22°53'W (1M SSE of Porto de Pedra de Lume)

Courses and distances
⊕ CV01 – ⊕ CV03 via ⊕ CV02 = 14M, 237° & 168° / 348° & 057°
⊕ CV01 – ⊕ CV05 = 11 5M, by eye
CV03 – ⊕ CV04 = 12 5M, by eye
⊕ CV03 – ⊕ CV06 (3M NW of Pta do Sol, Boavista) = 29M, 175° / 355°
⊕ CV03 – ⊕ CV12 (2M N of Pta Espechim, São Nicolau) = 78M, 269° / 089°
⊕ CV03 – ⊕ CV15 (2M S of Pta Vermelharia, São Nicolau) = 78M, 257° / 077°
⊕ CV03 – ⊕ CV23 (8M NE of Ilhéu dos Passaros, São Vicente) = 113M, 278° / 098°
⊕ CV03 – ⊕ CV36 (4M NNE of Pta do Lobo, Santiago) = 104M, 193° / 013°

Magnetic variation
10°10'W (2011), decreasing by 8'E annually. Local magnetic anomalies are reported to exist west of Ilha do Sal.

Tidal Streams
Tidal streams around Ilha do Sal are generally weak. However, allowance should be made for the current, which usually sets southwest at 0·5–1 knot but is strongly influenced in both rate and direction by the wind.

Charts
Admiralty *367* (1:200,000)
US *51520* (1:250,000)
Imray-Iolaire *E4* (1:500,000)

Lights
2925 **Amilcar Cabral airport (Monte Curral)**
Aero Al.Fl.WG.5s83m26M Airport control tower (operates only when an aircraft is due)
2919·75 **Ponta Norte** Fl(3)12s16m8M Metal column 5m
2923·5 **Pedra de Lume** Fl(5)20s28m8M Metal post with gallery 5m
2919·9 **Rabo Junco** Fl.4s15m8M Metal column 5m
2922 **Ponta do Sinó** Fl(2+1)15s11m8M 300°-vis-142° Square grey tower 9m

Coast Radio Station
Ilha do Sal 16°45' 3N 22°56' 3W (remotely controlled from São Vicente)
VHF Ch 16 (24 hours), 22, 79
DSC VHF Ch 70, MMSI 006170000

Irish-based Cape Verde Developments Ltd, who also have projects under construction on São Vicente, have featured the Murdeira Beach Marina Village on their website at www.capeverdedevelopment.com since 2009 or earlier. The development is apparently to include a 75–100 berth marina with its entrance at 16°40'N 22°56'·2W, but few other details are available. Mordeira Bay – locally spelled 'Murdeira'– is classified as a Marine Protected Area by the Worldwife Fund for Nature, and is a breeding site for whales and a hatchery for loggerhead turtles. Even so, after environmental consultants were brought in to modify the initial plans, by early 2010 the necessary paperwork was complete. Once again, lack of funds due to the worldwide recession meant that only foundations and general infrastructure were in place a year later, with no sign of work starting on the proposed marina.

The projected marina developments at Pedra da Lume and Porto Murdeira, both publicised on the internet in early 2010, were no longer in evidence a year later. The former was still advertised as a holiday village plus golf course, but of the marina aspect there was no mention.

Telecommunications

Mobile (cell) phone reception throughout Ilha do Sal is good, though note the limitation detailed on page 329. The country code for the Republic of Cape Verde islands is 238, with no individual island or area codes, and the telephone number always contains seven digits. If only six are given, add a 2 (for landlines) or 9 (for mobiles) at the beginning.

By 2010 the internet could be accessed at several places in Espargos and Santa Maria, with free Wi-Fi available at the airport and elsewhere, though note the warning on page 329.

Websites

The internet currently offers no websites devoted specifically to Ilha do Sal, though it has several pages on wikipedia.org/wiki/Cape_Verde and others on the excellent www.caboverde.com. The site of the four-star Morabeza Hotel in Santa Maria has some interesting photos of the town before it was taken over by tourism.

Approach

Much of the island is low, with a few isolated hills of which the highest, at 407m, is Monte Grande (Monte Vermelho) in the extreme northeast. Thus it can often be lost in haze until very close in. An offing of 0·5–1M is sufficient around the northern part of the island, but the southern part should be allowed a minimum of 1M due to the long sand spits which extend offshore in several places. The current in the vicinity of Ilha do Sal usually sets southwest at about 0·5 knots but may sometimes be much stronger, particularly when the northeast trades are blowing.

A pavement in Espargos incorporates tile and flooring offcuts to interesting effect

Harbours and anchorages

Porto da Palmeira

16°45'·16N 22°58'·91W (breakwater head)

Waypoint
⊕CV03 – 16°44'·8N 22°59'·9W (1M WSW of Porto de Palmeira)

Tides
Time difference on Dakar: 0000, on Mindelo (Porto Grande): +0045. Predictions for Porto da Palmeira are available via Admiralty *EasyTide* – see page 336
Mean spring range 0·8m
Mean neap range 0·4m

Plans
Admiralty *367* (1:12,500)
Cabo Verdean *21* (scale unknown)
Portuguese *67503* (1:5,000)
Imray-Iolaire *E4* (1:15,000)

Lights
2921·3 **Breakwater** Iso.R.4s11m5M
White tower, red bands 5m
2921 **Oil pipeline, Lts in line on 044°** (occas)
Fl.3 5s9/15m5/3M Red posts 7/11m (lights 95m apart)
Note Both the above pairs of lights in line indicate the oil pipeline and tanker berth – they are NOT leading lights
buoy **Tanker berth No 1**
buoy **Tanker berth No 2**
Both Fl.6s3M on metal ships' mooring buoys, plus other unlit buoys nearby

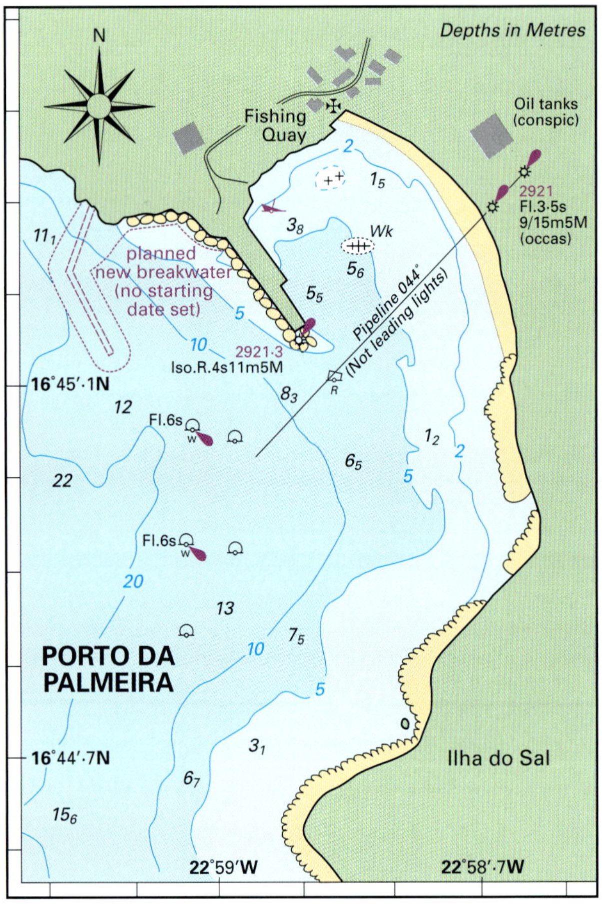

Anchorage behind extended breakwater

A deeply indented bay on the west coast of Ilha do Sal, Porto da Palmeira offers good shelter from northwest through east to south, further improved by the recently-extended breakwater. Work to reinforce the old breakwater and lengthen it by 120m began in 2009, and despite northwesterly swells destroying much of the work over the winter, by late the following year work was complete. The pale stone and concrete of the new southern section is said to be visible from well offshore, in contrast to the older north part which, being of local stone, tends to blend in with the background. The village is also clearly visible from a distance, with two prominent wind generators to the northwest (at 16°46'·1N 22°59'W) and a cluster of silver oil storage tanks to the southeast.

The anchorage can accommodate thirty or more yachts without serious overcrowding, but is somewhat bleak and often subject to swell. The village remains small and sleepy, and though some new building has taken place it has changed remarkably little over the past 17 years. Barefoot women still carry their loads in great baskets balanced on their heads, whilst children play in the streets. The roads are either cobbled, a legacy of Portuguese colonial times, or dirt tracks. Only the main road to the airport is of tarmac.

There appear to be few problems with security and it is not considered necessary to employ a yacht or dinghy 'watcher'. (Though see note page 324.)

The newly extended breakwater at Porto da Palmeira in November 2010, seen almost end-on, with the port hand buoy mentioned in the text in the foreground *Kai Brosmann*

Approach and entrance

Straightforward in daylight and feasible at night in good visibility, though note the warning on page 336 concerning the unreliability of lights throughout the archipelago. Only two of the four steel buoys marking the tanker berth are lit, both Iso.R., and it is best to avoid crossing the area as the discharge pickup buoy is often awash and difficult to spot. A safe-water mark lies about 200m south of the southwest tanker buoy, but if lit its characteristics remain unreported.

Looking southwest across the anchorage at Porto da Palmeira in February 2010, with the fishermen's quay at far right and waves breaking on the unfinished breakwater in the background

There is no obvious reason why a yacht arriving from the north should not enter between the breakwater and the northern pair of tanker buoys – the gap is almost 250m wide, with a port hand buoy positioned about 100m south of the breakwater head. Four starboard hand buoys are said to lie opposite, but though supposedly lit it would be most unwise to rely on this.

Following completion of the breakwater extension, plans have been drawn up to build a second, outer wall from a point slightly further west, with an angled arm creating a rectangular port area (see plan opposite). However this entails working in much greater depths than previously, and as of 2011 the *Capitão do Porto* had no idea when work might start.

Anchorage

Best anchorage is to be found in the northeast of the harbour in about 3–5m over sand and stones, though holding is variable (it seems that, once set, an anchor is generally secure). The inside of the mole is in continuous use by cargo boats, ferries and fishing boats and there is no possibility of lying alongside.

The remains of a 40ft steel motor-sailer lie inside the harbour at 16°45'·25N 22°58'·84W. Until 2007 its masts broke the surface, but by 2010 it had settled sufficiently to offer about 2m clearance at mean low water. Amazingly, it remains completely unmarked – take care! A second wreck, that of a large fishing trawler, lies on its side in the northwest corner of the harbour. However, it is clearly visible at all states of the tide so presents no real hazard. Both the above can be seen on current Google images, as can the extended breakwater.

Dinghies can be left at the small quay in the north corner of the harbour, though both consideration and a long painter should be employed as it is used extensively by local fishermen who are generally friendly but do not appreciate being impeded by flocks of dinghies on short painters. Catches are landed and gutted on the stones, often watched by tourists bussed in for day trips in a charter yacht. There is a small slipway at the west end of the quay where it might be possible to carry an engineless inflatable ashore, but beware its lower slopes which are extremely slippery.

Formalities

Palmeira is currently one of only four ports in the archipelago where inward clearance to the Republic of Cape Verde can be obtained – see Entry and regulations, page 333. Formalities appear to change relatively frequently, but in 2011 the situation was as follows:

On arrival: The skipper should visit the *Capitão do Porto* in his office near the small quay, taking ship's papers and crew passports. The office is totally unmarked, but look for a square, two-storey cream building with angular concrete 'arches' above the windows and a tell-tale VHF aerial. The *Capitão do Porto* occupies the first office on the right and is usually there from 0800–1600 on weekdays. If arriving at the weekend, visit on Monday morning. A crew list must be completed and the ship's papers will be held until departure. The adjacent office is occupied by the *Polícia Marítima*, who will carry out clearance if the *Capitão do Porto* is elsewhere. No charge is made and Armindo, *Capitão do Porto* for a number of years, is notably courteous and helpful with good English. The *Capitão do Porto* and *Polícia Marítima* are sometimes referred to collectively as the *Delegação Marítima*.

In the block beyond the *Delegação Marítima* lies the small office of the local police, labelled *Polícia de Ordem Publica*, where crew passports will be stamped on payment of CVE 200$ / €2 each. This office is claimed never to close, and though no English is spoken the atmosphere is relaxed and friendly. The *Polícia de Ordem Publica* do not have the authority to issue visas, for which it is necessary to visit the *Polícia de Fronteira* at the airport. These are normally issued on the spot on payment of CVE 2,500$, €25 or US$40, and will be needed by any crew members leaving the island by plane. A photocopy of their passport's information page, plus a couple of spare passport photos, should be available if required. Obtaining a visa should not be left until the last moment, as although the airport immigration desk is always manned when an

Fishermen land their catch on the quay at Porto da Palmeira

international flight is due, it may not be when one is due to depart – and without the correct entry and visa stamps in their passport they will **NOT** be allowed to board their plane.

On departure: Both offices need to be revisited. No charge is made for exit stamps in passports, but CVE 700$ / €7 is payable at the office of the *Capitão do Porto* when reclaiming the ships' papers. Visiting another anchorage on Sal is permitted, but if sailing to another island and planning to return it is necessary to clear out and then in again.

Facilities

Little is available in Palmeira itself and it is generally necessary to visit Vila do Espargos, about 2M inland, for more than routine needs. Athough taxis are rare in Palmeira, *aluguer* minibuses (see page 332) depart regularly from the edge of the town.

Boatyard Although in 2010 one yacht and several large fishing boats lay ashore on the north side of the harbour there is no boatyard as such, and no obvious means of hauling or launching. Unless desperate it would be far preferable to make for Mindelo.

Water By can from the *fontenario* – a blue concrete structure set back to the north of the main street – the only source of supply for many local people. It is locked at night and all day Sunday. Water comes by road tanker from the nearby desalination plant and is claimed to be safe to drink, though many will prefer to play safe and buy bottled water.

Showers A public shower block – painted blue and labelled *Sentina Municipal* – overlooks the quay and beach. Though nominally open 0700–1800 Monday to Saturday, in practice its hours appear variable and standards of cleanliness leave much to be desired.

Laundry Nothing in Palmeira other than the *fontenario*, where most local laundry appears to be done. There is said to be a laundry in Espargos near the football field east of the town – ask for Casa de Manuel – but it has not been checked.

Fuel Diesel is available by can from the Shell depot to the east of the harbour. However, they do not accept payment, so first it is necessary to visit the office in Espargos, located at the back of the Shell filling station about 200m down the road towards the airport. Vessel details are required together with payment in cash (at CVE 75$ per litre in 2011). Back in Palmeira cans will be filled on production of the printed receipt. There is a gate into the depot from the beach, so dinghy access is easy.

Bottled gas Camping Gaz cylinders can be exchanged at the tiny bakery (see below), or failing that at the filling station in Espargos. Other bottles may be refilled (with butane only) at the Shell depot – but only if the necessary adaptor is available. Unlike diesel, gas can be paid for in the depot office (where some English is spoken) and in early 2011 cost CVE 968$ for a 6kg refill.

Banks No bank or cash dispenser in Palmeira but three in Espargos (open 0830–1500 weekdays only), all in the centre near the church. Both Caixa Económica de Cabo Verde and Banco Interatlântico have exterior cash dispensers which accept Visa and other major credit cards. There are two more banks at the airport, both with accessible cash dispensers.

Shops/provisioning Several small grocery stores in Palmeira, plus bread from diminutive Padaria Dadô on the main square opposite the *Delegação Marítima* offices.

A much better choice is available in Espargos, where there are three or four *minimercados* with tinned goods, freezers and cold counters. The largest, The Central, also stocks some household items. Also two bakeries, clothes shops, small stationery store, etc., with several Chinese-owned general stores meeting any remaining needs.

Produce market In both Palmeira and Espargos. Note that most fruit and vegetables offered in shops will have been chilled so will not keep, making market purchases a better bet.

Cafés, restaurants & hotels Several bar/cafés and a single restaurant in Palmeira, with many more in Espargos where there are also hotels and other accommodation. In 2011 the pale green bar across the square from the fish quay was run by Carlos, a German ex-pat who is said to be an excellent source of local knowledge. Visitors might be wise not to use the bar on the fish quay itself, where petty theft has been reported.

Medical services Hospital in Espargos, plus an immaculately-kept pharmacy.

Communications

Post office In Espargos (open 0800–1200 and 1430–1800).

Telephones At the post office, with booths for international calls, and at Cyberspace (see below).

Internet access Small cybercafé in Palmeira, though note the warning on page 329. Free Wi-Fi is usually available in the main square in Espargos in the evenings, and all day at the airport a few miles south. Cyberspace in Espargos – a bright orange building a couple of streets south of the square – is open 0800–2200 daily and has ten computers, paid for by the minute. Suzy's Internet Café, also near the square, has been recommended as a place to plug in one's own computer (not an option at Cyberspace). It was closed when visited in 2010, with no indication whether this was temporary or permanent.

Car hire In Espargos and at the airport. See Road transport, page 331.

Taxis Readily available in Espargos, but it may be difficult to find one in Palmeira itself. *Aluguers* (see page 332) are available on an ad hoc basis, the chief pick-up point in Palmeira being near the edge of the village on the Espargos road. In 2011 the standard rate was CVE 50$ to Espargos or the airport.

Ferries Regular inter-island service from Porta da Palmeira.

Air services Amilcar Cabral Airport remains the largest and busiest in Cape Verde, with frequent inter-island and international flights. If needing to confirm a flight (recommended at least 48 hours before departure), note that the TACV office at the airport is open 0800–1130, 1400–1700 weekdays only.

Baía da Mordeira

16°41'·7N 22°58'·1W (NW anchorage)

Lights
2919·9 **Rabo Junco** Fl.4s15m8M Metal column 5m

Beautiful anchorage in wide bay

A very beautiful anchorage with clear water, Baía da Mordeira (Murdeira on local maps) is nearly 3M wide and almost semicircular. Situated on the southwest coast of Ilha do Sal, it gives good protection from northwest through northeast to southeast. The centre of the bay is a prohibited anchorage due to submarine cables which terminate at a red building on the shore – a line from this building to the northwest point of the bay (Ponta Pesqueirona) marks the northern limit of the cables.

Most yachts opt to anchor in the northern corner of the bay, where the bottom shelves gradually and fetch can be reduced by working into 5–6m over rock and sand. A tripline is advisable. There is excellent snorkelling, but take care when landing as a big surf runs on the beach. There are no facilities ashore, but buses to Palmeira or Santa Maria run along the main road a little to the east.

A tourist resort has been ceated around a small semicircular lagoon on the southeast shore of Baía da Mordeira, but entry is totally unsuitable even for dinghies – which in any case would probably not be welcome.

Baía de Santa Maria

16°35'·6N 22°54'·5W (anchorage)

Waypoint
⊕CV04 – 16°34'·1N 22°55'·4W (1M S of Pta do Sinó)

Plans
Admiralty *367* (1:20,000)
Portuguese *67503* (1:7,500)
US *51520* (1:15,000)

Lights
2922 **Ponta do Sinó** Fl(2+1)15s11m8M
300°-vis-142° Square grey tower 9m
2922·5 **Ponta de Vera Cruz**
Fl(5)R.20s6m5M 300°-vis-049°
White tower emerging from building

Rolly anchorage off excellent beach

Formerly a salt shipping port, Santa Maria is the archipelago's first serious venture into the tourist industry – and hopefully lessons will be learned from the apparently indiscriminate building which has mushroomed over the past decade and far outstripped the town's infrastructure. Nearly all the new construction is of hotels and holiday apartments, and in early 2010 many buildings sported tattered *Se Vende* (For Sale) notices, while others were abandoned and derelict. Most roads remain unsurfaced and unlit, and visitors' comments range from 'a building site' through a 'ghost town' to 'like something out of the Wild West'.

Having said that, the beach west of the rebuilt pier is outstanding. Windsurfers and scuba equipment are available for hire from several outlets and it is backed by a multiplicity of bars and restaurants. A long range of cream buildings with pink tiled roofs (the Morabeza Hotel) lies near the head of the bay and is easily seen from seaward.

The wreck of a large schooner has lain on the reef southeast of Ponta do Sino for more than a decade – which, if nothing else, says much for her construction. It should be noted that the south-going

Beautiful Baía da Mordeira, looking northwest towards the headland of Rabo Junco

IV. THE CAPE VERDES

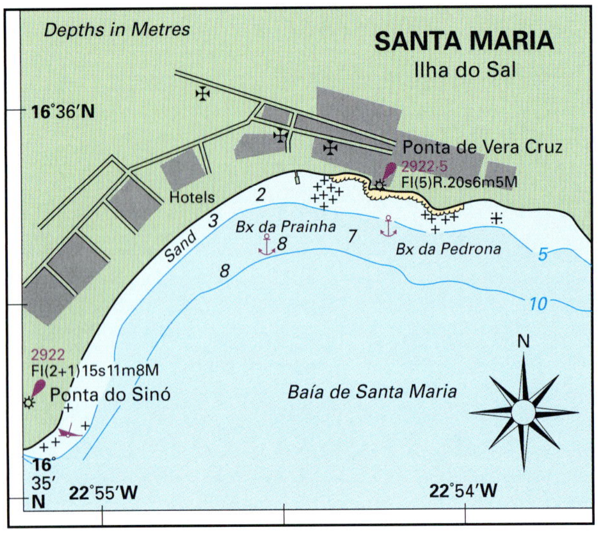

Looking west-southwest along the fabulous beach at Santa Maria towards the pier

current is gradually causing the sandbank off the headland to extend, leaving the lighthouse stranded some distance inland.

Anchorage

Shelter is good from southwest through north to east, though northeasterly swells frequently work into the bay and some rolling is almost inevitable. Best anchorage is in the middle of the bay southwest of the pier, outside the local boat moorings, but depths shoal suddenly so approach with care. Holding is good in 5m or more over sand, and some yachts favour a second anchor to hold them into the swell.

Landing on the superb white sand beach is likely to be a wet experience as there is nearly always some surf, making the renovated pier the only dry option. This is in constant use by fishermen and tourist traffic yet boasts a single stainless-steel ladder, well 'guarded' by local boys who in 2011 charged €5 to look after your dinghy. Even so, while the dinghy may be safe in their hands its contents will not, and nothing should be left in it to tempt the light-fingered.

The old customs house at Santa Maria, now converted into cafés and shops. The stone buildings on the left belong to one of the beachfront hotels

Facilities

Water Bottled water readily available in the shops and bars, but no tap to be seen, even on the pier.
Showers Several of the hotels have beach showers, for which a small charge is likely to be made.
Bank Several, open 0800–1500, with cash dispensers from which escudos can be drawn on a Visa card.
Shops/provisioning Several small supermarkets, plus a bakery at the east end of the main street (recommended for its excellent ginger biscuits which are said to last for months).
Produce market Small market – though much of it has been taken over by souvenir sellers – with fresh fish often available at the pier.
Cafés,restaurants & hotels Good choice of the first two, including several on the beach, plus accommodation at all levels.
Medical services Small health centre, with a hospital in Espargos.

Communications

Post office & telephones In the town centre.
Internet access Various possibilities, including GSM.SUD in a large blue building close east of the pier.
Car hire Hertz, Avis and other companies hire out both standard and 4-wheel-drive vehicles. See Road transport, page 331.
Taxis Plenty.
Buses Frequent *aluguer* minibuses to Espargos via the airport. In 2011 the standard rate was CVE 100$ each way.
Air services Amilcar Cabral Airport remains the largest and busiest in Cape Verde, with frequent inter-island and international flights. If needing to confirm a flight (recommended at least 48 hours before departure), note that the TACV office at the airport is open 0800–1130, 1400–1700 weekdays only. It takes about 20 minutes to reach the airport by taxi.

Porto de Pedra de Lume

16°45'·7N 22°53'·45W (molehead)

Waypoint
⊕ CV05 – 16°44'·8N 22°53'W (1M SSE of Porto de Pedra de Lume)

Plans
Admiralty *369* (1:18,000) (based on surveys dating from 1956; soundings in fathoms)

Lights
2923·5 **Pedra de Lume**
Fl(5)20s28m8M Metal post with gallery 5m
2923·6 **Quay** Fl.R.4m1M Column on round base 7m

Fascinating area best visited by road

On the exposed east coast of Ilha do Sal, Porto de Pedra de Lume provides shelter from south through northwest to northeast, but would be uncomfortable and probably dangerous when the northeast trades are blowing. The tiny inner harbour has little more than 1m depth. Parts of the bay are rocky, but when the wind shifts into the west it is possible to anchor south of the quay in 7–8m over sand and rock. In January 2005 a very experienced yachtsman reported finding good overnight anchorage in flat seas off Porto de Pedra de Lume, following several days of strong winds from the southwest. He was later told that conditions in Palmeira that night had been 'terrible'.

Porto de Pedra de Lume was the first settlement on Sal and for many years exported salt, which forms naturally in a nearby volcanic crater. Until less than a decade ago the rusting tugs and lighters employed in this trade remained hauled out on the beach, close to the antique and sadly dilapidated processing machinery. Salt production has now resumed, though largely as a tourist attraction, and it is also possible to swim in the very buoyant, salty water.

Little can have changed at the tiny Porto de Pedra de Lume since its heyday in the salt trade. Now, despite a few small fishing boats and an antique sheerlegs, it has an almost eerie atmosphere

The tiny harbour at Porto de Pedra de Lume. In 2010 a marina development was suggested for the area, a plan which now appears to have been shelved *Sue Thatcher*

In November 2007 visitors to Pedra de Lume (by road) were surprised to see hoardings announcing ambitious plans for the Pedra de Lume Marina and Golf Resort – a large development of houses, apartments and shops fronted by a marina located close east of the current harbour. Three years later a marina was still part of the plan, but all mention of it had been erased by 2011 even though the shoreside development was still being advertised.

There is reported to be a good beach-front restaurant, but otherwise facilities are effectively non-existent.

Despite the tropical climate, bougainvillea needs regular water and attention to thrive

Boavista

Between 15°58'N–16°14'N and 22°40'W–22°58'W

Introduction

Ilha da Boavista is the most easterly of the Cape Verde islands, lying just over 21M south of Ilha do Sal and 42M north-northeast of Ilha do Maio, and covering an area of some 620km². Much of the eastern part is high, reaching 390m at Pico Estância, but visibility is sometimes deceptively poor and the island hidden by haze until only a few miles distant. Until recently it was one of the least developed of the Cape Verde islands and still has the lowest population density, despite a rise from about 3,500 inhabitants in 1990 to more than 6,000 in 2010.

With its giant sand dunes and thousands of date palms, Boavista has aptly been described as 'a small piece of the Sahara adrift in the Atlantic Ocean', and it is well worth visiting the unexpectedly attractive interior. After centuries of being virtually ignored, its miles of white sand beach, excellent windsurfing and interesting diving (more than 200 known wrecks litter the shores of Boavista), now attract many thousands of tourists each year – enough to warrant the building of an international airport handling direct flights from northern European countries including the United Kingdom. Several enormous luxury hotels cater for the influx, and many tourist village developments were begun – though not all completed – before the global recession set in.

In addition to the anchorage off Porto de Sal Rei, between January and March it may be possible to anchor off the long white beach at Santa Monica on the south coast of the island, but later in the year swell makes this unpleasant or downright impossible. The so-called Porto Ferreira on the east coast is a port in name only, unsuitable for yachts and with very little ashore.

'Down at the waterhole' – the water tank and communal laundry near the beach at Vila de Sal Rei are a focus of village life *Sue Thatcher*

Telecommunications

Mobile (cell) phone reception is good in and around Sal Rei, though note the limitation detailed on page 329. The country code for the Republic of Cape Verde islands is 238, with no individual island or area codes, and the telephone number always contains seven digits. If only six are given, add a 2 (for landlines) or 9 (for mobiles) at the beginning.

Internet access is possible at several cybercafés in Sal Rei but is said to go down fairly frequently.

Websites

In addition to several pages on www.en.wikipedia.org/wiki/Cape_Verde and others on the excellent www.caboverde.com, the island has its own website at www.boavistaexperience.com. Though aimed primarily at those considering a holiday or property purchase on the island, it also includes unexpectedly comprehensive sections on the history, geography and economy of the Cape Verdes as a whole and Boavista in particular.

Approach

Ilha da Boavista is most likely to be approached from the north or east, both of which require particular care. Generous allowance must be made for the strong south or southwest-going current, and an offing of at least 4M maintained along the northeast coast to avoid the breaking reefs of Cabeça da Rifona. The island should be closed to within 1M only after Ponta do Sol comes abeam.

Navigation

Waypoints
⊕ CV06 – 16°15′·8N 22°57′·5W (3M NW of Pta do Sol)
⊕ CV07 – 16°11′·2N 22°57′·1W (1M NW of Ilhéu de Sal Rei, NW point)
⊕ CV08 – 16°02′·6N 23°01′·2W (3M W of Pta Varandinha)
⊕ CV09 – 15°59′·8N 23°00′·3W (3M SW of Pta Varandinha)
⊕ CV10 – 15°47′·7N 23°05′W (4M ESE of Baixo de João Valente)

Courses and distances
⊕ CV06 – ⊕ CV03 (1M WSW of Porto de Palmeira, Ilha do Sal) = 29M, 355° / 175°
⊕ CV06 – ⊕ CV07 = 4·6M, 175° / 355°
⊕ CV07 – ⊕ CV08 = 9·5M, 205° / 025°
⊕ CV08 – ⊕ CV09 = 3M, 163° / 243°
⊕ CV07 – ⊕ CV15 (2M S of Pta Vermelharia, São Nicolau) = 81M, 281° / 091°
⊕ CV08 – ⊕ CV35 (4M N of Pta Moreia, Santiago) = 56M, 227° / 047°
⊕ CV08 – ⊕ CV32 (3M NW of Pta Cais, Ilha do Maio) via ⊕ CV10 = 42M, 194° & 197° / 017° & 014°
⊕ CV08 – ⊕ CV36 (4M NNE of Pta do Lobo, Santiago) via ⊕ CV10 = 63M, 194° & 203° / 023° & 014°

Magnetic variation
10°10′W (2011), decreasing by 8′E annually. Local magnetic anomalies are reported to exist east of Boavista.

Tidal Streams
Although tidal streams as such are weak, generous allowance must be made for the strong south-southwest setting current in the channel between Ilha do Sal and Boavista.

Charts
Admiralty *366* (1:500,000)
US *51520* (1:250,000)
Imray-Iolaire *E4* (1:500,000)

Lights
2919·5 **Ponta do Sol** Fl(4)15s117m12M
017°-vis-272° Metal tower 7m
2914 **Morro Negro**
Fl.20s163m31M 163°-vis-035°
Square white turret on building 12m
2916 **Ponta Varandinha**
Fl(2)6s22m10M Lantern on red structure 7m
Racon *V* every 30s 310°-194° 24M

CAUTION
The maintenance of lights around Boavista appears consistently poor, even by Cape Verdean standards. In 2002 the *Capitão do Porto* took pains to stress their unreliability, and nine years later things had not changed. In April 2011 only one of Porto de Sal Rei's four lights was working, and that with characteristics quite different to those listed. Approaching the island in darkness, even with current charts and GPS, would be unwise in the extreme.

If departing Sal Rei's southern anchorage for Ilha do Maio or Santiago it is essential to leave on a bearing of not less than 220° in order to clear the Baixo Vauban, a reef running almost 1·5M offshore west-southwest of Ponta do Morro d'Areia.

Anchorages

Porto de Sal Rei

16°10′·67N 22°55′·51W (breakwater head)
16°09′·9N 22°55′·1W (southern anchorage)

Waypoint
⊕ CV07 – 16°11′·2N 22°57′·1W (1M NW of Ilhéu de Sal Rei, NW point)

Tides
Time difference on Dakar: –0020, on Mindelo (Porto Grande): +0025. Predictions for Porto de Sal Rei are available via Admiralty *EasyTide* – see page 336
Mean spring range 1·0m
Mean neap range 0·4m

Plans
Admiralty *369* (1:50,000) (based on surveys dating from 1905 and 1950, and seriously inaccurate; soundings in fathoms)
Portuguese *67503* (10,000)
Imray-Iolaire *E4* (1:30,000)

Lights
2919·6 **Breakwater** Iso.R.4s6m5M
Concrete column on wall 1m
(reported not working April 2011)
2918·1 **Ponta de Escuma (Ilhéu de Sal Rei, NW)**
Fl(5)G.20s9m7M Lantern on metal post 3m
(reported to be LFl.G.4s in April 2011)
2918 **Calheta do Velho (Ilhéu de Sal Rei)**
Fl(5)WR.20s28m11M 220°-R-355°-W-220°
Column close to grey building 8m
(reported not working April 2011)
2919 **Inner quay** Fl(3)R.12s8m5M
Red lantern on building 6m
(reported not working April 2011)
Communications tower F.R. Lattice tower
2917 **Ribeira de Rabil**
Fl(3)G.5s16m5M 010°-vis-120°
Metal column with lantern 5m
(situated at the airport about 1M inland)

Anchorage close to excellent beaches

Vila de Sal Rei, lying inside the island of the same name, remains a small town despite growing rapidly for the past decade – nearly all the new tourist developments take advantage of the beaches further south. There is a small concrete quay used by fishermen, but cargo is landed at the breakwater to the north.

In 2011 work was under way on a large, new outer breakwater which will much improve protecion in the northern anchorage – see plan overleaf.

The beautiful beaches south of Sal Rei are long, clean and almost deserted – other than where they front tourist hotels or other new developments – though landing is often difficult due to the swell. Sailboards are available for hire, and the area has a growing international reputation as an outstanding venue for the sport. There are also several PADI-accredited dive schools.

Approach and anchorage – southern

Visiting yachts normally anchor in the bight formed by the southern end of the island and the shore, sheltered from north through northeast to southeast, with some protection around to south.

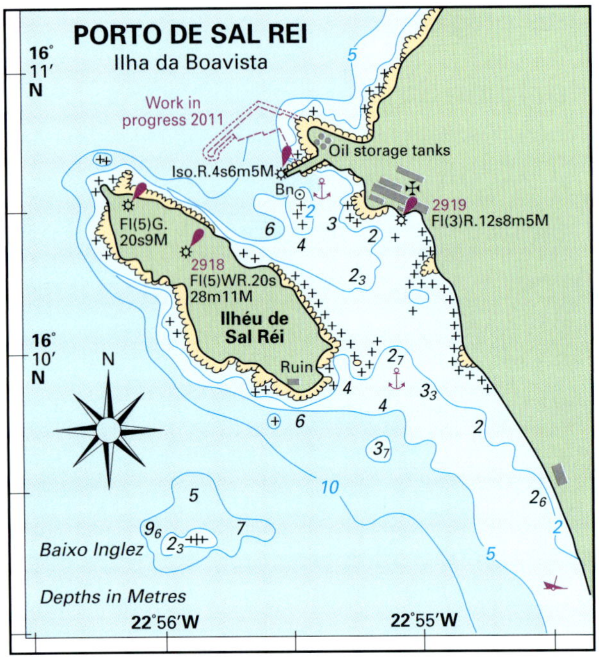

Approach in daylight only, keeping well offshore in 25m or more until Ilhéu de Sal Rei bears due east. A ruined chapel and large cross are clearly visible about halfway along the island. Then close the island to the 10m contour (some 400m offshore) and skirt its southern end, passing inside Baixo Inglez which lies 0·65M off the island at 16°09′·3N 22°55′·9W.

Turn east when the ruined fort comes abeam and hold this course until the town bears due north. Then turn northwards and work into a suitable depth for anchoring – the bottom shelves gradually but does vary – and 4–5m will be found about halfway between the southern point of the island and the shore. Holding is patchy, with rocks underlying the sand in some areas. Take care not to stray too far west as a reef parallels Ilhéu de Sal Rei, its shallowest point at 16°09′·96N 22°55′·27W. Behind it lies a small but excellent (and usually deserted) beach, where a dinghy can be left while exploring the island.

It is not possible to reach the village from the south by yacht due to shoals – access is via a dinghy passage carrying about 1m. Stone steps provide a convenient dinghy landing point, though the dinghy itself would be better left on the small beach just north of the old quay. There does not appear to be a security problem in Boavista, but even so a padlocked wire strop might be wise to deter 'borrowing'. If using an outboard, beware the floating lines used by moored boats tied off to the pier.

Particular care should be taken if visiting the area during summer or autumn when south or southeasterly winds are common. Though seldom strong, they can rise without warning and set up a heavy swell which makes it difficult if not impossible for a vessel to leave the bay. Even in winter when the northeast trades are established, gales further north may set up a northwesterly swell which runs down both sides of Ilhéu de Sal Rei, breaking heavily on Baixo Inglez, causing the reef between the island and the town to break all the way across, and even producing white water on the 3·7m patch south of the anchorage. The only thing to do in such conditions is to get out while it is still safe to do so – conditions offshore are likely to be much pleasanter.

Approaching Porto de Sal Rei from the northwest. Although the breakwater should be marked by a light, it very seldom works *Terry O'Brien*

The view southwest across the southern anchorage at Porto de Sal Rei, seen from the root of the old fishermen's quay. The harbour office can just be seen beyond the tree, while the blue building on the right is a bougainvillaea-shaded restaurant

Looking east across Porto de Sal Rei's north anchorage. The unlit beacon can be seen near the left side of the picture with its associated reef breaking in the foreground *Chris Smith*

Approach and anchorage – northern

Weather permitting and subject to space it may be possible for a yacht to anchor south of the new breakwater or even lie alongside, albeit briefly, in 3m or more. Extreme caution is needed, however, as the area can quickly become dangerous if the weather deteriorates and particularly if a northwesterly swell develops. The new outer breakwater – see plan opposite – should partially alleviate this problem.

Do NOT attempt entry other than in light winds and good daylight, even after work on the new breakwater is complete. Five silver fuel tanks visible from well offshore, lie close to the breakwater root. Approach the northwest end of Ilhéu de Sal Réi on a southerly bearing, alteringcourse for the entrance channel at approximately 16°11'N 22°56'·2W and keeping the (unlit) beacon which marks the central reef slightly open of the inner breakwater. Round the end of the latter about halfway between the two. A number of charter yachts and fishing boats are likely to be found in its shelter, either on moorings or multiple anchors, making a tripline a necessity. Note that all the buoys are private – should one be free a 'day trip' boat is almost certain to return to it before the evening.

The reef extends more than 200m south-southeast from the beacon, but the channel between it and the shore carries 3m or more at its northern end decreasing as one continues south – sufficient for an outboard nearly all the way to the old quay. Alternatively, there is a slipway on the south side of the breakwater where it might be possible to land by dinghy, as although the whole area is closed off by a gate complete with uniformed guard the attitude appears fairly relaxed.

Formalities

Boavista has recently joined the three other islands where inward clearance to the Republic of Cape Verde can be obtained – see Entry and regulations, page 333. Perhaps more importantly – since few cruising yachtsmen will choose it as an initial landfall – visas are issued at the airport, should a crew member be leaving the yacht.

On arrival, the skipper should visit the *Delegação Marítima* (harbour office) on the old quay, open 0800–1200 and 1230–1530 Monday to Friday,

Almost the reciprocal of the view above, with the beacon on the right and the northern part of Ilhéu de Sal Rei stretched out behind *Terry O'Brien*

IV. THE CAPE VERDES

Ilhéu de Sal Rei in the evening light, with the reef breaking in the foreground. The 'cross' on the skyline supports the small island's main light (*2918*), said to be as unreliable as its fellows *R Waber*

closed weekends. A fee of CVE 650$ / €6 is payable for a stay of any duration, irrespective of the size of yacht or number of crew, and the ship's papers are normally retained until departure. Provided that immigration clearance has already been obtained at a previous island there is no further paperwork.

Any crew member leaving the yacht by plane will need a visa, normally issued on the spot on payment of CVE 2,500$, €25 or US$40. A photocopy of their passport's information page, plus a couple of spare passport photos, should be available if required. Obtaining a visa should not be left until the last moment, as although the airport immigration desk is always manned when an international flight is due, it may not be when one is due to depart – and without the correct entry and visa stamps in their passport they will NOT be allowed to board their plane.

Facilities

In early 2011 the commercial harbour was being developed to the north of the breakwater. Local sources report that a boatyard is planned, together with several pontoons to be placed in the anchorage, though whether these will offer space for visitors or be purely for the use of local charter boats remains to be seen.

Water By can from a blue building on the road leading northwards out of the main square. Although it appears clean it would nevertheless be unwise to drink it without treatment – bottled water is available in every shop and is bought by all, including local people. Also distinctly cloudy water from an aluminium tank on the front just north of the old quay, next to a communal laundry building. Small charges are made at both facilities.

Showers Try one of the hotels.

Fuel By can from one of the two filling stations on the road south out of town. It may be possible to order larger quantities of diesel delivered to the breakwater by road tanker, but Palmeira and Mindelo are much better options for fuelling up. The large Shell depot close northeast of the breakwater is not a retail operation.

Bank Several around the main square, all open 0800–1500 Monday to Friday, with cash dispensers.

Shops/provisioning Several supermarkets of varying size with reasonably good stocks (though not, apparently, of UHT milk), plus small pharmacy, hardware stores, etc. There is a small tourist bakery, though bread rolls are usually available in the produce market – ask if they cannot be seen, as they may well be covered against flies.

Produce market Large, airy produce market on the main square. Stocks vary (depending on when the cargo ship last called) but generally include a reasonable variety of tropical fruits and vegetables. Take your own bags.

Restaurants A good choice, both European and locally owned. Booking is generally required, particularly for fresh lobster. Credit cards are unlikely to be accepted.

Hotel An ever increasing number at all levels, many Italian owned and run.

Medical services New and modern Health Centre, with limited hospital facilities, near the main square.

Communications

Post office In the northwest corner of the town.

Telephones At both the post offices.

Internet access Several internet cafés, though the link is reported to go down fairly frequently. Wi-Fi at the hotels, though not always available to non-residents.

Taxis Readily available, or negotiate with an *aluguer* driver for a day trip. Car hire is also possible, but given that Boavista's better roads are cobbled and the others no more than dirt tracks, most people will prefer to hire their car complete with local driver.

Ferries In theory the inter-island ferry calls every week, but poor weather – particularly northwesterly swell – may cause delays.

Air services The previously tiny airport 5km southeast of the town now handles direct flights to and from northern European countries as well as regular inter-island flights.

Baixo de João Valente

15°48'·7N 23°09'·2W

Waypoint
⊕ CV10 – 15°47'·7N 23°05'W (4M ESE of Baixo de João Valente)

Dangerous shoal, isolated and unmarked

This dangerous unlit shoal lies some 17·5M southwest of Ilha da Boavista, almost straddling the direct course to Ilha de Santiago. The shallowest part, itself divided into two distinct reefs, is said to have less than 2m over it at mean low water – not surprisingly, it breaks in all but the calmest weather. Depths of less than 10m extend nearly 2M to the north-northwest, with the 50m contour enclosing an area some 5M in latitude and 3M in longitude.

The bank is formed mainly of hard basalt rock with a thin covering of broken shells and sand. It is home to a wide variety of fish species and local charter boats visit for the diving, some claiming that it is the best dive site in Cape Verde. It is also a good place to sight whales on the surface.

São Nicolau

Between 16°29'N–16°41'N and 24°01'W–24°26'W

Introduction

São Nicolau, with an area of 388km², is the most easterly of the northwestern group of islands, lying only 9M from Ilhéu Raso but approximately 60M due west of Ilha do Sal. It is very mountainous, reaching 1,304m at Monte Gordo, and is thus wetter and more productive than most of the other islands with fruit, vegetables and sugar cane being grown. Much of the northern and western coastline terminates in sheer cliffs – in 2010 one yachtsman remarked that 'sailing along the north coast, the dramatic scenery was reminiscent of the island at the start of the King Kong film'.

The main town is Vila da Ribeira Brava, near the centre of the island, where nearly 5,000 of the island's 13,000 people live. For many years this was the seat of the Cape Verde diocese, later moved to Santiago, and was also a notable seat of learning in Portuguese colonial times.

Telecommunications

Mobile (cell) phone reception is good around both Porto do Tarrafal and the capital, Ribeira Brava, though there are almost certainly holes in some of the mountain valleys. Note also the limitation detailed on page 329. The country code for the Republic of Cape Verde islands is 238, with no individual island or area codes, and the telephone number always contains seven digits. If only six are given, add a 2 (for landlines) or 9 (for mobiles) at the beginning.

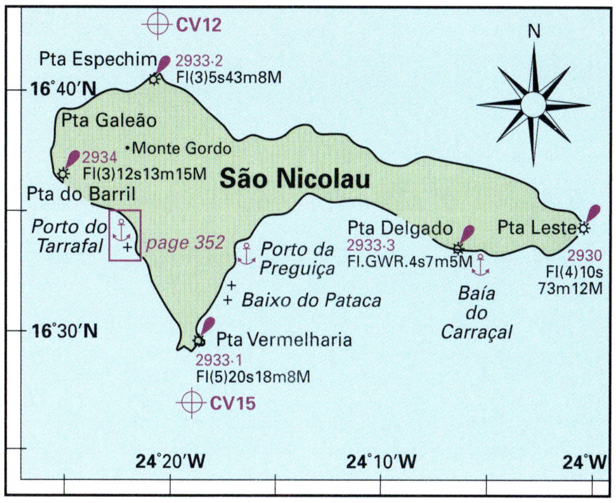

By 2010 the internet could be accessed at internet cafés in both Porto do Tarrafal and Vila da Ribeira Brava, but free Wi-Fi does not yet appear available.

Websites

The internet currently offers no websites devoted solely to São Nicolau, though it has several pages on www.en.wikipedia.org/wiki/Cape_Verde and others on the excellent www.caboverde.com. It also features on several of the general sites listed on page 330.

Parts of the north coast of São Nicolau are very productive, with maize, beans and sugarcane grown on the terraced slopes *Sue Thatcher*

Pounding grain is still a regular household chore, despite the fact that both ladies may well have mobile phones in their pockets *Sue Thatcher*

Navigation

Waypoints
⊕ CV11 – 16°34′·2N 23°59′·3W (2M E of Pta Leste)
⊕ CV12 – 16°42′·9N 24°20′·6W (2M N of Pta Espechim)
⊕ CV13 – 16°39′·9N 24°27′·2W (2M NW of Pta Galeão)
⊕ CV14 – 16°34′·1N 24°22′·2W (0·5M W of Porto do Tarrafal)
⊕ CV15 – 16°26′·8N 24°18′·9W (2M S of Pta Vermelharia)

Courses and distances
⊕ CV11 – ⊕ CV12 = 22M, by eye
⊕ CV11 – ⊕ CV15 = 8M, by eye
⊕ CV12 – ⊕ CV03 (1M WSW of Porto de Palmeira, Ilha do Sal) = 78M, 089° / 269°
⊕ CV12 – ⊕ CV13 = 7M, 245° / 065°
⊕ CV13 – ⊕ CV14 = 20·6M, by eye
⊕ CV13 – ⊕ CV23 (8M NE of Ilhéu dos Passaros, São Vicente) = 34·5M, 308° / 128°
⊕ CV14 – ⊕ CV16 (2M E of Ilhéu Raso) = 10·6M, 287° / 107°
⊕ CV14 – ⊕ CV18 (2M E of Pta dos Tarrafes, Santa Luzia) = 19·5M, 304° / 124°
⊕ CV14 – ⊕ CV38 (2M W of Pta da Janela, Santiago) = 95M, 160° / 340°
⊕ CV15 – ⊕ CV03 (1M WSW of Porto de Palmeira, Ilha do Sal) = 78M, 077° / 257°
⊕ CV15 – ⊕ CV07 (1M NW of Ilhéu de Sal Rei, Boavista) = 81M, 091° / 281°
⊕ CV15 – ⊕ CV14 = 8·5M, by eye

Magnetic variation
10°45′W (2011), decreasing by 8′E annually.

Tidal Streams
Tidal streams set west on the flood and east on the ebb at up to 2 knots.

Charts
Admiralty *366* (1:500,000)
US *51500* (1:250,000)
Imray-Iolaire *E4* (1:500,000)

Lights
2930 **Ponta Leste** Fl(4)10s73m12M
140°-vis-030° White column, red lantern 3m
2933·2 **Ponta Espechim**
Fl(3)5s43m8M Metal column 5m
2934 **Ponta do Barril** Fl(3)12s13m15M
Square white tower and building 9m
2933·1 **Ponta Vermelharia**
Fl(5)20s18m8M Metal column 5m
2933·3 **Ponta Delgado**
Fl.GWR.4s7m5M Metal column 5m

Approach

The exposed north coast should be given at least 1M clearance, increasing to 1·5M around Ponta Espechim. A generous 0·5M gives a safe margin along the south and southwest coasts, except if sailing from Ponta da Vermelharia towards Porto da Preguiça, when the shoals of Baixo do Pataca should be given a wider offing.

Harbours and anchorages

Porto do Tarrafal

16°34′·06N 24°21′·63W (breakwater head)

Waypoint
⊕ CV14 – 16°34′·1N 24°22′·2W (0·5M W of Porto do Tarrafal)

Plans
Cabo Verdean *31* (1:5,000)
Portuguese *67501* (1:5,000)

Lights
2932 **Breakwater**
Iso.R.4s8m5M Red post and lantern 5m

Popular anchorage off growing town

Situated on the southwest coast of the island, Porto do Tarrafal with its substantial breakwater provides shelter from north through east to southwest. A small village when visited in 1993, by 2010 it had grown into a sprawling town with wide cobbled

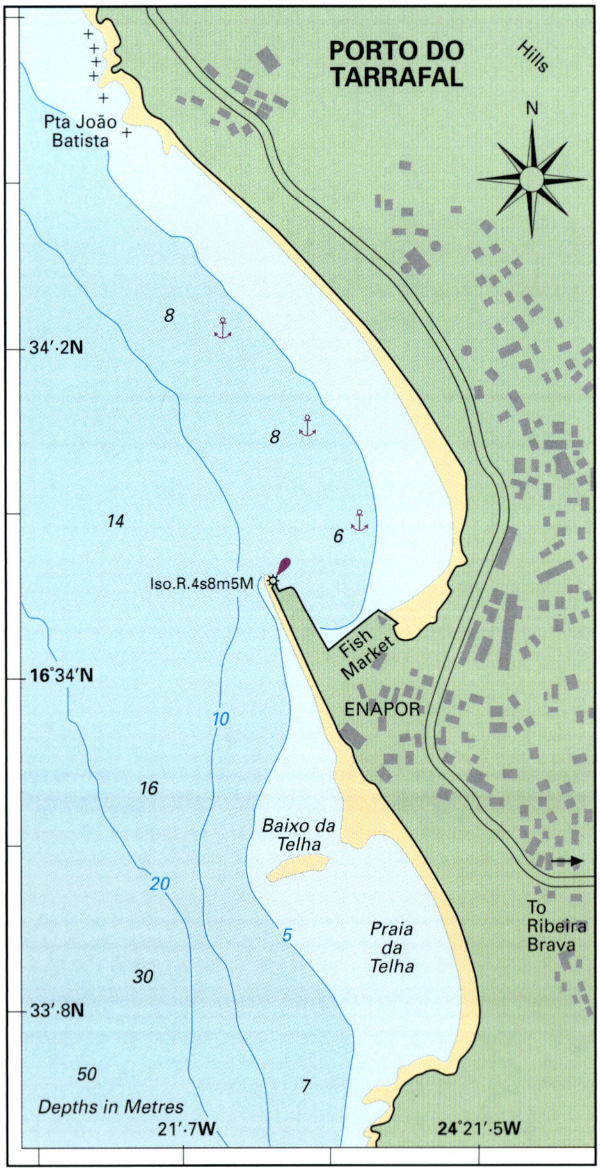

Yachts anchored below the spectacular cliffs at Porto do Tarrafal, looking north. Fierce squalls can funnel down the narrow ravines with little warning, so it is fortunate that the holding is good

streets, sporting a contrasting mixture of old and new buildings and able to meet all daily needs. Many yachtsmen familiar with the Cape Verde islands consider it their favourite anchorage.

The local economy revolves largely around fishing, with tuna and other large fish salted on the quay and a fishmeal processing plant (which generates surprisingly little smell) behind the beach. After years of discussion as to whether a tourist centre should be built to exploit the excellent sport fishing in the channel between São Nicolau and Santa Luzia, where a number of international records are held, construction finally started in 2007. However, by 2010 work appeared to have ground to a halt without much of the supporting infrastructure being in place.

Swimming in the harbour could be unwise, but there is a clean, dark sand beach (complete with local beach bar) five minutes' walk south. The local people are friendly and welcoming towards visitors, and security appears to be good.

Approach and anchorage

The breakwater and village are easily identified from offshore with no hazards on approach, though if coming from the south a minimum offing of 300m should be allowed around the Baixo da Telha. It would be wise not to close the breakwater until it bears northeast.

Holding is mainly good in 5–10m over black sand (fortunate, since fierce northeasterly squalls may funnel down the ravines with little warning) but there are reported to be a few soft patches. Consider laying a second anchor if leaving the boat unattended, even for a few hours. At other times a light onshore wind picks up, making it essential not to anchor too close in. When very crowded – and up to 50 yachts have occasionally been reported – it will be necessary to anchor further north, where holding is variable over rock, stones and black sand.

Ferries and small cargo boats as well as fishing boats use the breakwater and inner quay, and the *Capitão do Porto* rightly insists on yachts keeping well clear of the fairway. Most turn just north of the breakwater and back in, and if an anchored yacht leaves them insufficient space to manoeuvre it will be moved whether or not anyone is aboard. Even so, it might be possible to lie alongside for a limited time by prior arrangement, possibly to load water or fuel – consult the *Capitão do Porto*.

Dinghies can either be pulled up on the slipway at the root of the mole or left on the beach. The latter is likely to attract a posse of young 'boat minders' eager to 'guard' it all day for CVE 100$ / €1 or less. There seem to be even more children in Porto do Tarrafal than in most Cape Verdean towns, all competing to take the painter and demonstrate their skill at tying a bowline, or to help carry the dinghy up the beach. If using an outboard to land near the fish market beware submerged rocks and rubble; if relying on oars bear in mind that when strong northeasterly squalls are blowing it may be difficult or even impossible to make headway in an inflatable.

Formalities

The friendly 'one-stop' *Delegação Marítima* (harbour office) will be found off a short, tree-lined cobbled boulevard running up the hill from the harbour, its entrance up a flight of steps under an L-shaped building. The office is open 0800–1530 Monday to Friday. Entry is quick and straightforward, with some English spoken, and a standard charge of CVE 650$ / €6 payable for a stay of any duration, irrespective of the size of yacht or number of crew. Ship's papers normally retained

The wide bay at Porto do Tarrafal, looking west-southwest

Cruising yachts and local dinghies share the anchorage at Porto do Tarrafal *Chris Smith*

until departure. Provided that immigration clearance has already been obtained at one of the four specified islands – see page 333 – there is no further paperwork.

Facilities

Facilities in the town have improved vastly over the past few decades and the trend looks set to continue.

Engineers The generating station behind the cream wall opposite the beach also contains some engineering equipment, and maintenance staff might be willing to assist in an emergency (provided the language barrier could be overcome).

Water Taps just north of the square building on the beach, and again further up the road, both turned on at set times – enquire locally. Neither is of drinkable quality, but bottled water is readily available.

For larger quantities visit the ENAPOR office (open 0800–1530) at the top of the breakwater steps. A metered tap will be turned on, controlling a hose at the back of the steps.

Showers Try the Pensão Alice (a small green building opposite the beach) or anywhere else offering accommodation. A charge will, of course, be made.

Fuel By can from either of the filling stations on the road out of town. The Shell diesel pump on the quay does not serve yachts. It may be possible to get fuel delivered to the quay by road tanker – enquire at the ENAPOR office.

Bottled gas Camping Gaz from the Shell filling station (which maintains several other compounds around the town) but no facilities to refill other bottles.

Bank On the main square, open mornings only, closed weekends. There is understood to be a cash machine outside.

Shops/provisioning Several small supermarkets stocking basic provisions including eggs, fruit and vegetables. Fish can be bought directly from the boats as they unload at the quay – or sometimes from deck to deck on their way home. There is no produce market.

Restaurants & hotels A growing number of hotels and *pensãos* which serve meals to non-residents (some notice may be required) plus several local café/bars.

Medical services Hospital in Ribeira Brava.

Communications

Post office with telephones On the main square, open weekdays only.

Internet access Two cybercafés in the town as of late 2010, but no public Wi-Fi.

Taxis Congregate on the square near the *Delegação Marítima* office.

Buses Shared *aluguer* minibuses offer excellent value. The ride across the mountain ridge to Ribeira Brava shows a completely different side of São Nicolau and is highly recommended.

Ferries The inter-island ferry calls weekly on its way from Santiago to São Vicente.

Air services Small airport on the road between Ribeira Brava and Porto da Preguiça, with regular inter-island flights.

Looking south over Porto do Tarrafal from Monte Gordo, at 1,312m (4,304 feet) São Nicolau's highest point *Chris Smith*

Porto da Preguiça

16°33'·65N 24°16'·81W (molehead)

Tides
Time difference on Dakar: –0035, Mindelo (Porto Grande): +0010. Predictions for Porto da Preguiça are available via Admiralty *EasyTide* – see page 336
Mean spring range 0·8m
Mean neap range 0·4m

Plans
Admiralty *369* (1:12,230) (based on surveys dating from 1904; soundings in fathoms)
Portuguese *67501* (1:7,500)
Imray-Iolaire *E4* (1:8,500)

Lights
2936 **Porto Velho**
Fl(2+1)R.15s25m5M 285°-vis-016°
Red lantern on white building 7m

Possible anchorage off old quay

Once the main port of São Nicolau, with the building of a breakwater at Porto do Tarrafal the more exposed Porto da Preguiça has reverted to life as a small fishing village where boats are drawn up on the stony beach west of a small quay. A large white building on low cliffs to the east is conspicuous from offshore.

In favourable weather it is possible to anchor off in about 10m, and yachts have been known to go alongside the quay for short periods, though it would be wise to check first by dinghy for underwater obstructions. There are steps on the western side to facilitate landing by dinghy.

Any attempt to close the beach would be unwise due to moored boats and numerous floating lines. Not a harbour to be recommended, and with very little ashore beyond a couple of bars and a communal water tap.

Baía do Carraçal

16°33'·1N 24°05'W (anchorage)

Remote but interesting anchorage

Suggested as a possible anchorage in the *Africa Pilot* (see page 403) but not visited by the author. The following description was received from Jill Schinas, to whom grateful thanks:

> 'The south coast of São Nicolau is of unremitting orange-brown until one reaches Baía do Carraçal. Here a little clump of palm trees and acacias chokes the mouth and meeting place of two *ribeiras*. The sea has pushed its way into their mouth to form a tiny cove, and the village of Carraçal sits on either side. For a yacht on passage from Ilha do Sal to Tarrafal or vice-versa it would be a good place for an overnight stop.'

Other reports confirm that the village of white houses is easy to spot, but the bay is small with shoals on either side. Though offering shelter from the northeast trades it can be rolly in any swell. There is a disused tuna-canning factory on the shore.

Anchorage

Jill recommends:

> 'Anchor just outside the cove in about 12m, but beware of isolated rocks on either side. It is also possible to anchor inside the cove and take a line ashore (there is insufficient swinging room for normal anchoring). Landing is easy on the black sand beach, and the local people friendly without being pushy.'

Looking southwest along the south coast of São Nicolau past the old town of Preguiça and its tiny quay

Santa Luzia

Between 16°44′N–16°48′N and 24°41′W–24°48′W

Introduction

Santa Luzia is separated from São Vicente by the 4·5M wide Canal de Santa Luzia. At less than 12km long it is one of the smaller of the Cape Verde islands and has very little vegetation and no permanent inhabitants, though fishermen may stay for periods of a week or more, camping in the derelict village on the southwest coast. However it is said to be home to a variety of feral animals including donkeys, goats, cats and dogs (though possibly the latter had travelled to the island with the fishermen).

The southeast coast is flat, uninteresting and completely exposed, and the 'landing place' marked at Praia Francisco on BA *369* could only be usable in very light winds from north or northwest.

Having been unable to visit the island myself, I would particularly like to thank Jill Schinas for much of the following information, and Henry Buchanan and Chris Bates for confirming and adding to it.

Websites

Perhaps unsurprisingly, there appear to be no websites devoted solely to Santa Luzia, though it has a few pages on www.en.wikipedia.org/wiki/Cape_Verde. It is the only island without a page on www.caboverde.com, but does feature on several of the other general sites listed on page 330.

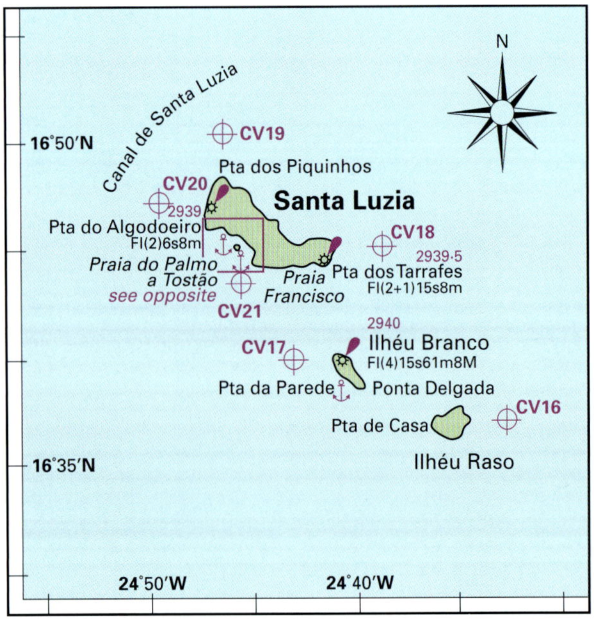

Navigation

Waypoints

⊕ CV16 – 16°37′·2N 24°32′·7W (2M E of Ilhéu Raso)
⊕ CV17 – 16°40′N 24°43′·2W (2M W of Ilhéu Branco)
⊕ CV18 – 16°45′·1N 24°38′·9W (2M E of Pta dos Tarrafes)
⊕ CV19 – 16°50′·4N 24°46′·6W (2M N of Pta dos Piquinhos)
⊕ CV20 – 16°47′·1N 24°49′·6W (2M W of Pta do Algodoeiro)
⊕ CV21 – 16°43′·5N 24°45′·5W (1M SW of Pta do Laje)

Courses and distances

⊕ CV16 – ⊕ CV14 (0·5M W of Porto do Tarrafal, São Nicolau) = 10·6M, 107° / 287°
⊕ CV17 – ⊕ CV26 (1M S of Pta Lombinho, São Vicente) = 16M, 290° / 110°
⊕ CV18 – ⊕ CV14 (0·5M W of Porto do Tarrafal, São Nicolau) = 19·5M, 124° / 304°
⊕ CV18 – ⊕ CV19 = 9M, 306° / 126°
⊕ CV18 – ⊕ CV21 = 6·5m, by eye
⊕ CV19 – ⊕ CV20 = 4·4M, 221° / 041°
⊕ CV20 – ⊕ CV21 = 5·3M, 132° / 312°
⊕ CV20 – ⊕ CV26 (1M S of Pta Lombinho, São Vicente) = 9M, 260° / 080°

Magnetic variation

10°55′W (2011), decreasing by 8′E annually.

Tidal Streams

Tidal streams can run strongly in the Canal de Santa Luzia, the northeast-going stream beginning about three hours before HW (though in practice the tidal stream overrules the ocean current only after very prolonged periods of light winds) and the southwest-going stream – which combined with the ocean current can reach 4 knots or more – beginning about two hours after HW.

Around the rest of the island tidal streams set west on the flood and east on the ebb at up to 2 knots.

Charts

Admiralty *369* (1:90,440) (based on surveys dating from 1952; soundings in fathoms)
US *51500* (1:250,000)
Imray-Iolaire *E4* (1:500,000)

Lights

2939 **Ponta do Algodoeiro**
Fl(2)6s8m Metal column 5m
2939·5 **Ponta dos Tarrafes**
Fl(2+1)15s8m Metal column 5m

Approach

The surrounding waters are poorly charted and the island should therefore be given an offing of at least 1M, particularly at its eastern end. Wind over tide plus the uneven and relatively shallow depths can make for very confused seas. At times the wind can blow right round Ilha da Santa Luzia, suddenly turning the prevailing northeast wind into a southerly.

Santa Luzia in unusually green mode in November 2010
Chris Bates

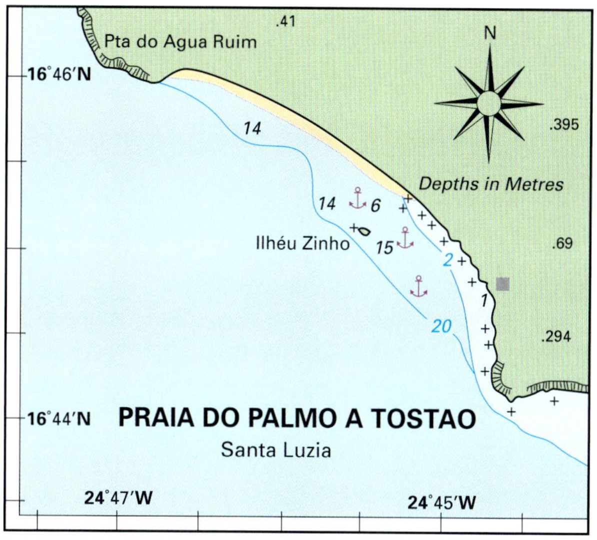

Anchorages

Praia do Palmo a Tostão

16°45′·1N 24°45′·5W (Ilhéu Zinho)

Tides
Time difference on Dakar: –0040, on Mindelo (Porto Grande): +0005. Predictions for Santa Luzia are available via Admiralty *EasyTide* – see page 336
Mean spring range 0·8m
Mean neap range 0·6m

Windy anchorage off deserted beach

A shallow bay on the southwest coast backed by a sandy beach, affording protection from northwest through northeast to southeast. The 12m Ilhéu Zinho, with outlying rocks, lies some 500m offshore in the centre of the bay and anchorage may be made either side of it, or between it and the shore, over good holding in about 6m. The shallow shelf broadens considerably towards the southeast end of the beach. There is no fresh water or other facilities.

The anchorage is prone to williwaws which may peak at more than twice the average wind speed, one yacht experiencing squalls in excess of 50 knots even though no more than 25 knots was encountered once on passage towards São Vicente. In compensation, there is almost limitless swinging room and another yacht reports laying 70m of chain after which 'the williwaws were not a problem'.

Landing by dinghy can be difficult due to surf, and sometimes only those prepared to swim ashore may be able to set foot on the island. The surf is reported to be least inside Ilhéu Zinho and just northwest of the small rocky shelf which extends towards it from the shore. This appears to have little to do with the island, however, and more to the fact that the area is sheltered from the northeast by a hill bracketed by deep ravines which channel the gusts to either side.

Praia do Palmo a Tostão backed by the arid hills of Santa Luzia, in November 2007.
Landing on the beach can be a wet experience! *Henry Buchanan*

Ilhéus Branco e Raso

Navigation

Tidal streams and charts
See under Santa Luzia, page 356.

Unihabited island nature reserves

Tiny islets both less than 3km long, Ilhéu Branco lies 4M southeast of Santa Luzia with Ilhéu Raso some 3·5M beyond. Neither is inhabited. Both are nature reserves and in theory permission is required to visit. Great care should be taken not to disturb birds or other wildlife, including the Cabo Verdean giant gecko. Both islets are high and generally steep-to, and can safely be approached to within 0·5M.

Anchorages

Ilhéu Branco

Bisected by 16°39'·5N 24°40'·2W

Waypoint
⊕CV17 – 16°40'N 24°43'·2W (2M W of Ilhéu Branco)

Lights
2940 **Ilhéu Branco**
Fl(4)15s61m8M Metal column 5m

Challenging island anchorage

Jill Schinas describes Ilhéu Branco as 'magnificent'. The oblong island emerges through the *harmattan* haze as a vast white triangle and only later, as it gets closer, does the surrounding rock come into view. The white patch (from which the island presumably gets its name) is of sand. The island's highest point reaches 327m, and much of the coast consists of sheer cliffs. As with Santa Luzia, fishermen visit and camp ashore, both to fish and to collect young birds for food – the latter causing a catastrophic collapse in the endemic Cape Verde shearwater population. Frigate birds also breed on the island.

It would be possible to anchor anywhere along the south coast of the island, in that it is shallow enough, but in normal trade wind conditions vicious northwesterly gusts (reportedly reaching 50–60 knots) may be encountered between Ponta da Parede and Ponta Delgada in the extreme southeast. More shelter should be found just west of Ponta da Parede in about 8m, where landing can be made on a small, stony beach just east of the white sand patch. The eastern extremity of Branco consists of a flat, low-lying sandy tail where, in very windless conditions, it might also be possible to anchor.

The occasional strong southwesterly gust should be anticipated when anchoring, and any variation on the usual northeast or east-northeast wind would probably allow a swell to work around one or other end of the island.

Ilhéu Raso

Bisected by 16°37'N 24°35'·5W

Waypoint
⊕CV16 – 16°37'·2N 24°32'·7W (2M E of Ilhéu Raso)

An island for birders

Ilhéu Raso consists of an 8km² plateau raised above the sea on a low cliff (less than 2m in places), surmounted by a number of dull, brown mounds, the tallest reaching only 164m. The southwestern area is flat and rocky, intersected by dry riverbeds. There is little vegetation. The island's only real attraction is the colonies of seabirds which nest there – including the brown booby, red-billed tropicbird, shearwaters and petrels – plus the Raso lark which is found nowhere else in the world and is thought to number no more than 40 pairs.

Visiting fishermen anchor off a tiny inlet with a ancient quay close northwest of Ponta de Casa at the southwest corner of the island, possibly in considerable depths.

Cape Verdes is proud of its diverse wildlife. Turtles – *tartarugas* – frequent the archipelago's waters and lay their eggs on some of the quieter beaches. The Iago sparrow is endemic to the Cape Verdes and was first described by Charles Darwin in 1832. It nests on most of the islands, including Ilhéus Branco e Raso

São Vicente

Between 16°46'N–16°55'N and 24°52'W–25°06'W

Introduction

Much of São Vicente's 227km² is hilly, in contrast to a low-lying peninsula on the northeast coast and extensive sand dunes south and east of Baía do Porto Grande on which Mindelo, the archipelago's second largest city, is situated. When seen from the northeast at 25–30M the western hills appear to be detached from the main mass centred around the 774m Monte Verde, the summit of which is often hidden in haze.

The entire island – including the optimistically named Monte Verde – is very lacking in both natural water and vegetation, and is largely of an unrelieved sandy brown. Almost all its 76,000 population live in Mindelo and its surrounding suburbs.

The island was discovered on 22 January 1462, the feast day of Saint Vincent, hence its name. Being unsuitable for agriculture it remained largely uninhabited until 1838, when a coal bunkering station was established to supply the early Atlantic steamers and Mindelo also became a focal point for transatlantic cables. The attractive old Portuguese customs house on the waterfront in Mindelo, modelled on Lisbon's famous Torré de Belem, still bears witness to the one-time importance of the port.

Carnaval celebrations, said to be the most lively in the Cape Verdes, take place in Mindelo during the days before Lent. Many shops, banks and other businesses are closed on the Tuesday and Wednesday, and some remain shut all week.

Mindelo in the early years of the 20th century, photographed from almost the same spot as the panorama on page 363

Telecommunications

Mobile (cell) phone reception is excellent in and around Mindelo, certainly as far as the airport, and is believed to cover the entire island, though note the limitation detailed on page 329. The country code for the Republic of Cape Verde islands is 238, with no individual island or area codes, and the telephone number always contains seven digits. If only six are given, add a 2 (for landlines) or 9 (for mobiles) at the beginning.

Wi-Fi is available at Mindelo Marina and in several parts of the city, including the main square. As of 2010 there was also at least one cybercafé.

Websites

In addition to several pages on both www.en.wikipedia.org/wiki/Cape_Verde and the excellent www.caboverde.com, Mindelo is served by www.mindelo.info, a newspaper-style site with reports on past and future events plus some island history. www.thinkcapeverde.com is the site of a property company based in Mindelo, with a little background information on the Cape Verdes as a whole but apparently nothing specifically about São Vicente. The island also features on several of the general sites listed on page 330.

Navigation

Waypoints
⊕ CV20 – 16°47'·1N 24°49'·6W (2M W of Pta do Algodoeiro, Santa Luzia)
⊕ CV22 – 16°53'·7N 24°49'·2W (3M NE of Pta do Calhau)
⊕ CV28 – 17°06'N 24°53'·7W (4M E of Pta da Tumba, Santo Antão)
⊕ CV23 – 17°01'N 24°55'·6W (8M NE of Ilhéu dos Passaros)
⊕ CV24 – 16°53'·6N 25°01'W (1M WNW of Mindelo)
⊕ CV25 – 16°50'·3N 25°07'·1W (2M W of Pta Machado)
⊕ CV26 – 16°45'·6N 24°58'·8W (1M S of Pta Lombinho)

Courses and distances
⊕ CV28 – ⊕ CV23 = 5·3M, 200° / 020°
⊕ CV23 – ⊕ CV03 (1M WSW of Porto de Palmeira, Ilha do Sal) = 113M, 098° / 278°
⊕ CV23 – ⊕ CV13 (2M NW of Pta Galeão, São Nicolau) = 34·5M, 128° / 308°
⊕ CV23 – ⊕ CV24 = 9M, 215° / 035°
⊕ CV24 – ⊕ CV25 = 7·5M, by eye
⊕ CV24 – ⊕ CV29 (0·5M SE of Porto Novo, Santo Antão) = 7·3M, 343° / 163°
⊕ CV25 – ⊕ CV26 = 9·2M, by eye
⊕ CV25 – ⊕ CV30 (2M S of Pta do Pesqueiro Fundo, Santo Antão) = 10·6M, 281° / 101°
⊕ CV25 – ⊕ CV35 (4M N of Pta Moreia, Santiago) = 118M, 137° / 317°
⊕ CV25 – ⊕ CV38 (2M W of Pta da Janela, Santiago) = 130M, 144° / 324°
⊕ CV25 – ⊕ CV43 (1·5M W of Vale de Cavaleiros, Ilha do Fogo) = 120M, 163° / 343°
⊕ CV25 – ⊕ CV44 (3M E of Ilhéu de Cima, Ilha Brava) = 116M, 164° / 344°
⊕ CV25 – ⊕ CV45 (3M W of Ilhéu Grande, Ilha Brava) = 114M, 169° / 349°
⊕ CV26 – ⊕ CV17 (2M W of Ilhéu Branco) = 16M, 110° / 290°
⊕ CV26 – ⊕ CV20 (2M W of Pta do Algodoeiro, Santa Luzia) = 9M, 080° / 260°

Magnetic variation
11°10'W (2011), decreasing by 8'E annually.

Tidal Streams
Tidal streams run strongly in both the Canal de São Vicente and Canal de Santa Luzia, the northeast-going stream beginning 3·5 hours before HW and the southwest-going stream about 2·5 hours after HW. The latter can reach 2·5 knots in the Canal de São Vicente and 4 knots or more in the Canal de Santa Luzia when combined with the southwest-going current.

Charts
Admiralty *366* (1:500,000), *367* (1:150,000)
US *51500* (1:250,000)
Imray-Iolaire *E4* (1:500,000)

Lights
2942 **Ilhéu dos Pássaros (Dom Luís)**
Fl(3)12s86m14M 057°-vis-091° & 196°-vis-258°
White pyramid, red lantern 5m
Note Obscured from offshore 091°-196° by Santo Antão and 258°-057° by São Vicente, but visible if passing between the two larger islands
2944·5 **Salamanza**
Fl(2)WRG.6s8m5M Metal tower 5m
2944·4 **Baía das Gatas**
Fl(3)R.12s9m6M Metal tower 5m
2944·6 **Ponta do Calhau**
Fl(4)WRG.15s9m5M Metal tower 5m
2946 **Ponta Machado (Dona Amélia)**
Fl.5s56m17M 302°-vis-172°
Square white tower and building 14m

Coast Radio Station
São Vicente 16°51'·5N 24°59'·1W
VHF Ch 16 (24 hours), 18, 19
DSC VHF Ch 70 MMSI 006170000 16°52'·1N 24°56'W
✆ 232 2158/2263 *Fax* 231 1882
Email s.movelmaritimo@cvtelecom.cv

Maritime Rescue Coordination Centre
16°52'·1N 24°56'W ✆ 238 4342/6475
Email capitaniasv@cvtelecom.cv VHF Ch 16, 70 (24 hours)
(This station does not accept public correspondence other than distress and safety traffic)

Navtex
Ribeira de Vinha, identification letters 'U' and 'P'. Transmissions in English (U) are on the standard Navtex frequency of 518kHz, those in Portuguese (P) are on 490kHz. Ribeira de Vinha 'U' transmits weather bulletins and navigational warnings in English at 0320, 0720, 1120, 1520, 1920, 2320 UT. Ribeira de Vinha 'P' transmits the same information in Portuguese at 0230, 0630, 1030, 1430, 1830, 2230 UT. (Several yachtsmen have commented on the unreliability of this station, which is sometimes off the air for extended periods and at others may transmit the same information for several days running.)

Carnaval in Mindelo caters for all age groups – here the junior prince and princess set off with their attendants

Approach
São Vicente is separated from Santo Antão to the northwest by the 6·5M wide Canal de São Vicente, and from Santa Luzia to the southeast by the 4·5M wide Canal de Santa Luzia. Both are deep and clear of dangers, but the strong tidal currents can build large seas, particularly on the flood. The small islet of Ilhéu dos Pássaros lies 0·75M northwest of Ponta João Ribeira, close north of Mindelo, and can be passed in deep water on either side. There is also good water close inshore all around São Vicente and an offing of 0·5M is adequate except in the vicinity of Ponta Viana on the east coast where at least 1M should be allowed.

Harbours and anchorages

Mindelo (Porto Grande)

16°53'·28N 25°00'·06W (outer breakwater head)

Waypoint
⊕ CV24 – 16°53'·6N 25°01'W (1M WNW of Mindelo)

Tides
Portuguese tide tables are available for Mindelo (Porto Grande), alternatively the standard port is Dakar – see Tides and tidal streams, page 336. MLWS is 0·4m above datum and time difference on Dakar: –0045. Predictions for Mindelo (Porto Grande) are also available via Admiralty *EasyTide* – see page 336
Mean spring range 0·8m
Mean neap range 0·5m

Plans
Admiralty *367* (150,000 and 17,500)
Cabo Verdean *41* (scale unknown)
Portuguese *66302* (10,000)
US *51500* (1:20,000)
Imray-Iolaire *E4* (1:20,000)

Lights
2943 **Cabnave Shipyard**
Fl.R.2s8m5M Metal post 4m
2944 **Breakwater, outer arm**
Fl.R.3s10m6M White column 8m
2944·2 **Breakwater, inner arm**
Fl.G.4s10m5M White column 8m
2944·3 **Ferry quay**
Iso.Y.4s6m5M Post 4m
Marina, outer pontoon
Iso.3s2m2M
Marina, access jetty
Iso.4s2m2M
2943·6 **Comando Naval Lts in line on 076°** (occas)
F.R.20/27m5M Buildings (lights 530m apart)
Note Not leading lights – see Entrance, below
Fishing harbour detached mole, W end
Fl.R.5s5m4M
Square white column, red lantern 2m
Fishing harbour detached mole, E end
Fl.G.5s5m4M
Square white column, green lantern 2m
2943·4 **Oil tanker berth Lts in line on 147°** (occas)
F.G.13/19m 5M (lights 790m apart)
buoy **Tanker berth No 2**
buoy **Tanker berth No 4**
Both Fl.6s3M on white pillar buoys, plus other unlit buoys nearby

Harbour communications
Port Authority ✆ 231 4492/4144 *Fax* 231 4281
VHF Ch 15
Marina Mindelo ✆ 230 0032, 991 5878, 997 2322
Email mail@marinamindelo.com or reserve@marinamindelo.com
www.marinamindelo.com VHF Ch 09 (0900–1830 Monday to Saturday, 0900–1200 Sunday from 15 October to 15 March, otherwise 0900–1230, 1430–1830 weekdays, 0900–1500 Saturday, closed Sunday)
boatCV ✆ 232 6772, 991 5878 *Fax* 230 0381
Email info@boatcv.com VHF Ch 09 www.boatcv.com
Cabnave Shipyard ✆ 232 1930 *Fax* 232 1935
Lusonave ✆ 232 7928

Well-protected harbour and thriving city

The harbour at Mindelo – still referred to on some charts by its 'colonial' name of Porto Grande – is amongst the finest in the eastern Atlantic, giving total protection from northwest through east to south, and partial protection (with a fetch of up to 2M) from south around to west. Very occasionally a westerly swell can set in but this is rare, and although strong northeasterlies can produce unpredictable gusts these have little fetch. More often cool breezes of 5–10 knots from northeast or east keep the area well ventilated.

The harbour has occasionally seen more than 100 yachts at anchor simultaneously, and with the opening of the long-awaited Marina Mindelo in 2007 the number of visitors passing through looks set to increase. Although the 120-berth marina has inevitably encroached on the anchorage, space for at least 50 yachts remains. It seems that the authorities took some convincing that a marina was a viable proposition, and it says much for the persistence of manager Kai Brosmann and his business partner Lutz Meye-Scheel that it ever saw the light of day. The support services – not to mention the local employment – which it provides continue to increase. There is now little reason for yachts to visit the fishing harbour on the southeast side of the bay – previously the only place where diesel and water tanks could be filled. If choosing to do so, however, note that although it has a least interior depth of 3m at all states of the tide, access is via the southwest entrance only – the northeast one is partially blocked by a wreck.

To the east of the anchorage lies the city of Mindelo, second largest in Cape Verde with a population estimated at more than 70,000. The tall buildings and narrow cobbled streets near the waterfront date back to colonial days, with an occasional patterned pavement in the style typical of older Portuguese towns, whilst the rapidly expanding suburbs separated by wide, tree-lined roads are a great improvement on the depressing shanty-towns which so often surround the cities of less developed countries.

The atmosphere in Mindelo has changed vastly since the first edition of this book was researched in 1987. While poverty clearly exists in some areas,

Looking northwest across the Canal de São Vicente towards Ilhéu dos Pássaros and the steep crags of Santo Antão, with the Mindelo – Porto Novo ferry in the foreground
Henry Buchanan

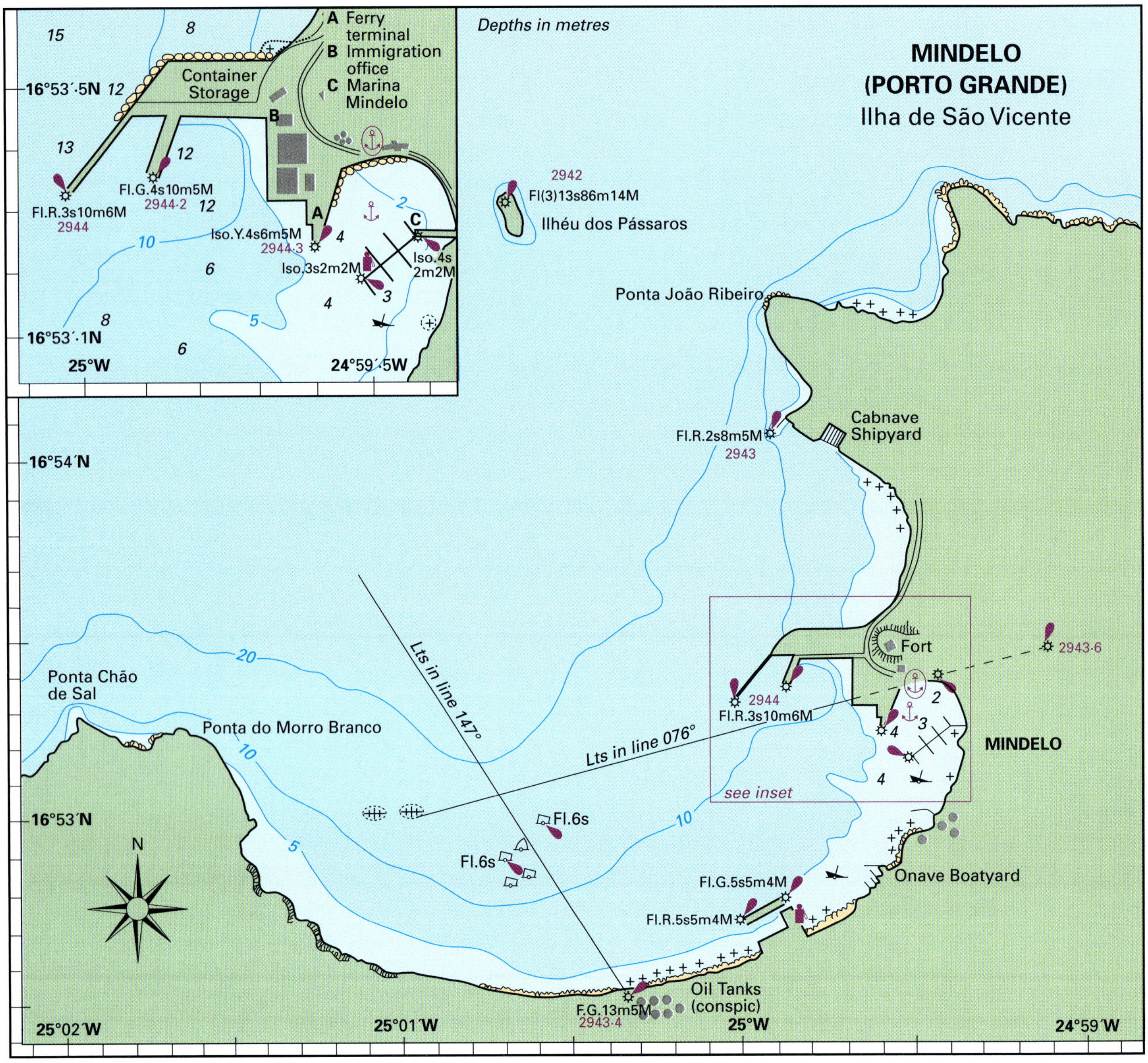

contrasting with the small percentage of ostentatiously rich residents, both are far outnumbered by a prosperous, educated middle-class. The population is young by European standards – around one-third are under 30 – which doubtless promotes the pace of change, and though a few yachtsmen may lament the growing commercialisation of the harbour-front, it is possible they did not experience the hordes of ragged children and starving dogs which used to greet every foreign visitor in hopes of a few escudos or some table scraps – after which even more would appear... There are doubtless areas of Mindelo where it would be unwise for a visitor to venture alone in darkness, but that is true of most cities in most countries. All in all, Mindelo now bears comparison with many of the more interesting cities of southern Europe. Those with an interest in culture should visit the *Museu de Arte Tradicional* on Praça Nova (open 0900–1700 weekdays, 0900–1300 Saturday) to admire its displays of Cape Verdean art and sculpture.

Yachts are not allowed to anchor overnight off the beach at Praia da Laginha, the long bay north of Mindelo, but it deserves mention as the nearest good swimming to the harbour. In settled weather it offers a pleasant if slightly rolly short-term anchorage in about 8m of clear water over sand and eel grass. Alternatively it is only a short walk to the beach whilst leaving the yacht in Mindelo.

An excellent view over the entire area can be obtained from the small hill immediately north of the anchorage, for many years the site of the island's prison but now being redeveloped as a luxury hotel. In early 2010 a Spanish project to build a second marina and redevelop the Lusonave (Onave) boatyard area was reliably stated to be under discussion. However, it was thought unlikely that a start would be made for at least five years.

Caution

The Canal de São Vicente, which separates São Vicente and Santo Antão, is notorious for its strong and gusty winds, the two islands combining to produce a classic venturi effect. Although true throughout the year, this is particularly noticeable between December and May, when the northeasterly winds may increase from 15–20 knots over the open ocean to gusts of 35–40 knots in the channel. Even during the less windy season from June to November, 10 knots elsewhere may increase to 25–30 knots between the islands. Surprisingly, this fact does not appear in the published statistics but has nevertheless been reported by many yachtsmen over the years.

Approach

The vast majority of yachts are likely to approach from the north, but it is straightforward from any direction. Ponta João Ribeiro and the breakwater sheltering the Cabnave shipyard to the north, and Ponta Chão de Sal to the west, may both be rounded at 200–400m, and Ilhéu dos Pássaros passed close on either side. Thence a direct course to the end of the grey stone breakwater clears all dangers, including two unmarked wrecks in the southern part of the bay.

In darkness, bright street lighting in Mindelo and the docks shows as a distinct loom in the sky above the hills when approaching from the north or northeast. The outer breakwater light should be identified without problem, and both the breakwater itself and some oil tanks on the southern shore are brightly lit.

Entrance

Entry in daylight should present no problems and, provided the current edition of Admiralty *367* is to hand, neither should entry in darkness even if – as is quite probable – not all the various lights are operating. Note in particular that the lights in line on 076° lead not into the yacht anchorage or to the marina but straight onto the corner of the substantial stone quay. While several of the potentially dangerous wrecks to the south of the entry line have been removed, slow speeds and a good bow lookout are still necessary to watch for the many anchored ships and unlit buoys and fish-holding pens.

The marina itself is lit, but the six small can buoys which divide it from the yacht anchorage to the north (starboard hand, green) and hazards to the south (port hand, red) are not. Take care if entering the anchorage in darkness. Equally, if approaching the southwest corner of the marina be certain to stay inside the red buoy which lies near it, as a semi-submerged wreck lurks not far to the south. Both buoys and wreck can be seen in the photographs below and on page 365.

Anchorage

Anchor in the northeast corner of the bay, with good holding in firm sand and some mud. Depths of 5–6m in the outer part of the anchorage shoal gradually towards the beach, where some patches of poor holding have been reported. Generous scope, preferably of chain, is required as the prevailing northeasterlies occasionally pick up to gale force (35–40 knots) in the gusts. The water appears to be fairly clean but is far from clear, with visibility seldom more than 2m and less after heavy rain when the entire bay turns brown. There is no charge for anchoring, and rumours that it would be forbidden once the marina was operational are groundless.

Security in the anchorage appears to be much improved, and local officials are reported to have made a serious effort to crack down on harassment and petty crime against visitors both ashore and afloat. Even so, the authorities require that someone is always on board at night. One skipper mentioned

Looking south-southeast over the yacht anchorage at Mindelo, with the marina beyond

the 'conspicuous, but not oppressive police presence around the marina and anchorage', and told how 'on the one night I returned late, I found the *Polícia Marítima* patrolling the anchorage in a RIB'.

Dinghies can normally be left at the marina dinghy pontoon close south of the office, for which CVE 400$ per day was charged in 2011 (a fee said to be necessary due to the amount of garbage transported ashore, for which the city levies high disposal fees). A reduction is available if two weeks are paid for in advance. The pontoon may become overcrowded in November/December, with tenders two or three deep and a boy employed to prevent dinghies from being tied up elsewhere. However, tenders left on the beach appear to be safe enough, possibly due to the *Polícia Marítima* office on the shoreward side of the marina building. If heading towards the beach from the anchorage beware the very solid lump which breaks surface from about half tide and could do serious damage to a dinghy propeller. The old photograph on page 359 shows what appears to be a wreck exactly where this lump still lies.

Berthing

Marina Mindelo accepted its first visiting yachts late in 2007, and contains 120 berths on six pontoons for vessels of up to 30m in length and 4·5m draught. Those to windward of the pontoon have a buoy but no pick-up line; those to leeward have a pick-up line but no buoy – think for a moment of the manoeuvring implications in an area where the wind is nearly always from the same direction and one realises immediately that this marina was designed by a yachtsman! Shore access is via the restored *Cais d'Alfandega Velha*, with the marina office on its outer tip and a security gate alongside, for which a card is obtainable against a CVE 1,000$/ €10 deposit.

Even if prior contact cannot be established on VHF Channel 09, yachts arriving in daylight are likely to be spotted, directed straight to a berth and have their lines taken – particularly helpful with the prevailing northeasterly wind taking the yacht sideways. RIB tow and push boats are available if required.

Approaching Mindelo from the northwest, with the city framed between Ponta João Ribeiro and Ilhéu dos Pássaros
Henry Buchanan

Some motion is nearly always evident, and the marina's own 'General Terms and Conditions' (listed in full on the website) mention 'the strong shear winds ... which appear frequently'. This is very hard on mooring lines, and snubbers (either rubber or steel) are essential, even for short stays. Once in place it would clearly be wise to reinforce the line through the buoy in chafe-resistant fashion.

Formalities

Mindelo is currently one of only four ports in the archipelago where inward clearance to the Republic of Cape Verde can be obtained – see Entry and regulations, page 333.

Entry formalities change from time to time and are best checked at the marina office (whether berthed there or not). There are currently no plans for the relevant officials to be based at the marina – the *Polícia Marítima* at the rear of the building are concerned with general harbour security, while the office between the showers and toilets is occupied by the marina master – often, and confusingly, referred to as the 'harbourmaster'. Neither need be visited by yachtsmen, who should talk to one of the helpful and efficient girls in the office at the top of the marina walkway (in English, French, German or Spanish as well as Portuguese).

On arrival: The two officials who do need to be visited are both in the main port area, in almost adjacent offices. Only the skipper need go, bearing the ship's papers, crewlist and passports. The *Polícia de Fronteira* (Immigration) office (also labelled *Polícia Marítima* and *Guarda Fiscal*), open 0800–1600 weekdays only, is the last on the left as one approaches the main gateway to the port. In 2010 CVE 500$ / €5 was charged for inward clearance. If arriving at the weekend one was expected to clear in on Monday morning.

Any crew member leaving the yacht by plane will need a visa, issued on the spot on payment of CVE 2,500$, €25 or US$40, so must obviously accompany the skipper, taking a spare photocopy of the information page of their passport plus a couple of passport photos, though neither are likely to be needed. Note that the office is closed at weekends, and without the correct entry and visa stamps in their passport they will **NOT** be allowed to board their plane.

Just beyond the *Polícia de Fronteira*, again on the left, is 'Gateway A', complete with uniformed guard. The *Polícia Marítima* (who also represents the harbourmaster) will be found behind the first door on the left in the first building on the left – all totally unmarked. Office hours are again 0800–1600 weekdays only, with the same relaxed 'Monday is fine' attitude to weekend arrivals. A form must be completed and the ship's papers will be held pending departure – unlike in Praia, a photocopy is not acceptable – but no charge is made for entry.

Mindelo Marina seen from due south, with the semi-submerged wreck described on page 363 in the foreground. Like most hazards in Cape Verdean waters it remains unlit *Chris Bates*

On departure: Both the above officials must be visited for the appropriate departure stamps, and the ship's papers reclaimed from the *Polícia Marítima*, for which CVE 650$ was payable in 2010. A receipt will be issued (and should be retained), together with a *Desembaraço de Autoridade Marítima* – particularly important if heading for the Caribbean where proof of one's port of departure is often required. If intending to leave at the weekend the formalities can be completed on Friday afternoon, otherwise one has the usual 24 hours.

If wishing to visit one or more of the smaller islands before leaving territorial waters, request a 'next port' (*próximo porto* or *porto seguinte*) document from the *Delegação Marítima* when clearing out – see page 333.

When visited in early 2010 both officials were pleasant and helpful, and spoke French plus a little English. The atmosphere was noticeably more relaxed than a few years previously and the entire process took no more than 20 minutes – plus the rather hot walk!

Charges

The berthing fee is calculated on a length x beam basis and in 2011 was set at €0.62 per m², including tax but not water, showers or electricity. Prices reduced considerably over longer periods, and discounts of 15% or more were available between April and September. Payment – which must be made on arrival – is accepted in all major currencies, as are credit cards including Visa and Mastercard, though use of a card incurs a surcharge. In common with most marinas, evidence of third party insurance is required.

Facilities

Boatyards/travel-lift Cabnave ✆ 232 1930 *Fax* 232 1935 *Email* cabnave@cvtelecom.cv, situated about 0·75M north of Mindelo, can haul and repair almost anything from a 3,000-tonne ship downwards. In 2010 it was said to no longer handle yachts, but this rule would probably be waived in the case of a megayacht.

Lusonave (referred to locally as Onave), ✆ 232 7928, situated about 0·5M south of the anchorage, no longer has a GRP moulding shed or, indeed, much else other than two marine railways, one with a carriage onto which a deep-keel yacht can be floated and lashed. Although rather decrepit at first sight, Lusonave hauls the boatCV charter fleet every year, so far without incident. Unless fluent in Portuguese it would be wise to ask boatCV to make the necessary arrangements. A travel-lift was still on the latter's wish list in 2011.

Fibreglass products – mat and resin – are available from Matexplas, ✆ 232 7928, on the south side of the Praça Estrela and also opposite the Lusonave entrance gate.

Looking southwest over Mindelo Marina with the dinghy pontoon in the foreground

Many of the buildings which line Mindelo's attractive waterfront date back to Portuguese colonial times. The building at far right, once the customs house, was modelled on Lisbon's famous Torré de Belem

Agents If needing to bring spares or other equipment in by air it is almost certainly worth using an agent, of which there are several in the town – the marina can advise.

Engineers Cabnave, Lusonave and boatCV all have diesel engineers, while the former has a metalwork shop which is said to be able to fabricate virtually anything. boatCV holds Volvo spares, though the mechanics will work on any engine, inboard or outboard. It also stocks a range of new outboards.

Electronic & radio repairs boatCV has a fully equipped electronics workshop and is a certified Raymarine service agent and distributor, though will work on any make. Kai Brosmann is a fully qualified marine electronics engineer and has had a vast amount of experience of fixing autopilots...

Sail repairs boatCV employees handle repairs on two professional machines, working from their homes, but do not make new sails.

Rigging boatCV has a swage machine for wire of up to 12mm, and a good stock of Norseman terminals including larger sizes. Should it be necessary, entire rigs can be ordered and set up.

Chandlery boatCV's Ship Shop (open 0900–1200, 1500–1800 Monday to Saturday), at the landward end of the marina building, holds some basic items including rope, shackles and common spares, with more in a warehouse ashore. Items not in stock can be ordered from abroad – delivery normally takes five days by DHL (very expensive), or four weeks by ordinary mail (usually no extra shipment cost). Visa and MasterCard are accepted.

Maripesca Lda, on Rua de São João stocks mainly fishing gear plus a little general chandlery. Several hardware stores selling electrical cable and fittings, piping, hose clips and other plumbing items, and all kinds of tools will be found in the city.

Charts boatCV stocks Imray-Iolaire charts of the Cape Verde islands and Caribbean. In addition a few charts – including those published locally by the *Direcção Geral de Marinha e Portos*, see page 336 – are normally available at the Casa das Bandeiras at Rua Governador Calheiros 14, though it appears to be a matter of luck what is in stock.

Courtesy flags Printed courtesy flags are available in the marina office for about CVE 1,500$ / €13. Fully sewn flags are made and sold in the African market on Praça Estrela by Mercy Cole at Stall 127 (near the restaurant end). She makes various sizes, a typical 30cm x 40cm courtesy flag costing CVE 800$, albeit without lanyard, and can make or repair any flag to order in an hour or so. Mrs Cole is Nigerian so speaks excellent English, and will normally be found at her stall from 0900–1830 Monday to Saturday.

Photocopying and printing Very cheap copying and printing in both A3 and A4 is available at the Jean Piaget University building just off the western end of the Praça Nova (the small square northeast of the harbour) though note that most charts and pilot books – including this one – are protected by international copyright.

Water On the marina pontoons and available to anchored yachts by arrangement, at CVE 2$ / €0.02 per litre. A storage tank has been installed to overcome the problem of the town's intermittent supply. Payment is via a prepaid card which those berthed in the marina can also use in the shower block.

Showers Smart new showers and toilets behind the marina reception area, available to marina users only. Payment is via prepaid card (see *Water* above), with an average shower costing well under one euro. The alternative is to use the adequate though elderly (cold) showers at the *Clube Náutico* at CVE 100$ a time.

Laundry No launderette is planned for the marina, but there are several full-service laundries in the city. The nearest is Lavanderia Mindelo Express (on the side of the prominent blue building southeast of the Cais d'Alfandega Velha, which charges by the kilo – about CVE 300$ for washing, drying and (optional) ironing. This normally takes 48 hours, but for an additional CVE 150$ one can have same-day turnaround. In late 2010 a new token-operated, self-service laundrette opened on the southeast side of the Praça Estrela, charging CVE 400$ to wash 4·5kg load, plus CVE 300$ for drying.

Electricity At all marina berths, charged by the day according to the load required – 6, 16, 32 or 63 amps.

Fuel The fuel berth (diesel only), operational since November 2009, occupies the western corner of the marina. Arrange times in advance at the office and note that a surcharge is made if paying by credit card. Hours are similar to those of the marina office, but closing 30 minutes earlier at the end of the day. Petrol – and small quantities of diesel, as the marina will not fill cans – is available by can from the Shell filling station on the waterfront south of the *Cais d'Alfandega Velha*.

Bottled gas Camping Gaz cylinders can be exchanged at the Shell filling station mentioned above. A standard 3kg exhange costs less than CVE 500$, with the cylinders visible appearing to be in a good state.

Other makes of cylinder must be taken to Enacol, at their large orange and grey building at the south end of town (open 0800–1300, 1400–1700 weekdays only) for refilling. Only butane is available. The staff, headed by Sr Carlos Costa, are helpful and Sr Costa speaks good English, but cylinders can only be refilled if the correct adaptors are available – the days of a length of rubber hose and two jubilee clips are long past. If filling proves possible it will be done in a matter of minutes, and prices are low.

Ice A freezer producing 'drinks quality' ice cubes is planned for the marina restaurant; meanwhile, cubes can be bought at the small Manafil supermarket behind the *Clube Náutico*, open 0830–1300, 1500–2100 Monday to Saturday.

Weather forecast Posted daily outside the marina office.

Clube náutico Long established in a low building with two gables, opposite the *Cais d'Alfandega Velha*. After a period of seeming neglect in the 1990s, by 2010 the *Clube Náutico de Mindelo* was thriving as a pleasant and shady yachtsmen's bar and restaurant – aptly described by one visitor as 'the Café Sport of the Cape Verde islands' – though without any sign of actual maritime activity. Local musicians play traditional music most evenings, for which a small charge is added to the bill.

Banks Plenty, including several branches of the Banco Comercial do Atlântico, all equipped with cash dispensers which accept Visa and other international credit/debit cards and can be accessed outside banking hours (not always the case in Cabo Verde). If drawing cash against a card inside the bank, or even changing currency, a passport will be required. See also Money, page 328.

Shops/provisioning Although vastly improved since the first edition was researched in 1987, the variety of foodstuffs available is more limited than in Praia. There are several small *supermercados*, including a couple open long hours – Fragata on Praça Nova is open 0900–1300, 1500–0000 from Monday to Saturday and 1800–0000 on Sunday and public holidays – but all have limited ranges and it may be necessary to visit several. Foodstuffs in particular are noticeably more expensive than in the Canaries. Of the several bakeries, the French-run Padaria Français opposite Chez Loucha on Avenida 12 de Setembro is particularly recommended.

Other shops include several pharmacies, photographic shops, footwear, clothing, booksellers and stationers – in fact very much what one would expect to find in a medium-sized UK town.

Produce market Bustling produce market in the renovated *mercado* building on Rua Libertadores de Africa, selling all kinds of fruit and vegetables, familiar and unfamiliar, plus every variety of beans and pulses known to (wo)man. With so much competition the quality is high. The surrounding booths contain several butchers, plus one cubicle apparently selling nothing but eggs (take your own box). Upstairs are assorted boutiques, souvenir and music shops.

The market is open Monday to Saturday from 0800 onwards, though many of the vendors leave by about 1400. Prices are higher than in Madeira or the Canaries and bargaining does not appear to be the custom. Carrier bags, if available, are unlikely to be free.

Fish market On the waterfront next to the old customs house. A good, though sometimes unfamiliar, choice at very reasonable prices is to be found in surroundings of somewhat dubious cleanliness (but it's going to be cooked...). Fish is also sold by roadside vendors on the ajacent streets.

Cafés, restaurants & hotels No shortage of eating places at all levels, many with live local music, and at least a dozen hotels and *residencials* of varying standards and prices. If intending to leave an anchored boat after dark it is essential to organise a watchman – who might well be a crew member from another yacht.

In January 2011 Marina Mindelo opened a floating bar/restaurant, the Marina Club, open 0900–2200 daily. Close south lies the Pont d'Agua complex, a Belgian/Cabo Verdean 'leisure club' containing bars, restaurants, boutiques and a small swimming pool.

Medical services Mindelo Hospital, ✆ 221 9082, is on the east side of the city and is reported to be of good standard. Many of the doctors and other staff speak some English.

Communications

Post office with telephones At the southern end of the Praça Amilcar Cabral. Open 0800–2200 weekdays, 0800–1130 and 1500–1700 Saturday, and 0800–1130 Sundays and holidays.

Mailing address The marina's postal address is: C.P. 1191 – Cais Alfândega Velha, Mindelo, São Vicente, República de Cabo Verde. It is **essential** that the name of the yacht is included. If ordering parts or other goods from abroad the marina office recommends using DHL – other carriers do not appear to be as reliable.

Internet access The marina offers Wi-Fi, in 2010 charging CVE 575$ / €5.22 for 64MB download, CVE 1,056$ / €8.54 for 128MB and CVE 5,750$ / €52.27 for 1GB, the only problem being no warning of when the relevant amount is about to expire. (If your computer is set up to make automatic downloads it will gobble your allowance, so disable them.) Should your computer be acting up, Kai Brosmann has a contact who is said to be a genius at fixing such things.

Free Wi-Fi is sometimes available on the Praça Nova (also known as the Praça Amilcar Cabral) where you can sit outdoors under the trees. It is reported to be most reliable in the evenings. Cybercafés come and go, but in 2010 the Restaurant Esplanada on Avenida 5 de Julho had two computers and charged CVE 300$ per hour or pro rata.

Car hire Several companies in the city and at the airport – see Road transport, page 331.

Taxis Both taxis and communal *aluguers* – see pages 331–2 – are available. As with car hire, rates should be agreed in advance.

Ferries Regular inter-island service, plus daily ferries to Porto Novo, Santo Antão. The ticket office, where timetables are also displayed, is on the ground floor of the imposing new building at the root of the *Cais Cabotagem* (ferry quay).

Air services Frequent inter-island flights from the airfield at São Pedro, 8km southwest of Mindelo, plus two or three flights each week to Lisbon (though it may be considerably cheaper to fly via Ilha do Sal). If needing to confirm a flight (recommended at least 48 hours before departure), note that the TACV office in Mindelo is open 0800–1200, 1430–1700, weekdays only.

The view westwards over Mindelo and the Canal de São Vicente, with Santo Antão showing clearly in the background *Andy O'Grady*

Baía de São Pedro

16°49'3N 25°03'·8W (anchorage)

Blowy beach anchorage

Just over 5M southwest of Mindelo, Baía de São Pedro offers shelter from northwest through northeast to southeast, though northeast winds may funnel down the wide valley and swells can work their way in from the east. Best anchorage is off the small village at the southeast end of the black sand beach in 8–10m over a flat sandy bottom with very good holding. The airport buildings can be seen about 0·5M inland (there are no flights at night) with the approach path over the bay marked by four red buoys. As my informant remarks, 'it may be advisable not to anchor just there'. A submerged wreck has been reported in the vicinity of 16°49'·1N 25°04'·6W. It is not known exactly how accurate this position is, nor the depths over the wreck, so the area should be treated with caution.

When deciding on anchor scope, allow for both the venturi effect created between the islands of São Vicente and Santo Antão – see Caution, page 362 – and that in the valley between Mindelo and São Pedro. Boardsurfing and speedsailing enthusiasts claim that the bay at São Pedro has the best wind in the world, and many records are set there.

A bar and small general store will be found in the village, together with a French-run restaurant and a daily baker's van – at 0600! The Fajã Branca Hotel complex at the western end of the beach caters for non-residents and provides a good buffet lunch (with free transport to/from Mindelo at weekends). Frequent *aluguers* make the trip into Mindelo, with taxis at the airport.

Baía das Gatas

16°54'·16N 24°54'·27W (molehead)

Lights
2944·4 **Baía das Gatas**
Fl(3)R.12s9m6M Metal tower 5m

Unpromising anchorage but good swimming

A small southeast-facing bay on the northeast coast of São Vicente, recently enhanced by a tiny harbour behind a short mole, Baía das Gatas has been suggested as a possible anchorage. With depths of little more than 2m on the rocky bar, however, it appears suitable only for shoal-draught yachts or multihulls willing to eyeball their way in – and then only when the northeast trades are down.

The Baía das Gatas is well worth visiting by road to enjoy a swim or to wander around the small fishing village. There are several cafés and restaurants, and the area is popular with Mindelo residents, some of whom own holiday homes in the area. An international music festival is held at the Baía das Gatas every August.

Santo Antão

Between 16°54'N–17°12'N and 24°58'W–25°22'W

Introduction

The northwesternmost island of the archipelago, Santo Antão is both second largest and second highest, reaching 1,979m in the far west at Tope de Coroa. Due to its greater rainfall it is the most productive island agriculturally of the entire group and lays claim to being the most beautiful, particularly in the north where there are deep, dramatic valleys and forests of pine, eucalyptus and cypress. In contrast, the southern part of the island is much lower and dryer, with scrub or desert vegetation.

The only true harbour on Santo Antão is at Porto Novo, where many of the island's 60,000 people live, and though it is possible to visit by yacht is it far simpler to visit by ferry from Mindelo. After many years during which the crossing was often a wet and windy affair, by 2011 two new ferries were in service providing two or three return trips each day. However, the timetable is somewhat flexible, particular regarding return times, so be sure to check the schedule before booking.

Spectacular scenery in northeastern Santo Antão, where even the precipices appear to have been terraced *Sue Thatcher*

Numerous *aluguers* meet the ferry at Porto Novo and set off for Ribeira Grande (also referred to as Povoação) and Ponta do Sol. Most public *aluguers* use the new east coast road – quicker, but much less scenic – making group hire of a minibus worth considering. The old, cobbled road runs through breathtaking mountain scenery which no visitor should miss.

Finally, check the water temperature at Ponta do Sol! Vulcanologists have been monitoring a steady rise since 1999 which may indicate a forthcoming eruption.

Telecommunications

Mobile (cell) phone reception is good around Porto Novo and Porta do Ponta do Sol, but has not been checked elsewhere, though note the limitation detailed on page 329. The country code for the Republic of Cape Verde islands is 238, with no individual island or area codes, and the telephone number always contains seven digits. If only six are given, add a 2 (for landlines) or 9 (for mobiles) at the beginning. There is, as yet, no public internet access point in Porto Novo though there is understood to be one in Ribeira Grande.

Fruit for sale under the shade of a tree near Porto Novo *Sue Thatcher*

Aluguers load up with goods and passengers on the quay at Porto Novo *Sue Thatcher*

Navigation

Waypoints

⊕ CV27 – 17°16'·4N 25°05'·5W (4M N of Pta do Sol)
⊕ CV28 – 17°06'N 24°53'·7W (4M E of Pta da Tumba)
⊕ CV29 – 17°00'·6N 25°03'·2W (0·5M SE of Porto Novo)
⊕ CV30 – 16°52'·4N 25°17'·9W (2M S of Pta do Pesqueiro Fundo)
⊕ CV31 – 17°02'·8N 25°23'·9W (2M W of Pta Mangrade)

Courses and distances

⊕ CV29 – ⊕ CV24 (1M WNW of Mindelo, São Vicente) = 7·3M, 163° / 343°
⊕ CV27 – ⊕ CV28 = 15·4M, 133° / 313°
⊕ CV27 – ⊕ CV31 = 23M, by eye
⊕ CV28 – ⊕ CV29 = 10·7M, by eye
⊕ CV29 – ⊕ CV30 = 17M, by eye
⊕ CV30 – ⊕ CV25 (2M W of Pta Machado, São Vicente) = 10·6M, 101° / 281°

Magnetic variation

11°15'W (2011), decreasing by 8'E annually.

Tidal Streams

Tides run strongly in the Canal de São Vicente. The northeast-going stream begins 3·5 hours before HW and the southwest-going stream about 2·5 hours after HW, with the latter reaching 2·5 knots when combined with the southwest-going current.

Charts

Admiralty *366* (1:500,000), *367* (1:150,000)
US *51500* (1:250,000)
Imray-Iolaire *E4* (1:500,000)

Lights

2952 **Ponta do Sol** Fl.4s15m9M
141°-vis-321° Metal tower 10m
2950 **Ponta da Tumba (Fontes Pereira de Melo)**
Fl(4)20s162m17M 141°-vis-321°
White octagonal tower and building 16m
2956 **Porto Novo** Iso.G.4s13m6M
Metal column on white base 6m
2955·1 **Tarrafal de Monte Trigo**
Fl(5)GWR.20s5M Metal column 5m
2954 **Ponta Mangrade**
Fl(2)10s112m13M 005°-vis-200°
White column, red lantern 3m
2955 **Cruzina da Graça**
Fl(2)6s5M Metal column 5m

Websites

Santo Antão has no website of its own, though it has several pages on www.en.wikipedia.org/wiki/Cape_Verde and others on the excellent www.caboverde.com. It also features on several of the general sites listed on page 330.

Approach

Much of the coastline consists of cliffs with deep water within 0·5M of the shore, though headlands should be allowed an offing of at least 1M. The mountains produce a windshadow extending up to 20M to the southwest.

Harbours and anchorages

Porto Novo

17°00′·92N 25°03′·6W

Waypoint
⊕ CV29 – 17°00′·6N 25°03′·2W (0·5M SE of Porto Novo)

Plans
Cabo Verdean *11* (1:5,000)
Portuguese *67501* (1:5,000)
Imray-Iolaire *E4* (1:10,000)

Lights
2956 **Breakwater** Iso.G.4s13m6M
Metal post on white base 6m

A port in name only

Porto Novo is the only harbour on São Antao. It is protected from the north by the land and from easterly swell by a stone breakwater used by the Mindelo ferry, small cargo boats and a few fishing craft, though most of the latter are drawn up on the beach. However, there is little shelter from northeasterly or easterly winds. In late 2010 work was said to be taking place on the mole, possibly to extend it.

Anchorage and berthing

Best anchorage is close west of the breakwater in about 6m, exposed only to the southwest. Be sure to allow sufficient room for vessels manoeuvring to and from the breakwater – and note that the ferry turns in its shelter on leaving. Allow also for the fact that the prevailing northeasterly wind may die during the night, or even blow onshore. The holding is generally poor.

It is sometimes possible for a yacht to lie alongside near the root of the mole in 3–4m, but there is constant surge and both lines and fenders suffer.

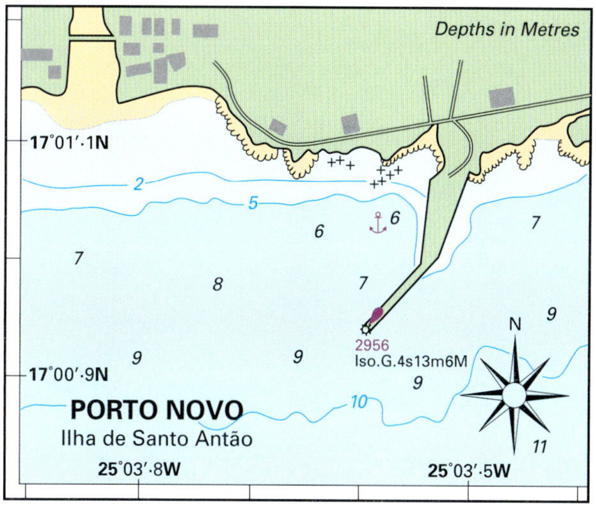

Facilities

Water No public tap – try the market or one of the cafés. Bottled water is readily available.
Fuel By can from the Shell filling station on the road leading inland from the harbour.
Bottled gas Camping Gas from the filling station, but no refills.
Bank At the western end of the town, open 0800–1400 Monday to Friday.
Shops/provisioning At least two small supermarkets plus numerous tiny general stores.
Produce market On the road which parallels the beach, plus separate fish market (though fish can often be bought direct from the boats).
Restaurants & hotels Several *residencials* together with the usual pavement cafés and small restaurants.
Medical services Small hospital.

Communications

Post office On the road leading inland from the harbour.
Car hire At least one company in Porto Novo, though the roads are such that a local driver may be preferable.
Taxis Plenty available, but somewhat expensive. Best value is obtained by group hire of a minibus.
Buses The usual public *aluguers* run a frequent service to Ribeira Grande and beyond.
Ferries Several crossings from/to Mindelo most days.
Air services The tiny airport at the north end of the island has been closed since 2003.

Porto Novo, with the ferry from São Vicente berthed alongside

Baía do Tarrafal

16°57'·2N 25°18'·8W (anchorage)

Tides
Predictions for Baía do Tarrafal do Monte Trigo (Baía do Tarrafal) are available via Admiralty *EasyTide* – see page 336

Plans
Admiralty *369* (1:12,000) (based on surveys dating from 1954; soundings in fathoms)

Lights
2955·1 **Tarrafal de Monte Trigo**
Fl(5)GWR.20s5M Metal tower 5m

Remote anchorage off welcoming village

In the extreme southwest of Santo Antão, the 2M long Baía do Tarrafal is reported to offer reasonable anchorage, with good holding in 9–12m along most of its length. Although protected from northeast through east to southeast (indeed, located in a complete windshadow so far as the trade winds are concerned) swell breaks almost permanently on the beach of large round boulders, and landing by dinghy is often difficult, particularly in winter. With a northwesterly Atlantic swell running in, the bay would swiftly become dangerous, and over the years several yachts have dragged their anchors and ended up on the beach.

Tarrafal, surrounded by green vegetation, is the first village seen when coming from the south. An isolated, semi-derelict building stands at the south end of the bay, which is very scenic with sea eagles and kites flying overhead.

My thanks to Don Goodspeed for this additional report:

> 'We visited Tarrafal in March 2002 and dropped anchor about 100m offshore in 9m. Two local fishermen were happy to take us ashore – we gave them CVE 500$ (about €4.50) for a round trip for which they also cleaned our propeller and waterline. Nestled in the trees is a new *residencial* run by an American/German couple who also provide drinks and meals for guests. They have running water (which the local people do not), a telephone and intermittent electricity.
>
> The locals now watch for visiting yachts and will row out to offer assistance and to sell fish and lobsters, so it is not necessary to launch a dinghy. They will also deliver water to the boat, and bottled gas refills are understood to be available. An *aluguer* makes the return trip to Porto Novo each day, leaving at 0600 and returning at 1300. We stayed for 48 hours, and managed to communicate with the friendly local people using French, Spanish and lots of sign language. We had a wonderful time and highly recommend Tarrafal as a not to be missed location.'

Baía do Monte Trigo

17°01'·3N 25°20'W

The westermost anchorage in the Cape Verdes

My thanks to Jill Schinas for the following information:

> 'Situated just north of Baía do Tarrafal, Baía do Monte Trigo is smaller and browner than its neighbour. It shares the same, almost permanent, windshadow. In theory it could become a dangerous lee shore if a southerly gale rose, but local people say that such a thing has never happened in this bay.
>
> The shore at Monte Trigo drops off steeply and what looks like a perfect spot to anchor, 100m off the beach in the corner of the bay, is actually off soundings. However there is a 15m patch just outside the breaker line at the west end of the village.
>
> Landing needs to be timed very carefully as the waves are even bigger than at Tarrafal and the beach is of equally unsympathetic large, round stones. However the people are wonderfully friendly, probably because they seldom see any visitors. There is no surfaced road and, as with Tarrafal, the only way out of Monte Trigo is a steep track up the valley – or by boat.'

In 2003 Mary Robinson added:

> 'We found about 10m over sand with good holding to the west of the village, in the area suggested by Jill Schinas. There is a conspicuous white mark on the rocks which looks a bit like a giant gingerbread man, and we anchored just below it. We were in a total wind shadow and needed 360° swinging room, but had no problems. Landing looked hazardous with surf over boulders and we didn't attempt it.'

There are a number of local fishing vessels and moorings to the west of the village close inshore.

Porto da Ponta do Sol

17°12'·22N 25°05'·65W (molehead)

Waypoint
⊕ CV27 – 17°16'·4N 25°05'·5W (4M N of Pta do Sol)

Tides
Time difference on Dakar: –0030, on Mindelo (Porto Grande): +0015. Predictions for Ponta do Sol are available via Admiralty *EasyTide* – see page 336
Mean spring range 0·8m
Mean neap range 0·5m

Plans
Admiralty *369* (1:18,000) (based on surveys dating from 1951; soundings in fathoms)

Lights
2952 **Ponta do Sol** Fl.4s15m9M
141°-vis-321° Metal post 10m

Small harbour best visited by land

A small and attractive village situated in the extreme north of Santo Antão. Its miniature harbour, the Boca da Pistola, is used by local fishing boats which

Sunlight and shadow as a local fishing boat enters the tiny Boca da Pistola ('gun's mouth') at Porto da Ponta do Sol

are then manhandled ashore. The harbour is totally unsuitable for yachts and, though it is possible to anchor off when the wind is from well east of northeast, this is another Cape Verdean harbour which is best visited by land.

Approach, anchorage and facilities

If approaching from north or east, allow an offing of at least a mile around Ponta do Sol – Admiralty *369* demonstrates why. Do not turn in towards the headland until it bears almost due east, when about 25m over rock and stones should be found some 300m southwest or west of the harbour entrance. The extensive reefs provide some protection from the northeasterly swell, but in the calmer conditions of summer the outer reefs do not break at all and even the reefs close to the shore are scarcely visible.

Landing by dinghy in the tiny harbour can be interesting – once again it is a matter of careful timing as the waves sometimes break across the entrance. However, only accept the help of local fishermen after careful negotiation – it has been reported that they may be very eager to offer lifts ashore, only to demand an exorbitant fee for the return journey.

Facilities are minimal, though there are several shops, a couple of cafés offering basic lunches, and at least one *residencial*. For a bank, post office and better shops it would be necessary to catch a minibus to Ribeira Grande.

A small fishing boat is carried ashore inside the Boca da Pistola. An *aluguer* waits in the background, possibly to take the catch to market in Ribeira Grande *Sue Thatcher*

IV. THE CAPE VERDES

Ilha do Maio

Between 15°07′N–15°20′N and 23°05′W–23°15′W

Introduction

Measuring 270km^2 or less, Ilha do Maio is one of the smaller Cape Verde islands and is also the most southeasterly, its nearest neighbour being Ilha de Santiago 14M to the southwest. Much of the island is arid and low-lying, though a small area in the centre around Monte Penoso (436m) is somewhat higher, and large stretches of the coast are fringed with fine sandy beaches. About 8,000 people live on the island, mostly in the vicinity of Vila do Maio, the only real town. Its name is derived from the date of its discovery – 1 May 1460.

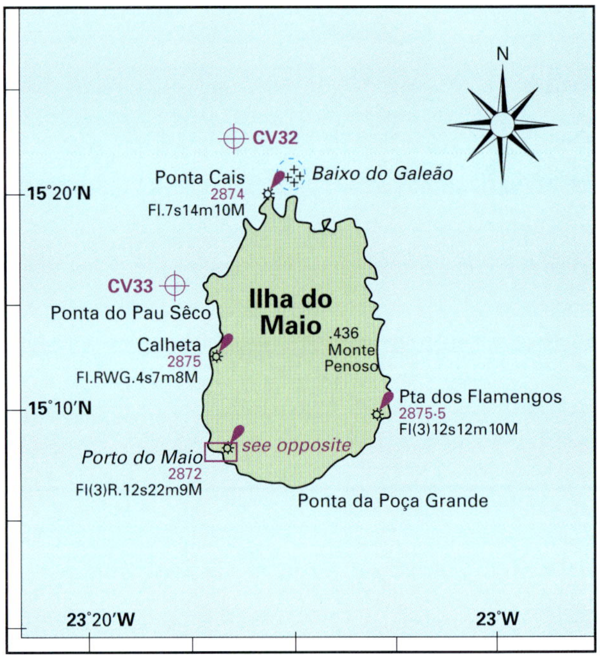

Telecommunications

Mobile (cell) phone reception is good around Vila do Maio, but has not been verified elsewhere. Note also the limitation detailed on page 329. The country code for the Republic of Cape Verde islands is 238, with no individual island or area codes, and the telephone number always contains seven digits. If only six are given, add a 2 (for landlines) or 9 (for mobiles) at the beginning. Two possiblities for internet access are listed on www.maiocv.com (see below).

Websites

Ilha do Maio boasts a surprisingly good website at www.maiocv.com. Though run by property development company Maio Cape Verde, the site has far more depth than is typical of the genre. The island also has pages on both en.wikipedia.org/wiki/Cape_Verde and on the excellent www.caboverde.com, as well as featuring on several of the general sites listed on page 330.

Approach

An offing of 1M is sufficient all around the island other than in the extreme north, where the breaking Baixo do Galeão extends more than 2M offshore, and the extreme south, where a potentially dangerous wreck lies about 1·25M south of Ponta da Poça Grande. Currents can be strong and erratic and, according to recent GPS readings, charted positions may be suspect. Swell tends to hook around the roughly oblong island, and 2·5m waves have been reported as breaking on the beach at Porto do Maio even in apparently calm conditions.

If approaching from the northeast, refer to the caution regarding Baixo de João Valente on page 350. If sailing at night note also that the light at Ponta Cais, described above, is unlikely to be working.

Navigation

Waypoints

⊕ CV32 – 15°22′·5N 23°13′W (3M NW of Pta Cais)
⊕ CV33 – 15°15′·8N 23°15′·9W (2M W of Pta do Pau Sêco)
⊕ CV34 – 15°07′·9N 23°14′·3W (1M WSW of Porto do Maio)

Courses and distances

⊕ CV32 – ⊕ CV08 (3M W of Pta Varandinha, Boavista) via ⊕ CV10 (4M ESE of Baixo de João Valente) = 42M, 017° & 014° / 194° & 197°
⊕ CV32 – ⊕ CV33 = 7·3M, 203° / 023°
⊕ CV33 – ⊕ CV34 = 8M, 169° / 349°
⊕ CV34 – ⊕ CV36 (4M NNE of Pta do Lobo, Santiago) = 10M, 247° / 067°

Magnetic variation

10°35′W (2011), decreasing by 7′E annually.

Tidal Streams

Tidal streams are weak, but the current around Ilha do Maio sets southwesterly at 0·5–1 knot, strongly influenced by the wind.

Charts

Admiralty *366* (1:500,000)
US *51540* (1:200,000)
Imray-Iolaire *E4* (1:500,000)

Lights

2874 **Ponta Cais** Fl.7s14m10M
038°-vis-292° Metal structure 7m
Racon *M* every 30s 038°-292° 20M
Note Light and presumably racon reported as 'temporarily extinguished' in April 1996 and still not operational 15 years later
2875 **Calheta** Fl.RWG.4s7m8M Metal column 5m
2872 **Porto do Maio (Forte de São José)**
Fl(3)R.12s22m9M 349°-vis-090°
Platform on tower of fort 7m
2875·5 **Ponta dos Flamengos** Fl(3)12s12m10M
038°-vis-292° Metal column 5m

Anchorages

Porto do Maio (Porto do Inglez)

15°08′·37N 23°13′·24W

Waypoint
⌖ CV34 – 15°07′·9N 23°14′·3W (1M WSW of Porto do Maio)

Tides
Time difference on Dakar: –0100, on Mindelo (Porto Grande): –0015. Predictions for Porto do Maio are available via Admiralty *EasyTide* – see page 336
Mean spring range 1·0m
Mean neap range 0·6m

Plans
Admiralty *369* (24,500) (based on surveys dating from 1902; soundings in fathoms)

Lights
2872 **Porto de Maio (Forte de São José)** Fl(3)R.12s22m9M 349°-vis-090° Platform on tower of fort 7m
2873 **Jetty** Iso.G.4s6m5M Rusty white metal post 3m

Local fishing craft share the beach at Porto do Maio with goalposts for the school football team

Rolly beach anchorage off 'desert' island

Porto do Maio, formerly known as Porto do Inglez due to the many English vessels which called to load salt, is little more than an open anchorage off a southwest-facing beach. There is nearly always some swell, making the anchorage rolly and landing difficult – though the beach itself is superb. The large church fronted by an attractive square is clearly visible from several miles offshore, with Forte de São José to the south and a long jetty, completed in 1997, to the north.

Anchorage

Best anchorage is to be found at the southern end of the beach in 4–8m over sand, directly off the town. If anchoring close in a stern anchor could be wise, as both wind and current may reverse direction with little warning.

Dinghies can safely be left on the beach – there is generally least swell near the low rocky cliff at its southern corner – or off the steps at the old quay, in which case a long painter and a holding-off anchor will be needed.

The jetty is built of ferro-concrete piles and elevated some 3–4m above sea level, making even

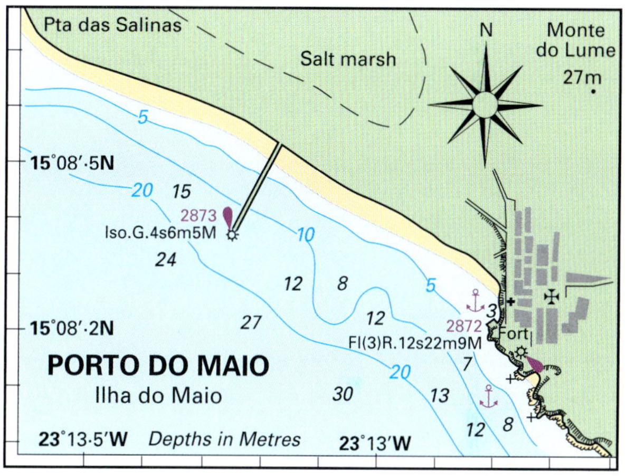

Azure waters off the long beach at Porto do Maio, looking a little north of west, with the jetty in the middle distance and the mountains of Santiago clearly visible behind

The pretty church at Vila do Maio, lovingly cared for inside and out

the small section which is solid almost to water level unsuitable for a yacht to lie alongside. There do not appear to be any ladders or steps. The cargo boat from Santiago normally calls each Tuesday.

Formalities

Visit the *Polícia* near the old quay – there is no *Delegação Marítima* (harbour office) in the town. Yachts are still very much a rarity at Porto do Maio.

Facilities

Water Public water supply just off the main square.
Showers May be possible at one of the *residençials*.
Fuel By can from the filling station on the north edge of the town.
Bank On the main square, open 0800–1300 Monday to Friday, plus cash dispenser.
Shops/provisioning The Mini Mercado Paulo Jorge – continue up from the church, right at the tiny roundabout, first left, first right and in a grey building on the left – is surprisingly well stocked and spotlessly clean. The Chinese-run general store overlooking the roundabout sells everything from clothes to oil lamps.
Produce market Near the main square. Informal fish market under a shade tree near the stone cross on the front, though fish and shellfish can often be bought direct from the boats at very good prices.
Cafés, restaurants & hotels Several cafés and restaurants, plus two *residençials* near the square.
Medical services Small health centre on the road overlooking the beach. Anything serious would undoubtedly mean evacuation to Santiago.

Communications

Post office with telephones Uphill from the church, beneath the telecom tower and aerials.
Car hire One company with a limited number of cars. See Road transport, page 331.
Taxis Available for day tours. Go for an all-terrain vehicle if possible.
Buses The usual irregular *aluguers*.
Ferries Weekly service to/from Santiago.
Air services Regular (but not daily) flights to/from Santiago from the airport north of the town.

Ponta do Pau Sêco

15°16'·4N 23°13'·6W

Remote anchorage with nothing ashore

A possible anchorage has been reported in the northeast corner of the bay just north of Ponta do Pau Sêco (locally, and somewhat confusingly, known as Porto Cais), as marked on US chart *51540*. The long bay south of the point is shallow and obstructed with rocks and coral.

The northern bay would plainly be at is best in wind and swell from east of northeast, and would become untenable in a northwesterly swell. The bottom appears to be of sand with coral and weed patches, but it has not been visited and would require careful eyeball pilotage in good light. It is surrounded by scrubland and acres of beach, but little else.

Selling fish, Maio style! *Sue Thatcher*

Santiago

Between 14°54'N–15°20'N and 23°25'W–23°47'W

Introduction

With a surface area of 991km² Ilha de Santiago is the largest island in the group by a considerable margin. Much of the central and northern parts are mountainous, the highest point being Pico da Antónia at 1,392m. Rainfall is higher in these areas than in the south, permitting the widespread cultivation of fruit, maize and sugar cane on the lower slopes and in the valleys.

Santiago was discovered around 1460 and was the first island in the Cape Verdes to be permanently inhabited. The first settlement, at Cidade Velha on the southwest coast – see pages 324 and 383 – was the earliest European colonial outpost in the tropics. Santiago is still the leading island commercially, with Cidade da Praia, the capital and seat of government, situated in the extreme south. It is home to more than half the archipelago's population – an estimated 240,000 in 2010, of whom about half live in and around Praia.

Much of the island is very attractive, with stark contrasts between the lush central mountain slopes and the flat and arid land further the south, and if anchored in Praia an excursion by taxi or *aluguer* is highly recommended – provided someone can be found to keep an eye on the boat. It seems a little strange that Santiago's largest tourist project, the Sambala Development about seven miles northeast of Praia, is situated in one of the least attractive parts of the island (proximity to the airport doubtless trumps other considerations). Plans for the development include the 'Porto Lobo Resort and Marina', though the site proposed for the latter looks most unpromising and it seems unlikely that it will ever berth cruising yachts. See www.sambaladevelopments.com for further details.

Telecommunications

Mobile (cell) phone reception is excellent both on the south coast of Santiago and around Baía do Tarrafal, though holes almost certainly exist in some of the mountain valleys. Note also the limitation detailed on page 329. The country code for the Republic of Cape Verde islands is 238, with no individual island or area codes, and the telephone number always contains seven digits. If only six are given, add a 2 (for landlines) or 9 (for mobiles) at the beginning.

By 2010 free Wi-Fi was available in the main squares of both Praia and Tarrafal, though the signal is sometimes poor. There was a single cybercafé in Praia – see page 382 – and understood to be one in Tarrafal also.

Websites

Despite being the largest island in the archipelago and the seat of government Santiago has no website of its own, though it has several pages on en.wikipedia.org/wiki/Cape_Verde and others on the excellent www.caboverde.com. It also features on several of the general sites listed on page 330.

Boat repairs on the beach at Praia

Navigation

Waypoints

⊕ CV35 – 15°24'·4N 23°43'·8W (4M N of Pta Moreia)
⊕ CV36 – 15°03'·9N 23°24'W (4M NNE of Pta do Lobo)
⊕ CV37 – 14°53'·3N 23°29'·2W (1·5M SE of Porto da Praia)
⊕ CV38 – 15°04'·4N 23°49'W (2M W of Pta da Janela)
⊕ CV39 – 15°16'·9N 23°46'·4W (1M W of Baía do Tarrafal)

Courses and distances

⊕ CV35 – ⊕ CV08 (3M W of Pta Varandinha, Boavista) = 56M, 047° / 227°
⊕ CV35 – ⊕ CV25 (2M W of Pta Machado, São Vicente) = 118M, 317° / 137°
⊕ CV35 – ⊕ CV36 = 28M, 137° / 317°
⊕ CV35 – ⊕ CV38 = 21M, by eye
⊕ CV36 – ⊕ CV03 (1M WSW of Porto de Palmeira, Ilha do Sal) = 104M, 013° / 193°
⊕ CV36 – ⊕ CV08 (3M W of Pta Varandinha, Boavista) via ⊕ CV10 (4M ESE of Baixo de João Valente) = 63M, 023° & 014° / 194° & 203°
⊕ CV36 – ⊕ CV34 (1M WSW of Porto do Maio, Ilha do Maio) = 10M, 067° / 247°
⊕ CV36 – ⊕ CV37 = 12M, by eye
⊕ CV37 – ⊕ CV38 = 23·5M, by eye
⊕ CV37 – ⊕ CV41 (3M NE of Pta dos Mosteiros, Ilha do Fogo) = 48M, 283° / 103°
⊕ CV37 – ⊕ CV42 (2M SE of Pta do Alcatraz, Ilha do Fogo) = 47M, 265° / 085°
⊕ CV38 – ⊕ CV14 (0 5M W of Porto do Tarrafal, São Nicolau) = 95M, 340°/ 160°
⊕ CV38 – ⊕ CV25 (2M W of Pta Machado, São Vicente) = 130M, 324° / 144°
⊕ CV38 – ⊕ CV39 = 13M, 011° / 191°
⊕ CV39 – ⊕ CV41 (3M NE of Pta dos Mosteiros, Ilha do Fogo) = 32M, 247° / 067°

Magnetic variation

10°40'W (2011), decreasing by 7'E annually.

Tidal streams

Tidal streams are generally weak, though a 2 knot east-going stream has been reported to occur close west of Porto da Praia at mid-ebb. The southwesterly-setting current is felt most strongly around the northern part of the island, where it may run at up to 1 knot.

Charts

Admiralty *366* (1:500,000)
US *51540* (1:200,000)
Imray-Iolaire *E4* (1:500,000)

Lights

2888 **Ponta Moreia**
Fl(5)20s97m10M 055°-vis-275°
Red lantern on white hut 4m
Porto Formoso
Fl(3)10s10M Metal column 5m
2883·8 **Calheta de São Miguel**
Fl(4)R.15s10m5M Metal column 5m
2883·7 **Pedra Badejo**
Fl.G.4s8m6M Metal column 4m
2883·5 **Praia Baixo**
Fl(3)G.12s10m6M Metal column 5m
2882 **Ponta do Lobo**
Fl(4)15s17m10M 190°-vis-292°
Square tower and building 9m
2876 **Ponta Temerosa (Dona María Pía)**
Fl(2)6s25m5M 258°-vis-095°
White octagonal tower and building 21m
Note Difficult to identify against shore lights
2883 **Mosquito** Fl(2)WRG.6s13m8M Grey tower 7m
2883·6 **Porto Rinção**
Fl(5)WR.20s9m8/5M Metal column 4m
2884 **Ribeira da Barca**
Fl(3)RGW.12s6m6M 080°-vis-121° Grey post 3m
2885 **Chão Bom**
Fl(2+1)WRG.15s7m6M
Metal column 5m
2890 **Ponta Pretá** Fl(3)12s34m8M
Square white building 6m

Coast Radio Station

Ilha de Santiago 15°02'·1N 23°37'·2W (remotely controlled from São Vicente)
VHF Ch 16 (24 hours), 20, 21
DSC VHF Ch 70, MMSI 006170000

Approach

The coast is generally steep-to with 0·5M offing sufficient, except on the east coast from Ponta da Corõa to Ponta do Lobo where at least 1M should be allowed.

The west coast of Santiago can form a wind shadow, and if unwilling (or unable) to motor it may be better to sail up the east coast if on passage between Porto da Praia and Baía do Tarrafal. At other times gusts funnelling down the ravines can create sudden squalls – one yacht encountered 55 knot gusts in a true wind strength of less than 30 knots off the west coast of Santiago.

If approaching from the northeast, most probably on passage from Ilha do Sal or Boavista, refer to the caution regarding Baixo de João Valente on page 350.

Local ladies still carry their vegetables to market in the traditional way

Harbours and anchorages

Porto da Praia

14°54'·48N 23°29'·98W (Cais Novo, head)

Waypoint
⊕ CV37 – 14°53'·3N 23°29'·2W (1·5M SE of Porto da Praia)

Tides
Time difference on Dakar: –0104, on Mindelo (Porto Grande): –0019. Predictions for Porto da Praia are available via Admiralty *EasyTide* – see page 336
Mean spring range 1·1m
Mean neap range 0·6m

Plans
Admiralty *367* (1:150,000 and 15,000)
Cabo Verdean *71* (scale unknown)
Portuguese *66301* (7,500)
US *51540* (1:15,000)
Imray-Iolaire *E4* (1:22,000)

Lights
2876 **Ponta Temerosa (Dona María Pía)**
Fl(2)6s25m5M 258°-vis-095°
White octagonal tower and building 21m
Note Difficult to identify against shore lights
2881 **Cais Novo, east end** Fl.G.4s10m5M
Lantern on round concrete structure 5m
2881·5 **Cais Novo, west end**
Fl.Y.4s4M Yellow metal column 2 5m

Harbour communications
Port Authority ✆ 261 2382, 260 2970 *Fax* 261 6133
VHF Ch 13, 16

Rolly harbour anchorage with mixed reputation

Porto da Praia lies at the head of a deeply indented bay and is well sheltered from winds from southwest through north around to east, though some swell nearly always works in. The main commercial and ferry quay lies on the east side of the bay with a mole extending southwest from its eastern end, while its western end has been extended to form a ferry and fishing harbour, in which yachts are normally able to leave dinghies (see Anchorage, below). There are plans to extend the eastern mole and reclaim some land beyond it, possibly for use as a container port, but other than possibly reducing the swell slightly this is unlikely to affect visiting yachts.

The older part of the city – known as 'O Centro' – stands on a steep-sided plateau about 30m above sea level to the northwest of the harbour, but building has spread in all directions over the surrounding lower land. The older areas are interesting, with several imposing churches, squares and official buildings as well as a bustling market. The city has long had a reputation for casual theft, and wallets and other tempting items should still be carried in a secure inner pocket or waist bag. However, most visiting yachtsmen now consider Cidade da Praia to be a pleasant place – visibly thriving, with well-stocked supermarkets and many new cars in evidence. Perhaps with these in mind, a two-lane highway has been built around the base of the plateau to connect the southern part of the town – which includes most of the better hotels, as well as embassies and other official buildings – with the harbour and airport. However, roads on the plateau are still mainly cobbled, and flanked by pavements which are irregular to the point of being dangerous. Watch your step!

Not to be missed while in Praia are the small *Museu do Cidade* on Avenida 5 de Julho (open 0800–1600), and the *Centro de Restauração e Museologia* – signed as the *Museu de Arqueologia* – www.arq.de, tucked away below the south end of the plateau on the Rua da Alfândega, behind the large, pale green *Arquivo Historico Nacional*, and open 0930–1600. Exhibits in both museums are well labelled in English, Portuguese and sometimes French, the former giving an idea of life ashore in the islands while the latter presents a fascinating selection of artefacts recovered from wrecks around their shores. Both charge CVE 100$ for admittance.

A major problem for the city authorities is its annual population growth rate, currently estimated at nearly 6%. Said to be a combination of improved health care (leading to lower infant mortality and much increased life span), immigration (mostly from West Africa), and a drift to the city from rural areas of Santiago as well as from neighbouring islands, it imposes a vast strain on fresh water, sanitation and housing. A large proportion of the foreign aid received is currently being spent on improving basic services.

Looking south-southwest over Porto da Praia with the city on its plateau at far right, Ilhéu de Santa Maria in the centre, the fishing harbour at centre left and the Cais Novo and main port facilities at far left

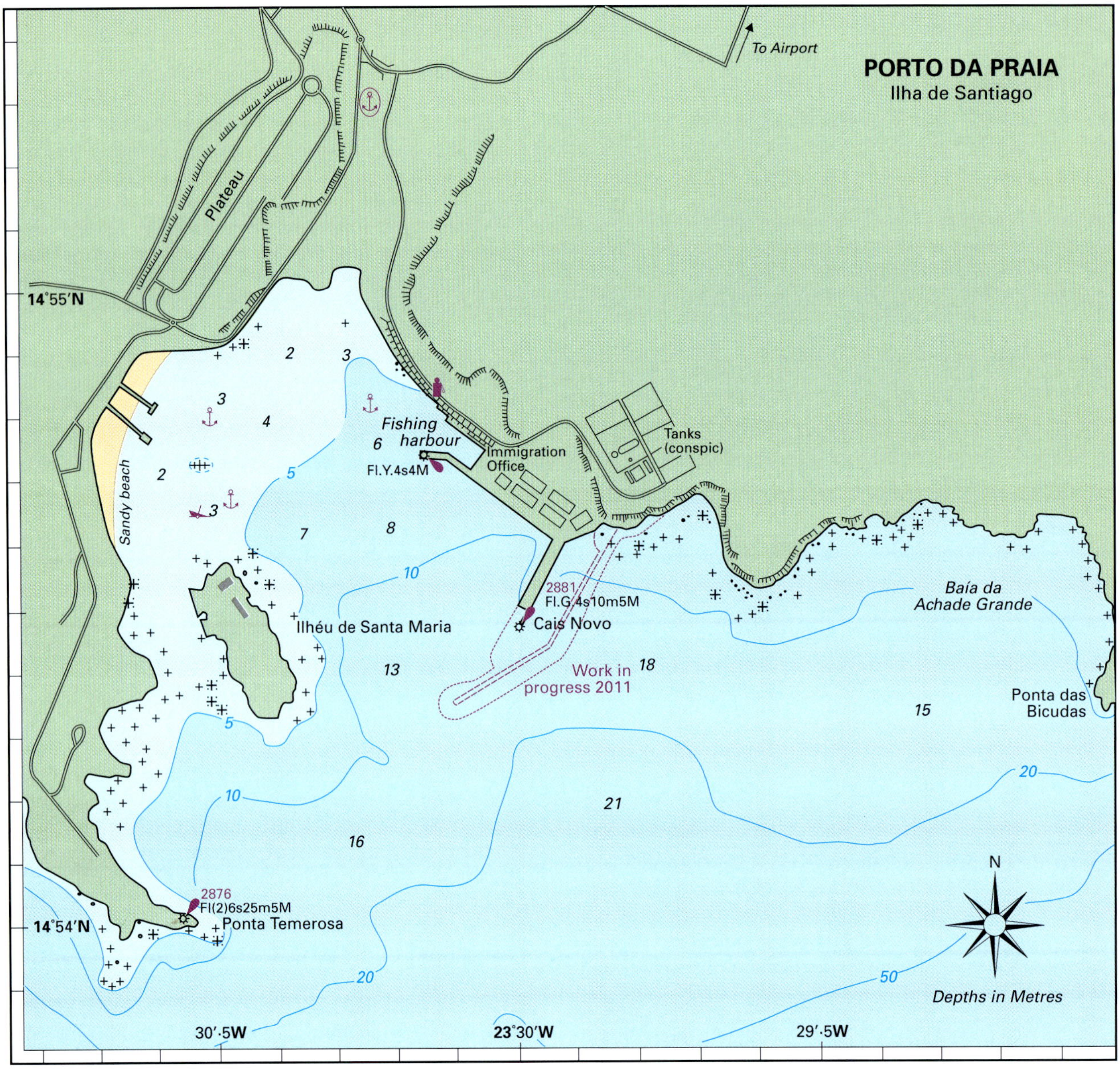

Approach

Entry in daylight is quite straightforward, with no dangers further than 400m offshore. Although entry after dark is not recommended, if necessary it could be made with the light on Cais Novo bearing between 286° and 031°. There is also considerable ambient light both on the *cais* and from the city itself.

Anchorage

After many years during which yachts were expected to anchor off the beach on the western side of the harbour – an area notorious for its long fetch, swell, indifferent holding and submerged wrecks – the authorities have now accepted that most prefer to anchor west of the fishing harbour. The cliffs to the northeast provide some shelter, though the trade winds still funnel down the valley of the Ribeira de Trinidade and the nearby harbour road creates a good deal of dust and grit. Depths vary from 5–6m and holding is good in firm, sandy mud.

Dinghies can normally be left at the northern end of the ferry/fishing harbour, a tip of around CVE 100$ being expected, though it may be wise to row ashore having left the outboard securely padlocked to the parent craft. Taxis are readily available if one does not fancy the dusty walk into town. There is a café in the Gare Maritimo building at the head of the harbour and a few roadside vendors, but little else nearby. If wishing to land on the west side of the bay, note that both piers are now too dilapidated to offer safe landing while the beach nearly always has a sizeable swell.

A ‘boat boy’ (often middle-aged) is likely to approach each newly arrived yacht to offer his services. Many speak good English and have repeatedly proved their worth in organising local services – particularly for those who speak little or no Portuguese – though it would be wise to ask to see references from other yachtsmen and agree payment, by the day or per ‘service’, in advance. A local man known as Tunuca (or Tanaka) has been

The yacht anchorage, with the open mouth of the fishing harbour and beyond it the Cais Novo, seen from the northwest

mentioned by several visiting skippers over the past five years, all of whom have commended his services. Even so, if a watchman is employed to stay aboard while the crew enjoy an evening ashore – the *Capitão dos Portos* recommends that yachts should not be left unattended after dark – it is essential that the yacht be securely locked.

Caution

If cruising the islands in August, September or October, be warned that strong southerlies are quite common and send a dangerous swell into the bay. It may be possible to seek temporary shelter inside the new fishing harbour, but it would be unwise to leave an anchored yacht unattended for more than a few hours at this time of year.

Formalities

Porto da Praia is currently one of only four ports in the archipelago where inward clearance to the Republic of Cape Verde can be obtained – see Entry and regulations, page 333. The rules appear to change every few years but are, very gradually, relaxing. Even so, they must be followed with care – any attempt to circumvent any part of the procedure is simply not worth the likely consequences. In early 2010 the sequence was as follows:

On arrival: Having come ashore at the fishing harbour, the skipper must first visit the *Polícia de Fronteira* (Immigration police) in their (unmarked) office near the entrance arch to the port. Walk down the little cul-de-sac to the right of the archway and theirs is the last door on the right. In 2010 the officials were pleasant, both spoke French and one also spoke English. The passports of all crew members will be required, and possibly the ship's papers, but there is no need for everyone to attend (though see below). If the boat has already cleared at Porto da Palmeira or Mindelo, and all the crew are remaining aboard and departing with her, the passports will be stamped and immigration procedures are complete. However, if not previously

Having a harbour of its own has allowed the Praia fishing fleet to grow in both number and average size

cleared into the archipelago the *Polícia de Fronteira* will visit and inspect the yacht, for which a charge will almost certainly be made.

Any crewmembers leaving the yacht by plane will need visas, which can be issued by the *Polícia de Fronteira* on payment of CVE 2,500$, €25 or US$40 each. They must obviously accompany the skipper there, and should have photocopies of the information pages of their passport plus a couple of passport photos each, although these are unlikely to be needed. Note that without entry and visa stamps in their passport they will **NOT** be allowed to board their plane to leave. The office is open 0800–1600 weekdays only, and if a yacht arrives at the weekend the *Guarda Fiscal* will notify the *Polícia de Fronteira* who will then come out to the yacht – charging for their services. It would be unwise to go ashore before they arrive, and tempting fate to rely on a visa being issued in time for a crewmember to leave on a weekend flight.

The second stage of the process is for the skipper to visit the *Capitão do Porto* (port captain) in his office at the *Instituto Marítimo e Portuário*, on the fourth floor of a modern building near the dry riverbed. (If on foot, walk towards the plateau, cross the road bridge, and take the second left off the roundabout just beyond. It is – currently – the second building on the left, and is clearly marked). Enter the air-conditioned outer office (*empurre* = push) and settle down to wait ... possibly for an hour or more. The original copy of the ship's papers must be produced, together with a crew list and all passports. The *Capitão do Porto* normally holds the ship's papers pending departure, but a clear photocopy may be accepted in lieu. This office is also open 0800–1600 weekdays only, and the weekend procedure seems a little confused. In theory it is necessary to notify the *Capitão do Porto* ✆ 261 2382, 260 2970 on the last working day before arrival – difficult, if not impossible, for most yachtsmen. In practice it would probably be best to consult the *Polícia de Fronteira* when they arrive to check the yacht, being suitably humble about causing so much trouble. Of course the ideal would be to time one's arrival to avoid the weekend altogether.

On departure: Both the above offices must be revisited (by any member of the crew), the *Polícia de Fronteira* to get exit stamps in the passports and the *Capitão do Porto* to reclaim the ship's papers (if left there) and pay a small exit charge – CVE 860$ / €8 in early 2010. They can be visited in either order. If wishing to clear out the day before leaving, be sure to make this clear so the exit date is entered accordingly.

If wishing to visit one or more of the smaller islands before leaving territorial waters, request a 'next port' (*próximo porto* or *porto seguinte*) document from the *Delegação Marítima* when clearing out – see page 333.

As of 2010 it was no longer necessary to visit the *Polícia Marítima* (maritime police) in their office near the beach on either arrival or departure.

Facilities

Chandlery No chandlery as such, though there are several hardware stores selling tools and plumbing items such as hose clips, etc. Similarly, non-specialist electrical items are readily available.

Water Filling tanks can be a problem, probably best solved with the aid of one of the 'boat boys' mentioned above. Even so, quality should always be checked before going ahead. Be wary of the taps on the Cais – some, if not all, deliver salt water. Bottled water is readily (and cheaply) available.

Showers Can often be had at one of the smaller hotels on payment of a fee.

Fuel By can from the Shell filling station on the road behind the beach. Alternatively it may be possibly to order large quantites of diesel for delivery by road tanker to the Cais Novo from either Shell or Enacol. Fuel prices are low, and payment will be required in advance.

As of early 2010 the fuel pontoon just north of the new fishing harbour, connected to a filling station on the road above, was no longer in place.

Bottled gas Most Shell filling stations exchange Camping Gaz bottles. Other cylinders can be refilled (with butane) at the Enacol plant overlooking the Cais Novo, provided the necessary adaptor is available.

Banks Several around the city, plus the Cotacâmbios currency exchange just north of the produce market (open 0800–1800 Monday to Friday, 0900–1300 Saturday) where cash can be drawn against a Visa card (passport required). As of February 2010 cash dispensers which accepted Visa and other international cards were installed at the Banco Interâtlantico and Banco Comercial do Atlântico on the main square, and inside the nearby Casa do Cidadão.

Shops/provisioning Several well-stocked supermarkets on the plateau, including the Supermercado Felicidade located beneath the hotel of the same name; the Palácio Fenícia near the corner of the main square (the Praça Alexandre Albuquerque) with an equally impressive 'department store' next door; and Calú & Ângela northwest of the market with electronic and household items on the upper floor. Open 0800–2000 Monday to Saturday and (unusually) 0900–1300 on Sunday. All have good ranges of everything from washing powder to breakfast cereal, spotless chilled and frozen meat counters, and shelves laden with alcohol of all kinds.

Produce market Colourful African-style market on the plateau, operating from 0700 or earlier seven days a week and selling a good variety of fruit and vegetables plus all kinds of beans, as well as meat and fish in the buildings in the corners. A greater variety of fish is available in the informal fish market on the Cais Novo, near where the fishing boats berth, and where it may also be possible to buy small quantities of ice-box grade ice.

The market area in Sucupira, where fish and meat were previously sold, now handles mainly clothes and shoes, but is also a good place to buy CDs or tapes of Cape Verdean music. All three are areas in which to watch one's purse.

Cafés, restaurants & hotels A wide range, with food to suit most tastes and pockets. There are more than a dozen hotels and *residençials* at all levels, with more being built each year, generally at the upper end of the price scale.

Medical services Hospital ✆ 246 2130 on the plateau, plus several pharmacies.

Communications

Post office On the eastern edge of the plateau, with telephone and fax facilities.

Telephones At the post office, plus many card-operated boxes.

Internet access In 2010 the only internet access for those without their own computers appeared to be at the Cybercafé Sofia on Praça Luís de Camões, the venues mentioned in previous editions having closed. Free Wi-Fi is available in the city's main square (the Praça Alexandre Albuquerque), though service is reported to be slow and fitful. It is necessary to log in with a username and password, both of which are provided on the welcome screen. Computer expendables, including inkjets, are available from Infotel, nearly opposite the post office.

Car hire Several companies, but inspect the vehicle carefully before signing anything. See Road transport, page 331.

Taxis Both taxis and communal *aluguer* minibuses cover routes all over the island. A trip through the mountains by *aluguer* is surprisingly cheap and gives a glimpse of a completely different world.

Ferries Regular inter-island service – see Transportation, page 331.

Free Wi-Fi is available in the main square at Praia, which is well provided with stone benches and shade trees

Air services Frequent inter-island flights from the airport east of Praia, and direct flights to/from Lisbon, Dakar and Bissau. There is a visible police presence, and the young taxi touts who used to frequent the airport – and often intimidate arriving passengers – are no longer in evidence. If needing to confirm a flight (recommended at least 48 hours before departure), note that the TACV office on the plateau is open 0800–1300, 1500–1800 weekdays only.

Cidade Velha

14°54'·8N 23°36'·5W (anchorage)

Anchorage off World Heritage site

Several yachts have mentioned anchoring off Cidade Velha to break the passage between Baía do Tarrafal and Porto da Praia. A rocky reef runs out from the southwest end of the beach, and as the water is generally clear it is very definitely a case of 'eyeballing' in. Holding is variable in 6–8m.

Cidade Velha was the site of the islands' first capital, at which time it was known as Ribeira Grande and was the first European-built city in the tropics. Despite being recognised by UNESCO as a World Heritage site, to the uninformed visitor little appears to remain of the 'old city' – after successive attacks during the 16th and 17th centuries, in 1712 the capital moved to the steep-sided plateau where Cidade da Praia now stands. All one finds now is a small village of thatched cottages with few facilities but some fascinating relics, including the imposing walls of the original cathedral and the surprisingly well preserved old church of Nossa Senhora do Rosário on the north side of the village with flagstone memorials dating back to the days of the *conquistadors*.

If not planning to visit by sea it is well worth an excursion from Cidade da Praia by taxi or *aluguer*. A bar in the square sells cold drinks, but there is little else.

Ribeira da Barca

15°08'·25N 23°45'·7W (anchorage)

Lights
2884 **Ribeira da Barca** Fl(3)RGW.12s6m6M
080°-vis-121° Grey post 3m

Anchorage off small fishing village

This small bay on the west coast of Ilha da Santiago, sheltered from north through east to south, is occasionally visited by yachts on passage between Baía do Tarrafal and Porto da Praia. A linked pair of breaking rocks lie in the middle of the bay, with another two rocks awash further south and slightly

The stony bay at Ribeira da Barca offers potential shelter on the passage between Baía do Tarrafal and Porto da Praia, but little more

IV. THE CAPE VERDES

inshore. Keep north of the visible pair, avoiding moored fishing boats and what appears to be a cargo-unloading float (keep a careful watch for submerged lines if heading in past it).

The northeast trades tend to funnel down the valley and there is usually some swell, and with holding patchy in sand and rock it is prudent to lay two anchors, possibly with a third to prevent the yacht swinging inshore if the wind drops. The northeast corner of the bay contains a small quay with steps where it would be possible to land from a dinghy.

There is a small fishing village ashore with a couple of bars, but otherwise facilities are minimal.

Baía do Tarrafal

15°16'·83N 23°45'·26W (molehead)

Waypoint
⊕ CV39 – 15°16'·9N 23°46'·4W (1M W of Baía do Tarrafal)

Tides
Time difference on Dakar: –0035, on Mindelo (Porto Grande): +0010. Predictions for Baía do Tarrafal are available via Admiralty *EasyTide* – see page 336
Mean spring range 1·0m
Mean neap range 0·6m

Plans
Admiralty *369* (18,500) (based on surveys dating from 1902; soundings in fathoms)

Lights
2890 **Ponta Pretá** Fl(3)12s34m8M
Square white building 6m

Rolly anchorage in attractive bay

Baía do Tarrafal, on the northwest coast of Ilha de Santiago, provides good shelter from north through east to south. The town with its distinctive blue and white church lies at the southeast corner of the bay, overlooking an attractive white sand beach backed by coconut palms. It has become a popular weekend venue for people from Praia and is regarded locally as Santiago's main tourist attraction. There are now more than 10,000 inhabitants, making it Santiago's second largest town.

Approach

If approaching from the south be sure not to confuse Baía do Tarrafal with Baía do Chão Bom, a wide shallow inlet some 2M further south. Ponto do Atum, which separates them, is comparatively low and can be difficult to identify from offshore. However, the white tower and brown roof of Ponta Pretá light to the north of Baía do Tarrafal is unmistakable, standing on a ledge some 30m above the water backed by a steep hill which continues upwards to 369m.

Enter the bay on a course just south of east. There are several shoal spots close in and careful watch should be kept both on the depth sounder and over the bow – the water is usually very clear. An increasing number of moorings for local fishing craft have been laid over recent years, with more hauled up on the beach.

Anchorage

Anchor off the beach in 5–8m, as close in as local moorings permit. The sand is thin in patches and much of the bottom rock and boulders, making a tripline a sensible precaution. Gusts come down off the hills in the evening or an onshore breeze may spring up, so two anchors are advisable, and in the unlikely event of a northwesterly ground swell building it would be wise to leave at once. Dinghies can normally be landed on the beach, but if much swell is breaking it may be preferable to use the steps on the inside of the mole.

Although previously a hassle-free anchorage, following a number of thefts it is now considered unwise to leave a yacht unattended after dark. By the same token, dinghies left on the beach appear to be relatively safe in daylight when there are plenty of people around, but the same may not be true in the evening. It is reported that reliable watchmen can be recommended by the owner of the beach bar.

The wide bay at Baía do Tarrafal seen from the southeast, with the old mole and its offlying rocks on the left and Ponta Pretá just right of centre

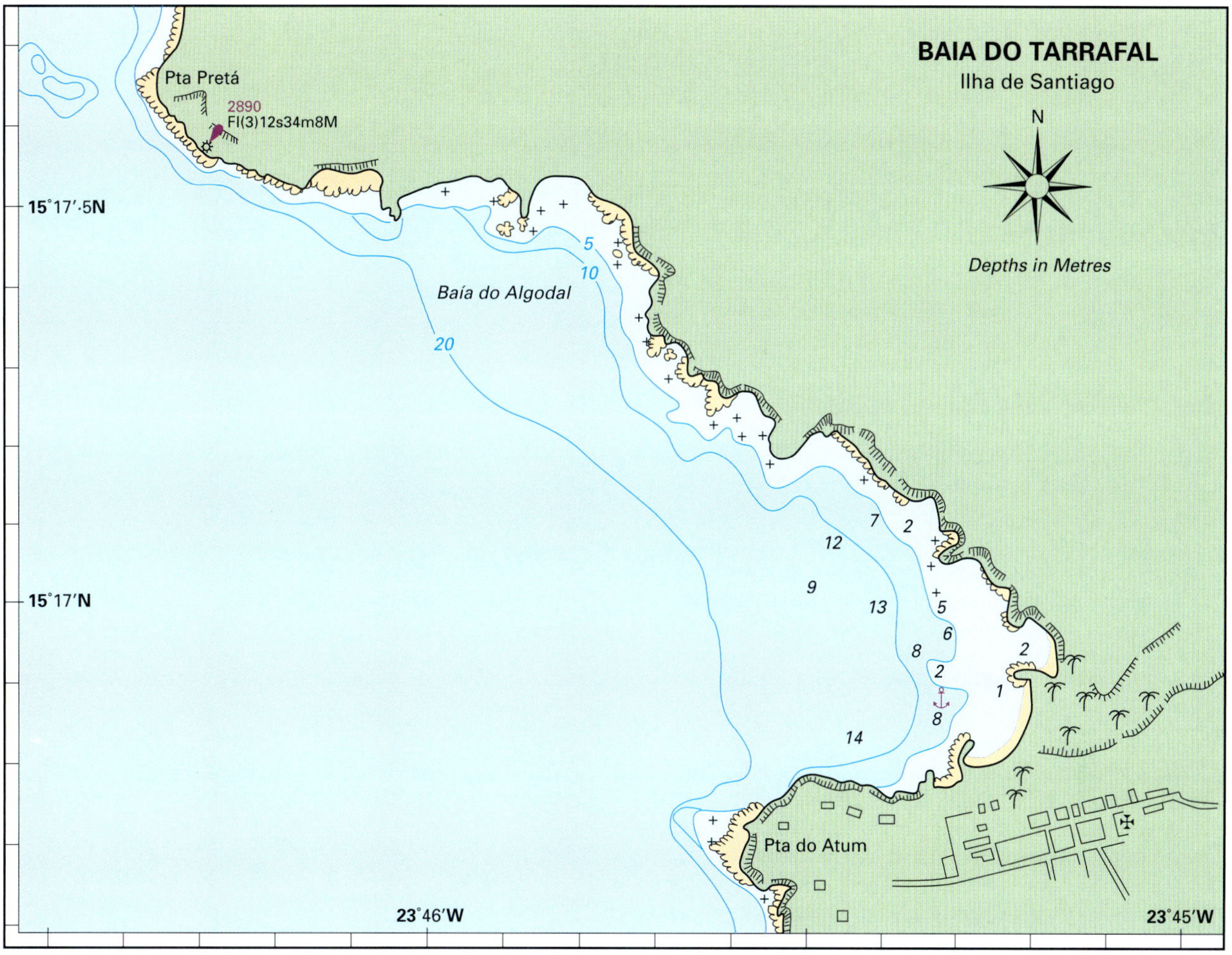

Formalities

The *Polícia Marítima* office is in the north end of an empty warehouse overlooking the mole. There is no sign, and although nominally open 0830–1200 and 1430–1600 Monday to Saturday, 0830–1200 Sunday, in practice the office is seldom manned. Mid-morning is probably the best time to catch someone. It appears that there is no longer a *Delegação Marítima* at the port.

Facilities

Water Usually available by can from a communal tap at the north end of the beach, or from one of the hotels/restaurants further south.

Fuel By can from the filling station just south of the town on the main Praia road.

Bank Overlooking the main square.

Shops/provisioning The usual limited range of canned and dried stores.

Produce market New and much enlarged market a little way down the main Praia road selling fruit, vegetables and fish (which may also be bought directly from the fishermen on the beach).

Cafés, restaurants & hotels Two hotels on the beach with several small *residencials* in town and the usual range of restaurants, café and bars.

Medical services Small hospital and pharmacy.

Communications

Post office On the main Praia road.

Internet access Free Wi-Fi in the main square, a cybercáfe in the town, or try one of the hotels.

Taxis and frequent *aluguer* minibuses to and from Praia and elsewhere.

The superb beach at Baía do Tarrafal, a favourite weekend spot for residents of Santiago

IV. THE CAPE VERDES

Ilha do Fogo

Between 14°49'N–15°03'N and 24°17'W–24°31'W

Introduction

Ilha do Fogo lies 30M west of Ilha de Santiago, the whole 476km² island comprising a classic and spectacular single volcanic cone. A crater nearly 8km in diameter occupies the middle of the island, with a small cone on its eastern side forming the highest point at almost 3,000m. The volcano's most violent eruption in recorded history occurred in the late 17th century and lasted for several years, during which flames and smoke were said to be visible for more than 100 miles. It was at this time that the island's name was changed from São Filipe to Fogo – 'fire' in Portuguese. Though largely quiet these days the volcano continues to have active periods – in 1951, when lava poured down the steep eastern slopes into the sea, and more recently from early 1995, when it spewed ash, lava and molten rock at intervals for over a year.

The 1995 eruption, which began on the night of 2 April, was largely confined to the interior of the massive crater. Lava flows and 'bombs' of molten rock covered the single access road across its floor and almost obliterated the small village of Boca Fonte, though the slightly larger villages of Portela and Bangaeira just escaped. Incredibly, no lives were lost as local people fled their homes. Much of the vine-growing area was destroyed, either by lava or by layers of volcanic ash, but despite being provided with new houses on the mountain's southern slopes many people have since chosen to return.

When approaching from the east the island looks totally desolate, but the western side is cultivated with much terracing, though still predominantly brown. Due to Fogo's height a wider variety of crops can be grown than on most of the other islands, including coffee, vines (though wine production has been much reduced since the eruption), and the usual fruit, vegetables, maize and sugar cane. The 55,000 population appear to be more evenly spread throughout the island than is often the case elsewhere in the Cape Verdes, though the majority live in and around the capital, São Filipe.

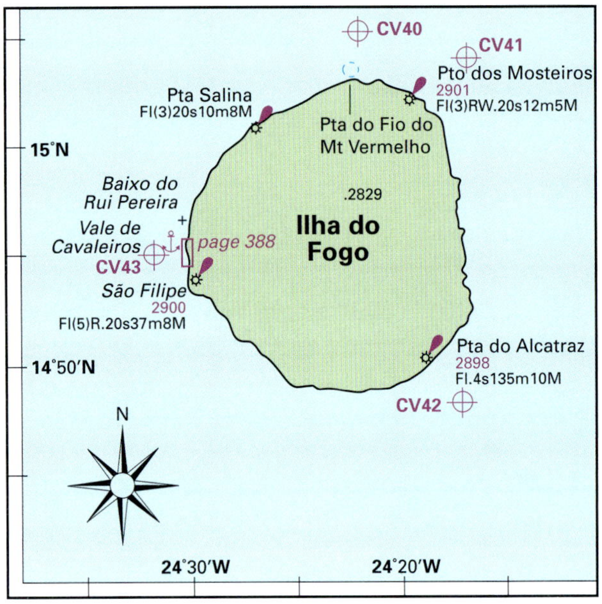

Fogo has long been popular with yachtsmen, with an excursion to the crater a highlight of any visit to the Cape Verdes. After more than a decade during which departure regulations effectively precluded a visit by yacht, in 2011 the law was relaxed – see page 333 – and private yachts may now request a next port' (*próximo porto* or *porto seguinte*) document from the *Delegação Marítima* when clearing out from Mindelo or Porto da Praia, and then visit one or more of the smaller islands before leaving territorial waters. It is still necessary to clear in and out with the *Delegação Marítima* in São Filipe – see page 388.

Probably the most common reason for calling at Ilha do Fogo – 'island of the fire' – is to see the volcano, which last erupted in 1995 after being dormant for more than 40 years

Telecommunications

Mobile (cell) phone reception is good around São Filipe and Vale de Cavaleiros, but has not been verified on the volcano itself. Note also the limitation detailed on page 329. The country code for the Republic of Cape Verde islands is 238, with no individual island or area codes, and the telephone number always contains seven digits. If only six are given, add a 2 (for landlines) or 9 (for mobiles) at the beginning.

There is at least one cybercafé in São Filipe, and the seafront gardens are said to offer free Wi-Fi.

Navigation

Waypoints
⊕CV40 – 15°06'·2N 24°22'·1W (3M N of Pta do Fio do Mt Vermelho)
⊕CV41 – 15°04'·1N 24°16'·9W (3M NE of Pta dos Mosteiros)
⊕CV42 – 14°49'N 24°17'·1W (2M SE of Pta do Alcatraz)
⊕CV43 – 14°55'·1N 24°31'·8W (1·5M W of Vale de Cavaleiros)

Courses and distances
⊕CV41 – ⊕CV37 (1·5M SE of Porto da Praia, Santiago) = 48M, 103° / 283°
⊕CV41 – ⊕CV39 (1M W of Baía do Tarrafal, Santiago) = 32M, 067° / 247°
⊕CV41 – ⊕CV42 = 15·5M, by eye
⊕CV41 – ⊕CV43 via ⊕CV40 = 21M, by eye
⊕CV42 – ⊕CV37 (1·5M SE of Porto da Praia, Santiago) = 47M, 085° / 265°
⊕CV42 – ⊕CV43 = 17 5M, by eye
⊕CV43 – ⊕CV25 (2M W of Pta Machado, São Vicente) = 120M, 343° / 163°
⊕CV43 – ⊕CV46 (1M E of Pta da Jalunga, Ilha Brava) = 7·6M, 258° / 078°

Magnetic variation
11°10'W (2011), decreasing by 7'E annually. Local magnetic anomalies are reported to exist near Ilha do Fogo.

Tidal Streams
Although tidal streams are weak, the southwest-going current may attain 1 knot around the north and northeast coasts of Ilha do Fogo, but is strongly wind-influenced.

Charts
Admiralty *366* (1:500,000)
US *51540* (1:200,000)
Imray-Iolaire *E4* (1:500,000)

Lights
2901 **Porto dos Mosteiros**
Fl(3)RW.20s12m5M White pyramid on wall 3m
2898 **Ponta do Alcatraz**
Fl.4s135m10M 225°-vis-045°
White column 3m
2900 **São Filipe (Fortim Carlota)**
Fl(5)R.20s37m8M
Red lantern on white column near large cream building 4m
Ponta Salina
Fl(3)20s10m8M Metal column 5m

Websites

The internet currently offers no websites devoted specifically to Ilha do Fogo, though it has several pages on en.wikipedia.org/wiki/Cape_Verde and others on the excellent www.caboverde.com. Some dramatic footage of the 1995 volcanic eruption is to be found on www.youtube.com, and the island also features on several of the general sites listed on page 330.

Approach

The coast is generally steep-to and 0·5M clearance is sufficient. However, more is required both north and south of Vale de Cavaleiros – see Approach and entrance, on this page.

Harbours and anchorages

Vale de Cavaleiros

14°55'·13N 24°30'·24W (breakwater head)

Waypoint
⊕CV43 – 14°55'·1N 24°31'·8W (1·5M W of Vale de Cavaleiros)

Tides
Time difference on Dakar: –0120, on Mindelo (Porto Grande): –0035
Mean spring range 1·1m
Mean neap range 0·6m

Plans
Imray-Iolaire *E4* (1:10,000)

Lights
2900 **São Filipe (Fortim Carlota)** Fl(5)R.20s37m8M
Red lantern on white column near large cream building 4m
Note There is a red daymark on the breakwater at Vale de Cavaleiros, but it is **NOT** lit, nor expected to be

Harbour communications
Port Authority ✆ 281 1264

Fogo's only harbour

Situated on the west coast of Ilha do Fogo about 1·5M north of the main town of São Filipe, Vale de Cavaleiros provides reasonable shelter from the prevailing northeasterly winds and swell. It is Ilha do Fogo's only harbour, used mostly by small cargo boats and the inter-island ferries, which visit several times each week.

Since the breakwater was repaired and extended in 2000, ships berth alongside. Even so, space in the harbour is very limited and if a second ship arrives any yachts at anchor may be instructed to leave immediately.

Approach and entrance

If coming from the north keep at least 1M offshore to avoid Baixo do Rui Pereira which has less than 2m. If coming from the south take care to avoid the reef about 0·5M south of the port, 'marked' by a very angular section of wreck which shows at all times. An offing of 0·75M is adequate.

The breakwater is not lit, though the end is marked by a red daymark, and night entry would be unwise.

Anchorage and berthing

Yachts normally lie south of the inner mole, with a long stern line to the mole (which features one large old bollard and numerous large angular rocks) and a bower anchor down in about 4m over sand and rock. Swell-induced chafe is likely to be significant, making a chain loop around the rocks ashore a wise precaution, with nylon or other springs on both anchor and stern lines.

A maximum of six yachts can be squeezed in, with the most comfortable spot about a quarter of the way in from the outer end. Be sure to remain well east of the end of the mole – most ships need the entire width between the breakwater and the mole to turn (either on arrival or departure), and while this is generally done with great skill there would almost certainly be no compensation were a yacht to be damaged in the process.

Dinghies can be landed either on the beach or on the slipway north of the inner mole (taking care not to impede local fishing boats), but in either case do not venture ashore unshod. Security does not appear to be a problem.

The breakwater is in frequent use by ferries and cargo ships, but it might be possible to lie alongside for a short period to take on water and/or fuel – consult ENAPOR in their office at the harbour, both for permission to lie alongside and regarding the water hose. Swell may be a problem, though the angled breakwater end gives some protection.

Be particularly vigilant if visiting Vale de Cavaleiros between June and November, a season when the wind may swing into the south without warning. Local people take this danger very seriously indeed, and ships generally move out of the harbour overnight due to the danger of being trapped by a southerly gale.

Formalities

All formalities are handled by the *Delegação Marítima* (harbour office) from premises on the southern edge of São Filipe (open 0800–1500 Monday to Friday), the port captain dealing only with commercial vessels. (To locate the office, take an *aluguer* into town and listen for the (noisy) electrical generating station. Continue past it and over a bridge, past a primary school and then take the second right. The *Delegação Marítima* occupy a small grey building opposite the secondary school, the Liceu de São Filipe). The officials are normally helpful and welcoming, and at least one speaks English.

The usual ship's papers, passports and crew list (giving name, passport number and place/date of birth) are required, though only the skipper need visit the office in person. A standard charge of CVE 650$ / €6 is payable for a stay of any duration, irrespective of the size of yacht or number of crew, and the ship's papers are held until departure, though a photocopy may be accepted. If intending to leave at the weekend the papers will be released on Friday, and again only the skipper need attend.

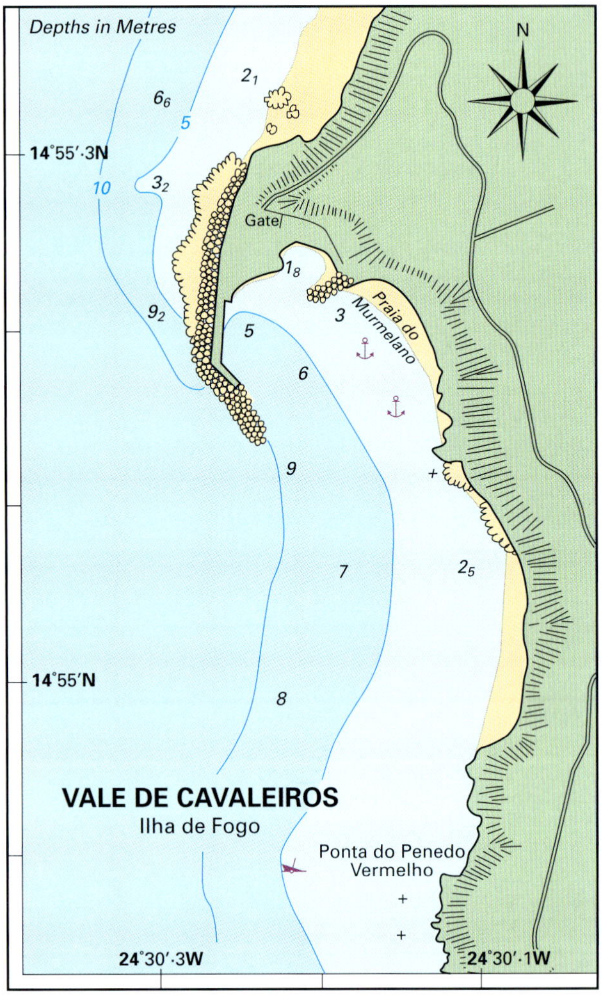

Facilities

Good drinking water from a tap in the gated area beyond the harbour offices, right under the cliffs against the eastern wall. Visiting yachtsmen are normally allowed to fill containers without charge, though as a security guard will need to unlock the gate it would be best to choose a quiet moment between ferries or other ships. It may be possible to arrange with ENAPOR – see above – for larger amounts to be taken aboard by hose.

Small amounts of fuel can be collected by can from one of the filling stations in São Filipe. It may be possible to arrange for large quantities of fuel (for one or more yachts) to be delivered by road tanker – a short (but hot) walk up the road from the harbour brings one to the main Shell depot and offices – but it would be far preferable to fuel up before leaving Mindelo or, failing that, Praia.

Vale de Cavaleiros, looking slightly south of west. The breakwater was rebuilt and extended in early 2000 after repeated storm damage

Yachts lie at anchor beneath the cliffs at Vale de Cavaleiros, with stern lines to the inner mole

There is virtually nothing else at the harbour other than a part-time bar (operational only when a ship is in) and the possibility of buying fish direct from the boats. It is necessary to walk some 3km south into São Filipe for shopping, though there is a good chance of getting a ride in an *aluguer* or a private car.

São Filipe

14°53'·7N 24°30'W

Poor anchorage but pleasant town

São Filipe is an open and exposed roadstead – the island is almost circular and the prevailing northeast wind and swell work right round it. It is generally untenable during the winter with heavy surf running, though it might be possible to anchor off its dramatic black sand beach in summer when the northeasterlies are light or the wind is in the south. Conditions are too unpredictable to leave a yacht unattended, and for the same reason it is unsuitable as an overnight stop.

São Filipe is Ilha do Fogo's largest town, identifiable by its large church and the old fortress of Fortim Carlota to the south. It is the oldest town in the Cape Verdes other than the largely ruined Cidade Velha in Santiago, and one of the most elegant. Many of the houses and official buildings dating back to Portuguese days are in good condition and there are several attractive public squares and gardens. The atmosphere is pleasantly relaxed and local people notably friendly towards visitors.

Facilities

Water Several taps in the town, in addition to that at Vale de Cavaleiros.
Showers Try one of the hotels or *residencials*.
Laundry Communal washing area with public taps and apparently unlimited water.
Fuel Small amounts by can from either of the filling stations. See above regarding larger quantities.
Bottled gas Shell Gas is available from the filling station in São Filipe and the Shell depot near the harbour, but bottles cannot be refilled.
Bank In the southwest corner of the town, open 0800–1500 Monday to Friday. The cash dispenser outside accepts Visa cards.
Shops/provisioning Several grocery stores plus at least one bakery, the former reasonably well-stocked with staples and canned goods, including canned butter and UHT milk, as well as highly drinkable Fogo wine. The bakery appears to sell out early, but bread is also available from a vendor near the market. The Shell Select shop (continue along the road which leads south from the harbour) is open on Sunday.
Produce market With a reasonable selection of fruit and vegetables, some locally grown. Several vendors also sell eggs, and/or fresh goats' cheese in small rounds wrapped in sisal leaves.
Cafés, restaurants & hotels Several restaurants and hotels, but a surprising lack of seafront cafés or bars. The Hotel Xaguate has a swimming pool which is available to non-residents for a small fee.
Medical services Small hospital on the road towards the harbour.

Communications

Post office Overlooking the main square, near the back of the older part of town.
Internet access At Eduteca Alf in the centre of the town, plus free Wi-Fi in the seafront gardens.
Car hire Available, though prices are relatively high. See Road transport, page 331.
Taxis Taxi trips to the volcano are expensive, but if the weather is clear the cost is more than justified. Several local taxi drivers speak good English.
Buses The usual *aluguers*, which leave from near the market.
Ferries Ferries call several times each week on their way to Praia, sometimes calling at Brava en route.
Air services Frequent departures to Santiago, less frequently to São Vicente and Ilha do Sal, from the small airport some 2·5km east of São Filipe. The old airport at Mosteiros is now closed.

Porto dos Mosteiros

15°02'N 24°19'·39W (molehead)

Lights
2901 **Porto dos Mosteiros**
Fl(3)RW.12s12m5M White pyramid on wall 3m

A complete misnomer…

Not a port by any stretch of the imagination – rather a gap in the rocks where a few fishing boats are hauled ashore. Fully open to the northeast trades and quite impossible so far as a yacht is concerned.

Ilha Brava

Between 14°48'N–14°54'N and 24°40'W–24°45'W

Introduction

Ilha Brava is the southwestermost island of the archipelago, separated from Ilha do Fogo by a 10M wide channel. With an area of only 67km² it is the smallest of the Cape Verdes to be permanently inhabited and is the only one where the population is decreasing – from about 6,900 when the first edition of this book was researched in 1987 to around 6,000 in 2011.

Very little of Isla Brava is low-lying, its highest point being Monte de Fountainhas at 976m. The capital, Vila de Nova Sintra, is situated in a small *caldeira* more than halfway up its northeastern slope. It is a very beautiful island – frequently described as the prettiest in the archipelago – and unique in that even the west coast, so often dry and desolate in the other islands, is green and fertile with coconut palms lining the shore and good drinking water.

Whether anchored at Porto da Furna or at Fajã d'Água it is worth catching an *aluguer* up to Vila de Nova Sintra, an attractive little town which is nearly always shaded by a cloudcap and, for much of the year, is remarkably green with splashes of red hibiscus and indigo-flowered creeper. The young man employed to dig weeds out of the cracks between the cobblestones must surely have a job unique in the Cape Verdes... If anchored at Furna, the walk back down the old cobbled road is highly

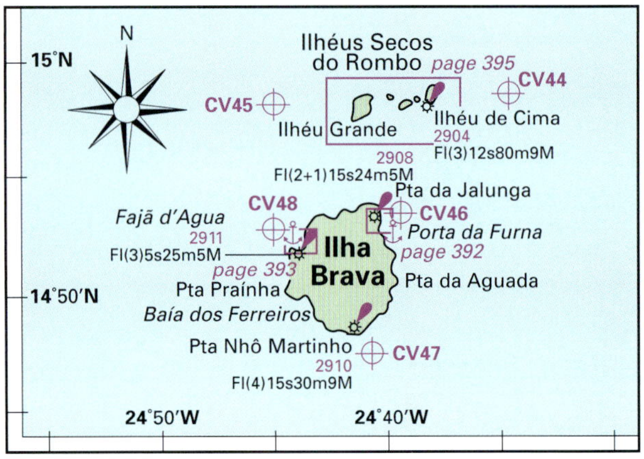

Ilha Brava is amongst the greenest of the Cape Verdes

Looking eastward over the rooftops of Vila de Nova Sintra, with the shadow of Ilha do Fogo in the distance *Sue Thatcher*

Navigation

Waypoints
⊕ CV44 – 14°58'·6N 24°34'·7W (3M E of Ilhéu de Cima)
⊕ CV45 – 14°58'·1N 24°45'W (3M W of Ilhéu Grande)
⊕ CV46 – 14°53'·5N 24°39'·4W (1M E of Pta da Jalunga)
⊕ CV47 – 14°47'·4N 24°41'·4W (1M SE of Pta Nhô Martinho)
⊕ CV48 – 14°52'·8N 24°45'W (1M WNW of Fajã d'Água)

Courses and distances
⊕ CV44 – ⊕ CV25 (2M W of Pta Machado, São Vicente) = 116M, 344° / 164°
⊕ CV44 – ⊕ CV46 = 7M, 222° / 042°
⊕ CV45 – ⊕ CV25 (2M W of Pta Machado, São Vicente) = 114M, 349° / 169°
⊕ CV45 – ⊕ CV48 = 5·3M, 180° / 000°
⊕ CV46 – ⊕ CV43 (1·5M W of Vale de Cavaleiros) = 7·6M, 078° / 258°
⊕ CV46 – ⊕ CV47 = 7M, by eye
⊕ CV47 – ⊕ CV48 = 8M, by eye

Magnetic variation
11°15'W (2011), decreasing by 7'E annually. Local magnetic anomalies are reported to exist near Ilha Brava.

Tidal Streams
Tidal streams are weak but the current sets southwest around Ilha Brava at 0·5–1 knot.

Charts
Admiralty *366* (1:500,000)
US *51540* (1:200,000)
Imray-Iolaire *E4* (1:500,000)

Lights
2904 **Ilhéu de Cima, summit** Fl(3)12s80m9M 047°-vis-252° & 304°-vis-010°
Square white hut and lantern 4m
Note Obscured from offshore 010°-047° by Ilha Brava and 252°-304° by Ilha do Fogo, but visible if passing between Ilhéu de Cima and its larger neighbours
2908 **Ponta da Jalunga**
Fl(2+1)15s24m5M 187°-vis-007°
Grey column and building 8m
2910 **Ponta Nhô Martinho**
Fl(4)15s30m9M 237°-vis-106 5°
Square white column, red lantern 4m
2911 **Ponta de Fajã d'Água**
Fl(3)5s25m5M Metal column 5m

Smiling local children at Fajã d'Água on Ilha Brava's west coast *Sue Thatcher*

Pawpaw growing in a garden in Vila de Nova Sintra, with hibiscus flowering in the background *Sue Thatcher*

recommended for those without knee problems, and offers a chance to admire the scenery at one's own pace. Only the very energetic would wish to walk back to Fajã d'Água, albeit the views are even more spectacular.

Following the relaxation in departure regulations detailed on page 333, private yachts may now request a next port' (*próximo porto* or *porto seguinte*) document from the *Delegação Marítima* when clearing out from Mindelo or Porto da Praia, and then visit one or more of the smaller islands before leaving territorial waters. It is still necessary to clear in and out with the *Delegação Marítima* in Porto da Furna – see page 392.

Telecommunications

Mobile (cell) phone reception is good in both Porto da Furna and Fajã d'Água, as well as up at Vila de Nova Sintra, but has not been checked elsewhere. Note also the limitation detailed on page 329. The country code for the Republic of Cape Verde islands is 238, with no individual island or area codes, and the telephone number always contains seven digits. If only six are given, add a 2 (for landlines) or 9 (for mobiles) at the beginning.

Public internet access, at broadband speeds, is available one street up from the harbour at the north end of the town in a clearly signed building. Computers are available or one can take one's own laptop. It is not clear whether connection is via Wi-Fi or cable, and whether a charge is made.

Websites

In addition to several pages on www.en.wikipedia.org/wiki/Cape_Verdes and others on the excellent www.caboverde.com, Ilha Brava has its own website at www.bravanews.com. In Portuguese only (which auto-translates poorly), it is presumably intended as much for the many islanders living abroad as for those at home and includes news, forthcoming events, ferry schedules, etc. A relatively new site, it is to be hoped that an English version soon be available.

Approach

The coast is generally steep-to with 0·5M clearance sufficient all round the island.

Harbours and anchorages

Porto da Furna

14°53′·2N 24°40′·7W (anchorage)

Waypoint
⊕ CV46 – 14°53′·5N 24°39′·4W (1M E of Pta da Jalunga)

Plans
Imray-Iolaire *E4* (1:9,750)

Lights
2908 **Ponta da Jalunga**
Fl(2+1)15s24m5M 187°-vis-007°
Grey column and building 8m
Note Resembles a farm building until close enough to see the lantern

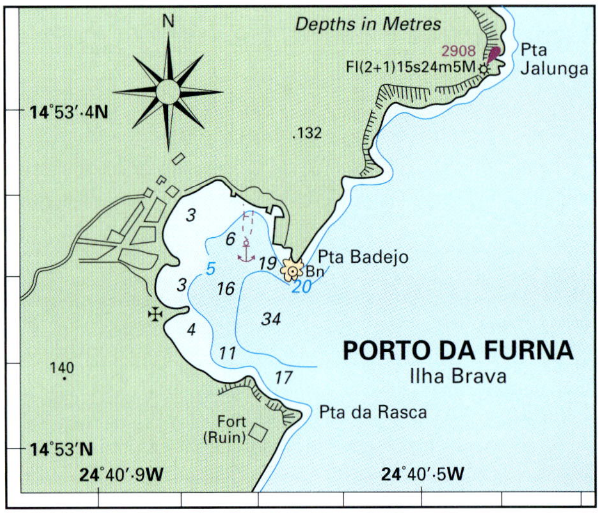

Small ferry harbour with little space for yachts

Porto da Furna lies 0·5M southwest of Ponta Jalunga and is well sheltered other than in a southeasterly. It is the island's main harbour and used by the inter-island ferries, one of which generally calls several times each week. The village lies at the head of the bay, from which a road runs the few kilometres up to Vila de Nova Sintra.

Security does not appear to be a problem, but some of the children are more persistent than in other harbours with demands for sweets, pens and money. A simple 'no' accompanied by a friendly smile is undoubtedly the best response, unless well-prepared with suitable small gifts.

Approach and anchorage

The white buildings of the village are visible from several miles offshore unless hidden by Ponta Badejo. The buildings associated with Ponta da Jalunga are more difficult to spot, but a single, large, white wind generator stands on the hill behind. Neither side of the entrance is lit and entry in darkness is out of the question.

Major construction work took place in the northern part of the harbour a few years ago and the inter-island ferry (or more accurately her after half) now berths alongside the quay inside Ponta Badejo. The rocks running south from the headland are marked by an unlit green post with a west cardinal ⧗ topmark.

The semicircular bay at Porto da Furna seen from the Vila de Nova Sintra road, looking almost due east

Unfortunately much of the space which might be available to visiting yachts has, for the past six years or more, been occupied by a large motorboat and an 18m yacht, both apparently unattended and semi-derelict. The area to the east of them is required for the ferry to manoeuvre, but there is room to the west for two or three yachts to anchor with lines run ashore. This spot is less protected than further east and sometimes uncomfortable, but is usually tenable, albeit with some movement. Note, however, that the surrounding hills may deflect the prevailing northeast trades around to southeast or even southwest within the harbour itself. Depths shoal close inshore, but 4–5m should be found a little further out. Dinghies can be landed on the slipway, where there is seldom much swell.

Formalities

If the *Capitão do Porto* does not appear seek him out at the *Delegação Marítima* (harbour office) in the first building on the right on entering the town – the entrance is up some stairs at the back. The office is seldom manned at weekends unless a ship is due. Ship's documents are not held by the authorities and the *Capitão do Porto* may be willing to issue inward and outward clearance in a single visit. There are no immigration authorities on Ilha Brava and no *Polícia* in the village, though an official will come down from Vila de Nova Sintra if required.

Facilities

Water may be had from a tap in the village, where there are several small stores selling dried and tinned foods. Little fresh produce is available other than bread and eggs, plus fish and shellfish directly from the boats. Public internet access, at broadband speeds, is available one street up from the harbour at the north end of the town in a clearly signed building. Computers are available or one can take one's own laptop.

Alternatively catch an *aluguer* up the road to the small but charming town of Vila de Nova Sintra. The bank now has a cash dispenser – though bear in mind that Cape Verdean currency cannot be

The ferry quay and northern headland at Porto da Furna. The unlit green beacon mentioned in the text can just be made out at the left end of the dark rock shelf

exchanged after leaving the islands – and a well-stocked grocery store with a reasonable range of frozen meats is situated two blocks west of the main square. The bakery, formerly opposite the bank, is now said to be difficult to find without directions, but the many street vendors of fruit, vegetables and eggs are normally happy to assist. There is also a post office with telephone and a small health centre.

Fajã d'Agua (Porto da Fajã)

14°52'·4N 24°44'W (anchorage)

Waypoint
⊕ CV48 – 14°52'·8N 24°45'W (1M WNW of Fajã d'Água)

Tides
Time difference on Dakar: –0135, on Mindelo (Porto Grande): –0050. Predictions for Fajã d'Agua are available via Admiralty *EasyTide* – see page 336
Mean spring range 1·2m
Mean neap range 0·6m

Plans
Admiralty *369* (1:17,500) (based on surveys dating from 1905; soundings in fathoms)

Lights
2911 **Ponta de Fajã d'Água**
Fl(3)5s25m5M Metal column 5m

The westernmost anchorage in the Cape Verdes

Fajã d'Água is a small bay sheltered from north through east to southwest, which offers a quiet and pleasant anchorage in the right conditions. The village of Lagoa fringes its northeast corner. In general both adults and children are friendly and helpful without being pushy, though little English is spoken. There are good natural swimming pools at the southern end of the bay.

In the late 1990s an airport was completed about 2km to the south, but unpredictable crosswinds combined with a very short runway proved such a dangerous combination that within a year or two it was closed – fortunately before an accident took place.

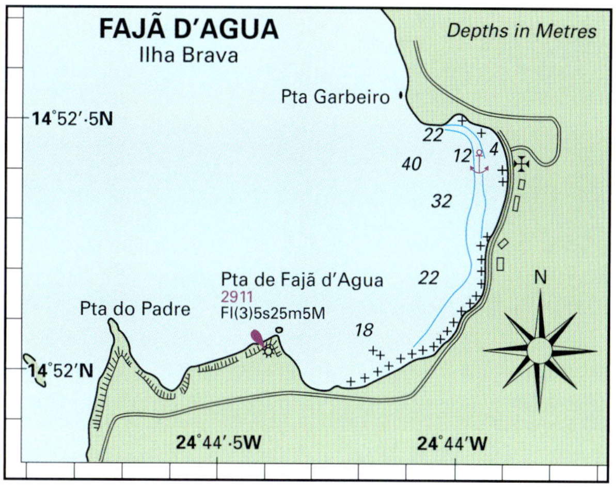

Approach and anchorage

Anchor off the village in the northeast corner of the bay, in 8m or less over sand with a few rocks. One or two local craft plus a few fishcages are moored off the small slipway. The seabed drops steeply to 20m or more offshore and it is essential to be well onto the shelf before anchoring. Swell can work its way right around the island, and the surrounding mountains frequently cause the wind to box the compass.

The beach is mainly boulders with some sand and getting ashore can be a damp experience, particularly with a heavy dinghy, though local fishermen often come to assist. The favoured places are either below the slipway (where a dinghy can safely be left), or further north in the shadow of the pale green church, according wind and swell.

Formalities

None – there is no *Delegação Marítima* (harbour office) or *Polícia* in the village.

Facilities

Facilities ashore are limited, but many yachtsmen will appreciate the opportunity to fill their tanks with good water, do their laundry and even take a (cold) shower. (Note that only the tap gives drinking

A fisherman pulls away from Fajã d'Água's somewhat inadequate slipway

The wide bay at Fajã d'Água, looking northeast. The 'bird table' on the left supports the area's only light

water – the supply to the showers and laundry sinks is brackish). All three facilities cost just a few escudos – ask around for the young man who holds the key.

A small general store sells the usual dry and canned goods, and a limited range of fruit and vegetables is generally obtainable from local people. Fish and fresh bread are sold from a bright green house almost opposite the slipway – it may also be possible to arrange with local fishermen for a langouste or two. More shops, including a relatively well-stocked general store, will be found some distance up the valley at Vila de Señora del Montaña. Taxis are available, though the energetic will enjoy the attractive walk.

Two small *pensãos* overlook the bay, and with prior arrangement a shower followed by meal ashore might be arranged.

Communications are limited to a single, card-operated, telephone and the occasional *aluguer*.

Fajã d'Água seen from the north, with the parapet of the narrow road in the foreground *Sue Thatcher*

Baía dos Ferreiros

14°49'·9N 24°44'·3W (anchorage)

Sheltered anchorage in remote, unspoilt bay

This deeply indented bay south of Ponta Praínha offers good anchorage in about 8m good holding over sand some 100m off the beach. Favour the eastern side, as there are reported to be rocks in the western part of the bay. It is open only to the south, with limited fetch for the prevailing northeast trades though gusts blowing down off the mountain might well be fierce. A breaking reef, clearly visible in good daylight, partially blocks the entrance.

There are no permanent homes at Baía dos Ferreiros and the road between it and the small village of Lomba, perched on a ridge high above, was only completed in 2010. Electricity is still a novelty, put to good use running a small ice plant to enable the villagers to send fish to the market in Vila de Nova Sintra. The village boasts one small shop and spectacular views, but little else. Even so, the climb up to the village is recommended as worth the effort, the descent being made 'along shady terraces beside irrigation channels to the adjacent valley, which is farmed and grows every fruit known to man – a true Garden of Eden'.

A dozen or more rowing boats are drawn up on the beach at Baía dos Ferreiros, reported as 'launching in the dark at about 0300, each lit by a flaming paraffin torch and crewed by entire families fishing – an amazing sight'. Few yachts visit, but when one appears the village children run down and swim out to it (towing the smaller ones on homemade rafts of empty water bottles!), while fishermen are eager to barter part of their catch for fuel or other necessities. More than one yachtsman has described their visit to Baía dos Ferreiros as the highlight of their time in the Cape Verdes.

Baía dos Ferreiros on the southwest coast of Ilha Brava offers sheltered anchorage and a warm welcome, but few facilities *Mary Robinson*

Ilhéus Secos do Rombo

Bisected by 14°58'·4N 24°38'·2W (Ilhéu de Cima) and 14°58'·1N 24°41'·5W (Ilhéu Grande)

Rocky islets with connecting reefs

This group of four tiny and two somewhat larger islets, all connected by reefs, lies about 3·5M north of Ilha Brava and 7·5M west of Ilha do Fogo, separated from them by deep-water channels. The largest and highest of the group are Ilhéu de Cima to the east at 77m, and Ilhéu Grande to the west at 96m.

None of the islets are inhabited, though Jill Schinas reports that the fishing is excellent and fishermen from Brava come out each day, principally working the reef-strewn area between Ilhéu Luiz Carneiro and Ilhéu de Cima. In rough weather they camp out (there is a small building) rather than make the journey to and fro in their small open boats. The entire group is a designated nature reserve, with large colonies of nesting seabirds including the rare Bulwer's petrel.

If on passage and not intending to stop at the islands, the entire area should be given an offing of several miles.

Anchorages

Two anchorages are marked on US *51540*. That south of Ilhéu Luiz Carneiro, the small central island, is said to be reasonable in normal conditions and easy to vacate by day or night should the need arise. The other, east of Ilhéu Grande (known locally as Ilhéu de Baixo) looks quite untenable, though there is said to be a spot off the southwest tip which is somewhat better. In either case getting ashore would be a problem as there is no beach.

Donald M Street describes a visit to the islands by chartered fishing boat, anchoring on the south side of Ilhéu de Cima in the saddle between two hills in 7–9m in good holding over sand. He regards it as unsuitable for an overnight stay but usable by day in settled weather.

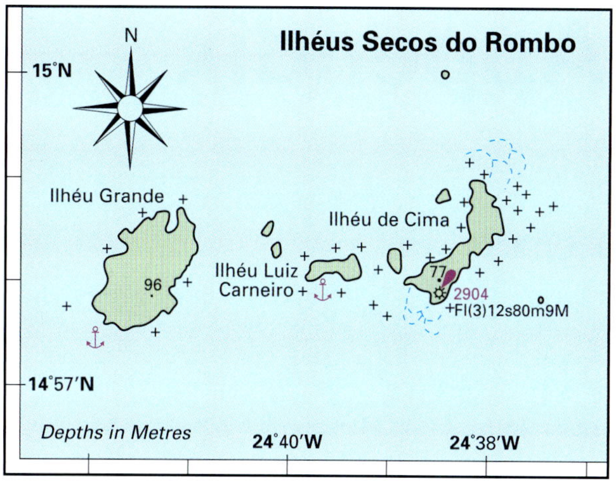

Navigation

Waypoints
⊕ CV44 – 14°58'·6N 24°34'·7W (3M E of Ilhéu de Cima)
⊕ CV45 – 14°58'·1N 24°45'W (3M W of Ilhéu Grande)

Courses and distances
⊕ CV44 – ⊕ CV25 (2M W of Pta Machado, São Vicente) = 116M, 344° / 164°
⊕ CV44 – ⊕ CV46 = 7M, 222° / 042°
⊕ CV45 – ⊕ CV25 (2M W of Pta Machado, São Vicente) = 114M, 349° / 169°
⊕ CV45 – ⊕ CV48 = 5·3M, 180° / 000°

Magnetic variation, Tides and Charts
See under Ilha Brava.

Lights
2904 **Ilhéu de Cima, summit**
Fl(3)12s80m9M 047°-vis-252° & 304°-vis-010°
Square white hut and lantern 4m
Note Obscured from offshore 010°-047° by Ilha Brava and 252°-304° by Ilha do Fogo, but visible if passing between Ilhéu de Cima and its larger neighbours

Ilhéu Grande, seen from Ilha Brava on a rather hazy day

The Ilhéus Secos do Rombo seen from the southeast

Appendix

I. Charts

Charts are listed in numerical order within each section. They and other publications may be updated on a regular basis by reference to online *Notices to Mariners* or the national equivalent:

Admiralty Notices to Mariners: published weekly by the UK Hydrographic Office
www.ukho.gov.uk

Avisos aos Navegantes: published monthly by the Portuguese *Instituto Hidrográfico*
www.hidrografico.pt

Avisos a los Navegantes: published weekly by the Spanish *Armada Española*
www.armada.mde.es

US Notices to Mariners: published weekly by the US National Geospatial-Intelligence Agency
http://msi.nga.mil

Imray Correction Notices: contain cumulative corrections for individual Imray charts.
Go to www.imray.com, enter the chart number in the home page 'search' box, and click on 'Latest corrections' at bottom left.

Charts produced by the Portuguese *Instituto Hidrográfico* may not be easy to obtain once in the Azores or Madeira, but can be ordered online before departure from J Garraio & Ca Lda in Lisbon (www.jgarraio.pt).

Charts produced by the Spanish *Instituto Hidrográfico de la Marina* are available from JL Gándara y Cía SA in Las Palmas (www.gandara-sa.com). See page 244.

Since June 2010 paper charts produced by the US National Geospatial-Intelligence Agency (formerly the NIMA/DMA) have not been available for public sale by the NGIA. However, nearly all are available from OceanGrafix LLC (www.oceangrafix.com) who print them as required, thus ensuring that charts are corrected to the date of despatch.

Attention is drawn to the notes regarding Horizontal chart datum on page 10, and on Chart datum and Satellite derived positions on pages 31, 141, 195 and 337.

Imray-Iolaire charts, as well as British Admiralty charts and publications, are available from:

Imray Laurie Norie & Wilson Ltd
Wych House, The Broadway,
St Ives, Cambs PE27 5BT, England
✆ 01480 462114 *Fax* 01480 496109
Email orders@imray.com
www.imray.com

Passage Charts

British Admiralty www.ukho.gov.uk

Chart	*Title*	*Scale*
3133	Casablanca to Islas Canarias, including Arquipelago da Madeira	1,250,000
3134	Islas Canarias to Nouakchott	1,250,000
3135	Nouakchott to Bissau and Arquipelago de Cabo Verde	1,250,000
4011	North Atlantic Ocean, Northern Part	10,000,000
4012	North Atlantic Ocean, Southern Part	10,000,000
4014	North Atlantic Ocean, Eastern Part	10,000,000
4103	English Channel to the Strait of Gibraltar and the Arquipélago dos Açores	3,500,000
4104	Lisboa to Freetown	3,500,000
4114	Arquipélago dos Açores to Flemish Cap	3,500,000
4115	Arquipélago dos Açores to the Arquipélago de Cabo Verde	3,500,000

US National Geospatial-Intelligence Agency
www.nga.mil (but see note above)

Chart	*Title*	*Scale*
103	English Channel to the Strait of Gibraltar including the Azores	3,500,000
104	Lisbon to Freetown	3,500,000
120	North Atlantic Ocean, Southern Sheet	6,331,100
121	North Atlantic Ocean, Northern Sheet	5,870,000
125	North Atlantic Ocean, Southeastern Sheet	5,281,950
126	North Atlantic Ocean, Northeastern Sheet	3,619,020

Imray Laurie Norie & Wilson Ltd www.imray.com

100	North Atlantic Ocean Passage Chart	1:7,620,000

The Azores

British Admiralty www.ukho.gov.uk

Chart	*Title*	*Scale*
1895	Ilha de São Miguel	150,000
	Ponta Delgada, São Miguel	10,000
1950	Arquipélago dos Açores	750,000
1956	Arquipélago dos Açores (Central Group)	175,000
1957	Harbours in the Azores (Central Group)	
	Canal do Faial	37,500
	Porto da Horta, Faial	10,000
	Vila da Praia, Graciosa	12,500
	Praia da Vitória, Terceira	12,500
	Angra do Heróismo, Terceira	12,500
1959	Flores, Corvo and Santa Maria with Banco Formigas	
	Ilhas Flores and Corvo	150,000
	Santa Cruz, Flores	25,000
	Lajes, Flores	20,000
	Ilha de Santa Maria with Banco das Formigas	150,000
	Vila do Porto, Santa Maria	12,500
	Bahia de Sao Lourenço, Santa Maria	12,500

Portuguese Hydrographic Institute
www.hidrografico.pt

Chart	*Title*	*Scale*
41101	Arquipélago dos Açôres	1,000,000
43101	Arquipélago dos Açôres – Grupo Ocidental	300,000
43102	Arquipélago dos Açôres – Grupo Central	300,000
43103	Arquipélago dos Açôres – Grupo Oriental	300,000
46201	Canal de São Jorge (Ilhas de São Jorge e Pico)	75,000
46401	Ilhas das Flores e do Corvo	75,000
	Porto das Lajes das Flores	5,000
	Porto de Santa Cruz das Flores	10,000
	Porto de Casa	5,000
46403	Ilha do Faial e Canal do Faial	50,000
	Porto da Horta	7,500
	Porto da Madalena	7,500
46404	Ilha Graciosa	50,000
	Vila da Praia	5,000
	Santa Cruz	5,000
	Folga	5,000
46405	Ilha Terceira	75,000
	Angra do Heroísmo	10,000
	Praia da Vitória	10,000
46406	Ilha de São Miguel	100,000
	Porto de Ponta Delgada	10,000
46407	Ilha de Santa Maria e Ilhéus das Formigas	
	Ilha de Santa Maria	75,000
	Porto de Vila do Porto	7,500
	Baía de São Lourenço	7,500
	Ilhéus das Formigas	75,000

Chart	*Title*	*Scale*
47501	Portos das Ilha de São Jorge e do Pico	
	Porto da Calheta, São Jorge	5,000
	Porto das Velas, São Jorge	5,000
	Porto de São Roque, Pico	5,000
	Porto das Lajes, Pico	5,000
	Porto de Santa Cruz das Ribeiras, Pico	5,000
47502	Vila Franca do Campo, São Miguel	7,500
	Ribeira Quente	5,000
	Porto Formoso, São Miguel	5,000
	Rabo de Peixe, São Miguel	5,000
	Porto de Capelas, São Miguel	5,000

US National Geospatial-Intelligence Agency
www.nga.mil (but see note above)

Chart	*Title*	*Scale*
51002	The Azores Archipelago	750,000
51041	Flores and Corvo	250,000
	Santa Cruz, Flores	25,000
	Lajes, Flores	20,000
51061	Faial, Graciosa, Terceira, Pico and São Jorge	250,000
51062	Plans in the Central Azores	
	Approaches to Horta, Faial	50,000
	Horta, Faial	10,000
	Approaches to Santa Cruz, Graciosa	50,000
	Santa Cruz, Graciosa	10,000
51064	Eastern Approaches to Terceira	50,000
	Angra do Heroísmo, Terceira	12,500
	Praia da Vitória, Terceira	10,000
51081	São Miguel and Santa Maria	250,000
	Vila Franca do Campo, São Miguel	20,000
	Vila do Porto, Sta Maria	10,000
51082	Approaches to Ponta Delgada São Miguel	50,000
	Ponta Delgada, São Miguel	10,000

Imray-Iolaire Series www.imray.com

Chart	*Title*	*Scale*
E1	Arquipélago dos Açores	750,000
	Vila das Lajes, Flores	20,000
	Horta, Faial	12,500
	Madalena, Pico	37,500
	Porto das Velas, São Jorge	7,500
	Vila da Praia, Graciosa	10,000
	Angra do Heroismo, Terceira	12,500
	Praia da Vitória, Terceira	20,000
	Ponta Delgada, São Miguel	10,000
	Vila Franco do Campo, São Miguel	15,000
	Vila do Porto, Santa Maria	10,000

The Madeira Group

British Admiralty www.ukho.gov.uk

Chart	*Title*	*Scale*
1684	Machico & Caniçal	7,500
1685	Ponta Gorda to	
	Ponta de Sao Lourenco	30,000
	Funchal	10,000
	Canical	10,030
1689	Ports in the Arquipelago da Madeira	
	Baia do Porto Santo	20,000
	Porto do Porto Santo	7,500
1831	Arquipélago da Madeira	150,000
3133	Casablanca to Islas Canarias, including	
	Arquipélago da Madeira	1,250,000
	Ilhas Selvagens	100,000

Portuguese Hydrographic Institute,
www.hidrografico.pt

Chart	*Title*	*Scale*
33101	Arquipélago da Madeira	350,000
36201	Ilha da Madeira e Ilhas Desertas	100,000
36401	Ilha do Porto Santo	50,000
	Baía do Porto Santo	15,000
	Porto do Porto Santo	5,000
36402	Ponta Gorda à Ponta de S. Lourenço	30,000
	Porto do Funchal	10,000
36403	Paul do Mar à Praia Formosa	30,000
	Câmara de Lobos e Praia Formosa	10,000
36406	Islas Desertas	50,000
	Doca (Carga da Lapa)	15,000
36407	Ilhas Selvagens	100,000
	Selvagem Grande	25,000
	Selvagem Pequena	25,000
37501	Portos da Ilha da Madeira	
	Portos do Machico e Caniçal	7,500
	Porto do Moniz	7,500
	Porto da Cruz	7,500

US National Geospatial-Intelligence Agency
www.nga.mil (but see note above)

Chart	*Title*	*Scale*
51261	Archipelago da Madeira	150,000
51263	Baía do Funchal and Praia Formosa	10,000
	Porto do Funchal	5,000
51342	Salvage Islands	103,640
	Selvagem Grande	20,625
	Selvagem Pequena and Ilhéu de Fora	20,700

Imray-Iolaire Series www.imray.com

Chart	*Title*	*Scale*
E3	Arquipelago de Madeira	170,000
	Baía de Porto Santo	25,000
	Ponta de Sao Lourenço	30,000
	Quinta do Lorde Marina	20,000
	Porto de Machico	7,500
	Água de Pena boatyard	5,000
	Porto do Funchal	10,000
	Porto de Recreio da Calheta	6,250
	Isla Deserta Grande – Anchorage	25,000

The Canary Islands

British Admiralty www.ukho.gov.uk

Chart	*Title*	*Scale*
886	Estrecho de la Bacayna	
	and approaches to Arrecife	75,000
	Puertos de Arrecife, Naos and	
	los Mármoles	12,500
1870	Lanzarote to Gran Canaria	300,000
	Approaches to Puerto del Rosario	75,000
	Puerto del Rosario	7,500
1847	Santa Cruz de Tenerife	12,500
1856	Plans in Gran Canaria	
	Approaches to Las Palmas de	
	Gran Canaria	75,000
	Las Palmas de Gran Canaria	12,500
	Puerto de Salinetas	15,000
1858	Approaches to Santa Cruz de Tenerife	
	and Santa Cruz de la Palma	
	Approaches to Santa Cruz de Tenerife	75,000
	Approaches to Santa Cruz de la Palma	75,000
	Santa Cruz de la Palma	10,000
	San Sebastián de la Gomera	10,000
1869	Gran Canaria to Hierro	300,000

Spanish Armada Española www.armada.mde.es

Chart	*Title*	*Scale*
60A	Lanzarote y Fuerteventura	200,000
60B	Fuerteventura y Gran Canaria	200,000
61A	Gran Canaria, Tenerife y La Gomera	200,000
61B	La Palma, La Gomera y El Hierro	200,000
505	De punta de Tostón a punta Amanay	50,000
507	Península de Jandía	55,000
600	De Arrecife a La Isleta con las islas	
	Alegranza, Montaña Clara y	
	La Graciosa	60,000
600A	Pasos entre las islas Alegranza,	
	Montaña Clara, La Graciosa y	
	Lanzarote	25,000
601	Costa occidental de la isla de Lanzarote	
	y costa norte de la isla de	
	Fuerteventura	60,000
601A	Estrecho de La Bocayna	25,000
604	Del puerto de Gran Tarajal	
	al puerto del Rosario	60,000
605	De Arrecife (Lanzarote)	
	a Puerto del Rosario (Fuerteventura)	60,000
	Puerto Calero	12,500
	Puerto del Carmen	12,500
610	Del cabo Descojonado	
	a la península de Gando	60,000
611	Del cabo Colorado a	
	la bahía de Melenara	60,000
612	Del puerto de Güimar	
	a la punta El Guindaste	60,000
613	Del puerto de los Cristianos	
	al puerto de Güímar	60,000
614	De punta Montaña Amarilla	
	a punta del Guindaste	60,000
616	Isla de la Palma	60,000
617	Isla de La Gomera	60,000
618	Isla de El Hierro	60,000
6010	Puertos de Arrecife, Naos y	
	Los Mármoles	10,000
6030	Puertos de Gran Tarajal y del Rosario	
	Puertos de Gran Tarajal	5,000
	Puerto del Rosario	5,000

Chart	Title	Scale
6100	Puerto de Las Palmas	12,500
6110	Puertos de Mogán, Arguineguín y Muelle Cementero	
	Puerto de Mogán	7,500
	Puertos de Arguineguín y Muelle Cementero	7,500
6120	Puerto de Santa Cruz de Tenerife	12,500
	Puerto Caballo	5,000
6140	Puerto de Los Cristianos	3,500
6150	Puertos de Santa Cruz de La Palma, San Sebastián de La Gomera y La Estaca	
	Puerto de Santa Cruz de La Palma	7,500
	Puerto de San Sebastián de La Gomera	7,500
	Puerto de La Estaca	7,500
D210	Gran Canaria	100,000
	Marina de Las Palmas	10,000
	Pasito Blanco	10,000
	Arguineguín	10,000
	Puerto Rico y Anfi del Mar	10,000
	Mogan	10,000
	Agaete / Las Nieves	10,000

US National Geospatial-Intelligence Agency, www.nga.mil (but see note above)

Chart	Title	Scale
51260	Islas Canarias (Western Group)	300,000
51341	Santa Cruz de Tenerife Harbour	50,000
	Santa Cruz de Tenerife	10,000
51343	Approaches to Puerto de Rosario	50,000
	Puerto del Rosario	10,000
51344	Ports in the Islas Canarias	
	Approaches to Puerto de la Luz	30,000
	Santa Cruz de la Palma	15,000
	Puerto de la Luz	10,000
51380	Islas Canarias (Eastern Group)	263,900

Imray-Iolaire Series www.imray.com

Chart	Title	Scale
E2	Islas Canarias	600,000
	Estrecho del Rio, Lanzarote	50,000
	Marina Rubicon, Lanzarote	25,000
	Puerto del Rosario, Fuerteventura	10,000
	Morro Jable, Fuerteventura	–
	Puerto de las Palmas, Gran Canaria	20,000
	Marina Tenerife, Santa Cruz de Tenerife	17,500
	Marina Santa Cruz, Santa Cruz de Tenerife	17,500
	Puerto de San Sebastián, Gomera	10,000
	Puerto de Santa Cruz, La Palma	12,500
	Puerto de la Estaca, Hierro	7,500

The Cape Verdes

British Admiralty www.ukho.gov.uk

Chart	Title	Scale
366	Arquipélago de Cabo Verde	500,000
367	Ports in the Arquipélago de Cabo Verde	
	Ilha do Sal	200,000
	Baía do Palmeira, Sal	12,500
	Porto do Santa Maria, Sal	20,000
	Approaches to Porto Grande, São Vicente	150,000
	Porto Grande, São Vicente	17,500
	Approaches to Porto da Praia, Santiago	150,000
	Porto de Praia, Santiago	15,000
369	Plans in the Arquipélago de Cabo Verde	
	Porto de Pedra de Lume, Sal	18,000
	Porto de Sal Rei, Bõa Vista	50,000
	Porto do Preguiça, São Nicolau	12,230
	Ilhas Sta Luzia, Branco and Razo	90,440
	Tarrafal do Monte Trigo, Sto Antão	12,000
	Ponta do Sol, Sto Antão	18,000
	Porto Inglez, Maio	24,500
	Porto da Santiago, Santiago	10,000
	Baía do Tarrafal, Santiago	18,500
	San Filipe and Encarnação anchorages, Fogo	10,000
	Porto da Fajã, Brava	17,500

Direcção Geral de Marinha e Portos, Cape Verdes

Chart	Title	Scale
11	Porto Novo	5,000
21	Porto da Palmeira, Ilha do Sal	–
31	Porto do Tarrafal, São Nicolau	5,000
41	Mindelo (Porto Grande), São Vicente	5,000
71	Porto da Praia, Santiago	–

Portuguese Hydrographic Institute, www.hidrografico.pt

Chart	Title	Scale
66301	Porto da Praia	7,500
66302	Porto Grande	10,000
67501	Portos das Ilhas de Santo Antão e São Nicolau	
	Porto Novo	5,000
	Tarrafal	5,000
	Porto da Preguiça	7,500
67503	Portos das Ilhas da Boavista e do Sal	
	Baía de Palmeira	5,000
	Santa Maria	7,500
	Porto de Sal Rei	10,000

US National Geospatial-Intelligence Agency, www.nga.mil (but see note above)

Chart	Title	Scale
51027	Baie Du Levrier to Cape Vert including Arquipelago de Cabo Verde	926,562
51500	Cabo Verde Islands:	
	Northwestern Part	250,000
	Porto Grande, São Vicente	20,000
51520	Cabo Verde Islands: Eastern Part	250,000
	Porto de Santa Maria, Sal	15,000
51540	Cabo Verde Islands: Southern Part	200,000
	Porto da Praia, Santiago	15,000

Imray-Iolaire Series www.imray.com

Chart	Title	Scale
E4	Arquipelago de Cabo Verde	500,000
	Baía da Palmeira, Sal	15,000
	Porto de Sal-Rei, Bõa Vista	30,000
	Porto da Preguiça, São Nicolau	8,500
	Porto do Tarrafal, São Nicolau	8,400
	Ilha de Sta Luzia	90,000
	Porto Grande (Mindelo), São Vincente	20,000
	Porto Novo, Sto Antão	10,000
	Porto da Praia, Santiago	22,000
	Cavaleiros, Fogo	10,000
	Porto da Furna, Brava	9,750

II. Waypoints

The Azores

Flores

⊕ A01 – 39°21′·3N 31°13′·9W (1M S of Pta da Rocha Alta: light weather)

⊕ A02 – 39°19′·3N 31°15′W (3M S of Pta dos Ilhéus: heavy weather)

⊕ A03 – 39°32′·6N 31°12′·4W (1M N of Pta Delgada)

⊕ A04 – 39°22′·2N 31°09′·4W (0·5M SE of Lajes)

⊕ A05 – 39°22′·8N 31°09′·3W (0·5M E of Lajes)

Corvo

⊕ A07 – 39°39′·3N 31°07′·7W (1M SSW of Pta Negra)

⊕ A08 – 39°44′·5N 31°07′·2W (1M N of Pta Torrais)

⊕ A09 – 39°40′·1N 31°06′W (0·5M SE of Vila Nova)

Faial

⊕ A10 – 38°36′·1N 28°51′·4W (1M W of Pta dos Capelinhos)

⊕ A11 – 38°30′·7N 28°45′·8W (1M SW of Pta do Castelo Branco)

⊕ A12 – 38°30′·5N 28°37′W (0·5M SE of Monte da Guia)

⊕ A13 – 38°32′N 28°36′·6W (0·5M E of Horta)

⊕ A14 – 38°32′·8N 28°35′·5W (0·5M E of Pta de Baía do Cavalo)

⊕ A15 – 38°35′·8N 28°35′·4W (0·5M E of Pta da Ribeirinha)

⊕ A16 – 38°39′·7N 28°42′·9W (1M N of Pta dos Cedros)

Pico

⊕ A17 – 38°32′·5N 28°32′·5W (0·5M NW of Madalena)

⊕ A18 – 38°32′·1N 28°18′·6W (0·5M NE of São Roque)

⊕ A19 – 38°24′·3N 28°00′·6W (1M ESE of Pta da Ilha)

⊕ A20 – 38°24′N 28°16′·2W (0·5M W of Lajes do Pico)

São Jorge

⊕ A21 – 38°45′·7N 28°20′·3W (1M WNW of Pta dos Rosais)

⊕ A22 – 38°40′·2N 28°12′·5W (0·5M SSW of Velas)

⊕ A23 – 38°35′·5N 28°00′·8W (0·5M SSW of Calheta)

⊕ A24 – 38°32′·8N 27°43′·4W (1M ESE of Ilhéu do Topo)

Graciosa

⊕ A25 – 38°59′·7N 27°55′·4W (1M SE of Ilhéu de Baixa)

⊕ A26 – 39°02′·7N 27°56′·8W (1M SE of Vila da Praia)

⊕ A27 – 39°05′·2N 27°59′W (0·5M ESE of Cais da Barra)

⊕ A28 – 39°06′·6N 28°03′·8W (1M NW of Pta da Barca)

Terceira

⊕ A29 – 38°37′·8N 27°13′·6W (0·5M S of Monte Brasil)

⊕ A30 – 38°38′·7N 27°12′·5W (0·5M SE of Angra do Heroísmo)

⊕ A31 – 38°35′·7N 27°06′·6W (1M S of Ilhéus Fradinhos)

⊕ A32 – 38°43′·5N 27°01′·7W (1M E of Praia da Vitória)

⊕ A33 – 38°47′·4N 27°03′·3W (1M NE of Ilhéu do Norte)

⊕ A34 – 38°46′·6N 27°23′·7W (1M NW of Pta Serreta)

São Miguel

⊕ A35 – 37°56′·6N 25°47′·7W (2M NNW of Pta da Bretanha)

⊕ A36 – 37°51′·7N 25°52′·6W (1M W of Pta da Ferraria)

⊕ A37 – 37°49′·2N 25°51′·6W (1M SW of Pta da Candelaria)

⊕ A38 – 37°42′·9N 25°41′·1W (1M S of Santa Clara)

⊕ A39 – 37°43′·9N 25°38′·9W (0·5M SE of Ponta Delgada)

⊕ A40 – 37°41′·9N 25°30′·6W (0·5M S of Pta da Galera)

⊕ A41 – 37°41′·9N 25°25′·2W (1M SSE of Vila Franca do Campo)

⊕ A42 – 37°43′·7N 25°09′·5W (1M SE of Fajã do Calhau)

⊕ A43 – 37°48′·5N 25°05′·5W (2M E of Pta Marquesas)

⊕ A44 – 37°52′·5N 25°06′·9W (2M NE of Pta da Ribeira)

Santa Maria

⊕ A45 – 37°00′·4N 25°12′·1W (1M WNW of Pta do Lobaio)

⊕ A46 – 36°56′N 25°08′·9W (0·5M S of Vila do Porto)

⊕ A47 – 36°56′·5N 25°06′·4W (0·5M SSE of Baía da Praia)

⊕ A48 – 36°55′·1N 24°59′·9W (1M SE of Pta do Castelo)

⊕ A49 – 36°59′·6N 25°02′·6W (0·5M ENE of Baía de São Lourenço)

⊕ A50 – 37°01′·4N 25°02′·4W (1M NE of Pta do Norte)

The Madeira Group

Porto Santo

⊕ M01 – 33°09′N 16°15′·2W (2M NE of Ilhéu de Fora)

⊕ M02 – 33°02′·8N 16°16′·2W (0·5M SE of Ilhéu de Cima)

⊕ M03 – 33°02′·3N 16°26′·5W (1·5M W of Ilhéu de Ferro)

⊕ M04 – 32°59′·2N 16°22′·9W (0·5M S of Ilhéu de Baixo)

⊕ M05 – 33°03′·1N 16°19′·1W (0·4M SSW of Porto Santo harbour)

Madeira

⊕ M06 – 32°42′·9N 16°34′·6W (1M SE of Ilhéu de Fora, Madeira)

⊕ M07 – 32°37′·6N 16°50′·8W (0·5M S of Pta do Garajau)

⊕ M08 – 32°37′·4N 16°56′·5W (0·5M S of Pta da Cruz)

⊕ M09 – 32°48′·8N 17°16′·4W (0·5M W of Pta do Pargo)

⊕ M10 – 32°44′·2N 16°41′·5W (0·5M SSE of Baía da Abra)

⊕ M11 – 32°44′N 16°42′·8W (0·5M S of Quinta do Lorde Marina)

⊕ M12 – 32°43′·6N 16°43′·7W (0·5M S of Caniçal)

⊕ M13 – 32°42′·6N 16°45′·2W (0·5M SE of Machico)

⊕ M14 – 32°38′·5N 16°53′·9W (0·5M ESE of Funchal)

⊕ M15 – 32°38′·2N 17°58′·5W (0·5M SSW of Linha Sextante Lda boatyard)

⊕ M16 – 32°40′·2N 17°05′·5W (0·5M S of Marina do Lugar de Baixo)

⊕ M17 – 32°42′·6N 17°10′·6W (0·5M SW of Porto de Recreio da Calheta)

⊕ M18 – 32°51′·9N 17°09′·2W (0·5M E of Porto Moniz)

Ilhas Desertas

⊕ M19 – 32°30′·2N 16°30′·7W (0·5M SSW of Carga da Lapa, Ilha Deserta Grande)

Ilhas Selvagens

⊕ M20 – 30°09′·9N 15°50′·1W (0·5M ENE of Baixo do Nordeste, Selvagem Grande)

The Canary Islands

Lanzarote

⌖ C01 – 29°29′N 13°30′·6W (4M N of Isla Alegranza)

⌖ C02 – 29°17′·1N 13°27′·7W (1M NE of Isla Graciosa)

⌖ C03 – 29°15′·6N 13°27′·9W (0·5M SE of Pta de Pedro Barba, Isla Graciosa)

⌖ C04 – 29°12′·5N 13°24′·3W (1M E of Pta del Palo)

⌖ C05 – 28°57′·5N 13°31′·3W (0·5M SE of Puerto de los Mármoles)

⌖ C06 – 28°56′·7N 13°32′·8W (0·5M SSE of Puerto de Arrecife)

⌖ C07 – 28°54′·4N 13°42′·4W (0·5M S of Puerto Calero)

⌖ C08 – 28°49′·8N 13°47′·2W (0·5M S of Pta Papagayo)

⌖ C09 – 28°51′·1N 13°49′·6W (0·5M SW of Marina Rubicon)

⌖ C10 – 28°50′·3N 13°52′·4W (0·5M S of Pta Pechiguera)

Fuerteventura

⌖ C11 – 28°44′·9N 14°02′·4W (2M NW of Pta Tostón)

⌖ C12 – 28°45′·2N 13°50′·8W (1M NE of Corralejo)

⌖ C13 – 28°47′N 13°48′·5W (1M NNE of Isla de Lobos)

⌖ C14 – 28°29′·2N 13°50′·8W (0·5M SE of Puerto del Rosario)

⌖ C15 – 28°23′N 13°51′·4W (0·5M S of Puerto del Castillo / Caleta de Fustes)

⌖ C16 – 28°12′·9N 13°56′·2W (1M SE of Pta Lantailla)

⌖ C17 – 28°11′·9N 14°01′·2W (0·5M SSE of Gran Tarajal)

⌖ C18 – 28°01′·7N 14°19′·9W (1M S of Pta de Morro Jable)

⌖ C19 – 28°02′·8N 14°22′·4W (0·5M SW of Morro Jable entrance)

⌖ C20 – 28°01′·2N 14°32′W (3M SSW of Pta Jandia)

Gran Canaria

⌖ C21 – 28°12′·3N 15°22′·3W (2·5M NE of La Isleta)

⌖ C22 – 28°06′·9N 15°23′·9W (0·5M SE of Las Palmas)

⌖ C23 – 27°59′·7N 15°20′·8W (1M NE of Pta Melenara)

⌖ C24 – 27°56′·6N 15°20′·6W (1M NE of Pta de Gando)

⌖ C25 – 27°51′·7N 15°21′·7W (1M E of Pta Arinaga)

⌖ C26 – 27°47′·9N 15°24′·6W (1M SE of Pta de Tenefé)

⌖ C27 – 27°42′·3N 15°34′W (2M S of Pta de Maspalomas)

⌖ C28 – 27°44′·3N 15°37′W (0·5M SSE of Puerto de Pasito Blanco)

⌖ C29 – 27°44′·8N 15°42′W (1M SW of Puerto de Arguineguín)

⌖ C30 – 27°46′·4N 15°43′W (0·5M SW of Puerto Rico)

⌖ C31 – 27°48′·5N 15°46′·2W (0·5M SW of Puerto de Mogán)

⌖ C32 – 28°05′·6N 15°43′·2W (0·5M SW of Puerto de las Nieves)

⌖ C33 – 28°11′·8N 15°43′·6W (2M NNW of Pta Sardina)

Tenerife

⌖ C34 – 28°38′·3N 16°09′·3W (2M N of Roque de Fuera)

⌖ C35 – 28°33′·3N 16°06′W (1M E of Pta de Anaga)

⌖ C36 – 28°29′·2N 16°12′·3W (0·5M SE of Dársena Pesquera, Santa Cruz de Tenerife)

⌖ C37 – 28°27′N 16°14′·5W (0·5M SE of Dársena de los Llanos, Santa Cruz de Tenerife)

⌖ C38 – 28°23′·5N 16°19′·3W (0·5M SSE of Puerto Radazul)

⌖ C39 – 28°21′·2N 16°21′·5W (0·5M SE of Puerto Deportivo La Galera)

⌖ C40 – 28°00′·7N 16°32′·1W (1M SSE of Pta Montaña Roja)

⌖ C41 – 28°00′·6N 16°36′·6W (0·5M SSE of Marina San Miguel)

⌖ C42 – 27°59′·9N 16°39′·8W (0·5M SSW of Las Galletas / Marina del Sur)

⌖ C43 – 27°59′·4N 16°42′·7W (1M SW of Pta de la Rasca)

⌖ C44 – 28°02′·4N 16°43′·4W (0·5M SW of Los Cristianos)

⌖ C45 – 28°04′·6N 16°44′·8W (0·5M WSW of Puerto Colón)

⌖ C46 – 28°15′·3N 16°50′·9W (0·5M NW of Puerto de Los Gigantes)

⌖ C47 – 28°21′N 16°57′·7W (2M W of Pta de Teno)

⌖ C48 – 28°25′·6N 16°49′·8W (2M N of Pta de Buenavista)

⌖ C49 – 28°36′·8N 16°19′·3W (2M N of Pta del Hidalgo)

La Gomera

⌖ C50 – 28°14′·2N 17°16′·2W (2M N of El Roguillo)

⌖ C51 – 28°04′·6N 17°06′·2W (0·5M SE of San Sebastián)

⌖ C52 – 28°01′·3N 17°11′·4W (0·5M SE of Puerto de Santiago)

⌖ C53 – 28°00′·2N 17°14′·6W (1M S of Pta del Becerro)

⌖ C54 – 28°04′·3N 17°20′·3W (0·5M SW of Puerto de Vueltas)

La Palma

⌖ C55 – 28°53′·5N 17°55′W (2M N of Pta del Mudo)

⌖ C56 – 28°51′·8N 17°45′W (2M NE of Pta Cumplida)

⌖ C57 – 28°44′·6N 17°42′·3W (1M E of Pta Sancha)

⌖ C58 – 28°39′·8N 17°44′·8W (1M SE of Santa Cruz de la Palma)

⌖ C59 – 28°26′·2N 17°50′·5W (2M S of Pta Fuencaliente)

⌖ C60 – 28°38′·3N 17°57′·2W (0·5M WSW of Tazacorte)

El Hierro

⌖ C61 – 27°53′N 17°55′·8W (2M N of Pta Norte)

⌖ C62 – 27°48′·6N 17°50′·8W (2M E of Pta Caleta)

⌖ C63 – 27°46′·2N 17°53′·1W (1M SE of Puerto de la Estaca, El Hierro)

⌖ C64 – 27°37′·4N 17°58′·4W (1M SSE of Pta Restinga)

⌖ C65 – 27°42′·1N 18°10′·4W (1M SW of Pta de la Orchilla)

The Cape Verdes

Ilha do Sal

⊕ CV01 – 16°55′·5N 22°55′·3W (4M N of Pta Norte)
⊕ CV02 – 16°51′·7N 23°01′·4W (3M NW of Pta Preta)
⊕ CV03 – 16°44′·8N 22°59′·9W (1M WSW of Porto de Palmeira)
⊕ CV04 – 16°34′·1N 22°55′·4W (1M S of Pta do Sinó)
⊕ CV05 – 16°44′·8N 22°53′W (1M SSE of Porto de Pedra de Lume)

Boavista

⊕ CV06 – 16°15′·8N 22°57′·5W (3M NW of Pta do Sol)
⊕ CV07 – 16°11′·2N 22°57′·1W (1M NW of Ilhéu de Sal Rei, NW point)
⊕ CV08 – 16°02′·6N 23°01′·2W (3M W of Pta Varandinha)
⊕ CV09 – 15°59′·8N 23°00′·3W (3M SW of Pta Varandinha)
⊕ CV10 – 15°47′·7N 23°05′W (4M ESE of Baixo de João Valente)

São Nicolau

⊕ CV11 – 16°34′·2N 23°59′·3W (2M E of Pta Leste)
⊕ CV12 – 16°42′·9N 24°20′·6W (2M N of Pta Espechim)
⊕ CV13 – 16°39′·9N 24°27′·2W (2M NW of Pta Galeão)
⊕ CV14 – 16°34′·1N 24°22′·2W (0·5M W of Porto do Tarrafal)
⊕ CV15 – 16°26′·8N 24°18′·9W (2M S of Pta Vermelharia)

Santa Luzia

⊕ CV16 – 16°37′·2N 24°32′·7W (2M E of Ilhéu Raso)
⊕ CV17 – 16°40′N 24°43′·2W (2M W of Ilhéu Branco)
⊕ CV18 – 16°45′·1N 24°38′·9W (2M E of Pta dos Tarrafes)
⊕ CV19 – 16°50′·4N 24°46′·6W (2M N of Pta dos Piquinhos)
⊕ CV20 – 16°47′·1N 24°49′·6W (2M W of Pta do Algodoeiro)
⊕ CV21 – 16°43′·5N 24°45′·5W (1M SW of Pta do Laje)

São Vicente

⊕ CV22 – 16°53′·7N 24°49′·2W (3M NE of Pta do Calhau)
⊕ CV28 – 17°06′N 24°53′·7W (4M E of Pta da Tumba, Santo Antão)
⊕ CV23 – 17°01′N 24°55′·6W (8M NE of Ilhéu dos Passaros)
⊕ CV24 – 16°53′·6N 25°01′W (1M WNW of Mindelo)
⊕ CV25 – 16°50′·3N 25°07′·1W (2M W of Pta Machado)
⊕ CV26 – 16°45′·6N 24°58′·8W (1M S of Pta Lombinho)

Santo Antão

⊕ CV27 – 17°16′·4N 25°05′·5W (4M N of Pta do Sol)
⊕ CV28 – 17°06′N 24°53′·7W (4M E of Pta da Tumba)
⊕ CV29 – 17°00′·6N 25°03′·2W (0·5M SE of Porto Novo)
⊕ CV30 – 16°52′·4N 25°17′·9W (2M S of Pta do Pesqueiro Fundo)
⊕ CV31 – 17°02′·8N 25°23′·9W (2M W of Pta Mangrade)

Ilha do Maio

⊕ CV32 – 15°22′·5N 23°13′W (3M NW of Pta Cais)
⊕ CV33 – 15°15′·8N 23°15′·9W (2M W of Pta do Pau Sêco)
⊕ CV34 – 15°07′·9N 23°14′·3W (1M WSW of Porto do Maio)

Santiago

⊕ CV35 – 15°24′·4N 23°43′·8W (4M N of Pta Moreia)
⊕ CV36 – 15°03′·9N 23°24′W (4M NNE of Pta do Lobo)
⊕ CV37 – 14°53′·3N 23°29′·2W (1·5M SE of Porto da Praia)
⊕ CV38 – 15°04′·4N 23°49′W (2M W of Pta da Janela)
⊕ CV39 – 15°16′·9N 23°46′·4W (1M W of Baía do Tarrafal)

Ilha do Fogo

⊕ CV40 – 15°06′·2N 24°22′·1W (3M N of Pta do Fio do Mt Vermelho)
⊕ CV41 – 15°04′·1N 24°16′·9W (3M NE of Pta dos Mosteiros)
⊕ CV42 – 14°49′N 24°17′·1W (2M SE of Pta do Alcatraz)
⊕ CV43 – 14°55′·1N 24°31′·8W (1·5M W of Vale de Cavaleiros)

Ilha Brava

⊕ CV44 – 14°58′·6N 24°34′·7W (3M E of Ilhéu de Cima)
⊕ CV45 – 14°58′·1N 24°45′W (3M W of Ilhéu Grande)
⊕ CV46 – 14°53′·5N 24°39′·4W (1M E of Pta da Jalunga)
⊕ CV47 – 14°47′·4N 24°41′·4W (1M SE of Pta Nhô Martinho)
⊕ CV48 – 14°52′·8N 24°45′W (1M WNW of Fajã d'Água)

Ilhéus Secos do Rombo

⊕ CV44 – 14°58′·6N 24°34′·7W (3M E of Ilhéu de Cima)
⊕ CV45 – 14°58′·1N 24°45′W (3M W of Ilhéu Grande)

III. Further reading

Passages and general information

Africa Pilot (NP 1) (UK Hydrographic Office) Madeira, Canaries and Cape Verdes only
Atlantic Crossing Guide, The Jane Russell (RCC Pilotage Foundation/Adlard Coles Nautical)
Atlantic Pilot Atlas, The James Clarke (Adlard Coles Nautical)
Birds of the Atlantic Islands: Canary Islands, Madeira, Azores, Cape Verde Tony Clarke (Helm Field Guides)
Bugs, Bites & Bowels Dr Jane Wilson-Howarth (Cadogan Guides)
First Aid at Sea Dr Douglas Justins & Dr Colin Berry (Adlard Coles Nautical)
Fishing Afloat Dick McClary (Royal Yachting Association)
Flight Identification of European Seabirds Anders Blomdahl, Bertil Breife & Niklas Holmstrom (Helm Identification Guides)
Ocean Birds Lars Löfgren (Cristopher Helm)
Ocean Passages and Landfalls Rod Heikell & Andy O'Grady (Imray Laurie Norie & Wilson)
Ocean Passages for the World (NP 136) (UK Hydrographic Office)
Reeds Maritime Meteorology Maurice Cornish & Elaine Ives (Adlard Coles Nautical)
Rough Guide Portuguese Phrasebook (Rough Guide Phrasebooks)
Rough Guide Spanish Phrasebook (Rough Guide Phrasebooks)
Rough Guide to Travel Health, The Dr Nick Jones (Rough Guides)
Seabirds, an Identification Guide Peter Harrison (Houghton Mifflin)
Seafarer's Guide to Marine Life, The Paul V Horsman (Cristopher Helm)
Spanish for Cruisers Kathy Parsons (Aventuras Publishing)
Travel Health Dr Jane Wilson-Howarth (Cadogan Guides)
West Coast of Europe and Northwest Africa (Pub 143) (US National Geospatial-Intelligence Agency)
Whales & Dolphins of the European Atlantic Dylan Walker & Graeme Cresswell (WildGuides UK)
Whales, Dolphins, and Porpoises Mark Carwardine (Dorling Kindersley Handbooks)
World Cruising Routes Jimmy Cornell (Adlard Coles Nautical)
Yachtsman's Ten Language Dictionary Barbara Webb & The Cruising Association (Adlard Coles Nautical)

The Azores

Açores em Vista Aérea / Azores in Aerial View Filipe Jorge, Isobel Soares de Albergaria & Rui Monteiro (Argumentum, Lisbon, Portugal)
Açores Flores (Azores Flowers) Erik Sjögren (Direcção Regional de Turismo, Horta, Faial)
Azores Guide for Tourists (Publiçor Lda, Ponta Delgada, São Miguel) Published annually
Azores David Sayers (Bradt Travel Guides)
Azores, The Claude Dervenn (George C Harrap & Co) Out of print, but sometimes available secondhand
Azores, The Robin Bryans (Faber & Faber) Out of print, but sometimes available secondhand
Azores, The Terry Marsh (Globetrotter)
Azores: Car Tours and Walks Andreas Stieglitz (Sunflower Books)
Azores: Globetrotter Travel Pack Terry Marsh (New Holland Publishers)
Destinazores Tourist Guide (Destinazores, Ponta Delgada, São Miguel) Available in several languages
Dolphins and Whales from the Azores Serge Viallelle (Espaço Talassa, Lajes do Pico)
Madeira and the Azores Claude Herve-Bazin (JPM Publications SA, Switzerland)
Operation Alacrity: The Azores and the War in the Atlantic N Herz (Naval Institute Press)
Parques e Jardins dos Açores / Azores Parks and Gardens Isobel Soares de Albergaria (Argumentum, Lisbon, Portugal)
Peter – Café Sport Jorge Alverto da Costa Pereira (Quetzal Editores, Lisbon)
West Coasts of Spain and Portugal Pilot (NP 67) (UK Hydrographic Office)
Winter in the Azores and a Summer at the Baths of the Furnas, A Joseph & Henry Bullar (The British Library)

The Madeira Group

Cruise of the Alerte, The E F Knight (Kessinger Publishing)
Faróis da Madeira / Lighthouses of Madeira Filipe Jorge & J Teixeira de Aguilar (Argumentum, Lisbon, Portugal)
Gardens of Madeira, The Gerald Luckhurst (Frances Lincoln)
Madeira & Porto Santo: Rough Guide Directions Matthew Hancock (Rough Guides)
Madeira and the Azores Claude Herve-Bazin (JPM Publications SA, Switzerland)
Madeira Plants and Flowers Antonio da Costa & Luis de O Franquinha (Francisco Ribeira, Funchal, Madeira)
Madeira: AA Essential Guides (Automobile Association)
Madeira: Baedeker (Mairdumont GMbH & Co)
Madeira: Berlitz Pocket Guides (Berlitz Publishing)
Madeira: Car Tours and Walks John & Pat Underwood (Sunflower Books)
Madeira: DK Eyewitness Top 10 Travel Guides Christopher Catling (Dorling Kindersley)
Madeira: Insight Guides (APA Publications Pte)
Madeira: The 50 finest levada and mountain walks Rolf Goetz (Rother Walking Guides)
Madeira: Thomas Cook Traveller Guides (Thomas Cook Publishing)
Walk! Madeira Shirley & Mike Whitehead and Ros & David Brawn (Discovery Walking Guides)
Walking in Madeira: 60 Routes on Madeira and Porto Santo Paddy Dillon (Cicerone Press)

The Canary Islands

Bananas About La Palma David M Addison (AuthorHouse)
Canary Islands Cruising Guide Jimmy Cornell, Juan-Francisco Martin & Andrew Bishop (World Cruising Publications)
Canary Islands: Lonely Planet Sarah Andrews & Josephine Quintero (Lonely Planet Publications)
Classic Geology in Europe: The Canary Islands Juan Carlos Carracedo & Simon Day (Terra Publishing)
Flowers in the Canary Islands Perez Juan Alberto Rodriguez (Editorial Everest)
Flowers of the Canary Islands Bruno Foggi & Andrea Innocenti (EG Bonechi, Italy)
Guanches Survivors, and their Descendants, The José Luis Concepción (José Luis Concepción)
History of the Discovery and Conquest of the Canary Islands, The Juan de Abreu Galindo (Elibron Classics) Facsimile of a 1764 publication
La Gomera: A Guide to the Unspoiled Canary Island Tim Hart (Colley Books)
La Gomera: Island of Columbus Kristine Edle Olsen (Thames & Hudson)
Tenerife and Its Six Satellites, or The Canary Islands Past and Present Olivia M Stone. Vol.1: Tenerife, La Gomera, La Palma, El Hierro; Vol.2: Lanzarote, Fuerteventura, Gran Canaria. (Adamant Media Corporation / Elibron Classics) Facsimile of an 1887 publication

Series:
AA Spiral/Essential Guides: Lanzarote; Fuerteventura; Gran Canaria; Tenerife (Automobile Association)
Berlitz Pocket Guides: Canary Islands; Lanzarote and Fuerteventura; Gran Canaria; Tenerife (Berlitz Publishing)
Car Tours and Walks: Lanzarote; Fuerteventura; Gran Canaria; Tenerife; Southern Tenerife and La Gomera; Palma and El Hierro Noel Rochford (all) (Sunflower Books)
Globetrotter Travel Packs: Canary Islands Andy Gravette; *Lanzarote* Rowland Mead; *Tenerife* Rowland Mead (New Holland Publishers)
DK Eyewitness Guides: Canary Islands Piotr Paszkiewicz & Hanna Faryna-Paszkiewicz; *Gran Canaria* Lucy Corne (Dorling Kindersley)
Pocket Guides: Lanzarote; Fuerteventura; Gran Canaria; Tenerife (Thomas Cook Publishing)
Rother Walking Guides: Tenerife; La Gomera; La Palma Klaus and Annette Wolfsperger (all) (Rother Walking Guides)
Rough Guide Directions: Lanzarote & Fuerteventura Emma Gregg; *Gran Canaria* Neville Walker; *Tenerife* Christian Williams (Rough Guides)
Walk! Lanzarote David & Ros Brawn; *Walk! Tenerife* David Brawn; *Walk! La Gomera* Charles Davis; *Walk! La Palma* Charles Davis (Discovery Walking Guides)
Walking on: Tenerife; La Gomera and El Hierro; La Palma, The World's Steepest Island Paddy Dillon (all) (Cicerone Press)

The Cape Verdes

Cape Verde Islands Berlitz Pocket Guide (Berlitz Pocket Guides)
Cape Verde Islands Aisling Irwin & Colum Wilson (Bradt Travel Guides)
Cape Verde Islands (Great Britain Foreign Office) Facsimile of a 1923 publication
Cape Verde Callie Flood (Other Places Publishing)
Cape Verde: Crioulo Colony to Independent Nation Westview Profiles: Nations of Contemporary Africa by Richard Lobban (Perseus)
Kapverdische Inseln: Der Nautische Revierführer Kai Brossmann, Nikolaus Hüwe, André Mégroz (MSK Mediaplanung Schott Klas GbR)
Street's Guide to the Cape Verde Islands Donald M Street (Seaworthy Publications)
The History of the Cape Verde Islands Abe Hall (Webster's Digital Services)
Travellers Cape Verde Sue Dobson (Thomas Cook Publishing)

IV. Glossary

A more complete list of translations can be found in the *Yachtsman's Ten Language Dictionary* compiled by Barbara Webb and the Cruising Association (Adlard Coles Nautical).

General and chartwork terms

English	*Spanish*	*Portuguese*
anchor, to	fondear	fundear
anchorage	fondeadero, ancladero	fundeadouro, ancoradouro
basin, dock	dársena	doca
bay	bahía, ensenada	baía, enseada
beach	playa	praia
beacon	baliza	baliza
beam	manga	largura, boca
berth	atracar	atracar
black	negro	preto
blue	azul	azul
boatbuilder	astillero	estaleiro
bottled gas	cilindro de gas, carga de gas	cilindro de gás, bilha de gás
breakwater	rompeolas, muelle	quebra-mar, molhe
buoy	boya	bóia
bus	autobús	autocarro
cape	cabo	cabo
car hire	aquilar coche	alugar automóvel
chandlery (shop)	efectos navales, apetrachamento	fornecedore de barcos, aprestos
channel	canal	canal
charts	cartas náuticas	cartas hidrográficas
church	iglesia	igreja
crane	grua	guindaste
creek	estero	esteiro
Customs	Aduana	Alfândega
deep	profundo	profundo
depth	sonda, profundidad	profundidade
diesel	gasoil	gasoleo
draught	calado	calado
dredged	dragado	dragado
dyke, pier	dique	dique
east	este	este
eastern	levante, oriental	levante, do este
electricity	electricidad	electricidade
engineer, mechanic	ingeniero, mecánico	engenheiro, técnico
entrance	boca, entrada	bôca, entrada
factory	fábrica	fábrica
foul, dirty	sucio	sujo
gravel	cascajo	burgau
green	verde	verde
harbourmaster	capitán de puerto	diretor do porto
height, clearance	altura	altura
high tide	pleamar, marea alta	preia-mar, maré alta
high	alto/a	alto/a
ice	hielo	gelo
inlet, cove	ensenada	enseada
island	isla	ilha, ilhéu
islet, skerry	islote	ilhota
isthmus	istmo	istmo
jetty, pier	malecón	quebra-mar
knots	nudos	nós
lake	lago	lago
laundry, launderette	lavandería, automática	lavanderia, automática
leading line, transit	enfilación	enfiamento
leeward	sotavento	sotavento
length overall	eslora total	comprimento
lighthouse	faro	farol
lock	esclusa	esclusa
low tide	bajamar, marea baja	baixa-mar, maré baixa
mailing address	dirección de correo	endereço para correio
marina, yacht harbour	puerto deportivo, dársena de yates	porto desportivo, doca de recreio
medical services	servicios médiocos	serviços médicas
mud	fango	lôdo
mussel rafts	viveros	viveiros
narrows	estrecho	estreito
north	norte	norte
orange	anaranjado	alaranjado
owner	propietario	propietário
paraffin	parafina	petróleo para iluminãçao
petrol	gasolina	gasolina
pier, quay, dock	muelle	molhe
point	punta	ponta
pontoon	pantalán	pontão
port (side)	babor	bombordo
Port of Registry	Puerto de Matrícula	Porto de Registo
port office	capitanía	capitania
post office	oficina de correos	agência do correio
quay	muelle	molhe, cais
ramp	rampa	rampa
range (tidal)	repunte	amplitude
red	rojo	vermelho
reef	arrecife	recife
reef, spit	restinga	restinga
registration number	matricula	número registo
repairs	reparacións	reparações
rock, stone	roca, piedra	laxe, pedra
root (e.g. of mole)	raíz	raiz
sailing boat	barca de vela	barco à vela
sailmaker, sail repairs	velero, reparacións velas	veleiro, reparações velas
saltpans	salinas	salinas
sand	arena	areia
sea	mar	mar
seal, to	precintar	fechar
shoal, low	bajo	baixo
shops	tiendas, almacéns	lojas
shore, edge	orilla	margem
showers (washing)	duchas	duches
slab, flat rock	laja	laje
slack water, tidal stand	repunte	águas paradas
slipway	varadero	rampa
small	pequeño	pequeno
south	sur	sul
southern	meridional	do sul
starboard	estribor	estibordo
strait	estrecho	estreito

APPENDIX

English	*Spanish*	*Portuguese*
supermarket	supermercado	supermercado
tower	torre	tôrre
travel-lift	grua giratoria, pórtico elevador	e pórtico, pórtico elevador, içar
water (drinking)	agua potable	água potável
weather forecast	previsión/boletin metereológico	previsão de tempo, boletim meteorológico
weed	alga	alga
weight	peso	pêso
west	oeste	oeste
western	occidental	do oeste
white	blanco	branco
windward	barlovento	barlavento
works (building)	obras	obras
yacht (sailing)	barca de vela	barco à vela
yacht club	club náutico	clube náutico, clube naval
yellow	amarillo	amarelo

Meteorology and sea state

English	*Spanish*	*Portuguese*
calm (Force 0, 0–1kns)	calma	calma
light airs (Force 1, 1–3kns)	ventolina	aragem
light breeze (Force 2, 4–6kns)	flojito	vento fraco, brisa
gentle breeze (Force 3, 7–10kns)	flojo	vento bonançoso, brisa suave
moderate breeze (Force 4, 11–16kns)	bonancible	vento moderado, brisa moderado
fresh breeze (Force 5, 17–21kns)	fresquito	vento fresco, brisa fresca
strong breeze (Force 6, 22–27kns)	fresco	vento muito fresco, brisa forte
near gale (Force 7, 28–33kns)	frescachón	vento forte, ventania moderada
gale (Force 8, 34–40kns)	duro	vento muito forte, ventania fresca
severe gale (Force 9, 41–47kns)	muy duro	vento tempestuoso, ventania forte
storm (Force 10, 48–55kns)	temporal	temporal, ventania total
violent storm (Force 11, 56–63kns)	borrasca, tempestad	temporal desfieto, tempestade
hurricane (Force 12, 64+kns)	huracán	furacão, ciclone
breakers	rompientes	arrebentação
cloudy	nubloso	nublado
depression (low)	depresión	depressão
fog	niebla	nevoeiro
gust	racha	rajada
hail	granizada	saraiva
mist	neblina	neblina
overfalls, tide race	escarceos	bailadeiras
rain	lluvia	chuva
ridge (high)	dorsal	crista
rough sea	mar gruesa	mar bravo
short, steep sea	mar corta	mar cavado
shower	aguacero	aguaceiro
slight sea	marejadilla	mar chão
squall	turbonada	borrasca
swell	mar de leva	ondulação
thunderstorm	tempestad	trovoada

General and chartwork terms

Spanish	*English*	*Portuguese*
Aduana	Customs	Alfândega
agua potable	water (drinking)	água potável
alga	weed	alga
almacéns	shops	lojas
alto/a	high	alto/a
altura	height, clearance	altura
amarillo	yellow	amarelo
anaranjado	orange	alaranjado
ancladero	anchorage	fundeadouro, ancoradouro
apetrachamento	chandlery (shop)	fornecedore de barcos, aprestos
aquilar coche	car hire	alugar automóvel
arena	sand	areia
arrecife	reef	recife
astillero	boatbuilder	estaleiro
atracar	berth	atracar
autobús	bus	autocarro
azul	blue	azul
babor	port (side)	bombordo
bahía	bay	baía, enseada
bajamar	low tide	baixa-mar, maré baixa
bajo	shoal, low	baixo
baliza	beacon	baliza
barca de vela	sailing boat, yacht	barco à vela
barlovento	windward	barlavento
blanco	white	branco
boca	entrance	bôca, entrada
boya	buoy	bóia
cabo	cape	cabo
calado	draught	calado
canal	channel	canal
capitán de puerto	harbourmaster	diretor do porto
capitanía	port office	capitania
carga de gas	bottled gas	cilindro de gás, bilha de gás
cartas náuticas	charts	cartas hidrográficas
cascajo	gravel	burgau
cilindro de gas	bottled gas	cilindro de gás, bilha de gás
club náutico	yacht club	clube náutico, clube naval
dársena de yates	marina, yacht harbour	porto desportivo, doca de recreio
dársena	basin, dock	doca
dique	dyke, pier	dique
dirección de correo	mailing address	endereço para correio
dragado	dredged	dragado
duchas	showers (washing)	duches
efectos navales	chandlery (shop)	fornecedore de barcos, aprestos
electricidad	electricity	electricidade
enfilación	leading line, transit	enfiamento
ensenada	bay, inlet, cove	baía, enseada
entrada	entrance	bôca, entrada
esclusa	lock	esclusa
eslora total	length overall	comprimento
este	east	este
estero	creek	esteiro
estrecho	narrows, strait	estreito
estribor	starboard	estibordo
fábrica	factory	fábrica
fango	mud	lôdo
faro	lighthouse	farol

Spanish	English	Portuguese
fondeadero	anchorage	fundeadouro, ancoradouro
fondear	anchor, to	fundear
gasoil	diesel	gasoleo
gasolina	petrol	gasolina
grua giratoria	travel-lift	e pórtico, pórtico elevador, içar
grua	crane	guindaste
hielo	ice	gelo
iglesia	church	igreja
ingeniero, mecánico	engineer, mechanic	engenheiro, técnico
isla	island	ilha, ilhéu
islote	islet, skerry	ilhota
istmo	isthmus	istmo
lago	lake	lago
laja	slab, flat rock	laje
lavandería, l. automática	laundry, launderette	lavanderia, l. automática
levante	eastern	levante, do este
malecón	jetty, pier	quebra-mar
manga	beam	largura, boca
mar	sea	mar
marea alta	high tide	preia-mar, maré alta
marea baja	low tide	baixa-mar, maré baixa
matricula	registration number	número registo
meridional	southern	do sul
muelle	breakwater, pier, quay, dock	quebra-mar, molhe, cais
negro	black	preto
norte	north	norte
nudos	knots	nós
obras	works (building)	obras
occidental	western	do oeste
oeste	west	oeste
oficina de correos	post office	agência do correio
oriental	eastern	levante, do este
orilla	shore, edge	margem
pantalán	pontoon	pontáo
parafina	paraffin	petróleo para iluminaçao
pequeño	small	pequeno
peso	weight	pêso
piedra	rock, stone	pedra
playa	beach	praia
pleamar	high tide	preia-mar, maré alta
pórtico elevador	travel-lift	e pórtico, pórtico elevador, içar
precintar	seal, to	fechar
previsión/boletin metereológico	weather forecast	previsão de tempo, boletim meteorológico
profundidad	depth	profundidade
profundo	deep	profundo
propietario	owner	propietário
Puerto de Matrícula	Port of Registry	Porto de Registo
puerto deportivo	marina, yacht harbour	porto desportivo, doca de recreio
punta	point	ponta
raíz	root (e.g. of mole)	raiz
rampa	ramp	rampa
reparacións	repairs	reparações
repunte	tidal range, stand, slack water	águas paradas, amplitude
restinga	reef, spit	restinga
roca	rock	laxe
rojo	red	vermelho
rompeolas	breakwater	quebra-mar, molhe
salinas	saltpans	salinas
servicios médicos	medical services	serviços médicas
sonda	depth	profundidade
sotavento	leeward	sotavento
sucio	foul, dirty	sujo
supermercado	supermarket	supermercado
sur	south	sul
tiendas	shops	lojas
torre	tower	tôrre
varadero	slipway	rampa
velero, reparacións velas	sailmaker, sail repairs	veleiro, reparações velas
verde	green	verde
viveros	mussel rafts	viveiros

Meteorology and sea state

Spanish	English	Portuguese
calma	calm (Force 0, 0–1kns)	calma
ventolina	light airs (Force 1, 1–3kns)	aragem
flojito	light breeze (Force 2, 4–6kns)	vento fraco, brisa
flojo	gentle breeze (Force 3, 7–10kns)	vento bonançoso, brisa suave
bonancible	moderate breeze (Force 4, 11–16kns)	vento moderado, brisa moderado
fresquito	fresh breeze (Force 5, 17–21kns)	vento frêsco, brisa fresca
frêsco	strong breeze (Force 6, 22–27kns)	vento muito fresco, brisa forte
frescachón	near gale (Force 7, 28–33kns)	vento forte, ventania moderada
duro	gale (Force 8, 34–40kns)	vento muito forte, ventania fresca
muy duro	severe gale (Force 9, 41–47kns)	vento tempestuoso, ventania forte
temporal	storm (Force 10, 48–55kns)	temporal, ventania total
borrasca, tempestad	violent storm (Force 11, 56–63kns)	temporal desfieto, tempestade
huracán	hurricane (Force 12, 64+kns)	furacão, ciclone
aguacero	shower	aguaceiro
depresión	depression (low)	depressão
dorsal	ridge (high)	crista
escarceos	overfalls, tiderace	bailadeiras
granizada	hail	saraiva
lluvia	rain	chuva
mar corta	short, steep sea	mar cavado
mar de leva	swell	ondulação
mar gruesa	rough sea	mar bravo
marejadilla	slight sea	mar chão
neblina	mist	neblina
niebla	fog	nevoeiro
nubloso	cloudy	nublado
racha	gust	rajada
rompientes	breakers	arrebentação
tempestad	thunderstorm	trovoada
turbonada	squall	borrasca

APPENDIX

General and chartwork terms

Portuguese	*English*	*Spanish*
agência do correio	post office	oficina de correos
água potável	water (drinking)	agua potable
amplitude, águas paradas	tidal range, stand, slack water	repunte repute
alaranjado	orange	anaranjado
alfândega	customs	aduana
alga	weed	alga
alto/a	high	alto/a
altura	height, clearance	altura
alugar automóvel	car hire	aquilar coche
amarelo	yellow	amarillo
areia	sand	arena
atracar	berth	atracar
autocarro	bus	autobús
azul	blue	azul
baía, enseada	bay, inlet, cove	bahía, ensenada
baixa-mar, maré baixa	low tide	bajamar, marea baja
baixo	shoal, low	bajo
baliza	beacon	baliza
barco à vela	sailing boat, yacht	barca de vela
barlavento	windward	barlovento
bôca, entrada	entrance	boca, entrada
bóia	buoy	boya
bombordo	port (side)	babor
branco	white	blanco
burgau	gravel	cascajo
cabo	cape	cabo
calado	draught	calado
canal	channel	canal
capitania	port office	capitanía
cartas hidrográficas	charts	cartas náuticas
cilindro de gás, bilha de gás	bottled gas	carga de gas, cilindro de gas
clube náutico,	yacht club clube naval	club náutico
comprimento	length overall	eslora total
dique	dyke, pier	dique
diretor do porto	harbourmaster	capitán de puerto
do oeste	western	occidental
do sul	southern	meridional
doca	basin, dock	dársena
dragado	dredged	dragado
duches	showers (washing)	duchas
e pórtico, pórtico elevador, içar	travel-lift	grua giratoria, pórtico elevador
electricidade	electricity	electricidad
endereço para correo	mailing address	dirección de correio
enfiamento	leading line, transit	enfilación
engenheiro, técnico	engineer, mechanic	ingeniero, mecánico
esclusa	lock	esclusa
estaleiro	boatbuilder	astillero
este	east	este
esteiro	creek	estero
estibordo	starboard	estribor
estreito	narrows, strait	estrecho
fábrica	factory	fábrica
farol	lighthouse	faro
fechar	seal, to	precintar
fornecedore de barcos, aprestos	chandlery (shop)	apetrachamento, efectos navales

Portuguese	*English*	*Spanish*
fundeadouro, ancoradouro	anchorage	fondeadero, ancladero
fundear	anchor, to	fondear
gasoleo	diesel	gasoil
gasolina	petrol	gasolina
gelo	ice	hielo
guindaste	crane	grua
igreja	church	iglesia
ilha, ilhéu	island	isla
ilhota	islet, skerry	islote
istmo	isthmus	istmo
lago	lake	lago
laje	slab, flat rock	laja
largura, boca	beam	manga
lavanderia, l. automática	laundry, launderette	lavandería, l. automática
laxe	rock	roca
levante, do este	eastern	levante, oriental
lôdo	mud	fango
lojas	shops	almacéns, tiendas
mar	sea	mar
margem	shore, edge	orilla
norte	north	norte
nós	knots	nudos
número registo	registration number	matricula
obras	works (building)	obras
oeste	west	oeste
pedra	rock, stone	piedra
pequeno	small	pequeño
pêso	weight	peso
petróleo para iluminãçao	paraffin	parafina
ponta	point	punta
pontáo	pontoon	pantalán
Porto de Registo	Port of Registry	Puerto de Matrícula
porto desportivo, doca de recreio	marina, yacht harbour	puerto deportivo, dársena de yates
praia	beach	playa
preia-mar, maré alta	high tide	pleamar, marea alta
preto	black	negro
previsão de tempo, boletim meteorológico	weather forecast	previsión/boletin metereológico
profundidade	depth	profundidad, sonda
profundo	deep	profundo
propietário	owner	propietario
quebra-mar	jetty, pier	malecón
quebra-mar, molhe, cais	breakwater, pier, quay, dock	muelle, rompeolas
raiz	root (e.g. of mole)	raíz
rampa	ramp, slipway	rampa, varadero
recife	reef	arrecife
reparações	repairs	reparacións
restinga	reef, spit	restinga
salinas	saltpans	salinas
serviços médicas	medical services	servicios médicos
sotavento	leeward	sotavento
sujo	foul, dirty	sucio
sul	south	sur
supermercado	supermarket	supermercado
tôrre	tower	torre

Portuguese	*English*	*Spanish*
veleiro, reparações velas	sailmaker, sail repairs	velero, reparacións velas
verde	green	verde
vermelho	red	rojo
viveiros	mussel rafts	viveros

Meteorology and sea state

Portuguese	*English*	*Spanish*
calma	calm (Force 0, 0–1kns)	calma
aragem	light airs (Force 1, 1–3kns)	ventolina
vento fraco, brisa	light breeze (Force 2, 4–6kns)	flojito
vento bonançoso, brisa suave	gentle breeze (Force 3, 7–10kns)	flojo
vento moderado, brisa moderado	moderate breeze (Force 4, 11–16kns)	bonancible
vento fresco, brisa fresca	fresh breeze (Force 5, 17–21kns)	fresquito
vento muito fresco, brisa forte	strong breeze (Force 6, 22–27kns)	fresco
vento forte, ventania moderada	near gale (Force 7, 28–33kns)	frescachón
vento muito forte, ventania fresca	gale (Force 8, 34–40kns)	duro
vento tempestuoso, ventania forte	severe gale (Force 9, 41–47kns)	muy duro
temporal, ventania total	storm (Force 10, 48–55kns)	temporal
temporal desfieto, tempestade	violent storm (Force 11, 56–63kns)	borrasca, tempestad
furacão, ciclone	hurricane (Force 12, 64+kns)	huracán
aguaceiro	shower	aguacero
arrebentação	breakers	rompientes
bailadeiras	overfalls, tide race	escarceos
borrasca	squall	turbonada
chuva	rain	lluvia
crista	ridge (high)	dorsal
depressão	depression (low)	depresión
mar bravo	rough sea	mar gruesa
mar cavado	short, steep sea	mar corta
mar chão	slight sea	marejadilla
neblina	mist	neblina
nevoeiro	fog	niebla
nublado	cloudy	nubloso
ondulação	swell	mar de leva
rajada	gust	racha
saraiva	hail	granizada
trovoada	thunderstorm	tempestad

V. Abbreviations used on charts

Spanish	*Portuguese*	*Meaning*
Lights		
F.	F.	Fixed
D.	Rl.	Flashing
Gp.D.	Rl.Agr.	Group flashing
F.D.	F.Rl.	Fixed and flashing
F.Gp.D.	F.Rl.Agr.	Fixed and group flashing
Ct.	Ct.	Quick flashing
Gp.Ct.	Ct int.	Interrupted quick flashing
Oc.	Oc.	Occulting
Gp.Oc.	Oc.Agr.	Group occulting
Iso.	Is.	Isophase
Mo.	Morse	Morse
Colours		
am.	am.	Yellow
az.	azul.	Blue
b.	br.	White
n.	pr.	Black
r.	vm.	Red
v.	vd.	Green
Seabed		
A.	A.	Sand
Al.	Alg.	Weed
R.	R.	Rock
F.	L.	Mud
Co.	B.	Gravel

VI. Conversion tables

1 inch = 2·54 centimetres (roughly 4in = 10cm)
1 centimetre = 0·394 inches
1 foot = 0·305 metres (roughly 3ft = 1m)
1 metre = 3·281 feet
1 pound = 0·454 kilograms (roughly 10lbs = 4·5kg)
1 kilogram = 2·205 pounds
1 mile = 1·609 kilometres (roughly 10 miles = 16km)
1 kilometre = 0·621 miles
1 nautical mile = 1·1515 miles
1 mile = 0·8684 nautical miles
1 acre = 0·405 hectares (roughly 10 acres = 4 hectares)
1 hectare = 2·471 acres
1 gallon = 4·546 litres (roughly 1 gallon = 4·5 litres)
1 litre = 0·220 gallons

Temperature scale

t°F to t°C = $\frac{t°F - 32 \times 5}{9}$

t°C to t°F = $\frac{t°C \times 9}{5} + 32$

So:

70°F = 21·1°C   20°C = 68°F
80°F = 26·7°C   30°C = 86°F
90°F = 32·2°C   40°C = 104°F

APPENDIX

Index

INDEX